MW01630031

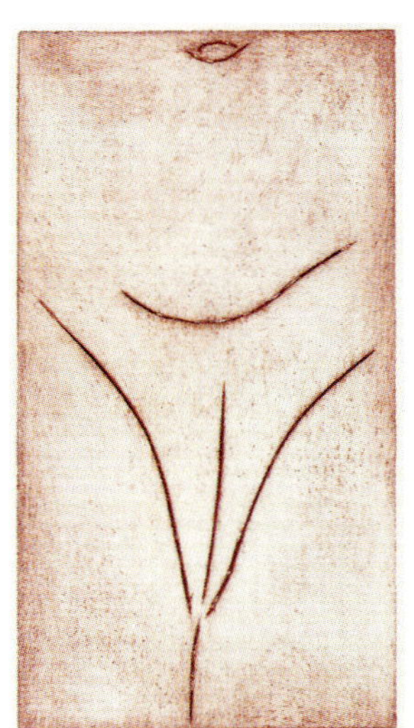

PICASSO
Érotique

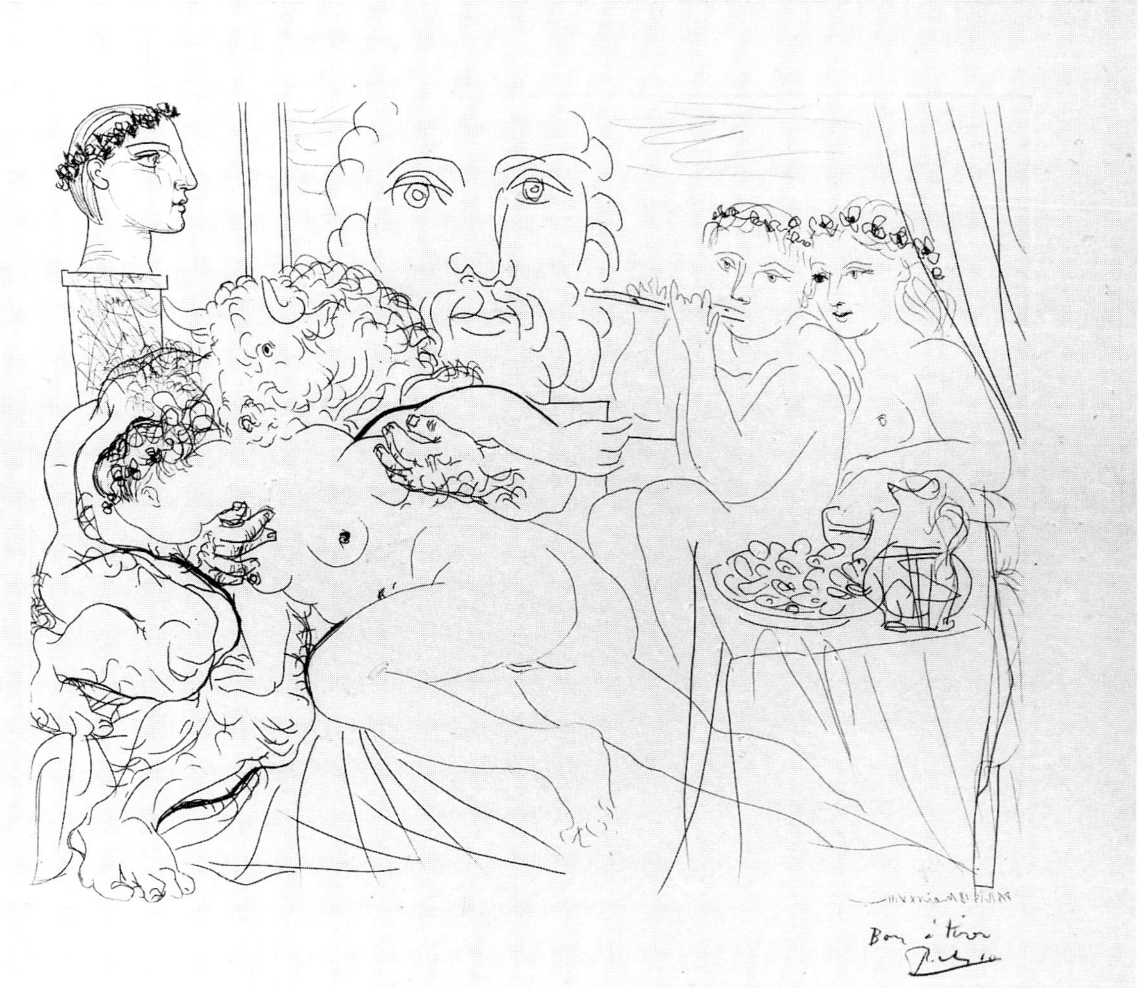
Bon à tirer

PICASSO *Érotique*

Edited by Jean Clair

With contributions by
Jean Clair, Annie Le Brun,
Pascal Quignard, Jean-Jacques Lebel,
Patrick Roegiers, Malén Gual,
Maria Teresa Ocaña,
Robert Rosenblum,
Brigitte Baer, Marie-Noëlle Delorme,
Dominique Dupuis-Labbé,
Marilyn McCully

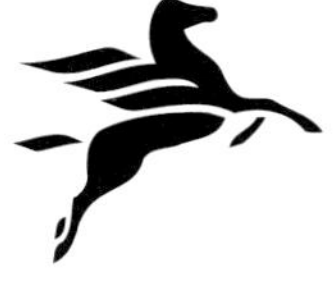

Prestel

Munich · London · New York

This exhibition was organized by
the Réunion des musées nationaux and the
Musée national Picasso, Paris, and co-produced
with the Galerie nationale du Jeu de Paume, Paris,
the Montreal Museum of Fine Arts
and the Museu Picasso, Barcelona.

The Paris exhibition was produced in partnership
with Air France and Dauphin
with the support of Pierre Bergé, Yves Saint Laurent
and the Centre de documentation Yves Saint Laurent.

General project coordination was provided by
the Département des expositions, Réunion des musées nationaux.

For the English edition © Prestel-Verlag, Munich, London, New York/
Musée des Beaux-Arts du Canada, 2001
For the French edition © Éditions de la Réunion des Musées Nationaux, 2001
49, rue Étienne-Marcel, 75001 Paris
© Succession Picasso, 2001
© ADAGP, Paris, 2001
© Estate Brassaï, 2001

Cover and Page 1:
Fragment of a Female Body, 28 December 1960
Illustration for P. A. Benoit, *Les Livres de Picasso réalisés par PAB*, May 1966
Burin on plastic matter, 16.5 x 9 cm
Paris, Musée Picasso, MP 3578

Page 4:
Self-Portrait, Three Forms: Crowned Painter, Bust of Sculptor and Amorous Minotaur,
18 May 1933
Etching on copper; trial proof; 30 x 36.7
Paris, Musée Picasso, MP 1982-143

Prestel-Verlag
Mandlstrasse 26
D-80802 Munich
Germany
Tel.: (89) 38 17 09-0
Fax: (89) 38 17 09-35
www.prestel.de

4 Bloomsbury Place
London
WC1A 2QA
England
Tel.: (020) 7323 5004
Fax: (020) 7636 8004

175 Fifth Avenue, Suite 402
New York
NY 10010
U.S.A.
Tel.: (212) 995-2720
Fax: (212) 995-2733
www.prestel.com

Library of Congress Card Number: 2001086283

Prestel books are available worldwide. Please contact your nearest bookseller
or any of the above addresses for information concerning your local distributor.

Translation from the French: Services d'édition Guy Connolly, Montreal,
except for "The School of Darkness" by Jean Clair translated by Mark Hutchinson
Editing and proofreading: Services d'édition Guy Connolly
Design: Philippe Ducat, Paris
Typesetting: Meike Weber, Munich

Origination: IGS, L'Isle-d'Espagnac
Printing and binding: Aubin, Ligugé
Printed in France

ISBN: 3-7913-2561-2 (hardcover)
ISBN: 3-7913-2530-2 (paperback)

Curators of the Exhibition

Jean Clair
Chief Curator
Director, Musée national Picasso, Paris

Dominique Dupuis-Labbé
Scientific Curator
Curator, Musée national Picasso, Paris

Guy Cogeval
Associate Curator
Director, The Montreal Museum of Fine Arts

Nathalie Bondil-Poupard
Assistant Curator
Chief Curator, The Montreal Museum of Fine Arts

Jean-Jacques Lebel
Guest Curator for The Montreal Museum of Fine Arts

Maria Teresa Ocaña
Associate Curator
Director, Museu Picasso, Barcelona

Daniel Abadie
Director, Galerie nationale du Jeu de Paume

We wish to express our deepest gratitude to all of the institutions and private collectors,
as well as those lenders who wish to remain anonymous, whose generous contributions
have ensured the success of this exhibition in Paris, Montreal and Barcelona:

Musée des Beaux-Arts, Amiens
Musée Réattu, Arles
Stadthalle, Balingen
Museu Picasso, Barcelona
Fondation Beyeler, Riehen, Basel
Galerie Beyeler, Basel
Öffentliche Kunstsammlung, Kupferstichkabinett, Basel
Donation Maurice Jardot, Belfort
Staatliche Museen zu Berlin, Nationalgalerie, Heinz Berggruen Collection, Berlin
Museum of Fine Arts, Boston
The Albright-Knox Art Gallery, Buffalo
The Cleveland Museum of Art, Cleveland
Galerie Gmurzynska, Cologne
Museum Ludwig, Cologne
Statens Museum for Kunst, Copenhagen
Musée des Beaux-Arts, Dijon
Marina Picasso Collection, courtesy Galerie Jan Krugier, Ditesheim & Cie, Geneva
LS Art, Geneva
Konstmuseum, Göteborg
David & Leslee Rogath, Greenwich, Connecticut
The Israel Museum, Jerusalem
James Roundell, London
Centro de Arte Reina Sofía, Madrid
Fondation Socindec, courtesy Fondation Pierre Gianadda, Martigny
Landau Fine Art, Montreal
The Montreal Museum of Fine Arts, Montreal
Musée des Beaux-Arts, Nantes
Marina Picasso Collection, courtesy Jan Krugier Gallery, New York
The Metropolitan Museum of Art, New York
The Museum of Modern Art, New York
Bibliothèque nationale de France, Département des Estampes et de la Photographie, Paris
Centre Georges-Pompidou/Musée national d'Art moderne, Paris
Musée d'Art moderne de la Ville de Paris
Musée national Picasso, Paris
Galerie Louise Leiris, Paris
Galerie Vallois, Paris
Musée d'Art moderne, Saint-Étienne
Musées de Strasbourg
The Art Gallery of Ontario, Toronto
Galerie Art Focus, Zurich
Galerie Pels-Leusden AG, Zurich

This project would not have seen the light of day without the contribution
of the professional and technical staff of the Musée national Picasso in Paris.
Ms. Colette Giraudon and Ms. Odile Michel, Musée national Picasso, were responsible
for documentation, general coordination and the catalogue.
Mr. Hubert Boisselier, Musée national Picasso, supervised the transportation
of the works.
Ms. Marie-Christine Enshaian and Ms. Claire Bergeaud, Mr. Yann de Saint Maurice
and Mr. Patrick Mandron restored and mounted the works
from the Musée national Picasso collection.
Mr. Franck Besson and Mr. Vidal Garrido, installation technicians,
Musée national Picasso, framed and installed them.
We extend warmest thanks to them.

The Montreal Museum of Fine Arts thanks its teams for making possible
the presentation of this exhibition.
The Museum extends special thanks to Mr. Jean-Jacques Lebel, on whose
initiative the Montreal venue of the exhibition was organized.

This project would not have been possible without the scientific
and technical contributions of the staff of the Museu Picasso, Barcelona:
Mr. Lluís Bagunyà, Associate Director, Ms. Sonia Villegas, Exhibition Assistant,
Mr. Malén Gual, Superintendent, and his assistant Ms. Anna Fàbregas, as well as
Mr. Claustre Rafart (communications and cultural activities), Ms. Margarida Cortadella
and Ms. Montserrat Torras (copy-editing), and Ms. Margarita Ferrer (photographic
archives).

The presentation of the exhibition in Paris would not have been possible without the
collaboration of the team at the Galerie nationale du Jeu de Paume:
Ms. Arlette Singer, Secretary-General, and Ms. Élisabeth Galloy, Coordinator, assisted
by Ms. Caroline Ferreira d'Oliveira; Mr. Jean-Luc Delest (transportation of the works),
assisted by Ms. Cécile Allouis; Mr. Walter Pellevoisin (installation); Ms. Françoise Bon-
nefoy, Publications Director; Mr. Michel Baudson (cultural service); Ms. Eva Bechmann
and Ms. Maya Salem (press relations); and Ms. Laurence Lissac (partnerships);

along with the team at the Réunion des musées nationaux: Ms. Ute Collinet,
Secretary-General, assisted by Ms. Laurence Robin; Ms. Bénédicte Boissonnas, Director,
Exhibitions Department; Ms. Marie-France Cocheteux and Ms. Hélène Flon, project
coordinators, assisted by Ms. Anne Giani; Mr. Jean Naudin and Ms. Céline Peyre
(transportation of the works); Ms. Béatrice Foulon, Publications Director; Ms. Dagmar
Rolf and Ms. Julie Bénet, publications managers; Ms. Évelyne David (photographs
management); as well as Mr. Alain Madeleine-Perdrillat, Ms. Florence Le Moing and
Ms. Cécile Vignot (communications and press relations).

The text of the English edition of the catalogue was prepared in Montreal by
Services d'édition Guy Connolly, under the direction of Ms. Françoise de Luca and with
the collaboration of Mr. Michael Gilson, Ms. Diana Halfpenny, Ms. Cynthia Kelly,
Mr. Donald McGrath, Ms. Maryse Ménard and Ms. Vanessa Nicolai, to whom we
extend our thanks.

Very special thanks are due to Mr. Pierre Bergé and Mr. Yves Saint Laurent for their personal involvement in supporting the presentation of this project in Paris.

Our thanks also to all of those who, through their cooperation at various stages in the preparation of this endeavour, have helped make it possible:

Sally F. Addams, Jean-Jacques Aillagon, Claude Allemand-Cosneau, Jean-Pierre, Angremy, Ruth Apter-Gabriel, Juliette Armand, Ida Balboul, Anne Baldassari, Jacques Beauffet, Laure Beaumont-Maillet, Sylvain Bellanger, Heinz Berggruen, Ernst Beyeler, Juan Manuel Bonet, Paloma Botín, Mme Bourgin, Laura Catalano, Joaquín Cervera, Hugues Charreyron, Christie's, London, Los Angeles and New York, Gilles Courtois, Christophe Cousin, Piero Crommelynck, Pierre Daix, Martine Dancer, Roland Doschka, Jacky Drouet, Philippe Ducat, Bernd Dütting, Paloma Esteban Leal, Pierrot Eugène, Hélène Fauré, Evelyn Ferlay, Björn Fredlund, Sylvie Fresnault, Jean Gautier, Marie-Jeanne Geyer, Léonard Gianadda, Kristina Gmurzynska, Joëlle Gouel, Claire Guérin, Joseph C. Handricks, Tim Hardacre, Mme Hartmann, Béatrice Hatala, Allis Helleland, Fabrice Hergott, Alexandra Holz, Catherine Hutin-Blay, Lucilia Jeangeot, Beda Jedlicka, Konrad Klapheck, Caroline Klein, Caroline de Lambertye, Anne Latournerie, Quentin Laurens, Brigitte Léal, Annie Le Brun, Anne Levesque, William Lieberman, Glenn Lowry, Sylvie Lucas, Laurence Madeline, Sophie Mayoux, Hanne Møller, Philippe de Montebello, Michèle Moutachar, Dr. Christian Müller, Marcus Muller, Jacqueline Munck, Susanne Orlando, Alfred Pacquement, Suzanne Pagé, Paul-Hervé Parsy, Kim Paschko, Véronique Patard, Claude Picasso, Marina Picasso, Paloma Picasso, Robert Poujade, Stéphanie Poux, Jean-René Quentric, Dr. Katherin Reid, John Richardson, Jennifer Roberts, Brigitte Robin-Loiseau, Bill Robinson, Malcom Rogers, Cora Rosevear, Dominique Rossi, James Roundell, Maître Ruellan, Bernard Ruiz-Picasso, Christine Ruiz-Picasso, Walter Ryser, Isabelle Sauvage, Suzanne L. Schenton, Dr. Katarina Schmidt, Dr. Angela Schneider, Douglas G. Schultz, Prof. Peter Klaus Schuster, Hélène Seckel-Klein, Maître Lucien Solanet, Sotheby's, London and New York, Emmanuel Starcky, Simon Studer, Jeanne-Yvette Sudour, Matthew Teitelbaum, Paolo Toeschi, Sylvie Vautier, Bernard Venet, Martin Veyl, Marta Volga de Minteguiaga, Maître Jean-Marie Vuilliemin, Dr. Kenneth Wayne, Evelyn Weiss, Maya Widmaier-Picasso, Florence Wrobel, Pierre Zécri.

PREFACE

Picasso's oeuvre—and this is a given—is purely, entirely erotic. His was a genius in which the creative gesture was fused with the sexual impulse. There is nothing novel about such an observation.

Yet a quick perusal of bibliographical sources reveals that exhibitions devoted to this central theme have been scarce, as though the very idea of addressing it were enough to cause a general retreat. To be sure, there have been a few generalized studies of "the erotic in art," but they have in most cases been mundane and lacking in rigour, aimed only at a popular readership. Some comic strips, occasionally quite delectable, like those of Massimo Rotundo, narrating in images the sex life of Picasso in the lower depths of Barcelona and on the upper slopes of Montmartre. A few learned studies of his suites of prints: *347* and *La Célestine*. But comprehensive attempts to examine such an omnipresent aspect of this singular genius have been virtually non-existent. In other words, this exhibition is here, now, to fill a void. A space where something has been lacking. Could we not have dared do so earlier? And might we no longer dare do so tomorrow? When, at the close of the century, all signs point to the return of a moralist order on the Western shores of the Atlantic (where, already, Picasso's erotic works are no longer shown), it becomes hard to deny that places in which we are fortunate enough to enjoy such liberty—not to say libertine thought—are becoming few and far between.

Every artist has been, is, or will be erotic—another commonplace assertion. From Corot, with his *œuvres libres*, to Francis Bacon and his candid confessions, they have always been so… but each in his own way. Picasso's eroticism has nothing to do with contemplation; it does not proceed from amorous transfixion, nor from thwarted desire. It is an immediate action, born of covetousness and accomplished without delay. It has to do with tension, erection, the bow stretched taut—precise and cruel—from which fly the lines of a graphic style that recalls the snare as much as it does the arrow. Here, the supple and reticulate line that envelops forms, there the stroke of the remorseless archer who strikes them down. It is the art of the retiarius as well as that of the picador. The games of the Circus Maximus as well as the *corrida*. Médrano, the saltimbanques, the fragile funambulists in pink tights, yes, of course—but also the blood, the sweat, the tears of the athletes and of the horsebreakers with their stinging crops. Apollinaire and his *Onze Mille Verges*, but also Tod Browning and his *Freaks*. A fantastical killing, glimpsed, not without fear and quaking, in the daily frissons of the *petite mort*, "that infinite accessible even to poodles," in the words of Céline. From the very first drawings done at age eight, revealing a precocious fascination for the female form, to the very last accomplished a few days before his death, dislocated, pathetic visions of a sex, the destiny of the twentieth century's greatest artist was to unfold under the sign of Eros —and of Thanatos.

All of Picasso's visual art (to say nothing of a literary corpus that ranges from the surrealist farce *Desire Caught by the Tail* to licentious poetry) is thus guided by a specifically Spanish eroticism, a medley of sensuality and tenderness, of scatology and gluttony, of which the most august example in literature is Fernando de Rojas's tragicomedy *La Celestina* (1499, soon thereafter suppressed by the Holy Office), but that we also find in the writings of Ramón Gómez de la Serna, that marvellous creator of *Senos*, those of Rafael Alberti and, in the Spain of *la movida*, of Juan Manuel de Prada, author of *Coños*.

We are delighted to have produced this modest introduction to an Art of Loving, to which lenders, both public and private, amateurs and lovers, *dilettanti* and specialists, erudite libertines and those with a fetishistic flair for detail, have provided such invaluable assistance. May they be thanked for having done so.

Guy Cogeval

Director,
The Montreal Museum of Fine Arts,
Montreal

Jean Clair

Director,
Musée national Picasso,
Paris

Maria Teresa Ocaña

Director,
Museu Picasso,
Barcelona

Note
The following abbreviations have been used in referring to catalogues raisonnés: G./B. and Baer
(for Brigitte Baer); Spies (for Werner Spies); and Z. (for Christian Zervos). Full references may be found
in the Bibliography.
Unless otherwise indicated, all works illustrated are by Picasso.
For a work not travelling to all three museums on the exhibition itinerary, the symbols [P] (for Paris),
[M] (for Montreal) and [B] (for Barcelona) at the end of the catalogue entry indicate where it
is being shown. An asterisk following the lender´s name or the inventory number denotes the
provenance of the specific etching reproduced.
All dimensions are given in centimetres.

CONTENTS

THE SCHOOL OF DARKNESS

Jean Clair

"All beings move around inside one another….
Every animal is more or less of a man; every mineral is more or less of a plant;
every plant is more or less of an animal….What is a being?
The sum of a certain number of tendencies." Diderot

Suppose we begin with Philippe Sollers: "In the whole of modern art, there was only one name I cared for: Picasso…. Carefully concealed, invisible in broad daylight, aristocratic to the very end and always in perfect taste even when the clashing of colours could hardly be uglier? A faultless composer? Each volume in place, no mysterious searching, no afterlife, no symbols, no idle daydreams: the sexual diagnosis, each time monumentally transposed, bang on target."[1]

You don't care for Sollers, one of the few picaresque writers left at the end of the century? Then listen to some old-world humanism, to what Jean Leymarie has to say: "About twenty years ago, I was asked to give a talk on art and sexuality. I went to see Picasso and I asked him: 'What should I say?' and he replied: 'They're the same thing.' Picasso was fascinated by sexuality, he lived it to the full in his art and in his life. Every time there was a new woman, there was a new norm, a new vision, because he literally possessed the woman in everything he saw; he himself changed."[2] "New norm," "new vision," "sexual diagnosis… transposed, bang on target," "possessed the woman in everything he saw": it all points to a consistently clinical outlook, what Diderot would have called an experimental physiology, that in its cold-heartedness takes no account of the sentimental side of love.

Let us try and examine, regardless of temperament, this uncompromising vision, different each time, for each woman in turn, in which the anatomy is exposed to the gaze, laid bare, examined and probed the way an old-fashioned doctor would move his stethoscope about, listen, rub gently with his fingers, consider almost absent-mindedly, through half-closed eyes, the freshness of the complexion or the tenor of the skin, the crimped appearance of a hair, the pupils of the eyes; listen to the beating of the heart, the pulsing of an artery, the wheezing of the larynx—then, tracing all these scattered observations back to the ideal image of a body, not only offer a diagnosis but predict a future. The future of this particular body, the accidents and mishaps embedded in its morphology, the marks and scars betokening a long life or a brief existence. In the same way, Picasso the painter, with his dark eyes, his small short hands, his skin, his hair, his pores, would take the most striking characteristics of each new woman who

1 Philippe Sollers, *Portrait du joueur* (Paris: Gallimard, 1984), p. 184–85. (Free translation.)
2 Jean Leymarie, "Normes et déviances," *3es Rencontres internationales de Genève* (La Baconnière: Neuchâtel, 1988), p. 127. (Free translation.)

revealed herself to him (with, in the background, the perfect paradigm, the ideal woman always denied) and out of them assemble something new, a makeshift and unprecedented construction of limbs and organs which gradually, in the darkness of the body and the warmth of the mucous membranes, sealed a fate. A fate not governed by chance, but forced on the painter by necessity… Such is the power of Picasso's art in its muscular and laborious struggle for *operanti*, its roots reaching deep into the entrails of vision.

And what an admission of stupidity on the part of his biographers, today bent on portraying him in the guise of the ogre, the dark demon, the wife-eating Minotaur—or even more simply a superman who cast off the women in his life once he had worn them out. It would be truer to say of Picasso what a woman once wrote, before feminism poisoned relations between the sexes, of Don Juan: "Not the profaner of love, but the hero of profane love."[3]

Passion feeds on sacrifice. Sacrifice is Passion. You have to be American and naively believe that art is useful for educating small children and cleansing adults of their sins, and indispensable therefore to the welfare of an enlightened society, to believe in the innocence of art. An artist is a criminal, an outlaw, a pervert, the only difference being that he pays a high price for his crimes, and in a different coin from that used to sell his works in the auction room once he is dead. What else is an artist's genius if not the right he claims to see for himself, a claim that lesser mortals have never been able to stake? That is why images are taboo in so many religions.

Seeing for Oneself
To see for oneself, then. Sacred love and profane love. Let us turn to another giant, Titian, whom Picasso most certainly had in mind only a year before his death, at a time when his faculties were waning, his senses one after the other taking leave, his body deserting him, and he set about painting, in April 1972, his *Musicians*.

A twilight serenade, a short, secret duet before dying, a small flute held between the fingers or sounding a few last notes beneath the lips, a last musical exchange between a small ithyphallic faun and a Venus in a lace mantilla.

And a final allusion to two works: *The Three Ages of Man*, likewise concerned with flutes and how they are played; and, more importantly, *Venus and Cupid with an Organist*, which can be seen in the Prado in Madrid, where Titian beats a cunning little tattoo on all five portals of the body: sound (the organ), touch (the small dog), smell (the hay in the nearby meadow), taste (the iridescent autumn fruit) and, last but not least, sight, sight itself, embodied in the gaze the musician fixes on the lap of his delightful listener. The way his body pauses for a second, this momentary hesitation in the flow of chords as he looks round from the body of the instrument to see this other gash, long and fleecy but similar in form to the

---

3 Micheline Sauvage, *Le Cas Don Juan* (Paris: Seuil, 1953).

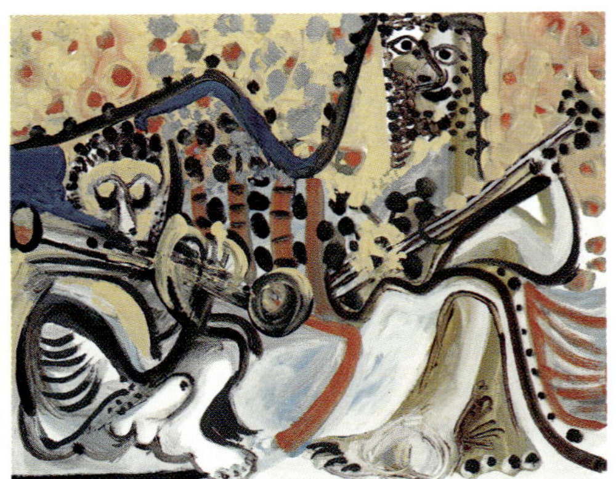

Fig. 1: *Musicians*, 11 April 1972
Oil on canvas; 73 x 92.5
Paris, Musée Picasso, MP 1990-49

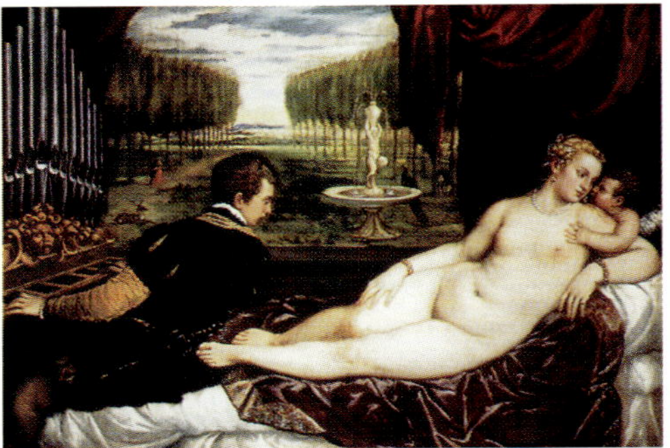

Fig. 2: Titian, *Venus and Cupid with an Organist*, 1548
Oil on canvas; 148 x 217
Madrid, Museo del Prado, MP 1990-49

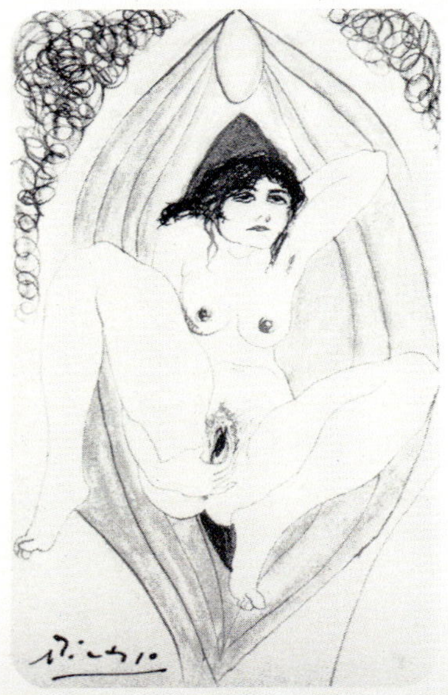

Fig. 3: *Vaginal Environment*, 1902
Ink and coloured pencil on cardboard; 13 x 9
Private collection

almond-shaped openings at the base of the organ-pipes, might indeed be described as an "organ point" or fermata.

Sight, then, the crime, the passion, the unremitting catastrophe of having to move back and forth from the eye, and by means of the eye, to the vulva, the vagina—not the garrulous vagina of the psychoanalyst's couch, but the silent vagina, inward, delightful, terrifying, the vagina which speaks with the voice of silence, all that the "mouth of darkness" does not say, that eternal silence which strikes fear in men's hearts, the *selva oscura*. And then—as though the experience of seeing involved a new birth each time, sending you back along the path you had once come, as though the artist gifted with vision, born again each day, was the *eu genos*, the "well-born," blessed with the powers that attach themselves to those who are twice-born—to pass on from the small, dark, speechless hole of the vagina to everything else, to the world, to the sum total of all the bodies on earth. The earth and only the earth, but the earth in its entirety. To paraphrase Racine: "*Physis tout entière à sa proie attachée.*"

And you think it's funny, or educational, or good for enlivening after-dinner conversation, this passion for seeing things, for seeing them well, for seeing them all, this voyeurism with its compulsive need to *see for oneself*, to check everything, fold after fold, hair after hair, to open it all out, to note it all down, line by line, to examine it all in detail, to see right through to the bone—and each time conclude there's *nothing* there, "not even a harmonica" as Henry Miller would say, not even another "self" poking its head up from the bottom of the hole. No, nothing but nature, self-regulating but demanding just the same that you set your sights on it. Asking you to be attentive, to pay attention, both in the old French sense of *attentif*, of "being subject to the orders of one's superior" and in the military sense of "standing at attention" (this more aggressive, sadistic sense is also found in certain usages of the word "gaze," as when we speak of God's "piercing" gaze); but also in the modern sense of "attentive to the needs of," "considerate," where the infinite, minutely detailed attention paid to the object in question is a sign of infinite consideration.

Nothingness and All

What, incidentally, would the iterative of the verb "to see" (*voir*) be that stands in the same relation to the act of seeing as "dictate" (*dicter*) does to the act of "speech" (*dire*)? In other words, how is the repetition, the reiteration, the obsession of seeing to be expressed? How are we to express this libido of seeing which gradually turns into a libido of knowing, of knowing everything that the world holds up to the gaze? How are we to express this mania for knowing women, for nourishing the senses, for keeping awake? This capacity, time and again, to give a start or jump up or let out a roar? This refusal to face the fact that we start dying the moment we set foot on earth? Delicious, this maddening itch to see? Scandalous, this refusal, in old age, to turn aside from the gaze the way one turns aside from war? No, over the entrances to museums should be placed the inscription Dante read over the entrance to Hell.

At twenty, Picasso attached so much importance to his beloved eyes that he painted blind people. Poor people, beggars, cripples, every one of them blind. He also painted blind musicians, the very antithesis of the love-struck organist. In the same way that lovers would sometimes have a blind musician play for them to heighten the pleasures of their frolicking? In the same way that, in the prints of Outamaro, where the vagina is as accurately and outrageously detailed as in the late engravings of Picasso, there is always a young witness to hand, trying hard to look the other way? Not to see is a form of damnation. It is also the most primitive form of castration. Freud has spoken well of this "terrifying infant fear of going blind." He was writing about Hoffmann's Sandman, who plucks out children's eyes. Every night, as he lies in bed, the young Nathanael hears the heavy steps of Coppelius echoing along the hallway as he comes to visit his father. Coppelius and the father: the two men have work to do, are in league with one another.

For how can we fail to suppose between the Sandman and the Father a common tie, what psychoanalysts call the Law—that bond which serves to counteract desire and protect the mother? In the secret game they play together in the dark, two antagonistic aspects of the paternal *imago* are at work: the good father, the one who protects, instructs, sustains, the paedophore Saint Christopher, the kindly blond giant carrying the small body in his arms; and the evil father, the one who threatens, imposes taboos, mutilates. There is something more powerful in this duality than the good and evil breast of Melanie Klein; regarding Picasso, at least, the relationship seems more apt.

Perhaps the strangest painting of his old age in this respect is *The Painter and Child* of 1969. On the right is the father, recumbent but shored up, as it were, by a triangle; that same triangle at the centre of which, in other paintings from this period, an eye is often found. Here, it is occupied by a handful of paintbrushes, arranged horizontally (it's all one of them can do to lift its head and detach itself from the bundle). On the left is a young child hardly out of his diapers, waving the instrument discarded by his father. But who today remembers Picasso's father, that blond, blue-eyed giant, Don José Ruiz? The painting is also a small, dark, mirror image, sixty or eighty years on, of Picasso grown old in his turn and passing on the flame to his son, the old fogey as an impotent voyeur handing on to posterity, to childhood (whose hair is once more blond) responsibility for carrying on the family business, in keeping with that "formidable machinery of repetition" that Pierre-Jean Jouve talks about in Mozart's *Don Juan*.

"The greatest pleasure in the world is buggering one's dying father," wrote Picasso in 1960. He was nearly eighty years old when he scrawled these powerful words in Spanish, his mother tongue, in red crayon on a drawing.[4] Was it his own father he had in mind? Or was he thinking, on the contrary, of his children?

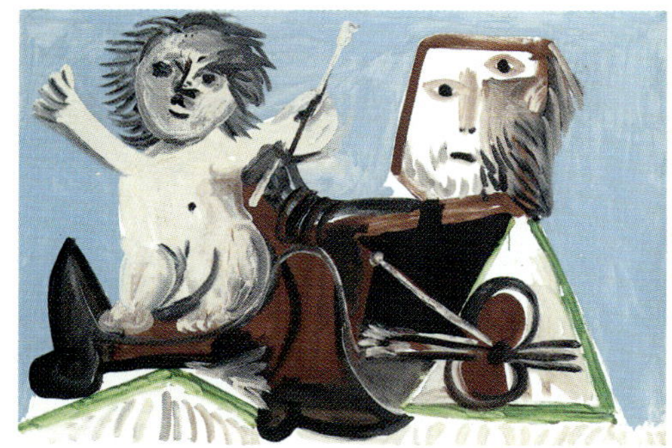

Fig. 4: *The Painter and Child,* 21 October 1969
Oil on canvas; 130 x 195
Paris, Musée Picasso, MP 1990-36

4 *"El mayor placer en este mundo es darle por el culo a su padre moribundo."* Marie-Laure Bernadac and Christine Piot, *Picasso: Écrits* (Paris, Gallimard, 1989), p. 375. English ed. *Picasso: Collected Writings* (New York: Abbeville Press, 1989).

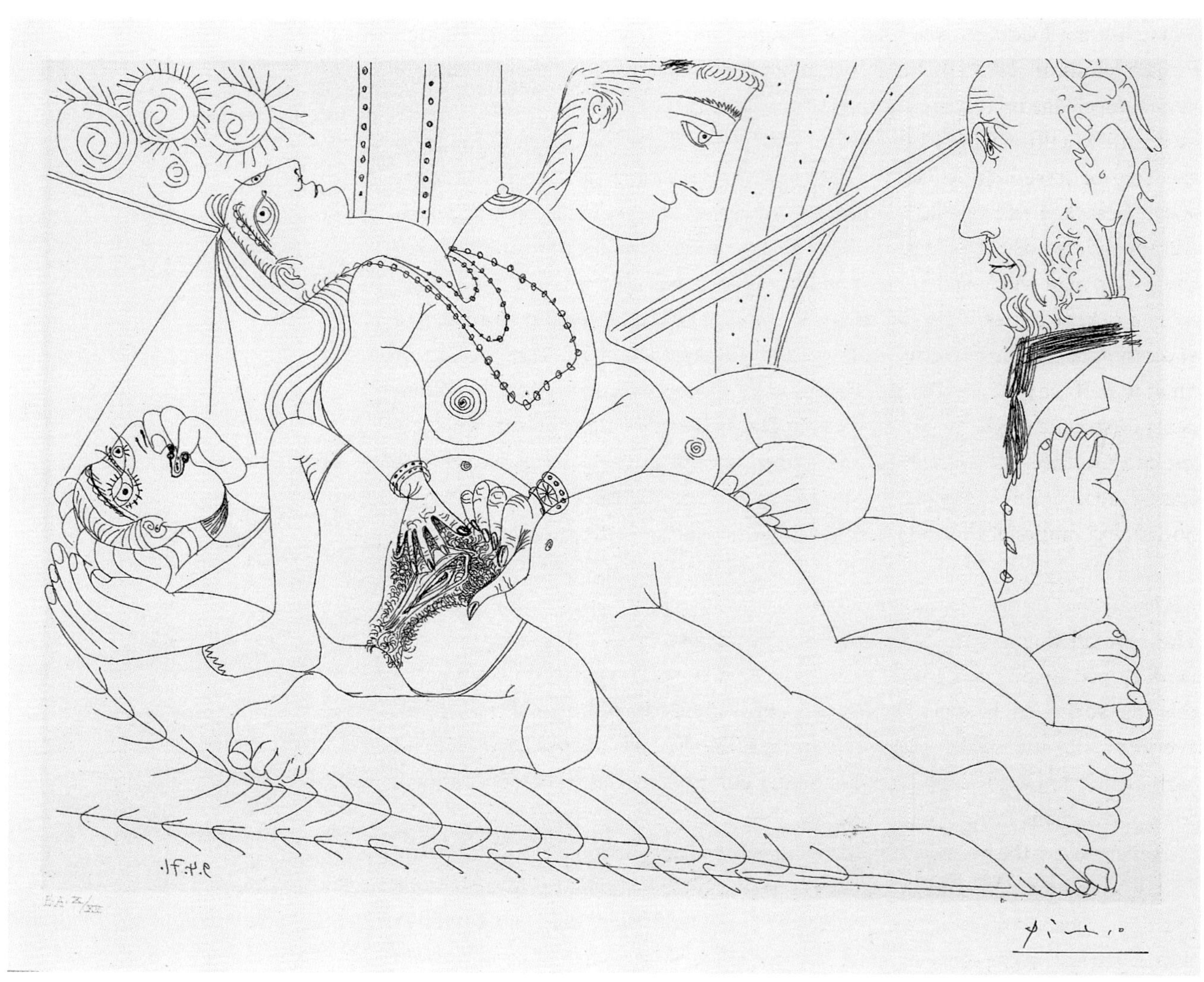

304 The Maison Tellier. Girls to Themselves. Degas Flabbergasted, 9 April 1971

Etching on copper; 36.7 x 49.4
Paris, Musée Picasso, on deposit at the Musée d'Art moderne, Saint-Étienne, MP 1990-311* [P]
Paris, Bibliothèque nationale de France, Département des Estampes et de la Photographie [M]
Barcelona, Museu Picasso, MPB 112.225 [B]

We are not looking at the final scene in a *dramma giocóso*, however. Though Picasso hands on the flame to his son, there is no echo of the *Dammi la mano in pegno*, no pledge made to a clinging, ice-cold Commander who will send you into everlasting hellfire. Rather the reverse: born out of the bosom of the father, as in the Tree of Jesse depicted in stained-glass windows, this little doll of fidgety, warm flesh is a reminder that life goes on. Knowledge is handed down, power transferred, the art of *pennellatura* given in gift and a guarantee provided that the young man will keep his eyes open and possess both women and fame.

The risk, of course, as in Hoffmann's tale, is of reducing women to dolls, to a succession of creatures whose heads, eyes and legs can be taken off and stuck back on at will. If we need to ward off the threat of Coppelius, do we not also need to learn to become mechanics? It is not love that is at issue here, that strange abnegation of self we call "falling" in love, but the frantic renewal of desire, the constant regeneration of the humours of the body and the manifold procedures a human hydraulics of this kind requires.

Mille e Tre
They are all there, then, these women who in giving their shape to Picasso's work helped shape that work; and it is because they were themselves so different that his work is so diverse. "He loves and lusts after everything, and having had everything, he knows how to go without it all. The women and the young girls in particular are in his head, but they can't get out any more, they can't move on," as the marvellous Prince de Ligne wrote of Casanova in his *Memoirs*.

Nevertheless, the eye must be unusually supple, unusually gentle and flexible, if each of these qualities in each of these women is to be given its due. Each line must be probed with the fingers, each joint tested, each particularity observed — "particularity" in the sense in which Lavater spoke of faces whose "parts" did not fit together properly. For the real challenge, every bit as important as taking the doll apart, is reconciling the parts with the whole, breaking down the whole into so many parts, then piecing the parts together again as a whole. Painting as a "sum of destructions," as Picasso said. I will return to this later.

In the meantime, there is the first of these women, Madeleine, by whom he almost had a son (who would have been sixty-four in 1968, he later confided with alarm).[5] And there is the last, Jacqueline, with her unforgettable effigy. Between them is a long line of faces that seem to fall away in two directions. On the one hand, there is the mourning face, from melancholy Olga to weeping Dora (on whom, as I saw with my own eyes, death had lain the marble mask of an ancient Greek divinity). This is the dark face that the Andalusian in Picasso would often fall back on. The other face — sun and moon, light and milk — goes from Marie-Thérèse, whom I imagine as rather similar to Paul Morand's Aïno, "a short-haired Eve from before the Fall, without embarrassment or shame, stretching out

---

5 Cited by Pierre Daix in *Picasso créateur : La vie intime et l'œuvre* (Paris: Éditions du Seuil, 1987), p. 52. English ed.: *Picasso: Life and Art* (New York: Icon, 1993)

arms lined like those of swimmers with long slender muscles,"[6] to Françoise. Slipping in and out between these two groups are the fleeting passions, Lee Miller, Nusch already a shade among the shades, Geneviève, and all those whose names we have never known. Each was a world of her own, with its liberties and laws, its rules and surprises. Each was empowered to create a mood, an atmosphere, a climate and ultimately a style.

Style

In the old days, a style meant the proportions of the female body, examined then readjusted, reduced to this or that mathematical arrangement which artists then took as their model. Who, after Panofsky, will ever write that strange story in which the learned artist, the disciple and rival of the physician and geometer, drew up identical proportions for the endless diversity of the body, an ideal anatomy that allowed him to construct a painting—or a temple, a table, a wine glass—that could withstand both the passage of time and that subject of time, desire? From Polyclitus's Canon to the Venuses of Cranach, and on up to the beginning of the 20th century, the history of form was the history of these unusual but regular deformations imposed on the body in the name of abstract beauty.

Picasso exploded this tradition of the *homo bene figuratus*. To hell with symmetry, proportion, eurythmics. And the revolution he brought about—and it really was a revolution—not in the forms themselves but in the way they are organized (in the sense in which we speak of "organized" life) is contemporary with two other revolutions in the history of ideas, one in biology, the other in psychology. Body and soul, in other words.

Briefly, the first decade of the 20th century saw the triumph of the theory of evolution, refuting once and for all that immutability of the species on which the theory of ideal beauty was founded. And the embodiment of that ideal beauty, at the top of the *scala naturae*, was man, the physical appearance of man.

The earliest outline for this perpetual variation of forms, the still uncertain idea that all things are in a permanent state of flux, is probably older. Diderot, whose Eros is remarkably similar in many respects to that of Picasso, had already noticed that "the world is constantly beginning and ending; at any moment it has its beginning and its end: it never had, and never will have, any other."[7] In this perpetually fleeing universe, the only reality that thought can grasp is the possible; the only fixed form the eye can capture, metamorphosis: "All beings move around inside one another, consequently all species… everything is in a state of permanent flux… Every animal is more or less of a man; every mineral is more or less of a plant; every plant is more or less of an animal. There is nothing precise in nature. …What is a being? The sum of a certain number of tendencies… Can I be something other than a tendency? No, I move towards an end."[8]

6   Paul Morand, "La Nuit nordique," *Ouvert la nuit* (Paris, Gallimard, 1957).
7   Denis Diderot, *Le Rêve de d'Alembert* (Paris: Didier, 1951), p. 55–56. (Free translation.)
8   Diderot, p. 69–71. (Free translation.)

He might almost be describing Picasso sitting behind the glass in Clouzot's film, a joyous demiurge forever changing plants into animals, animals into women, in a series of "unnatural" couplings that serve to illustrate a surprising new genesis that is forever starting out afresh. But Diderot embodies an optimistic *Naturphilosophie* founded on a sort of fecundity principle, a universal pansexuality that in its constant mutations tirelessly engenders the billions of children conceived during these couplings.

If we really want to see Picasso, as some of his biographers have done, as an erotomaniac bent on destroying his conquests, it is to Sade we must turn in seeking an echo of Diderot's thoughts. We might put in the painter's mouth the complacent words spoken by the Marquis de Bressac to the appalled Sophie, a foolish incarnation of Mademoiselle de Lespinasse listening to d'Alembert: "As for the destruction of one's fellow man, rest assured, Sophie, that it is purely chimerical. Power to destroy is not granted to man, at the very most he has power to vary forms, but not to annihilate them; and since all forms are equal in the eyes of nature, nothing is lost in the immense crucible in which her variations are performed, each portion of matter thrown therein being constantly renewed in another shape. …What does it matter to eternally creative nature that this mass of flesh which today takes the shape of a woman will tomorrow be reproduced in the form of a thousand different insects?… And if the degree of attachment, or indifference rather, is the same, what difference can it make to her that through what is called one man's crime another be changed into a lettuce or a fly?"[9]

The final sentence ("And if the degree of attachment," etc.) is important, for we can safely assume that in this melting pot of a natural order where nothing is lost and nothing created, in this heaving mass of constantly changing forms, the painter is on the side of life. The thousands of crushed insects Picasso painted to either side of the double doors on the walls of Dora Maar's house were not painted with the same eye that gave us the erotic portraits, painted over the same period, of his mistress.

In the second decade of the 20th century, however, as Darwinism moved into the ascendant and Picasso experimented with his *dolce stil nuovo,* an astonishing book, D'Arcy Wentworth Thompson's *On Growth and Form,* was published. At a time when appearances were breaking up everywhere and the immutability of the species was slowly going down like the *Titanic,* the book put forward a new Pythagorean canon, as it were, a new mathematical framework for what we see. The book came out in 1917. It sought — and Panofsky was the only one to notice its importance — to set out a new theory governing the proportions of life forms, laying the foundations for a morphogenesis governed by geometrical transformations that brought out similarities between related species. It was the first attempt to move beyond confusion and found a new order within the Creation.[10]

9   The Marquis de Sade, *Les Infortunes de la vertu* (Paris: Gallimard, coll. "Bibliothèque de la Pléiade,"1998), Vol. II, p. 35. (Free translation.)
10 D'Arcy Wentworth Thompson, *On Growth and Form,* abridged ed. John Tyler Bonner, pref. Stephen Jay Gould (London: Cambridge University Press, 1992).

Three years earlier, in 1914, Picasso, weary of Cubist experimentation, had returned with *The Painter and His Model* to a more "regular" form of painting, rather hastily labelled a "return to classicism."

Eros, Nomos, Thanatos

In the meantime, just to complicate the picture, another revolution was under way in the realm of the psyche, as I mentioned earlier. In his *Studies on Hysteria*, Freud found himself confronted with the enigma of a patient body that flouts all the normal laws of anatomy. What diagram of the body does the hysteric obey that allows her to violate the laws of anatomy? To what extent does a fit of hysteria, the form usually taken by erotic madness, create a wholly new body that, in displacing its pleasures and emotions, makes a mockery of neurophysiological localizations? The hysteric is literally mad about her body; she pioneers a stupefying malleability of the body organs.[11]

A crisis in representation, theories of the proportions of the human body put to flight—orthopedics had once more ceased to exist, and the pretensions of Lombroso or Richet to found a new Laocoön on science looked utterly Utopian.

Freud, as we know, having originally drawn on Plato and his theory of the energy of Eros (in which the libido is a principle of union, fusion, aggregation) to develop his theory of instincts or drives, was tempted at the end of his life to make these obscure emanations of the psyche, these *Triebe*, a principle of disorganization and disintegration bent on destruction and a return to the organic—in other words, death. This is more like Sade philosophizing on human beings turning into lettuces or flies than the gentle Diderot rejoicing in the boundless profusion of the life-principle present in all natural creatures.

Whichever vision of Eros Picasso subscribed to, it is worth noting that in the years in which his style was being forged any idea that creatures and things were stable entities had been shattered by the advance of the ideas of Darwin and Freud. After them, the canvas became, as I mentioned earlier, a "sum of destructions."

All organized life, as we know, is based on symmetry. In the earthworm as in man, an invisible mirror reproduces on the right-hand side what is found on the left. A bilateral or sagittal symmetry that intersects with a second plane of symmetry in the direction of motion. Every organized life form is a plan, it has a front and a back, a head and a snout; in short, it is going somewhere. Above all, it develops, it grows in segments—or, as biologists would say, "metameres." This is as true of the earthworm with its rings as it is of man with his vertebrae. Let us also note that the more complex the life form is, the more limited and restrictive the symmetry becomes. Organisms that are immobile or of limited mobility, from plants to sea urchins and radiolaria, possess radial symmetry, for example. Further down on the evolutionary ladder, rocks and crystals often possess

11 Jean Clair, "Anatomie de l'âme," *Éloge du visible: Fondements imaginaires de la science* (Paris: Gallimard, 1996), p. 66–67.

symmetries brought about by lateral displacement. In other words, the greater the symmetrical constraint on life, the richer the variety of forms.

Plato, when he imagined two creatures joined together prior to the division of the sexes in the form of a perfect sphere, was applying to the idea of life a radical homeopathics also found in the theory of the Five Bodies. The Platonic Eros, like the Platonic cosmology, is a crystalline dream. Picasso, on the other hand, fiercely homophobic and fiercely bent on the heteronomy of the sexes, shatters the Platonic sphere, changing the smooth, gentle, binding libido of the Platonic Eros, the union of like with like, into a furious libido that nothing can assuage, the impossible union of two permanently different bodies. The gendered being is both a profusion of forms brought about by the constraints of symmetry and the death of the individual in the name of the safeguarding of the species.

The Beautiful and the Ugly

Symmetry is a fact of nature, playing around with symmetry a fact of art. To get round symmetry or avoid the effects of symmetry, to surprise the gaze by shifting accents or upsetting the balance of things is an act of artifice. In the same way that the blind were once thought to have superhuman powers, the lame, the hunch-backed, the unicorn and the narwhal were looked on as freaks of nature. The painter, presumably, sides with this anti-nature, father of monsters.

Yet as we know, the divinities Priapus and Baubo are deformed.[12] *Kakómorphos* (mishapen), *ámorphos* (formless, unattractive), *aiskhrós* (disgracefully ugly) are the terms used of Priapus, son of Aphrodite, the goddess of immeasurable beauty (*Kállos amétrèton*). *Choïros* (little pig, piglet) was the name given by the Ancient Greeks to the vulva. In modern slang it's called "the beard." It is one of those trivial and undignified things, like "hair or mud or dirt," of which Plato speaks in the *Parmenides*. Whether male or female, phallus or vulva, the genitals, having no fixed form or size, no distinct proportions, sometimes too little, sometimes too big, always disproportionate, are beyond measure. By the same token, they are beyond the realm of art. They belong with those *turpia visa* that make you blush with shame. And which stimulate desire.

Picasso plays off desire—disproportionate, *ámorphos, kakómorphos*—against art and the proportions of art. For if symmetry, etymologically speaking, is the right proportions, or just measure (*su metron*), then Picasso certainly goes out of his way to avoid symmetry. To the law of nature he opposes the fantasies of art; to the rule of biological evolution, the "misrule" of desire. Twisted, chopped up, unrecognizable, the body astonishes and surprises us like that day in our teens when we saw a naked body for the first time. It is this initial shock of nudity that the canvas must reproduce: that is the law of man-made art, which is not the same as the creation of the gods.

12   See Maurice Olender, "Priape le mal taillé," in "Corps des Dieux," *Le Temps de la réflexion*, VII (Paris: n.p., 1986) and "Aspects de Baubô," *Revue de l'Histoire des Religions*, Vol. CCII, fasc. 1, Jan.–Mar. 1985.

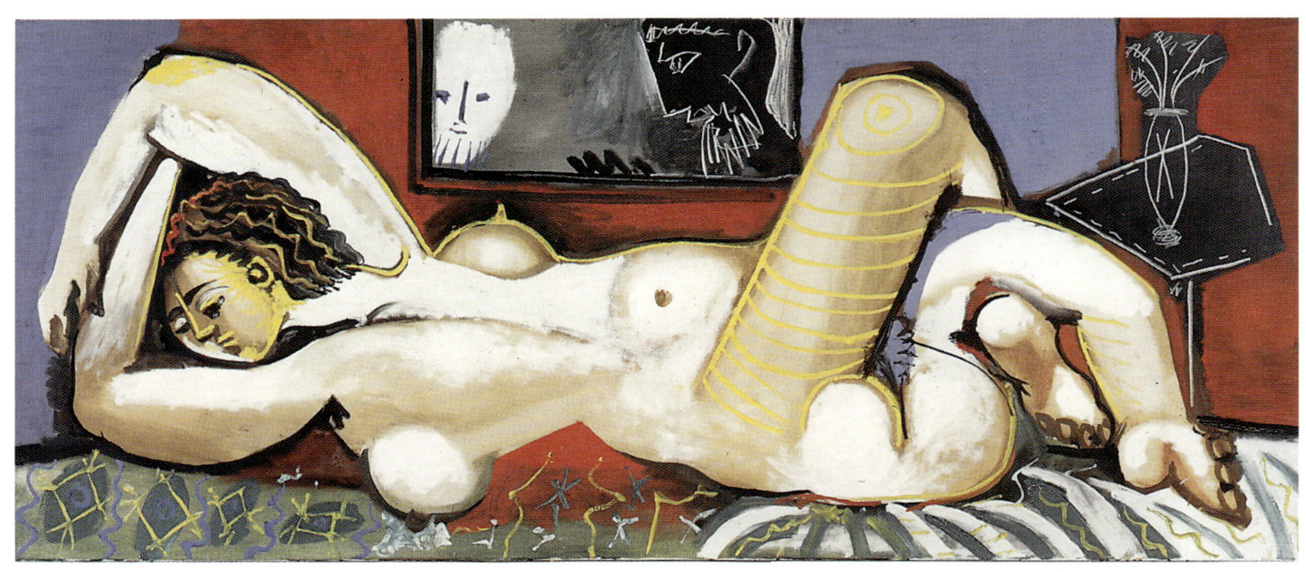

207 Susanna and the Elders, 24 August 1955
Oil on canvas; 80 x 190
Paris, Private collection [P]

The body being what it is, what can we do to ensure it goes on surprising us and holding our attention? Desire and death are closely bound up with one another, like death and fashion (as Leopardi's dialogue tells us). Fashion outmanoeuvres death when it avoids the deadly traps of symmetry. In this respect, the painter is also a fashion designer, a milliner, a corset maker, a draper who, with a stroke of the pencil or some dazzling colour or unexpected harmony, upsets the body's symmetry in the same way that a wrinkle, a crease, an unusual cut in the material disrupts the harmony of a toilette. The form of the skirt, sometimes reaching down around the ankles, sometimes pulled up around the pelvis; the waist, never in the right place, either down around the hips or hiked up under the breasts; the pants, sometimes a kind of petticoat hiding the tops of the thighs, sometimes short and tightly clinging, narrow about the hips or pulled up to the waist so as to draw out the legs, now covering the buttocks, now, on the contrary, a G-string leaving them exposed—these are just a few, brief examples of the ways in which fashion constantly transforms the body.

Fashion is transformation. As long as it "refashions" things, it stops us from seizing up, nodding off, growing bored. And what is true of fashion is also true of painting. It plays around with the natural articulations of the body in order to conjure up new ones. Of a universal object that, apart from the genitals, hardly varies in the relation of the parts to the whole, it makes a collection of partial objects, stitched, stuck or welded together in surprising, often shocking, always disturbing ways.

There is almost no limit to the ways in which these different pieces can be reassembled by the artist. Sometimes he dismantles them, cutting to the quick what the body holds together as one, severing the trunk from the face, disarticulating the ribs, shortening a femur; sometimes, on the contrary, he brings together fragments that anatomy tells apart. These collages and rearrangements are dictated, not by a concern for form, but by desire. It is physical desire, not artistic canons of beauty, which makes him put a face and a profile side by side, allowing him to delight in two incompatible angles of vision, or—still more astonishing— arrange on the same plane what the body separates out on two different sides.

The splendour of *Susanna and the Elders*. While the elders are reduced to little more than silhouettes, one a face, the other a profile, ghostly beings lacking substance and flesh, powerless to embody their desire, Susanna displays her body gorged with water, developing it in all three dimensions at once, rolling from side to side, alluring them with a forcible distortion of the torso and suddenly holding up for inspection her breasts, her belly, her backside, the instep and sole of her feet, her genitals and her anus, all at the same moment.

The star-shaped anus of the final canvases, that marvellous piece of drawing, a star anise, part hyphen, part exclamation mark, summing up in two dark splashes that sexual graffiti which is a constant source of fascination to children and was photographed by Brassaï (and which adults in my youth still scrawled on lavatory doors)—the painter's erotic typography continued toying with these sensual metaphors right up to the last months of his life. It is the union of two bodies, of course, which makes these "joinings" and "cut-ups" so utterly incandescent, improbable, delightful, bewildering, so ever-increasingly unique. "We have succeeded in being the most perfect image of the never-ending/I live in her and she live [sic] in me," wrote Picasso, beside himself with the love he had found in Marie-Thérèse.[13] It's a far cry, indeed, from the ogre… The symbiotic life is not the life of cannibals.

Picasso the deformer, the mutilator, the iconoclast—Picasso the liquidator, as Roger Caillois called him—was arguably the first artist to respect, and to take into account, the ineradicable difference of each human being; each woman, each of the sexes, he would refuse to insert in some overall scheme. In this he showed himself loyal to his country and fiercely patriotic (to compensate, no doubt, for the murder of the father). There are not many nudes in Spanish painting. The ones that are there, however, are extremely striking, like the nude we see for the first and last time in the farewell murmured to a "passing woman." They are desirable because they are vulnerable. From the diversity of human life the Ancients defined a style; on the singularity of human life Picasso founds the diversity of a style. Who can say whether Picasso met Olga because he needed that melancholy, classical ideal he had rediscovered in Italy, or whether it was the other way round, the chance meeting that brought about the change in style? And what does it matter in the end? At eighty years of age he painted an exorbitant gaze peering down into this bottomless pit, moss-like, fleecy, curling about the edges, this precipice where all his life, like Axel in Jules Verne's novel, he had schooled himself in darkness.

13   Bernadac and Piot, p. 374, n. 4. (Free translation.)

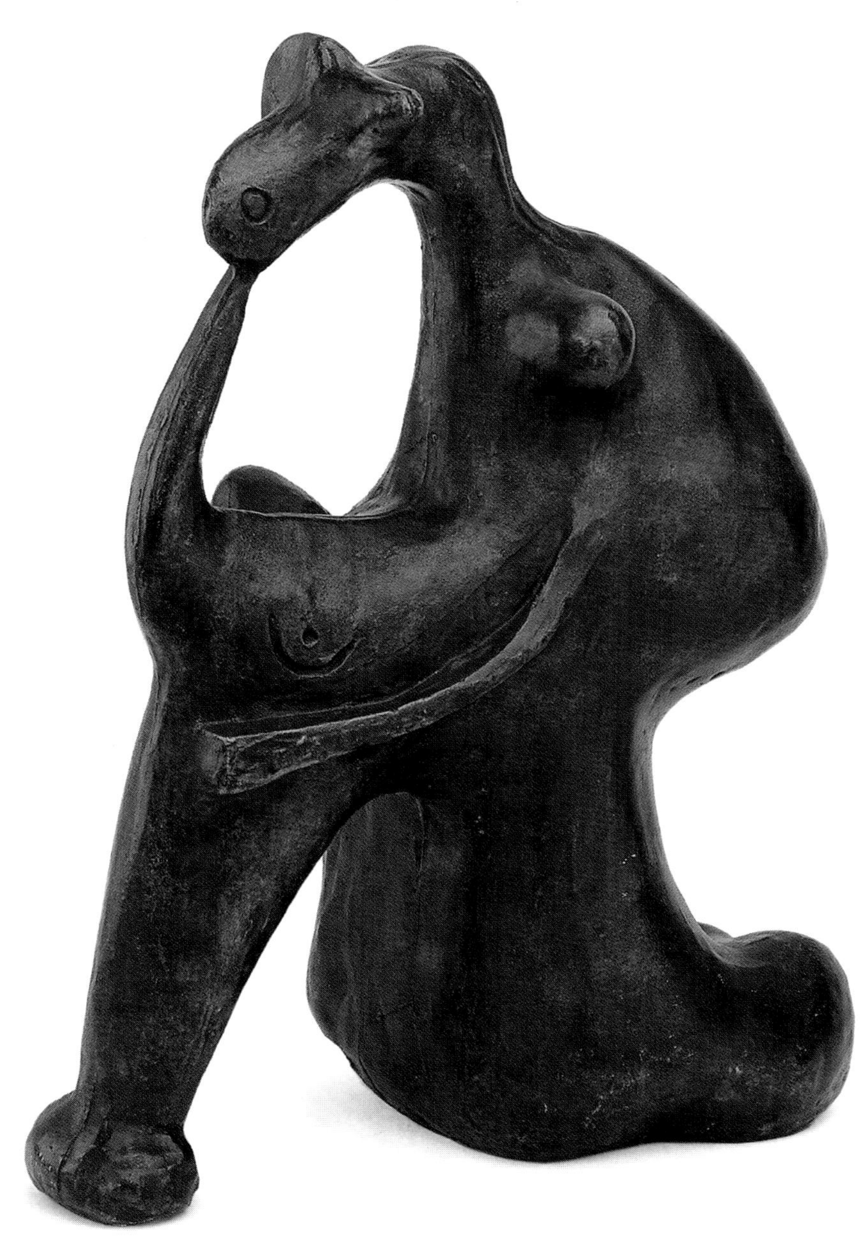

94 Metamorphosis I, 1928
Bronze; 22.8 x 18.3 x 11
Paris, Musée Picasso, MP 261 [MB]

PAINTING
IN THE BEDROOM [1]

Annie Le Brun

No sooner do we discover myriad new stars in the Milky Way than it becomes enriched with countless secret shimmerings. Although nothing there may have actually changed, our discovery changes everything.

Putting Picasso's erotic work into perspective is a phenomenon of the same order. It reveals, above and beyond his obvious interest in things erotic, that he was obsessed with these to such a degree that they appeared to coincide for him—from the beginning of his career through to the very end—with the enigma of representation. As if, more so with him than with any other person and perhaps like never before, the invention of form had to do essentially with the arousal of desire.

Still, however exceptional Picasso may have been, it could be said that his concern with the representation of amorous play is precisely the point at which he shows affinities with many other painters. I want to speak now of that studio tradition in which the nude escaped the pose to become nature in the raw, a convulsive nature (when it did not slip into humour or caricature). Our initial impulse might be to draw a line from this tradition to the first erotic works of Picasso, who derived as much pleasure from drawing his girlfriends as he did from sketching the boarders of Barcelona brothels, either alone or with their clients, who were often his own friends—that is, when he wasn't in the picture himself. To do this, however, we would have to pass over the twenty or so *Embraces* he executed between 1899 and 1907 in the form of drawings, pastels or watercolours. And we would certainly not be paying attention to the extraordinary variety, not of styles but of approaches ranging from the lyrical to the caricatural, and from realism to expressionism, that Picasso drew upon at the time, as if impelled by the need to thwart, by all and any means, a traditional disregard for the erotic. And this despite the continual flowering of those amorous images—the wild grasses or somewhat sombre copses—that line the royal ways of plastic expression running from Callot to Baldung Grien, Michelangelo to Rembrandt, Fragonard to Fuseli, Rodin to Klimt, and from Maillol to Schiele—not to mention the spectacular *Private Notebooks* of Ingres, who from his early youth had busied himself with carving out that space which he would, at eighty-two, crown with the triumph of voluptuousness known as *Le Bain turc*.

---

1 I would like to thank Dominique Dupuis-Labbé and Hélène Seckel who, in their separate ways,
   facilitated access to the world of Picasso.

Side by side with an often anonymous body of work that has become increasingly specialized in the suggestive evocation of amorous play are centuries of disagreement over what must be contextualized and framed, even if this means it must sometimes surreptitiously intrude on some mythological, historical or religious pretext. Thus it is with Dürer's *Temptation of Saint Anthony*, Aldegrever's *Anabaptist Bath* and Raimondi's *Nymphs and Satyrs*, which perpetuate the equivocal representation of the seven deadly sins, ostensibly for the viewer's edification. And one could also adduce the *Last Judgment* by Michelango who, in depicting the sin of sodomy, sprinkles the ceiling of the Sistine Chapel with the nude bodies of his lovers.

Little by little, however, a strange turbulence began to take over the margins, even if the margin tended more and more toward marginality in every sense of the word. For was it not as illustrations of clandestine texts that erotic representation became a genre unlike any other, one where Romain, Raphael and Titian, for example, found themselves in the service of Aretino? Equally marginal were the contributions made by Watteau, Boucher and Fragonard to the sexual education of young kings, before social criticism led to the resurgence, on the margins of the city, of images and attitudes that the latter reproved.

So much so that it was in the greatest secrecy that Courbet's *Origin of the World* (1866) maintained its place at the heart of painting: to contemplate it one had to (as we read in Edmond de Goncourt's *Journal* entry for 29 June 1899) "unlock a painting whose outer panel showed a village church in snow, and whose hidden [inner] panel was the one that Courbet did for Khalil Bey, which showed a woman's groin with a black and pronounced mound of Venus over a slightly parted pink cunt."

Which still leads us to wonder, more than a century later, what could have made possible this exhibition, which was so secretive and remained so, at least as far as the general public was concerned, until recent years. As for me, I am too much of a believer in hidden passageways not to be persuaded that *The Origin of the World* would have remained permanently buried under snow if, three years earlier, in 1863, the visible part of the abyss—by that I mean the nude stripped of all religious, mythical or historical alibis—had not, thanks to Manet, surfaced twice to refocus the landscape (both inner and outer with, respectively, *Olympia* and *Luncheon on the Grass*) on the scandal of light made flesh.

Nudity, with all its dazzle, had deployed its power of hypnosis to evoke yet hide the great darkness of sexuality, which it covertly restored to its place at the heart of representation. And this is undoubtedly what accounts for the considerable air of scandal surrounding these two paintings by Manet, which together inaugurated the uniquely violent struggle that apparently ensued between erotic representation and what gives rise to it. Indeed this is one of the key issues underlying modernity and its continual fluctuation between the lyrical and the mechanical. Should one represent the object of desire, or desire revealing itself through its representations? Picasso seems to me to have outstripped all others in the intensity with which he sought to answer the question of what it is that makes us dream, love or die—a question that extends, and internalizes, the famous one posed by Gauguin: "Who are we, where do we come from, where are we going?"

Hence it is odd that, while critics eventually did not have any great difficulty appreciating, for example, Duchamp's reflections on the overlapping mechanisms of desire and representation, there seems to have been the greatest reluctance to recognize a similar merit in the work of Picasso. A Picasso crazy about painting was obviously fine, as was a Picasso in love with love; but on the subject of what it is that, above and beyond the clichés, brings these two activities together in the depths of existence and feeds their common flame to produce mighty explosions, prolonged tremors—nothing but silence. It is true, of course, that Picasso strenuously refrained from giving explanations or information on his working procedures, unlike Duchamp, who did so with such irony in his notes on *The Bride Stripped Bare by Her Bachelors, Even*. But the almost tragic tenacity with which Picasso returned to the subject of the erotic in the last ten years of his life has led (if not obliged) critics on both sides of the fence to reconsider his life and work in this light. And if they have willingly complied, they have too often done so in accordance with psychological, psychoanalytical and aesthetic considerations that are not particularly illuminating, particularly now that the erotic has become a category of aesthetics.

There was, of course, *Les Demoiselles d'Avignon*. We must be grateful to Hélène Seckel for the exhibition she devoted to it in 1982,[2] and for which she assembled, as so many proofs, the mass of drawings and preliminary notebooks that supported the non-formalist interpretation of the painting made by Leo Steinberg in the 1960s and further developed by William Rubin. According to this interpretation, *Les Demoiselles d'Avignon* is first and foremost a depiction of a scene in a brothel and, as such, this image represents a major upheaval in the history of representation.

I need only refer to these critics' highly pertinent analyses, although I am inclined to shore them up somewhat more by pointing to a certain conjunction of dates which, to my knowledge, has strangely enough been neglected. For 1907, the year in which Picasso put the finishing touches on this tumultuous composition, was also the year in which Guillaume Apollinaire's astounding erotic novel *Les Onze Mille Verges* appeared anonymously. In this novel, the imagination is swept up in sexual violence that still has the power to shock whoever takes the time to read it, and does not see it (as has too often been suggested) as a fantasy written for pecuniary reasons.

In this regard, it may very well be that the painting and the book were suppressed in a like manner, which consisted in not acknowledging the revelation of a sexual fury that they both unwittingly showed to exist at the heart of all representation, be it in poetry or painting.

---

2 See *Les Demoiselles d'Avignon* (Paris: Réunion des musées nationaux/Musée Picasso, 1982).

Hence, that intolerable quality which accounts for the modernity of both, and about which everything may already have been said—in connection, at least, with *Les Demoiselles d'Avignon*; for critics have failed to see that curious pendant to the painting which we have in *Les Onze Mille Verges*, that "novel of modern love" (as it is described in advertising copy discovered by Louis Perceau, and in all likelihood revised and corrected by Apollinaire himself, which stresses the "barely believable boldness" of this novel where "scenes of pederasty, sapphism, necrophilia, scatomania and bestiality are combined in the most harmonious manner"[3]). A harmony whose origin (which is chaotic, to say the least) calls to mind the troubling coherence that undergirds *Les Demoiselles d'Avignon*.

It is not that I want to place Picasso's painting and Apollinaire's book on the same level, since the impact of the latter does not even begin to approach that of the former. But it is impossible to disregard the fact that Picasso repeatedly stated that, in his view, *Les Onze Mille Verges* was Apollinaire's masterpiece. This is attested to in the preface written anonymously for the 1930 edition by Louis Aragon, who takes this opportunity to highlight the unique contribution of Picasso's irreplaceable friend: "What constitutes Apollinaire's greatness is undoubtedly this curiosity, which often took the admirable form of the image, and to such an extent that one could say that his poetry is, first and foremost, a curiosity about the unknowable. And that his greatest curiosity was reserved for the world of morals."[4]

We also know that Apollinaire unfailingly shared this curiosity of his, ensuring that his friends had access to erotic literature, which he was the first to defend and publish (between 1908 and 1913, in the *Maîtres de l'amour* series). Whether we are talking about Sade, Baffo, Nerciat or Aretino, to Apollinaire belongs the incomparable merit of having taken them out of the shadows where some people had tried to forget them without even suspecting what they were losing in the process. And we must also concede Aragon's perspicacity when in the same anonymous preface he writes: "Such a clear awareness of the links between poetry and sexuality, which is the awareness of a profaner and a prophet—this is what places Apollinaire at that singular moment in history when the age-old pretences of rhyme and insanity brutally break apart."[5]

This is the person to whom Picasso gave or sent some fifteen drawings, sketches and erotic caricatures between 1905 and 1907, not to mention the marvellous love scene of 1905 that he dedicated to "my dear friend Guillaume Apollinaire." And how indeed could he not feel an affinity with this "profaner" who also dwelled in that sensitive depth in which both came to a recognition of the central fire contained in the amorous embrace?

3   Quoted by Michel Décaudin in his introduction to *Les Onze Mille Verges* in Guillaume Apollinaire, *Œuvres en prose complètes* (Paris: Gallimard, coll. "Bibliothèque de la Pléiade," 1977–1993), Vol. 3, n. 1319. (Free translation.) English ed.: *Les Onze Mille Verges or The Amorous Adventures of Prince Mony Vibescu*, trans. N. Rootes (New York: Taplinger Publishing Company, 1979).
4   Décaudin, p. 1319. (Free translation.)
5   Décaudin, p. 1320. (Free translation.)

From this perspective, *Philosophical Brothel*, the first title of *Les Demoiselles d'Avignon*[6]—given, perhaps, by Apollinaire (which is likely since he, of all Picasso's friends including Max Jacob and André Salmon, surely had the best knowledge of Sade's work)—introduced a very important reference to Sade's *Philosophy in the Bedroom*.

For this reference would tend to confirm (as the preliminary drawings suggest) Picasso's successive distancings from the various evocations—realistic, anecdotal, symbolic, allegorical—of the brothel. And this to the extent that it sheds light on the eventual disappearance of the two male figures, the medical student and sailor, that Picasso included in his initial plans for the painting, at a time when he found that he was no longer satisfied with that purely female atmosphere which he had surely appreciated in Toulouse-Lautrec's *Salon on the Rue des Moulins*. (The artist painted it in 1894 but could only show it in private.) Picasso's erotic drawings and sketches from Barcelona and his first years in Paris are ample evidence that he had grasped the sensual attraction of this atmosphere heavy with objectless desire, in which carnal promiscuity and erotic vacancy operate within an intermediary time that suspends, as if in a dream, the immediate utility of actions and attitudes.

That Picasso's extraordinary eye gradually came to discern in this a sort of sexual stupor, one that converts to a staggering power capable of usurping all and any representations (previously, only the boldness of Sade had revealed anything comparable, but in a context well beyond the image)—this is the terrible discovery attested by *Les Demoiselles d'Avignon*, as we can see from a perusal of the preliminary drawings. In this respect, the elimination of the student and the sailor is of the greatest significance. For, however emblematic of the brothel the client's presence may be, both consumer and observer are condemned to assume the role of bothersome witnesses, should they venture into the depths of this sexual theatre, more and more persuaded (as was Picasso—and this in the course of two years spent in proximity to Apollinaire) that something else entirely is going on.

Something else entirely that, in 1958, would prompt Picasso to move heaven and earth in order to acquire seven monotypes by Degas,[7] something he had been unable to do fifty years earlier. Something else entirely that, purely and simply, turned perspective inside out and made Degas' famous dancers, for example, into caricatures of the brothel denizens to whom the artist paid the finest and most ferocious tribute in his monotypes. Whether they are at *The Proprietress's Party*, *At Rest*, *On the Bed*, *In the Salon* or *Waiting*, their presence is an organic proof that overturns everything, to the point of intruding upon every female representation.

6 According to André Salmon in *La Jeune Peinture française* (Paris: Société des Trente/Albert Messein, 1912), and later in *Propos d'atelier* (Paris: G. Crès et Cie, 1922); see also Leo Steinberg, "The Philosophical Brothel, Part I," *Art News* 71, No. 5 (Sept. 1972).
7 On this subject, see Seckel, *Picasso collectionneur* (Paris: Réunion des musées nationaux, 1998), p. 111–21.

In this connection, commentators have not failed to point to a female animality that Degas was fond of painting, in the light of what he said about women at their *toilette*: "I show them stripped of coquettishness, in the condition of animals cleaning themselves."[8] Although the comparison rings true, it in no way accounts for the sexual gravity that Degas' genius forces us to feel deep within ourselves. I should speak more, perhaps, about the pent-up *sexual charge* that takes representation far away from all aesthetic considerations—as if it were no longer a question of representing, but of going beyond the forces that act upon us, however terrifying they may be.

That Degas arrived at this point within the secrecy of this preserve does not unburden his official work, which became the mask of what obsessed him. And this is exactly what Picasso put all his energy into avoiding during the development of *Les Demoiselles d'Avignon*. For to make the sexual charge appear, he had to eliminate all witnesses as well as all traces of a form of representation for which this brothel gradually became the place of execution.

A brothel, then, that was no more philosophical than the one where Sade brought about the unprecedented revolution of putting philosophy *into* the bedroom, while the most freethinking of his contemporaries were concerned merely with putting the bedroom into philosophy. Thus one could say that Picasso, impelled by the need to protect representation from the instinctive violence from which it normally draws its sustenance (yet in the process neutralizes this violence), does nothing but *put painting into the bedroom*. With the important consequence that the bedroom or brothel, both of which had remained on the margins of Western aesthetics, were instituted as the centre threatening all representation, like a new mental space where forms take on meaning. A totally different meaning, of course. That which Courbet, Manet and Degas had anticipated, and which Gauguin had won and lost in his solitude, Picasso threw in the world's face with the rosy obscurity of *Les Demoiselles d'Avignon*.

One immediately understands why Picasso would have said, "Negro art? I know nothing about it!"[9]—especially when one keeps in mind the shock he claimed to have experienced during his first visit to the Trocadéro museum: "The masks weren't just like any other pieces of sculpture. Not at all. They were magic things.... If we give spirits a form, we become independent. Spirits, the unconscious (people still weren't talking about that very much), emotion—they're all the same thing. I understood why I was a painter. All alone in that awful museum, with masks, dolls made by the redskins, dusty manikins. *Les Demoiselles d'Avignon* must have come to me that very day, but not at all because of the forms: because it was my first exorcism-painting—yes absolutely!"[10]

One also sees more easily the full depth of the bond between Picasso and Apollinaire, who was *at one and the same time* the "inventor" of the *Maîtres de*

---

8   According to Georges Janniot, *La Revue universelle* (15 Oct. 1933). (Free translation.)

9   In response to an enquiry published by *Action* (1920); quoted in Seckel, *Les Demoiselles d'Avignon*, Vol. 2, p. 632, n. 1. (Free translation.)

10 André Malraux, *Picasso's Mask* trans. June Guicharnaud and Jacques Guicharnaud (New York: Holt, Rinehart and Winston, 1976), p. 10–11.

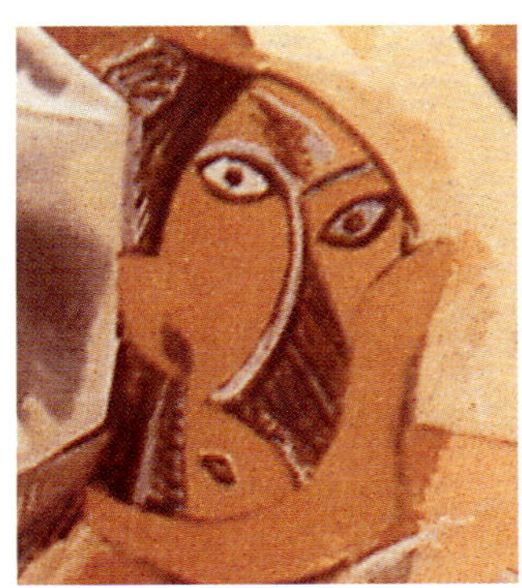

Fig. 1: *Les Demoiselles d'Avignon*
(detail), 1907
Oil on canvas; 244 x 234
New York, The Museum of Modern Art

l'amour series and "primitive" art (fascinated as he was by the latter's comparable power over us). I would even go so far as to claim that Picasso and Apollinaire owe their respective statures as artists mainly to their shared conviction that only this rapprochement between erotic imagination and the "primitive" could give rise to that which now continues to dispel the lie of aesthetics. Each knew intuitively that, in the secrecy of love as in that of initiation, one has to give shape to the enigma before one can dare to confront it.

Knowing this, one is even more struck by the series of drawings that Picasso executed on trade cards between 1901 and 1903. In these drawings, which appear to hold a middle ground somewhere between dreams and caricature, Picasso creates an extraordinary *mise en abyme*[11] involving an amorous figure framed by the sex organs of a young woman opening her vagina, in the depths of which one just might discern the gaze of the same young woman opening her vagina, in the depths of which… And one is struck not only because Picasso rediscovers here the immemorial figure of the personified vulva, which Georges Devereux analysed in relation to *Baubo*, the Etruscan Gorgon,[12] but, also and especially, because this *mise en abyme* of a woman's vulva (titled, moreover, *Vaginal Environment*) determines in a way both premonitory and metaphorical the space of what would become *Les Demoiselles d'Avignon*, once erotic representation was restored to the place from which it emerged and where it would endlessly reappear.

It is in this light that we must consider the extraordinary profusion of erotic scenes (in all genres) that Picasso collected between 1903 and 1907, and with such success that they, in their extreme concentration, imploded in his mind to create the violent space of *Les Demoiselles d'Avignon*. Thus when Leo Steinberg rightly states that the brothel reverts to the jungle[13] in this painting, we must be careful not to see in it a recovered savagery that comes to a sudden end in a formal brand of primitivism. If there is a jungle, it is the one in which five naked women (each in her own irremediably ferocious manner and in a display that is, paradoxically, obscene because—although nothing obscene is actually shown—one cannot help thinking of the kind of displays that brothel dwellers put on to show their various specialties) constitute an affront to all conventional representations of nudity. The fact that they do not relate to each other in any way, that each appears within her prison of solitude, supports the sense one has of the solidity and rigidity of this new space, which is constructed less from planes than from blocks of aggressive impulse directed at the viewer.

So we are quite far from those celebrated "viewers" who, for Duchamp, "make the painting" what it is. Because what we have here is a dazed and stupefied nakedness that looks out at us from the canvas. What is more, it is these women who, side by side and one after the other, challenge the viewer to withstand the gaze directed at them.

11 Translator's note: Originally a term in heraldry designating a shape within a shield that reproduces in miniature the shape of the shield itself. By extension, any such device in painting or drawing.
12 Georges Devereux, *Baubô, la vulve mythique* (Paris: Jean-Cyrille Godefroy, 1983).
13 Steinberg, "Le Bordel philosophique," Seckel, *Les Demoiselles d'Avignon*, Vol. 2, p. 332, n. 2.

The second consequence of the revolution undertaken by Picasso is this: that henceforth it would be the sexual drive that would determine representation (and would do so as much through its extreme peculiarities as through its innocent violence). In this connection I would stress the disarming innocence which the often disparaged face mask (in the far right side of the painting) acquires close up, as if it were the finest of adornments. And I would even go so far as to ask whether people have been so preoccupied with the perceived formal discrepancies or even inconsistencies—which some believe to have greatly harmed the unity of these "demoiselles"—that they cannot see that, from one figure to the next, these very "inconsistencies" release, as if by osmosis, those principles of condensation, reversibility and interchangeability that Hans Bellmer would reveal a half century later (in his *Anatomy of the Image*) as characteristic of an untiring desire that reinvents the image of the body. (After having discovered them himself, of course, with his series of *Poupées* [dolls], his "articulated minors.")

While Bellmer was intent on bringing out the extraordinary resources of these same principles, endlessly tilling the "lyrical fields" of erotic representation, Picasso seems to have made a firm decision to make these the principles underlying the revolution of the image that he himself had instituted. In fact this might explain his almost total abandonment, from 1907 onward, of conventional erotic subjects (lascivious positions, brothel scenes) in favour of embraces, which, while unceasingly refusing to disclose their secret, increasingly became a recurrent theme in a body of work that seemed to let nothing stand in its way.

It is hardly the least of paradoxes that, in an approach carried along by an eagerness to always find oneself different, one always comes up against the enigma of eroticism. "Legs spread around the middle of the secret number,"[14] wrote Picasso on 12 April 1936, a time when, in the throes of an artistic and personal crisis, he had stopped painting. There is something touching about his lifelong perusal of the entire spectrum of love, running from the most tender embrace to rape, from kisses to violation and from caresses to bacchanalia. And, moreover, to see him using every approach, going back over all styles in a quest so essential that it seems to determine the violence of a relationship to creatures and things in which curiosity vies with insatiability.

Thus it becomes difficult not to think of the *super male*, that extraordinary hero of the 1902 novel by Alfred Jarry, who set himself the task of reinventing love by both calling it into question and putting it to the question. And it certainly no accident that Picasso was keen on having Hermann-Paul's portrait of Jarry in his collection. "One can imagine the importance he attached to owning a portrait of one of the authors who was essential to him, both in his youth and throughout his lifetime," says Hélène Seckel, adding that, "from his time in Paris, Picasso would be marked by Jarry's iconoclasm, and acquired a thorough knowledge of his work through the literary circles he frequented."[15] All this to suggest,

---

14 Marie-Laure Bernadac and Christine Piot, *Picasso: Écrits* (Paris: Réunion des musées nationaux/ Gallimard, 1989), p. 119. English ed.: *Picasso: Collected Writings* (New York: Abbeville Press, 1989).
15 Seckel, p. 140, n. 7. (Free translation.)

finally, that *Les Demoiselles d'Avignon* of 1907 owed much to someone who would never see it.

How could one not be struck by the resemblance between this portrait of Jarry (executed between 1901 and 1903) and the self-portrait that Picasso painted in 1903 and gave to Apollinaire? The hair and moustache are the same, but more importantly there is that same gaze of darkness and solitude that enable each of them to plunge into the night of eroticism where they had to confront a sexual criminality that lay at the very origin of desire.

Finally, one need only recall the dazzlingly provocative and accurate opening sentence of Jarry's novel ("Love is an act of no importance since one can perform it endlessly") to recognize what may be a key to Picasso's behaviour and reiterative manner. For with these he did not set out to exhaust this or that woman, form or idea, but—quite the contrary—to conquer not only the prey they represented but also the shadow of what they were yet to become. And let us not again hear the retort that we are dealing with an approach with affinities to the kind of formalism exhibited by Gertrude Stein and her "A rose is a rose is a rose." Indeed, Picasso does just the opposite, urging the colour rose to become more rose than rose when, on 11 January 1936, he writes: *"si le rose pâle colore sa rose du plus rose pâle encore et le rose rosit de rose en un rose plus rose encore du rose rose rosissant son rose rose rose rose dans le plus rose le rose qui s'enflamme à la soif de boire l'or qui saupoudre son rose enflammé au feu de l'or qui brûle ses joues ardant de son rose incandescent que l'or fondu au rouge blanc brûle."*[16]

Indeed it is here that he finds the principle of excess in desire, which constantly reawakens from its own gratification in order to probe the horizon, though it be from the edge of the abyss—even if, in this matter, Picasso did not often let go of his link with reality.

The fact is that by putting painting into the bedroom with *Les Demoiselles d'Avignon*, Picasso turned perspective inside out. But if he succeeded brilliantly in making the point that the studio blends into the brothel, he was not afraid to subsequently add the *corrida*, the mythological scene, so as to bring in the public. One could at this point ask whether something is not lost because of distance, a distance that Sade and Jarry made irremediable in relation to the world as it is. We know that, with Picasso, things did not turn out the same way. Perhaps the reason for this lies in an admission he made on 18 April 1935. "I can no longer stand this miracle that is knowing nothing in this world and having learned nothing but how to love things and eat them alive."[17]

It is in this equally splendid and tragic light that we must consider the theatre he has left us, this drama of an unprecedented unmasking in which women, forms and life itself are stripped bare, not by their "bachelors" but by their lover, who could just as well be not only the one who will devour them but also their murderer.

Still, something of major importance was at work—and continues to operate—in the space between the two vistas that Picasso and Duchamp opened up at

16 Bernadac and Piot, p. 88, n. 13.
17 Bernadac and Piot, p. 9, n. 13.

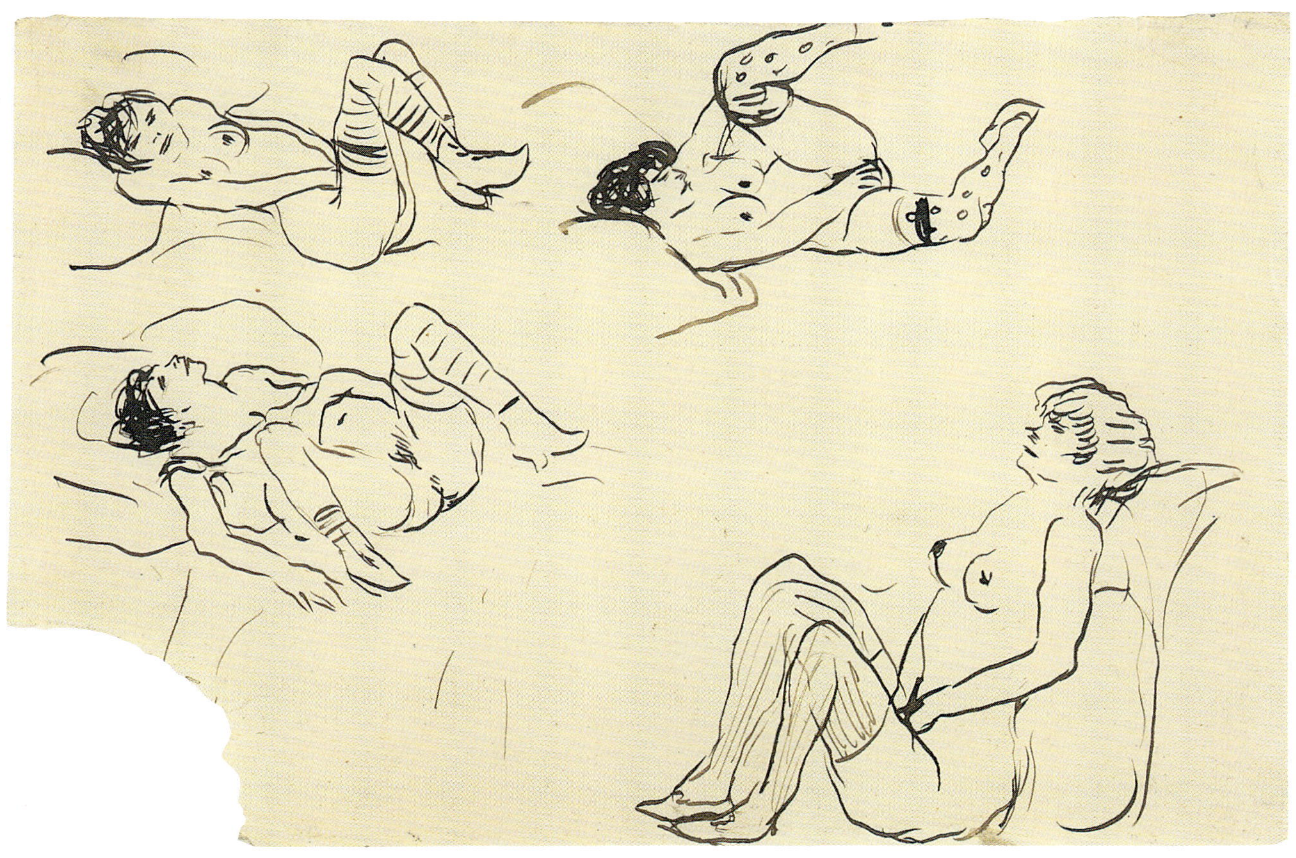

23 Women with Striped Socks, 1902
India ink on paper; 20 x 31
Paris, Private collection

the start of the 20th century, so that we might see there the unlikely encounter of our ways of loving and thinking. While Duchamp obliges us to remain quite literally behind the door of *Étant donnés…* (a work exhibited posthumously), bringing us face to face with a sexual shock that he worked his whole life to dodge if not deny (which gives one pause), it is apparently a happier circumstance that Picasso spent *his* last years bringing together his friends (and certainly not the least among them, but Rembrandt, Manet, Ingres, Degas, etc.) in order to show everyone the stuff they were made of, that shared erotic passion that consumed them and in the light of which people began to see. This is no small feat and should in fact be accepted as a final gift, like the "carnal love at night with its gloves of laughter" that Picasso announced on 6 December 1935.

A question of temperament, one might say—to avoid having a curtain come down on one of the liveliest perspectives of the 20th century. But on the condition that we do not forget this confidence of Picasso: "Love does not yet exist. Later people will find something about this in what I have written and in what people call my poems." Even if we are not done with finding something about this in what people call his painting.

HEADSTRONG IMAGES

Pascal Quignard

A singular force arises from within us, constraining us, in turn, to act, desire and dream. This stubborn force is sexual, antitemporal. It seeks to reproduce and succeeds in bringing back the same figures again and again. Something irrepressible shapes and colours our destiny, giving rise to the most heartrending occasions and abruptly transfiguring places. This is a destiny that is not owing to us. The singularity in us is not our own doing.

In 1819 the Brothers Grimm published a tale entitled *The Stubborn Child*. It goes like this:

> Once upon a time there was a stubborn child who never did what his mother told him to do. The dear Lord, therefore, did not look kindly upon him and let him become sick. No doctor could cure him and in a short time he lay on his deathbed. After he was lowered into his grave and was covered up with earth, one of his little arms suddenly emerged and reached up into the air. They pushed it back down and covered the earth with fresh earth, but that did not help. The little arm kept popping out. So the child's mother had to go to the grave herself and smack the little arm with a switch. After she had done that, the arm withdrew, and then, for the first time, the child had peace beneath the earth.[1]

Nothing is more heady than sexual difference. The signs in which it ponders itself precede the letters we learn to write. So it is that, behind everything that is made with letters, difference continues to haunt us—sexuation beneath language. Myths, tales, legends, proverbs, commandments, missals, codes and history books all attempt to bury nature under language, to stamp down the animal under the human, the child under the adult. He who still holds fast to the frontier of silence must speak forthwith.

Yet he continues to keep silent.

Yet the arm of the stubborn child continues to rise up even after his death.

Like Gongsun Long during the Warring States period, looking only at the pointing finger and not at what it was pointing at.

---

1 *The Complete Fairy Tales of the Brothers Grimm,* trans. Jack Zipes (New York: Bantam Books, 1992), p. 422.

Like Picasso, keeping his gaze fixed on open female genitalia, endlessly deforming the formless.

Obstinacy pushes forward.

Like the bull against the red cloth.

The gaze came to an abrupt stop when it fell upon the two Babylonian elders. In the tree's shade, under their eyes, Susanna grasps that other cloth halfway between a blouse and a veil, and slowly lifts it up to enter the water. It is midday. She uncovers her groin, origin of men and not of the world, and slides it into the lapping water.

One of the two elders goes so far as to open the garden gate and cries out with all his might in Babel, calling down a verdict of adultery.

A raised finger. An arm rising up. A groin low-crouched in the shade of a tree.

Only the child Daniel will know if this tree is an aspen.

Or if it is an acacia.

An intractable force constrains us to reimmerse ourselves in a more ancient condition. *The Stubborn Child* by the Brothers Grimm is taken from Hans Sachs's 1522 ballad *The Dead Boy of Ingolstadt*.

> A boy from Ingolstadt hit his mother and died. He was buried. But the hand that had hit his mother emerged, straight as a whip, from the earth. And when they reburied the hand, it popped back up.
>
> The mother had to hit the hand of her child until it was completely covered in blood.
>
> When his hand was drenched in red, the child drew it back into the earth and buried it in it his grave.[2]

Be it the version of the Brothers Grimm, or that of Hans Sachs, death is not capable of putting an end to stubbornness.

There is a stubbornness stronger than death.

Sexuality goes beyond death. It reproduces the dead sexually. Their figuration goes beyond death via the mystery of the *spitting image*.

There is a figuration stronger than divine aniconicism.

There is a figuration stronger than the abstraction of language.

A figuration stronger than every event that must be interpreted in order to be experienced.

An inadmissible, sullying, veracious, verifying, inflexible figuration stripped of meaning. A figuration more peremptory than any commandment of velation or invisibility.

One cannot but think: it is sexual desire and not the human will that keeps art inside figuration.

It may be that pornography alone is non-decorative.

2 Free translation.

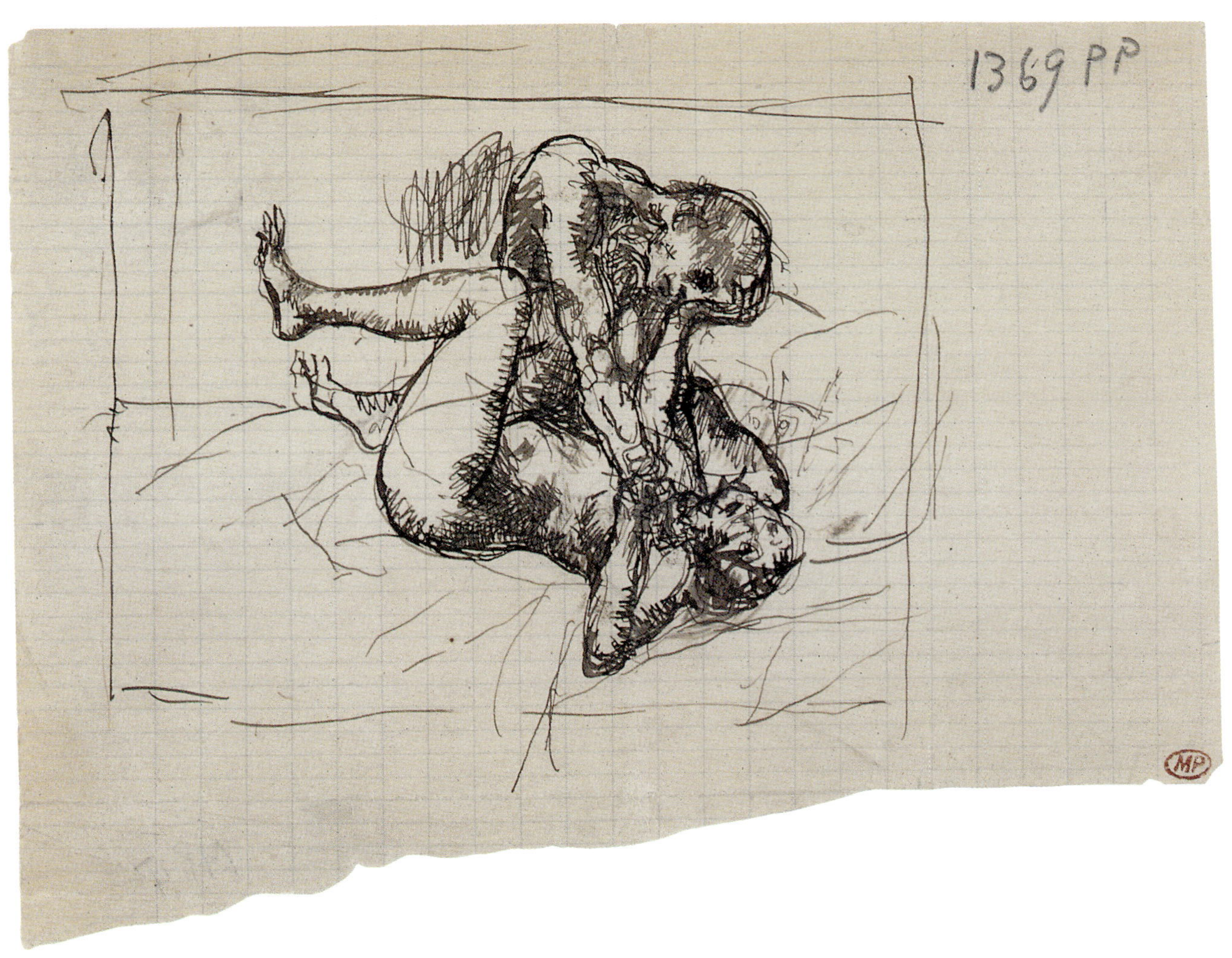

42 The Woman Strangled, circa 1904

Pen and brown ink on quadrille paper; 16 x 21
Paris, Musée Picasso, MP 462

Cannot be contemplated.

Is contagious.

The child who, living or dead, never obeys, is also *the only one who remains faithful to the sexual desire that produced him.*

Whichever version we turn to, *The Stubborn Child* or *The Dead Boy of Ingolstadt*, the tale is a true marvel: in the duel between mother and child, a duel that takes place in total silence since it involves a child who does not yet possess language, the child loses (dies) but also wins. Because from the other side of death he continues to raise his hand (Sachs) or arm (the Brothers Grimm). He does not compromise. He cries out forever in his silence.

An endless duel.

An endless duel between what was wild and what can never be tamed, contained in the stupefying brevity of a tale that forswears all dialogue and that does not amount to ten full lines. This—the unending sexual duel—is what appears continually in the works of Picasso. And this is why figuration never withdraws from these works, regardless of what the painter may wish or want; because in figuration three other figurations overlap, pile up on top of one another in layers of earth, stone and rods (the magic wand and the switch used to discipline the child). A threefold figuration that precedes humanity.

That goes to its head in dreams. That haunts it in reproduction. That kills it in fascination.

What does the strongheaded child have in mind? The scene that bodies him forth, the primal scene, is also the figurative scene. The invisible scene is in the process of embodying those whom it brings together in that which they ignore even though they reproduce.

There are rebellious images, images that are not only refractory to all discourse, that no amount of breeding could tame, but that rise up from below humanity. Which, all of sudden, in the course of the events that make up its history, encounters them yet does not recognize them.

Images that not only do not die but that kill.

In this respect the version of the Brothers Grimm is more radical than that of Sachs, which is merely symmetrical (the hand of the mother which hits the hand that hit the mother). This raised arm is akin to the gesture of giving the finger. No, it implies, I will not respect prohibitions, be they maternal, social or divine. The sex in me will be stronger than the mother who gives orders rod in hand, stronger than the language she claims to teach, and stronger than prohibitions, morality or even death.

And in the struggle against death, it dies.

There exists *an irresistible figuration to which life can abandon itself unto the point of death.*

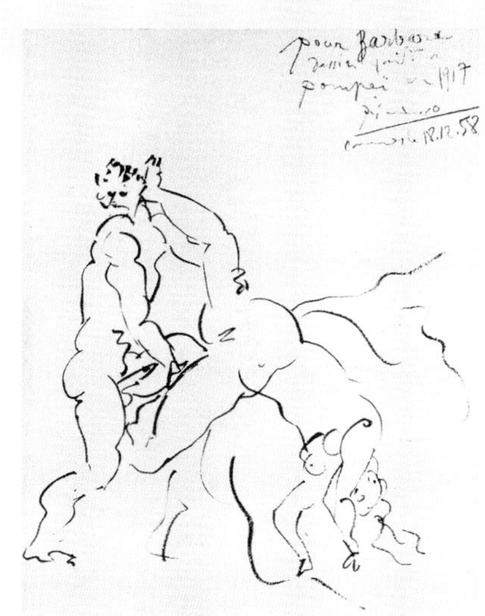

Fig. 1: *Erotic Drawing*, 1917
Ink on paper; 26.5 x 20
Private collection

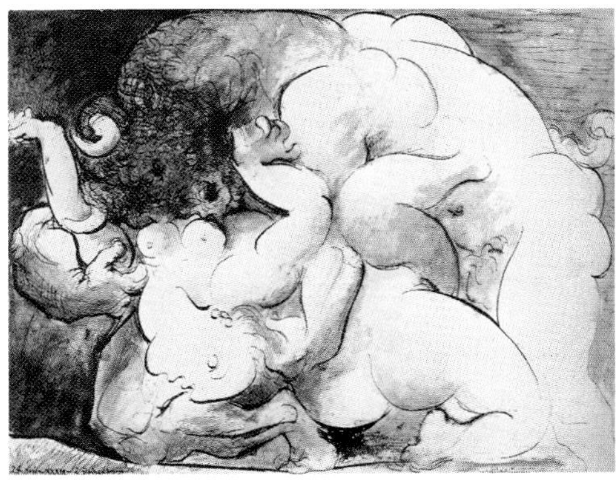

Fig. 2: *Minotaur and Woman*, 24 June 1933
Pencil and ink on blue paper; 48 x 62.8
Chicago, The Art Institute of Chicago, Gift of Margaret Blake

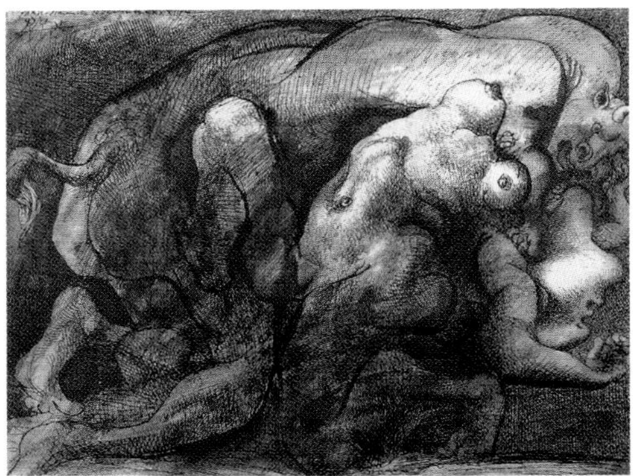

Fig. 3: *Bull and Woman*, 10 December 1933
India ink on paper; 36 x 49.5
Zurich, Private collection,
Courtesy Galerie Thomas Ammann Fine Art

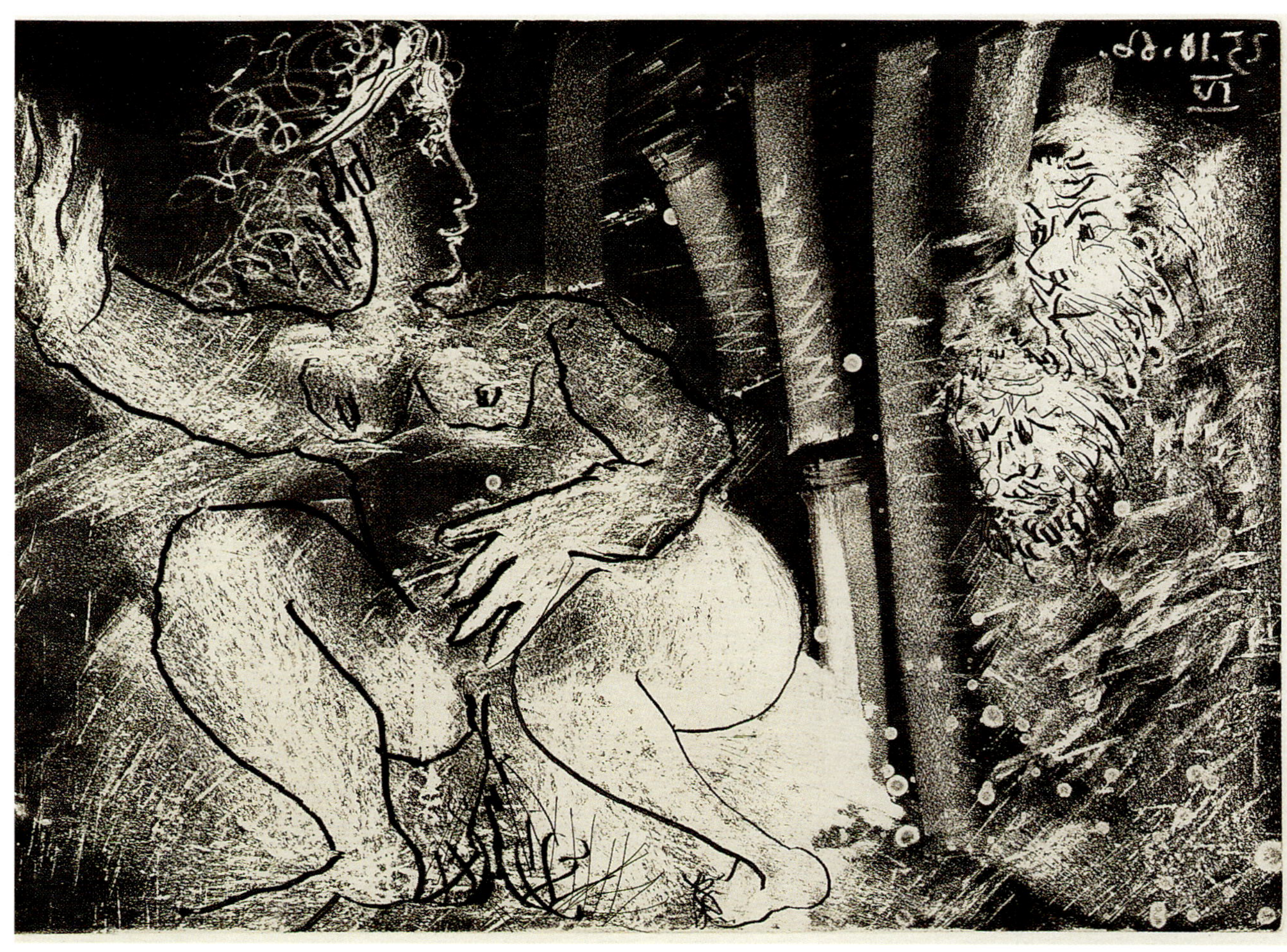

228 Woman Pissing Surprised by Two Old Men, 25 October 1966
Aquatint and etching on copper; 27.2 x 37.6
Paris, Bibliothèque nationale de France, Département des Estampes et de la Photographie [P]
Paris, Private collection* [M]
Barcelona, Museu Picasso, MPB 70.510 [B]

In the animal world forms devour other forms.

We call this fascination. The object of this is a piece that fits snugly into the face watching it and devours itself there. It is an automanduction of the large form comprised of the two petrified animal forms that observe one another in the fright of their mutual lying in wait.

The fascinating face swallows up the fascinated one in the same way that the paramecium devours itself in the paramecium next to it.

It devours itself in the same way as it subdivides.

What is the origin of the word "fascination"? The Romans used *fascinus* to designate the erect penis and *fascinatio* for the irresistible movement of the eyes ordained by its exposure—a movement extending, too, to the petrifying and erectile metamorphosis it undergoes as a result of fright.

What is fright? To be frightened is to remain nailed to the spot. A figure nailed to the spot in the *irrégrédient in exactly the same way as a picture nailed to a wall.*

There is, in German, a magnificent word for stubbornness: *Eigensinn*. A fixed sign, like an *idée fixe*, with a single, strict, rigid and fanatical meaning. *Eigenhändig*: something that is "by one's own hand." A sign made by the hand of the cadaver of the dead boy from Ingolstadt. An autographic and authentic sign. Heidegger derives *das Ereignis* from *Eigen*. Picasso wished to produce *authentic signs*.

But the French word for stubbornness, *entêtement*, is extraordinary in itself. (The first attestation for the earlier *entestement*, a written form, dates back to 1642.) It says that there is something inside the head (*tête*) that is not swept away by the acquisition of language. That there is, within the skull, a force stronger, more stubborn and heady than conscience (which is nothing more than that half-maternal, half-collective inner voice that is suddenly triggered like a tape loop around the age of seven, and that comes to accompany all one's actions).

Something external to language has somehow remained stuck inside the head and cannot be dislodged.

There is, inside the head, a rebellious head that is older, stubborn and voiceless.

This head, in the state of pure rebellion, produces dreams.

Oneiric hallucinations, which have developed among numerous animal species, are more virulent that all of the paintings ever made by human hands.

There is an involuntary figuration more violent than all decoration, aesthetics, styles or periods. An uneducable, uncivilized and uncultured figuration that enables us to respond to the oldest images as well as to morphologies that precede our own.

There is an irremediable and incurable form of pornography that has no specific boundaries and for which the billions who have died over many millennia pose no obstacle; in which comprehension is already understood; and which

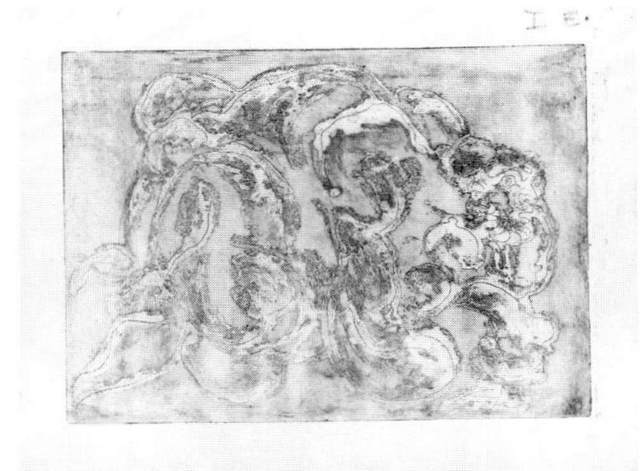

Fig. 4: *Couple Making Love*, 2 November 1933
Etching, scraper and drypoint on copper;
State I; 19.8 x 27.9
Paris, Musée Picasso, MP 2552

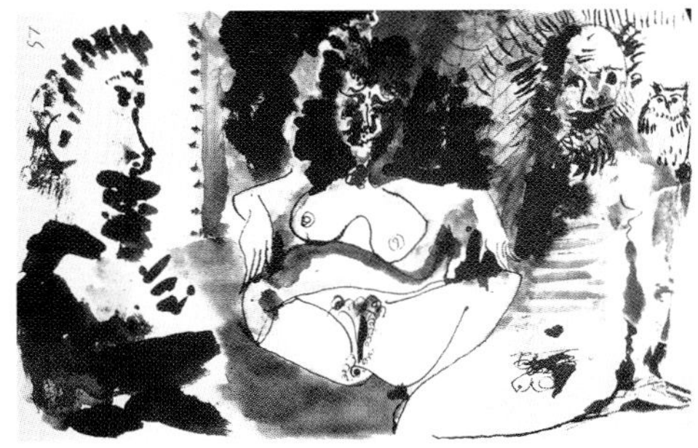

Fig. 5: *Suzanne Flanked by Two Old Men
in Joachim's Garden*, 1972
India ink wash on paper; 22.5 x 35.5
Private collection

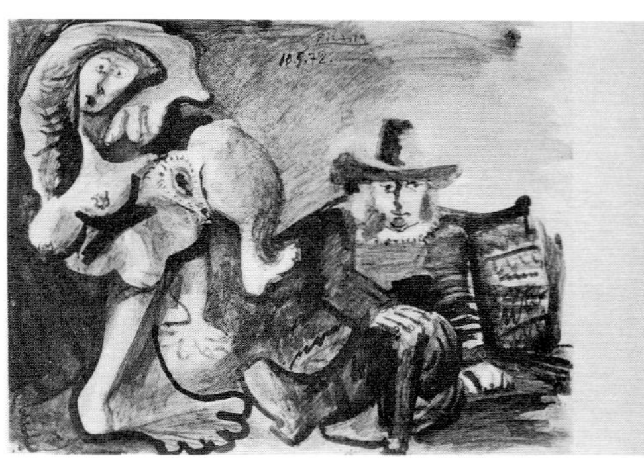

Fig. 6: *Seated Musketeer and Dancing Nude,* 18 May 1972
India ink wash on paper; 59.8 x 77
Private collection

is immediate, in other words, wholly impervious to contemplation because it is immediately efficient. There is no clear difference between figuration or reflection, images, shadow, flesh.

An erection accompanied by involuntary images persists stubbornly in dreams. Each time that "bygone days" return, an animal drives the human Eros, which becomes fascinated and rears its head. Bygone days, as untractable as the incorrigible child. A figuration that resumes its full dimensions in our heads as soon as night falls. Inaccessible to maternal language, to the laws of culture, to the Voice that, once God, comes to dominate. Impervious to light. Uneducable. It can be found equally in the heart of the jungle and in cities, on mountaintops, in the Bible, in the 21st century. It is as present in women as it was in the bulls of Crete. As frequent in the musketeers of King Louis XIII as in the elders of Babylon.

It is found as much in the cat as in the bird who spies its death in the cat's gaze and its end in the cat's leap.

It is prior to all the images ever painted since the glaciers withdrew from the caves and stripped their walls bare.

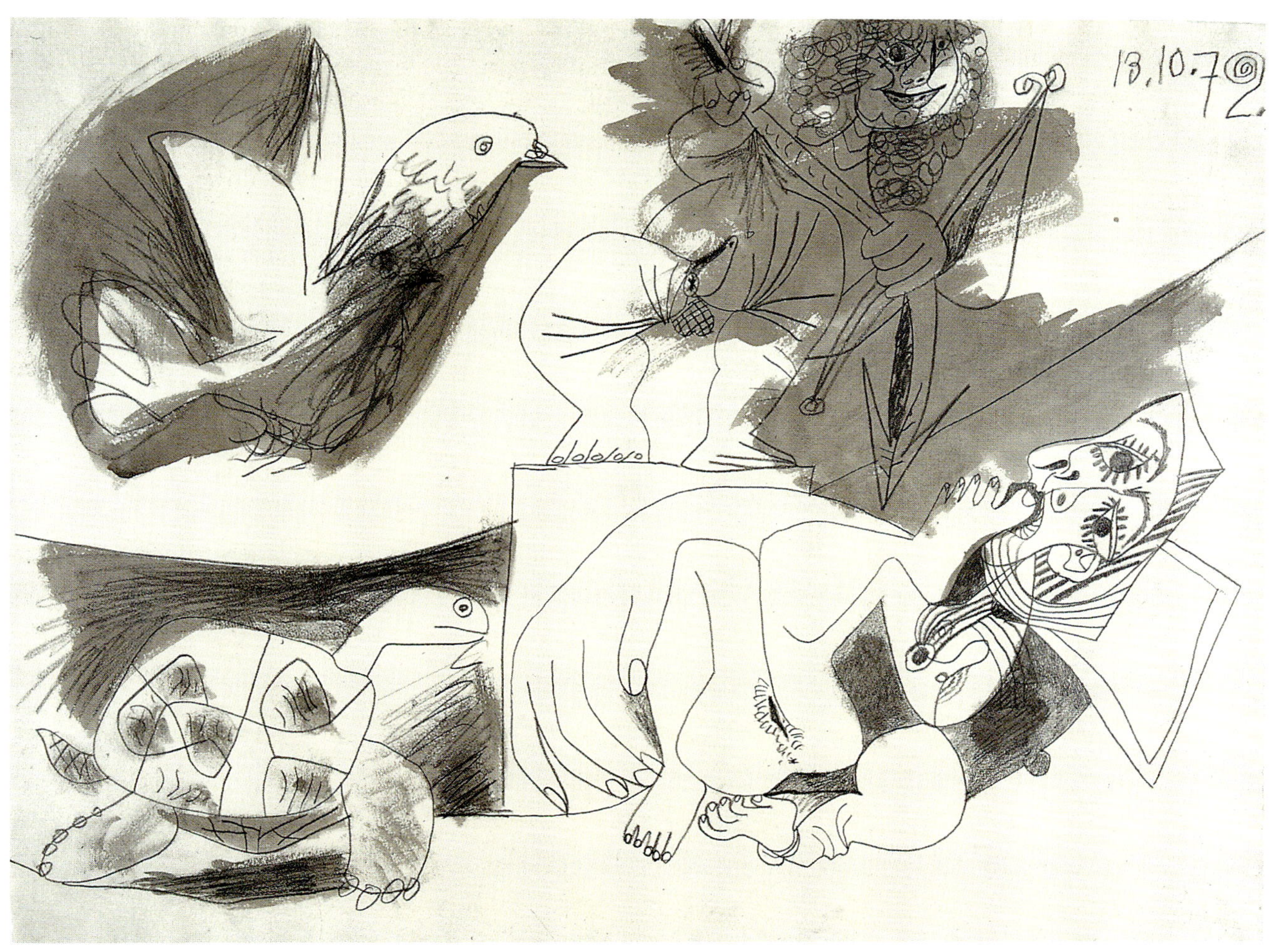

336 Dove, Cupid, Tortoise and Reclining Nude, 13 October 1972

Pencil, black crayon and India ink wash on paper; 57 x 77.5
Paris, Musée Picasso, MP 1541

PICASSO'S (EROTIC) GAZE

Jean-Jacques Lebel

"New peeps through old holes"   Georg Christoph Lichtenberg[1]

No comment necessary as to the archetypal invariance of "old holes"—which are certainly archaic yet still always desiring, at least in painting; but what exactly did Lichtenberg, philosopher of Enlightenment if ever there was one, mean by "new peeps"?

This is one of the main questions to be raised and, if possible, clarified by the *Picasso érotique* exhibition—an exhibition designed (why hide it?) to put an end to inevitable sidesteps and ideological/religious prohibitions that have lasted far too long. The event will provide an opportunity for connoisseurs, even more so than for specialists (who are too often blinded by their university degrees), to interrogate the drives that led the co-inventor of Cubism to modify and renew ways of looking (i.e., peeping) in the way that Lichtenberg meant.

In these times it is, perhaps, worth remembering that the history of art is not and should not be simply the history of the art market, nor even the history of conflicts that have continually pitted artists (be they rebellious or obliging) against the institutional superego. The history of art is also—and, let us hope, especially—the history of ways of looking.

To date, very little attention has been paid to the typology of gazes in the work of Picasso, who, along with Duchamp, was one of the prime discoverers of what first came to light in the 20th century—I mean its *jamais vu*. And Picasso was also a master of the eternal return to the *déjà vu*. In both directions, the path of the gaze describes a large spiral that returns exactly (or almost exactly) to its point of departure—just like a Möbius strip. Picasso's gaze followed a few basic patterns of obscenity which will outlast and outshine the dulling effect of the hundreds of exhibitions devoted to his work throughout the world each year. One wonders whether their ultimate and unstated goal is to make us sick of Picasso's work, and thereby continue to conceal and deny the existence of the most subversive elements of his hyperprolific career. What if the so-called Xsara Picasso —that obnoxious gadget produced and marketed by the carmaker Citroën, which kidnaps Picasso's trademark signature—were also intended to block the road to freewheeling desiring machines much less enslaved to merchandising?

Picasso himself was so perversely ambivalent in this regard that advertising industry pundits, reasoning in terms of market share, would almost be justified

---

1   Georg Christoph Lichtenberg, *Aphorismes,* pref. André Breton (Paris: Jean-Jacques Pauvert, 1980). (Free translation.)

in affirming that there is ultimately no solution of continuity between the Xsara Picasso and the artist's infamous homage to Stalin, published with the artist's full consent (in *Les Lettres françaises*) on the dictator's death in 1953. The goods may change, but the marketing tactic is the same.

Strategies of politics, art marketing and desire… How does one interpret the gaze that Picasso directs at Stalin (of whose nameless crimes he was undoubtedly aware)—as it appears, for instance, in a period photograph of the artist standing in front of an Italian Communist Party poster showing the mask-like features of the Soviet czar? What is the difference between this gaze—unfathomably and cynically ambiguous—and the way Picasso looked at the bodies of female models, or at the landscapes, still-lifes and skulls (*vanitas*) that appear throughout his work? And what of the gaze he brought to bear on the works of artists he admired yet often set out to pull apart? It is plain to see that the creative force of his erotic gaze intensified considerably from 1966 on—when he was over 85 years old and was drawing ever closer to the oldest of all "black holes"? "The eye was in the grave, fixed upon Cain," wrote Victor Hugo. What if, for Picasso, the grave in question was none other than the *Origin of the World* (as painted by Courbet) and its end?

Without prying into Picasso's private life—although the "star system" he so expertly indulged in depends on a steady supply of more-or-less accurate personal details—we must ask ourselves why, at such a ripe old age and with an ardour reminiscent of his whoring Barcelona days, he embarked on several series of paintings, drawings and etchings that are now considered erotic masterpieces. What we are dealing with here is, if not an enigma, then at least a key question that undoes rationalization and forces it to abandon its pseudoscientific platitudes. Whether historiography is favourable or hostile to the artist, it will not get away with its few facile pronouncements on the lechery of an old man forced to sublimate his libido (even if he does sometimes appear to invite such equivocal interpretations).

A case in point is the very laconic, and at the same time very symptomatic, view expressed concerning an exhibition held at the Jan Krugier gallery in Geneva in June 1996: "All of Picasso's work is bathed in an eroticism that appears to intensify with age. The artist is often present in these representations, as a voyeur, through the theme of the painter and his model, or in a series inspired by Degas and dedicated to brothels. As Picasso himself confirmed: 'Age forces us to give up smoking, but the desire remains. It is the same thing with making love.'"[2]

This perfunctory paragraph does not, strictly speaking, tell any untruths; moreover, it could be applied to other great artists such as Titian or Duchamp. However, in refusing to see what is blatantly obvious in Picasso's erotic work, the commentary is a perfect example of institutionalized evasiveness.

Although Picasso was sporadically fascinated by the erotic throughout almost all his life, the two periods in which he most intensely, systematically and

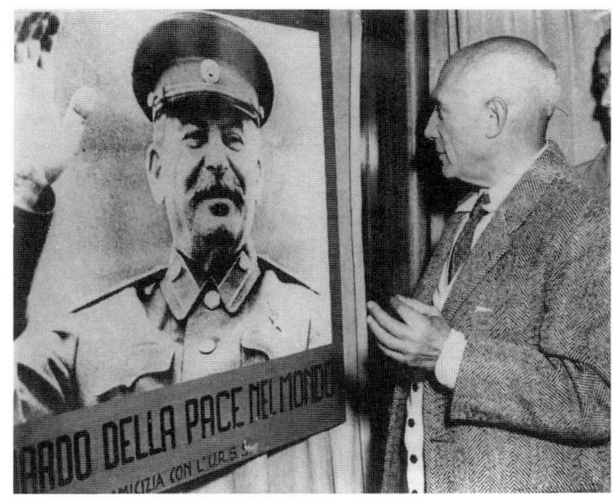

Fig. 1: Picasso face to face with a portrait of Stalin, 1951
Press photograph

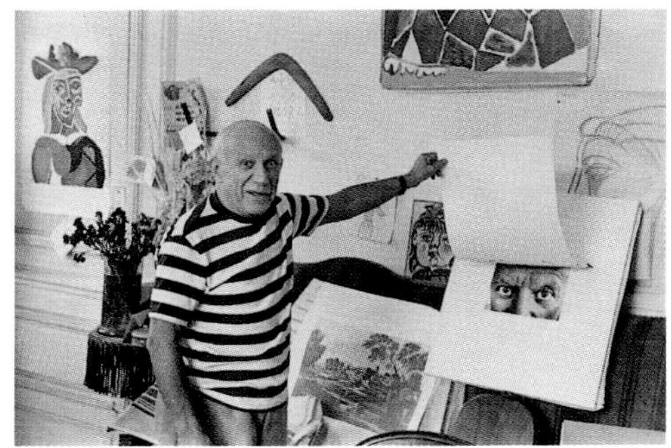
Fig. 2: Picasso unveils his own gaze, 1957
Photograph: René Burri

2 *Beaux-Arts magazine,* No. 146 (1996). (Free translation.)

explicitly devoted himself to such themes were at the beginning of his life (1901 to 1908) and at the end (1966 to 1972). The works from these periods reveal a wide variety of framing, viewing angles and staging techniques, as well as a return to certain recurrent, indelible images: the continual confrontation with Courbet's *Origin of the World*, the intrusive witness, scatology, the delegation of power, the penetrating gaze, the "scopic" vagina. We will return to these later.

Visitors who are invited into the intimacy of these series are given an enormous range of viewing roles to choose from. As always, Duchamp's *mirroric returns* win the day; nothing is decided ahead of time.

In *La Monnaie vivante*,[3] arguably the best 20th-century treatise on erotic theatricality, Pierre Klossowski defines the rule to which Picasso passionately subscribed, albeit late in the game: "In the impulsive perspective, producer and consumer become one."

But before becoming one, they examine and size each other up; they are reflected in each other's gaze. The erotic offering is primarily visual and, in Picasso's work from 1966 on, it reaches an almost inimitable level of exuberance. Amorous display in the visual arts was certainly not new to Europe, but never before had the sexual organs and other *bijoux de famille* (anatomical treasures) of both genders been paraded so openly, exhaustively and methodically. The innumerable drawings and etchings as well as the few paintings from this period seem to teleologically grant the erotic wishes voiced by Giorgio Baffo in his five sonnets titled *Ad un pittor*. Baffo, who was Casanova's role model and who was considered by Guillaume Apollinaire (chief rediscoverer and translator of his works) to be "the greatest libertine poet of all time," commissioned an imaginary painter to produce a series of obscene compositions, daringly crude down to the slightest detail. He dreamed of creating an ideal museum dedicated to Eros—a dream that Picasso, two centuries later, appears to have shared.

We must come back to the anticipatory vision of poets like Apollinaire who initiated both Picasso and Duchamp—another point they held in common—to the notion of hallucinatory perception. How can or could the fantasies of the desiring subject and the spectacles of the desired object (really and truly played on the Other Stage of the unconscious) be combined in images? How could the operations of the mental gaze of each party be visually portrayed? These themes of reflection and pictorial development date back to the beginning of creative expression in prehistoric times, and apparently continue to operate in every contemporary art form worthy of the name.

Picasso and Duchamp approached the materialization of the mental gaze, which is present at the heart of the image, in a very different yet fairly complementary manner. In *The Large Glass* and *Étant donnés...*, Duchamp constructed highly complex optical and conceptual/intellectual devices for "optician-eyewitnesses" (*témoins oculistes*). Picasso, on the other hand, preferred to broach the

---

3 Pierre Klossowski, *La Monnaie vivante* (Paris: Joël Losfeld, 1994).

problem with the more traditional techniques of the painter, and we must view his erotic works—even the most outrageous—in this context, because they are firmly entrenched in the cultural movement that, from the first European religious paintings to the pagan and philosophical revival of the Renaissance, considered art to be an instrument of pleasure and food for thought, not a commodity. While most of Picasso's visual plots are more rudimentary and less sophisticated than Duchamp's installations, they are no less thought-out or significant.

Let us briefly examine the way in which religious painting, from the very beginning, coded visual manifestations of the love tie—that is, as rays of golden light, as a sort of "sundust," like beams of daylight streaming through the stained-glass windows of a cathedral. This was the device used to portray the passionate ties joining the eyes of the devout to the heart of the Holy Spirit and vice versa. In the *Très Riches Heures du Duc de Berry* (Chantilly, Musée Condé) the miniature of Paradise shows God, duly haloed with light, glaring at the naked bodies of Adam and Eve, who have presumably just committed the Original Sin. A beam of seven rays connects the stare of the superego to the "dirty" sinful organs that have incurred His wrath.

The judgmental eye of religious sentiment gradually gave way to the mind's eye, but the pictorial procedure remained the same. The Louvre has an excellent example of a pagan rendition of sublime erotic love expressed through the same rays of golden light used by religious painters. The subject of the work is the Hellenistic cult of Venus, but it is composed and executed as if it were an altarpiece. Painted on wood in the 15th century and attributed to an Italian artist known as the Master of the Prise de Tarente, the work is titled *The Triumph of Venus Vener- ated by Six Legendary Lovers*. It is a dodecagonal panel serving as a tray of fruits and sweets for a new mother (similar panels were attributed to Masaccio, Benozzo Gozzoli and countless other Renaissance artists). The six lovers in attendance are Achilles, Tristan, Lancelot of the Lake, Samson, Paris and Troilus.

Venus holds court in the centre of the sky (the position occupied by the Virgin in Catholic mythology), and is flanked by two strange cherub youths with birds' feet. Completely naked, she stands in her womb-like mandorla, opening its sides—in the same way that some of Picasso's or Bellmer's female figures hold open their vaginal lips. Her serene face emits sparkling rays, at once defensive and expansive. Kneeling in the grass at her feet, in a *garden of love*, her six paramours fixedly gaze at the same spot: the *mons Veneris* of…Venus. The artist has portrayed erotic desire mingled with philosophic ardour, almost religious in its ritualized representation, by using the famous rays of golden light, all of which converge on the goddess's sex.

The nudity, or quasi-nudity, of Christ clearly does not have the same meaning as that of Venus. The love he inspires, in painting at least, is of another order. All the same, a number of scenes showing adoration, fervour and flagellation would fit quite well in contexts less chaste than churches or museums. Take, for instance, *Christ after the Flagellation Contemplated by the Christian Soul* by

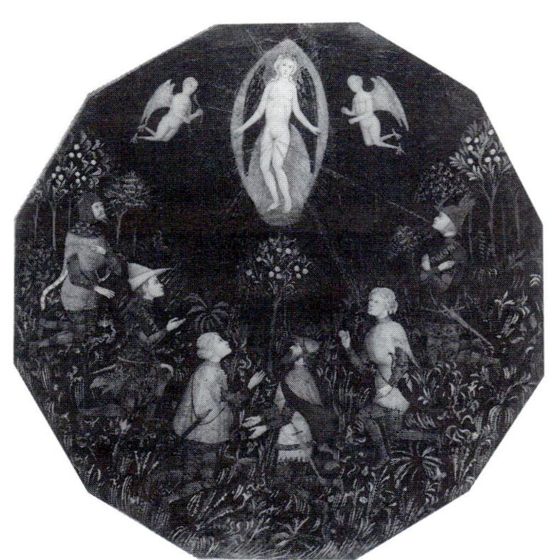

Fig. 3: Master of the Prise de Tarente
*The Triumph of Venus Venerated
by Six Legendary Lovers*, first half 15th C.
Oil on dodecagonal panel; diam. 51
Paris, Musée du Louvre

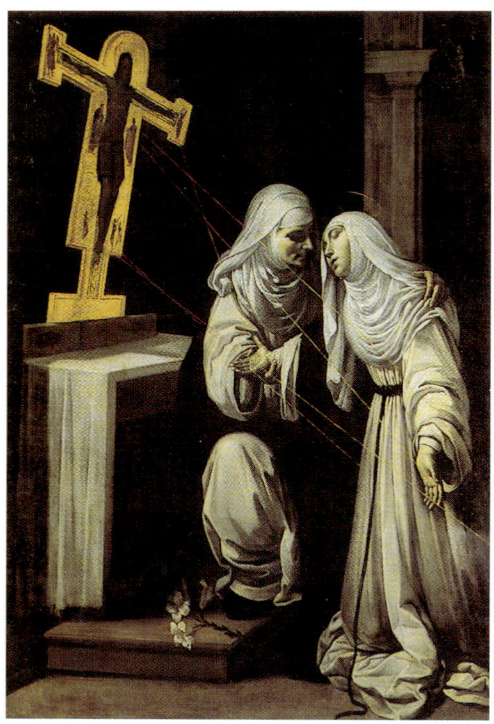

Fig. 4: Rutilio Manetti
The Stigmatization of Saint Catherine of Siena, circa 1630
Oil on canvas; 150 x 119.5
Private collection

Velázquez (London, National Gallery), which shows a flash of recognition between the young boy kneeling in prayer and the wounded expression of Christ, who is attached to a column with his torturers' instruments displayed before him. A very thin thread of golden light—so fine that it probably escapes the notice of most visitors to the museum—represents what, for want of a better name, we could call the mental gaze of the child as he contemplates Christ and internalizes His suffering.

A similar mystical fusion occurs in *The Stigmatization of Saint Catherine of Siena* by Rutilio Manetti, a contemporary of Velázquez who was equally meticulous in his portrayal of the Passion. Christ, on an altar cross against a golden Sienese background, leans toward the saint who, swooning in ecstasy, is held up by another nun. Rays of light, at first blood-red and then golden, pass from the wounded hands and feet of the crucified Christ figure to pierce the palms of the ecstatic.

Surprising as it may seem, the themes in this painting, or in those of Velázquez and the Master of the Prise de Tarente, are not far different from the themes out of which some of Picasso's figures evolve. The visual means he uses to depict their ecstasy, suffering and ways of beholding are likewise similar. Prayer and desire are often rooted in the same passions.

A number of 20th-century artists have revived this visual convention to portray the desiring gaze. Take, for instance, Paul Klee's *The Eye of Eros*, an emblematic drawing in which the male's sensual attraction to the female body is depicted by three pairs of straight lines projected from his lustful bulging eye to the tips of the breasts and the buttocks of the reclining woman who, naked but for shoes, seems to be revelling in the attention.

In a similar vein, Picasso produced an etching, dated 9 April 1971 (Cat. 304), showing a complex cluster of shapes in which three tangled naked female bodies can be made out, as well as three faces, perhaps three times the same face, which could indicate three successive stages of the same theme. One of the bodies is turned toward us, the viewers, and two hands with painted fingernails are shown carefully opening the lips of a figurative vagina. Also facing the viewer is her highly detailed anus, beside hairy genitals and between two widely opened thighs. To add an additional layer of complexity, the observer in the piece is called Degas, and the erotic landscape—a brothel reminiscent of Madame Tellier's establishment made famous by Maupassant—is much more explicit than in other works.

This image, at once clear and enigmatic, deserves closer attention. Once again the erotic display is aimed at us, the external viewers, and not at the spectator in the work itself. Degas' gaze, represented by four straight lines, falls into the void behind the three tangled women's bodies. Although framed in the same composition and context (that of the brothel), the three women and Degas have no visual or, *a fortiori*, erotic contact with each other. It is a non-love story.

In another etching (number IV, 26 June 1968), also situated in a brothel setting (that of *La Celestina*), Picasso artfully uses the same pictorial strategy to portray desiring gazes, but in a different way with very different intentions. The background reveals a dark, unpleasant, mercantile presence—none other than Celestina, the crafty, conniving madam or *dueña*, that eternal pivotal figure who derives advantage—and surplus gratification—from her skilful manipulations of other people's bodies. On the wall is an effigy of the bearded man (either a hanging portrait or an apparition in the window) who, from the first series of Barcelona drawings, commonly appears in Picasso's work. The man's face is ravaged and anguished. Does he reflect something of the artist's compulsions?

The *Tragicomedy of Calisto and Melibea*, the original title of Fernando Rojas's play *La Celestina*, is a dramatic exploration of the classic brothel *ménage à trois* (client/prostitute/madam) that Picasso transposes in different ways, permutating roles and changing the course of gazes and desires, as in the *Raphael and La Fornarina* series. Here, things are more clear-cut.

In the foreground, the handsome hidalgo reappears, this time directly entering the bedroom of the professional seductress on his elegant steed. His face (under a wide-brimmed black hat) and his bearing recall the courtiers and courtesans of Góngora or Velázquez. He pulls on the reins, causing his horse to raise its right hoof to salute the beautiful woman, who is completely naked except for her shoes. We have already seen her hundreds of times in Picasso's paintings, drawings and etchings. Calm and serene, she lies on the bed against a large pillow, arms crossed above her head. Her thighs are opened wide, inviting the horseman—and us—to admire the sexual display intended for his and our eyes. This is an exceptional instance in Picasso's work, where we are privy to an exchange of desiring gazes. Each figure consents to the other's desire: the visual rays establish direct ties between them—between the cavalier's eyes and the breasts or inner thighs of the woman, and between her eyes and the heart or (one presumes) sex of the cavalier. There is a fit, indeed an interchange, between subject and object. Their bodies remain distant but their gazes, shot like luminous rays from two facing movie projectors, are crossed, joined and mingled together. Picasso takes us through the enactment of an erotic spectacle. Exceptionally, both protagonists find themselves in an intimate love scene where the reciprocal offer meets the equally reciprocal demand. The gazes they exchange are neither indifferent nor penetrating; they are inviting.

Picasso shows such astounding energy in the cycles dedicated to Degas, Celestina and Raphael, and such an insane combinatorial genius in the notebooks and drawings from his so-called Surrealist period, that the works preceding 1907 risk being overshadowed. However, the almost superhuman virtuosity he shows in later life should not lead us to conclude that the erotic Barcelona drawings, watercolours and paintings—largely, though not exclusively, inspired by his brothel experiences—are not up to scratch! That is simply not true. Picasso had started making references to art history very early on in his work and, by his Barcelona phase, he had started becoming obsessed with the idea of a continuum, wanting to renew and extend the works of painters he admired. This much becomes apparent starting with *The Origin of the World, Le Déjeuner sur l'herbe*

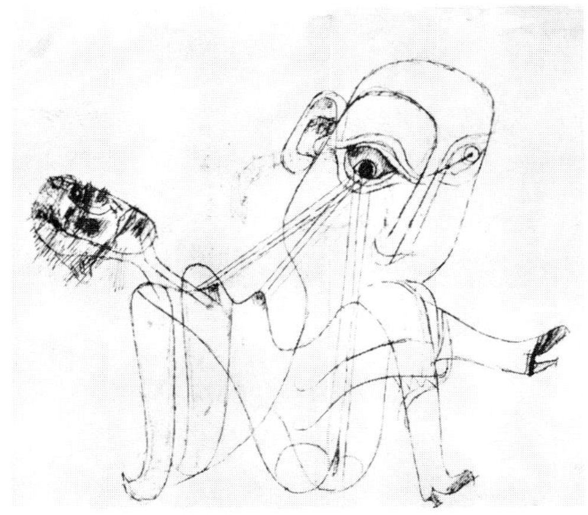

Fig. 5: Paul Klee, *The Eye of Eros*, 1919
Ink on paper mounted on cardboard, 13.3 x 21.6
Chicago, Morton G. Neumann collection

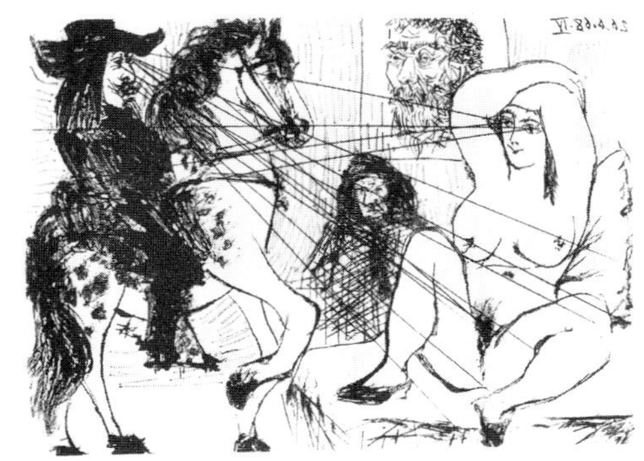

Fig. 6: *Calisto and Melibea*, 26 June 1968
Etching on copper; 19.7 x 25.7
Private collection

and *Women of Algiers*; even in *Olympia*—a figure explicitly referred to by the 1901–02 watercolour *Two Figures and a Cat* (Cat. 28). It is worth noting, in this piece, the ellipse that reduces the content of the images (both Manet's and Picasso's) to "next to nothing." The nondescript title completely ignores the cunnilingus the woman is enjoying, not to mention the impressive sculpted headboard presiding over the couple's lovemaking. The face of this guardian spirit is made up of ithyphallic penises and, already, eye-like vulvae, lending to an erotic activity a ritual solemnity that borders on the comic. The "bouquet of cocks" that appears in the Picasso writings of 1935 had already been present in his work for quite some time.

Several of the elements that were to make up the overflowing imaginative richness of Picasso's later works are already found here: iconoclastic humour, the bestial crudity of sexual impulses, complex staging, historic references, even serial production!

Optical and conceptual borrowing and reframing have been a consistent feature of Western and Eastern art since their beginnings. All the less reason to separate Picasso and Duchamp (who have been too hastily, superficially and mechanically opposed to one another) from their predecessors. Clearly the recurrent voyeur motif in Picasso's work, where the seer (young or old) stands behind a curtain—from the Barcelona drawings to the etchings of the 1970s—stems from an interminable questioning of the observer's position per se. In Picasso's 1941 play *Desire Caught by the Tail*, the character called The Curtains leaves the stage saying, "Night of thunder in my incongruous belly. (laughing and farting.)"[4]

Partly through Cubism, we have learned that familiar objects have a soul, but here they have a *body* and *voice* as well! The curtains are not only something we hide behind. They speak. Like the *Raphael and La Fornarina* etchings; like the green curtains behind which Khalil Bey hung Courbet's *The Origin of the World*; or the concealing door that André Masson painted, at the request of Jacques Lacan, to hide the same painting; or the sliding mechanism that allowed Goya's *The Nude Maja* to be revealed by lifting up *The Clothed Maja*. These rudimentary devices might pale beside *The Large Glass* and *Étant donnés…*, but we should never neglect the cross-fertilization of works we admire for fear of lessening their originality. Picasso was frequently subject to negative appraisal on the part of imperceptive specialists. Incidentally, his extensive studies and finished works depicting the "act of viewing" have an important predecessor in Thomas Rowlandson, who worked extensively in the area of optic, panoptic and/or conceptual machinery, anticipating the staging activities of both Picasso and Duchamp. Rowlandson's irrepressible fascination with imaging (or staging) sexual behaviour takes on proportions that have rarely been rivalled—except, of course, by

---

4 Pablo Picasso, *Le Désir attrapé par la queue*, Act 1, Scene II (Paris: Gallimard, coll. "L'imaginaire", 1989), p. 16. English ed.: *Desire Caught by the Tail*, trans. Sir Roland Penrose (London: Calder and Boyars, 1970), p. 22. The translations here have been slightly reworked to conform to Picasso's typographical idiosyncrasies.

Picasso. One could consider the former artist as having paved the way visually for Picasso to stage or orchestrate his similar fascination with the mind's eye.

Let us examine a specific example of Rowlandson's work—the watercolour titled *Exhibition <u>Stare</u> Case*—a veritable *mise en abyme* of the museum-as-institution in general, and of that displaying erotic works, in particular. The scene takes place in London, in part of the double winding staircase of Somerset House (a bastion of academic culture in the 17th century and currently home to the Courtauld Institute of Art). Formerly, the staircase led to a temple in the basement. There, in a niche, Rowlandson places a copy of the *Callipygian Venus*, or perhaps it is the original borrowed from the National Archeological Museum of Naples. In any event, it is the "Venus of the beautiful buttocks," the absolute prototype of Venusness. Her splendiferous backside holds its own with those so willingly displayed by Picasso's enticing seductresses. The staircase itself is a theatrical avalanche of flesh. Crowds of corpulent bourgeois men and women, as well as a few pretty, feathered *demi-mondaines*, fall over one other, catching sight, as if by accident, of several naked buttocks, inner thighs and legs. Not surprisingly, some of them take advantage of the situation to seize on a "prey," while a dog, a clergyman, a turbaned Turk and an enormous, pot-bellied bureaucrat ogle at the spectacle. Even more astonishing is the painting's title. "Exhibition" refers not only to the museum display but to the obscene activity of the exhibitionist. The artist makes the point explicit by underlining the wordplay "stare" as in "staircase," whence the emblematic significance of the Venus figure. Rowlandson paints the Royal Academy—a supremely respectable institution for the display of art works—as a privileged venue for peeping toms. The Academy's staircase becomes a meeting place for voyeurs and exhibitionists to give or get an eyeful, as in a bordello.

This universe is extremely close to that of Picasso. I am thinking not only of the caricature from his youth, *Vernissage*, in which similarly fat visitors parade naked in front of the art works, but also of the true exhibitions of sexual acts and organs that he ceaselessly portrayed from so many angles.

From the start, Picasso threw himself into the problem of instituted modes of perception vis-à-vis pictorial work. He immediately perceived the inanity of the "specialist's" eye and just as soon denounced it in a very concise portrait, dated 1889–90 and called *Un sabio* ("A connoisseur"). The bespectacled subject, dark and sinister, is shown examining the drawing of a nude without realizing that it is placed *upside down* on the easel—a clear sign that Picasso understood, or anticipated, that although the essential nature of the body might be displayed to the viewing public, it would undoubtedly remain incomprehensible (invisible) to the majority. All the more reason for him to focus much of his creative energy on such subjects.

From before *Les Demoiselles d'Avignon*, Picasso had ceased to explore, in a purely frontal manner, the difficulty of visually portraying ways of looking. The possibility of a more rounded vision, of a panoptic or all-encompassing gaze (the Cubist vision), had already taken form. Picasso and his painter friends altered the

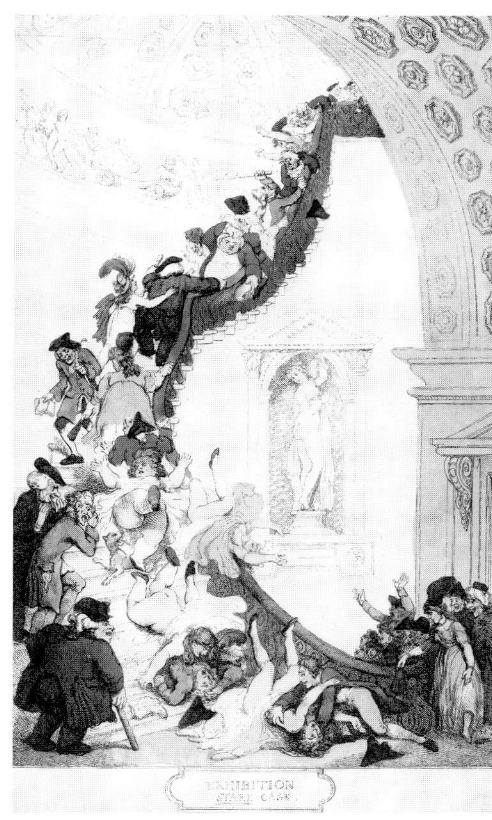

Fig. 7: Thomas Rowlandson
Exhibition <u>Stare</u> Case, circa 1800
Watercolour
London, Courtauld Institute

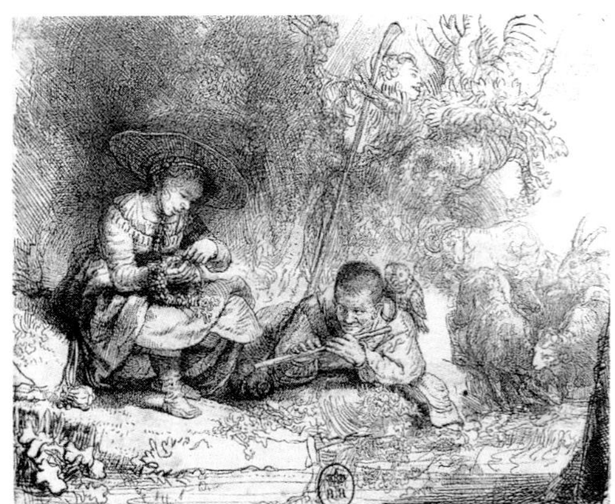

Fig. 8: Rembrandt, *The Flute Player*, 1642
Etching and drypoint
Paris, Bibliothèque nationale de France,
Département des Estampes et de la Photographie

viewing strategy and register. One must not, however, skip an important stage in the process: before the all-encompassing gaze, there was the *diagonal gaze* (already advocated by Aristophanes in *The Clouds*), an excellent means of side-stepping academic obstacles, particularly in the area of erotic art.

It is worth noting that certain stock images or provocative memories could, at some point, have opened up the path Picasso ended up taking. Let us start with an etching by Rembrandt, dated 1642 and titled *The Flute Player*. Etchings such as this show the strong sense of mischievousness and even the strategy of the desirous gaze that Picasso was to take so much further. Without analysing metaphors such as the delicately fingered wind instrument or the owl of Minerva sitting on the captivated musician's shoulder in broad daylight; without discussing the mirroring stream or the nearby billy goats and she-goats; or even the falsely innocent look of the peasant girl weaving a crown (for whom?)—certain tensions become obvious. The girl knows what is going on and imperceptibly opens her legs in response to the flute player's unvoiced request—which does not mean she intends to make his task any easier. On the contrary, she wants to make him bow down even further before giving him what he desires. In this etching by Rembrandt, as in many etchings and drawings by Picasso, as well as a painting by Tintoretto which will be discussed shortly, one senses a struggle or conflict of interests (real or imagined) which results in the protagonists confronting, ignoring or, much less frequently, joining one another. Throughout its history, erotic art has persistently asked the same set of questions: how far is A willing to go to get what s/he wants from B? To what degree do A's actions give pain or pleasure to C? What is the true nature (often unspoken and misunderstood) of the transaction that brings them face to face, as they size one another up? For Picasso, as for Duchamp, the flagrant obscenity of such acts and visions is a game that involves a lot more than pure sexual appetite.

It is now time to examine Tintoretto's *Susanna and the Elders*. In this painting, as is frequently the case in Picasso's erotic etchings, "false innocence" reaches the height of narcissism. The two aging voyeurs are mesmerized, not only by Susanna's nudity, but by the fact that she is secretly looking at herself in a mirror placed at a sufficiently low and "indecent" angle to suggest that she is admiring her own sex. The competing gazes and reflections lead the first old man (who could have been "borrowed" from one of Picasso's erotic etchings) to twist himself into an absurd position on the ground, while the outcome of his approach remains uncertain. As in Picasso's work (or as in Fragonard's *L'Escarpolette* and afterwards in Jean Renoir's *Une Partie de Campagne*), one cannot be absolutely sure in this painting what the protagonists have seen. It is an exemplary although not totally convincing attempt to experiment with the diagonal gaze—a gaze that Picasso undoubtedly reflected on and tried out, judging from the techniques used in some of his drawings.

If there is reason to believe that Picasso had examples from Rembrandt and Tintoretto in mind when exploring this angle, it would not be as safe to assume that he knew of two other predecessors, just as skilled although less-often-cited proponents of *diagonal gazes, grovelling gazes* and the *position of a viewer lying flat on the ground*. I am thinking of some drawings (Warsaw, Literary Museum) by the great Polish writer and artist Bruno Schulz, and of Jean Eustache's double cinematic masterpiece *Une sale histoire* ("A dirty story").[5] This film explores the grounded gaze of the quasi-professional "artist"/voyeur whose ultimate goal is not to share what he has managed to see, but to tell us, in intimate detail, how he goes about tracking down and "catching" the displays that fuel his passion.

Once again, we are at the heart of Picasso's erotic works, listening to the tale of an ever-renewed, ever-changing fascination with the *radical obscenity of the Other*. To get a sense of the awkwardness involved in Picasso's works—which some people may deem to be unbearable, in comparison to the less indecent, more commonplace situations evoked in Rembrandt, Tintoretto, Fragonard, Jean Renoir, Eustache and Schulz—I suggest we analyse his drawing number III, signed and dated 13 July 1972. Here, the register changes; the "things get tough," so to speak. We are confronted by one of those troubling, enigmatic scenes that Picasso created to exorcize his terror of the ultimate great black hole. Unlike many other erotic works, we know that in this case there will be a winner and a loser, but we do not know what is a stake in the amorous battle. All we see is the head of the observer, held captive under a Big Foot (the use of uppercase letters will soon become clear), which locks it in a kind of judo grip. This distorted big foot refers not only to the disproportionate members that both Miró and Picasso often used in their paintings, but also to the character who supposedly represents the author in *Desire Caught by the Tail*. The staring eyes and open mouth of the observer, pinned to the ground, presumably indicate that he is waiting, fearing, desiring something. Could that something, as his position and that of his dominatrix might suggest, be a Duchampian *waterfall* and *illuminating gas*? (i.e., Duchamp's installation *Étant donnés…*)?

Such an interpretation could explain the strange positions of both characters. Big Foot's co-actor and lover in the play is called The Tart and, as we all know (or should know), her "shameless behaviour [is that of] a prostitute dragged into Big Foot's sewer-studio by lecherous desires."[6] The Tart runs onto the stage, crying: "Good morning! Good evening! I bring you an orgy I am buck naked and am dying of thirst."[7] How many times have we seen her thus in Picasso's drawings? In other words, the position in which Big Foot finds himself—if indeed it is he who is held captive under the magnified, hairy, gaping orifice next to the plump and equally hairy anus of The Tart (if indeed it is her)—is not exactly a relaxed one. Even more so because this urinary hole and anus, clearly visible and very close to him given the position of The Tart's lifted left leg, would lead one to believe that something is about to happen. But what? Even more excruciating

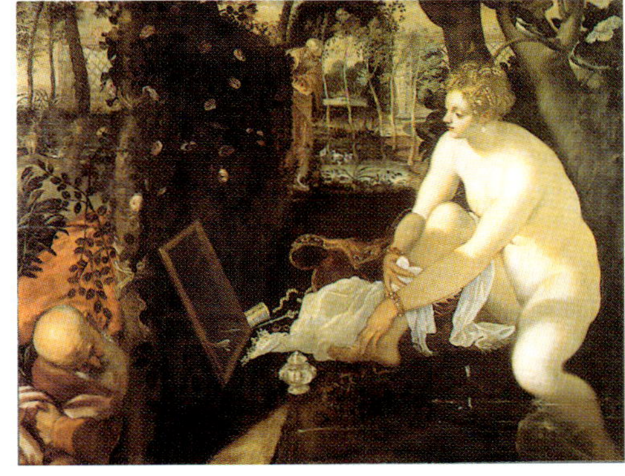

Fig. 9: Tintoretto
Susanna and the Elders, circa 1560
Oil on canvas; 193 x 243
Vienna, Kunsthistorisches Museum

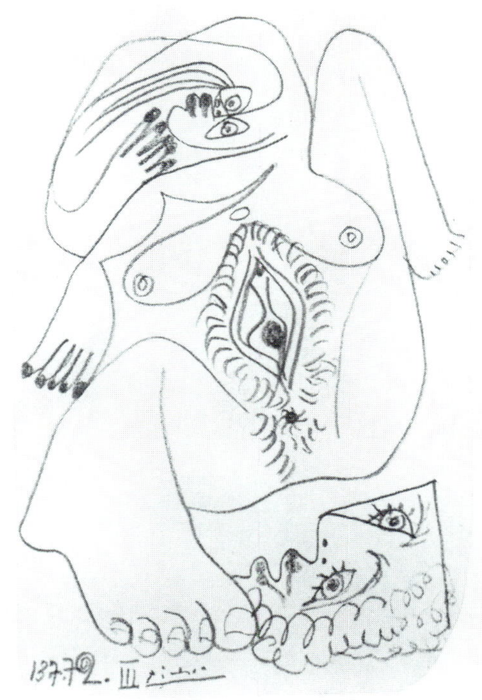

Fig. 10: *Reclining Nude and Head*, 13 July 1972 (III)
Pencil on paper; 20.2 x 13.5
Private collection

---

5   In Eustache's film, the story is first filmed with its true protagonist, Jean-Noël Picq, then a second time, with an actor (Michel Lonsdale) playing the role of the voyeur. The off-screen narration is the same in both cases.

6   Picasso, *Le Désir*, n. 4, Act V.

7   Picasso, *Le Désir*, n. 4, Act V.

than the uncertain anticipation of the prostrate character is the view of the scopic, vertically oriented, overbearing vagina, directly above him. We have already noted that the eye-vulva theme appeared very early in Picasso's work and would remain central to the end—until the precise moment when *The Origin of the World* and its end began, for him, to merge. This late drawing, clumsy by purely aesthetic standards, is far less refined than those of the Cubist, Neoclassical or "Surrealist" periods. To my mind, however, it remains a work of key importance due to the themes it addresses and the questions it raises. Once again, I would like to emphasize the structural analogies that link this type of drawing with Duchamp's masterpiece installation at the Philadelphia Museum of Art.

Yes! *Desire Caught by the Tail* would have made a perfect title for this exhibition—not quite museum-like, perhaps, but certainly ideal for conveying the element in Picasso's work that has triumphed, to date, over political correctness and other societal, political or religious institutions. Dated 1941, this play is one of the works that have most effectively resisted, and continue to resist, the trend toward spineless and mindless consensual submission to the puritanical norm.

The Tart, mentioned above, reappears in several different forms and characters. At one point, she is the *Woman Pissing on the Beach*, a major painting from 1965, first owned by Zette and Michel Leiris and now housed at the Centre Georges-Pompidou. It is worth noting that Rembrandt's famous little etching, completed in 1631, which supposedly inspired Picasso's painting, not only portrays a "pisser," as its deceptive title might lead one to believe; for she is also and above all a "shitter"—a detail that certainly did not escape Picasso's keen eye!

I have explored the rootstalk of the mental gaze as well as those of the obscene stagings and the scopic vagina. I have yet to look at what might be called the "excremental vision," to borrow Norman O. Brown's phrase in his discussion of a love poem by Jonathan Swift, which contains the leitmotif "Celia Shits." (Rrose Sélavy's aphorism "DOUCHE IT AGAIN"[8] comes to mind.)

The Tart also resurfaces in 1945 among the tiny drawings and cut-out silhouettes on paper tablecloths in the Parisian restaurant *Le Catalan*, where Picasso invited his friends and family during the Nazi Occupation. These drawings are reminiscent of the little statuettes of shitting figures, called *caganers* ("crappers"), which are part of Catalan folklore and may be still be found in the Ramblas. As early as 1896, Picasso was drawing these figures (see, for instance, *Muchacho defecando*, Barcelona, Museu Picasso). Nor should one forget the explicitly scatological passages scattered throughout Picasso's writings, superbly collated and presented by Marie-Laure Bernadac and Christine Piot.[9] Or one of the artist's most outspoken childhood friends, the painter Joan Ossó, whom Picasso painted in a Jarryesque watercolour (Cat. 31) that shows him serving a

8 Marcel Duchamp, *Rose Sélavy* (Paris: Éditions G.L.M., 1939).
9 Marie-Laure Bernadac and Christine Piot, *Picasso: Écrits* (Paris: Gallimard, 1989). English ed.: *Picasso: Collected Writings* (New York: Abbeville Press, 1989).

roast chicken on a platter with his right hand and masturbating with his left, at the same time defecating with his pants down around his ankles! It would be interesting to count the number of times this work has been exhibited or reproduced, both in the United States and Russia (during the Stalin era or since the fall of the Berlin Wall).

Furthermore, Michel Décaudin has found an acrostic by Apollinaire around Picasso's name, around which is dedicated to·him and puts him into competition with Mony Vibescu, the erotomaniac and scatological prince and hero of all excesses in *Les Onze Mille Verges* ("The Amorous Adventures of Prince Mony Vibescu"). Apollinaire's brief poem speaks volumes of the type of relationship he enjoyed with Picasso:

Prince Mony of Romania was obsessed with love.
In serving the princes of Love he perished, and is
Certainly deserving of a glorious title.
At every chance he used his dick,
Selflessly earning the right to whip the gods,
Surrounded by a fat ass-halo we call the moon—
Oh Pablo, tell you'll do better some day…

G. A.[10]

When, thanks to Michel Leiris, I had the opportunity to meet Picasso in 1966 to discuss *Desire Caught by the Tail* (which I was planning to stage the following year), I asked him about *Les Onze Mille Verges*, which, according to Louis Aragon's anonymous 1930 preface, he considered a masterpiece. Not trusting Aragon, I asked Picasso what he thought of the novel, upon which he confirmed Aragon's assertion. Not surprisingly, *Desire Caught by the Tail* and *Les Onze Mille Verges* have many points in common.

Apollinaire devotes one of the most "indecent" and inspired episodes in his novel to a sort of fecal ecstasy, not unlike one described by Laure in a text called *Le Sacré*.[11] Apollinaire's heroine is called Culculine d'Ancône. After a wild copulation session, she "got up to piss. She took a bowl, stood over it with her legs astride, lifted up her skirt and pissed copiously; then, to blow away the last drops that were dangling in her pubic hair, she let out a discreet and delicate little fart, which considerably excited Mony."[12]

Let us now turn to the fifth act of Picasso's play:
(BIG FOOT takes her into his arms and they fall to the ground.)
    THE TART. (Getting up after the sexual embrace)
You're smart enough at giving and taking, I'm covered with snow and shivering. Bring me a hot brick!

10 Guillaume Apollinaire, *Les Onze Mille Verges* (Paris: J'ai lu, 1973). English ed.: *Les Onze Mille Verges or The Amorous Adventures of Prince Mony Vibescu*, trans. N. Rootes (New York: Taplinger Publishing Company, 1979). This poem is not included in the published translation, and has been freely translated here.
11 Cf. *Écrits de Laure* (Paris: Jean-Jacques Pauvert, 1985).
12 Apollinaire, p. 35, n. 10.

(She squats in front of the prompter's box, facing the audience, pisses and
pisses scalding hot for a good ten minutes.)
THE TART
Oof! I feel better now!
(She farts, farts again, tidies her hair, sits down on the floor and begins a
clever demolition of her toes.)[13]

The text of *Les Onze Mille Verges* continues with an excremental apocalypse
where Mony, Culculine and her girlfriend Alexine Mangetout shine in their most
squalid, outrageous colours. Picasso does not immediately take up Apollinaire's
challenge in the acrostic, but later on, in *Desire*, Thin Anxiety has no reservations
about shouting the following to her sister, Fat Anxiety:
THIN ANXIETY. (Shouting down the sewerhole of their bed)
Sister! Sister! Come here! Come and help me to lay the table and to fold
this dirty linen stained with blood and excrement![14]

I feel that should be enough to convince you that there is a lot more to Picasso
than meets the eye, both in his visual and written works. You have been fore-
warned: art historians have not even come close to explaining everything. So
much the better.

Legend has it that, during the period he lived on rue La Boétie, in the same
building as his dealer, Paul Rosenberg, Picasso brought the latter a fairly "risqué"
nude of Marie-Thérèse. Rosenberg was reputedly outraged and asked him to take
back his painting, protesting: "I don't want any assholes in my gallery!" This
argument is still advanced by many, particularly in the United States. Mayor
Giuliani of New York, for one. Whence the repetitious series of paintings that
have received the museums' stamp of approval and are suitably "toned down" for
public display to please Senator Jesse Helms, Christian crusaders and the like.

Between pornographic images considered vulgar and the sophisticated erotic
art works by great masters that we are occasionally allowed to admire in a museum, there is a vast and extremely rich "no-mans-land," of which the current
exhibition is a fine example. It is a continually expanding *Wunderkammer* cabinet where thousands of objects and all sorts of images tend to end up. It is the
type of space where one can find great quantities of old pornographic images
ennobled by the passage of time; kitsch that has been transformed and validated
by the process of the ready-made; silent porn films; and erotic toys that have all
become collectors' items. In other words, works of art. Picasso, like anyone else,
ceaselessly drew inspiration from this immense collection, whether consciously
or not. There is an entire study to be done on the ways in which he used popular
culture in Barcelona and porn imagery during the 1960s and '70s. Future experts
have their work cut out for them.

---

13 Picasso, *Le Désir*, n. 4, Act V.
14 Picasso, *Le Désir*, n. 4, Act VI.

One of the most recurrent, re-presented erotic scenes (probably one of his fondest and most persistent brothel memories) involves a simple, indeed almost simplistic, staging: a woman (dressed or naked) spreads her legs to display her sex to a voyeur (young or old, resembling the artist or unlike him). This repetitive sequence haunted Picasso throughout his life, right up to the last drawings of 1972. It is, however, a cliché in every sense of the term; a mainstay of the most banal pornography appearing in literally hundreds of different forms. One of these, dating from the beginning of the 20th century, was a set of popular serial postcards showing two elegant hookers wearing hats and open blouses, sitting at a table, probably at the Bagatelle gardens in Paris. A dandy with a monocle, top hat, waistcoat and cane passes by. The sassier of the two ladies immediately places her left leg on a chair, lifting up her skirts to offer the future client a full view, not only of her fine breasts, but also of her hairy sex and anus, both very alluring. (Oh, I almost forgot to mention the mug of beer on the table!)

The title under the image is not without its charm: *Maud and a Friend Angling*. So here we have it: what women continually do, again and again, in Picasso's erotic drawings and paintings, is angle; not only in the sense of a fisherman baiting his hook, but also in the cinematic sense of "angling a shot," or in the literary sense of finding an "angle for a story."

We are only too familiar with these angling women whom Picasso drew and painted. Whoever, like him, has spent lots of time in brothels, has seen them mechanically repeating the same gesture over and over, a blank expression on their faces, always rewinding to the beginning, to *The Origin of the World* or its more popular versions, those cut out of porn magazines and taped to the wall of prisoners' cells, "beaver shots." From beginning to end, this image flashes before our eyes like a familiar refrain, an obsessive fear, a protective spirit and (I hazard, at the risk of appearing cynical) a womb-like icon.

From 1902, the astonishing series called *Vaginal Environment* (Cat. 33 a) shows the dark-haired, heavy-lidded model from Barcelona, squatting with her legs open wide, opening the lips of her vulva with her right hand. She is nestled inside a mandorla like that of the Virgin Mary or Venus, except that, unlike most Catholic mandorlas, this one is hairy and layered and boasts an enormous clitoris.

Seventy years later, on 5 November 1972, Picasso began his farewells by drawing himself in front of a mirror—a sad, tired old man, deliberately turning his back on the woman who persistently tries to light a spark in his "old eyes" by lifting and opening her legs and her "old holes" like an automaton. His heart was no longer in it—that much is clear.

There is a sharp poignancy in the fact that one of the last erotic images, dated "25.7.72" (in oversized numbers, as if to emphisize the length of the artist's prodigiously fertile career) is a small wash drawing showing a quick, but very precise and remarkably skilled sketch: the umpteenth version of *The Origin of the World*, close up, with hair, urinary orifice, clitoris, lips and anus in full view. All magnificently "underlined" by an Oriental brush stroke, the exquisite finishing touch! To the left, a small Spanish-looking man, who does not physically

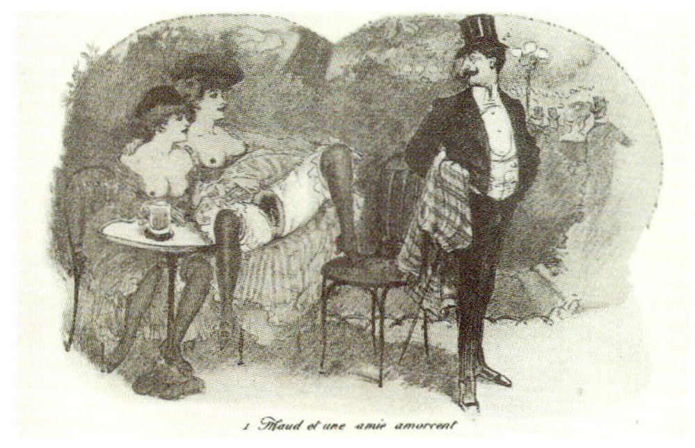

Fig. 11: *Maud and a Friend Angling*
French postcard (1978) reproducing a drawing
by an anonymous artist (circa 1905)

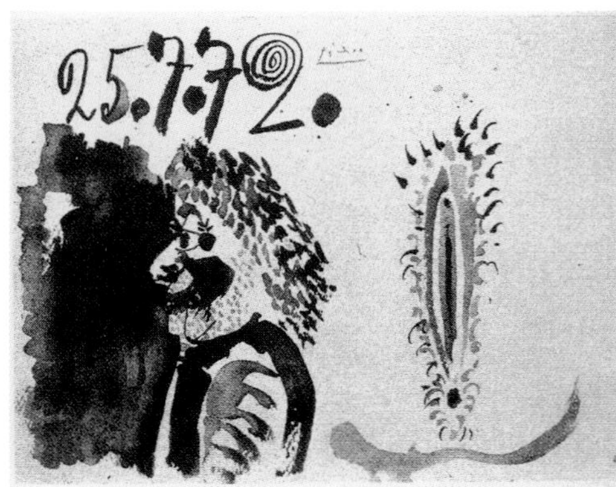

Fig. 12: *Bust of Man and Female Sex*, 25 July 1972
Wash on paper; 22.8 x 30
Private collection

resemble Picasso but who fully represents him, turns his back on the *Origin*, making his way, open-eyed, into the absolute night. He is taking his leave of the womb and its universe. He is taking his leave, period. Time is running out. In just a few months, he will have stepped over to the other side of darkness. End of love story.

All the prints from the *Raphael and La Fornarina* series are cryptic and referenced, giving them a specific, ritual and reiterative weightiness. We are almost embarrassed to be allowed to share, if only partially, in their secret. One of them is marked "31.08.68—III" (backwards, of course). It is no longer a question of fornication, but rather of an erotic offering made to the inhabitants of an invisible world, perhaps the members of an erotic Pantheon reserved for the great figures of art history. The print portrays a mystical/erotic ravishment, an ecstatic trance. The lovers are not resting but praying. The "Great Priapic Painter" has the superhuman ability to stay erect forever. His brushes, sex and gaze are pointed toward the sky, toward an ineffable orgasmic Beyond.

The mythic model, whose open thighs, sex and anus are calmed as if by a miracle, is graced with two eyes in the same orbit, like the double profile portraits of Dora Maar, whose memory is evoked here. Like *Dora Pro Nobis*, her gaze is turned upward towards Heaven.

The eye of this petrified cyclone is shifted toward the right, where a large hand draws open a vaginal curtain, as if on a stage. We recognize the master, each time different and yet always The Same, for whom the theatrical representation is taking place. He personifies the scopic impulse; he is the famous "Duchampian observer," integrated into the structure of the image. With two wild, staring and superimposed eyes, he personifies the hero. This anatomic feature indicates that he is not simply a passing voyeur, nor even a regular spectator, but rather the author and director of the scene occurring before us: the surpassing and transfiguration of Eros. It is almost a horrifically explicit remake of Giorgione's *The Tempest*. In fact, we are confronted by an *athanatophany*—an apparition of the spirits of Raphael and La Fornarina, a séance reminiscent of those in which Aeschylus, Aristophanes or Androcles dictated long rhyming strophes to Victor Hugo, or that in which the latter conversed with Shakespeare. "Ghosts write the works of the Living," Hugo remarked of these mediated sessions. Here, after Degas, Manet, Delacroix and Velázquez, Picasso reveals that he is inhabited by Raphael and his ghostly member is invested with the infallible phallic power of the Jarryesque *super male*. The hero of this artistic and sexual Renaissance agrees to incarnate the fantasies of he who directs/promotes the dramatic pictorial work. The one who keeps a close watch from behind the curtain, now as Polyphemus, now as a senile and wrinkled old monarch, now as the Pope on his pot, now as a statued clown, now as a grumpy Charlemagne dubbed by a second bearded man lying in wait under the bed where mythical lovers are fornicating (or have finished fornicating)—impassive porn actors born out of the mental gaze of an 86-year-old adolescent cinematic genius who documents their acts without a camera or film.

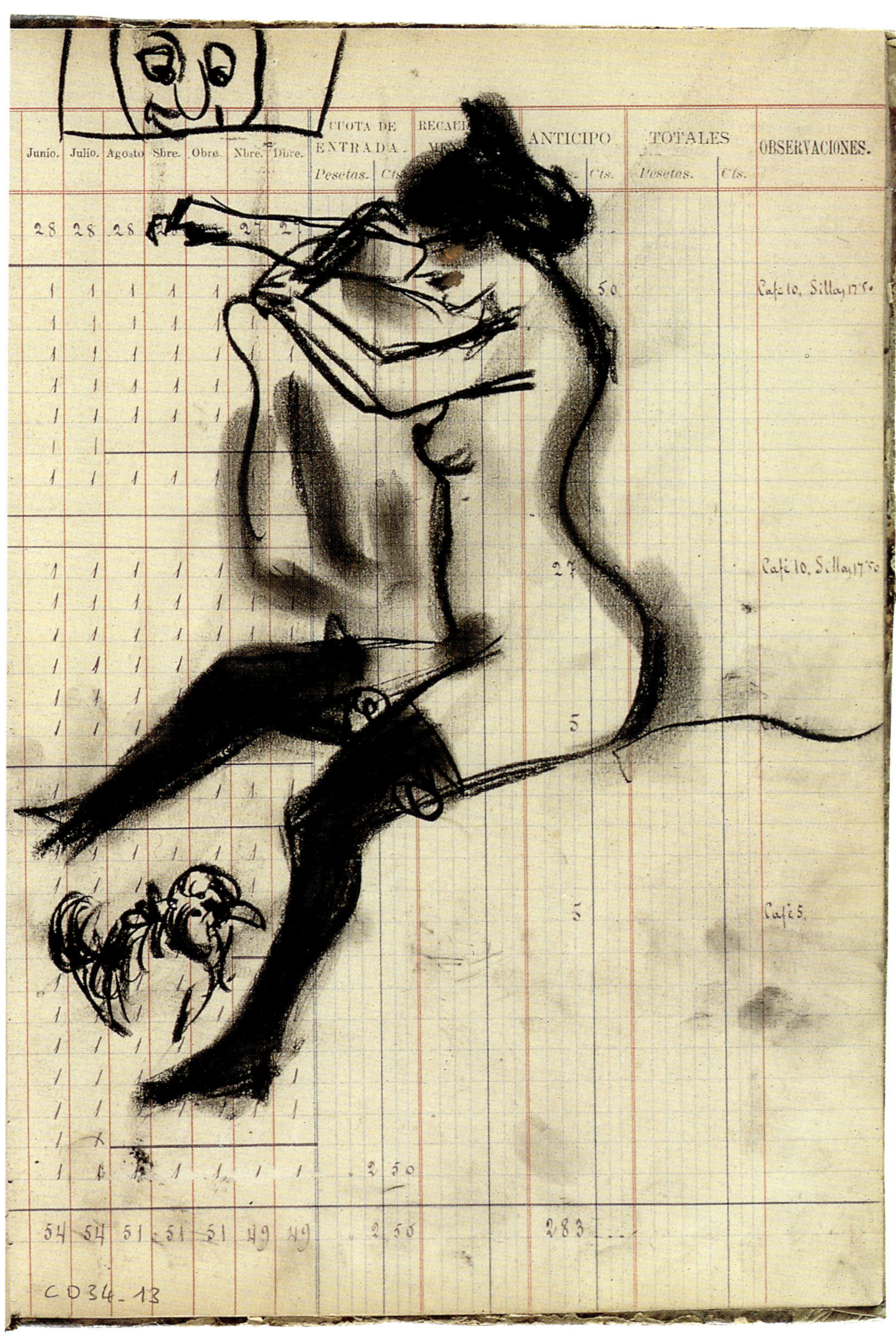

6 b Barcelona Sketchbook, Winter 1899–1900

Woman with Black Stockings Undressing (f° 8 r°)
Charcoal with oil highlights on paper; 31.5 x 22
Paris, Musée Picasso, MP 1990-93

All of which brings to mind an unforgettable scene from the film *Viridiana*, in which a group of beggars burst into the castle's fancy dining room and sit down in the owners' seats. After guzzling the fine wines and gorging themselves on luxury food, they amuse themselves by playing out Leonardo's *Last Supper*, with Buñuel himself in the role of Christ. One of the female beggars asks the others to pose for a photo. They get ready. Then someone asks: "What do you think you're going to take your photo with? You don't even have a camera!" To which she replies, moving to face the group, "Oh yes I do! I have this little camera that God gave me!" She then lifts up her skirt and a flash goes off as she snaps the photo with her cunt. A scopic vagina posing as a Kodak—a scene that could have been taken straight out of Picasso's work.

"Have a painter's eye. The painter creates by looking," wrote Robert Bresson, the master of film narrative, in his *Notes on the Cinematographer*.[15] What is this magic instrument that might appear to work like Dziga Vertov's Kino Eye, in its simultaneous shooting and editing of the image? By doubling the equipment, in other words, the visual capacity of La Fornarina and her spiritual master, Picasso gives a new meaning to the "painter's eye."

The splitting or reduction of the organs of sight is by no means new; on the contrary, it appears throughout the history of art in Europe and elsewhere, for instance in Africa and Melanesia. Originally born out of mystical preoccupations and magical beliefs, it involved seeing the invisible, dealing with the spirits. Picasso explicitly referred to the magical function of African masks and the process of exorcism involved in *Les Demoiselles d'Avignon* in a conversation with André Malraux during a visit to the Musée de l'Homme (Museum of Mankind). Malraux recorded this conversation in *Picasso's Mask*[16] and Jean Clair cited it in the brilliant essay he wrote on the genesis of the *Demoiselles*.[17] In the context of Western art, Picasso was aiming to represent the mental gaze or, to borrow the expression used by Gilles Deleuze in his discussion of the texts and drawings of Artaud, he aimed to represent "hallucinatory perception." Some of Picabia's paintings directly address these experiences: *L'Œil cacodylate* ("stink eye") (1921), *Échynomie livide* (1923), *Idylle* (1925), *Les Trois Grâces* (1927) and *Adam et Ève* (1927). This last painting was inspired by the multiple eyes dotting the Gothic seraphim's wings in the church of Santa Maria d'Aneu, near Barcelona

—a work Picasso was also familiar with. Man Ray has offered a rather different but no less disconcerting example of the wild-eyed/hallucinating stare with his

15 Robert Bresson, *Notes sur le cinématographe* (Paris: Gallimard, 1975). English ed.: *Notes on the Cinematographer*, trans. J. Griffin, intro. J.M.G. Le Clézio (Los Angeles: Sun & Moon Press, 1997). In a recent discussion at the Sarlat festival (cited by J.-M. Frodon in *Le Monde*, 12–13 Nov. 2000), Jean-Luc Godard offered an insight that might help us understand the role of the director and the position of the "Kino Eye" in some of Picasso's erotic scenographies: "I always feel that the camera has to go to wherever we don't see, that it must be positioned to help us see." Picasso often used this viewing strategy, which is why Michel Leiris called him a "show-all" (in his preface to the *Écrits*, n. 9).

16 André Malraux, *La Tête d'obsidienne* (Paris: Gallimard, 1974). English ed.: *Picasso's Mask*, trans. June Guicharnaud and Jacques Guicharnaud (New York: Holt, Rinehart and Winston, 1976).

17 Jean Clair, *Le Nu et la norme: Klimt et Picasso en 1907* (Paris: Gallimard, 1988).

famous photographic portrait of the Marquise Casati—actually the result of a marvellous mistake that was integrated into the creative process—showing the beautiful opium addict's ectoplasm portrayed with two pairs of staring eyes. In Northern Ethiopia, certain shamanic healing practices use protective parchments bearing the multiple painted eyes of divinities such as Gog and Magog.

This is certainly not a terrain one would have expected to find Picasso exploring, which is why, I believe, the works he uses to do so are so important. Take, for instance, a painting dated 24 October 1969, titled *The Kiss* (Cat. 279), where the hallucinating, visionary observer, hidden by his half-open curtain, is reduced to a simple stare represented by a long pointed triangle with a paradigmatic, sovereign eye that transforms the carnivorous embrace before us into an animalistic sacrificial spectacle.

If we compare the dramatic and visual structures of the early erotic scenes drawn or painted during the brothel period in Barcelona with those of the 1960s and '70s, we notice a qualitative mutation, both in the relations among the different actors and in the absolute preponderance of the scopic function that appears in the later period. The young voyeur, standing at the window or behind some kind of drapery, has taken control, thus metamorphosing himself into the role of director. Over the years, the passive and cunning witness has been transformed into the main recipient of the erotic action. Henceforth, it is toward him that all the obscene displays are directed. And it is for him that, through their fantastical and anatomically impossible acrobatics, the models simultaneously reveal *all* their charms and, in a single sculptural twist, make him a pansexual offering. It is to him, the artist and observer, that all the detailed close-ups and bestially obscene orifices (probably inspired by the stream of porn films and magazines churned out at the time) are shown. It is for him, back in his favourite spot behind the half-open curtain, that all the coded embraces, the mechanical adulterous carnival, the fabulous copulations are enacted. Spectacles in which he can participate simply by looking, and to which his presence lends a tragic air and pictorial finality.

Gone are the quick glances above the door; the furtive voyeur has been transfigured. He has entered the field to assume his melancholy but uncontestable reign over the erotic show. From now on, he holds an essential place at the heart of the image. He has become the observer, director and producer of the show. This fundamental mutation, a libidinal and pictorial role change, is what constitutes the unseen (not to say the blind spot) of Picasso's late erotic works.

In light of the above, the inanity of the cigarette-love metaphor, in which only desire remains, becomes clear. We realize the need to consider how the painter's gaze has undergone a fundamental metamorphosis; he is now both the subject and object of the image-making process. It is quite obvious that in certain explicitly or implicitly erotic works by artists such as Picasso, Duchamp, Magritte, Bellmer, Molinier, Courbet, Klimt, Schiele, Rodin, Boucher, Titian or Giorgione, the roles of painter and model are interchangeable. It is not by accident that the word "exhibition" refers both to the display of artworks and to the exhibitionist's wares. The question of the penetrating gaze is of the same order.

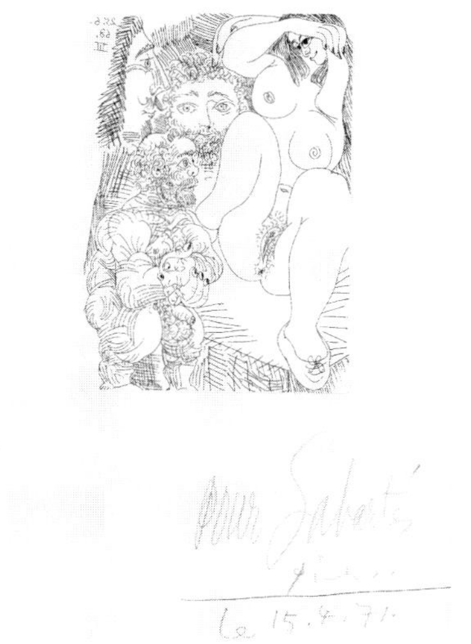

Fig. 13: *Young Courtesan with a Gentleman, a Sculptor and a Lecherous Old Man*, 25 June 1968 (III)
Etching on copper; 12.5 x 9
Barcelona, Museu Picasso, MPB 112.011

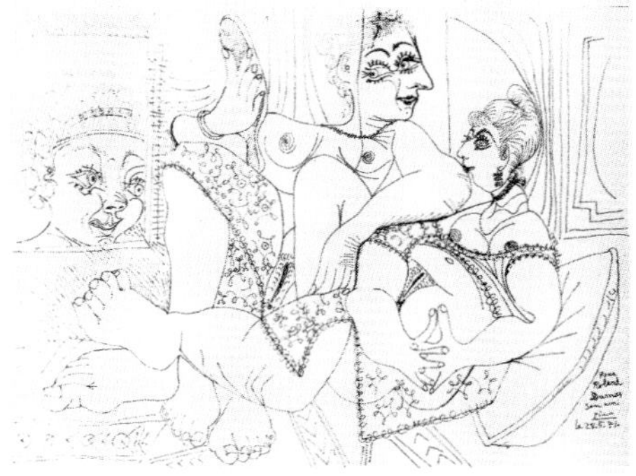

Fig. 14: *The Juvenile Voyeur*, 25 May 1971
Inscribed to Roland Dumas
Private collection

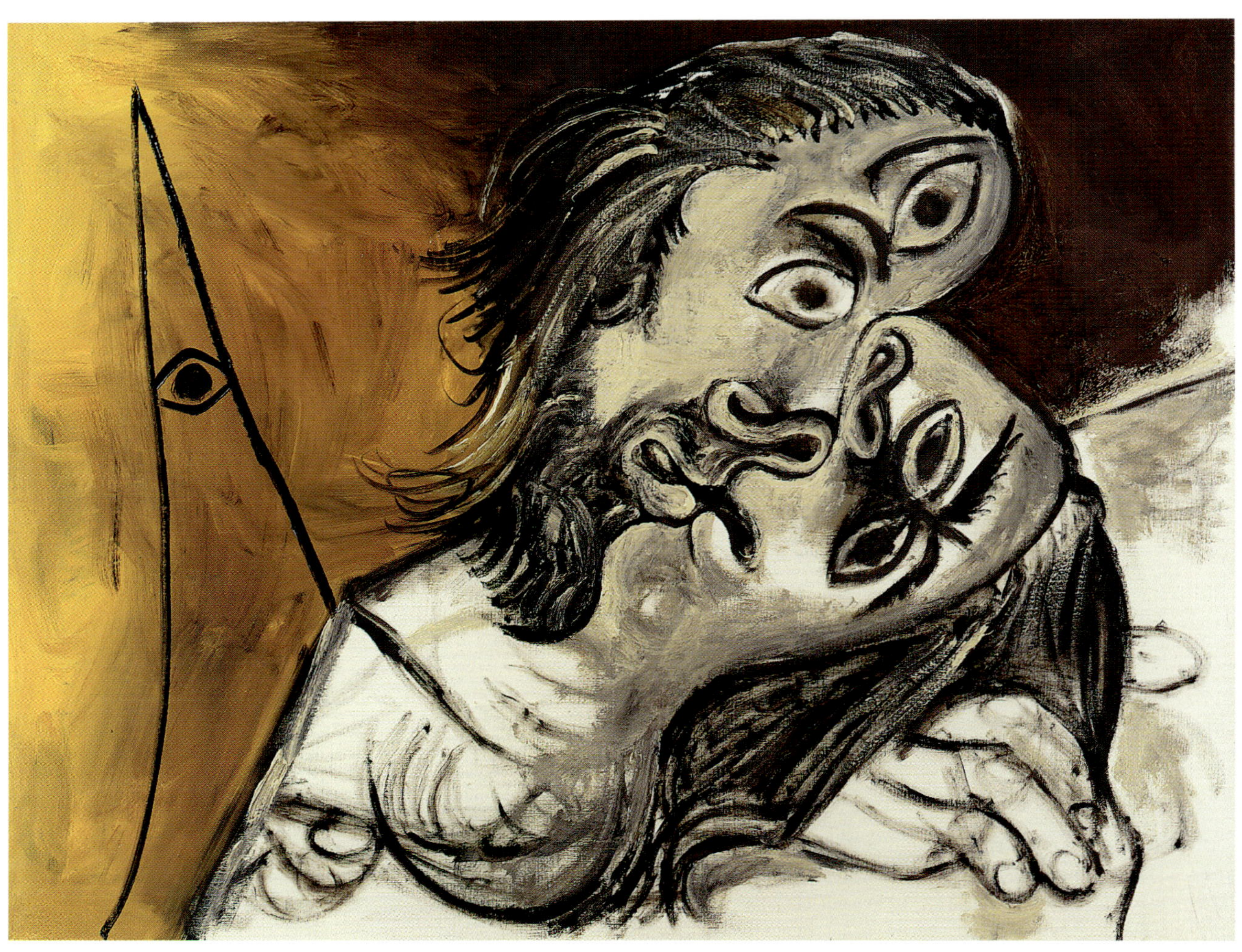

279 The Kiss, 24 October 1969
Oil on canvas; 97 x 130
Bermuda, Private collection

In the *Phaedo*, Plato puts into the mouth of a woman, "Diotima, the wise woman of Mantinea," a pertinent observation on the mental gaze that might shed further light on the mutation discussed above: "In truth, the mind's eye only begins to see clearly when the eyesight begins to fail."

In Duchamp's work, the transmutation of retinal painting into "grey matter" painting happened much earlier, even preceding the biological process evoked by Diotima. His last masterpiece, *Étant donnés…*, developed in secret for 20 years, was the result of a long process that started before *The Large Glass*. In Picasso's work, the maturing process appears to have occurred much more rapidly and to have been more closely tied to contemporary circumstances (a lessening of sexual and visual powers). Perspective disappears and is replaced by close-ups and flat surfaces; pencil lines waver, chairs collapse; and yet it is undeniable that the thinking eye and the resulting hallucinatory perception threw Picasso into a new phase of intense creativity, comparable in importance to his Cubist or "Surrealist" phases. The artist's creative juices gushed forth, drowning the voices of detractors like John Berger, who thought he was entirely disheartened and destroyed by his long and sad enslavement to the Communist Party's Stalinist politics.[18]

Such simplistic and disgruntled critics were over-hasty in proclaiming the inescapable decline and even the terminal pessimism of the emblematic "Greatest Painter of the Century." Picasso, on the contrary, was experiencing a burst of new energy. It is astonishing to note, *a posteriori*, how this erotically inspired sexual and pictorial renewal coincided with the gestation and explosion of the student movement in May 1968. I am not suggesting there was a relationship of cause and effect between the two outbursts; rather, I see them as simply concomitant, exhibiting, perhaps, a sort of objective chance or parallel ("rhizome-like") dynamic. It is not wise to attach too much importance to dates (a charge that is justifiably brought against the most obtuse art historians); however, there is a sufficiently striking synchronicity between the two developments to merit our attention. The student protest began at the University of Nanterre in 1967 with the explosive action of an anarchist group which, influenced by Wilhelm Reich's ideas about the "sexual struggle of youth," tore down the wall separating the women's dormitory from the men's. The time was ripe for change. It was a symbolic, destructive act that unwittingly unleashed the libidinal fury of an entire generation—and also of a glorious lonely old man, holed up in his studio on the Mediterranean.

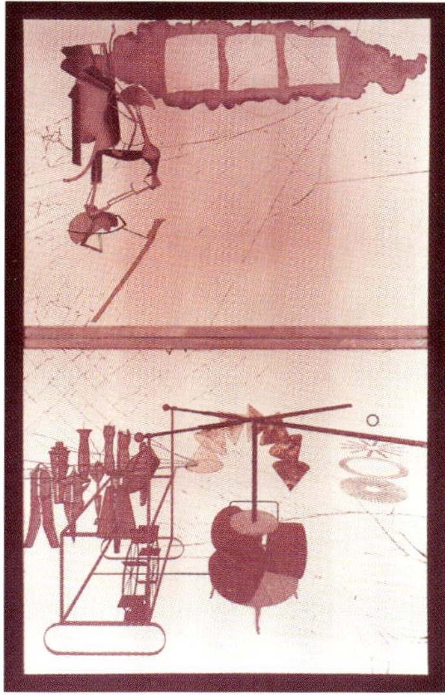

Fig. 15: Marcel Duchamp, *The Bride Stripped Bare by Her Bachelors, Even (The Large Glass)*, 1915–23
Philadelphia, Philadelphia Museum of Art, Louise and Walter Arensberg collection

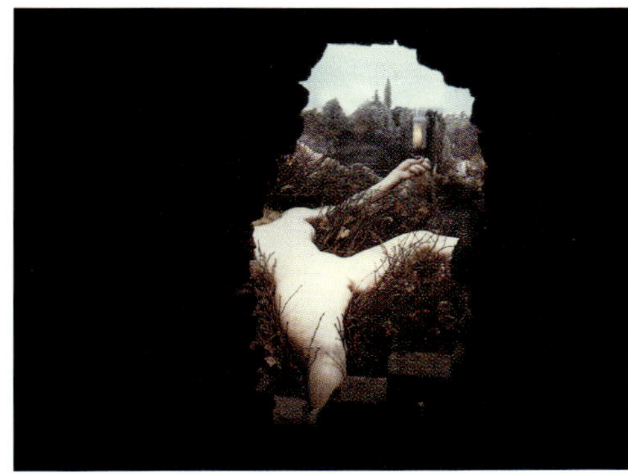

Fig. 16: Marcel Duchamp
Étant donnés…: 1. The Waterfall. 2. The Illuminating Gas, 1946–66
Philadelphia, Philadelphia Museum of Art, Louise and Walter Arensberg collection

---

18 In 1965, Berger published a harsh appraisal titled *The Success and Failure of Picasso*. A year later, translated sections of the book appeared in the *Quinzaine littéraire* under the title "L'échec de Picasso" (Picasso's failure), handing down a sentence that became widely accepted. "However favourably one judges Picasso's work since 1945," writes Berger, "it cannot be said to show any advance on what he created before. To me it represents a decline. … Perhaps this last large painting of Picasso's [*Las Meninas*] is a comprehensive admission of failure" (p. 183–85). In precisely the same year the French version of this denunciation appeared, Picasso's gaze mutated and his surprising erotic resurgence took place. One wonders whether he knew of Berger's book…

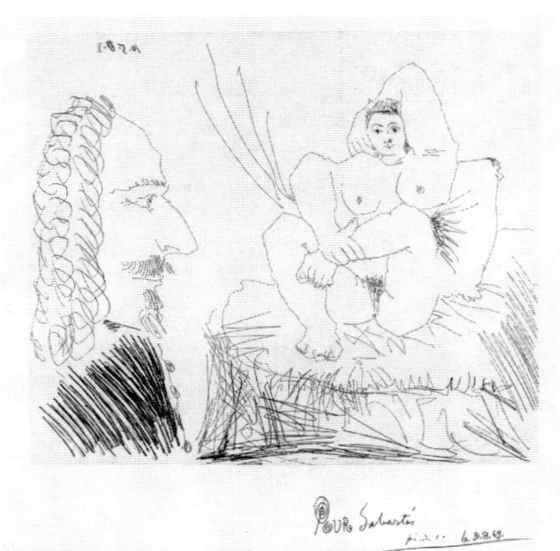

Fig. 17: *Courtesan in Bed with a Visitor*, 10 May 1968 (II)
Etching on copper; 41.3 x 48.9
Barcelona, Museu Picasso, MPB 70.608

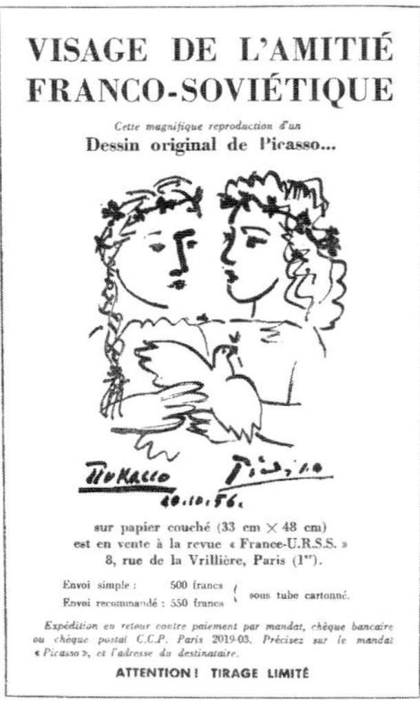

Fig. 18: *Visage de l'amitié franco-soviétique*, 10 October 1956
Propaganda drawing with double signature in Cyrillic and Latin characters; 33 x 48
Advertising page from *Recherches soviétiques*, Issue 7, 1957 (Paris: Éditions de la Nouvelle Critique)

Consider the etching on copper completed in Mougins and dated 10 May 1968. The chaste, almost prudish title given it—*Courtesan in Bed with a Visitor*—by no means reflects the contents of the piece; on the contrary, it hides them. The scene is probably one of the many inspired by Fernando de Rojas's *La Celestina*, a work that greatly inspired Picasso. As always, what the title *does not say* is more important than what it does say. The courtesan is naked, deliberately displaying her charming sexual wares to us, the viewers. The angle of her pose is important, because the dashing hidalgo, archetype of the Iberian macho and nobleman, is drawn in profile in the foreground, making it impossible for him to enjoy the spectacle revealed to us. He would have to turn his head toward the exhibitionist, which, of course, he cannot do. His gaze is fixed on something else, outside and beyond the frame of the picture. The client stands firm, indifferent to the treasures that are so indiscreetly displayed before his eyes. Although they are both included in the same frame and scene—one in the foreground, the other in the background—the courtesan and hidalgo remain in their separate spheres. Another non-love story. Art enthusiasts will immediately, almost automatically, see the parallel between the alluring courtesan in this etching and in many similar figures drawn, painted or etched by Picasso, and Courbet's *The Origin of the World* (once again)—the painting that seems to keep a relentless grip on our collective cultural memory. While the postures of the models are slightly different, they have a similar intention: to catch the eye, to attract and captivate the desiring energy of the spectator—male or female. And finally, to arouse the penetrating gaze—only to prevent it from going any further. A most perverse and typically whorish strategy, one that Duchamp beautifully captured by setting up an impassable wall (equipped with a crack or peephole) between the observer and his ideal erotic happenings. This image-trap, a remarkable example of one of the hundreds of parallels, if not exact similarities, between Picasso's and Duchamp's respective points of view, is the result of their ongoing experimentation with the possible manifestations and limitations of the mental gaze. We are very far removed from a purely retinal art form.

These were the reality of Picasso's creative endeavours on 10 May 1968. That same afternoon, a thousand kilometres away, hordes of enraged activists, from a variety of sociopolitical and cultural backgrounds (all with clearly playful Marxist overtones, of the Harpo variety), stormed the police-held Sorbonne. An inexplicable energy was unleashed, and the joyous, disorganized crowds began erecting huge barricades with whatever objects they could find, throughout the Latin Quarter and other parts of the city. These tremendous constructions, which had no military or practical purpose whatsoever, looked like a series of collective street installations. In the early morning hours, the rue Gay-Lussac, strewn with overturned, charred and stripped cars, was like the largest and certainly the most beautiful open-air sculpture museum the world had ever seen. The same tempestuous creative energies had been released during the night in the streets of Lyon, Bordeaux, Toulouse and other cities. The art of borrowing and appropriation invented and perfected by Duchamp, Picabia, Schwitters and, of course, Picasso, had once again made its mark, transforming urban space into a huge communal art lab. Whether Picasso was aware of these events is irrelevant; the seeds he had scattered by brilliantly revolutionizing the gaze, particularly in the erotic domain, continued that night to bear fruit…

When discussing the timeless, limitless and germinating force that has criss-crossed all cultures, eras, political regimes, religious spheres, economic systems and the life and work of Picasso, Duchamp and so many others—what I would call the erotic visual tradition—it is useless to try to establish a hierarchy of values. Fantasies do not vary significantly from one period or civilization to another. All that varies is the degree of freedom with which artists, poets and filmmakers may or may not express them, as well as the social contexts (institutional or private, public or clandestine) in which their fantasies may circulate. One can certainly assign values to works of art, albeit arbitrarily, because the Beautiful by nature is changeable and arbitrary, but we cannot arrange the sources of these works in a hierarchy. We know that Courbet, for instance, took his inspiration for *The Origin of the World* not only from a specific and very real woman nicknamed Jo, the Beautiful Irish Woman, who posed for him, but also from many of Auguste Belloc's so-called pornographic snapshots, which showed, very soon after the invention of photography, anonymous models adopting the same obscene pose. Like Duchamp, Bellmer, Grosz and so many others, Picasso clearly wondered about the sequel to *The Origin of the World*. What would happen next? Presumably, the woman's hands would move down to her sex to gently open and caress it. Incidentally, in 1997, two young Serbian artists, Zoran Naskowski and Vesna Pavlovic, made a video in which this *a posteriori* action is partially carried out. Bearing the same title as Courbet's icon, the video was shown opposite a painting by Tapiès dedicated to the same theme, as part of the *Garden of Eros* exhibition held in Barcelona in 1999. Picasso, like many others, followed Courbet's train of thought, working out an imaginary sequel in an astounding number of drawings and washes. There is a colour ink drawing, dated 23 August 1971, that I think could immediately follow on Courbet's archetype, even though the wider framing does not correspond at all to that of the original. The drawing seems especially appropriate since I found, in a collection of old erotic photographs that once belonged to Michel Simon and was, incidentally, put up for auction in the 1970s, a photo—attributed to the excellent libertine poet Pierre Louÿs—taken around 1895 in a brothel and showing a naked young woman in an armchair, making exactly the same obscene gesture, her head leaning (to the other side) with the same smiling expression on her face. Of course, there is no proof that Picasso was inspired by this photograph, nor that he ever saw it—unless, while going through his archives, somebody happens upon such evidence one day—but the photograph does prove something much more important. Namely, that artists of genius, like all others, always depict variants of images that have already been painted, drawn, photographed or filmed, or that are already present, in an uncensored, uncoded state, in all our minds.

Including yours, I hope.

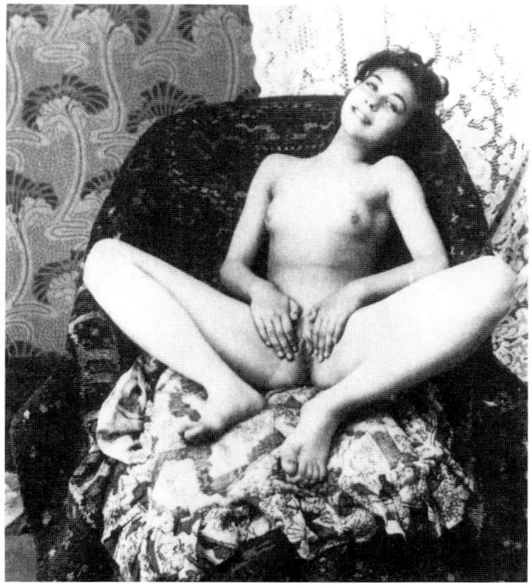

Fig. 19: Photograph attributed to Pierre Louÿs, circa 1895
Private collection
(formerly part of the Michel Simon collection)

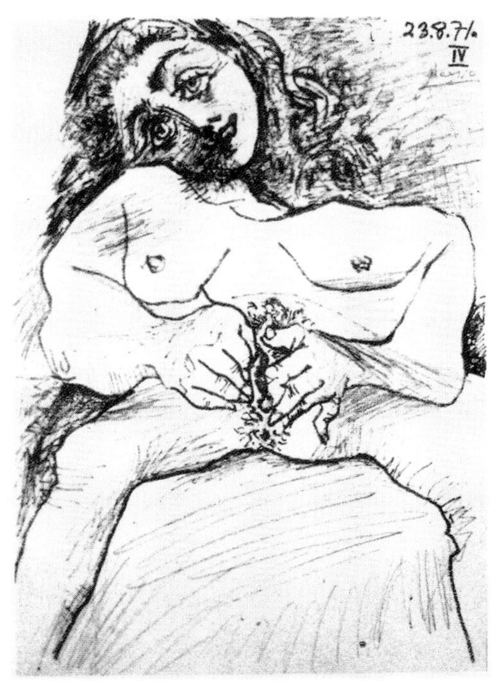

Fig. 20: *Nude*, 23 August 1971 (IV)
Pencil and coloured ink on cardboard; 30.7 x 22
Private collection

THE BODKIN, THE VULVA AND THE EYE-POPPING GAZE OF THE PAINTER

Patrick Roegiers

Installed in Isidro Nonell's sparsely furnished Montmartre apartment on rue Gabrielle, Pablo Picasso, who had just turned twenty, was living a life that was as penniless as it was joyful. He would sometimes cover up to three canvases a day and had already painted *The Death of Casagemas* as well as the caustic portrait of Gustave Coquiot that prefaced his exhibition with Iturrino at the Galerie Vollard. Picasso, who said he drew "better than Raphael," was also adept at dashing off spirited, free and spontaneous first-draft sketches that were not necessarily studies. Sensitive to stroke, Picasso worked to expand his sense of line in his drawing technique and was not averse to producing erotic drawings and lewd sketches. Allusions to his private life abounded in these works, where, quite naturally and with good humour, free from taboos or prejudice, he depicted scenes of his loves and his mistresses as in his paintings and sculptures. As far as Picasso was concerned, no subject was off limits. One simply had to know how to draw. He held on to even his most insignificant drafts and took pleasure in exploring his innate gift for caricature. Caricature was a humorous outlet that allowed him to transpose his secret thoughts or his most repressed desires onto paper, to give shape to the demons of his subconscious and rid himself of them.

The man whom Gustave Coquiot called a "frenetic lover of modern life" produced a series of India ink sketches entitled *Women with Striped Socks* (1902), using a classic technique, executed not in a series of strokes but in one, continuous line. In this series, the nude women—possibly Odette, Picasso's lover in Paris, Germaine, Casagemas's former lover, or Blanche, about whom nothing is known— display themselves, seated or lying down in three-quarters and profile positions, willingly spreading their legs and engaging in fondlings that transform these harmless little sketches into randy little scenes. As usual, Picasso undertook these drawings without any *a prioris*, in styles evoking Forain as much as Degas, Toulouse-Lautrec, Steinlen, the master of caricature who so impressed Picasso that he imitated his signature several times, or Rops, the refined pornographer. Among these quickly rendered scenes of arousing nude nymphets indulging in various pleasures, there is a rather hot and enthusiastically executed depiction of Sapphic fellatio, the obvious precursor of *Two Figures and a Cat*,[1] a brothel scene in watercolour and graphite on paper illustrating intense, sensual cunnilingus. This more

---

1 Maria Teresa Ocaña, *Picasso: La formació d'un geni, 1890–1904* (Barcelona: Lunwerg Editores, 1997).

aesthetically detailed piece shows a kitten that is the mute witness of a young girl whose pussy is being licked, lapped and thoroughly glottalized. Picasso produced an even more explicit ink wash depiction in which a woman blindfolds herself (1902), and a "sixty-nine" cunnilingus sketch, entitled *Sex and Death* (1901). In his realist canvas from 1903 entitled *Portrait of the Artist Making Love*[2] (Cat. 40), the barely identifiable artist is being indulged in buccal onanism, his hands resting behind his head. And there is another cunnilingus scene, drawn around 1905, jotted down on a piece of study paper along with some other naughty doodles, including one that depicts a girl exposing one cheek of her buttocks to an obscene, wealthy-looking man seated on a perch overhanging some fornicating pigs.[3]

These licentious Parisian sketches, which could either be viewed as Picasso's tall tales of sexual prowess or as puerile, schoolyard jokes, are entirely congruent with the sketches that Picasso produced upon his return to Barcelona in 1903. At this time, he produced a series of nine drawings that were parodies as much as they were fantasies, or even phantasmagorical evocations, drawn à la William Blake or in the Art Nouveau style of Aubrey Beardsley, on small business cards or advertising tracts bearing the trademark of the Junyer Vidal brothers. The brothers, Carles (an art and theatre critic) and Sebastià (later suspected of producing counterfeit art), were heirs to a prosperous dry goods store, and Picasso viewed them as patrons of sorts. In a parody of Manet's *Olympia*, Picasso poses beside a bed where a nude woman lies. He is nude, viewed in profile, his penis relaxed. Carles is on the other side of the bed. These sketches resembled the postcards and popular illustrations for sale under the overcoats of petty street hucksters. They were shameless, pre-surrealist scenes, with symbolist touches, in which Picasso gave free reign to his most intimate desires, as in his scene of a nude naiad, shown in profile with her hands behind her head, piously fellating the glans of an erect phallus. In *Sex in the Head*, a hetaera with her head upside down and her body contorted reaches her right hand toward the zipper of a hideous bourgeois man whose skull is adorned with a hairy vulva and who, in turn, is reaching over to touch her. Another illustration, entitled *The Phallus* (Cat. 36), depicts a nude mademoiselle with long hair, prostrate with her arms open, seated on the testicles of a penis erected before her like a stela and ornamented with a sacred-looking, smiling face.

The vulva, as we will see, and the phallus were the taboo subjects of the little scenes Picasso began sketching at the dawn of the Blue Period, and were recurrent motifs, if not leitmotifs, featured in several media and produced in a wide variety of styles during various periods to follow. Like works include a sketch depicting a young woman seated facing a snake, her tongue as forked as that of the reptile, and another of a young lady dancing beside a male member that stands upright

2 John Richardson (with the collaboration of Marilyn McCully), *A Life of Picasso, Vol. 1, 1881–1906* (New York: Random House, 1991), p. 258.
3 *Les Demoiselles d'Avignon*, Vol. II (Paris: Réunion des musées nationaux/Musée Picasso, 1988), ill. 196, p. 477.

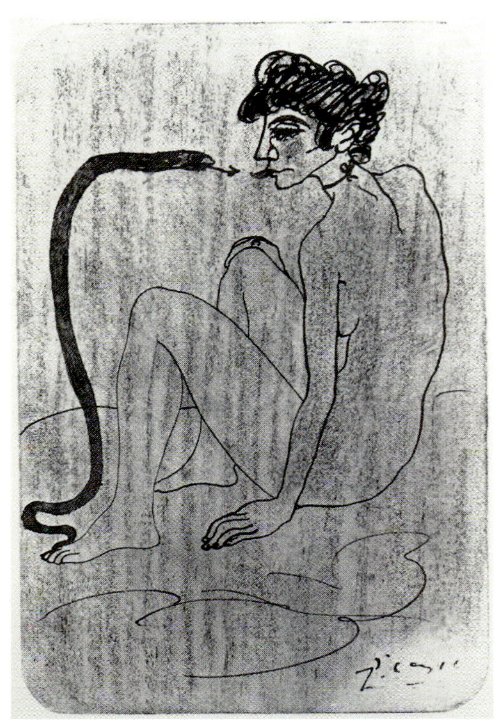

Fig. 1: *Nude Woman Facing a Serpent*, 1900
Pen and pencil; 13 x 9
Private collection

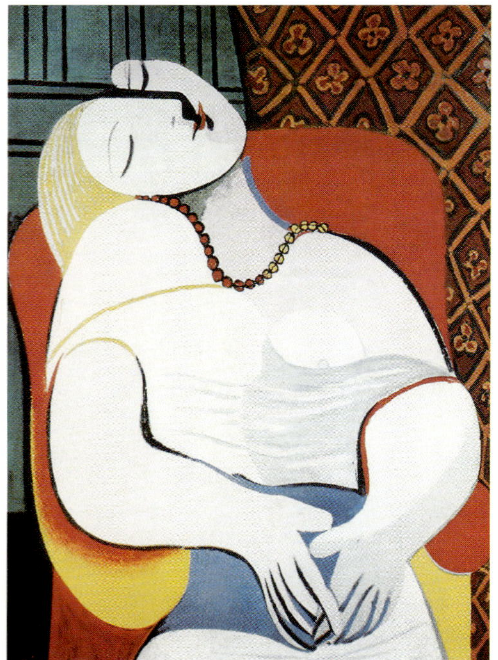

Fig. 2: *The Dream* (Portrait of Marie-Thérèse Walter),
24 January 1932
Oil on canvas; 130 x 97
Private collection

like a tulip. There is also the harmoniously proportioned penis in *Nude Study of José Roman* (1895), a work in charcoal and pencil based on a photograph, and other academic studies of nudes, in which we see the wee willy of a young ephebe (1906) or the diminutive member of a slightly recumbent, shaved giant in *The Harem* (Cat. 59, also 1906), beside four representations of Fernande. The giant's member is charmingly attractive, like that of a eunuch, and is rendered even more conspicuous by the vulgar, ersatz sausage placed beside him on a platter of refreshments. Or the depiction of the former smuggler Josep Fontdevila, pointing to the precise location of the penis on the human body; the organ is as slim in its resting state as that presented in *The Two Brothers* (1906), or as the slender tube of the *Young Boy with Crayfish* (1941). Picasso's penises are more often present as appropriately positioned, at the base of the abdomen, than are his noses, whose phallic and erectile qualities were caricatured in *The Dream* (Portrait of Marie-Thérèse Walter, 1932), priapic across the front of the subject's face, visibly flushed and disproportionately stretched like the neck of a horse. Later, in aquatint etchings like *Under the Footlights: Young Girl with Two Bearded Phalluses* (Cat. 232, 1966), the penis, hard as a bowling pin, appears as strongly constituted as Picasso's lady-love's buttocks are large. Given the repressive Catholicism in Spain at the time, one must salute the audacious amorality displayed in the sepia ink and watercolour drawing on "chickpea" yellow paper entitled *Isidro Nonell and a Female Figure* (Cat. 29, 1902–03). Isidro Nonell was the son of a pasta merchant who painted goitrous *cretinos* (cretins) and, like Picasso, divided his time between Barcelona and Paris. Nonell died at age 38 of typhoid contracted from his contact with gypsies. In this piece, he is being fellated by a kneeling, fair-haired young woman. Devised, according to John Richardson, to entertain the Junyer Vidals,[4] this comical and heartily executed scene should be unequivocally read as a send-up by Picasso, who was making fun of his friend, just as he lampooned Sabartés by drawing him as a "decadent poetess," or Apollinaire, who he depicted as an academic. Picasso also unabashedly magnified himself as a Minotaur, born of unnatural relations between woman and beast, as in his etching *Seated Minotaur with Dagger* (Cat. 142, 1933), whose sexual symbolism is augmented by the phallic representations of the pointed knife, the pointed horns and the member protruding from beneath a hairy torso, still perceived in 20th-century Spain as a shameful part of anatomy—as was the case among Christians with regard to the exposed arms of women.

The vulva is every bit as resplendent as the phallus in the series of erotic sketches, drawn on 13.3 x 9 cm trade cards, where women-flowers are gathered up in an Art Nouveau style. Was it not Picasso who maintained that "Different motifs demand different methods"? In *Vaginal Environment* (Cat. 33 a), a ravishing dark-skinned woman, her breasts pointed at their tips, has her legs open with her left arm—armpit hair plainly visible—folded under her head and her right arm, slipped under her thigh, brings her hand close to her gaping genitals, which

4 Richardson, p. 505, n. 22.

she clutches, presses and half-opens. The power of the vulva, with its bristling bush, is duplicated into another vulva, matrix, chrysalis, seashell, scar—an all-encompassing arabesque, encircled with pencilled-in curls of hair, that forms the box that contains the curled-up model. Vulva of a vulva, this unfathomable representation reminds us how the female genitalia are themselves a body. But they are also like a frame. Picasso took great pleasure in producing variations on this motif, in *Erotic Nude* (1902), a watercolour and blue ink illustration. In the same series of cards, another tantalizing muse has her sex sucked at by the tentacles of a grotesque animal (snail, scarab beetle), which also gores into the emaciated body of a screaming old woman whose mane of hair stands on end. In keeping with his famous dictum "I don't say everything, but I paint everything," Picasso would later forbid his models to shave, and continued to poke fun at his fantasies and play with stock phrases in pieces like *The Mackerel* (Cat. 33)—a facile play on words: "maquereau" means both *mackerel* and *pimp* in French—wherein a woman has her vulva sucked by a fish. A stigmata of sin?

Whether it is the wide-open cleft in his India ink wash *Suzanne Flanked by Two Old Men in Joachim's Garden* (Fig. 5, p. 43), or those in *Reclining Nude* (1967), in *Reclining Nude and Man Playing Guitar* (Cat. 287, 1970), in the light pencil sketch *Woman Wiping Her Feet* (Cat. 61, 1907), or in the beautiful drawing dated "28.12.1938," and dedicated "to Dora," Picasso's work is brimming with ripped vaginas: wailing vaginal mouths, gaping crevasses, unfathomable breaches, cracks, fissures, cloacae, womb-like chasms or suction cups, incandescent caverns and craters, and the *vagina dentata* of Eros in Spain—repugnant, obscene and filthy. Picasso pointedly derides these kinds of representations in his caricature *Ángel Fernández de Soto with a Woman* (Cat. 30, 1902–03). Ángel Fernández de Soto was a layabout and the unwilling drudge of a spice merchant whom Picasso met in Barcelona in 1899 ("On faisait la bringue ensemble!": "We used to raise hell together!")—an intransigent, elegant ne'er-do-well who swaggered around at the theatre in extravagant attire, which inspired Picasso's caricature. In it, the blessed "de Soto" (later to perish in the Spanish Civil War) is depicted with a jutting chin and a pipe in his mouth, holding a prostitute. She is clothed only in red stockings, and masturbates him with one hand while holding a cup of champagne in the other. Her drinking companion is half undressed, proud as a peacock, with his index finger delicately inserted in the pretty vamp's open charms (Eros is life!).

Views of the vulva became much more realist when Picasso, the high priest of live sexuality, held out his arm and brandished his paintbrush—a surrogate penis—its bristles as supple and downy-soft as a curly tuft of pubic hair, and trained his "too-black eyes" on models whose vulvas were neither oysters nor flowers nor figs nor seashells, but organic entities, drawn in their anatomical functionality, from a quasi-gynecological vantage point. Gertrude Stein called Picasso's sexuality "dirty." Without a doubt, she was not so much targeting Picasso's orgy of women, exhibited in provocative or indecorous poses, as she was one particular depiction of anonymous female genitalia, crudely perceived as a

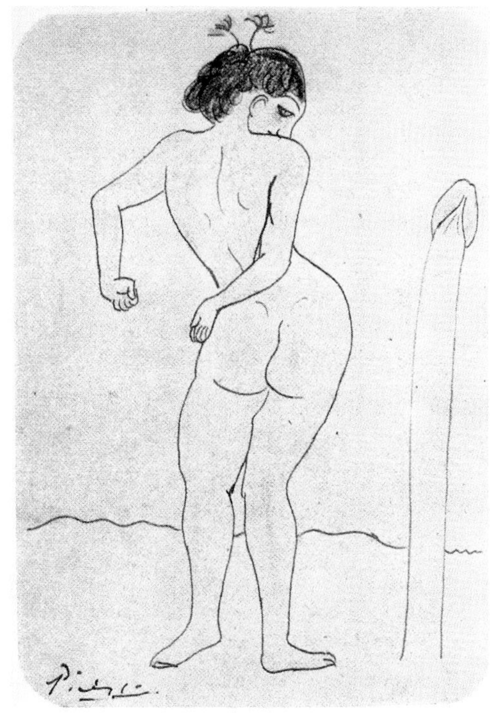

Fig. 3: *Erotic Caricature*, 1901
Ink and coloured pencil on paper; 13 x 10
Private collection

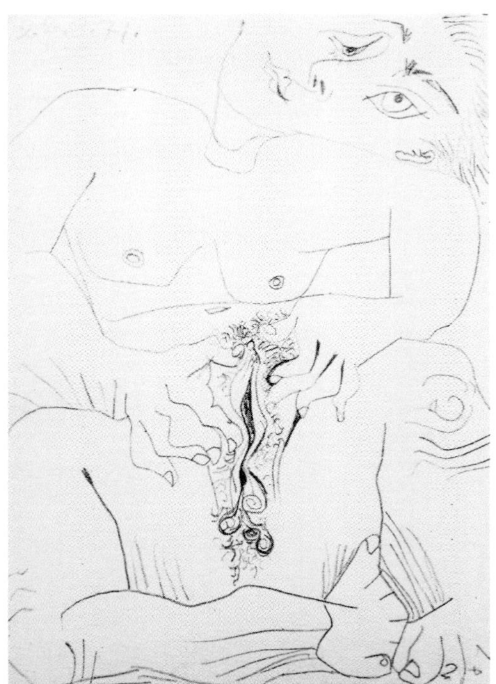

Fig. 4: *Nude*, 22 August 1971
Pencil on grey paper; 31 x 22
Paris, Galerie Louise Leiris

mouth, a hole, triturated by the fangs of two feverish, paw-like hands, physically palpable, lascivious and appalling, stunning, beatific, racked, convulsing and hastily sketched on cardboard in a very close-up perspective—*Untitled* (1971). The piece belonged to the Galerie Louise Leiris and was an ironic nod to Gustave Courbet's *The Origin of the World*, a surreptitious glance, but drawn as closely to the bone as possible. The subject resembles a coarse mound of pulp, a jagged-edged slug or a hedgehog, bristling its spines.[5]

"The gaze is the erection of the eye," wrote Jean Clair,[6] apropos, in his substantiation of the idea that the eye socket is an extension of the penis (Eros is vision!). With this premise in mind, one is naturally compelled to consider the white, wounded, mortified, castrated, gouged, enucleated, mutilated, glazed, invaginated iris of the celebrated Celestina, the one-eyed, one-legged prostitute and procuress who lived at 12 carrer Conde del Asalto in Barcelona and was a major character in works from Picasso's younger years—he first depicted her in March 1904. The real model was Carlota Valdivia, an ancient wench whose eyes were shaped like big, round peepholes. Valdivia was a witch-like streetwalker and the madam of a brothel in Barcelona that would have resembled the one Pablo frequented at age fourteen with his good friend Manuel Pallarés, in the *barrio chino*, the poorest area of the port city. With her penetrating, viscous eyes, this keyhole *voyeuse* and expert reliever of virile members spied on the vicious patrons who would line up to get theirs undisturbed, behind closed doors, from the women Picasso called *poutains* ("hookers") in his poor French. An unnatural, prurient mother, an ugly, aged harlot whose life was devoted, body and soul, to the service of *foutra* (fornication), this illustrious whorehouse proprietress was painted by Picasso as a venerable and virtuous parent, adorned with a chaste mantilla and draped in a prudish black coat. Celestina, a Goyaesque, archetypal and literary figure under the quill of Fernando de Rojas, takes all of Picasso's erotic works under her wing. Curious about everything, with piercing, all-seeing eyes, he was, apparently, haunted by blindness throughout his life. Indeed, a mortal fear of empty eye sockets left him petrified when he happened upon a hollow-eyed African statuette. Picasso, who was gifted with a unique vision, knew better than anyone that the eye is a substitute for the penis, a tool of visual rape, and that the lunar eye, extinguished, scarred, marred by leukoma, veiled by an opaque egg-white coating, opposes the solar eye. He knew that blindness is a metaphor for castration and that the eye, erogenous zone par excellence, is also the prism of inner vision. "Why not put sexual organs in place of the eyes and eyes between the legs?" he once wondered.[7] *La Celestina* was a crucial work of the Blue Period, the procuress's waxing eye a kind of eyeball with foreskin, casting a vigilant, vaginal gaze upon the shameless sexual romps of the young, fiery-eyed painter. For Picasso, a woman was a pleasure for the eyes, just as art was submitted to the pleasure principle. Like all Andalusians, he was obsessed by the

5 *Érotique de l'art* (Paris: Taschen, 1993), p. 56.
6 Jean Clair, *Méduse* (Paris: Gallimard, 1989), p. 79.
7 Richardson, p. 10.

mirada fuerte ("strong gaze"), which may have been symbolically represented by the "gigantic" bull's-eye window in the Barcelona attic that, for a time, served as the artist's studio.[8]

Coitus, connected with a stirring of the senses and with instinctual impulses, was Picasso's true painterly subject, as evidenced by the inscription on one drawing of a female nude in 1902: "*Quando tengas ganas de joder, jode!*" ("When you feel like fucking, fuck!").[9] Altogether unburdened of "shame," a Christian concept, Picasso wanted to paint the pleasure, the violence and the frenzy of the sexual act, the actual odour of bodies, and the intense delight of orgasm—since, for him, painting and making love were the same thing. Sexuality—just how does one define the sex of painting?—is indissociable from artistic creativity, and the grand design of Eros is physical union, the merging and symbiosis of two beings. "Art is never chaste," said Picasso, who set about producing representations of feverish copulation very early on in his career, as shown in *El Virgo* (Cat. 32, 1902–03), a stylized, scathingly ironic caricature of a man taking a woman from behind.

The first phase of copulation is *The Kiss*, recurrently studied and painted in 1925, 1929, 1931, 1943, on 7 October 1967, and in 1969, always under the same title. The fantasies of devouring and cannibalism are expressed in the artist's savage mixtures and raw depictions involving two facies that melt together and eat, suck on, ingest, swallow and devour each other, not so much with their eyes as with their bloodsucker lips, their intertwined tongues, and their phallic, copulating noses. In representing the stages preceding this frisky exchange, Picasso shows a recurrent obsession with duos, exploring their many facets in an infinite number of settings and circumstances, from the oil on canvas *Couple in the Retiro Park*, a chaste and blissfully happy representation of a prim and proper couple, to the pastel on paper, and later a more expressionist oil on canvas, *Lovers in the Street (The Kiss)* of 1900, dedicated to Lluis Vilaro[10] and visibly inspired by the sight of lovebirds embracing in the street as represented by Steinlen. It should be borne in mind that romance was as sinful as nudism was immoral during this era. *The Embrace (The Beast)*, also called *Bestial Embrace* (Paris, 1900), was Picasso's tribute to lovers who defied orthodoxy and society's conventions of virtue, and embraced each other in public. A piece under the same title, *Embrace* (Barcelona, 1903),[11] is an unambiguous interior scene, also produced in pastel, depicting a full-body view of a naked couple in a contrite pause that brings to mind Adam and Eve. In *The Embrace* (Paris, 1905), an oil on cardboard, dedicated to Apollinaire, two lovers clasp each other, lying down; *The Lovers* (Cat. 43, August 1904) precedes this work, with great purity in its line, while in *The Rape* (Cat. 9, c. 1900), the devil stands with darkly scribbled features, seizing his pretty woman with gusto.

8   Brassaï, *Conversations avec Picasso* (Paris: Gallimard, 1964), p. 227.
9   Richardson, p. 244, n. 2.
10 Richardson, p. 92.
11 Ocaña, p. 237.

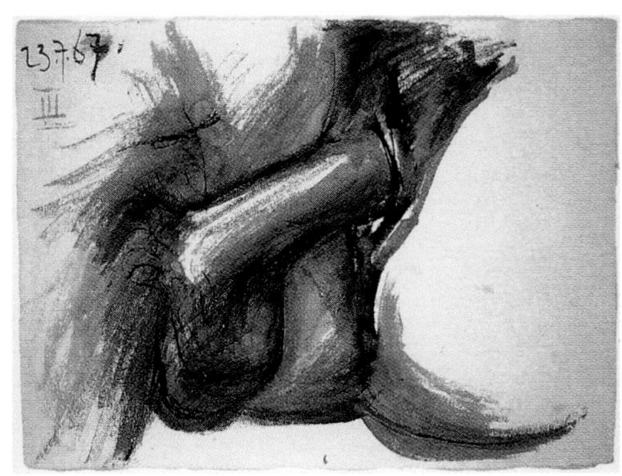

Fig. 5: *Untitled*, 23 July 1967
Wash on paper; 56 x 75
Private collection

Over the years, psychology annihilates itself and wipes itself out in the physiological realm served by the evocation of voluptuous embraces, delineated or brushed into existence with convulsive strokes intended to express, in infinite variations, the curves and counter-curves of the body and the flesh. Such was the laborious exercise in style undertaken by Picasso, whose attention was devoted above all, to line, to posture and to his models. Picasso evoked the act of sex in long, filanderous lines or snaking strokes that gradually transformed into a real body-to-body encounter, almost a wrestling match, in the true sense of a fight. The sexual violence of the embrace, of physical union, not merely seen but genuinely felt, became the focus of the activities Picasso depicted with such barbaric intensity. His male-female confrontations were not academic studies or illustrations of mythological heroes, Callipygian Venuses, centaurs or minotaurs, but flesh-and-blood human beings with their genitalia as clearly endowed as they were differentiated. From *Couple Making Love* (1902, 1905, 1917, 1933) to the innumerable variations on *The Embrace* (1925, 1933, 1955, 1963, 1970), India ink washes, etchings, aquatints or paintings, and even *Embrace and Kiss* (19 November 1969) and *Coupling* (1963), soon only an amassed relationship of shapes and corresponding strengths emerged, interweaving the whole and its parts. Orifices, folds and swells interlock, volumes and reliefs mingle, foreground and background blend together, the fronts and backs of anatomical parts agglutinate into one compact, sculpted block, impenetrable from the outside, a two-headed monster engulfing itself, a magma of meat and a jam of mucous, tongues, cheeks, bellies, buttocks, thighs, navels, armpits, holes, ravines, hills and bumps.

In this act of union, where identities were not readily distinguishable, orgasm would undergo a treatment at once obscene and distanced, boiling and mechanical, burning and barbaric, energetic and lustful, organic and sensitive, transforming bed and bedroom into a battleground, as though the paintings were produced through a somersaulting of chaos. Among the splayed thighs, the brandished phalluses, the tortured members and the anamorphic, liquefied, dislocated flesh, Picasso surrendered with delight and fury to his predilection for deformations and improbable physical contortions, fired by the vehemence of his solid tones and the exuberance of his colours, celebrating with unmatched energy, in a thousand positions, the coupling of bodies exhibited as living matter, clusters of abstract or dismantled shapes, of muscles and kidneys, the fruit of a primal, eye-popping gaze upon the annihilation of the world.

Copulation was an archetypal scene that Picasso scrutinized throughout his life with dogged insistence, captivated as he was by the urges of passion and by the physical commingling of bodies, as evidenced in a drawing dated "23.7.67."[12] This anatomical description of penetration features a confrontation and mutual devouring of lover-wrestlers at war that is reduced to a very raw close-up of the body parts at work. As a recurrent exercise, reproduced in an infinite number of

12 Marie-Laure Bernadac and Bernard Marcadé, eds., *Masculin-Féminin: Le Sexe de l'art* (Paris: Centre Georges-Pompidou & Gallimard/Électra, 1999), ill. 313.

media, the depiction of copulation was so fascinating to Picasso that he devoted his entire life to exploring it. It was both a fertile theme and the main thread of his work, and he approached it with swaggering pride and total impunity from a tender age, producing reformulated variations ad nauseam — everywhere: on the boulevard Raspail, at Céret, Sorgues, Avignon, the Bateau-Lavoir, Mougins, Vallauris and Vauvenargues. In the end, his collection of female bodies, assembled from each of the women he loved, became as one, continuously reformulated. Through all these variations in Picasso's work, we may glimpse Fernande Olivier, his first great love and companion until 1911, Olga, the "castrator," Eva, whom he called his "pretty one," as well as other "flower-women" or "second mothers," Marie-Thérèse Walter, his muse for 15 years, Dora Maar, Françoise Gilot, whom he met in 1943, and Jacqueline Roque, who became his wife in 1961.

At twenty years of age, a young Pablo Picasso intoned, "A woman who is loved becomes omnipresent." At that early date, he was still too much of a neophyte, with his accumulated canvases, prints and drawings before him, depicting all his lovers bustled, piled up, cancelling each other out and indiscriminately overlapping until they morphed into one body, clad in many modes of attire, exposing their alluring features, embraced a hundred thousand times with stupefying virtuosity and drive while his own, solitary body was still the same. "The passion of love is a true labour," the wild young fellow with the brooding eyes must have reflected, striking his typical pose, arms crossed, standing firm on his short but powerful legs. Already he was a man of deep-seated jealousy, instigating spiralling, gale-force liaisons, and proving that he possessed exceptional talent in drawing. It was through drawing that he would learn to master line and that his obsessions would blossom, unfettered. And while it is true that some of his obsessions may have been more admirable than others, Pablo Picasso stood firm in his conviction that no subject was unworthy of being represented. Some subjects he would only depict once, at breakneck speed — speed being one of his cardinal virtues — in off-the-cuff sketches. But it was his erotic sketches and the barefaced, boastful *pochades* he created during his formative years that would play a primordial role in the genesis of pieces he would continue to produce, even as an inspired nonagenarian, albeit in a marginal register and despite the fact that they were, incorrectly, deemed to be minor works.

THE YOUNG PICASSO'S INITIATION

Malén Gual

While painting and drawing were always the expression and affirmation of Picasso's life events and experiences, we must look to his first drawings to understand the awakening of his sexuality, a process which coincided with the emergence of a powerful propensity for curiosity and exploration.

In his conversations with John Richardson, Picasso maintained that he had never gone through adolescence in his life or in his work and that he had made a direct transition from childhood to sexual maturity.[1] However, the nude, sensuality and eroticism make a progressive, faltering appearance in his work, and their first manifestations are steeped in academic overtones, or are caricatural and very often infused with crude, scatological jokes commonly told by children and adolescents.

Picasso's sexual awakening took place during the years he spent at La Coruña (1890–95), from age ten to fourteen, as we can see in the sketches and the caricatures he drew in his schoolbooks and sketchbooks at that time. Based on details of his personal life provided by Picasso himself, several authors believe his first brief romances took place in La Coruña. For example, quoting some conversations with Picasso, Antonio D. Olano[2] asserts that the artist's first love was a young Galician girl named Carmiña, the daughter of fishermen and the model for *La Fillette aux pieds nus*.[3] However, John Richardson would say that Picasso's first romance was with Ángeles Méndez Gil,[4] a fellow student at the Instituto da Guarda in La Coruña, whose name appears in the margins of a few of his schoolbooks and in some drawings from this period.[5] But let us put aside these hypotheses on childhood crushes and attempt to retrace Picasso's slow, timid journey toward sexual awareness by analysing the content of his very first drawings.

Four schoolbooks have been preserved from Picasso's student years at the Instituto da Guarda; the margins are copiously illustrated with drawings, caricatures and inscriptions. The first book, *Literatura perceptiva. Retórica y poética*,[6] used by

1 John Richardson (with the collaboration of Marilyn McCully), *A Life of Picasso, Vol. 1, 1881–1906* (New York: Random House, 1991), p. 48

2 Antonio D. Olano, *Las Mujeres de Picasso* (N.p.: n.d.), p. 41.

3 Musée Picasso (Paris) collection, No. 2.

4 Richardson, p. 55.

5 See drawing MPB 110.367, featuring the annotation: *Ángeles/ Méndez/ Gil*; the textbook used by Picasso during the 1893–94 school year, *Literatura perceptiva. Retórica y poética* MPB 110.927, p. 97: *Sta. Ángeles Méndez Gil*; and the book used in 1893–94, *Ejercicios de análisis literario* MPB 110.928, p. 256: Ángeles.

6 Emilio Álvarez Giménez, *Literatura perceptiva. Retórica y poética* (Pontevedra: n.p.,1889), MPB 110.927.

the young Picasso during the 1893–94 school year, is full of drawings with childish themes, such as guns, knives, animals and caricatured heads. At the end of the book is *Donkey and She-Ass*, a pencil drawing of two asses in the act of mating, accompanied by a rhyme that was likely chanted by his schoolmates: *Sin más ni más ni más/la burra levanta el/ rabo sin más ni más ni más/el burro le mete el nabo* ("Get on, get it on, get it on/ she-ass lift up/ your tail get it in, get it in, get it in/ the he-ass puts in his prick"). Picasso and his chums sang these verses and crude songs. Indeed, these kind of ditties were so frequent in Spanish literature that, from the popular *romanceros* to major authors like Quevedo, there are references to coitus and comparisons between the members of animals and those of humans. As Sabartés said years later: "The inscriptions placed under the drawings often simply claim to elucidate the intention of the painter or to provide a commentary but, generally, words are used to translate the content of the imagination more quickly, thereby using drawings and the pictorial explanations more sparingly since it is not always easy to translate ideas into a drawn line. Moreover, we have already seen that in Picasso's work, each object claims a distinctive form and any means are valid, when used at the right time, to express the artist's thought. …With Picasso, words directly precede ideas; he draws on impulse, and then his drawing suggests more to him: words therefore come as a complement to finish the image that is sketched using lines or through any other means of expression."[7]

We find additional indications of this puerile curiosity, this approach to the human body, in the same schoolbook and others containing diverse sketches of characters defecating, as well as humorous mathematical operations with clear scatological references. The discovery of the female body, however, was still forbidden to Picasso during the entire La Coruña period: female nudes appear, along with several male nudes (often, these were academic studies), in only two sketches, one of which features scarcely recognizable female forms.[8]

When Pablo's father, Don José, was hired as a professor at Escuela de Bellas Artes de Barcelona (the School of Fine Arts, Barcelona, known as *La Llotja*), the entire Ruiz-Picasso family left La Coruña. For the young Pablo, the move meant a considerable change of lifestyle and customs. He found himself in a prosperous, ever changing and rapidly expanding city where architecture and the other arts were seeking and finding new forms of expression. Fashions and customs were becoming more liberal and followed the trends and news from abroad. Following in the footsteps of his father, Picasso was enrolled at La Llotja and made the acquaintance of other boys, sometimes older than himself, like Manuel Pallarés. These friends not only helped him enter Barcelona's artistic milieu but also showed him some of the more recreational aspects of the Catalan capital. Some Picasso biographers speak of Pallarés as a rabid skirt chaser who introduced Picasso to brothels, despite his young age.[9]

7 Jaime Sabartés, *Picasso: Retratos y recuerdos* (Madrid: Afrodisio Aguado, 1953), p. 109–10.
   (Free translation.)
8 MPB 111.416r and 111.504r, both produced in 1894–95.
9 Richardson, p. 68.

Pablo, who attended his courses regularly at La Llotja, as evidenced by his many academic studies, made very quick and considerable technical progress, acquiring a sure sense of line and a great compositional rigour. His academic drawings began to abound with female nudes. They include some representations of Venuses, copies of moulds in plaster,[10] sketches of women posing in contrived positions, like models for a composition drawn facing forward or backward, all still bereft of sensuality but whose curves and shadows already denote an attentive and prolonged observation of their anatomy.[11] Although it had played a determining erotic role from the very beginnings of artistic representation, in the 19th-century academies the nude was presented as an artistic theory, and a foundation of teaching methods. Therefore it is understandable that Picasso's first nudes lacked an erotic charge and that, during this period, they had not yet gained any distance from the chill of academe.

In keeping with the philosophy of La Llotja and encouraged by his father, during the 1896–97 school year the young Picasso cultivated his skills in historical and religious painting. Don José's ultimate goal was for his son to make a name for himself in the official painting milieu and, along with other teachers, he passed on the means and ideas that Pablo would need to develop themes of high moral value. Apart from his best known and most successful compositions from this period,[12] and their draft studies, Picasso attempted other scenes such as annunciations, apparitions of the Sacred Heart and scenes of martyrs as simple exercises in composition or figure studies. In one *Annunciation*[13] the irreverent insolence of the young artist is plain to see as, in the margin of the scene, an inverted inscription can be deciphered, making reference to copulation: "*saque por Dios déjemela V. Dentro.*" The full version of this verse appears on a page from one of his sketchbooks: "A very pretty young girl had a tooth/ that hurt and she went to the dentist/ to see if he would pull it out and when the poor little thing/ saw the instrument she said to the/ dentist Don't take it out, for God's sake leave it/ in me."[14] The double reference to penetration and the size of the "instrument" (member) must have provoked outbursts of laughter among Picasso and his friends. On another sheet in the same book is an inscription that combines a reference to masturbation with the kind of anticlerical derision that was common among all peoples of Spain: "My village priest/ died from scratching too much/ He was a good priest and he knew how/ to scratch himself."[15] In a magnificent study of eroticism in Spanish literature, Camilo José Cela has published several anticlerical satirical verses collected from various areas of the peninsula.[16] At the end of the 19th century,

10 For example, MPB 110.392, 110.856, 110.876.
11 See MPB 110.264r, 111.456.
12 *La Primera Comunión* (MPB 110.110.001) and *L'Escola* (musée de Montserrat), from 1896.
13 MPB 110.903.
14 "*Una niña muy bonita tenía una muela / picada y fue a casa de un dentista / para ver si se la sacaría y la pobrecita / niña al ver el instrumento le decía al / dentista no me la saque por Dios déjemela / V. Dentro.*" MPB 111.096r from sketchbook 110.911, worked on during the 1896–97 school year.
15 "*El cura de mi lugar / murió de una rascadura / Ese sí que era un buen cura y / se sabía rascar.*" MPB 111.804 from sketchbook 110.911.
16 Camilo José Cela, *Diccionario del erotismo*, Vol. II (Barcelona: Grijalbo, 1988), p. 272, 566.

traces of erotic-satirical poetry are apparent in literary and political verse. Several renowned artists wrote diatribes against the dominant classes and against the clergy, either in their own name or anonymously. According to Cela, these verses were widespread in the cafés of Madrid, and likely in Barcelona, printed on tracts that were passed around by customers.[17] Whether or not Picasso read these lampoons, as a young jokester he was sufficiently amused by the humour and double meanings of popular culture jokes to take note of them in his sketchbooks.

A few drawings done during the 1895–96 school year have been preserved, bearing witness to Picasso's observations of street life, his erotic awakening and his premature knowledge of the laws of romance and seduction; they depict the farewells of a soldier and his fiancée[18] or the delicate coquetries of a young girl between two boys, which the artist himself sagaciously entitled *Entre dos fuegos* (*Between Two Fires*).[19]

Madrid 1897–98

Encouraged by the first success of his son in official art circles, and further inspired by an honourable mention for Pablo's allegorical canvas *Science et Charité* in 1897, Don José decided to send his son to Madrid, to the Real Academia de Bellas Artes San Fernando (San Fernando Royal Academy of Fine Arts), for the 1897–98 school year. Pablo, who had just celebrated his sixteenth birthday, had found a way to escape the tutelage of his father. We know that the young artist was almost immediately disappointed with the education provided at the Madrid academy, as he himself recounted in a famous letter to his friend Joaquín Bas. His rejection of the academy compelled him to visit the Prado museum, walk the streets and frequent typical Madrid cafés, armed with his sketchbooks. At the Prado, he discovered the great masters of the past and copied works by Velázquez, El Greco and Goya. His copies of Goya's art included a few drawings from *La Tauromaquia*[20] and *Los Caprichos* No. 25 and No. 17.[21] He made the copies from drawings and not from engravings, as confirmed by Xavier de Salas: "… in the copy of the *Caprice* (No. 17), there is the detail around the edge of the brazier, clearly drawn, with some curved embellishments that can be seen in the drawing rather than in the shadow, as is the case in etchings."[22] The copy of this Goya *Caprice*, entitled *Bien tirada está* ("This is well drawn") (Fig. 1), marks the appearance of a character destined to figure in Picasso's art until the end of his days: Celestina. Picasso, who was a long-standing lover of picaresque Spanish literature, saw in the free and independent personage of the *pícaro* his alter ego, a nonconformist, self-made hero. He had a particular liking for Fernando de Rojas's *Tragicomedia de Calixto y Melibea*, published in 1499. The central character, an old procuress named Celestina, became

17 Cela, p. 716.
18 MPB 110.620.
19 MPB 110.364, 110.376, 110.376r, 110.663.
20 See sketchbook, MPB 110.917.
21 Respectively, MPB 111.517 and 111.369.
22 Xavier de Salas, *Carnet Picasso: Madrid, 1898* (Barcelona: Gustavo Gili, 1976).

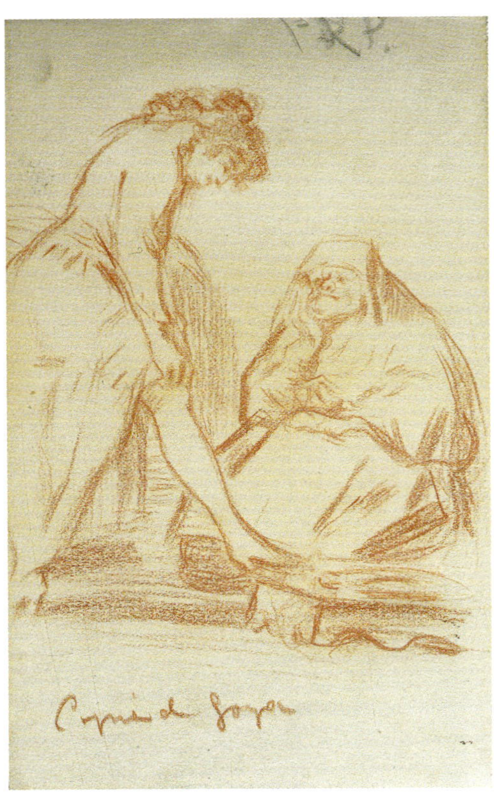

Fig. 1: *This Is Well Drawn*, 1898
Sanguine on paper; 17.5 x 10.5
Barcelona, Museu Picasso, MPB 111.369

such an important figure that she effectively replaced the original title of the work, and her name was used in antonomasia. Picasso, who inherited the character of Celestina from Spanish literature and painting, claimed her for himself, placing her in contemporary scenes, in brothels or cafés, or alone, reserving a lead role for her in one of the most famous paintings of the Blue Period.[23] The first Celestina to appear in a freely inspired drawing, contemporaneous with the copy of Goya's *Caprice*, is that in *Interior Scene*,[24] in which the old procuress offers a potbellied bourgeois man a young girl, who is sitting on a divan with her breasts bared. Picasso modernized the subject, but Celestina and her clothing were faithful to the customs of the 18th century, as represented by Goya, and would remain so in all of the painter's works: Celestina is an elderly, stooped woman with an amorphous body, her head covered by a hood or veil.

According to Pío Baroja, at the end of the century Madrid was all lightness and optimism, and there was an unbridled drive to escape conventions. "At that time, the area of Puerta del Sol was full of taverns, dives and cheap restaurants, which made our *plaza central* a kind of Court of Miracles. Around the Puerta del Sol were more than ten gambling houses, open all night long. …"[25] Picasso was no stranger to the nightlife and his drawings testified to his visits to cafés, taverns and gambling houses.[26] He drew the most classic places and characters in Madrid, especially women, enveloped in their capes or elegantly attired. A drawing of one of these women, sketched in a few strokes, was accompanied by the inscription *"What do you want?/ Give me a package of envelopes from London,"*[27] plainly revealing the artist's preoccupation with all things sexual. At the end of the 19th century, condoms were called "envelopes from London" in Spain (much like the English expression "French letter") because they were purportedly invented, or at least perfected, by the English. The condom appeared fortuitously in Spanish literature the same year (1898), with the first printing of a book entitled *El Arte de las putas*, by Nicolás Fernández de Moratín.[28] The book's title and content must have been a favourite subject of conversation in the cafés of Madrid: "This was how the condom was invented;/ afterward, the very subtle and philosophical/ English of the century improved it/ and reduced the thickness of its membrane … / and the prostitutes of London are fined/ if they fail to offer entire platters of condoms. …"[29]

23 Musée Picasso (Paris).
24 MPB 110.389.
25 Pío Baroja, *La Dama errante*, cited by José Carlos Mainer in *Modernismo y 98* (Barcelona: Ediciones Crítica, 1979).
26 See MPB 111.355, 111.357, 110.681.
27 *"¿Que quiere Vd?/ Deme un paquete de sobres de Londón,"* MPB 111.364r.
28 Cela, p. 648.
29 *"El condón de este modo fue inventado;/ después los sutilísimos ingleses/ filósofos del siglo, lo han pulido,/ y a membrana sutil lo han reducido…/ y las putas de Londres son multadas/ si no ofrecen bandejas de condones…."* Cela, p. 77.

With the exception of one isolated nude, erotic themes did not reappear in Picasso's work before his return to Barcelona in 1899. By this time, Don José found his son to be a more independent, mature and resourceful young man, who had no intention of accepting any paternal tutelage in either his artistic or his personal life. The first signs of revolt in Picasso came to light when he refused to pursue his schooling at La Llotja and enrolled at the Cercle Artístic liberal academy, where teaching was more avant-garde and in step with the French academies. Picasso was also looking for a studio in which to work outside his family home. Among the academic exercises preserved from this period there are several female nudes.[30] Although they suggest a considerable improvement, compared to drawings executed two years previous, in the artist's freedom of stroke and his skill in capturing volumes, in the importance of line and in the disappearance of shadows, they show that Picasso had not yet abandoned academic poses; we are far from the carnality and sensuality of other, more spontaneous drawings from the same period. The most erotic and suggestive nudes Picasso produced were perhaps the sketches he provided as illustrations for his friend Joan Oliva Bridgman's poem *El Clam de les verges* ("The lament of the virgins"),[31] published in *Joventut* of 12 July 1900.

Sharing a studio with other artists his own age (the Cardona brothers) not only meant that Picasso was distancing himself from his family, but also that he was widening his circle of friends beyond his classmates at La Llotja. Besides Pallarés and the Cardonas, Picasso associated with Carles Casagemas, the Fernández de Soto brothers and, a little later, with Sabartés. As Sabartés says in his memoirs: "I am a useful friend for conversation, someone who will not niggle over a personal point; someone who is in there for the long haul, all the way to Tibidabo or elsewhere, without showing any sign of fatigue. A friend to have fun with when one has no money to spend. Others accompany Picasso to see the bullfights on *corrida* days, go to cafés every evening, and, every night, to the Edén Concert and the bistros of Paralelo, or to see girls. Picasso is a discerning arbiter of various trends and tastes. … Some friends are used for one thing and others for other things."[32] In discussing the years of his youth, Picasso confirmed to Richardson that he frequented the *barrio chino* (the "hot" quarter of Barcelona) with Ángel Fernández de Soto—"On faisait la bringue ensemble!" ("We used to raise hell together!")[33]— and with Casagemas. Casagemas was his drinking companion in the Catalan capital and during Picasso's brief stay in Málaga, where the two friends proceeded

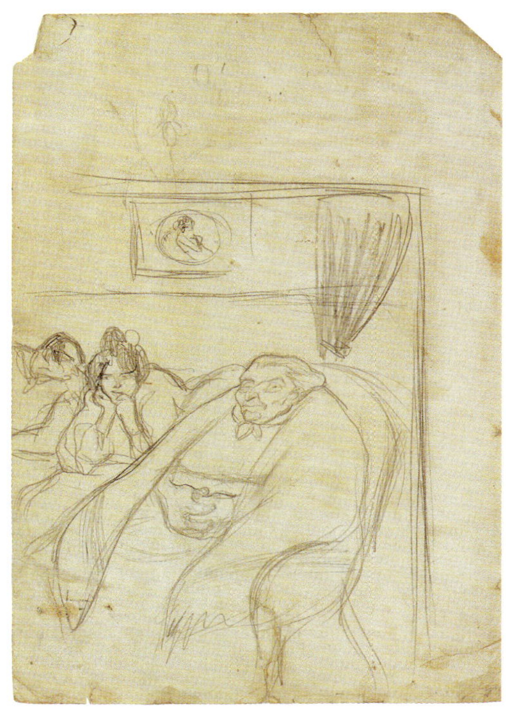

13 La Celestina with a Couple, 1901
Graphite stick on paper; 33.1 x 24
Barcelona, Museu Picasso, MPB 110.356 [PB]

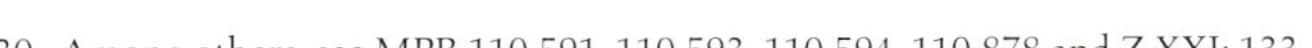

30 Among others, see MPB 110.591, 110.593, 110.594, 110.878 and Z.XXI: 133.
31 MPB 110.341, 110.669.
32 *"Yo soy el amigo que sirve para sostener una conversación porque no pone empeño en imponer su discrepancia; el que aguanta una caminata, montaña del tibidabo arriba, o adonde sea, sin dar muestras de fatiga. El amigo con quien uno puede distraerse sin gastar dinero cuando no hay dinero que gastar. Otros van con él a los toros, los días de corrida; al café cada tarde y cada noche; al Edén Concert y a las tabernas del Paralelo, o a otros sitios adonde les conduce su despreocupada juventud. Picasso sabe distinguir gustos y aficiones. …Unos amigos sirven para una cosa y otros para otra,"* Sabartés, p. 27. Tibidabo is a mountain northwest of Barcelona that takes its name from the evangelical scene of the Temptation of Christ.
33 Richardson, p. 116.

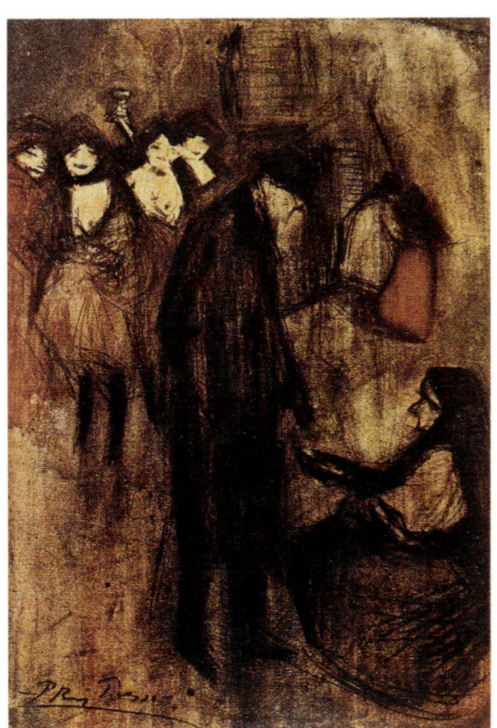

Fig. 2: *Alms-giving*, 1898
Coloured drawing with spirit dilution on paper; 47 x 32
Private collection

to scandalize the Picasso family. One of Picasso's sketchbooks, signed *PRP/ Málaga*, contains the following inscription: *Calle Grava-2-Casa d'amor* ("Calle Grava-2-House of Love"),[34] a clear indication of the two friends' preferences.

From these incursions into the *barrio chino*, into the taverns and brothels, the artist has left us some splendid drawings in which the theme of prostitution is treated with marked crudeness by the young seventeen/eighteen-year-old. In *El Diván* (Cat. 4) Celestina reappears, lurking in the background of a room as she keeps her eye on a couple, busy cuddling on a divan in front of a table on which a bottle is set. Above the divan are an oval mirror and a painting of a female nude—a typical feature of fin de siècle brothels. In the drawing *La Celestina with a Couple*[35] (Cat. 13) the procuress is more prominently featured, sitting in a chair in the foreground. The couple in the background, and old Celestina, look straight ahead toward the young artist who is painting them. Because of her literary connotations, or perhaps a morbid attraction to her as a character, Celestina is more important to Picasso than her protégées. At this juncture, Picasso had produced only one portrait of an emaciated prostitute, *La Chata*.[36] Also preserved—torn out of a sketchbook—is a portrait of Rosita,[37] long considered to be a prostitute until Richardson identified her as the "amazon" Rosita del Oro, Picasso's mistress at the time.[38]

Eager as ever to capture new scenes and impressions, the artist chose the theme of brothels, and filled numerous sheets and notebooks with sketches and notes in which curvaceous women, clothed only in stockings and skirts, exhibit themselves before their clients in suggestive poses.[39] In other depictions, the negotiations have been concluded and the couples begin their carnal exchanges.[40] Another series of very dark drawings with touches of red and yellow, no longer belonging to brothels but rather to the world of street prostitution, represents the juxtaposition of pleasure and misery that existed in the seediest areas of the city. Amid beggars and forsaken women, half-naked prostitutes, grimacing and obscene, attempt to attract the men passing by on the street; when they succeed, they form couples and retreat, entwined, to the end of the street, escaping our view (that of the spectator)[41] (Fig. 2). For all his vitality and erotic potential, Picasso could not escape being influenced by the dim, miserable and condemning view that 19th-century Spanish society took of prostitution; nor could he avoid attributing a certain moralistic overtone to his charcoal rendering of 1899[42] in which the legend of Eve after the Fall provides the framework for a portrait of an old, not very attractive woman who symbolizes the unfortunate consequences of practising the oldest profession (Fig. 3).

34 Arnold Glimcher and Marc Glimcher, eds., *Je suis le cahier: The Sketchbooks of Picasso*
     (New York: The Pace Gallery, 1986), No. 18, p. 307.
35 MPB 110.356.
36 MPB 50.486, 110.568.
37 MPB 110.653r.
38 Richardson, p. 68.
39 MPB 110.564, 110.604r, 110.287.
40 MPB 110.258r, 44r from MP Sketchbook No. 1.
41 MPB 110.592r; Z. I, 379, Z. VI, 229, Z.XXI: 90.
42 Z.VI: 176.

It was with even greater innocence that Picasso approached the theme of be-trothal (far removed from the ambiance of brothels) in several sketches of couples dressed in popular attire—courting each other on a patio, in the middle of the road or on the road to the *corridas*. For the first time, he produced a portrait of two fiancés kissing, describing in several sketches the approach to the kiss and ensuing loss of propriety, from an innocent kiss stolen from a resistant young girl[43] to a naively accepted kiss[44] (Fig. 4). Bodies and faces approach each other slowly before melting into an embrace in which the lovers' bodies become as one (Fig. 5). But it was not until the year 1900, in Paris, that the kiss and the embrace acquired the full intensity of sexual desire, encouraged by an expanded permissiveness in customs and inspired by scenes in rue de Steinlen, and probably by Munch's *The Kiss*. Picasso's work was subsequently invaded by very expressionistic oils and pastels, representations of couples clasped in fond embraces below Montmartre (Cat. 11), or holed up in bedrooms—where desire manifested itself much more brutally.[45] The premises of this violent sexuality are also manifest in some draw-ings done in May, in Barcelona,[46] that resonate with the expressionism of contem-porary Parisian painters: a horrified woman escapes a violent attack from a man who, in his brutality, ends up turning into a satyr.[47]

In a series of drawings with lighter and more humorous overtones, the artist comes closer to voyeurism and to "insinuation via the gaze." In a park, a governess is breast-feeding a baby and an old, smiling man draws nearer so that he can get a closer look at her enormous bosom.[48] The man is wearing a Catalan cap, a *barretina*, and Picasso has placed a green stain on his face as an allusion to the expression *viejo verde* ("green old man") the Spanish name for an older man who seduces or lusts after young girls. The saucy yet innocent look of the old man in the park turns into a grimace: a lecher, now of deformed proportions and bulging eyes, leers hungrily at a nude woman. The letters "PU" are written at the bottom of the drawing to suggest the vocation of the young receiver of the old man's hungry gaze (Fig. 6).[49] In the spring of 1901, in another sketchbook, the word *poutain* ("hooker") appears written this time in full, as the title of a portrait of a woman no longer young, her breasts drooping and her face withered, showing prostitution in its darkest light.[50]

Paris 1900
Following the example of most of the painters who frequented *Els Quatre Gats*, Picasso went to Paris with Casagemas for the *Exposition universelle* in October 1900, moving into the studio vacated by Isidro Nonell at 49 rue Gabrielle, near

43 MPB 110.724.
44 MPB 110.754, 110.804r.
45 PALAU 500.
46 MPB 110.296r, 110.268, 110.295.
47 MPB 110.342r.
48 MPB 110.756r, 110.781, Z.XXI: 60.
49 MP, Sketchbook No. 1, 33 V°.
50 MP, Sketchbook No. 1, 8 V°.

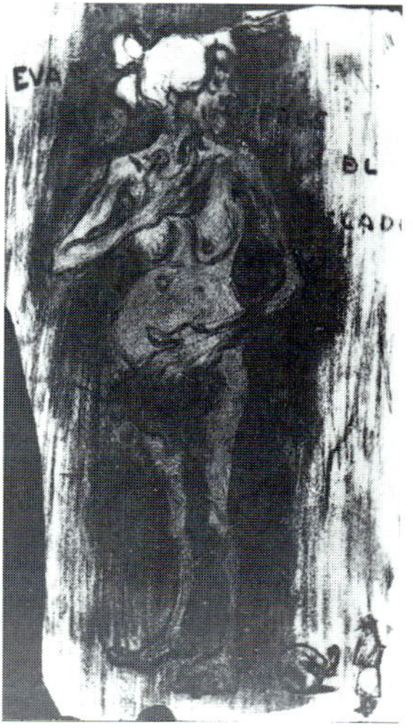

Fig. 3: *Eve after the Fall*, 1899
Charcoal and Conté crayon on paper; 28.7 x 16.5
Private collection

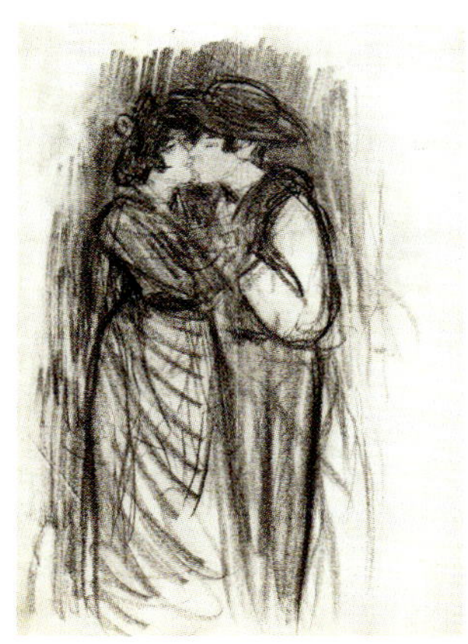

Fig. 4: *The Kiss*, April 1899
Conté crayon on paper; 22.8 x 16.7
Barcelona, Museu Picasso, MPB 110.375

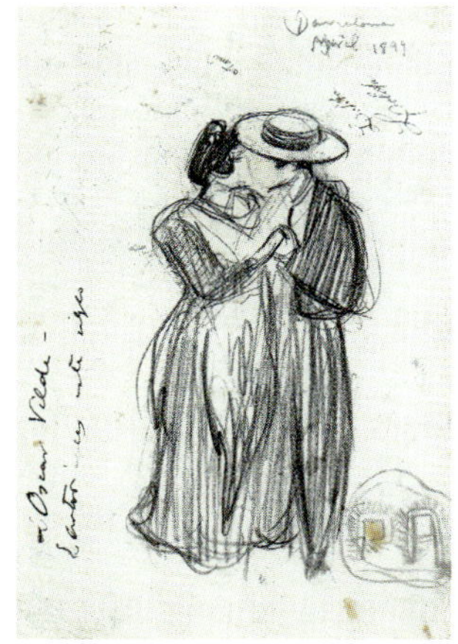

Fig. 5: *The Kiss*, April 1899
Conté crayon and pencil on paper; 31.5 x 22
Barcelona, Museu Picasso, MPB 110.754

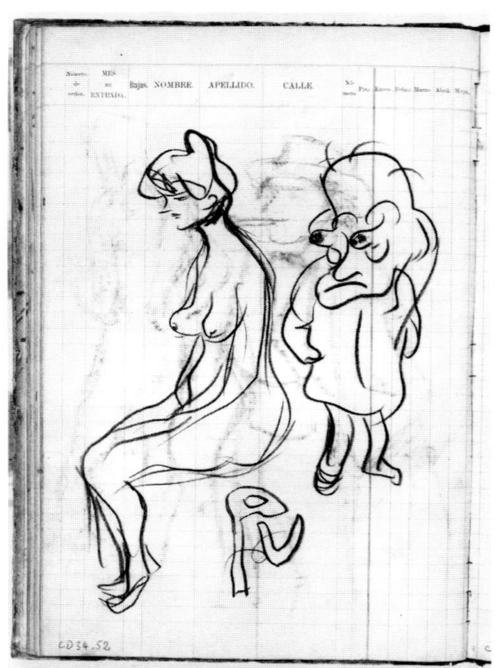

Fig. 6: *Barcelona Sketchbook*, Winter 1899–1900
Seated Nude Watched by a Character
with Eyes Popping Out of His Head (f° 33 r°)
Charcoal with oil heightenings on paper; 30.5 x 21
Paris, Musée Picasso, MP 1990-93

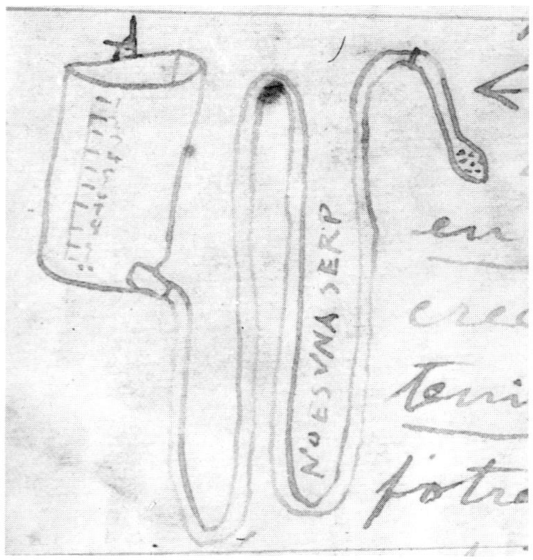

Fig. 7: Detail of a letter to Reventós, 25 October 1900
Collection of Dr. Jacint Reventós Conti

Sacré-Cœur. A few days later, Pallarés joined them. The three friends found Paris to be a relaxed and euphoric place at the time, both because of the Exposition and the excitement generated by the turn of the century. Human relations were infused with greater freedom. Above all, artists found a new kind of painting in Paris that was more colourful and revolutionary, less literary and corseted. As always with Picasso, the change of atmosphere and the shock of the new did not lead to an immediate shift in his work[51] but, because of his artistic hypersensitivity, his work during this period did become far more polychromatic, and his treatment of line was freer. Picasso's work reflected nightlife in Paris, with its extravagant characters, cabarets and *cafés-concerts*, sketches of street denizens and landscapes of Montmartre—all testimony to his constant perambulations in search of new sources of inspiration.

A series of letters that Picasso and Casagemas sent to the Reventós brothers reveals much about their relationships and how wild their lives were.[52] In his first missive to Ramón Reventós on 12 October 1900, Picasso writes seriously of the artistic projects and the canvases he is working on at the time. In the letters that Casagemas and Picasso wrote together thereafter, the tone is lighter and more jovial. They recount day-to-day anecdotes and describe their affairs with three models they have met through Nonell: Germaine, Odette and Antoinette, lovers of Casagemas, Picasso and Pallarés, respectively.[53]

On 25 October they sent a letter to Reventós containing a written portion from Casagemas and several illustrations from Picasso.[54] Casagemas recounts how their life is unfolding in the French capital, how they work and how they play, recounting their outings to the theatre, to *cafés-concerts*—in particular to the Cabaret de Bruant—and expressing their serious intention to work. They set to work in the early morning when the model arrives and devote themselves to their various projects: "At nine o'clock, the model arrives. A very nice girl of natural breeding, a perfect Parisian, although a little common. … Since we have been in Paris, we have only been to see the hookers once and we are not doing the model for the moment."[55] From this sentence it is obvious that, even though the young artists had a serious will to work, when a pretty model came into their studio, she soon became an object of temptation too difficult to resist. Among their other stories, Casagemas provides an exhaustive inventory of the objects in the studio and mentions with curiosity: "We even have a mysterious utensil for private use *by ladies only*. I don't know what it's called [see Fig. 7] but I believe it's used to clean oneself where one gets dirty *in coitus* and in addition I believe it's used to

51 Pierre Daix, *La Vie de peintre de Pablo Picasso* (Paris: Seuil, 1977), p. 38.
52 The content of these letters has been analysed by Maria Teresa Ocaña in "Una crònica des de Paris," *Picasso i els 4 Gats* (Barcelona: n.p.,1995) and in "Els anys de l'eclosió: Barcelona-Madrid-París 1900-1904," *Picasso: La formació d'un geni, 1890-1904* (Barcelona: Lunwerg Editores, 1997).
53 Josep Palau i Fabre, *Picasso vivent, 1881-1907* (Barcelona: La Polígrafa, 1980), p. 203–04; English ed.: *Picasso, the Early Years: 1881–1907* (New York: Rizzoli and München, 1981).
54 Ocaña, p. 318. See also Marilyn McCully, ed. *A Picasso Anthology: Documents, Criticism, Reminiscences* (London: Arts Council of Great Britain/Thames and Hudson, 1981 [reissued 1982]), p. 27–30.
55 *"A les nou ve la model qu'es/ una noya molt simpática y sobre tot/ molt de raça, es una Parisin per-/fecte encar que una mica ordinarieta. … D'ensa que som a Paris/ no mes hem anat una vegada de puta. Y no'ns tirém la model/ per ara."*

prevent having babies—that is to say, if you put it in your cunt it's the opposite of putting your head in the pot of Nuria."[56]

The following excerpt is from a letter written by both Casagemas and Picasso, dated 11 November.[57] It shows that, despite their most ardent resolutions, the friends devoted their days and nights to carousing, having sex and entertaining themselves, which explains Picasso's slow production at this time. Casagemas recognizes his love for Germaine, "who is for the time being the woman of my thoughts," and mentions that Odette (Picasso's girlfriend) is "beginning to get raucous because of [her] good habit of getting drunk every night." Confronted with the money problems that their carefree existence has brought to bear, the artists decide to put some order in their lives, and, after seeing their mistresses, they decide that "neither [the women] nor we will go to bed later than midnight, and every day we'll finish lunch by one. After lunch we'll dedicate ourselves to our paintings and they'll do women's work, that is, sew, clean up, kiss us, and let themselves be 'fondled.' Well, this is a kind of Eden or dirty Arcadia." Picasso continues the letter and assures Reventós that other than making love to models, he has been working: "All this about women, as seen through our letters and as Utrillo must be telling you, seems or must seem to take all our strength, but no! Not only do we spend our lives 'fondling,' but I've almost finished a painting—and, to be frank, I think I have it just about sold." Later on, he maintains that "we'll even try to fondle at regular hours."

While a few sales did improve their precarious financial situation, Picasso's promises to go home to his family before Christmas and Casagemas's desperate love life (the reason behind his constant suicide threats) led both to return to Spain on 20 December. After brief stays in Barcelona and Málaga, Picasso moved to Madrid, where he devoted himself to the adventure of publishing the *Arte Joven* magazine. Casagemas returned to Paris, where, as promised, he ended his days.

When Picasso returned to the French capital in June 1901, on the occasion of his exhibit at the Galerie Vollard, he rekindled his old friendships, as evidenced in a letter sent to Miguel Utrillo. Picasso's arrival and his liaison with Germaine provoked jealousy in Manolo Hugué and in Odette, who was indignant to find her former lover in bed with her friend (Fig. 8). For a short period, Picasso's life in Paris, both personal and artistic, was the extension of the happy period he had experienced before with Casagemas, but several practical and sentimental factors were to divert his work toward a more personal and intimate style, and his emotional life, toward other, more stable—and perhaps more mature—relationships.

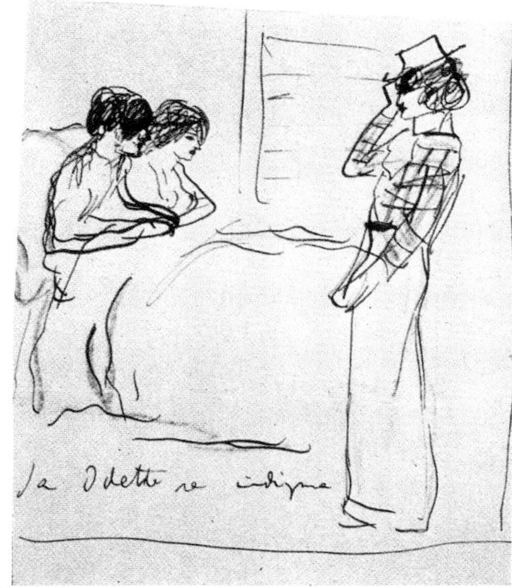
Fig. 8: Detail of a letter to Utrillo, June 1901
Private collection

---

56 *Hasta tenim una eyna misteriosa d'us privat, solo para señoras que no/ se com se diu pró qu'es axis y crec que/ serveix per sentarse/ alló que sels hi embruta/ en el coito, y ademés/ crec que serveix per no/ tenir criatures es a dir que/ fotras aixó al cony es al/revés que fotra'l cap a l'olla de Nuria."*
57 Ocaña, p. 319. See also McCully, p. 30–31.

DEL "MAL AMOR," 1902–1904

Maria Teresa Ocaña

During his Blue Period, Picasso was struggling to blaze a trail and establish a framework that would ground his painting, aspiring to join the inner circle of the art world's most innovative figures. Between 1901 and 1905, he fought to create "sincere work" that would satisfy him, help build a career and allow him to resist the temptation of easy money that might have compromised the authenticity he wanted for his art.

On the arduous path he took, where personal experiences commingled with his solemn, symbolically charged paintings, Picasso produced a series of minor works in which erotic play weaves a web of short narratives. These narratives were the harbingers of important paintings he would produce during this period.

Eroticism was present in Picasso's work from the time of his childhood. It also flourished in the Spanish literary tradition, where sins of the flesh figured prominently, notably in two key works: *Libro de Buen Amor* ("Book of Good Love") by the Archpriest of Hita, and *La Celestina* by Fernando de Rojas. As Camilo José Cela explains, these sins were deemed "quite tolerable and have never been known to cause anyone's physical or spiritual ruin. Bawdy, rowdy and joyfully coarse, one could almost say these healthy sins are an entreaty to the simple, patriarchal life."[1]

It was these carnal sins that Picasso was relating; sins he had glimpsed since his childhood, sins featured in popular romances and sins that provided endless material for the saucy jokes he knew so well. This was the "evil love" (*mal amor*) that the Archpriest of Hita contrasted with "good love," founded on the Christian spirit of the love of God. It is the hidden meaning in a *double entendre*, the inflamed passion behind the most intimate desires.

Thus, while shaping his own pictorial language, Picasso endeavoured to pull together a masterpiece that would capture all of the anxious restlessness he felt at that time, a feat he presumably accomplished only in 1905 with *The Family of Saltimbanques*. However, in the course of his lengthy endeavours, he produced two important allegorical works: *Evocation* (*The Burial of Casagemas,* Cat. 20), completed in 1901, marking his shift to blue monochrome and symbolism after his colourful postimpressionist phase, and *La Vie*, which he produced in 1903. As

---

1 Camilo José Cela, *Diccionario del erotismo*, Vol. I (Barcelona: Grijalbo, 1976 and 1982), p. V. (Free translation.)

Théodore Reff remarks, both of these works explore the allegorical contrast between two traditional forms of love: the "sacred" and the "profane."[2]

In this article, I wish to discuss the erotic connotations that emerged in the interval spanning the gestation of these two paintings—the alpha and omega of the reflections surrounding the personal crisis Picasso experienced vis-à-vis the death of his friend Carles Casagemas. Major themes were already emerging in several drawings that expressed Picasso's obsessions and restless worries. Some of these themes took form as major paintings; others simply remained as sketches.

Evocation clearly represents the confrontation between sacred and profane love—a duality that finds its resolution in the two halves of the composition. In the bottom portion of the painting, sacred love is conveyed through a reminiscence of the Christ-Casagemas figure descended from the cross with his grief-stricken mother and friends keeping vigil. By way of contrast, the upper portion of the painting, depicting "profane love," shows his soul ascending to heaven on a white horse and being embraced by a young woman, while off to the side are three *demi-mondaines* wearing only gaudy-coloured gartered stockings (an iconographic reference frequently used in drawings and small paintings in the years to follow).

Significantly, while Picasso was living in Barcelona between 1902 and 1903, a female nude with long hair made her appearance as the protagonist in a series of drawings. This voluptuous, "unwholesome" female weaves a thread through a framework in which allegorical scenes are interspersed with scenes probably culled from Picasso's personal life.

Two drawings, *Allegorical Sketches*,[3] portray a winged deity—in the first, she is a sort of mother goddess protecting a couple lying together, while in the second, she is transformed into a paternal god (probably the artist himself), protecting the woman-Eve and man-Adam in his arms. In another drawing, *The Phallus* (Cat. 36), the winged deity becomes a god in the shape of a phallus (a reference to Romanic images) who encloses the woman-Eve in his scrotum. This phallic god towers, with all his procreative might and main, above a half-submissive, half-defeated woman who nestles up into his scrotum like a foetus taking shelter in a mother's womb. While this female figure's identity is uncertain,[4] she clearly held the artist's abiding interest; from the initial drawing in May 1902 (depicting a couple under the protective figure of the mother goddess) Picasso continued to delight in depicting her. Not only does her image exude sensuality; it also has personal implications, since the artist represents himself and the young woman together, making love. It seems that, through the elements that bind these

---

2 Théodore Reff, "Temas de amor y muerte en las obras juveniles de Picasso" ("Love and death themes in Picasso's youthful works"), in *Picasso 1881–1973* (Barcelona: Gustavo Gili, 1974), p. 24.
3 MPB 110.522, 110.523.
4 Although the young girl's face is reminiscent of Cécile, also known as Geneviève Acker, whom Picasso identified as Geneviève (Max Jacob's only true love) in a photograph of a drawing shown to him by Richardson. See John Richardson (with the collaboration of Marilyn McCully), *A Life of Picasso, Vol. 1, 1881–1906* (New York: Random House, 1991), p. 260.

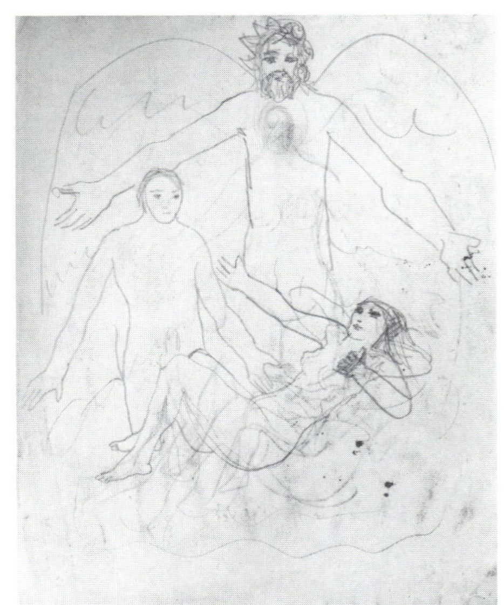

Fig. 1: *Allegorical Sketch*, 1902
Pencil on paper; 28 x 22.5
Barcelona, Museu Picasso, MPB 110.523

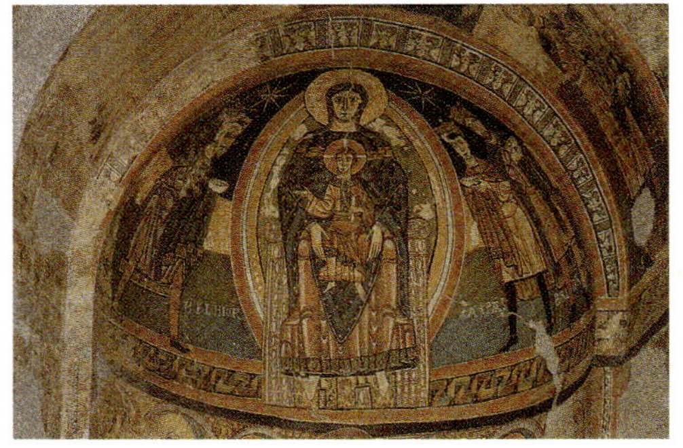

Fig. 2: Apse, Santa Maria de Taüli, 13th C.
Catalonia, Museum Nacional d'Art

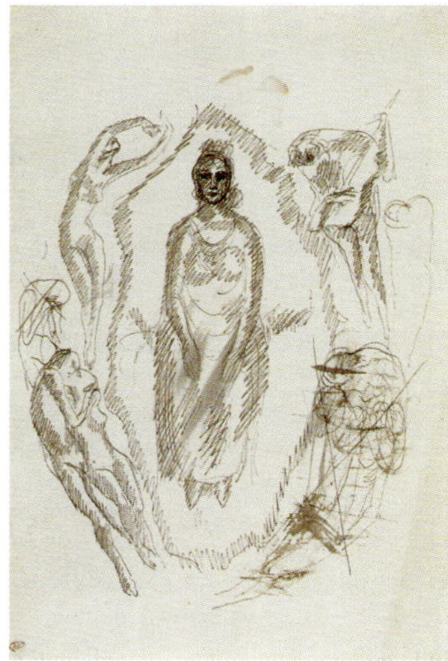

Fig. 3: *Woman Haloed by Figures*, 1903
Pen and brown ink on paper; 33.6 x 23.1
Paris, Musée Picasso, MP 471

drawings together (Fig. 1),[5] Picasso was teasing out a narrative in which, I dare say, he and the young woman share something beyond the simple sexual act. From this group of erotic/biographical drawings, we know of only one oil painting, *Portrait of the Artist Making Love* (Cat. 40), which shows the young woman fellating a reclining Picasso figure.[6]

As Picasso continued to focus his attention on this figure between 1902 and 1903, personal connotations faded away until it was transformed into an archetype. He used the resulting iconography again in the background painting of *La Vie*, which shows the woman figure hugging a despondent man.

It could almost have been a beautiful love story with a melancholy touch, had Picasso not, with his cutting humour, recreated the most sordid aspects of erotic play, subjected to the cruel passage of time. It sums up the indignation of a young man struggling to clear a path to the pinnacle of innovative artistic careers; a man seeking to create a work of art that would establish him as one of the best—a work in which he would have no qualms about incorporating anecdotes from his own personal life, since personal experience was for him the most authentic source of inspiration.

As in *The Phallus* (Cat. 36), the deification of the male member—the representation of nature's supreme reproductive force—was abundantly explored by the artist in a series of scenes in which the erect penis is standing up in front of a woman who is subdued by, or drinks from, this fount of virility.[7] The phallus is sometimes used as an ornamental motif to adorn a young woman's bed (Cat. 28).[8] As John Richardson[9] notes, several of Picasso's allegorical representations may have been influenced by his friend Max Jacob's fascination with palmistry and Tarot cards. Take, for instance, the drawing *Sex and Death* where, around a couple in the "sixty-nine" position, are a skull (symbolizing the frailty of our earthly existence) and a half-moon, which in Tarot signifies invention, imagination and magic.

The alternating duality between the sacred and the profane in *Evocation (The Burial of Casagemas)* can be found throughout Picasso's work from these years, in which solemn and anecdotal themes engage in a fluid dialogue. The symbolism characteristic of the Blue Period underlies all of the iconography that Picasso attributed to the abovementioned female nude, the eternal incarnation of Eve; and, the hasty execution of many of these sketches notwithstanding (most were drawn behind the store belonging to Picasso's friends, the Junyer Vidal brothers), solemnity and anecdote are presented side-by-side in several pieces. In *Nude with Mirror*,[10] the symbolic weight of a hand-held mirror, symbol of truth and an

5 Z.XXI.408, 409; Z.VI.405.
6 This work was shown at Dalmau's gallery in Barcelona as part of Picasso's 1912 exhibition. See Richardson, p. 258.
7 *Mujer desnuda acostada y falo* ("Nude Reclining Woman and Phallus"), 1902–03; *Falo y mujer* ("Phallus and Woman") (Richardson, p. 288).
8 MPB 50.492, 110.534.
9 Richardson, p. 270.
10 Z.XXI:343.

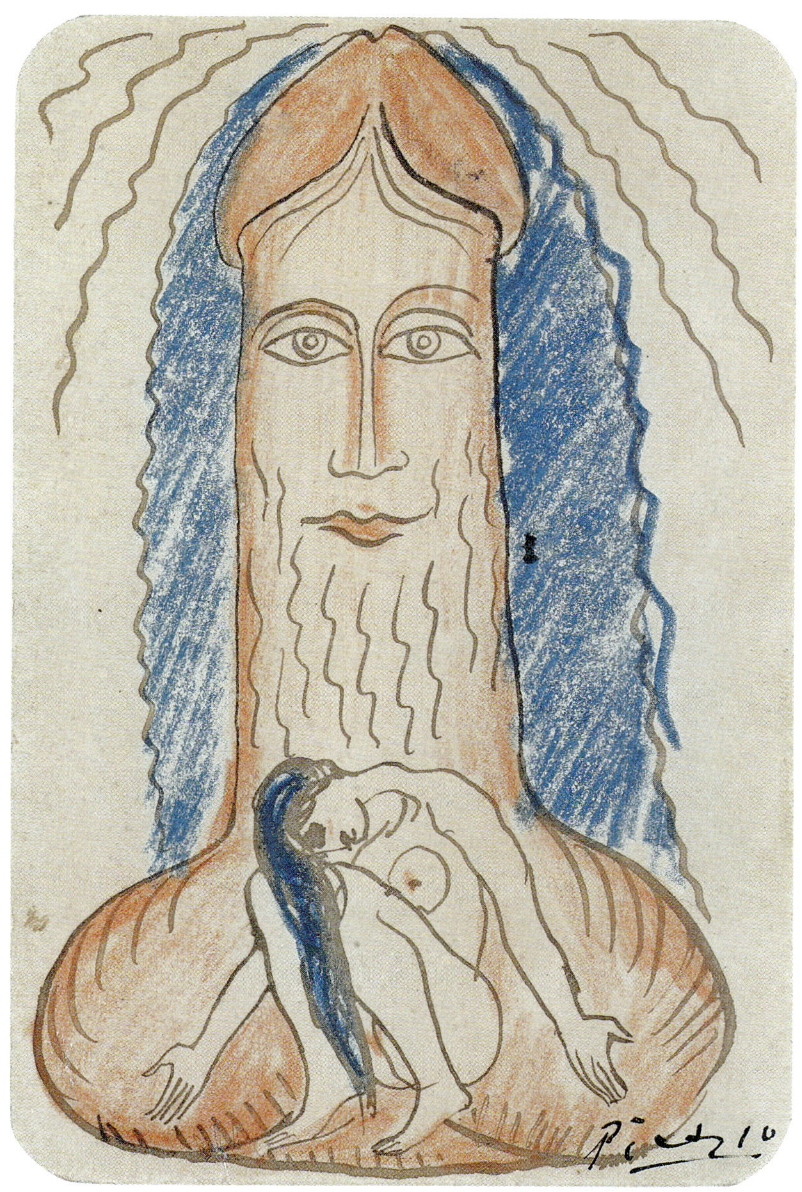

36 The Phallus, circa 1903
Ink and coloured wax crayon on paper; 13 x 9
Cologne, Private collection, Courtesy Galerie Gmurzynska

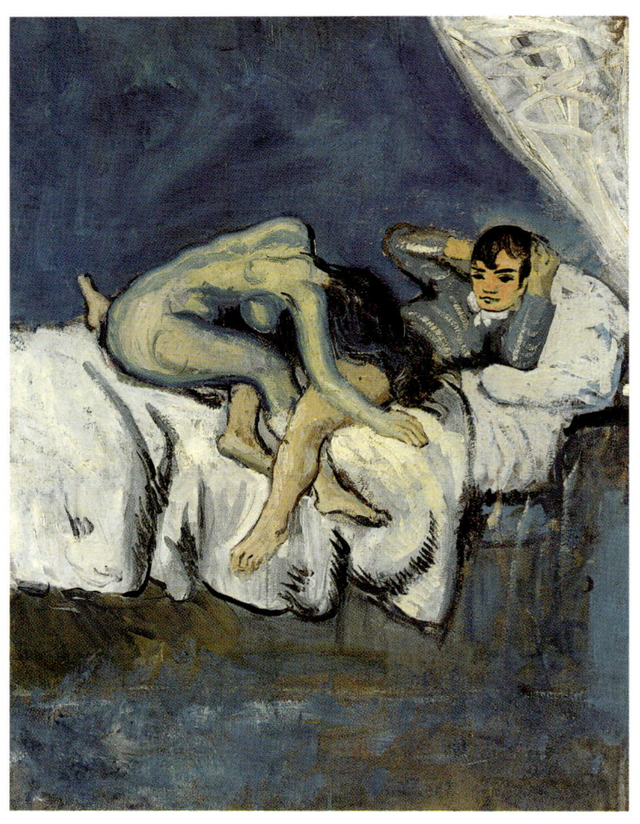

40 Portrait of the Artist Making Love, 1903

Oil on canvas; 53.3 x 37.3
New York, The Metropolitan Museum of Art,
Bequest of Scofield Thayer, 1984 [PM]

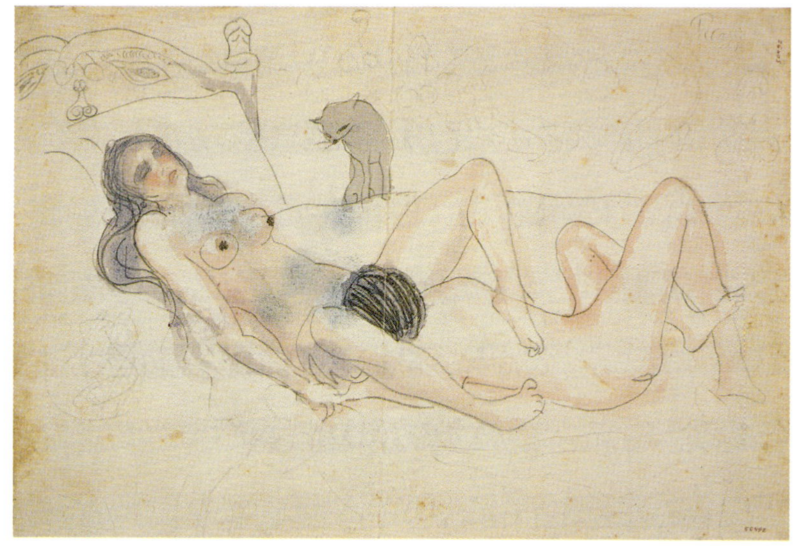

28 Two Figures and a Cat, 1902–1903

Pencil, watercolour and coloured pencil on paper; 18 x 26.5
Barcelona, Museu Picasso, MPB 50.492

obvious reference to the myth of Narcissus, contrasts with the vulgarity of the work's inscription—"When you feel like fucking, fuck!"—evocative of the *carpe diem* dictum that the artist seemed to epitomize in his zestful youth. In drawings like *The Mackerel* (Cat. 33) and *The Octopus*[11] there is also a double meaning in the zoomorphic "maquereau" (mackerel/pimp), who tongues the woman, placidly passive as she allows her body to be used. Here, Picasso borrows elements from the tradition of erotic art, but avoids any crude connotations. In the same vein, two noteworthy sheets of sketches[12] feature two female nudes whose sexual organs have blossomed. The allegorical meaning of these sketches, in which the vulva is assimilated into the "virginal whole," is reinforced by the delicate outlines of the nudes. In another sketch, *Vaginal Environment*, a female nude is shown masturbating inside a mandorla-shaped vulva (Fig. 3, p. 16).[13]

The source of the erotic charge in Picasso's work likely lies in the symbiosis between profane and sacred love, between the "good love" and "evil love" described by the Archpriest of Hita and portrayed in two exemplary sketches from 1903.[14] In the first, *Seated Woman*, the female figure of the Assumption is haloed by a series of nude couples forming a mandorla—probably an allusion to the vagina. The depiction of the couple with the woman hugging the man is reminiscent of the background couple in *La Vie*. The second sketch is very similar in composition, but the Assumption motif is replaced by a Crucifixion.[15] At Christ's feet, alone or in pairs, the nudes from *Seated Woman* are shown enacting a Deposition, a scene that anticipated the studies Picasso completed in 1929 for the painting *The Crucifixion*, and served to support the sexual nature of his religious themes. Richardson points out that these two sketches were also influenced by two Tarot cards: the Wheel of Fortune and the World.[16]

In another series of sketches, it is the artist's satirical tone that predominates. Once again, in this series, Spain's rich literary and artistic traditions indirectly inspired images that did much to revive the character of Celestina. In his rigorous study "Las primeras Celestinas de Picasso,"[17] Francisco Rico was the first to articulate the cultural significance of Celestina in Spain at the end of the 19th century. According to Rico, in the last decade of the past century, *La Celestina* was far from being considered one of Spanish literature's uncontested masterpieces (unlike today). Nonetheless, Picasso would certainly have been familiar with the character. Indeed, Celestina was more than just a literary work. She had entered into common parlance and iconography—amply depicted, for instance, by Francisco de Goya in his series *The Caprices*, which Picasso knew well.

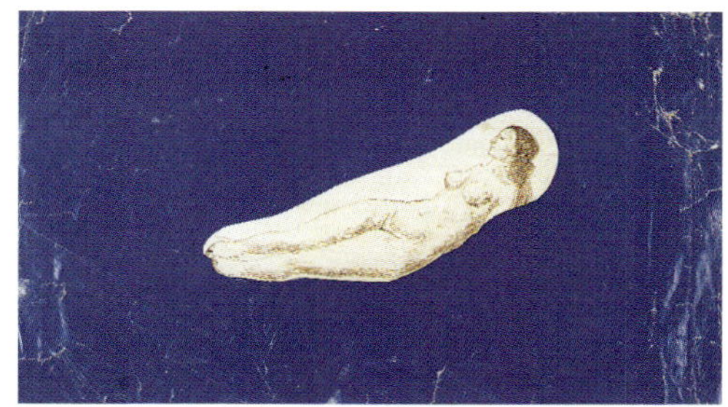

Fig. 4: *Female Nude*, 1902–1903
Pen on blue-gouached paper; 19.3 x 33.8
Barcelona, Museu Picasso, MPB 110.533

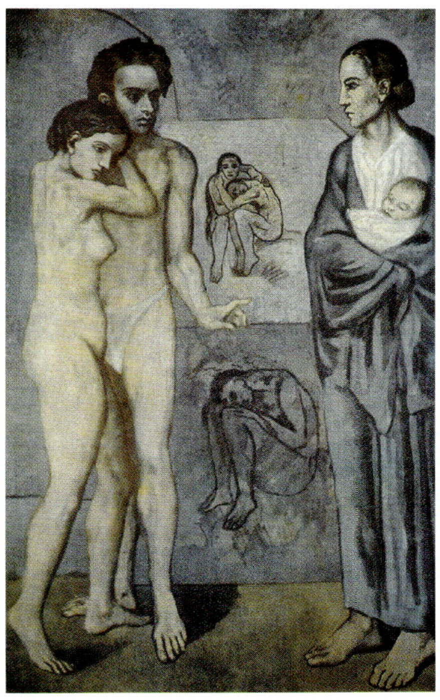

Fig. 5: *La Vie*, 1903
Oil on canvas; 196.5 x 128.5
Cleveland, The Cleveland Museum of Art

11 Richardson, p. 280.
12 Z.VI:438; MPB 110.482.
13 Richardson, p. 280.
14 Z.XXII:5, 6.
15 Z.XXII:6.
16 Richardson, p. 270.
17 Francisco Rico, "Las primeras Celestinas de Picasso" ("Picasso's first Celestinas"),
     Papers del Minotaure, (Barcelona: Museu Picasso, 1999), p. 59–67.

During his stay in Barcelona between 1903 and 1904, Picasso completed a series of sketches around the character of Celestina, inviting viewers to numerous erotic/satirical imaginings. The elderly woman in the background of *El Diván* (Cat. 4) is a case in point. Although not always present, Celestina hovers over these minor but nonetheless significant and creative artistic exercises. In *Two Women*,[18] a young woman is primping in front of a mirror in the presence of the madam as elsewhere, couples are flirting. While the woman Picasso depicts in these sketches is always young and fresh, her suitor is rarely in his first youth[19]; rather, he typically plays the role of a "dirty old man" (*viejo verde*). From this archetype, the artist gave himself free rein in a tangential series of obscene/satirical renderings, designed to egg on the lively banter with his friends behind the Junyer Vidal family store. In one of these sketches, the head of a libidinous old man opens up into the shape of a vagina as he watches the contortions of a young woman[20]; in another, the same man who is kissed by a woman in *The Kiss*[21] is represented with his eye sockets shaped like vulvas and his tear ducts like clitorises.[22] The old man appears in two other sketches. In the first, his skull is pecked at by a vulture[23] and in the second, his head is grabbed by a sort of android creature. The lewdness of all of these drawings find their origins in the dream-like subjectivity and irrationality that, years later, would feed the creative process of the Surrealists and of Picasso himself.

In contrast to these drawings, the magnificent portrait of Celestina (whose living incarnation was Carlota Valdivia, an elderly woman rooming in the same building as the Edén Concert) completed in March 1904 contains no erotic overtones whatsoever and is shrouded in a kind of solemnity. Accompanying this major work is a series of drawings depicting Sebastià Junyer Vidal and Picasso beside Carlota Valdivia as Celestina. These drawings are simply variations on a common theme that Picasso produced for his friend and faithful partner in binging and carousing during his last period in Barcelona, before they both left for Paris in April of the same year.

Picasso's circle of friends is depicted with uninhibited playfulness in drawings such as *The Brothers Mateu and Ángel Fernández de Soto, with Anita* (Cat. 34), *Isidro Nonell and a Female Figure* (Cat. 29), *Ángel Fernández de Soto with a Woman* (Cat. 30) and *The Painter Joan Ossó* (Cat. 31). All allude to his closest friends at the time and to their visits to the brothels of Barcelona. The illicit activities of Mateu and Ángel Fernández de Soto, and of the painter Isidro Nonell and the prostitutes he frequented, inspired humorous scenes that strike an ironic note regarding the atmosphere in which the youngest generation of Catalan artists

18 Z.I:176.
19 Z.I:177.
20 Richardson, p. 281.
21 Z.I:524.
22 Z.VI:148.
23 Z.VI:149.

was evolving. In point of fact, these were the same artists who ensured Picasso's contact with the city's most innovative artistic circles. Although the caricatures he produced of his friends were predominantly light-hearted, at times Picasso could also be tauntingly sarcastic, as in the two caricatures he produced of Santiago Rusiñol, the father of Catalan art and intellectual life and head of the Catalan Modernist movement. In *La Gloria-criti* (Cat. 37), Picasso depicts Rusiñol grabbing the hand proffered by a naked woman (Glory), while he is sodomized by a man (Criticism), who is also nude. In the same vein, another small drawing[24] shows a winged figure (Art) crowning Rusiñol with a wreath of the "chosen ones."

It would be a mistake to take a reductionist view of the role played by these diverse minor works and dismiss them as banal and superficial. While it is true that they were produced for their entertainment value, their erotic portent is palpable as we examine more closely how they served to gather up and expand the veiled sensuality that Picasso subsequently brought to his major works. Indeed, these drawings, completed in Barcelona between 1902 and 1904, provide us with a reading of the "small print" inscribed in the intense symbolic charge of the Blue Period. They are the deconstruction of themes that barely graze the surface of the artist's major paintings—the inside story on the illicit deeds that breathed life into Picasso's works of "mal amor."

24 Richardson, p. 257.

LES DEMOISELLES D'AVIGNON
AND PICASSO'S EROTIC THEATRE

Robert Rosenblum

Of the countless ways the *Demoiselles* shocks the viewer, one is its dramatic unveiling of a clandestine spectacle (Fig. 1). We seem to be in a theatre when, lo and behold, curtains are parted to reveal a sexual tableau. Already in 1905, in his unique interpretation of the most popular femme fatale of the fin de siècle, *Salome* (Cat. 47), Picasso had invented an erotic performance that is in full view of Herod, who commanded this licentious dance, but that can only be partly observed by us, the audience, who must look at the wanton princess from behind. Only he can see, as we cannot, Salome's shameless exposure of her sex. For Picasso, this particular kind of voyeurism was a motif familiar to the years 1905–07, when he painted and drew an abundance of wide-spread female thighs, to be looked at either head-on, as would so often be the case in the gynecological candour of his late work, or to be seen only in our erotic imagination, as in the case of the squatting "demoiselle" who, like Salome, turns her back to us. And in a related print, *The Danse Barbare* (Cat. 48), we are presented with another performance, a dance of grotesque nudes who attempt to entertain the languid spectators, Salome (in the pose of Ingres's *Grande Odalisque*) and Herod. But in the case of the *Demoiselles*, it is we, not Herod, who become the audience, facing a scene of sexual abandon on what now appears to be a stage space, defined front and back by curtains. One curtain, in the left foreground, is held by a standing nude who pushes it aside as if she were under the proscenium of a theatre. The other curtains, in the right background, are brusquely parted by a nude who looks at the scene from the wings and who, with her abrupt entrance, contributes to the sense of immediacy, as if a play had just begun.

As is now well known, the scene is set in the parlour of a *maison close* in which the whores are being displayed to a prospective client.[1] It is a narrative moment made clearer in many of Picasso's studies for the painting, in which a sailor or a medical student enters the brothel interior through a curtain. With his usual genius for conjuring up a rich genealogical table for his most ambitious canvases, Picasso here evokes a repertory of images in which a spectator, either inside or outside the picture, confronts a display of sexual offerings. There are, of course, many 19th-century prototypes, whether exotic harem scenes set in the Arab world or brothel interiors from the world of modern prostitution. To this

---

1 For the fullest account of the evolution of the *Demoiselles*, see William Rubin et al., *Les Demoiselles d'Avignon, Studies in Modern Art 3* (New York: The Museum of Modern Art, 1994).

ancestry, many famous artists contributed. Guys's and Degas's scenes of Parisian prostitutes in which sailors or gentlemen make their modern Judgment of Paris were surely known to the young Picasso[2]; and both Ingres' and Delacroix's Orientalist visions of harems and baths were established classics. And pertinently for the *Demoiselles*, in January 1907, the Louvre, following the wishes of Clemenceau, hung side by side two major representatives of these complementary displays of supine female flesh, one set in contemporary Paris, the other in a timeless Arab world, namely, Manet's *Olympia* and Ingres's *Grande Odalisque*, a painting Picasso would translate into the language of the *Demoiselles* in the very same year. In both these works, parted curtains contribute to that sense of private, theatrical disclosure so conspicuous in the *Demoiselles*. And there was, of course, Delacroix, whose *Femmes d'Alger* would famously inspire Picasso in the 1950s. During his first trip to Paris, Picasso would have encountered not only the first version (1834) in the Louvre, but also the second version (1849) (Fig. 2), which he must have seen at the *Exposition universelle*, where it hung in the Centennale Exhibition of French Art, 1800–89.[3] Indeed, in this later variant, the standing black servant who, with an upraised right hand, pushes aside the curtain to reveal the indolent women of the harem seems reborn, as a mirror image, in the curtain-raising figure at the left of the *Demoiselles*.

Curtained spaces were essential to these traditions of creating a private theatre of sexual delight. Ingres used them again and again, a fact that must have become particularly apparent to Picasso in 1905, on the occasion of the master's large retrospective at the Salon d'Automne. Ingres, of course, could use the magic of parted curtains to evoke the most high-minded religious experiences, as in his paraphrase of Raphael's *Sistine Madonna* for the dazzling disclosure of the cloud-borne Virgin and Child in his *Vow of Louis XIII* (1824). But usually, curtains served as erotic props, enforcing the fantasy of a stealthy, private view, especially in his many variations on a nude bather, frequently seen, like the squatting "demoiselle," from behind. The *Baigneuse de Valpinçon* (1808), curtained in foreground and background like the *Demoiselles*, is a classic example (Fig. 3); and Picasso may even have been thinking of it as a source of parody when, in 1906–07, while inventing the robustly masculine anatomy of his whores, he seems to have imagined how Ingres's voluptuously feminine nude might have looked when seen from the other side and unveiled by a curtain, now at the right

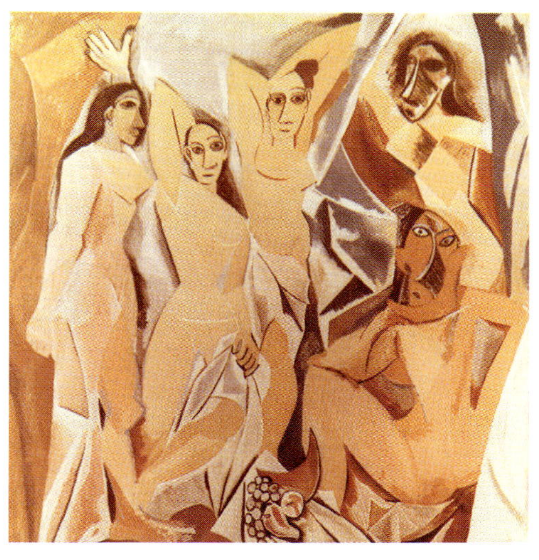

Fig. 1: *Les Demoiselles d'Avignon*, 1907
Oil on canvas; 244 x 234
New York, The Museum of Modern Art

---

2   The particular relevance of Guys's depictions of modern life, including brothel scenes, is emphasized in John Richardson, *A Life of Picasso, Vol. II: 1907–1917* (New York: Random House, 1991), p. 13–14. As for Degas's monotypes, illustrations for Maupassant's *Maison Tellier*, they were surely known later to Picasso, who bought one, and perhaps as early as 1907, a possibility suggested in Robert Rosenblum, "The Demoiselles Sketchbook No. 42, 1907," in *Je Suis le Cahier: The Sketchbooks of Picasso*, Arnold Glimcher and Marc Glimcher, eds. (New York: The Pace Gallery, 1986), p. 58.

3   *Exposition universelle de 1900; catalogue officiel illustré de l'Exposition centennale de l'art français de 1800 à 1889* (Paris: Ludovic Baschet, 1900), No. 218.

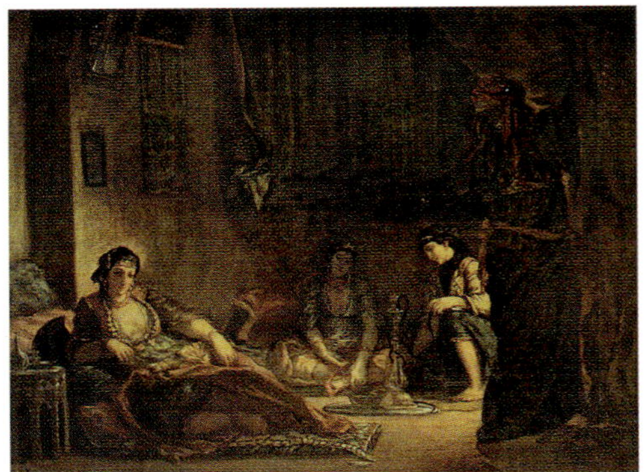

Fig. 2: Eugène Delacroix
Femmes d'Alger, 1849
Oil on canvas; 84 x 111
Montpellier, Musée Fabre

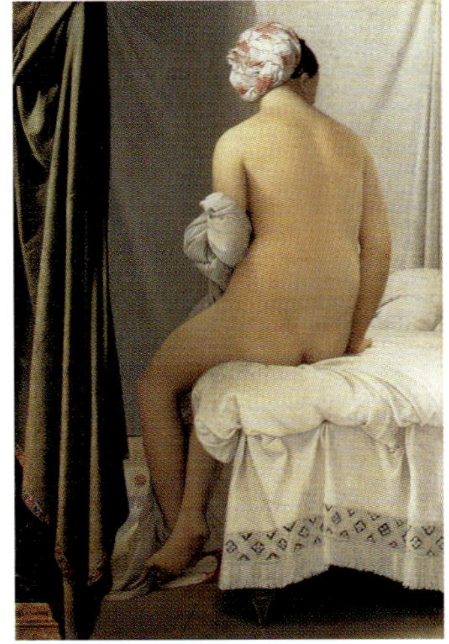

Fig. 3: Jean-Auguste Dominique Ingres
Baigneuse de Valpinçon, 1808
Oil on canvas; 146 x 97.5
Paris, Musée du Louvre

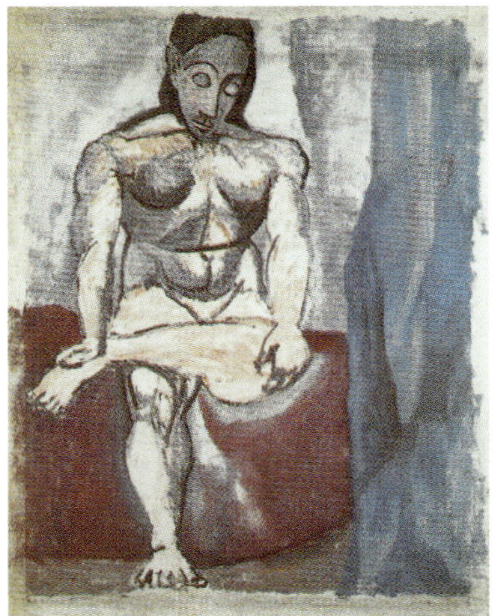

Fig. 4: *Seated Nude*, 1906–1907
Oil on canvas; 131 x 104
Paris, Musée Picasso, MP 10

(Fig. 4). In Ingres's later variant of this figure (1828) (Fig. 5), where more exotic bathers are introduced, the pair of curtains is parted symmetrically to reveal the view, here an almost blasphemous adaptation of Raphael's theatrical presentation in the *Sistine Madonna* that Ingres had piously quoted four years before. And it should be mentioned, too, that in the original, square version of the *Bain turc* (1859), before Ingres transformed it into a tondo, a curtain at the upper left was included, as if to emphasize the secrecy of this erotic theatre. As for the *Bain turc*, whether curtained or, in its more familiar form, uncurtained (Fig. 6), it provided Picasso with a trigger for the private erotic fantasies he invented in Gósol, where he spent the summer of 1906 with his new mistress Fernande Olivier.[4] In one of these, *Young Girl with Goat* (*Jeune fille à la chèvre*) (Fig. 7), he presents a strange trio of performers—an animal, a young girl, and a boy.[5] Entering an imaginary theatre through an imposing pair of parted white curtains, as if crossing a threshold that divides innocence from experience, they conjure up classical prototypes of a strongly erotic charge. The slender, self-involved girl, combing her hair like the new-born Venus, is a delicate image of an adolescent becoming aware of her sexual nature. In this, she is assisted more emphatically by the goat, traditionally associated with the satyr's rampant sexuality, and by the little boy who, with his small genitals profiled against the curtain and with an earthenware pot on his head like a classical canephorus, plays the role of Cupid. Leading the group through the white curtains, he follows what evokes a ceremonial path of sensuous pink. They might well be on their way to *The Harem* (Cat. 59), in which Picasso creates another low-budget production of Ingres's sumptuous surfeit of female flesh, appropriate to the rustic simplicity of the Pyrenean village. Beginning with the three confining planes of the *Bain turc*'s architecture, a corner view of what might be a stage with a steeply tilted floor, he then takes Ingres' rich inventory of sensual poses—nudes dancing, caressing, stretching, eating, perfuming hair—and reduces them to a minimal cast of four, undoubtedly inspired by the compliant model at hand, Fernande. And he adds two spectators, front and back, to this simple quartet. One, crouched in the corner, seems to play the role of an old procuress, a "celestina." The other, watching from a vantage point closer to ours, is a strangely androgynous figure, occasionally identified as a eunuch, who usurps the languorous roles of Herod and Salome as they watch the entertainment in the earlier *Danse Barbare*. Moreover, this muscular yet effete male, with emphatically small genitals, appears to be a transsexual mutation of the nudes in the lower right quadrant of the *Bain turc*. The parody is compounded by the still life beside him, a peasant repast of bread, cheese, sausage and a phallic *porrón* of

4   The comparison between Ingres's *Bain turc* and Picasso's *Harem* (as well as the *Demoiselles*) is often made. See, for example, Robert Rosenblum, "Picasso in Gósol: The calm before the storm," *Picasso: The Early Years, 1892–1906*, exh. cat. (Washington: National Gallery of Art, 1997), p. 263–75.

5   For the fullest account of this painting (by Hélène Seckel), see Richard J. Wattenmaker et al., *Great French Paintings from the Barnes Foundation: Impressionist, Post-Impressionist, and Early Modern* (New York: Alfred A. Knopf, 1993), p. 198.

red wine that makes a joke of Ingres's exquisite, miniature still life, a spatially precarious passage that Picasso reinvented once more in *Les Demoiselles d'Avignon*, where the fruit seems about to tumble into the spectator's lap.

Picasso, so often a voyeur in his art, could even stage his own sex life as a ribald memory of the old masters. In the smirkingly bawdy self-portrait of 1903, in which the young Bohemian flaunts his latest bout of oral sex (Cat. 40), he assumes the passive, but totally defiant posture of Goya's *Maja Desnuda* (a prototype he would use again in 1906 for the erotic set-piece of Fernande, naked on a bed, her hands behind her head).[6] Once more, the theatrical device of a curtain raised over the bed emphasizes our conspiratorial role as the audience for this lewd tableau, a confrontation intensified by Picasso's staring eyes that seek out a spectator to watch his sexual conquest.

The *Demoiselles* synthesizes many of these conventions of erotic entertainment, and absorbs as well the stagelike formats used to depict bordello life by painters working during Picasso's own youth. There is, for one, Émile Bernard's *Les Trois Races* of 1898 (Fig. 8) which, in turn, combines, on one hand, the romantic remoteness and sensuality of Ingres's and Delacroix's Orientalist harem scenes with, on the other, the brash contemporaneity of Manet's *Olympia*. Living in Cairo from 1893 to 1903, Bernard often depicted modern brothels in the city, and here, the result is closer to a scene of poverty-stricken Western prostitution than to a fiction from the *Arabian Nights*.[7] Within the familiar confines of a curtained interior, the three whores stare at us, the would-be client, in a realist preview of the *Demoiselles*'s demonic frontal gazes. And the French colonial variety of skin colour typical of the local Egyptian mix (Caucasian white, Arab brown, African black) looks not only back to Ingres's own harem fantasies but also forward to the changing racial features and skin colour that mark the whores in the *Demoiselles*.

Still closer in time and culture to Picasso is a brothel scene painted in 1906 by his Andalusian compatriot Julio Romero de Torres. Titled *Vividoras del Amor*, i.e., "those who live by love," it confronts us with a vignette of prostitution in Córdoba, the artist's native city (Fig. 9). The scene is again a kind of stage set, with a flight of stairs leading to the upper floors and, most startlingly at the left, a doorway through which a whore suddenly appears, like the one who bursts through parted curtains in the *Demoiselles*. Against the darkness of their skin, the whiteness of their eyes, seeking their next client on the audience side of the painting, again suggests an earthbound preview of the ferocious, apocalyptic stares of the *Demoiselles*. It is even likely that Picasso knew Romero de Torres's painting, a *succès de scandale*. In Madrid in 1906, it was rejected by the jury on moral grounds, and was exhibited with other offensive works in a little gallery, as a kind of Salon des Refusés called "*Rechazados por inmorales en la Exposición*

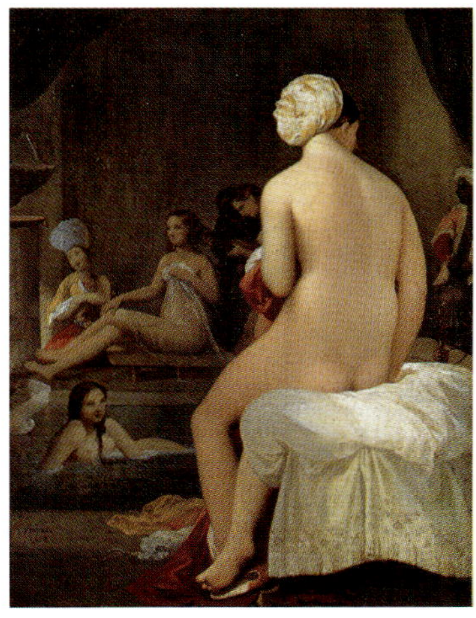

Fig. 5: Jean-Auguste Dominique Ingres
La Petite Baigneuse, 1828
Oil on canvas; 36 x 27, Paris, Musée du Louvre

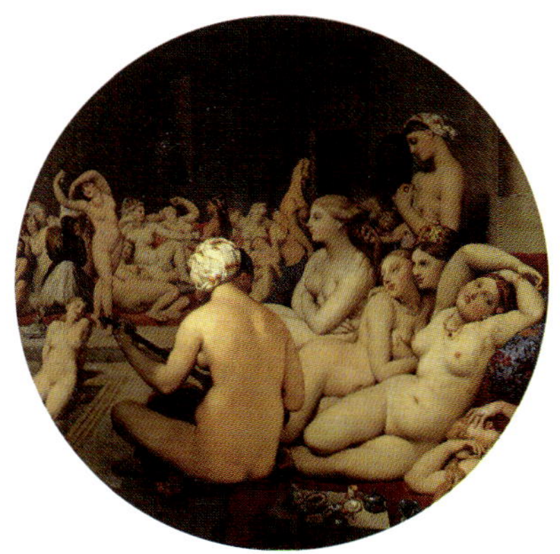

Fig. 6: Jean-Auguste Dominique Ingres
Le Bain turc, 1859–1863
Oil on canvas; diam. 108
Paris, Musée du Louvre

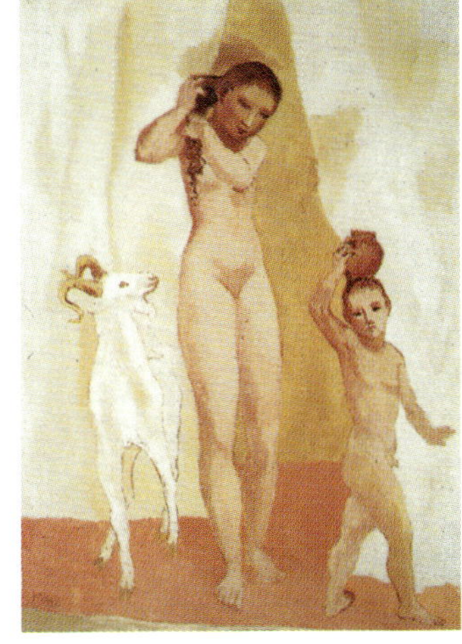

Fig. 7: *Young Girl with Goat*, 1906
Oil on canvas; 139 x 102
Merion, Pennsylvania, Barnes Foundation

---

6 Rosenblum, p. 267.
7 For a selection of these Cairene brothel scenes, see Jean-Jacques Luthi, *Émile Bernard: Catalogue raisonné de l'œuvre peint* (Paris: Éditions SIDE, c. 1982).

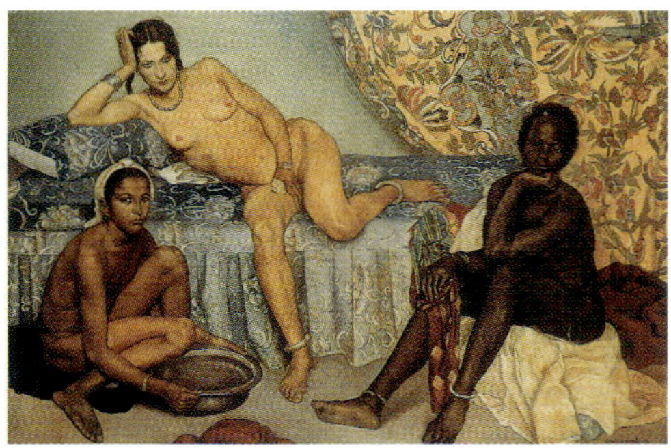

Fig. 8: Émile Bernard
Les Trois Races, 1898
Oil on canvas; 119.5 x 80.5
Los Angeles, Los Angeles County Museum of Art

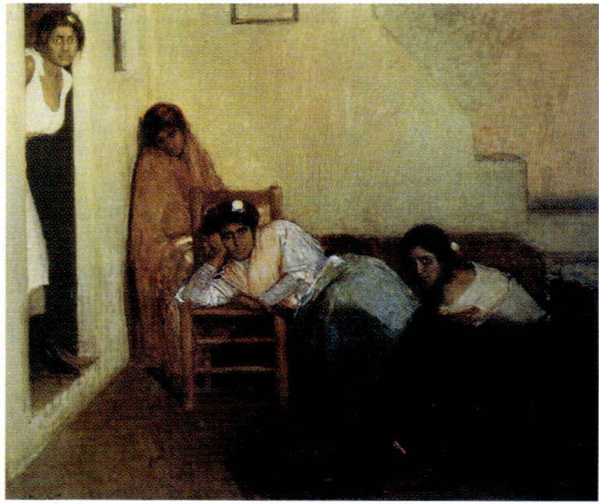

Fig. 9: Julio Romero de Torres
Vividoras del Amor (Those Who Live by Love), 1906
Oil on canvas; 129.5 x 182.9
Private collection

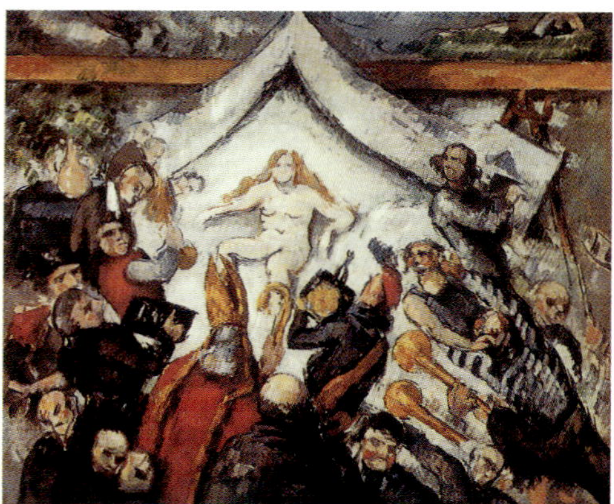

Fig. 10: Paul Cézanne
L'Éternel féminin, circa 1877
Oil on canvas; 42.2 x 53.3
Malibu, The J. Paul Getty Museum

Nacional de Bellas Artes." News of the scandal was international, reaching France and England; in fact, the painting was shown in Paris in 1907.[8]

But in the case of Picasso, and especially for the *Demoiselles*, a work that absorbs and digests a multitude of images and traditions, possible sources of inspiration continue to proliferate. One that comes from more familiar territory, Cézanne, may also be suggested here as a preview of the sexual theatricality of the *Demoiselles*, namely, the small but erotically charged painting, probably from the late 1870s, now titled *L'Éternel féminin* (Fig. 10), but known in Picasso's youth, when it belonged to his dealer Ambroise Vollard, as *Le Veau d'or*, the title under which it was exhibited in 1907 at the Salon d'Automne's Cézanne retrospective.[9] Here, in the strange turbulence of Cézanne's sexual anxieties, a theatrical tableau is presented in which we join the diverse ranks of male humanity (from bishop and banker to soldier and circus performer) in order to salute, with trumpets, the dramatic unveiling of a carnal female nude under the proscenium of curtains parted over a wide bed. With semi-parted thighs and a lethal gaze from blood-red eyes, she holds the male world in her dangerous thrall. Three decades later, her shameless display of gross anatomy and raw sexuality would find more than its match in the *Demoiselles*. And Picasso, so often a parodist, may well have had in mind Cézanne's tribute to female sexual power when, in spring 1909, possibly for St. Gertrude of Nivelles's Day on March 17,[10] he invented an equally theatrical homage to Gertrude Stein, the most improbable of all candidates for a nude, especially a heterosexual femme fatale (Fig. 11). Behind the parted curtains, heralded by attenuated angels and a trumpet blast that evokes Cézanne's fanfare, she fortunately appears not in person but in first name only, inscribed on a caricature of a baroque cartouche.

Like everything else in Picasso's universe, his role as an impresario, directing sexual displays and performances, was hardly limited to his youthful years of sexual adventure. The *Demoiselles*, to be sure, marks the spectacular climax of this era, but Picasso's theatre of sex never closed. Most poignantly, it was revived with the most febrile, voyeuristic fantasies during the last decades of his long life, during the 1950s and '60s, when, for a man in his seventies and eighties, sexual activity must have been more fiction than fact. It was then, for example, that he invented, as if Vasari had been reborn as a pornographic playwright, the secret sexual biographies of such famous artists as Raphael and Degas. Raphael appears as he was interpreted by Ingres (who made many versions of the divine master's earthly passion for La Fornarina), but far transgresses the propriety of Ingres's painting by performing sexual acrobatics behind the inevitable curtain, which,

8   My information about this painting comes from a sales catalogue: *Important 19th Century European Paintings and Sculpture*, Sotheby's, New York, 5 May 1999, Lot 148A.

9   For more on this painting, see John Rewald, *The Paintings of Paul Cézanne: A Catalogue Raisonné, Vol. 1*, (New York: Harry N. Abrams, 1996), No. 299; and Françoise Cachin et al., *Cézanne*, exh. cat. (Philadelphia: Museum of Art, 1996), No. 42.

10 This explanation is suggested in Pierre Daix and Joan Rosselet, *Picasso: The Cubist Years, 1907–1916: A Catalogue Raisonné of the Paintings and Related Works* (Boston: New York Graphic Society, 1979), No. 248.

with equal predictability for the often blasphemous Picasso, hides a voyeur, the Pope himself (Cat. 249). Degas appears as another fully clothed voyeur, visiting his own bordello scenes, much as the sailor and medical student had done in the preparatory studies for the *Demoiselles*. In his old age, even more than in his youth, Picasso went on staging the sexual dramas that teemed in his imagination.

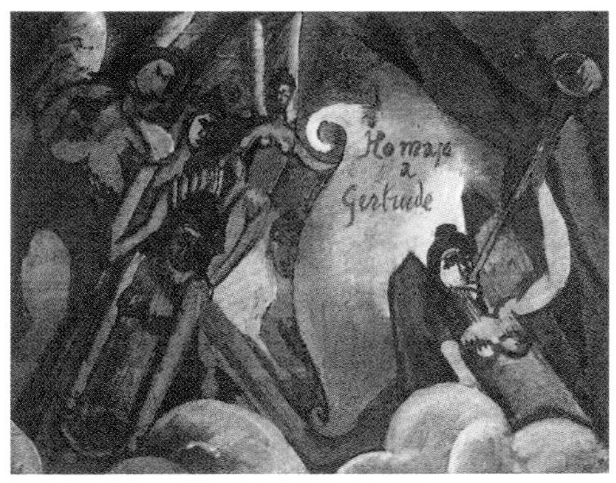

Fig. 11: *Homage to Gertrude*, 1909
Tempera on panel; 21 x 27
New York, Private collection

EARLY 1933
THE SCULPTOR AND HIS SCULPTURE
AND THEN THE MODEL

Brigitte Baer

The photograph that Brassaï took of the inside of the barn—the sculpture studio—in Boisgeloup is a marvel. And not only because of its poetry and beauty, which some would say was accidental: the harsh frontal light cast by the headlights of the Hispano-Suiza. This photograph "speaks." The large female plaster heads of 1931 stand guard, and one can make out the details of the rather strange forms, almost the sculptor's hand. Behind them steals the "large figure," only fragments of which remain; the plaster, transformed by art, suggests the praying mantis of which the Surrealists were so fond. This photograph makes quite a few things clear. First, it is obvious that it is the plasters that are the sculptures. The bronzes, cast during the war, have nothing to say; they are sombre, small, "vague," cold and eminently "silent." But the plasters! These are—aside from any considerations of plastic beauty—magical objects, magical in the true meaning of the word, magical and alive. They speak to us of spells, of hypnotism, of the spell cast and of the struggle against this bewitchment. They convey the uncontrollable voluptuousness of their birth from the hand of Picasso, as well as his fear of the dependency created by that other momentary sensual delight that we commonly refer to as the *grand frisson*. Fear is involved in the expression. Granted, Picasso worked quickly, but the work that went into one of these large female heads lasted longer than the "ecstasy" (if ever it does exist) that crowns the act of lovemaking.

My idea, my impression (which, of course, neither invalidates nor even weakens any of the other learned interpretations or elucubrations around this subject) is that for this artist, and particularly around this period, in 1931, eroticism (whatever the meaning of the word) resided mainly in the work, and more particularly in the "modelling"[1] of these large plasters. The hand, in applying, squeezing and spreading the plaster, in caressing it to create swellings, tumescences and the texture or smoothness of skin, could not fail to produce a sensation and a sensuality stronger than those produced when it kneaded or caressed flesh that already existed in and of itself. For the hand in this case appropriates the object, makes it its own forever, in actual fact and in the head, mind, psyche —as one likes to call that something that is ourselves—even if a catastrophe, some fire or war, were to destroy the material creation (one could almost say "creature").

1 Adrian Stokes, *The Critical Writings*, 3 vols. (London: Thames and Hudson, 1978).

The phallic appearance of these erect necks and the tumescent swellings of the heads initially evoke the onanism implied by the sculptor's actions. But we must be careful not to oversimplify, especially when we are dealing with someone as complex, private and indeed hidden as Picasso. These heads have very little in common with the "phallic" rocks of Chinese or Japanese prints, or with sculptures like Brancusi's *Mademoiselle Pogany*. Picasso did have a sense of humour, but it is absent here. This is a representation not of an erect penis, but of blended flesh, his own, and the head (obviously a synecdoche) of Marie-Thérèse (Fig. 1).

It is at this point that the magic comes in: these statues are evocative of spells and intoxication, of addiction to a hard drug. On the evidence of the works, one would say that it was only around 1930–31 that this fifty-year-old man experienced true physical pleasure, and not only that associated with conquest, tenderness, the joy of giving pleasure and simple physiological relief. (Why? How? Who knows? But this is not what we are interested in here.) This after several years of physical love with the same object of desire. Obviously, the supple *garçonne* who at seventeen resembled a willow shoot and whom the artist, in one of his sketchbooks, depicted as undulating branches of foliage, had broadened out and, to go by the famous photograph which shows her clad in a bathing suit and holding a ball in her hand, had become "sturdy," fleshy, solid, somewhat masculine and athletic. Like the statue that Picasso portrayed her as in his etching of 3 May 1933,[2] she had the muscles of a gymnast, although enveloped in the fat that characterized the physiques of the men and women of those years, and which was necessary if she was to stay warm during her long swimming sessions in often icy water.

Of course other explanations are possible. This pair must have found a meeting place in eroticism. But for a man of fifty, such an experience leads to a sort of revolution. He had his family, his work, his friends. It is certain that this experience sparked his creativity: it was Eros, the polar opposite of Thanatos, which is also the acute depression that empties the world both inside and out and that makes creation impossible (Picasso was familiar with that as well). In the ancient theogonies, Eros is the cohesive force that ensures the solidity of the Cosmos and its survival, not the plump-cheeked lad who scatters his arrows here and there. He was born at the same time as the Earth …

But if he is desirable, he is also terrifying. And these large plasters are at the same time "erotic" and terrifying. To produce their effect, they have to be set up close together the way they are in the photograph, instead of being scattered among bronzes and other sculptures. But perhaps then, they would be really and truly frightening. I have seen men, both painters and poets, in their mature years and hence with a fair measure of learning and sensibility, flee from the room in the Musée Picasso where they were shown. (It must be said that the room also contained all the various states of the 1933 print *Sculpture: Head of Marie-*

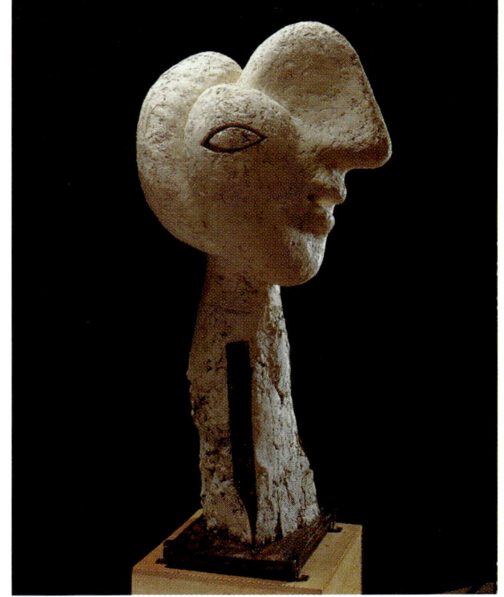

Fig. 1: *Head of a Woman*, 1931
Plaster and wood; 128.5 x 54.5 x 62.5
Paris, Musée Picasso, MP 301

---

2 Bernhard Geiser and Brigitte Baer, *Picasso peintre-graveur: Catalogue raisonné de l'œuvre gravé et des monotypes*, Vol. II (Berne: Kornfeld, 1992) (G./B. 344).

Thérèse.[3]) This is white magic: these sculptures are to varying degrees apotropaic, intended, of course, to preserve this creative *élan vital* and the pleasure it generates, but also to escape the dependency that inevitably exists when a single object in this world can, if we simply look at it or touch it, create this dramatic transformation of ourself. Many people dream of this experience without ever knowing it: they would undoubtedly be unable to stand it.

The plaster heads are magic. The insides, from the neck down, or even from the head down to the bust (as is the case for the one that goes as far as the breasts) are very strange. Already, in the lower studio of Notre-Dame-de-Vie, they were clustered almost as we see them in the photograph, but most of the necks were broken, the heads being too large and heavy for the upper neck where the narrow, teepee-shaped scaffoldings (made of bits of board bound together at the top with ropes, or with the kind of packing string that skins the fingers) came to a stop. Inside this hollow neck were all sorts of ordinary objects that could in no way help to make them stronger: dead leaves, tow, straw, old crumpled newspapers, dust and even dry earth—all, in any case, vegetable matter, and not the bones, teeth and shells one sees embedded in objects from Polynesia. White magic, then. One could argue that this jumble was simply lying around in the barn, but Picasso, remember, was superstitious and left nothing to chance. And Marie-Thérèse loved flowers, plants, grass, etc.

The artist had to maintain this driving force of Eros that did, during this period, make him the greatest creator of the century; therefore he had to preserve his love and his desire for this woman. But all this had to become more human and livable—in other words, he had to regain his personal autonomy.

Making these plaster pieces—and, perhaps, viewing them through other eyes, those of Brassaï in 1932 (Fig. 2)—had the desired effect, although this may have come about unconsciously. Moreover, as we know, the experience we are talking about does not last forever, magic or no magic. In any case, early in 1933, the prints of the *Vollard Series*, which feature the sculptor and his model, tell another story, one that is nostalgic yet calm. The sculptor is the true hero of the *Vollard Series* and of the other prints made around the same time—the ones that Vollard did not pick. The famous Minotaur, which came later, is but one aspect of the man-sculptor, namely the "animal" part. He is not wicked, far from it; he knows pleasure and pain but the sculptor, or the tiny sailor that stands in for him, has kept his head. The man loves Marie-Thérèse, has tenderness in abundance for her in addition to desire—but a desire that does not shake him up or make him dependent on it. She has her own little ways and he makes concessions to them, but what he has now is love and not that "need" that turned everything upside down.

All human beings are familiar with dependency, even if most of them no longer recall what it feels like. I mean the dependency of the newborn's first weeks, when the breast appears on demand, as if it were a part of the child itself

3 G./B. 288.

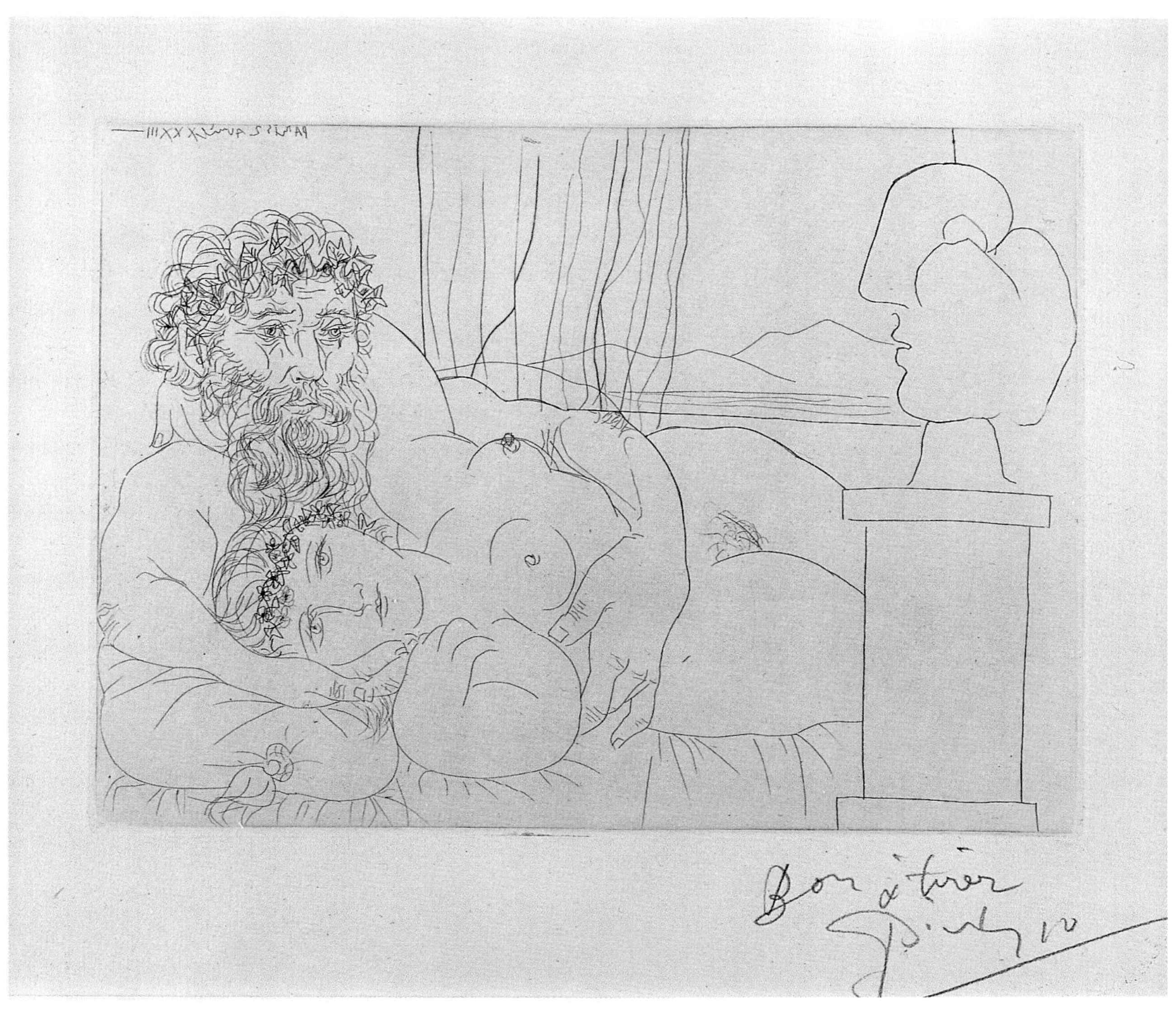

141 Sculptor and His Model with Sculpted Head of the Model, 2 April 1933

Etching on copper; trial proof; 19.3 x 26.8
Paris, Musée Picasso, MP 1982-121 [B]

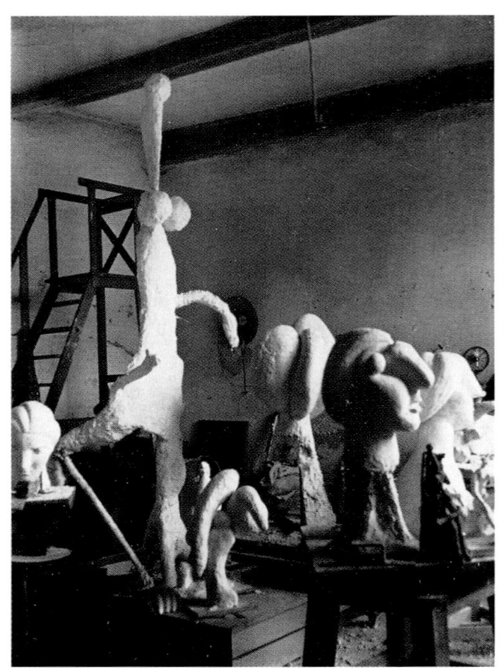

Fig. 2: Brassaï
The Sculpture Studio at Boisgeloup, 1932
Paris, Musée Picasso, MP 1966-241

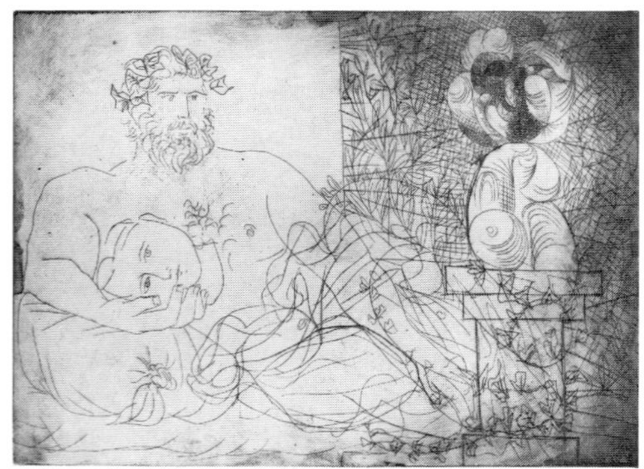

Fig. 3: *Sculptor and His Model with a Bust on a Column*
31 March 1933
Etching on copper; 19.4 x 26.7
Paris, Musée Picasso, MP 2605

and not some external object. But the mother will not always be available and, if the weaning process is gradual and the child adapts well to it, dependency is not felt. The breast simply becomes an external object, one that is sometimes absent but will come back. So the child slowly acquires a life of its own, as well as its autonomy. For some human beings and maybe for all, this first experience remains indelible. Of course Picasso did not think through or analyse this whole matter; rather, for a period of time he relived it with a blend of delight and terror. Two years later, if we go by the prints (which always seemed to be what enabled Picasso to reflect, to attempt to understand), it would appear that the detoxification process was complete. Yet the "drug" had also produced an intense and devastating pleasure.

The prints from the first months of 1933 almost always deal with the same theme: the sculptor is at rest while the model, who is often unidentified, not necessarily pretty and does not look at all like Marie-Thérèse, looks off somewhere with a drowsy, dreamlike air, her head on the knees of the man, who is looking not at her but at his sculpture, or thinking about it. Here we are dealing generally with the first head, which resembles that of a classical Greek goddess. It is it[4] that synthesizes all the others (Cat. 141). However, the sculpture is, at least in one instance, a sort of bust covered in tumescent swellings, a kind of erect penis that the sculptor stares at while the model is obviously bored (Fig. 3). The couple evokes the idea of *post coïtum, animal triste*. Yet one senses throughout these relatively repetitive images a latent, subterranean and languid eroticism that is certainly more present than in the various couplings and rapes which, by virtue of their graphic style, assume a bestial quality practically devoid of emotion. Whatever its stamp, eroticism without emotion is not eroticism.

Why, one might ask, does the face of the model have such an expression of indifference? Perhaps it is because it is the sculpture that is her face, perhaps because Picasso never worked directly from the model, or maybe it is to show that the model is wholly unimportant and that what counts is emotion (this word came easily to Picasso). The desire to avoid stirring up jealousy in Olga was undoubtedly another reason. Whatever the case, what we see in these multiple "images" of the bearded sculptor and his young languid model is that the sculptor's sensuality and desire go to his sculpture, even after lovemaking, and not to his companion. She feels this intuitively and her intuition also tells her that nothing can be done about it. She was made to be a lover and, more often than not, had to be content with the role of muse. Hence the nostalgia found in these images: that of the model and of the sculptor who, despite his consolations, still misses the intoxications of the past.

Other prints (Fig. 4) seem to indicate that the sculptor is trying to compare his sculptures to pseudo-antique groups — his are exceedingly free recollections of his brief visits to the Vatican — and is wondering if his art "holds up." But

4 Werner Spies and Christine Piot, *Catalogue raisonné de l'œuvre sculpté: Picasso sculpteur* (Paris: Centre Georges-Pompidou, 2000) (Spies 128).

another question arises at this point. His heads were born from a burning desire for a body that was both living and invented. What form of "eroticism" could have served as the trigger for these groups? In creating them, did the unknown sculptors of old experience the same type of sensuality? And if not, what *were* their feelings? He understood quite well the fighting and coupling horses, the bull disembowelling a mare, and an orgiastic Rape of Europa; but there is also the struggle of the ephebes and the boy picking up a switch before mounting his mare. These sculptors obviously found their erotic pleasure in their work—because it has ever been so and because art cannot do without it. But where, what, how?

However the case may be, the sculptor thinks only of his work, the supreme pleasure … while the model is bored. It would be hard to be more absent from one another than these two are with their lackadaisical physical contact. The artist thinks, attempting to put the pieces back together: the emotions, the past and the present, flesh and plaster. He has a meditative look, is elsewhere. The model, meanwhile, cares only for the present and has no use for an art that takes away her lover. Yet a sort of cloudy eroticism, heavy if intangible, permeates these prints and that is why we take such pleasure in looking at them.

Later, on 2 March 1934,[5] Picasso, for reasons unknown, returned to his ruminations and maybe to his past as well—Olga, remember, was a dancer. He did a highly personal version of Carpeaux's *Dance*, with what could easily be a caricature of the latter, but this was an exception at this period. And nostalgia for the true past shows through in the etchings of 7 and 8 April 1933. It would appear that Picasso was revisiting the time when he met the young Marie-Thérèse (undisguised here but for the brown curly hair). The bowl of anemones, the first (or almost first) flowers to appear in the spring in Greece, evokes Persephone's return to earth. Seated, the sculptor looks with amused tenderness upon a young, barely pubescent girl whose breasts have yet to sprout, who has the head and especially the ears of a faun and who, the day after, will fill out into a young girl. Marie-Thérèse admires herself in narcissistic fashion in a mirror: but the mirror is leaning against a sculpted sculptor's head and she, herself, without knowing it, is beginning to take shape in the sculptor's head. Which explains, perhaps, the tenderness and the note of pity in his contemplation of her. There is tenderness here rather than voluptuousness or eroticism. And yet…

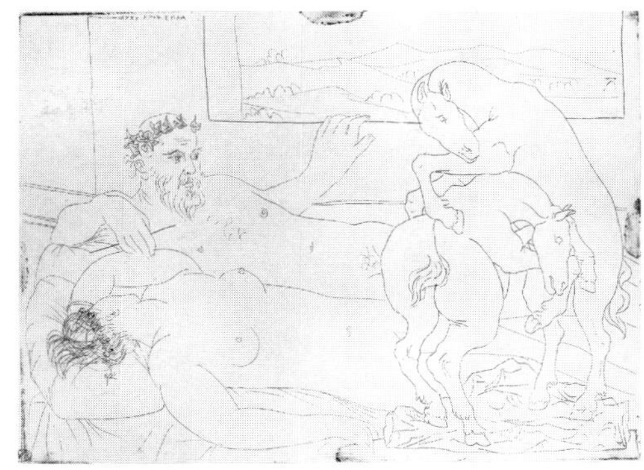

Fig. 4: *Old Sculptor and Model Dozing with Sculpted Group Representing Battling Horses*, 3 April 1933
Etching on copper; 19.4 x 26.7
Paris, Musée Picasso, MP 2617

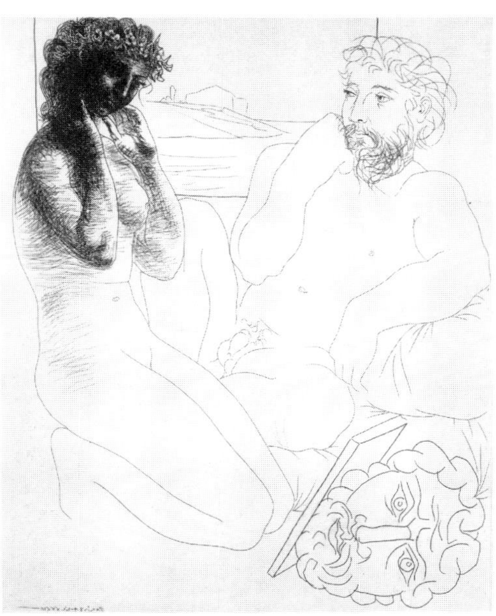

Fig. 5: *Sculptor and His Model Looking at Themselves in a Mirror Leaning against a Sculpted Self-Portrait*, 8 April 1933,
Etching on copper; 36.8 x 29.9
Paris, Musée Picasso, MP 2623

5 G./B. 421.

"DIAMOND MADE OF
ALL THE LOVE
OF THE LOVES OF BLOOD"[i]

Marie-Noëlle Delorme

"the only thing that saddens me right now is not being able to be with her and not being able to say to her let's go and walk in the garden like this morning and let's go buy cheese and bread and let's go eat them sitting on the bench in front of the big tree"[ii] (31 October 1935).

Picasso in love—he often was. Picasso yearning, unhappy, dreaming of his loved one—that did not happen quite as often. Between him and his brushes, pencils and chisels step his wife and the alluring pregnant child-woman, Marie-Thérèse.[1] The crisis is serious: he stops painting; he starts to write.[2]

"white ribbons that tie my lips so that they never again say anything but how much I love her now that she's asleep and I can see nothing from afar but her honey through the crystal doors of the rooms that separate us and poor soul that I am I write…"[iii] (21 October 1935).

Picasso-the-romantic sighs.

"…tell me you who know tell me if it is possible that this afternoon the moist memory of her face could be raining inside me"[iv] (18 April 1935).

At the root of his desire/need to write is a conjugal/love conflict,[3] and it is through the portrait of a poet, Paul Éluard, that he will emerge from this season in hell, punctuated by the birth of Maya on 5 September 1935.

"The baby girl ate up the fingers of the cold paintbrush,"[v] he notes on 1 December, but not for long; even though "the cries of a little shell girl"[vi] (29 March 1936) disturb the silence, after a while he cannot resist the pleasure of dashing off intimate sketches of daughter and mother. His pictorial silence lasts only three months.[4]

Thus at Boisgeloup, on 25 April 1935, Picasso was transported by an uninterrupted stream of words spilling from his pen. His first text was long, difficult, compact and obscure, punctuated with a ritornello, fed by love, blood, smells, delicacies and excrement, not to mention bullfighting and sacrosanct religion. Writing that André Breton would describe as "semi-automatic," although Picasso

i   "diamante hecho de todo el querer de los quereres de la sangre" (6 Jan. 1936). See p. 116, n.3

ii "la seule chose qui dans ce moment me chagrine c'est de ne pouvoir être avec elle et de ne pouvoir lui dire sortons nous promener au jardin comme ce matin et allons acheter du fromage et du pain et allons les manger assis sur ce banc qui est en face du grand arbre"

iii "cintas blancas que atan mis labios para que nunca más me digan otra cosa que cuanto yo la quiero que ahora que duerme y no veo más que su miel desde lejos a través de los cuartos que nos separan pobre de mí que escribo"

iv "y dime tú que lo sabes dime si puede ser que esta tarde aún llueva en mí el recuerdo húmedo de su cara"

v "la niña se comió los dedos del pincel frío"

vi "les pleurs d'une petite fille coquillage"

1 Picasso's relationship with his legitimate wife, Olga, was very belligerent; he never divorced her, and thus was forced to declare his children as having an "unknown father."

2 See Marie-Laure Bernadac and Christine Piot, *Picasso: Écrits* (Paris: Gallimard, 1989). English ed.: *Picasso: Collected Writings* (New York: Abbeville Press, 1989).

3 In an interview, Picasso challenged the idea that his family problems coloured his writings. See Roberto Otero, *Forever Picasso: An Intimate Look at His Last Years* (New York: Harry N. Abrams, 1974).

4 See *Picasso intime*, exh. cat., Musée de l'Athénée, Geneva, 4 July–6 Sept. 1981.

always impugned the Surrealists' quest for surges from the unconscious.[5] Despite his obvious affinities with Surrealist poetry, Picasso always wrote in an utterly original way off and on until 1959 (the date of the last known text). Words are linked to one another, leaping from one image to another, from one sound to another—he plays on words, plays with signs. Complex writing where threads enjoy getting tangled up, stories intertwine with no apparent grammar or logic, as if their author had suddenly been beaten to the punch by all the stimuli around him (smells, colours, reflections, shapes, sounds) and had layered several stories into a single text—as if many mirrors had shattered, carrying in their thousand shards the scenes they reflected, and Picasso had assembled them in an instant, in a sort of "verbal simultaneity." Too many contradictions dwell in him, his brush cannot keep up, only writing[6] allows him to compress onto a single page the myriad sensations, feelings, images overlapping with memories, the guts of a dead horse, the smell of stew and the fanned legs of a languid belle. Truly polyphonic writing,[7] in which themes and motifs speak to one another in a single text, and from one text to another, forming a labyrinthine whole. A remark made by Carl Einstein in 1928 in *Documents* applies perfectly to the painter's writing: "The important thing: Picasso is not subject to the retrograde tendencies of the imagination, because his paintings represent psychological elements that are not yet adapted and that overtake biological conservatism."[8]

Picasso himself places his texts in their relationship to drawing.

"the soup of the tangled hair of the narrative sweeping away the light that hides under the drawings feigning indifference to the proper words pointing to the gaping maw of things"[i] (20 February 1937).

Even more than in his paintings, time and space are exploded and no longer obey the principles "imposed by a stinking slavish rotting logic chained and sticky that traps the tongue if a real scream blossoms on it"[ii] (29 March 1936).

Pierre Daix[9] has rightly noted that Picasso found greater freedom to pour out his feelings in writing than in drawing, which was always controlled by his perfect mastery of the medium; an observation the artist himself confirmed.

"we sprinkle on top tiny aniseed sweets of every colour painted in front of the mirror of family memories which have that taste for me and which my mother at

---

5 "80 carats … mais une ombre" ("80 carats … with a single flaw") André Breton, *Combat*,
   2 Nov. 1961, repr. in Breton, *Le Surréalisme et la peinture* (Paris: Gallimard, 1965) p. 116–118;
   trans. Simon Watson Taylor, *Surrealism and Painting* (New York, Harper and Row, 1972).

6 Sometimes Picasso played the game of variation, using additions, collages and distortions—the best-
   known example being "Langue de feu" ("tongue of fire") published by Christian Zervos in *Cahiers
   d'art*, February 1936. This technique of dilating his writing is not unlike the swelling of the bodies of
   his *Bathers*. On other occasions, his texts came out in a single spurt—short impromptus or apho-
   risms. Most of the time, he filled his pages with compact writing in India ink, with many deletions,
   resumptions, scribblings and re-copyings. Of course, he sometimes used lead pencil or coloured
   crayons; his sketchbooks are interspersed with texts that have no apparent relation to the drawings.
   He also enjoyed the pleasure of transcription and beautiful calligraphy. A few manuscripts (often
   reproductions) are adorned with drawings such as the horse accompanying the texts of 7 and 15 June
   1935, the third state of the 7 June text and the first state of the 15 June text (MP 1054). There are also
   his lithographic poems. His two plays, *Desire Caught by the Tail* (14–17 Jan. 1941) and *The Four
   Little Girls* (24 Nov. 1947–13 Aug. 1948) have not been considered in this study.

7 Some groups of texts lend themselves more to methods of musical, rather than literary, analysis.

8 No. 1, Feb. 1929. (Free translation.)

9 Pierre Daix, *Dictionnaire Picasso* (Paris: Robert Laffont, 1995).

i *"la soupe des cheveux emmêlés du récit
   balayant la lumière qui se cache sous
   les dessins affectant l'indifférence aux
   mots propres désignant la gueule
   ouverte des choses"*

ii *"imposés par une logique puante
   esclave en décomposition enchaînée et
   gluante poissant la langue si un cri
   véritable la fleurit"*

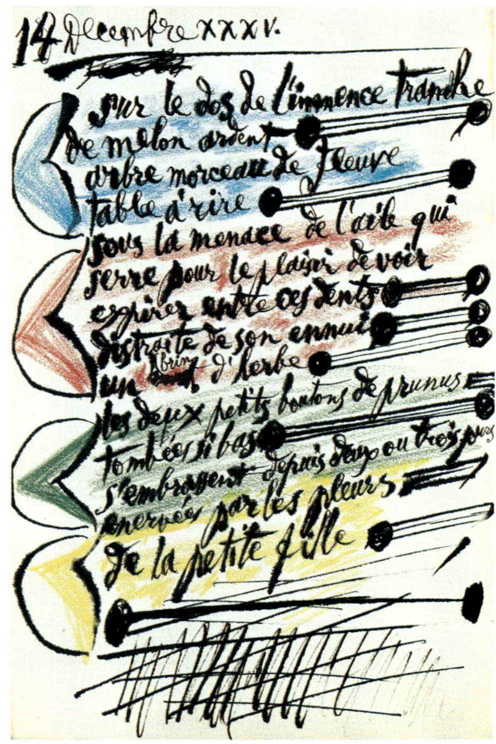

Fig. 1: *Sur le dos de l'immense tranche de melon ardent
(On the Back of the Immense Slice of Ardent Melon)*,
14 December 1935
India ink and coloured pencil on paper; 25.5 x 17.1
Paris, Musée Picasso, MP 1146

times sent to me knowing how much I liked those things when I was still a child so long ago and that now at eight minutes past one in the morning of January twentieth XXXVI lying in the bed of my room that looks out on the garden at number 23 rue La Boétie in Paris I don't know why I remember all this which has nothing to do with what I'm writing or which is perhaps only the apparent embroidery of the threads that run thrilled to float free without letting themselves be broken by the design imposed by the ticklings of the *mono sabio*"[i] (19 January 1936).

These threads "thrilled to float free" reveal the pleasure that Picasso took in writing, just as he took pleasure in everything else. With a typically Spanish exuberance, reminiscent of Góngora or even Rabelais, Picasso blends all kinds of language, shit and the Host, the blue of the sky and the stench of urine, peppering his texts in Spanish with Catalan or Andalusian slang. Is to play with words not the same as to take pleasure from them? Are not words caresses as soft as kisses?

"and squeezing its juice onto his tongue sees coming out of the landscape's mirror without a scratch the naked body of the blue sheet flapping its wings caught in the nets of greenery. Calls him and stretched out at his feet caresses him with its softest words and licks him"[ii] (19 March 1937).

The room is reflected in a large wardrobe mirror; in it, the poet-painter-voyeur's gaze surprises his lover's body, captures its movements, its kisses. Moving lines, the body becomes part of the intimate landscape and blends with bed, sheet, wallpaper, furniture and foliage. This indirect gaze, mediated by a mirror, transforms the vision, remodels volumes, shadows and lights; it establishes new relations among the objects and body parts reflected.

"she is drawn alive in her opening out of tenderness killing the curtain on the carpet that a wave of sheets coils round on the floor the mirror has imprisoned the corner of the room seen from the open door hidden in the gloom of the corridor and smashing to smithereens the fanned legs on the silk armchair"[iii] (18 April 1935).

The reality of love is often evoked through this fragile, quivering reflection of a mirror; a mirror that also has the ability to move and set the geometry of lines in motion, which makes the drawing more complicated.

"the raging toothache of grimacing colour and those very mathematical[ly] convolutions of tributes planted so skilfully at chance meetings in the shadow of the attitude taken by the drawing caught on the wing by the light crushing with its heavy thumb the line dazed by the reflection of the vase gives a nudge of the shoulder ransacking the desired order and spits all its disdain over the edge"[iv] (6 February 1936).

With all of his words the poet expresses the painter's problems, and perhaps the secret to many of the paintings can be found in these mirror-games and their abruptly broken forms. Games of shadows and light take flight on their own.

"in strips all the shadows lift off the bodies with the haste of holiday departures and go to lie faithfully by the rendezvous of light in the thickness of the smoked glass"[v] (4 May 1936).

i   *"se les echa por encima anisitos muy pequeños de todos los colores pintados delante del espejo de recuerdos de familia que tienen para mí este gusto y que mi madre a veces me ha mandado sabiendo lo que tanto me gustaban estas cosas cuando yo era aún niño hace ya tanto tiempo y que ahora a la una y ocho minutos de esta noche del día veinte de enero del XXXVI acostado en la cama en mi cuarto que da al jardín en la rue La Boétie número 23 en París no sé por qué me acuerdo de todo esto que no tiene nada que ver con lo que escribo o que quizás es solamente el bordado aparente de los hilos que corren locos de contento de flotar libres sin dejarse amaestrar por el dibujo que le hacen las cosquillas del mono sabio"*

ii *"et presse son jus sur sa langue voit sortir du miroir du paysage sans une blessure le corps nu du drap bleu agitant ses ailes pris dans les filets du feuillage. L'appelle et à ses pieds étendu le caresse de ses mots les plus doux et le lèche"*

iii *"se dibuja vivo en su expansión de cariño asesinando la cortina sobre la alfombra que una ola de sábanas rodilla en el suelo el espejo se trae prisionera al ángulo del cuarto visto desde la puerta abierta escondida en el negro del pasillo y haciendo añicos al abanico patas abiertas en la butaca de seda"*

iv *"la rage de dents de la couleur grimaçante et ces bien mathématiquement circonvolutions d'hommages plantés si adroitement au hasard des rencontres à l'ombre de l'attitude prise par le dessin pris au vol par la lumière écrasant de son gros pouce la ligne endormie par le reflet du vase renvoie d'un coup d'épaule chambarder l'ordonnance voulue et crache tout son dédain par-dessus bord"*

v   *"par lambeaux toutes les ombres se détachent des corps avec la précipitation des départs en voyage et vont s'étendre fidèles au rendez-vous de la lumière dans l'épaisseur du cristal fumé"*

This deconstruction of the visual plane goes further. It is an "untamed" eye that Picasso turns on objects reduced to shapes and colours, dissociating them from the laws of gravity, the physical ties that bind them. A Cubist collage, to be sure, but also a search for that primitive naïveté in looking which knows no rules. We "know" before we see, we interpret shadows, shapes, colours and light as a coherent system. Thus we "see" the beautiful woman lying in her bath, but why not "see" the water and bathtub hanging from her neck? Why cannot it be her reflection that holds the mirror into which she gazes as well as the wardrobe?

"wearing knotted around her neck like a scarf a bathtub full of boiling water"[i]

"wearing knotted around her neck like a scarf a wardrobe with a mirror filled with dirty laundry wearing knotted around her neck like a scarf the dining-room table laid for lunch the tablecloth in flames"[ii] (11 October 1936).

A surrealist image, to be sure, but one that also signifies a total liberation on the visual plane which allowed Picasso, particularly in sculpture, to use anything and everything to forge a new articulation. This skill at discovering new relationships between objects and their hidden forms is analogous to that which, in his poems, governs the relationships between the lover's body and her bed, the sheets or the chair in which she sits.

"the sheet gets up from the bed and right away its wheels laughing loudly tear the skin to shreds"[iii] (1 March 1940).

Unless…the objects themselves become flesh-and-blood lovers. A sexually charged emotional complicity pervades the familiar.

"as long as the chair doesn't come and give me its usual friendly tap on the shoulder and the kitchen table doesn't snuggle up in my arms"[iv] (7 November 1935).

"the table the chairs far more outgoing far more skilful in their caresses and so reserved taking you by the throat with the softness of their velvet paws[v] (20 February 1937).

This is the inverse, in writing, of the *Anatomies* of February 1933, where the bodies of women are transmuted into objects, tables or chairs (Cat. 136–138).

But what no painting or drawing will exude are smells: smells of flowers and underarms; smells of farts permeating the bedroom; kitchen smells rising out of pots; smell of rubbish and smell of steaming entrails; smell of the sky, smell of blue clasping the sun's neck, smell of silence and smell of time.

"the nose sniffing the hole in the lavatory and smelling the bouquet of roses already in their prime"[vi] (21 October 1951).

For Picasso, the nose is undeniably a source of sexual pleasure, and sticks itself everywhere.

"adjoining sun poking its nose into the asshole of dawn"[vii] (2 March 1951).

Of course, this olfactory sensibility is not present in Picasso's visual works but is compensated for by an enlargement of the nasal appendage, which becomes a male sexual organ. Marie-Thérèse's nose-phallus speaks volumes about these pleasures and their symbolic meaning. The metamorphosis of Marie-Thérèse's face is certainly erotic in origin, but also comes from the play of shadows on the sleeping

i   *"portant nouée à son cou en écharpe une baignoire remplie d'eau bouillante"*

ii *"portant nouée à son cou en écharpe une armoire à glace remplie de linge sale portant nouée à son cou en écharpe la table de la salle à manger servie pour le déjeuner la nappe en flammes"*

iii *"le drap se lève du lit et immédiatement ses roues en riant à gorge déployée déchirent en lambeaux la peau"*

iv *"tant que la chaise ne vienne me taper comme toujours si familièrement sur l'épaule et que la table de la cuisine ne se blottisse dans mes bras"*

v   *"la table les chaises autrement entreprenants autrement adroits dans ses caresses et si réservés vous prenant à la gorge par la douceur dans leurs pattes de velours"*

vi *"le nez au trou des cabinets et sentant le bouquet des roses déjà mûres"*

vii *"soleil mitoyen mettant son nez au trou du cul de l'aube"*

beauty, as for instance in *The Dream*. The nose-phallus changes the face of both men and women and even transforms itself into a revolting snout in *Dreams and Lies of Franco*. But the proliferation of the phallus doesn't end there: in some sculptures, the entire structure of Marie-Thérèse's face becomes an interweaving of male genitals.

"I shouldn't say that the head points to everything that lies under the bedspread"[i] (18 April 1935).

The sex-face is certainly not unique to Picasso—the cover of *What Is Surrealism?*, which appeared in 1934, shows a fine rendition of the same theme by Magritte.

After the head, the phallus appropriates the entire bust, as in the hilarious *Anatomies* —phalluses with legs and testicles for breasts.

"at twenty to one in the morning my grandmother's balls are potatoes with tomatoes"[ii] (8 December 1935)—an allusion to a popular song. The parts of the male-female body become geometric forms or fluid lines that intertwine and become entangled in the embrace "to the mathematical point of love," as in those giddy pirouettes where round shapes pretend to be breasts, balls, buttocks or bellies in "the square of desire."

The circle and square in a field full of flowers are coupled, transported by the "geometric flights of desire"[iii] (7 June 1936), arms and legs flailing in the wind like huge, fringed scarves. In these charming somersaults, the head of the lady becomes a heart made of two little buttocks with a dark crack and, at the end of a long handle (neck), takes the shape of a penis.

The eye, identical in men and women, permits the shift from one sex to the other, a passageway between masculine and feminine, inside and outside.

As eye, it is the oval female sex, it engulfs, swallows; it is the theatre of life and death; as gaze, it becomes male, bursting with seed—"the erect eye"[iv] (15 July 1940)—and is projected outside itself, like "the winged eye flying like a bullet without stopping from sky to earth and earth to sky"[v] (13 August 1940). It is the gaze of the painter, the obsessive eye that haunts Picasso's work. The gaze that connects the painter with his model:

"look at me since you're looking at me look at me since you're looking at me look at me since you're looking at me look at me since you're looking at me if since me since look that you're looking at me since if you're looking at me and if looking at her since looking at her if since look at her if her her if me if her me if if me if her if"[vi] (20 January 1936).

The eye is the androgynous zone where the canvas is played out; " the tongue-flick of its gaze wakes the tragic mishmash of the flies' ballet"[vii] (September 1936), aided by the sticky tongue-flicks of light. Georges Bataille, like Buñuel, associates the eye with cutting, while for Picasso the eye is whipped, stung by a crop.

"eyes made of stings of crops"[viii] (4 April 1936).

"sting of crop straight in the eyes"[ix] (26 March 1936).

To the toothed vagina of the Surrealists, Picasso responds with a toothed eye.

i "no debería decir que cabeza es para todo lo que viene detrás de la colcha"
ii "a la una menos veinte de la noche los cojones de mi abuela son patatas con tomates"
iii "vols géométriques du désir"
iv "el ojo en erección"
v "ojo alado volando como una pelota sin parar del cielo a la tierra y de la tierra al cielo"
vi "mírame ya que me miras mírame que ya me miras mírame que me ya miras ya mírame que me miras si ya me ya mira que ya miras que si me miras y si la mira ya la mira si ya mira la si la la si mi si la mi si si mi si la si"
vii "le coup de langue de son regard éveille la ratatouille tragique du ballet des mouches"
viii "yeux faits à coups de cravache"
ix "coup de cravache reçu en plein dans ses yeux"

"eyes biting with all their teeth of their jaw the morsel of coal in the toothless mouth vomiting its mass of hair"[i] (11–17 October 1936).

The text is accompanied by a drawing of eye-jaws: the "head" sprouts sketches of eyes with eyelash-teeth; from these serrations about the eyes, Picasso moves to a jaw that clenches an eye, showing precisely the details of teeth, iris and pupil, while the toothless mouth is a sex whose lips spit out hair-threads. Is this eye-in-the-mouth not an inverted illustration of, and Picasso's answer to, the eye-in-the-vagina of Georges Bataille's *The Story of the Eye*? The "eye of the egg"[ii] (8 and 20 May 1935) is the exact echo of the dialogue between Simone and Sir Edmond: "Do you see the eye? It's an egg."[10] But is this "eye of the egg," a blind eye, not also the clouded eye of *La Celestina*, the empty eye of the *Demoiselles d'Avignon* and of the blind Minotaur?

The mouth is sex, the sex is eye, the eye is sun—the shift occurs in the visual works as well as in the writings.

The mouth, narrow oval and hairy crack, truly a woman's sex in *The Kiss* of 1925 (Cat. 88), becomes a pair of threatening jaws that confront each other like castrating saws in *The Kiss* of 1931 (Cat. 117), "a mouth edged with man-trapping fishhooks"[iii] (4 March 1940).

The mouth, an "open wound showing its teeth at the well-hole"[iv] (11 February 1941), sometimes round (a toothed vagina), sometimes gaping and misshapen, ejaculating a scream or a tongue like an aggressive spear, appears as a sex that crushes and engulfs.

"your open mouth is ready—to swallow the sun…"[v] (4 November 1935) —the sun itself is a cannibal armed with huge teeth.

"raging toothache in the sun's eyes stings"[vi] (20 February 1937).

"surrounded by the teeth of the sun's jaw sunk into his flesh"[vii] (6 February 1938).

And, like an echo of the popular expression "poils aux dents, poils aux fesses," teeth are also covered in hair, "teeth covered in the hair of the hollow oranges of the gums"[viii] (19 March 1938).

The sky, too, is a nest of hair: "between the hairs of the sky"[ix] (23 February 1942), "hairs covering the clouds"[x] (24 July 1937), "solar hairs"[xi] (1 May 1941). Though a myriad hirsute hair-rays often bristle in Picasso's suns like eyes bordered by lashes, this hairy sky is a distinct feature of his writings, and exudes a strong scent of the bedroom.

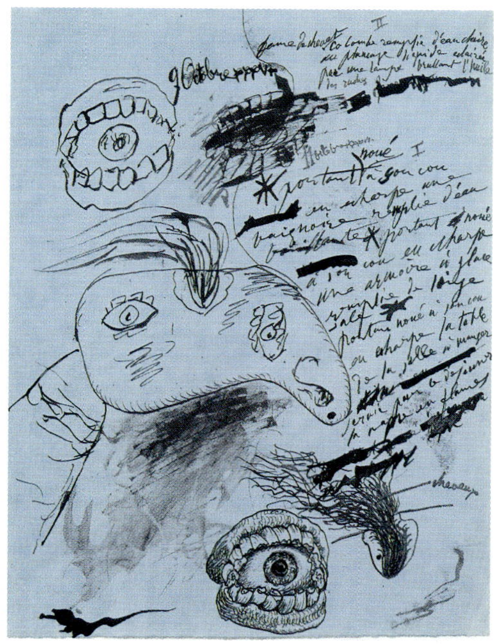

Fig. 2: *Studies: Head of Woman; Poems in French*,
9 and 11 October 1936
Pen, India ink and wash on paper; 27 x 21
Paris, Musée Picasso, MP 1171

10 (*"Tu vois l'œil ? C'est un œuf."*) Why would Picasso only converse with painters and not with his writer friends? It would be amusing to try to track down answers or playful remarks to his poet friends in his writings. Although it is not the subject of this study, there is a certain eroticism hidden in such a poetically ethereal expression as "aurora borealis," which recurs frequently in Picasso, but which Éluard, too, employs in *The Immaculate Conception* to indicate one of his Kama Sutra positions: "hydrangeas glued to the lilac wall-hanging covering the aurora borealis of the room" (*"des hortensias collés à la tenture lilas tapissant l'aurore boréale de la chambre,"* 9 Mar. 1951); "the aurora borealis of the closed fan of her mane" (*"l'aurore boréale de l'éventail fermé de sa crinière,"* 27 July 1947).

  i *"yeux mordant de toutes les dents de leur mâchoire le morceau de charbon dans la bouche édentée vomissant sa chevelure"*
 ii *"l'œil de l'œuf"*
iii *"bouche bordée d'hameçons piège à loup"*
 iv *"blessure ouverte montrant ses dents au trou du puits"*
  v *"ta bouche ouverte est prête – à avaler le soleil"*
 vi *"rage de dents aux yeux du soleil pique"*
vii *"entouré par les dents de la mâchoire du soleil plantées dans sa chair"*
viii *"les dents couvertes des poils des oranges creuses des gencives"*
 ix *"entre les poils du ciel"*
  x *"des poils recouvrant les nuages"*
 xi *"poils solaires"*

And yet writings and drawings are forged from the same coals, the fiery tongue, metal tongue. The "tongue trapped inside his mouth full of hairs"[i] (19 March 1937) spurts forth the fiery tongue of "the mouth stuck on the tap of the flame"[ii] (15 March 1937). A burning tongue "that hangs on its eye swallowing the spit of the flames"[iii] (1 May 1941), it invades painting; "the portrait is drawn in leaping tongues of fire"[iv] (18 March 1942): the body extended on the bed, distorted, "body hung by the tongue in the discreet flame of the shower of the sun-seeds of the artificial ardour of the palette kicked over the traces and defrocked unwinds the bobbin of rainbow threads and cuts out the drawing of the profile of the head on the stone"[v] (15 May 1936).

This tongue shoots forth like a phallus or a turd from the toothed crack of the face; licking or probing, it pierces or dribbles with caresses. *Figure at the Seashore* (Cat. 171) walking "on the tiptoes of its tongue"[vi] (29 July 1940). A terrifying cockleshell in pinkish and purplish hues, this monstrous sea-ear advances as in "a procession of mouths knocking at the door with their tongues"[vii] (7 July 1940). This gaping tumescent mouth on two legs, with its three teeth, its two protruding eyes, its spear-tongue and its odd floating strands of hair—is this the final mutation of the *Anatomies* of women (Cat. 136) or perhaps some androgynous creature, a primitive phallic cavity from before the separation of the sexes?

Nor should we forget that the mouth is the seat of a primordial pleasure: suckling, sucking, stuffing our fingers in our mouth, sensing the excitement of our taste buds is our most primitive manner of ingesting the other when we are newborn. I love you, I want to be you, so I eat you.

"I can no longer stand this miracle that is knowing nothing in this world and having learned nothing but how to love things and eat them alive"[viii] (18 April 1935). Picasso-the-sober, Picasso-the-frugal stuffs his texts with food, steaming soups, hearty stews washed down with great glassfuls of wine. So many memories of the tastes of childhood, so many delicious recipes, including one for a painting: "cut out the drawing of the profile of the head on the arum lily stone and rub her gaze with garlic and onion and untie the ribbons on her hands with the heat of the ball made from the melted mirror that seals in the immaculate image of the leap of the bull"[ix] (5 May 1936).

But there is no royal feast without steaming entrails, those of the painting or those of the bull.

"the words of love and the warning cries tear apart with their teeth the guts ripped from the canvas placed in a bier drying on the quay in its frame of longings and desires"[x] (19 July 1937).

Food and paint mix together in the fragrant kitchen of love.

When it lost its original sacred character, eroticism became a transgression and a stain; the supreme transgression being cannibalism and the kill, which we find in Picasso in a metaphorical mode. Picasso, like Bataille, intimately blends love and the stain of sin but in a natural, playful manner. Sweat, urine, vomit and farts are all part of his love vocabulary, truculent and humorous, as in the popular medieval farces where shit and bawdy love make fine bedfellows.

i *"lengua prisionera dentro de su boca rellena de pelos"*
ii *"la bouche prise au robinet de la flamme"*
iii *"qui pend à son œil en avalant la bave des flammes"*
iv *"le portrait se dessine en hautes langues de feu"*
v *"corps pendu par la langue au feu discret de la pluie des graines de soleil de l'artificielle ardeur de la palette jetée par-dessus les moulins aux orties déroule la bobine des fils de l'arc-en-ciel et découpe le dessin du profil de la tête sur la pierre"*
vi *"a punta del pie de su lengua"*
vii *"la procesión de bocas que llaman a la puerta con sus lenguas"*
viii *"no puedo más de este milagro que es el no saber nada en este mundo y no haber aprendido nada sino a querer las cosas y comérmelas vivas"*
ix *"découpe le dessin du profil de la tête sur la pierre des arums et frotte à l'ail et à l'oignon son regard et dénoue les rubans de ses mains à la chaleur de la boule faite du miroir fondu qui enferme l'image immaculée du saut du toro"*
x *"les mots d'amour et les cris d'appel déchirent à belles dents les tripes arrachées au tableau mis en bière séchant sur le quai dans son cadre d'envies et désirs"*

"shit and shit plus shit equals all shit multiplied by shit mucosal meanderings fetid breath of the rose of the wind from his anus double cream cocoon spun by the perfect love clinging to his pustules simmering on the so soft fire of his eyes"[i] (15 February 1937).

The pleasure of words and repetition explodes shamelessly. Father Ubu is not far off.[11]

"stupid old age curses and frightens between the skirts of the farts"[ii] (18 December 1935).

Here his writings make a radical break from his visual works, which include very few scatological or nauseating scenes. The famous *Woman Pissing* is more an homage to Rembrandt than a woman urinating.

Beyond this saucy humour lies another aspect of Picasso's sensibility. That which elicits desire is erotic; that which is repugnant is what we see as such. The criteria for beautiful and ugly, dirty and desirable, are interchangeable. For Picasso, shit is not excrement; it is a substance, a material like any other. There is neither provocation nor philosophical claim-staking; nothing to do with those little bags of excrement exhibited in the odd Parisian gallery. One need look no further than "Picasso dans son élément" ("Picasso in his element"), published by André Breton in *Minotaure* in 1933, where he recounts his visit to the painter's studio: "Came across a little unfinished canvas, the same size as the butterfly one, with only a large impasto occupying the centre. Making sure it was dry, he explained to me that the subject of this canvas was to be a piece of shit, as would become obvious once he'd put the flies on. He regretted only that he had to use paint instead of real dried shit and most precisely one of those *inimitable* ones that one might catch sight of in the countryside in the days when children bit into cherries without bothering to discard the seeds."[iii]

It is possible, without disrespect or an unduly scatological imagination, to see some of the *Reclining Bathers*, drawings and sculptures executed in 1931, as assemblages of turds.[12]

Picasso does not imprison himself in our well-bred rules. It is the freedom to feel, to think, to create that is manifest here. His pantheism explodes in a love of everything, of everything we see, smell, breathe, hear, touch, even what is horrible to our eyes. Thus about the neck of his lovely one he fastens several necklaces:

"necklace of smile"[iv] (10–12 February 1936).

"necklace at the neck made of onions and of cough drops and of pan pipes"[v] (21 April 1936).

"necklace of burning salt"[vi] (9 August 1940).

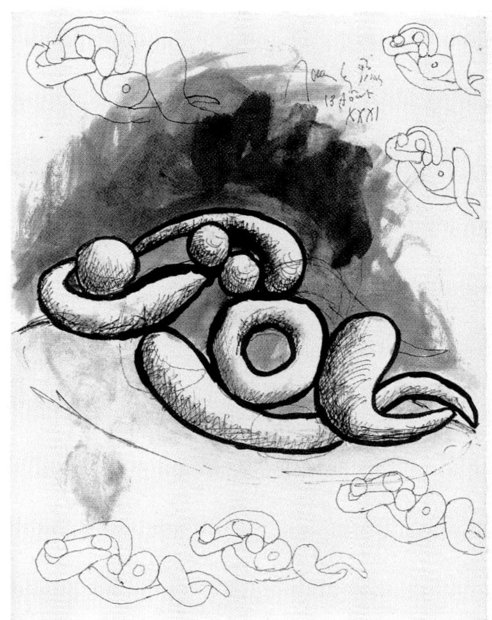

Fig. 3: *Reclining Bather*, 13 August 1931
Pen, India ink and wash on paper; 32.5 x 25.5
Paris, Musée Picasso, MP 1058

i   *"merde et merde plus merde égale à toutes merdes multipliées par merde glaires de gloses haleine pestilentielle de la rose des vents de son anus double crème cocon filé par le parfait amour accroché à ses pustules mijotant sur le feu si doux de ses yeux"*
ii *"la estúpida vejez carajea y espanta metida entre las faldas a los pedos"*
iii *"vint à passer une petite toile inachevée, du format de celle au papil-lon, et dont seul un large empâtement occupait le centre. Tout en s'assurant de sa sécheresse, il m'expliqua que le sujet de cette toile devait être un excrément, comme cela apparaîtrait du reste lorsqu'il aurait disposé les mouches. Il déplorait seulement d'avoir dû suppléer par la couleur au manque d'un véritable excrément séché et très précisément d'un de ceux, inimitable, qu'il arrive de remarquer à la campagne à l'époque où les enfants croquent les cerises sans prendre la peine de rejeter les noyaux."*
iv *"collier de sourire"*
v   *"collier au cou fait d'oignons et de pastilles pectorales et des flûtes de pan"*
vi *"collar del sal ardiendo"*

11 Picasso owned the manuscript of *Ubu cocu* ("Ubu cuckolded").
12 MP 1058, MP 1061 and especially the plaster *Reclining Bather*, MP 290, as well as the two plasters of *Head of a Woman*, MP 291 and MP 292.

"necklace of the sky"[i] (5–6 October 1940).

"necklace undone and free from the plate of fried onions"[ii] (7 November 1940).

"necklace of excrement"[iii] (28 November 1938).

Different places, different customs. There was a time when going to the latrine was a social activity of the well bred. It should not be forgotten that in the Sahara dried camel droppings were strung like pearls to make jewellery.

Besides, is not the work the artist's "excretion"?

There is no light without shade, no passion without hate nor desire without death.

"the knife that leaps contented has no other recourse but to die of pleasure"[iv] (5 December 1935).

Every birth bears inside itself its own death, every love its own destruction. The pregnant arrow, expectant mother, which Picasso would sculpt during Françoise's pregnancy in 1949, had already taken wing at the birth of Maya; "pregnant arrow pierces in mid-flight the flaming rose of death"[v] (19 January 1936).

This "flaming rose of death" finds her most beautiful blossoming in the "flesh of the square arena,"[vi] which is the "square of desire", (6 February 1938) where death is both spectacle and sexual climax.

Through their sacred origin, eroticism and tauromachy[13] become one in an ultimate sacrifice, where the pleasure of death invites a communion in the same ritual of bull, horse, matador and spectators. Instead of the ballet of the cape whereby the beast is lured, seduced, led finally to impale itself, head lowered, on the fatal *pica*, Picasso prefers the brutality of the *rejón de muerte*, that bloody close combat of the days of his youth when the caparison was not in fashion. This is not the "clean" bullfight whose *suertes* had been codified by Pepe Illo[14] and which the intellectuals revel in; it is not the death where the blood trickles timidly from the bull's mouth, when the *estoque* has been aimed straight to the medulla—"the sword quivers striking right to the heart of the Host"[vii] (26 January 1936)—that fascinates Picasso. No, it is the brutal ritual of bloody sacrifice, the fascination of blood shed, not the seductive aesthetics of the dance.

The bullfight is pagan festival, a blend of cries of joy, suffering, and stains.

The killing of the bull is supplanted by the disembowelment of the horse.

"the bouquet of flowers of the viscera of the horse wounded on its back caress the ear and ass of light"[viii] (7 November 1940).

Picasso's writings exude a nostalgia for the smell of entrails.

"and at the bull's first shove against the horse the curtain rises and all the boats full of firework footlights light up … the bull searches with his key for the

i   "collar del cielo"
ii   "collier défait et libre du plat d'oignons frits"
iii "collier d'excréments"
iv   "el cuchillo que salta de contento no tiene más remedio que morir de placer"
v   "flecha encintada viene a picar al vuelo de la rosa encendida de la muerte"
vi   "rose enflammée de la mort trouve son plus bel épanouissement dans la chair du carré de l'arène"
vii "la espada salta haciendo blanco en medio de la hostia"
viii "el ramo de flores de las tripas del caballo herido a cuestas acarician la oreja y culo de la luz"

13 See Bernadac, "Le Christ dans l'arène espagnole : le thème de la corrida dans les écrits de Picasso" ("Christ in the Spanish bullring: The theme of the bullfight in Picasso's writings"), *Cahiers du musée national d'Art moderne*, Winter 1991, p. 59–75.

14 José Delgado, alias Pepe Illo, wrote the first treatise on bullfighting, *La Tauromaquia o el arte de torear* ("Tauromachy, or, The art of bullfighting"), in 1786. Picasso illustrated an edition published by Gustaveo Gili in 1959.

eagle-eye of the drum that rattles at the call of the horn in the pandemonium of his stomach like the deliberate pealing of the delicate fine feast pleasure party of death and opens wide the door to the dance of the paunch of the mare raises the curtains and uncovers the feast"[i] (20 January 1936).

This festival of entrails is the literary echo of the bull-Minotaurs, devourers of entrails who figure in drawings and engravings of 1934.[15] Here, Picasso breaks from his *aficionado* friends to join in more ancient rites, the fragrant and viscous frothing of the cult of Cybele and the pleasure of wallowing in bloodiness. Certainly Picasso and Barcelona are inseparable, but let us not forget that the painter was born on the wilder shores of Málaga, closer to Carthage, Phoenicia and Gilgamesh than to urban civilities. The knife that plunges into the wound, the sword that buries itself in the medulla, the horn that gores the stomach—so many primitive pleasures, so many "sweet pleasures" of childhood haunt the writings of Picasso. This fine feast to which Picasso invites us brings together, in a single ritual, entrails, love and death.

"what a party and what a feast in the guts of the sky fallen to its knees on the ground and what a laugh shakes its belly in piercing the heart the horn of plenty of the beast struck dumb with love and glazed with bliss biting at the lips of the crazed bouquet"[ii] (15 February 1937).

A key figure in his love mythology, this disembowelled horse, its neck erect, stretched out in its blood at the foot of the spectators' stand, haunts Picasso's bullfight imagery.[16] The great many representations of embraces between horse and bull are mimicked in the bloody intertwinings of his writings. It must be said that Picasso-the-Minotaur frequently dons "the bull suit" to thrust his horn into the belly of the mare, split into a feminine sex-oval,[17] this mare who, even in death, plays the flirt.

"but what horse lugs its guts with so much grace sending so many kisses and smiles and so many inflaming glances and so many flatulencies so fragrant and perfumed with so many aromas at the moment of death"[iii] (18 February 1937).

Could this killing of the horse, this savouring of entrails, be for Picasso-the-cannibal a way of consuming-devouring the women he loves?

"the blue bride's dress that burns on the fire the black lace blouse her stockings and her jewellery overflow with the feast of her body"[iv] (3 May 1941).

In 1933 comes the *Death of the Female Toreador*[18]; the bull clasps in a last embrace the dying *torera*,[19] listless, stripped bare, abandoned, in a languorous sexual joust in which the horse sometimes participates.[20] This erotic Death given in a fatal kiss by an amorous Minotaur has no equivalent in the writings.

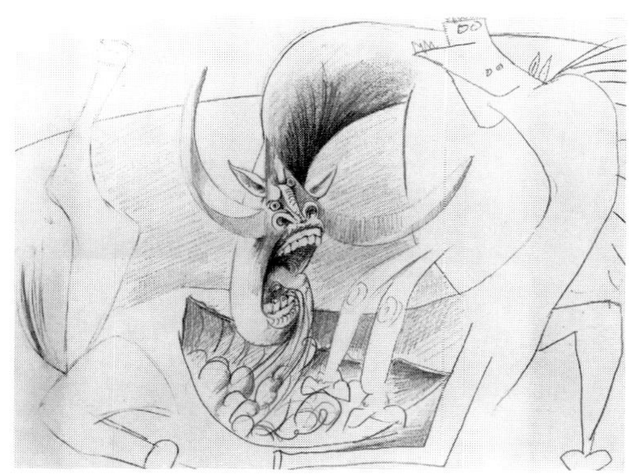

Fig. 4: *Bull and Horse*, 24 July 1934
Pencil on paper; 26 x 34.5
Hamburg, Klaus Hegewisch collection

15   *Bull and Horse*, 14 July 1934, Klaus Hegewisch collection; *Woman with a Candle, Fight between Bull and Horse*, 24 July 1934, Z.VIII:215, MP 1136.
16   *Dying Horse*, 1917, MPB 110 012; *Bullfight*, 1923, Z.V:146.
17   See the notebook of 17 July–12 Sept. 1927, MP 1874.
18   *Bullfight: Death of the Female Toreador*, Boisgeloup, 6 Sept. 1933, MP 144.
19   *Female Toreador. Last Kiss?*, 12 June 1934, etching, Baer II:426.
20   *Bull with Deathblow, Horse and Naked Woman*, 10 July 1934, Z.VIII:226. The erotic trio of bull, woman and horse does not figure in the writings.

i   *"y al primer rempujón que le da el toro al caballo levanta el telón y se encienden todas las barcas llenas de candilejas al fuego artificial y el toro con su llave busca el ojo de águila del pandero que resuena al golpe dado por el cuerno en el jolgorio de su vientre como el intencionado repique de la juerga convite fino y delicado de la muerte"*

ii   *"quelle fête et quel festin dans les tripes du ciel tombé à genoux par terre et quel rire ne secoue sa panse en traversant le cœur la corne d'abondance de la bête du coup muette d'amour et glacée de bonheur mordant aux lèvres du bouquet en folie"*

iii   *"mais quel cheval traîne ses tripes avec tant de grâce envoyant tant de baisers et sourires et tant d'œillades incendiaires et tant de ventosités si odorantes et parfumées de tant d'arômes au moment de la mort"*

iv   *"la robe bleue de mariée qui brûle sur le feu la chemise de dentelles noire ses bas et ses bijoux regorgent du festin de son corps"*

After the sacrifice of the horse, the sacrifice of the *torera*, comes that of the matador, who also succumbs to a fatal kiss.

"explodes like a kiss on the mouth of the horn blood of torero"[i] (4 July 1940).

In the *square of desire*, the roles are reversed; victim and executioner give and receive death in a single climax.

"dressed in garden—here is the matador—bleeding his joy among the folds of the cape"[ii] (7 August 1935).

Picasso-the-Minotaur, bull and bullfighter trade garments[21]; a game of metamorphoses that calls to mind the sliding of sex into eye, of eye into sun, of sun into bullring in the geometry of desire where the bull triumphs, "diamond made of all the love of loves of blood flag shaken by the olés of the cluster of hearts flapping their wings at the muzzle brandishing its beauty"[iii] (6 January 1936).

In the writings, the rapes and the most inflamed embraces[22] are related to bullfighting. No matter how great the love, a languid belle will never satisfy the infinite climax of the bull; "Javanese caresses will never fill the depth of a sigh…nor all desires"[iv] (12 July 1937).

Love "dribbling with caresses" breathes boredom.

"miserable shagreen clasping the torn body of love that bleeds so cramped in the crown of its nest of thorns miserable memory"[v] (3 October 1936).

Replying to the dialogue of the lover and his lady who tires so soon is "the dialogue of the bull and the horse despite the obviousness of the drama that is played out and repeated in a thousand different ways and that I shall have to go and tear out from the depth of the gaze of each spectator"[vi] (7 November 1935).

For it is through the gaze that desire is born, it is in the gaze that the game of love and death is played out.

"awakens egg sun more resplendent than the sun become a man bull Host surrounded by twenty-six wings of white eagles enveloped in circles of irises that grow larger when others appear and grow infinitely large and infinitely others and others that appear also grow on the India ink of infinity"[vii] (19 January 1936).

Only the spectacle of death opens upon the infinity of desire.

This study was greatly facilitated through the use of a linguistics software application developed by Ernest Grandjean within the scope of the *Picasso autrement* research group at the Centre National de la Recherche Scientifique, France. All of the citations in this text are taken from Marie-Laure Bernadac and Christine Piot's remarkable collection of Picasso's writings, *Picasso: Écrits* (Paris: Gallimard, 1989.) This enormous editorial undertaking anthologized all of Picasso's known texts at the time—written in either Spanish or French—with indications as to the various states and versions of the manuscripts. The Spanish texts were translated into French by Carol Volk and Albert Bensoussan. The original versions of both the Spanish and French texts are provided in the notes.

i   "estalla como un beso en la boca del cuerno sangre torera"

ii   "vestido de jardín –aquí está ya el torero– sangrando su alegría entre los pliegues de la capa"

iii   "diamante hecho de todo el querer de los quereres de la sangre bandera sacudida por los olés del racimo de corazones agitando sus alas al hocico que asoma su belleza"

iv   "les papouilles javanaises ne combleront jamais la profondeur du soupir… ni tous les désirs"

v   "misérable peau de chagrin serrant le corps déchiré de l'amour qui saigne si à l'étroit dans la couronne de son nid de ronces misérable souvenir"

vi   "le dialogue du toro et du cheval malgré l'évidence du drame qui se joue et se répète de mille façons différentes et qu'il me faudra aller arracher au fond du regard de chacun des spectateurs"

vii   "se despierta huevo sol más brillante que el sol hecho un hombre toro hostia rodeado de veinte y seis alas de águilas blancas envuelto de círculos iris que se van agrandando cuando otros aparecen y se agrandan infinitamente y que infinitamente otros y otros que aparecen se agranda también sobre la tinta china del infinito"

21   "the matador's suit that the bull at last has donned the wings of the horse sweep the rain" ("*l'habit de toréro que le taureau enfin a mis les ailes du cheval balayent la pluie,*" 4 Dec. 1935); "if matador if he still has not the grace to don his bull disguise with his suit of lights lighted colliding with lance" ("*si toréro s'il n'a pas encore la grâce de passer son déguisement de taureau avec son habit de lumières allumées heurtant pique,*" 19 Dec. 1935).

22   The terms "embrace" and "rape" are not used in the writings.

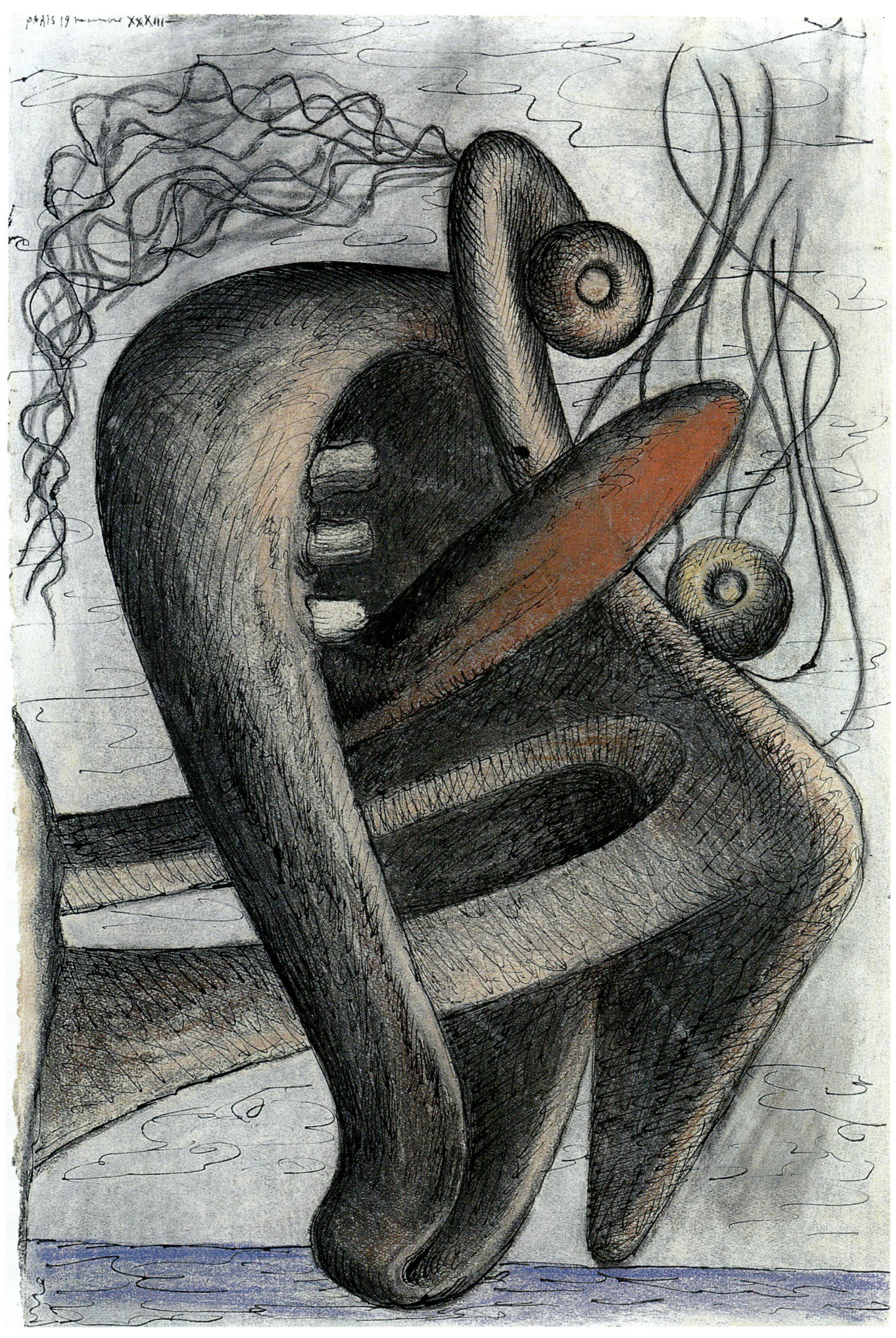

171 Figure at the Seashore, 19 November 1933

Pastel, India ink and charcoal on paper; 51 x 34.2
Paris, Musée Picasso, MP 1116

RAPHAEL AND *LA FORNARINA*

Dominique Dupuis-Labbé

"A man must not remain indifferent before a work of art that he passes by, negligently casting a glance at it. … He must vibrate with it, be moved by it, and in so doing, himself engage in creation, through his imagination if not in fact. … The spectator must be ripped out of his torpor, shaken, grabbed by the throat so that he can become aware of the world in which he lives—and, to do that, one must first get him out of this world. …" Pablo Picasso[1]

The suite of *347* prints begins on 16 March 1968, with a copper etching entitled *Picasso, son œuvre, et son public*. In this signal piece, Picasso, surrounded by a magician, a circus strongman and a young woman stretched out at his feet, naked, facing backward, is clearly indicating what was in store until 5 October of the same year: a representation of a circus, a role play, a step-right-up dramatization of life's illusions before our very eyes, right there, for the first time in his work— or evoked later on, in an allusive fashion, through a voyeur. The artist was giving us the huge universe to which he had given birth: a multitude of characters— both imaginary and rooted in his private life—living, loving, suffering, dying in a world where, to quote Paul Éluard, "he seeks to conquer through violence all that is gentle, and through gentleness, all violence." The series was a rich and complex private journal that condensed his reflections on life, love, sex, death and art, a day-by-day overview of his deepest emotions, the questions he was asking himself and would never cease to ask himself and us, about desire, pleasure, suffering, separation, the fear of growing old and of dying, creation, all of the things embodied in the image of a couple, a couple whose presence articulates the work of art, whether it is a couple representing love with its procession of seduction, embraces, copulations and rapes, a couple representing the artistic relationship (painter and/or sculptor and model, accompanied or unaccompanied by an admirer), or a couple representing battles and death: bull and horse. Love everywhere, sex everywhere, indissociable and antagonistic. "In the end, there is only love. Whatever kind of love it may be," Picasso tells us—but the impassioned stirring of the senses, the freeing of instincts, of impulses, and the near-permanent violence in his work is more evocative of a merciless battle in which one combatant will remain beaten on the ground than of idyllic sharing; this is the register of sensuality and sexuality in which the etching, and in particular the *Suite 347*, becomes a confidence, a testimony, an outlet and perhaps even a kind of therapy, constituting Picasso's "story in images." What do we see in it? An evocation meant to say everything about his early years and themes: the circus and its travelling performers, acrobats or stripped-down circus riders, voluptuous odalisques in the style of Ingres, picaresque Spain, strangely populated by Rembrant-like musketeers whose sole occupation is the pursuit and ravishment of women, regardless of whether they consent (what does it matter if they say "yes" when

---

1 Cited by Geneviève Laporte in *Si tard le soir, le soleil brille* (Paris: Plon, 1973), p. 98. (Free translation.)

you can always rape them?), the *majas* with their heavy mantillas who let their black dresses slide down to uncover their breasts or their vulvas, women who are as much prey as predators—Picasso represented a thousand and one different ways to use and abuse women or to be abused by them. Eroticism is omnipresent in the atmosphere of a brothel where young, shameless, sensual, full-bodied women offer themselves to the concupiscence of a voyeur who sizes them up and wastes no time, so it seems, in cashing in on his purchase from the sniggering old madam, Celestina. And the presence of an old man, shooting like a sharp pain through the scene; he is a buffoon, a pitiful clown, an old painter. Then there is the intriguing presence of a voyeur, a voyeur at work or at play, hidden or active, who then adds another dimension to the scene, played out from that point on for his benefit—the reciprocal pleasures of voyeurism and of exhibitionism, not solitary, stolen pleasures. The Picasso voyeur is above all the observer of a woman alone; contrary to established "norms," he does not spy on her without her knowledge; we do not partake of a violation of her privacy, but in the receipt of what she has to offer; we are not part of a practice of seeing in which the eye inflicts imaginary humiliation—the real source of pleasure—but in the midst of mutual erotic tension. The insistence on the visual excitement that precedes love, the moment when the sword anticipates gliding into the sheath, is even more remarkable since it is missing its natural conclusion: the embrace. It is as though Picasso was bound and determined to show us tender or brutal foreplay—the man, the woman, the desire—but not the pleasure of penetration, despite the very best efforts of a woman who unremittingly contrives to excite the male, to no avail. Thus the sexual act is absent from this series until its triumphant appearance in the *Raphael and La Fornarina* episode, the "priapic epic" in which an ithyphallic Raphael at last makes love to his model—something she and we have been awaiting for a long time—without letting go of his brush and palette, whose positions echo those of his impressive penis! The *Suite 347*, which, up to that point, feels as much like a fantasy as an evocation of paradises lost, at last takes on its full significance and—with its preponderant member, the reappearance of the Harlequin, Picasso's double, and the omnipresence of the painter—prompts us to question what reflections the artist might have undertaken regarding painting and its nurturing, the relationships between art and reality, love and flesh as driving forces of art, *amor magister artium et gubernator*, to quote the Neoplatonic theory that he very likely knew. Picasso was certainly no Apelles—the painter at the court of Alexandria, swooning before Campaspe, the model who so smote him he gave up his paintbrush and bowl of colour to contemplate her—but in reproducing the theme of Raphael and his curvaceous model, he was most certainly pondering his lot, since, as we know, this theme was recurrent in his work: "The fact that the artist at work—almost always the [male] Painter and his model, which in Picasso's work, has been a major theme for some time—has become, if not his only theme, at least his most recurrent one, shows just how important the very act of painting has become in Picasso's eyes. And might not this predilection lead us to think that, despite the fact that the vast majority of his

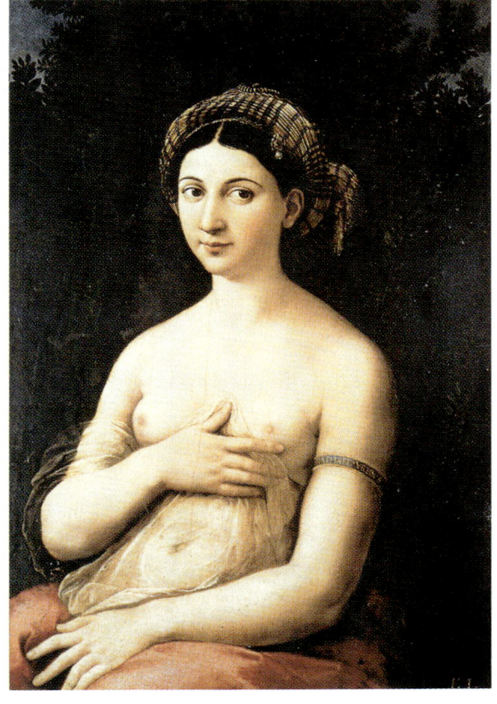

Fig. 1: Raphael
La Fornarina, circa 1518–1519
Oil on canvas; 87 x 63
Rome, Galleria Nazionale d'Arte Antica Palazzo Barberini

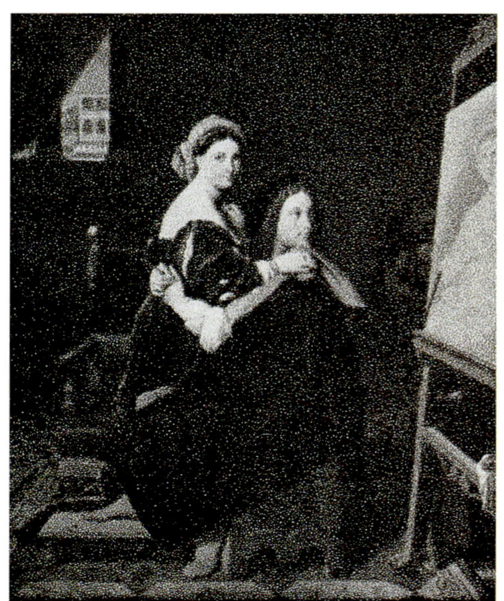

Fig. 2: Jean-Auguste Dominique Ingres
Raphaël et la Fornarina, circa 1845
Oil on canvas; 68 x 55
Cambridge, Fogg Art Museum

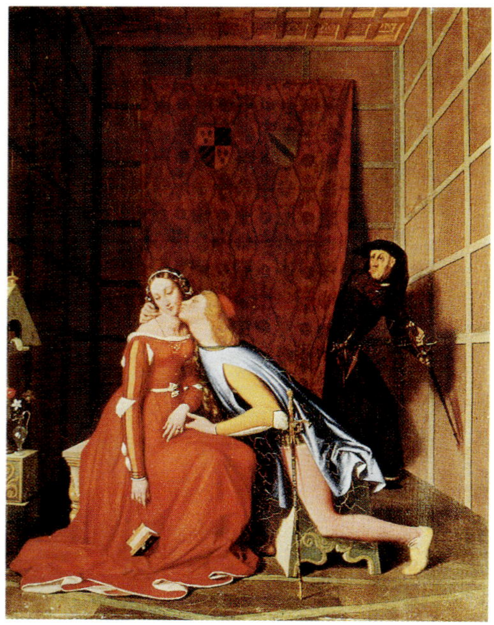

Fig. 3: Jean-Auguste Dominique Ingres
Paolo et Francesca surpris par Gianciotto, 1814
Oil on canvas; 48 x 39
Angers, Musée des Beaux-Arts

work is autobiographical in nature (not only due to motivations supplied by his heart but because, wanting to describe what he knows best, he paints mainly what is familiar to him), for him the true subject is—over and above any circumstantial or other kind of meaning—the painting itself that must be painted, or, rather, the one way among many others that it can be done?"[2] Clearly, the relationship of the painter and the model is established, and there can be no innocence, no neutral gaze, from the moment the painter stands before the female nude.

On 29 August 1968, then, Picasso approached the theme of Raphael and La Fornarina, combining two major paintings by Ingres[3]: *Raphaël et la Fornarina* (Cambridge, Fogg Art Museum) and *Paolo et Francesca surpris par Gianciotto* (Angers, Musée des Beaux-Arts). The life of Raphael fascinated the artists[4] and the public of the 19th century; his romantic relationships, which Vasari mentioned in his *Vite*—citing the famous portrait of a scantily clad woman, La Fornarina, thought to be Raphael's mistress—fired people's imaginations. So Raphael was also a red-blooded human being? While it may seem like a given, it had the effect of a revelation at the time, and the supposedly tumultuous life of this genius was freely embellished upon. Indeed, the combination of art and love sets the mind alight. In a now forgotten play, *Raphaël: Comédie historique en trois actes, en vers* (1851), Joseph Méry pointed up the painter's inability to work on the decoration of the Villa Farnesina so long as his patron had not provided the means for his woman companion to join him and renew his zest for life: "A smile, sensual pleasure, that is what ignites me / That is what makes me an artist!"

Alfred de Vigny penned a poem in the same vein: "La Fornarina—O mistress of Raphael, you saw him exhaust himself in your arms. What have you done, o woman! What have you done? With each kiss an idea flowed out onto your lips…"[5] This was fertile ground for art historians: "And Raphael himself, in his last days, was no longer without human love, murderous love, for La Fornarina. Ideals and love are two passions that are fired by each other: they are therefore infallible for art, but fatal. To dominate the senses in our attachments, we must have a heroism of ideas, as did Michelangelo and Beethoven. But such is not the case with precocious natures yet in the bud. In Raphael, as in Mozart, the intoxication of their senses was in proportion to the fervour of their genius. In their tender youth they lived one thousand lives, only to die, quickly consumed by them."[6] The cause of death is understood: Raphael died because he loved love too much and La Fornarina was responsible for it. She became the symbol of the devouring, alienating woman, the woman of love with a smiling face who paradoxically leads to death, the woman that drags a man into a fever of the senses,

2 Michel Leiris, "Préface," *Picasso, peintures 1962-1963*, exh. cat. (Paris: Galerie Louise Leiris, 1964). (Free translation.)
3 See Brigitte Baer, ed., *Picasso peintre-graveur: Catalogue raisonné de l'œuvre gravé et des monotypes, 1935-1968*, Vol. VI (Berne: Kornfeld, 1994).
4 Among them Léon Bénouville, Achille Devéria, Hyppolite Flandrin, Jules Salles.
5 "La Fornarina – Ô maîtresse de Raphaël, tu le vis s'épuiser dans tes bras. Qu'as-tu fait, ô femme ! Qu'as-tu fait ? Une idée par baiser s'écoulait sur tes lèvres…" Alfred de Vigny, *Œuvres complètes* (Paris: Gallimard, 1948), Vol. II, p. 992–93. (Free translation.)
6 A. Dumesnil, *L'Art italien* (Paris: Giraud, 1854), p. 180–81. (Free translation.)

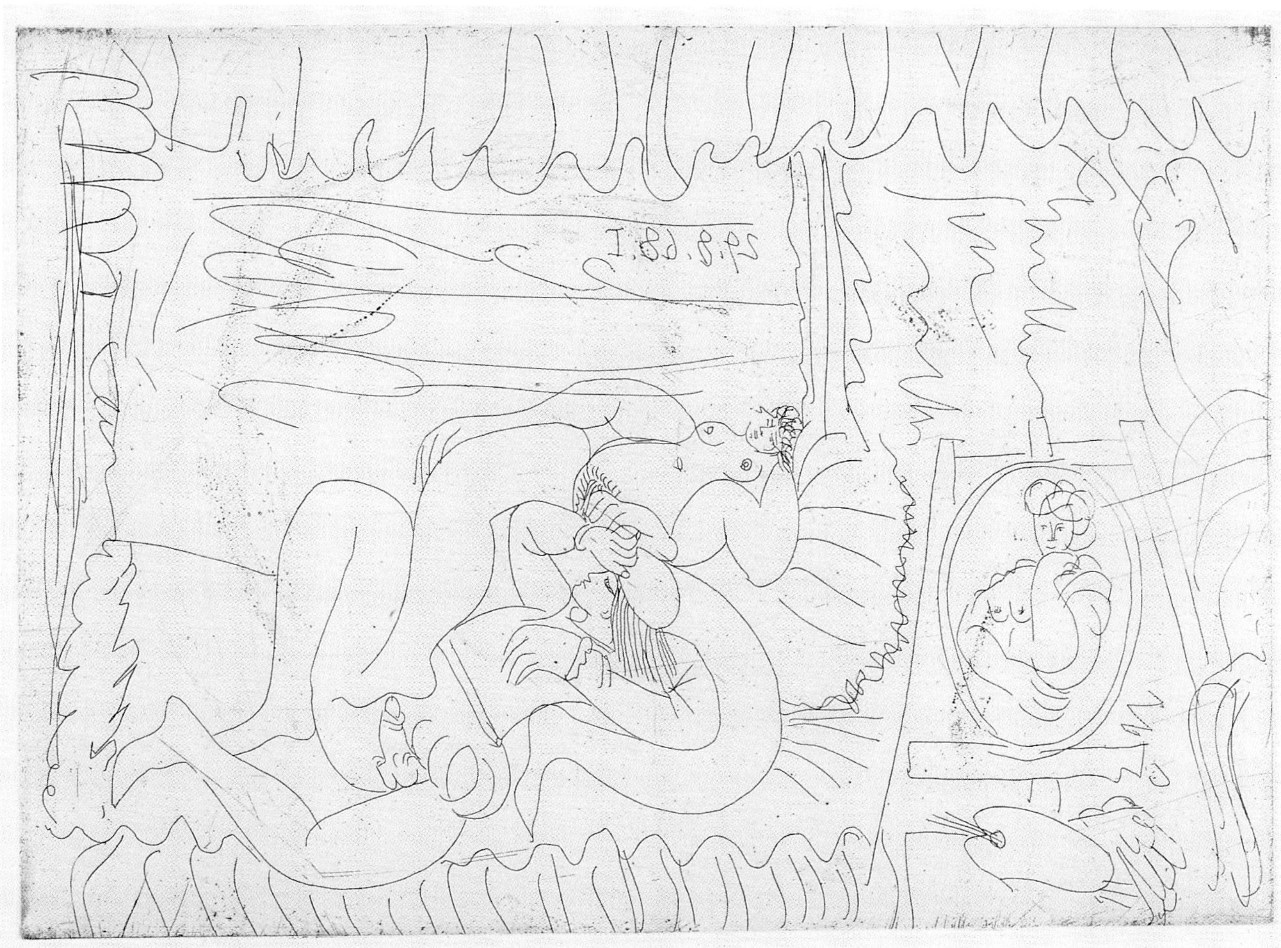

247 Raphael and La Fornarina I, 29 August 1968

Etching on copper; 27.9 x 38.9
Paris, Bibliothèque nationale de France, Département des Estampes et de la Photographie [P]
Paris, Private collection* [M]
Barcelona, Museu Picasso, MPB 70.593 [B]

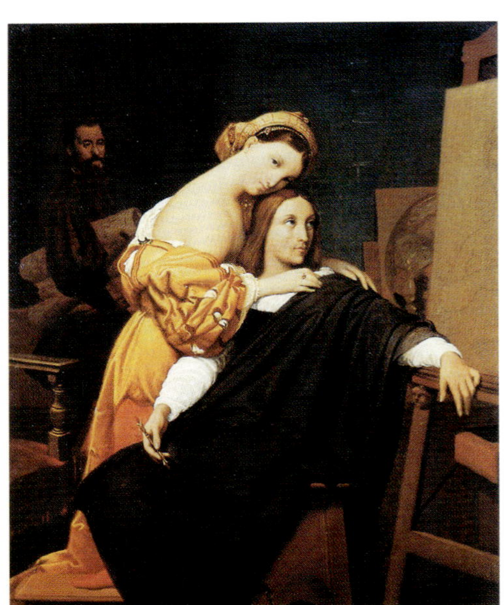

Fig. 4: Jean-Auguste Dominique Ingres
Raphaël et la Fornarina, 1814
Oil on canvas; 32 x 27
New York, Private collection

where he forgets himself, loses himself, loses his very ability to create—she appropriates the phallic paintbrush to her own ends.

The Ingres-like Raphael is in love, for even as he gazes melancholically upon a painting, he seems in no hurry to attack it. The dilemma: Must an artist love? Can he love? Are art and sexuality compatible? Ingres answers these questions: A man is there, in the shadow, casting a dark, disapproving glance at some lovers in a fond embrace. As for Picasso, he had no intention of depriving himself of either world and he, whose insatiable appetite and triumphant virility also contributed to his renown, took it upon himself to parody a painter who died from loving too much at age thirty-seven. We cannot help but imagine the fun he must have had in bashing the image of another genius painter, with whom he had serious scores to settle. For although we may remember Picasso's famous statement "When I was their age, I could draw like Raphael,"[7] another of his utterances is perhaps less well known: "They say I paint like Raphael: very well. But now that they know it, they should leave me the hell alone when I do other things."[8] Picasso did do other things, but he returned to Raphael. Why? Because Raphael was the painter archetype, because his aura was considerable and because Picasso, who was born in 1881, certainly must have felt that way about him, though it may seem strange to us, who may be blinded today, seeing him only as the creator of the *saint-sulpicienne* imagery that brought him to so much grief. Picasso deliberately chose the path of what could have been termed "obscenity" at that time, but which has become entirely relative in our time—although the power of the images to upset and disturb has remained intact.

"A phallic erection of Picassian power smashes the spectre of Eros to pieces. … Apparently the erect phallus delimits, for what was considered to be art of the elite, a zone beyond which the field of the forbidden would seem to extend, a reserved domain that sexuality, the obscene and pornography seemingly share in equal measure."[9] Picasso could have steeped the lovemaking of Raphael and La Fornarina in the kind of tender sensuality found in some of the episodes in his *Suite Vollard* but, on the contrary, in this work he recounts, from foreplay to orgasm, the building of excitement and its conclusion, sparing us no details, in a playful atmosphere, no less; not only is sex fun in Picasso's depiction, but it is happy—what could be more irreverent! Picasso was proclaiming, before the man who was Christian morality incarnate, that pleasure has its place. But what kind of pleasure? That of the painter or that of the lover? The voyeur allows us to understand the meaning of this amorous jousting.

Lurking, at first, behind a curtain, the voyeur takes his place close by the lovers, who are not timid about pursuing their passionate embrace. The man has a beard. "Every time I draw a man, involuntarily, I am thinking of my father. …

7 Cited in Antonina Vallentin, *Picasso* (Garden City, N.Y.: Doubleday & Co., 1963).
8 Cited in Robert Desnos, *Écrits sur les peintres* (Paris: Flammarion, 1984). (Free translation.)
9 F. Bayl, "L'art obscène et la provocation hédoniste," *Opus*, 1970. (Free translation.) Bayl saw eroticism as a principle that allowed for an evasion of the sexual content of the image in favour of spirituality, as though the carnal aspect of love was daunting to art criticism.

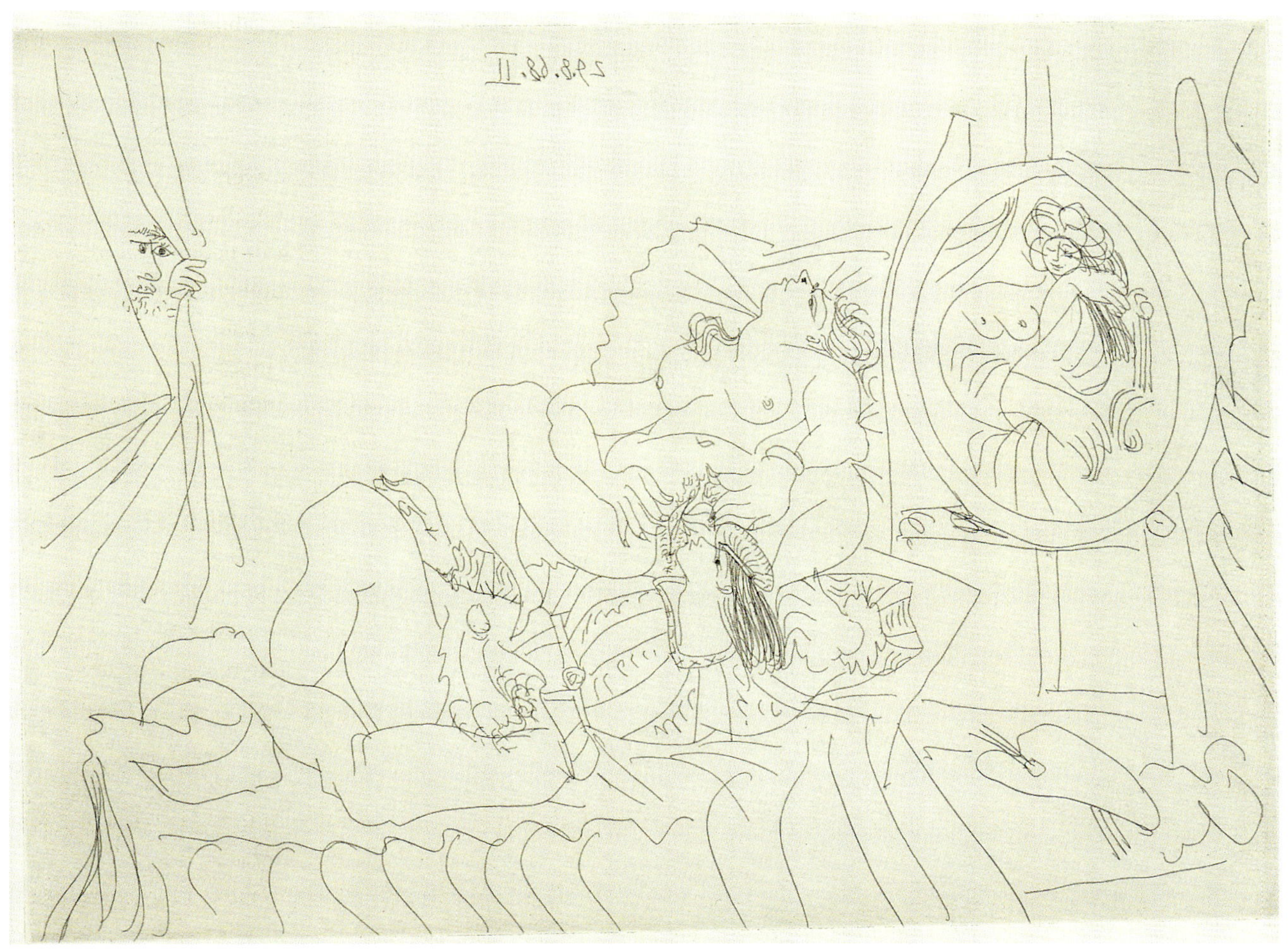

248 Raphael and La Fornarina II, with a Hidden Voyeur, 29 August 1968

Etching on copper; 27.9 x 38.9
Paris, Bibliothèque nationale de France, Département des Estampes et de la Photographie [P]
Paris, Private collection* [M]
Barcelona, Museu Picasso, MPB 70.594 [B]

For me, every man is Don José, and that will be so all my life. ... He wore a beard. ... All of the men I draw, I see them more or less with his features."[10]

Pope Julius II, patron of the artwork in the Sistine Chapel and the Chambers of the Vatican, sometimes seated on his "throne," looks on and delights in the scene before his eyes; he is not a voyeur full of repression, hate, or fear of castration. Nor is he, as some have perceived, an avatar of Picasso, forced to leave the scene of a battle (sex) from which he so often emerged victorious and cocksure in his derision of male impotency. Nothing is more dramatic for a man than to experience impotency, whatever the cause, and age brings no relief: it is a torture, never ironic, but rather, painful—as evidenced in the disembodied aspects of the *Embrace* of 26 September 1970, a piece suggestive of a man's inability to honour the woman he loves and desires. Picasso's supposed serene detachment in this regard was certainly deceptive; to consider that he was expressing this drama through the intermediary of the voyeur is unquestionably simplistic. Such was not the case. There was more to it.

Some have also chosen to interpret this work as an archetypal scene: the male infant who takes his mother in front of his father or, conversely, the half-terrified, half-delighted child who discovers the secret of parental sexuality; but the voyeur is not Picasso and, if he is the father, he is not witnessing the lovemaking of his son and his spouse.

The voyeur with whom we are concerned is not satisfied with catching a woman in the act of undressing, or who is nude. He is not a musketeer; he is watching the torrid tryst of a young couple upon whom he bestows his benediction. The voyeur is the *sine qua non* of the show that is played out for his benefit, and which exists through him. The father—note the similarity between *papa* (Pope) and *papá* (father) in Spanish—is the agent who gives the young child the possibility of entering into the world. The mother, either consciously or unconsciously, holds her child back, close to her. The father, in this case, is Don José Ruiz Blasco, the man who one day gave up producing his own art to let his young genius son take over, leaving him his paintbrushes and his colours; a rite-of-passage moment, the equivalent of the tauromachic alternative, through which he would enable his son to eroticize colours, those theatrical cosmetics that race across the canvas. Sabartés had thoroughly grasped the nature of Picasso's painterly action: "His gesture is that of a man in love as he coats the silks of the paintbrush with the oily paste of colours to mix them and spreads them across the canvas, all of his senses concentrated on one sole purpose, as though he has fallen under a spell."[11] His painting, whatever the subject, was always sexual in origin, a moment of erotic intensity derived from the simple act of spurting colour onto canvas. The embrace of the painter and of the model is, above all, an image of delight with the painting; the Pope, at first waiting in the wings, then taking the stage to play the role expected of him, is not only there to

10 Cited in Brassaï, *Conversations avec Picasso* (Paris: Gallimard, 1964). (Free translation.)
11 Jaime Sabartés, *Picasso: An Intimate Portrait*, trans. Angel Flores (New York: Prentice-Hall, 1948).

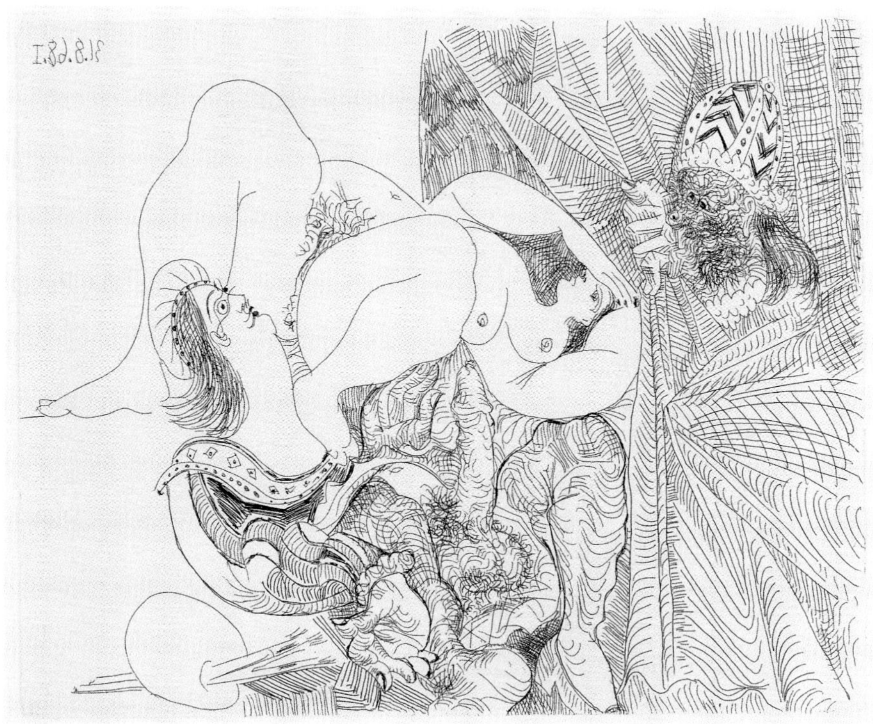

249 Raphael and La Fornarina III, with the Pope as Hidden Voyeur, 31 August 1968

Etching on copper; 16.7 x 20.8
Paris, Bibliothèque nationale de France, Département des Estampes et de la Photographie [P]
Paris, Private collection* [M]
Barcelona, Museu Picasso, MPB 111.886 [B]

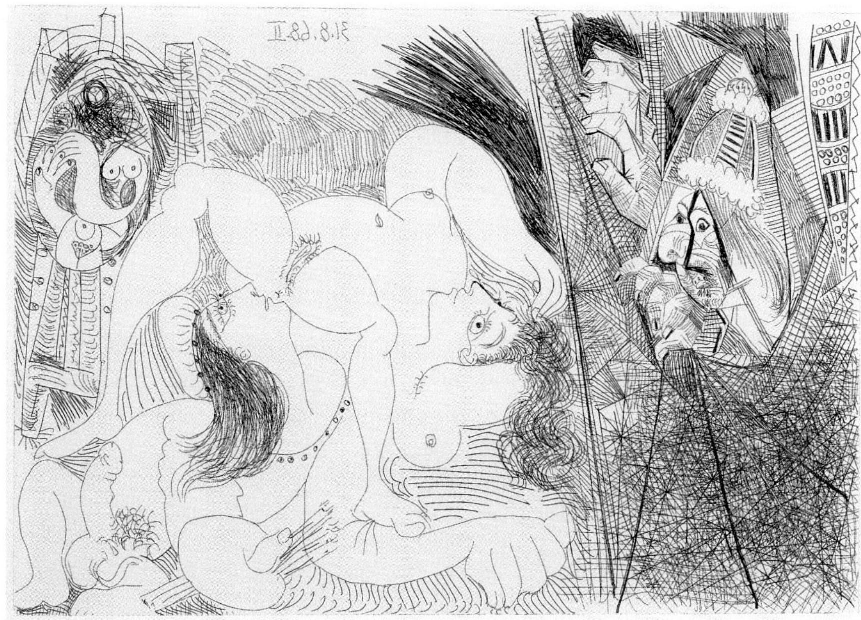

250 Raphael and La Fornarina IV, with the Pope Drawing the Curtain, 31 August 1968

Etching on copper; 23.2 x 33.1
Paris, Bibliothèque nationale de France, Département des Estampes et de la Photographie [P]
Paris, Private collection* [M]
Barcelona, Museu Picasso, MPB 70.599 [B]

catch the mystery of creation in the act but also to see it, admire it, contemplate it—because what is creation worth if it is not shown? The father is there, he looks on, and he approves: from that moment on, the painter has the right to create.

Why not imagine that the young woman is the Painting in person, that nudity is the stripping away of all artifice, all anecdote—that the painter's gesture, as he allows himself to go tease the tip of her breast with the end of his paintbrush, is not only love play or an erotic metaphor, but an illustration of the act of painting itself, the painter "attacking the virgin canvas"?[12]

The appearance of Piero Crommelynck, the printer of the series, along with his brother Aldo, in the scene depicted on 8 September, in which he closes the curtains in front of us, seems to reinforce the hypothesis that Picasso's treatment of art is for the voyeur who is present by the couple's side, while associating us with it through a double subterfuge.

The voyeur, be he the Pope, a Cardinal, or a simple fellow, does not, if we take his position into account, have nearly the same advantageous point of view as that afforded us. At times the anatomical contortions of La Fornarina deprive him from seeing the most delightful moments of the exhibition—which is to our advantage, for we are conspiring voyeurs, represented by the character hidden under the bed.

Michelangelo, jealous of Raphael and his success, a symbol of homosexuality literally disappearing under a bed shaken by the jolts of lovemaking, is the character that takes us as his witness to the incredible scene that he can overhear, but that others have the privilege of seeing. This is "the latent truth, at last captured, of the painter and his model: coitus is openly shown ever after."[13] What we suspected, from the erotic drawings of Barcelona through the bestiality of the 1930s to the last *Embraces*, is confirmed in this piece: Picasso never ceased to focus his work on libido, the inner life force, which he carried to its highest level of expression—because it was, for him, the one and only means through which he explored with us the question of representation, and because the enjoyment he derived from both libido and art was of the same nature.

> From the palms of the caulkers spring perfect vessels
> What did Raphael know of virginity
> Ere he slept with La Fornarina?[14]

12 Several prints (24 April, 7, 19, 20 May, and 26 June 1968) reflected Raphael's gesture depicting a scene that included a painter (sometimes a musketeer) painting directly on the model, or a painter directly facing a model without his easel: *Peintre, modèle et spectateur*, Baer, 1546; *Vieux Peintre, modèle et spectateur*, Baer, 1564; *Peintre peignant le sein de son modèle*, Baer, 1662; *Peintre et modèle sur un lit*, Baer, 1667; *Peintre peignant la nuque de son jeune modèle*, Baer, 1684.

13 Guy Scarpetta, "Picasso après-coup," Marie-Laure Bernadac, ed., *Le Dernier Picasso 1953-1973*, exh. cat. (Paris: Centre Georges-Pompidou, 1988). (Free translation.)

14 "Aux paumes du calfat gisent de parfaites marines;/ Que savait Raphaël de la virginité/ Avant d'avoir couché avec la Fornarine ?" A. Salmon, *Peindre* (Paris: Éditions de la Sirène, 1921), p. 51. (Free translation.)

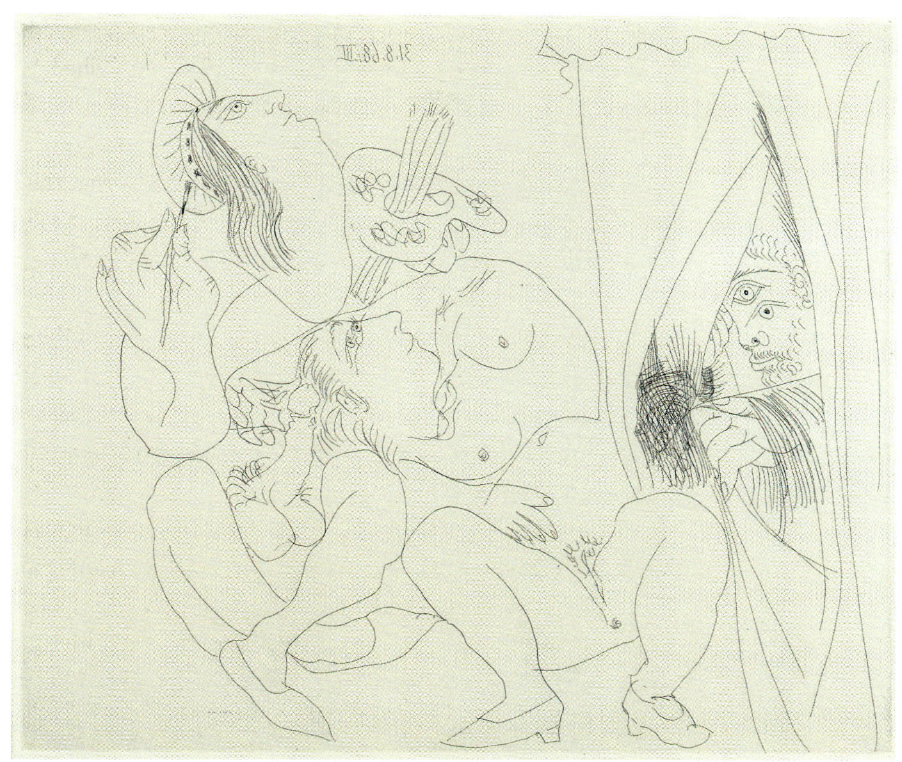

251 Raphael and La Fornarina V, with Voyeur Parting the Curtain, 31 August 1968

Etching on copper; 41.4 x 49.5
Paris, Bibliothèque nationale de France, Département des Estampes et de la Photographie [P]
Paris, Private collection* [M]
Barcelona, Museu Picasso, MPB 70.634 [B]

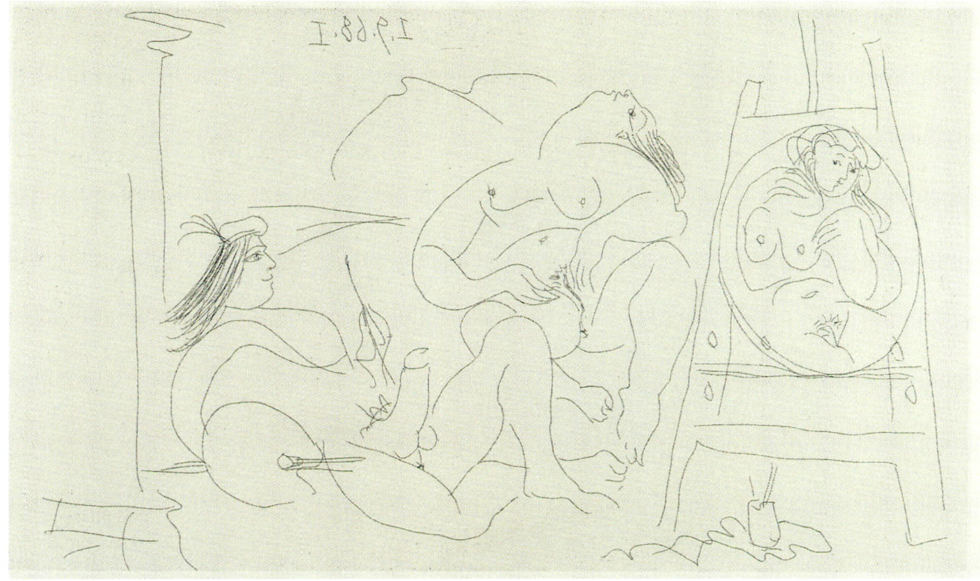

252 Raphael and La Fornarina VI: Alone at Last!, 1 September 1968

Etching on copper; 29.6 x 51.4
Paris, Bibliothèque nationale de France, Département des Estampes et de la Photographie [P]
Paris, Private collection* [M]
Barcelona, Museu Picasso, MPB 70.635 [B]

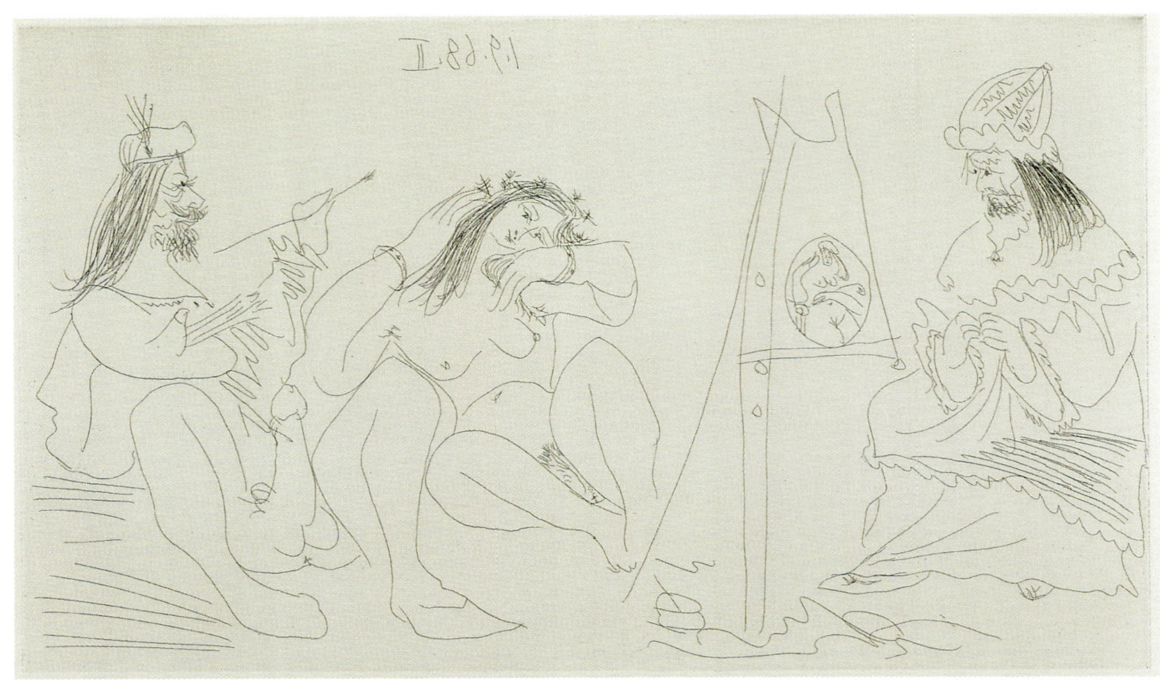

253 Raphael and La Fornarina VII: The Pope Is There, Sitting, 1 September 1968

Etching on copper; 29.7 x 51.4
Paris, Bibliothèque nationale de France, Département des Estampes et de la Photographie [P]
Paris, Private collection* [M]
Barcelona, Museu Picasso, MPB 70.636 [B]

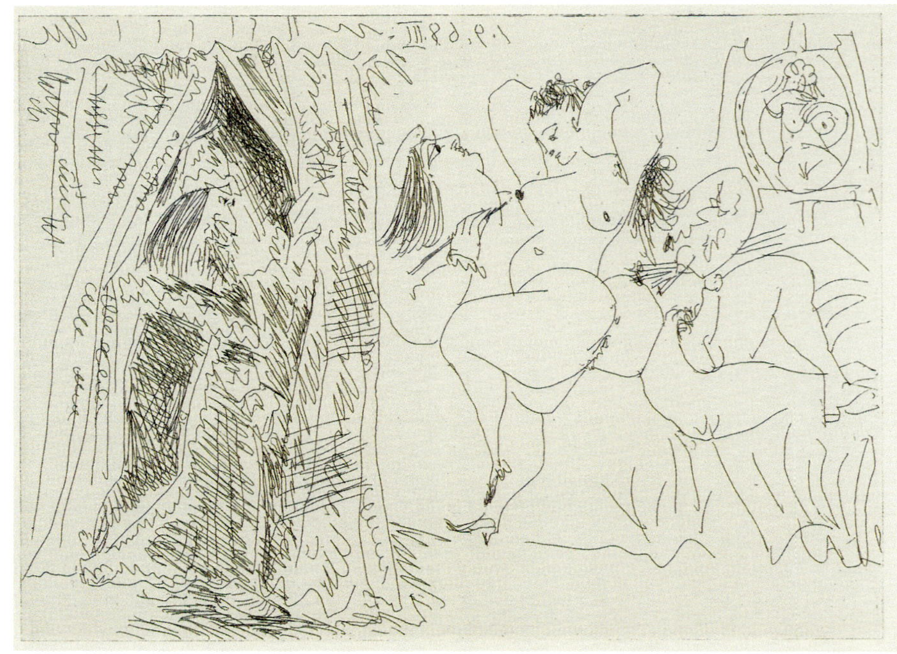

254 Raphael and La Fornarina VIII: The Pope Enters, with a Slick Smile, 1 September 1968

Etching on copper; 14.8 x 20.9
Paris, Bibliothèque nationale de France, Département des Estampes et de la Photographie [P]
Paris, Private collection* [M]
Barcelona, Museu Picasso, MPB 111.940 [B]

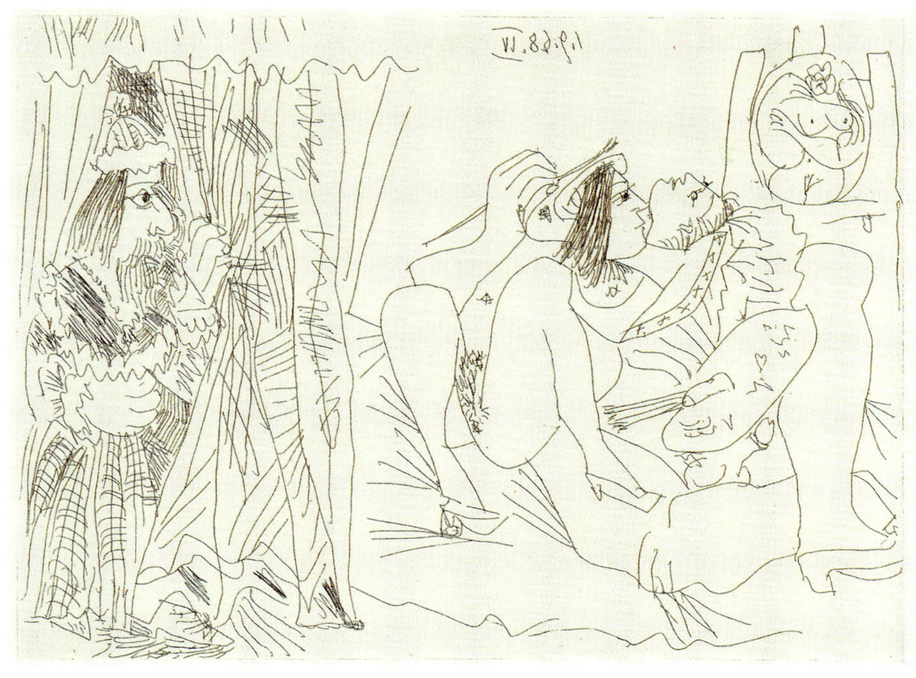

255 Raphael and La Fornarina IX: The Pope Arrives, 1 September 1968

Etching on copper; 14.8 x 20.9
Paris, Bibliothèque nationale de France, Département des Estampes et de la Photographie [P]
Paris, Private collection* [M]
Barcelona, Museu Picasso, MPB 111.941 [M]

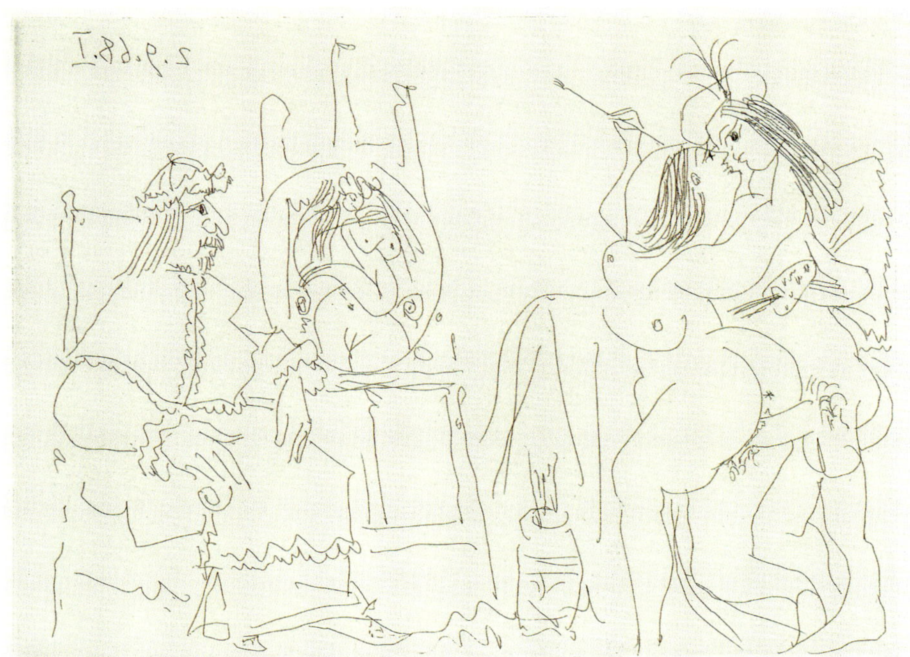

256 Raphael and La Fornarina X: The Pope Has Had His Armchair Brought, 2 September 1968

Etching on copper; 14.8 x 20.9
Paris, Bibliothèque nationale de France, Département des Estampes et de la Photographie [P]
Paris, Private collection* [M]
Barcelona, Museu Picasso, MPB 111.942 [B]

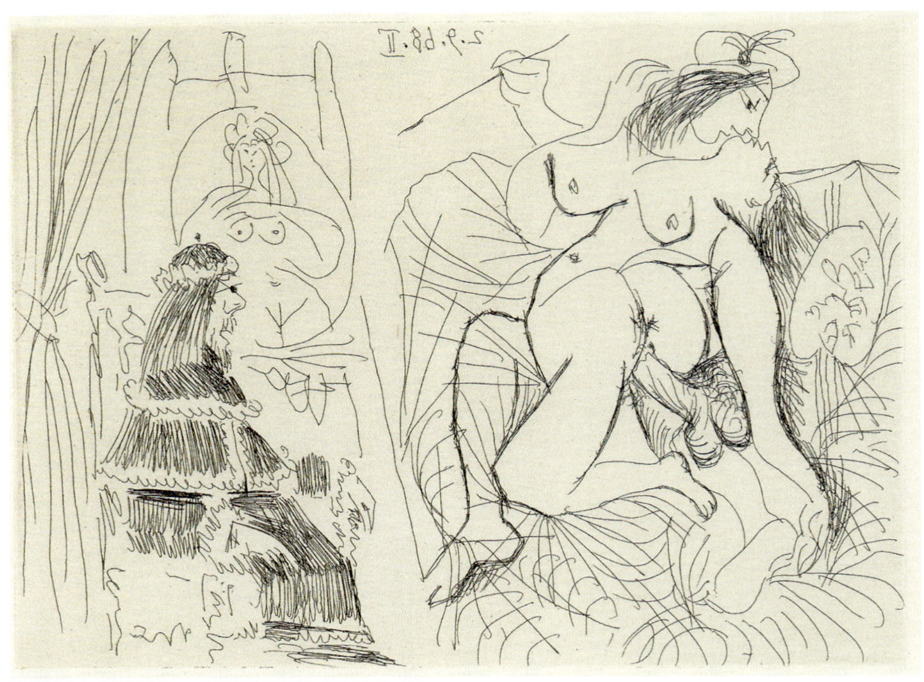

257 Raphael and La Fornarina XI: The Pope Is Open-Mouthed in His Armchair, 2 September 1968

Etching on copper; 14.8 x 20.9
Paris, Bibliothèque nationale de France, Département des Estampes et de la Photographie [P]
Paris, Private collection* [M]
Barcelona, Museu Picasso, MPB 111.943 [B]

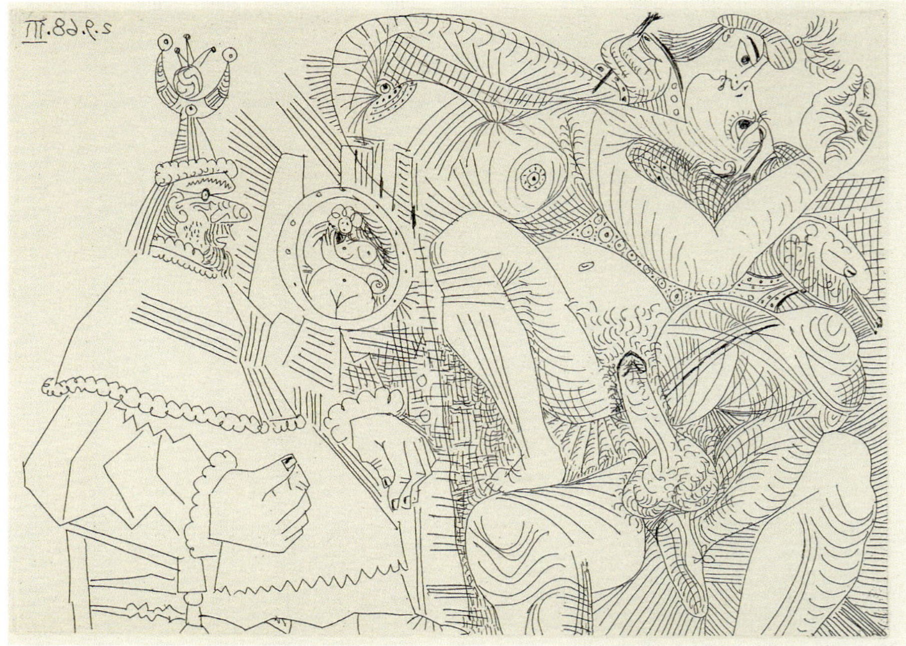

258 Raphael and La Fornarina XII: In His Armchair, the Pope Feels Cuckolded, 2 September 1968

Etching on copper; 14.8 x 20.9
Paris, Bibliothèque nationale de France, Département des Estampes et de la Photographie [P]
Paris, Private collection* [M]
Barcelona, Museu Picasso, MPB 111.944 [B]

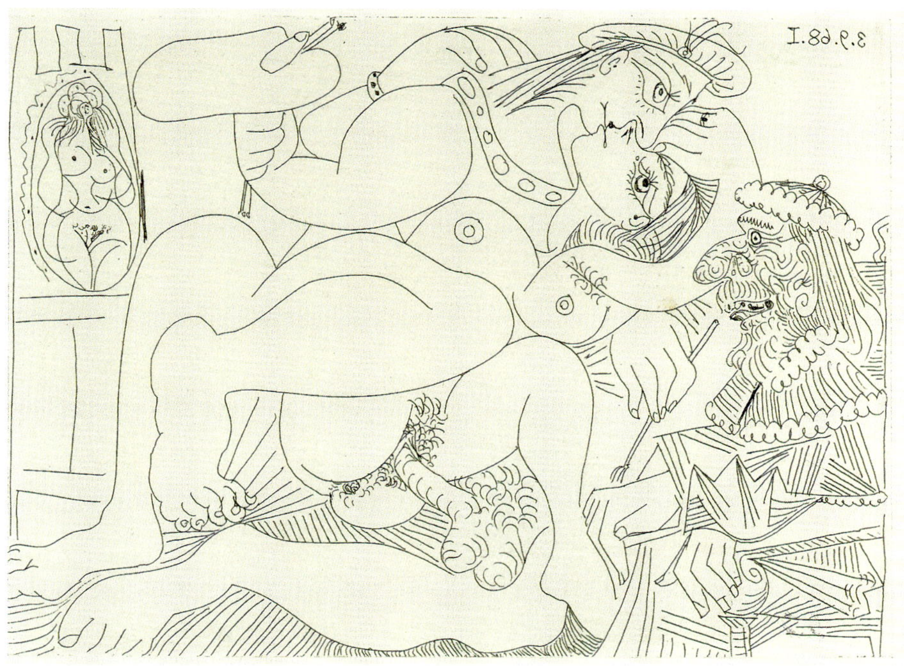

259 Raphael and La Fornarina XIII: The Pope Sticks Out His Tongue at the Whole Thing, 3 September 1968

Etching on copper; 14.8 x 20.9
Paris, Bibliothèque nationale de France, Département des Estampes et de la Photographie [P]
Paris, Private collection* [M]
Barcelona, Museu Picasso, MPB 111.945 [B]

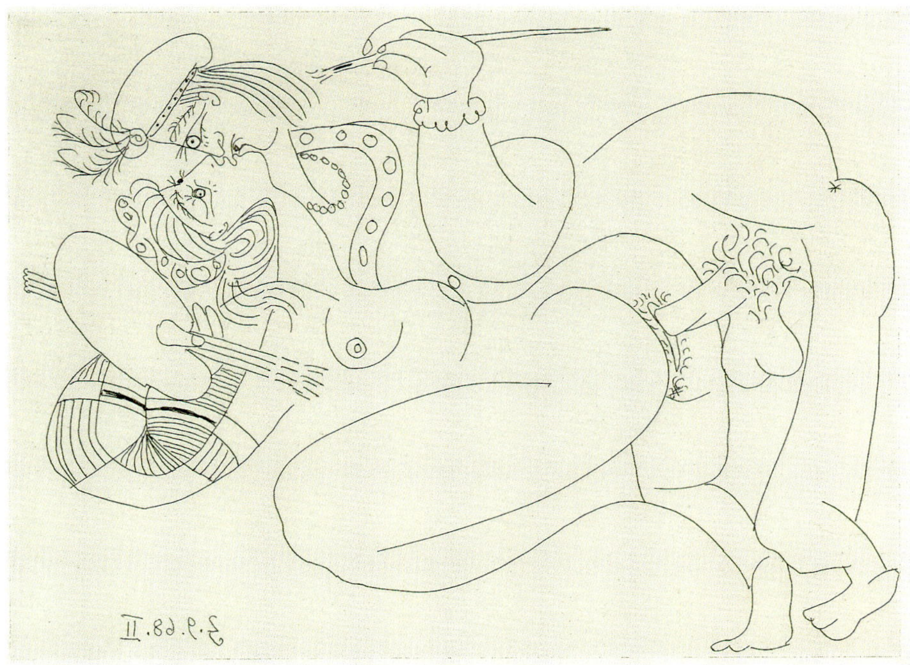

260 Raphael and La Fornarina XIV: The Pope Has Slipped Away, 3 September 1968

Etching on copper; 14.8 x 20.9
Paris, Bibliothèque nationale de France, Département des Estampes et de la Photographie [P]
Paris, Private collection* [M]
Barcelona, Museu Picasso, MPB 111.946 [B]

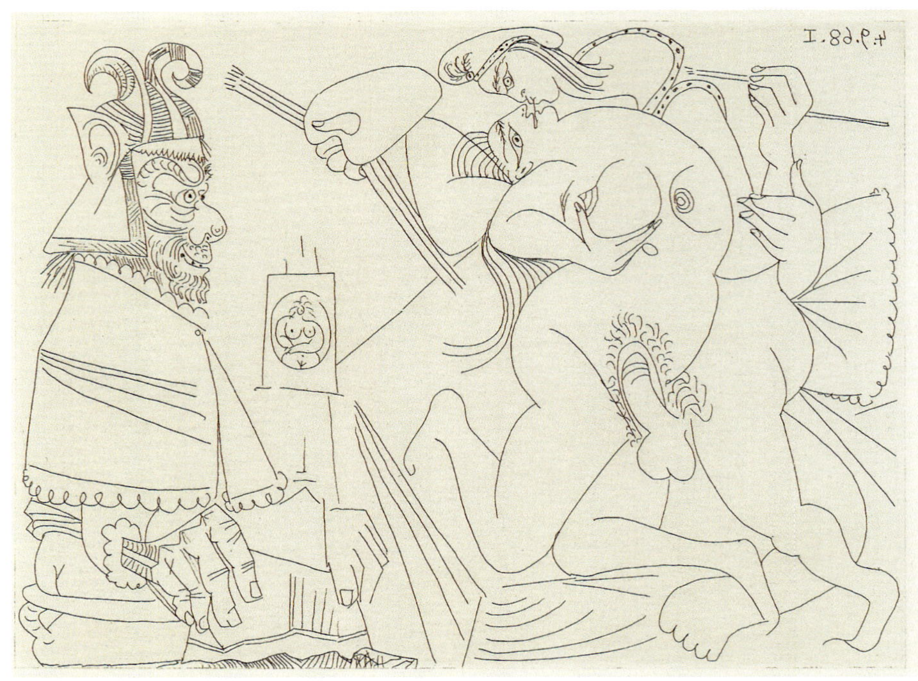

261 Raphael and La Fornarina XV: The Pope Is Back, on His Chamberpot, 4 September 1968

Etching on copper; 14.8 x 20.9
Paris, Bibliothèque nationale de France, Département des Estampes et de la Photographie [P]
Paris, Private collection* [M]
Barcelona, Museu Picasso, MPB 111.947 [B]

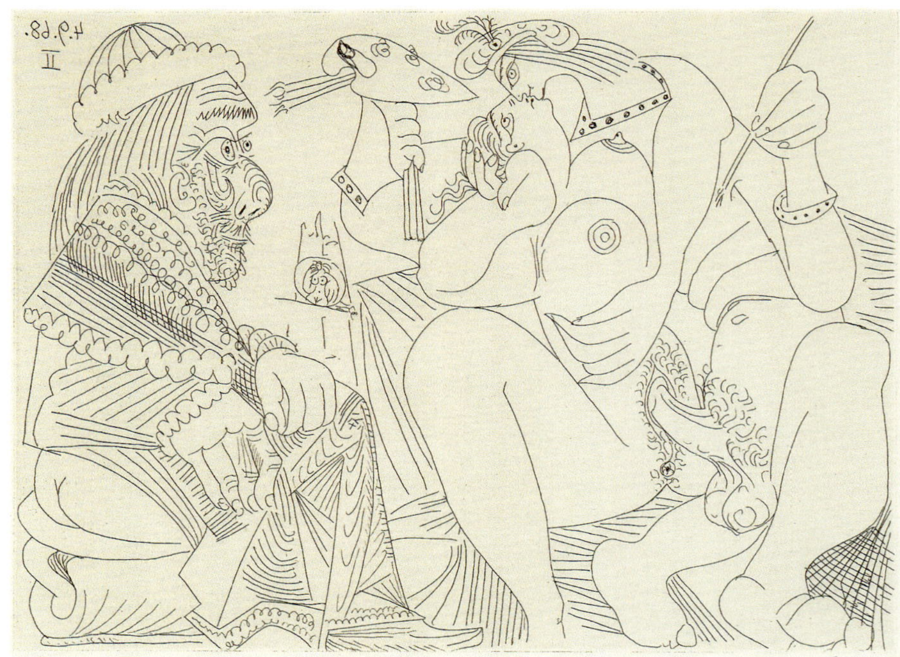

262 Raphael and La Fornarina XVI: The Pope Is Still on His Chamberpot, Pondering, 4 September 1968

Etching on copper; 14.8 x 20.9
Paris, Bibliothèque nationale de France, Département des Estampes et de la Photographie [P]
Paris, Private collection* [M]
Barcelona, Museu Picasso, MPB 111.948 [B]

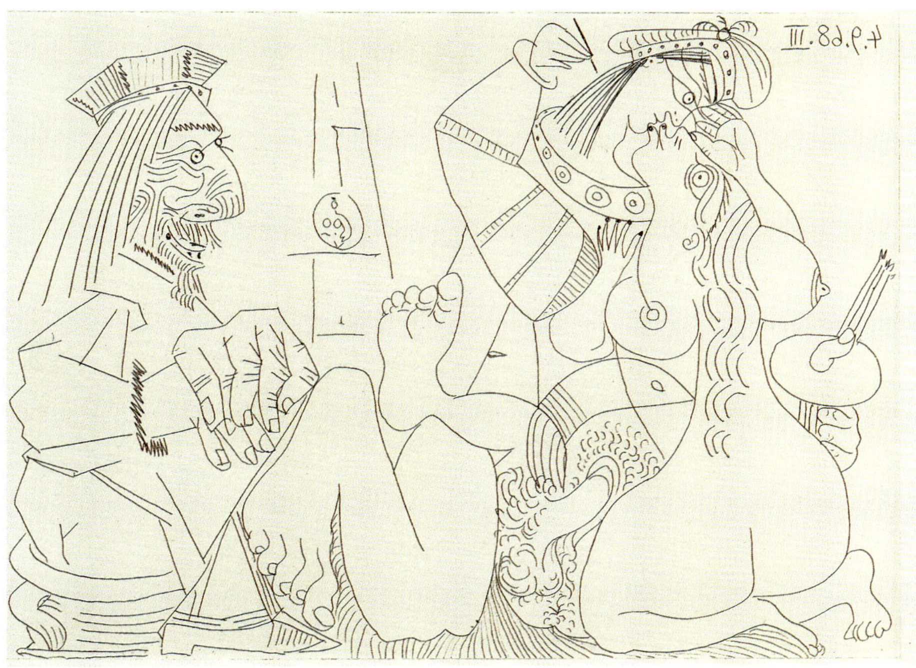

263 Raphael and La Fornarina XVII: On His Chamberpot, a Cardinal, Tickled, Laughs, 4 September 1968

Etching on copper; 14.8 x 20.9
Paris, Bibliothèque nationale de France, Département des Estampes et de la Photographie [P]
Paris, Private collection* [M]
Barcelona, Museu Picasso, MPB 111.949 [B]

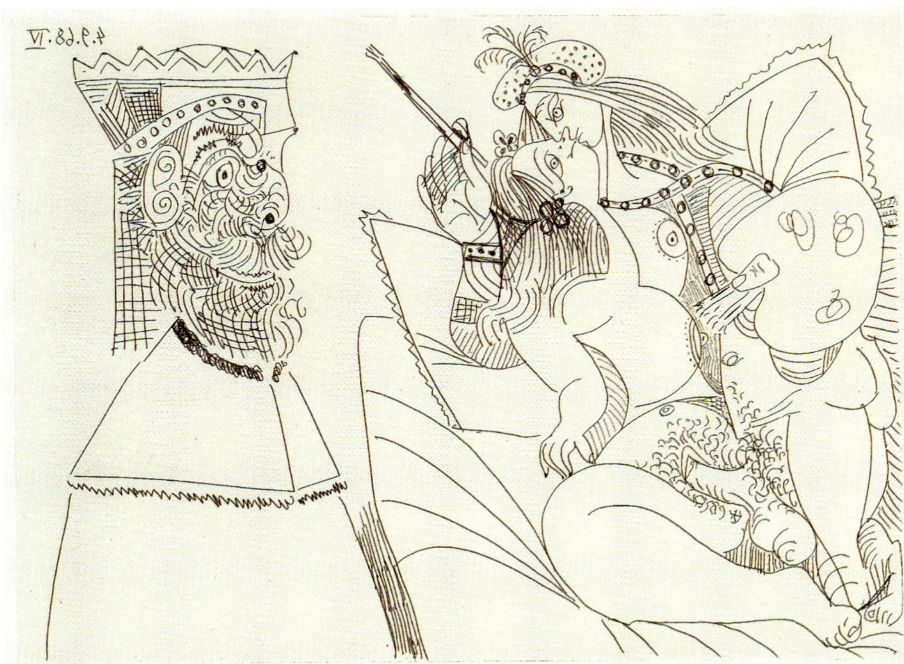

264 Raphael and La Fornarina XVIII: The Pope Is Oddly Coiffed, 4 September 1968

Etching on copper; 14.8 x 20.9
Paris, Bibliothèque nationale de France, Département des Estampes et de la Photographie [P]
Paris, Private collection* [M]
Barcelona, Museu Picasso, MPB 111.950 [B]

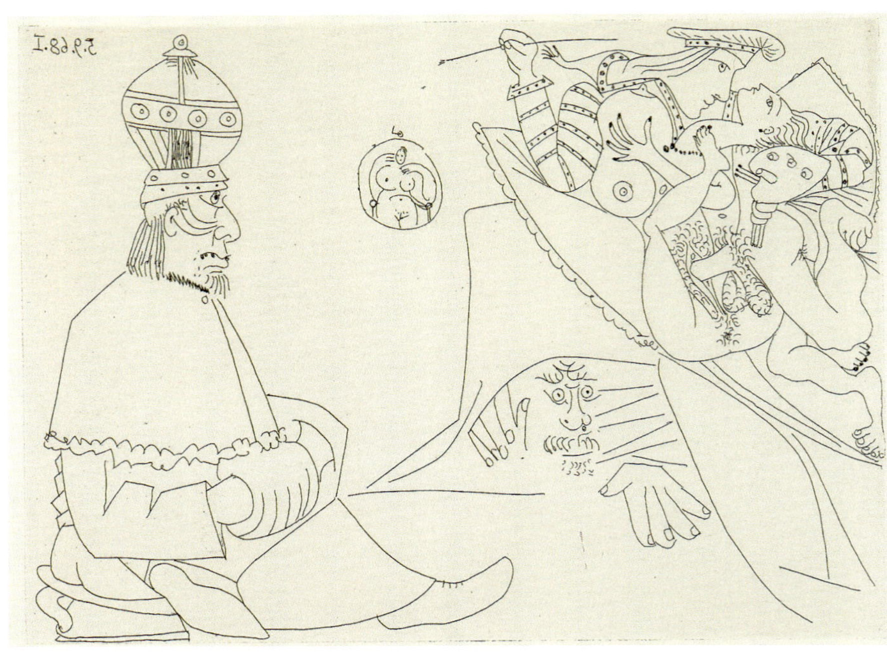

265 Raphael and La Fornarina XIX: Pope on His Chamberpot, with Tiara and Muff;
Michelangelo Is Hiding under the Bed, 5 September 1968

Etching on copper; 14.8 x 20.9
Paris, Bibliothèque nationale de France, Département des Estampes et de la Photographie [P]
Paris, Private collection [M]
Barcelona, Museu Picasso, MPB 111.951 [B]

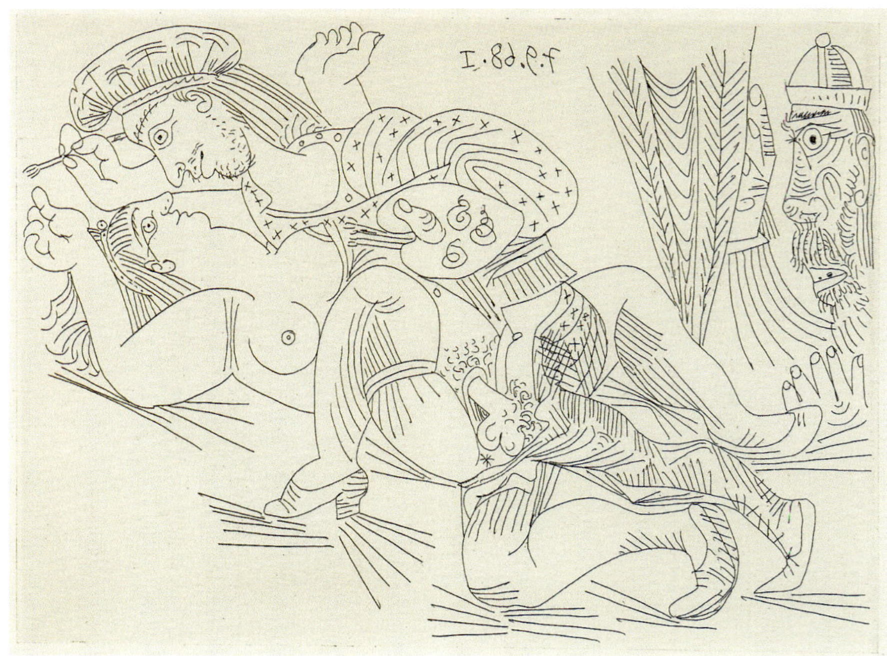

266 Raphael and La Fornarina XX: Exit the Pope, 7 September 1968

Etching on copper; 14.8 x 20.9
Paris, Bibliothèque nationale de France, Département des Estampes et de la Photographie [P]
Paris, Private collection* [M]
Barcelona, Museu Picasso, MPB 111.952 [B]

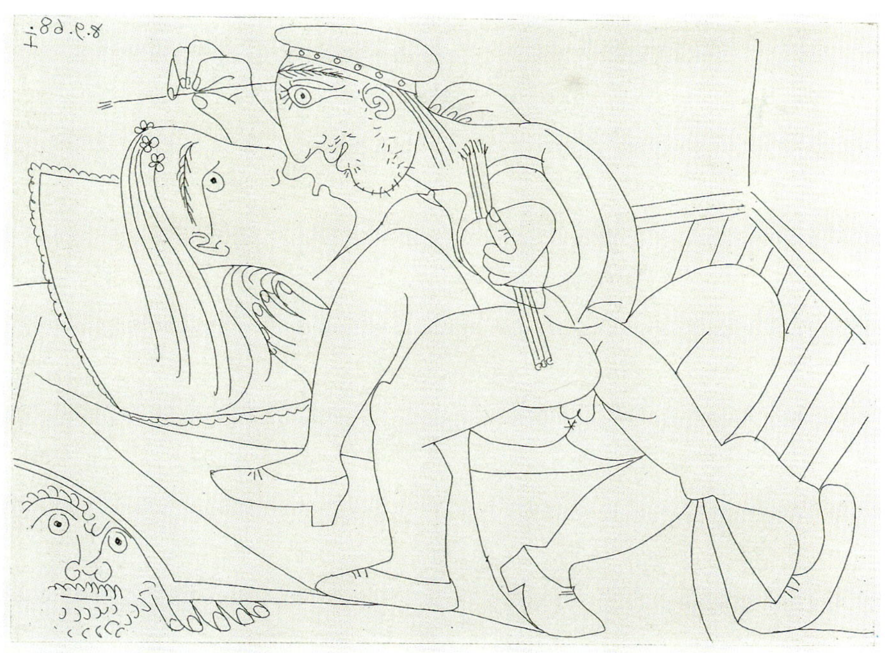

267 Raphael and La Fornarina XXI: Michelangelo Is Hiding under the Bed, 8 September 1968

Etching on copper; 14.8 x 20.9
Paris, Bibliothèque nationale de France, Département des Estampes et de la Photographie [P]
Paris, Private collection* [M]
Barcelona, Museu Picasso, MPB 111.953 [B]

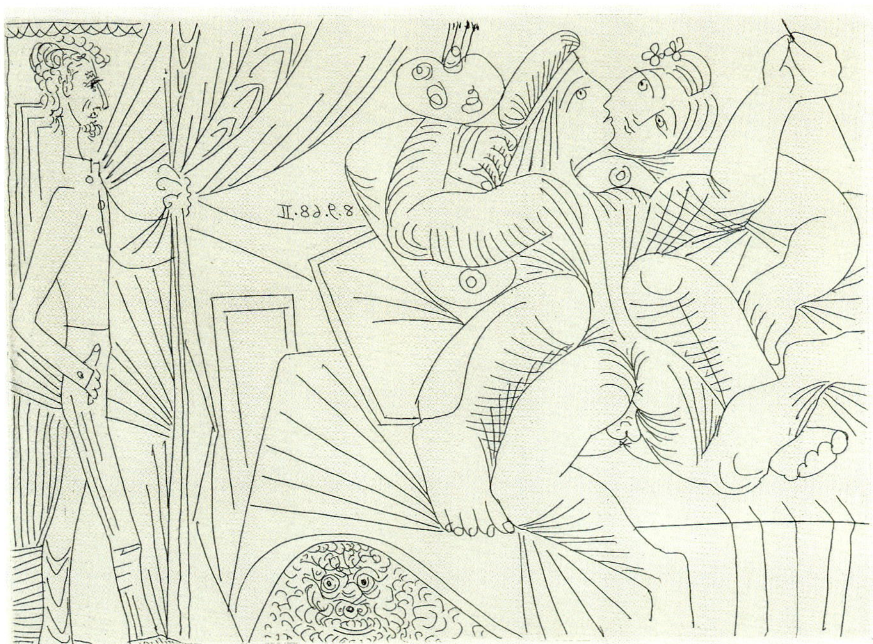

268 Raphael and La Fornarina XXII: Michelangelo under the Bed: Enter Piero Crommelynck, 8 September 1968

Etching on copper; 14.8 x 20.9
Paris, Bibliothèque nationale de France, Département des Estampes et de la Photographie [P]
Paris, Private collection* [M]
Barcelona, Museu Picasso, MPB 111.954 [B]

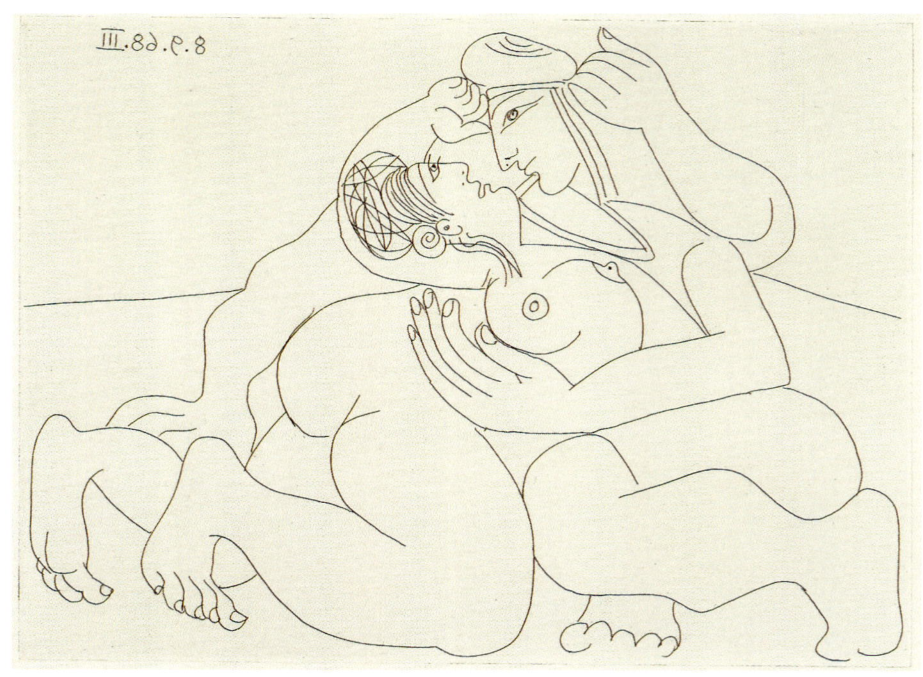

269 Raphael and La Fornarina XXIII: Alone, Embracing on the Ground, 8 September 1968

Etching on copper; 14.8 x 20.9
Paris, Bibliothèque nationale de France, Département des Estampes et de la Photographie [P]
Paris, Private collection* [M]
Barcelona, Museu Picasso, MPB 112.022 [B]

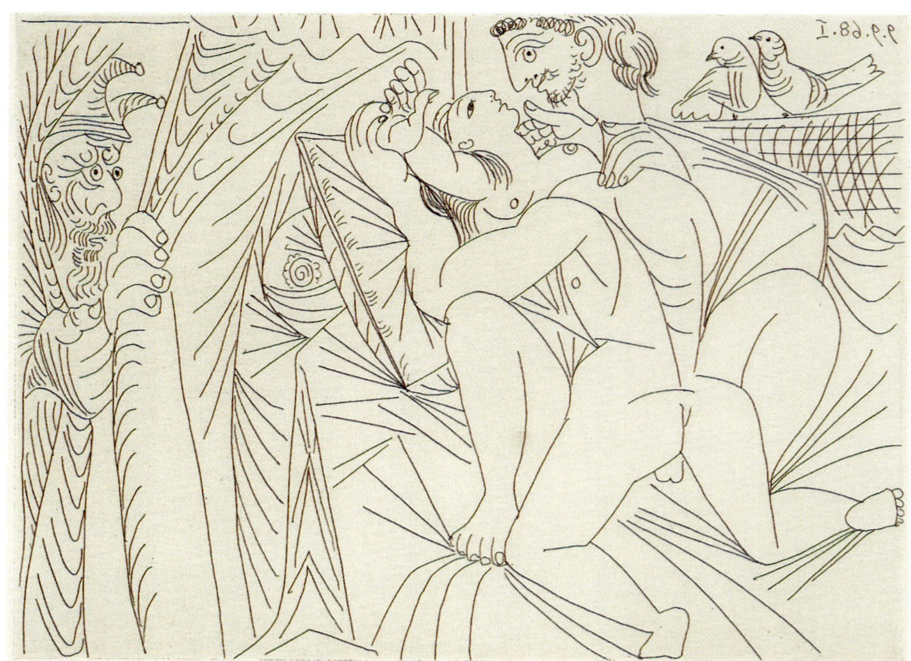

270 Raphael and La Fornarina XXIV: With Voyeur Wearing a Two-Horned Hat, and Two Pigeons, 9 September 1968

Etching on copper; 14.8 x 20.9
Paris, Bibliothèque nationale de France, Département des Estampes et de la Photographie [P]
Paris, Private collection* [M]
Barcelona, Museu Picasso, MPB 111.955 [B]

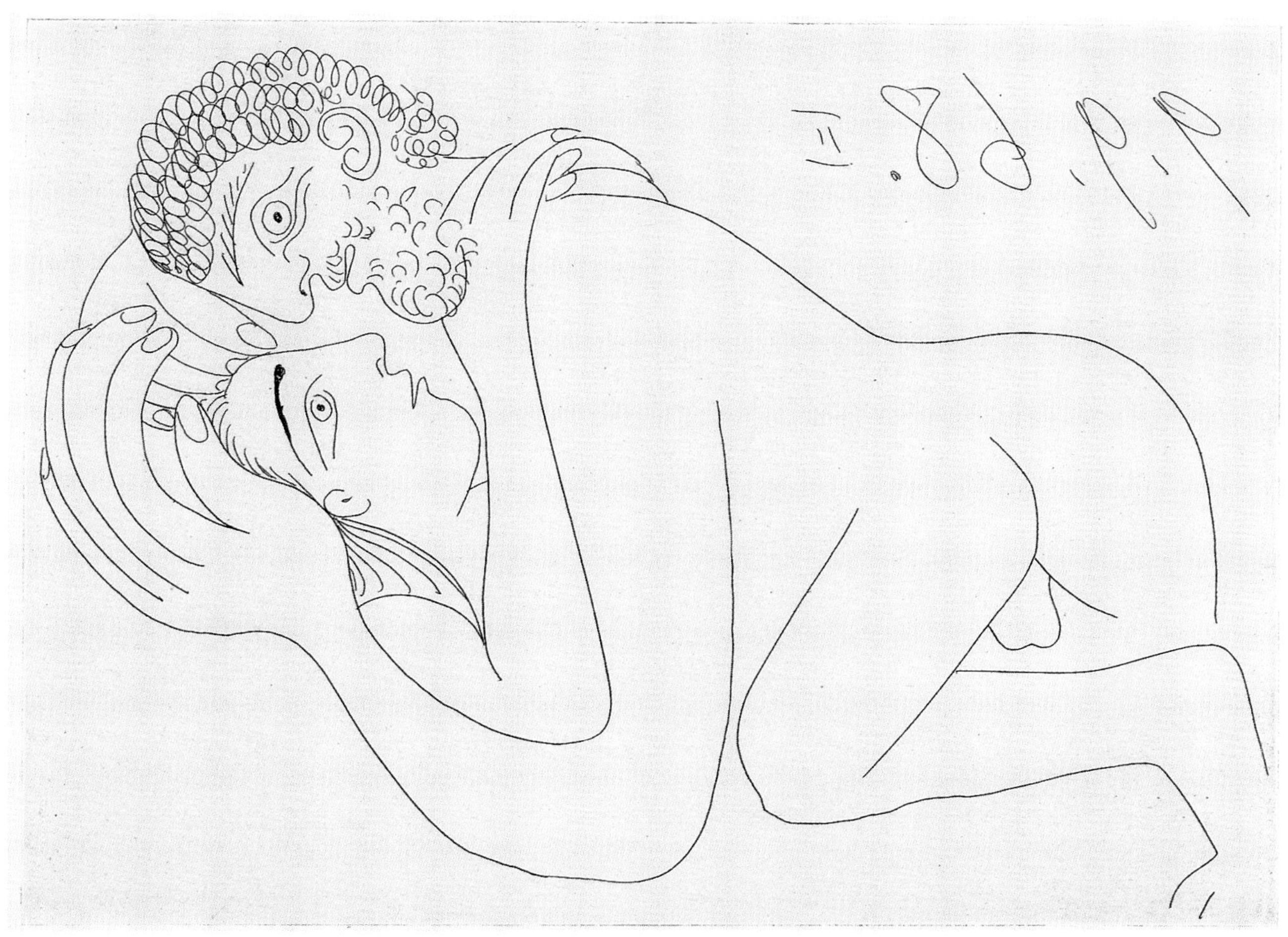

271 Amorous Couple (Raphael and La Fornarina: The End), 9 September 1968

Etching on copper; 14.8 x 20.9
Paris, Bibliothèque nationale de France, Département des Estampes et de la Photographie [P]
Paris, Private collection* [M]
Barcelona, Museu Picasso, MPB 111.956 [B]

BOISGELOUP:
PICASSO'S OLYMPUS

Marilyn McCully

For Bernard and Almine Ruiz-Picasso

Picasso bought a small chateau and several acres of land, enclosed by stone walls, at Boisgeloup, near Gisors, in June 1930. The principal reason, he told his friend Brassaï, was that he had become tired of "carrying back to Paris every year, from Dinard, from Cannes, from Juan-les-Pins, the cumbersome harvest of his summer; of packing and unpacking canvases, paints, brushes, sketchbooks, all the paraphernalia of his travelling studio. At Boisgeloup, he could leave everything."[1] But there were other compelling reasons. For one thing, Picasso wanted to realize modelled sculpture on a large scale, and he found an ideal space for this by converting the row of outbuildings across from the chateau into studios. For another, he needed somewhere to escape the irritating, jealous behaviour of his wife Olga, who would surely prefer their bourgeois apartment in Paris to the unheated, poorly furnished chateau. Even more, Picasso wanted greater freedom to carry on his hidden affair with the young Marie-Thérèse Walter and to express the passionate sexuality of their secret encounters in his art. Picasso's artistic production at Boisgeloup, especially in his graphic work and in sculpture, is focussed on Marie-Thérèse, on the theme of sex — often with associations of violence or death — and on his godlike power to transform objects and beings in the natural world into something transcendental, into art. The recently mooted plan for Picasso to illustrate Ovid's *Metamorphoses,* the collection of classical myths of the gods' seductions and transformations, perfectly matched his mood and his artistic preoccupations.

Boisgeloup is only 45 miles northwest of Paris, and Picasso would have been able to make the journey in his chauffeur-driven Hispano-Suiza in just over an hour. From dated works and correspondence he received there, it is clear that he spent a great deal of time at Boisgeloup over the next five years, sometimes with Olga, their son Paulo, and friends, but often on his own or with Marie-Thérèse. Nevertheless, he generally went to the Mediterranean in the summers, and he was also working regularly during this period in his painting studio on rue La Boétie in Paris.

Although he did not set up his studios at Boisgeloup until the autumn of 1930, Picasso immediately moved some of his things into the chateau and seems to

---

1 Brassaï, *Picasso & Company,* trans. Francis Price, pref. Henry Miller, intro. Sir Roland Penrose (New York: Doubleday & Co., 1966), p. 17.

have escaped there for a time. In a letter of 25 June 1930, his dealer Paul Rosenberg addressed him as "My dear evaporated and invisible friend, lord of Bois Geloux and other places, you are becoming even rarer than the triangular stamps of the Cape of Good Hope."[2] Picasso's old friend Julio González, with whom he was at that period collaborating on welded sculptural projects in Paris, appears to have visited him at Boisgeloup, probably to advise him on the requirements for setting up a sculpture studio. If Marie-Thérèse was at Boisgeloup when the Catalan sculptor visited, he was unaware of her presence. Picasso was intent on keeping her under cover, not only from his wife but also from his closest friends. A sketchbook (MP 1990-109) Picasso had with him at the chateau in July includes not only González's Paris address but three pencil drawings of a nude done by the sculptor himself. Most of Picasso's drawings in the sketchbook, two of which are dated 20 July at Boisgeloup, are devoted to his complex project for a monument, the so-called *Figure of Man's Head Brandishing Rods*. Only the metal head of this creature (Spies 80) was realized (in collaboration with González), but the drawings reveal that Picasso was contemplating adding to the head a monumental, volumetric body. In all the drawings the male genitals figure prominently, and in some they take the place of the torso of the figure.

Picasso, who would turn fifty in 1931, had begun his affair with Marie-Thérèse Walter several years earlier, when she was still a minor.[3] The overriding sexuality of their relationship had released a strong vein of eroticism in his work, although, apart from a few pencil and lithographic portraits,[4] his references to her in the late 1920s had been done primarily in code. It was not until 1930, the year in which Marie-Thérèse turned twenty-one, that her clearly recognizable physical characteristics—classical profile, blonde hair and sensuous body— began to appear undisguised in his work across all media. Her presence is certainly felt in the classically inspired series of *Metamorphoses* prints, which seems to have been his first major project undertaken at Boisgeloup, beginning in September 1930.[5]

Sometime earlier, probably the previous year, Picasso had been approached by the young Swiss Albert Skira to do an illustrated book for the publishing house he had recently established in Lausanne. Skira first proposed that Picasso illustrate a text about Napoleon, but that idea was flatly turned down. As the story

2   "Cher évaporé et invisible ami seigneur de Bois Geloux et autres lieux, vous devenez plus rare que les timbres triangulaires du Cap de Bonne Espérance." *Archives Picasso* (Paris: Musée Picasso). (Free translation.)
3   Marie-Thérèse was born on 13 July 1909. For the date of her first meeting with Picasso—sometime between 1925 and 1927—see Pierre Daix's summary of the conflicting evidence in *Dictionnaire Picasso* (Paris: Robert Laffont, 1995), p. 901–902.
4   G./B. 243, 244; and the drawing reproduced in Bernhard Geiser and Brigitte Baer, *Picasso peintre-graveur: Catalogue raisonné de l'œuvre gravé et des monotypes, 1935-1968* (Berne: Kornfeld, 1990), Vol. I, p. 389.
5   Lisa Florman's book *Myth and Metamorphosis: Picasso's Classical Prints of the 1930s*, scheduled to be published in November 2000 by MIT Press, was not available for consultation at the time of writing this essay. Florman's analysis of Picasso's prints in the context of Surrealist texts and art historical sources will surely add much to the study of the illustrations for Ovid's *Metamorphoses*.

goes, "one day, when Picasso was relating his dreams of women transforming themselves into fish, Pierre Matisse (the painter's son) said: Why don't you illustrate Ovid's *Metamorphoses?*"[6] The suggestion appealed to both Picasso and Skira. The publisher used Georges Lafaye's French prose translation of the text and underlined those stories that he believed would be most appropriate to illustrate. Ovid's compilation of ancient myth and legend, originally written in hexametric verse, was divided into 15 books. Skira asked Picasso to make 30 etchings in all: 15 full-page illustrations of the episodes he had chosen from each book, and 15 half-page illustrations to serve as chapter headings.

Some months passed before the project got underway; Skira confirmed in a letter of 30 April 1930 to Picasso that he wanted to go ahead with the book, although a few details remained to be sorted out. On the same day the printer Louis Fort sent the artist a bill for 21 varnished copper plates, presumably ordered for the *Metamorphoses* project.[7] Picasso took some of the plates with him to Juan-les-Pins, where he spent several weeks at the end of the summer with Olga and Paulo. While he was there he did a preliminary version of *Death of Orpheus* for Book Eleven (G./B. 173), though in the end this was not used. Once back in Boisgeloup,[8] he immediately set up a print studio and began work in earnest. Starting on 18 September and finishing on his birthday, 25 October, he produced the 15 full-page etchings, in addition to 14 alternative versions, which were unused in the publication.[9]

One of the parallels that can be drawn between Picasso's illustrations for the *Metamorphoses* and his personal situation — particularly the secret sexual relationship he shared with Marie-Thérèse — is the relish he took in depicting erotically charged scenes, ranging from seductions to violence and death. The first episode that Picasso worked on at Boisgeloup was the rape of Philomela. In his sixth book Ovid relates the story of the warrior-king Tereus, a descendant of Mars, who had married the daughter of Pandion, King of Athens, and taken her with him to Thrace. After five years his wife, who was lonely for her family, urged him to fetch her sister to visit her. To please his wife, Tereus travelled to Athens to bring back the girl, whose beauty, Ovid wrote, "was like the descriptions that one often hears of the naiads and dryads who haunt the depths of the woodlands… a flame of desire was kindled in Tereus's heart when he saw her." En route to Thrace, Tereus overcame the struggles of his defenceless sister-in-law, raped her and thereafter kept her prisoner in the forest.

6　Sebastian Goeppert et al., *Pablo Picasso: The Illustrated Books,* orig. publ. as *Pablo Picasso: Catalogue raisonné des livres illustrés* (Geneva: Patrick Cramer, 1983), p. 54.

7　Geiser and Baer, Vol. I, p. 241, n. 4.

8　A drawing (MP 1037) of a woman's profile and the head of a bull is inscribed and dated "Boisgeloup, 10 September 1930."

9　Practically every publication about the *Metamorphoses* project claims that the etchings were printed on Louis Fort's press, which was installed at Boisgeloup. However, as Baer has established, this press (which Picasso indeed acquired) was not installed there until 23 April 1934; see Baer, *Picasso: The Engraver,* exh. cat., (New York: The Metropolitan Museum of Art, 1997), p. 55. The printing of the *Metamorphoses* was surely done after all the plates were completed in 1931, on Fort's press in Paris.

Picasso did three versions of the rape scene, the first of which (Baer 179, Cat. 104) shows the bearded king overcoming the girl with force. The victim's head is thrown back so that we do not see her face, but a worked-out drawing of a head resembling Marie-Thérèse on the border below is shown in three-quarters view. The third plate (G./B. 153), which was chosen for the publication, shows the rape, with the legs of Philomela overlapping the lines that define the body of Tereus. The second plate (Cat. 105), also unused, is the most expressive of the three. The struggle is emphasized by the radiating lines beneath the girl at the lower right and by the details on the margins of heads, gestures and figures, which echo the force of the brutal encounter.

The scene for which Picasso executed the most versions, all six done on 25 October, was devoted to Jupiter's seduction of Semele, the daughter of King Cadmus, an episode which occurs in Book Three. When the queen of heaven Juno, wife (and sister) of Jupiter, found out about her husband's deceit, and especially when she learned that Semele was pregnant with the god's child, she was enraged. Disguised as the girl's old nurse, Juno convinced Semele that she should demand to see Jupiter, the father of her child, in all his glory. He had to grant Semele her wish, but when she saw him with thunderbolts in hand, she succumbed to the vision and was burned to ashes. The child, still unborn, was snatched away from his mother's womb. The artist might well have been tempted to portray the aggrieved wife's anger as if Juno were Olga, but he chose instead a quiet but erotically suggestive scene of the lovers Jupiter and Semele entwined in each other's arms, their bodies joined (Fig. 1).

Picasso finished the half-page etchings, including the *Fragment of a Female Body* (Cat. 119), for the *Metamorphoses* in the spring of 1931 in Paris.[10] Pierre Cabanne claims that because Skira was nervous that Picasso would not finish the job, the publisher had set up an office, which he shared with his associate, the Greek editor Tériade, next door to the artist's studio on rue La Boétie. To keep Skira happy, Picasso later related: "Each time I finished one of the copper plates, instead of going to the phone, I took my bugle and went to the window, to blow *Ta-ta-ti, ta-ta-ti, ti-ta-tati-ta-ta*—and presto! There was Skira!"[11] The book with Picasso's etchings, which was to make Skira's name as an art publisher, was published exactly a year after the Jupiter and Semele plates had been etched, on 25 October 1931—the artist's fiftieth birthday. For Picasso the project represented a fresh departure into the world of mythology and, for the first time, he produced book illustrations that depicted specific incidents in the text. His immersion in Ovid gave him a deep appreciation of the power of myth and of the archetypal theme of the gods' ability to harness the creative and destructive forces of love and death—just as the artist can harness them—through the act of metamorphosis; changing one thing into another.

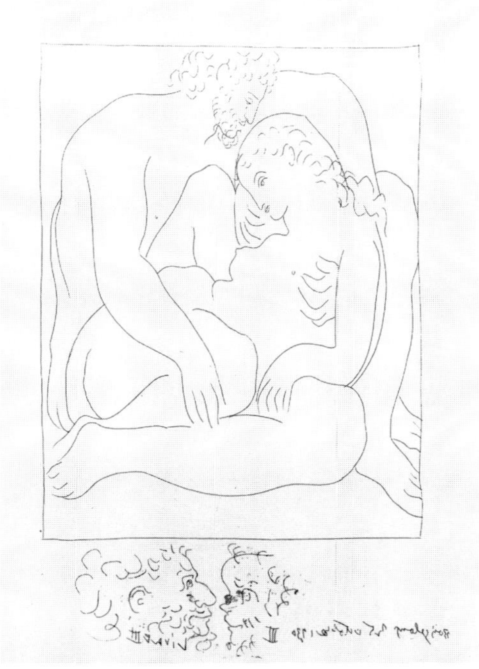

Fig. 1: *Jupiter and Semele* (Plate III),
25 October 1930
Etching on copper; State II; 31.2 x 22.4
Paris, Musée Picasso, MP 2122

---

10 According to Geiser and Baer, Vol. I, p. 241, n. 4, Skira wrote his son on 23 May 1931, announcing
    that Picasso had finished the etchings for Ovid's *Metamorphoses*.
11 Pierre Cabanne, *Le Siècle de Picasso*, Vol. II (Paris: Denoël, 1992), p. 680. (Free translation.)

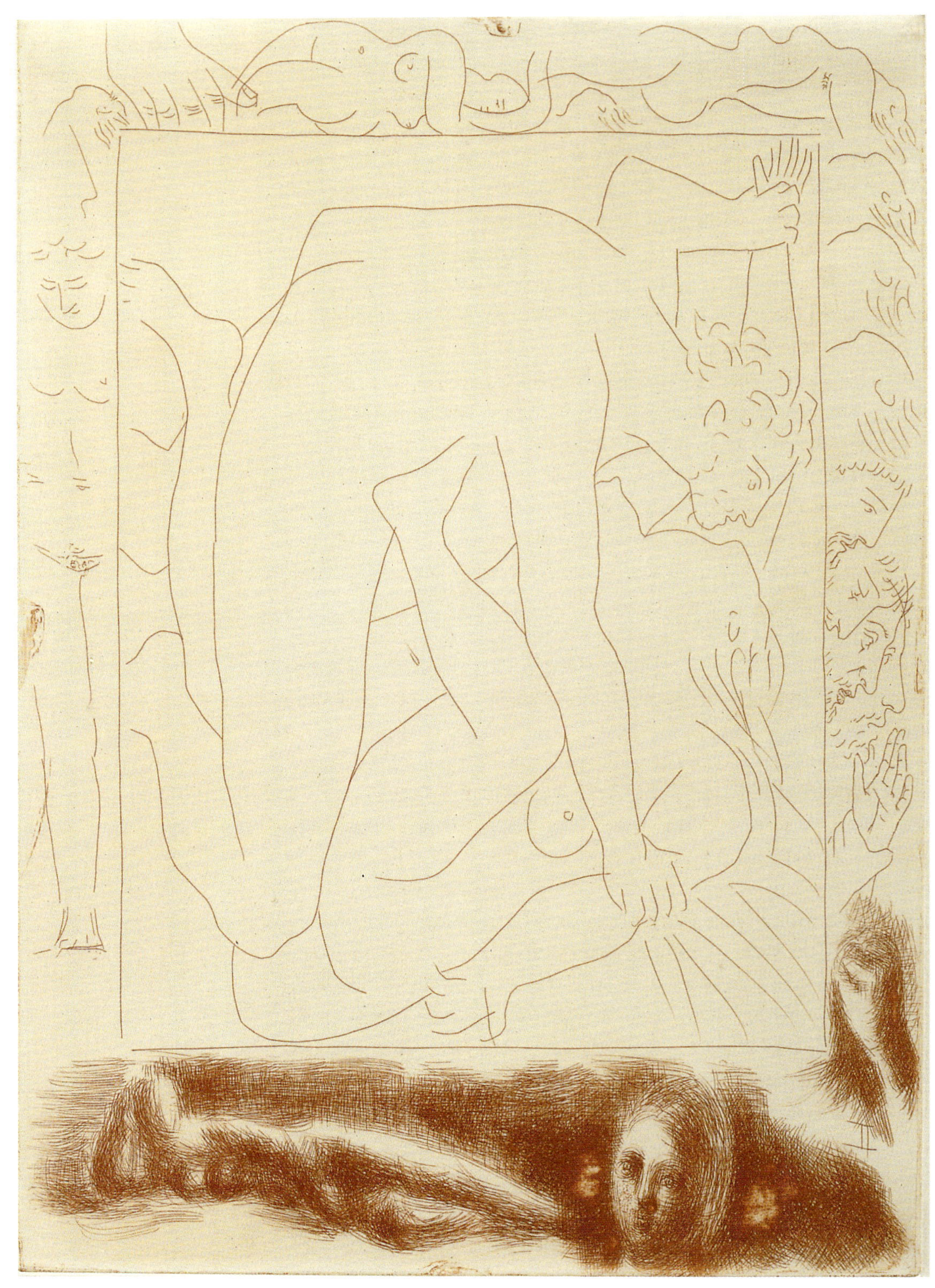

105 Struggle between Tereus and His Sister-in-Law Philomela (Plate II), 18 October 1930
Etching on copper; 31 x 22.3
Paris, Musée Picasso, MP 2156 [B]

Picasso's illustrations for the *Metamorphoses* are notable for their purity of line and the way in which the different compositions are fitted closely into the available space. In these respects Picasso's etchings recall engraved Etruscan mirrorbacks, and this emphasizes the classicism of the treatment. As Baer has pointed out, the process of etching was straightforward and simple enough for Picasso to use working on his own at Boisgeloup,[12] and the linear draftsmanship that he achieved with etching suited his purposes perfectly for the Ovid project. Compositionally, the rapes and seductions are remarkably close to other scenes, not obviously erotic, such as *Eurydice Bitten by a Serpent* (G./B. 162, 176) in Book Seven, in which Picasso portrayed death and violence. Nude figures tumbling forward, limbs intertwined, the domination of one figure by another, animals and men alike—the distance in imagery between lovemaking and violence, and even death, was very narrow indeed. The unifying theme that Picasso found in Ovid was that of the creative, transforming force of the immortals quickening the natural rhythm of the mortal world, in which love and death both lead to a renewal of the cycle. Picasso shared the fascination of his old friend Apollinaire for the association of sex and cruelty in the work of the Marquis de Sade, and it was with Sade in mind that Georges Bataille later wrote: "Although erotic activity is in the first place an exuberance of life, the object of this psychological quest, independent … of any concern to reproduce life, is not alien to death."[13]

Bataille, who had belonged early on to the Surrealist movement, was now one of the leaders of the breakaway *Documents* group, but Picasso was revered by both camps. The artist's work of this period has been discussed widely in the context of Surrealism, notably the Surrealists' emphasis on the creation of art and literature that could draw upon the unconscious in order to release the suppressed erotic impulses that Freud had used to explain human behaviour.[14] Picasso had been in touch with and promoted by a number of French Surrealists, notably André Breton, since the mid-1920s, and their relationship was a complex one. Many Surrealist preoccupations, especially the mining of symbolic material provided by the study of ancient cultures, ethnography, mythology and ritual, had been anticipated in Picasso's own work earlier in the century. In a special issue of *Documents* devoted to Picasso in 1930, Bataille discussed the artist's enthusiasm for the bullfight in the light of Mithraic ritual and primitive worship of the sun, and during this whole period the ideas of the Surrealists confirmed in the artist his intuitive understanding of the role of metamorphosis and the magical and shamanistic power of art.

12 Baer, *Picasso: The Engraver*, p. 59 n. 9.
13 Georges Bataille, *Eroticism* (London: Marion Boyars, 1997), p. 11.
14 See Robert Rosenblum's groundbreaking essay "Picasso and the anatomy of eroticism," *Studies in Erotic Art*, Theodore Bowie and Cornelia V. Christenson, eds. (New York: Basic Books, 1970) and Lydia Gasman's five-part dissertation "Mystery, Magic and Love in Picasso, 1925–1938: Picasso and the Surrealist Poets" (Columbia University, 1986). Although still unpublished in book form, Gasman's dissertation remains one of the richest sources and most original studies of Picasso's work in the context of Surrealism.

Picasso stayed on at Boisgeloup until mid-November 1930, and then returned to Paris. He had installed Marie-Thérèse in an apartment at 44 rue la Boétie, down the street from number 23, where he lived with Olga and Paulo. The artist and his young mistress still carried on their affair in secrecy, experimenting in sexual practices that, according to Marie-Thérèse, were freed from all taboos.[15] Passion and eroticism flared up in Picasso's works of the winter, notably in compositions set at the seashore, some of which recall the drawings for bone-like sculptures he had made in Dinard two summers earlier, when Marie-Thérèse had been secretly installed near the artist in a local pension. By summoning up the place — the beach — which had triggered the eroticism of the Dinard drawings, the scenes of lovers done in early 1931 in Paris reflect Picasso's desire to create painted or sculptural equivalents of the sexual obsession and power that he experienced in his continued relationship with Marie-Thérèse.

In *Figures at the Seashore* (Cat. 116), a large oil painted on 12 January 1931, Picasso rendered the grappling limbs of the figures as if they were carved sculptural elements, made smooth by the action of the waves. The dagger-shaped tongues echo the forms of the limbs and also refer to the two smaller paintings (Cat. 120) of interlocking, kissing heads that Picasso painted on the same day. The large composition is set against a backdrop of the sea, with a beach cabana in the background.[16] The breasts of the female creature occupy the space between the two figures and serve as a kind of pivotal point between the interlocking limbs. The idea of reassembling body parts, or at least shifting them around to achieve a formal balance — here, implying an equilibrium of sculptural weight — while still conveying the intensity and eroticism of a sexual encounter, stimulated the artist's ideas when he turned to realizing similar forms in three dimensions.

Because of the cold and lack of electricity at Boisgeloup, Picasso did not return to work there until the spring, probably again accompanied by Marie-Thérèse, whose portrait, dated 16 May 1931, appears along with a self-portrait among the pages of another sketchbook[17] he had with him there. In late May Picasso also started work in his sculpture studio. In a letter of the 20th June, the sculptor González wrote the artist in Boisgeloup: "You must tell me when I see you about your latest pieces, the first ones and the most recent."[18] Among the earliest works that Picasso made were the plasters *Head of a Woman* and *Bust of a Woman (Marie-Thérèse)* (Spies 132, 131), both of which appear in the sketchbook in a drawing, done on 13 June 1931, showing these works mounted on a sculptor's

15 Gasman, Part 1, p. 64.

16 For an in-depth discussion of the beach cabana as a sexual symbol in Picasso's work, see Gasman, Part 1, p. 7–448.

17 Arnold Glimcher and Mark Glimcher, eds., *Je suis le cahier: The Sketchbooks of Picasso* (New York, The Pace Gallery, 1986), No. 101.

18 Marilyn McCully, "Julio González and Pablo Picasso: A documentary chronology of a working relationship," *Picasso: Sculptor/Painter*, exh. cat. (London: The Tate Gallery, 1994), p. 217.

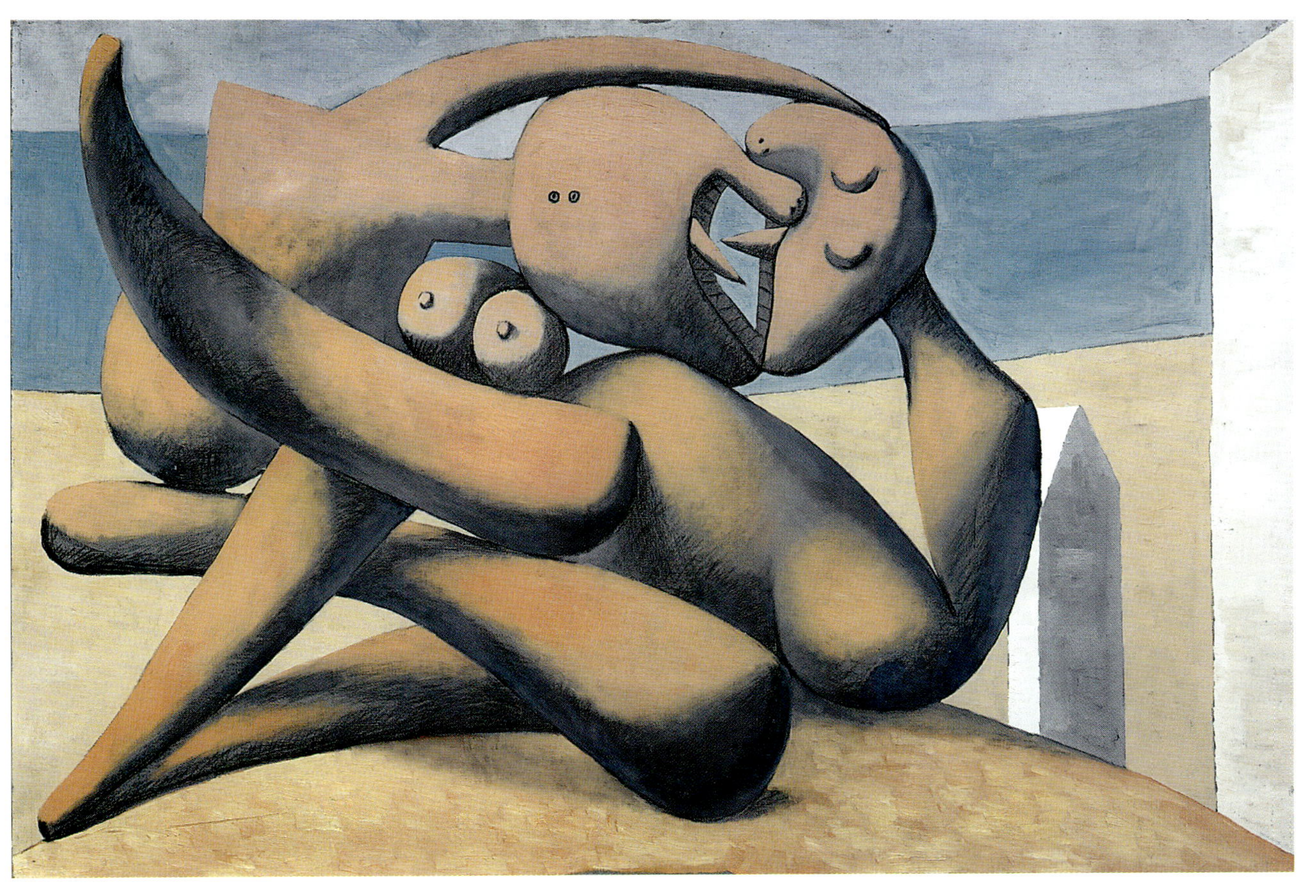

116 Figures at the Seashore, 12 January 1931
Oil on canvas; 130 x 195
Paris, Musée Picasso, MP 131

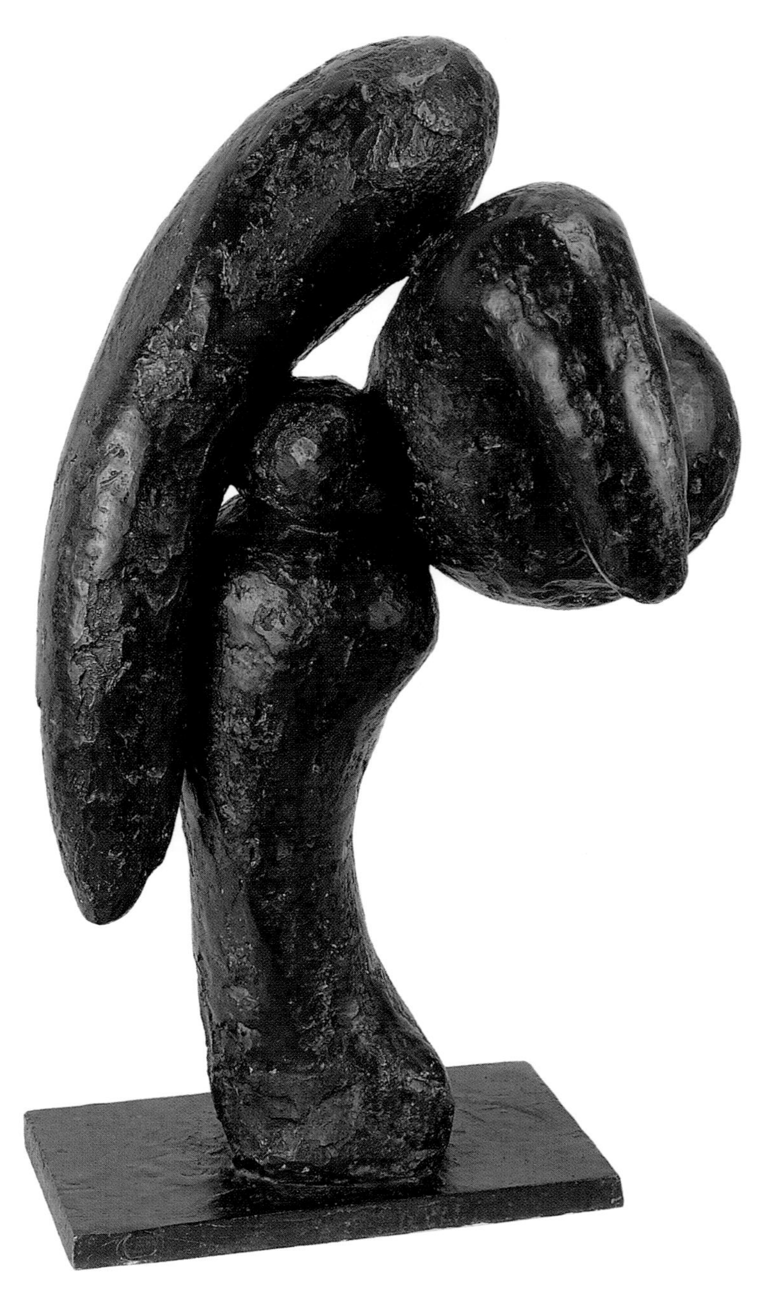

114 Head of a Woman, 1931
Bronze; 71.5 x 41 x 33
Paris, Musée Picasso, MP 292 [MB]

stand in the artist's studio.[19] The erotically inspired *Head of a Woman* (Cat. 114), which shares some of the same formal experiments with reassemblage of body parts that appear in the painting *Figures at the Seashore* (Cat. 116), was also made around the same time. Cowling has noted that Picasso apparently had a more complex scheme in mind when he began this particular sculpture, but later abandoned the idea because it was unworkable. A sheet of drawings, dated 26–27 June, shows "several views of a multi-part sculpture of a half-length reclining woman, who leans her head on her right arm, and whose left arm (which is detached and treated like a giant sausage) curves round and encloses her two perfectly spherical breasts. The phallic connotations of the work in this form are even more pronounced than in the definitive sculpture."[20]

Whereas Picasso had used the male genitals to form part of a male body in the drawings he had done at Boisgeloup the previous year, he now transformed these into a series of monumental female heads and figures. The erotic force of the plaster sculptures, in which the nose of Marie-Thérèse appears as if it were a phallus attached to her forehead, is derived from this extraordinary metamorphosis. The reassemblage of human attributes, especially erogenous ones — breasts and genitalia — results in all manner of forms imbued with sexuality.

One of Ovid's stories that Picasso had illustrated was the myth of Deucalion and his wife Pyrrha, who as sole survivors of the great flood were instructed by the goddess Themis to throw behind them "the bones of their mother." They obeyed, throwing stones (representing Mother Earth), which when they struck the ground "began to lose their hardness and rigidity ... once softened they acquired a definite shape. When they had grown in size ... a certain likeness to a human form could be seen ... they were like marble images, begun but not yet properly chiselled out, like unfinished statues." In his etching (G./B. 144) for Book One, Picasso had portrayed Deucalion and Pyrrha embracing a child as a means of illustrating this legend of the renewal of the human race. The impact of the story, however, was far greater when it came to his sculpture, for, like the softening, unchiselled stones described by Ovid, Picasso's Boisgeloup plasters embody and communicate both through their handling and their forms — caught in the process of becoming human — the force of their own creation.[21]

When Picasso returned to Paris for the winter, he set about producing a group of new paintings to be included in the large retrospective exhibition that was being planned at the Georges Petit Gallery for the following June (1932). Among them were a number of large paintings devoted to Marie-Thérèse, which are characterized by a vibrant palette, curvilinear forms (some of which make reference to the Boisgeloup sculptures) and, in all of them, a pervasive eroticism.

19 Elizabeth Cowling, "Catalogue," *Picasso: Sculptor/Painter*, exh. cat. (London: The Tate Gallery, 1994), p. 269.
20 Cowling, p. 269
21 Gasman has related the story of Deucalion and Pyrrha to Picasso's bone-like sketches made in Dinard in 1928 (Gasman, p. 325).

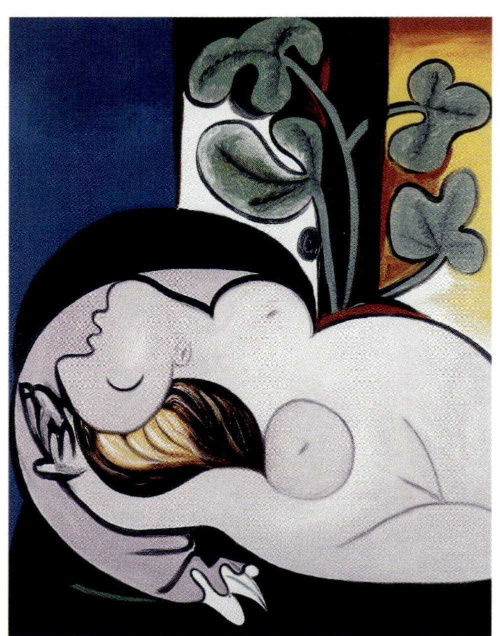

Fig. 2: *Nude with Black Armchair*, 9 March 1932
Oil on canvas; 162 x 132
Private collection

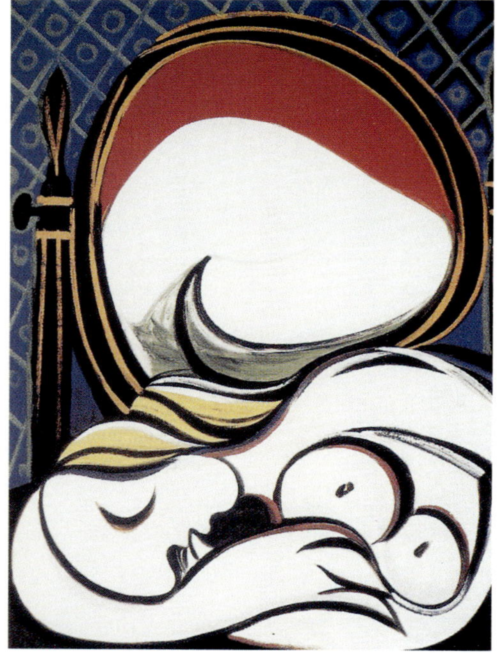

Fig. 3: *The Mirror (Marie-Thérèse)*, 14 March 1933
Oil on canvas; 130.7 x 97
Private collection

In *The Dream (Marie-Thérèse)* (repr. p. 70), for instance, painted on 24 January 1932, Picasso portrays Marie-Thérèse asleep in a chair, with a book falling open suggestively on her lap. Her face is divided into a double profile, with the upper part appearing as a phallus. As Richardson has written of this painting, "sex is literally on the dreamer's mind. This is what gives this seemingly lyrical image its erotic charge."[22]

For many of the paintings and drawings he did of Marie-Thérèse, beginning in 1932, Picasso envisioned the whole of her body as a kind of curvilinear assemblage—plant-like and sculptural at the same time. In *Nude with Black Armchair* (9 March 1932) (Fig. 2), the artist paints her as if she were a philodendron: her head rests on the curve created by her linked arms, and the gap between the neck and centrally positioned breasts is filled with flowing hair. The form continues with a second curve that follows her round hips and tapers off in the direction of her legs. In this composition, Picasso has turned Marie-Thérèse into a metamorphic image of a sleeping nymph who seems to seems to be sprouting leaves— from the hand beneath her and above her at the waist.

The artist's former dealer D.H. Kahnweiler, who was asked to lend works to the Georges Petit show, visited Picasso's studio on 17 March. He wrote the Surrealist writer Michel Leiris: "We saw two paintings at his place which he had just finished. Two nudes, perhaps the most moving things he's done. 'A satyr who had just killed a woman might have painted this picture,' I told him. It's neither cubist nor naturalist. And it's without painterly artifice: very alive, very erotic, but the eroticism of a giant. … We left feeling quite overwhelmed."[23]

Another of the paintings that would have been in the artist's studio at the time was *The Mirror (Marie-Thérèse)* (Fig. 3), painted on 14 March. In this composition, the reclining head faces downward, nestling into the arms, which enclose the breasts at the right. Reflected in the mirror is a rhyming curvilinear form showing the buttocks of the nude. One can see why Kahnweiler was at a loss to describe the new approach. The reflection allows two views of the body to be seen at the same time. The flowing yellow hair, the green reflection and the red of the mirror echoing the highlights on the woman's breasts all link the forms, lending not a "naturalist," but an organic, sublimely sensual quality to the whole.

Nineteen paintings done in 1932 were shown at the Georges Petit retrospective in Paris in June and later at the Kunsthaus Zurich in that year. Because of the presence of so many images of Marie-Thérèse, Richardson has suggested that the artist's wife became aware for the first time of a new woman in Picasso's life after seeing this show.[24] Others in Picasso's circle, including Kahnweiler, pro-

22 John Richardson, "Picasso," Michael Fitzgerald, ed., *A Life of Collecting: Victor and Sally Ganz* (New York: Harry N. Abrams, 1998), p. 30.
23 Pierre Daix, *Picasso: Life and Art* (New York: Icon, 1993), p. 221–22.
24 John Richardson, "Picasso and l'amour fou," *New York Review* (19 Dec. 1985), p. 66.

fessed ignorance of the affair until much later.[25] At any rate, husband and wife did not spend the summer together—Olga and Paulo went to Juan-les-Pins, while Picasso and Marie-Thérèse returned to Boisgeloup.

One of the most remarkable series of drawings on the theme of metamorphosis from this period in Picasso's oeuvre exists in a Boisgeloup sketchbook (present whereabouts unknown) begun at the end of the summer (8 August–8 October 1932). In page after page (Z.VIII 1–28, 30–33, 36, 39), Marie-Thérèse appears, sometimes merging with a jug (anticipating Picasso's dazzling ceramics of the late 1940s and 1950s), sometimes turning into a plant, or even a bird. According to Françoise Gilot, to whom the artist later confided details of his various affairs, Marie-Thérèse represented for Picasso a real creature of nature. She "haunted his life, just out of reach poetically, but available in the practical sense whenever his dreams were troubled by her absence. She had no inconvenient reality; she was a reflection of the cosmos. If it was a beautiful day, the clear blue sky reminded him of her eyes. The flight of a bird for him the freedom of their relationship."[26] On the last pages of the sketchbook are several drawings of Marie-Thérèse nude on the beach. Sometimes she is watched by other figures, sometimes she is rowing a boat, and on one sheet she is being chased by a naked man. The series is completed by several classically inspired scenes that foreshadow the great *Aubades* of the mid-1960s, in which a bearded pipe player serenades a sleeping nude.

At the end of 1932 Picasso introduced a dramatic event into his beach scenes: the rescue of a drowning swimmer (Cats. 130–132). Over a period of some weeks, he devoted his efforts to drawing, painting and engraving a group of compositions, the majority of which show Marie-Thérèse with other female bathers —most of whom resemble her—swimming, diving, playing with a beach ball or pulling an unconscious figure from the sea. When Picasso was geographically far from water, he sometimes depicted swimmers either to evoke a classical, Mediterranean setting or the presence of an absent mistress.[27] The drama inherent in the rescue scenes, however, has prompted a number of theories as to why this anguish entered Picasso's work at this time. Daix has suggested that it has to do with the angry Olga's return to Paris from her summer holidays, while Golding believes that it refers more generally to the deterioration of the marriage.[28]

Although Marie-Thérèse is not always portrayed in Picasso's compositions as the drowned figure, Baer has linked the subject of the rescue directly to an illness

25 Cabanne, Vol. II, p. 702–03, n. 11.
26 Françoise Gilot and Carlton Lake, *Life with Picasso* (New York: McGraw-Hill, 1964), p. 235.
27 Gilot recounts that "often when he was at Boisgeloup with Olga and family friends, he pictured Marie-Therese bathing in the Seine near Paris" (Gilot, p. 235).
28 Daix, *Picasso: Life and Art*, p. 224; John Golding, "Introduction," *Picasso: Sculptor/Painter*, exh. cat. (London: The Tate Gallery, 1994), p. 29. Gedo has unconvincingly suggested that there was some private disaster in Picasso and Marie-Thérèse's relationship—either an abortion or miscarriage; see Mary Mathews Gedo, *Picasso: Art as Autobiography* (Chicago: University of Chicago Press, 1980), p. 149.

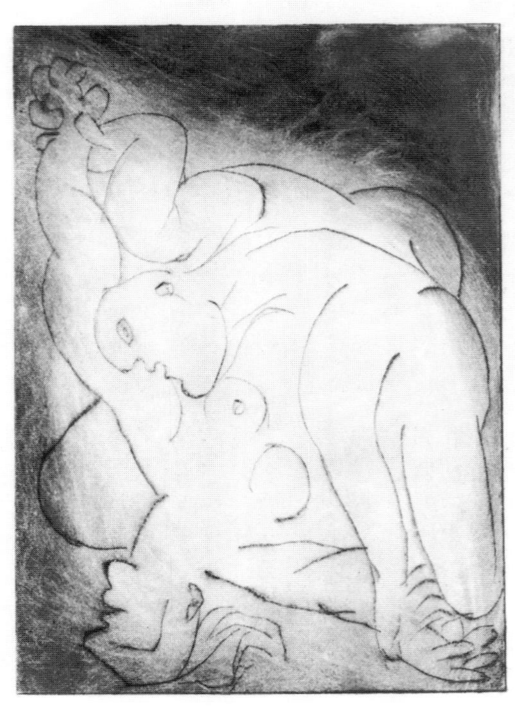

129 The Rape, 21 November 1932

Drypoint on copper; 12.3 x 9.1
Paris, Musée Picasso, MP 2202* [P], MP 2203 [M] and MP 2204 [B]

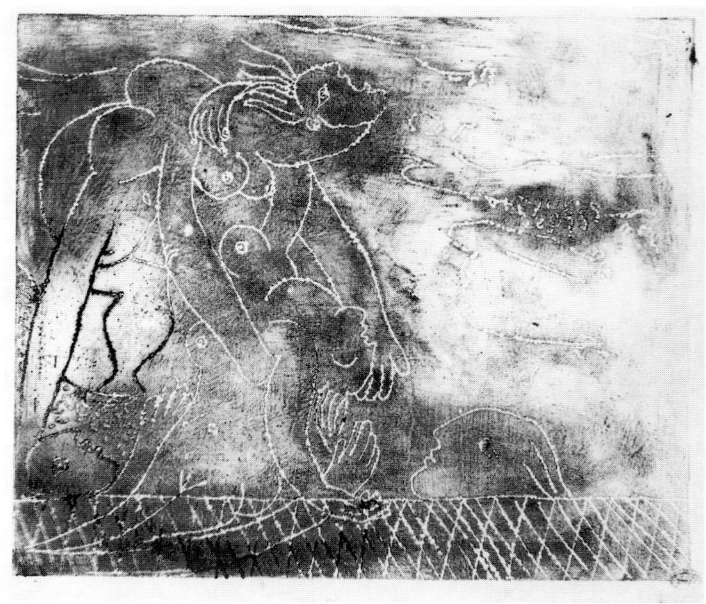

130 The Rescue of the Drowning Woman I, 17 December 1932

Etching on copper; 15.8 x 19.4
Paris, Musée Picasso, MP 2228 [M] and MP 2229 [B]

Marie-Thérèse contracted around this time while swimming in the Marne.[29] After being hospitalized with a high fever, which caused the loss of her blond hair, Marie-Thérèse was convalescent during the first months of 1933. In her absence Picasso often referred to her in his work, stirring up the erotic nature of their relationship in scenes showing rapes, nude bathers and, now, a drowning. It may well be that Marie-Thérèse was actually a witness to such an event and even participated in a rescue, but the subject that unfolds in Picasso's hands takes on different meanings in different media.[30]

In Ovid's *Metamorphoses* water is sometimes the medium in which transformations take place—mortals are turned into fish or even into the water itself. Hermaphroditus was seduced by a nymph who tempted him into a pool of clear water, where he succumbed to her passion as she wrapped herself around him. As a result of their sexual union in water, his body was forever changed. Richardson has noted that "Picasso held the sea in a veneration which was nothing if not erotic. Sex and swimming are often seen in terms of each other: witness those paintings of the mid-thirties which evoke Marie-Thérèse—often in the presence of her adored sister of whom Picasso was apparently jealous—cavorting in the waves and playing at life-saving."[31]

What might have begun as a game of life-saving in Picasso's narrative turns into a dramatic event filled with latent eroticism.

One of the compositional links between Picasso's representations of sex and the rescue scene can be found in the series of prints that he worked on in late 1932. On 21 November he did a drypoint depicting a rape (Cat. 129), in which Marie-Thérèse is portrayed as the victim. The head of the figure has her characteristic profile, and her curvaceous body is thrown to the ground by a bald male figure who holds her down with force. A few weeks later, in the rescue compositions, the artist shows a similar scene (Cat. 130), although now we see a naked rescuer lifting a drowned (also naked) figure from the sea, aided by one or two swimmers, all of whom share Marie-Therese's profile. The position of the lifeless body, her head and arms thrown back, revealing her round breasts, is strikingly similar to the figure in the rape scene, but in this composition it is the rescuer rather than the rapist bending over her.

29 Baer, *Picasso: The Engraver*, p. 33, n. 9. Maya Widmaier Picasso confirmed to Rosenblum that her mother had contracted spirochetal disease in the infected waters of the Marne, near her family's home at Maisons-Alfort, a suburb outside Paris; see Robert Rosenblum, "Picasso's blond muse: The reign of Marie-Thérèse Walter," *Picasso and Portraiture*, exh. cat. (New York: The Museum of Modern Art, 1996), p. 383, n. 64.

30 Another explanation for the subject of the rescue has been made by Reinhold Hohl in his analysis of *The Rescue* in *Fondation Beyeler* (Munich: Prestel, 1997), p. 90. He suggests that, because of the association of the white flowers in the painted version with a figure submerged in water, this particular composition refers to the story of Narcissus. However, Hohl does not take into account the other works in the series, in which flowers do not appear, nor the drama involving other people surrounding the rescue. He also insinuates that Marie-Thérèse, like Narcissus, was self-obsessed, a personality trait for which no other evidence is given.

31 Richardson, "Picasso and l'amour fou," p. 66. Marie-Thérèse actually had two older sisters, one of whom later recalled to Schwarz that she was present on the day that Marie-Thérèse first met Picasso; see Herbert T. Schwarz, *Picasso and Marie-Thérèse Walter, 1925–1927* (Inuvik, N.W.T., Canada: Éditions Isabeau, 1988), p. 119.

When Picasso introduced the Minotaur, the beast with the head of a bull and body of a man, into his work in 1933, he added a new dimension to the sexual and symbolic dynamics of his imagery.[32] The artist had been asked by the founders of the new review *Minotaure* to design a cover for the first issue, which appeared in June of that year.[33] The name of the review had been suggested by André Masson and Georges Bataille, both of whom were interested in the bull-men of Greek and Iranian mythologies. "For the surrealists," the photographer Brassaï later wrote, "the name invoked dark and cruel myths: the monstrous union of Pasiphae with the white bull, the labyrinth built by Daedalus, where the Minotaur devoured the young men and girls of Athens, myths which Freud reclaimed from legend and made part of the subconscious."[34] The cover that Picasso designed for the review did not, however, identify the beast with violence or unbridled liberty. The seated creature does hold an upraised dagger as his attribute, but in the maquette that Picasso carried out as a collage he placed his drawing of the beast against a backdrop of paper lace and foliage, implying through juxtaposition the ambivalence of the creature's motives and desires.

Soon after he had finished his work for *Minotaure*, Picasso added the beast to the cast of characters that he depicted in a series of prints devoted to the subject of the sculptor in his studio. In an etching begun on 18 May 1933 (Cat. 157), he showed the curly-haired creature holding a champagne glass in one hand, with the body of a naked model tumbling head-first over him. The bearded (and equally hairy) sculptor at the right holds a second model and returns the toast of the beast with his champagne. While both of these characters have been identified in various compositions as Picasso, each takes on a different role, reflecting different aspects of the artist's conscious will and subconscious desires as the narrative of his work unfolds. The beast, whose identity hovers ambivalently between man and animal, has none of the cruel associations of the Surrealists' monster. He seems rather to represent Jupiter, seducer and King of the Gods, in his guise as a bull. As Jupiter, the minotaur can also stand for Picasso, the artist with the gods' gift for metamorphosis.

In June 1933 Picasso returned to Boisgeloup and there he once again unleashed the erotic side of his art. In a series of forceful pen and inkwash drawings of a Minotaur ravishing a woman (repr. p. 41), he explores expressive new ways of conveying the power and bestial nature of the creature in the act of overcoming the yielding, soft flesh of the nude. The compositional similarity of these scenes with those of sex and violence in earlier works is striking: the woman, still with the body and profile of Marie-Thérèse, is bent back double

---

32 For an excellent discussion of the significance of the Minotaur in Picasso's work of the 1930s, see Gasman, Part 3, p. 1311–546.

33 A selection of photographs taken by Brassaï at Boisgeloup in December 1932 of Picasso's sculptures, in addition to a series of drawings by Picasso after Grünewald's *Crucifixion* and a sketchbook of Surrealist-inspired drawings entitled *An Anatomy* (Cat. 136–138), were reproduced in the first issue of *Minotaure.*

34 Brassaï, p. 9.

under the weight of the beast. The fury of the attack is mirrored in the intensity of line and shadows that defines the creature's head and their surroundings. Later in the year Picasso treated the same subject in several bold drawings (Z.VIII.145–146), but instead of mounting his victim, who appears to have fainted, the Minotaur pulls her up toward him, in a gesture that calls to mind the earlier scenes depicting the rescue of the drowned woman.

Picasso spent the remainder of the summer of 1933 with Olga and Paulo, first in Cannes and then in Barcelona. When he returned to Boisgeloup in September, he did a bullfight drawing (Cat. 162) that transforms the Minotaur into a *toro bravo*, and his victim, Marie-Thérèse, into a *rejoneadora* (a female bullfighter who fights on horseback). The woman's body falls across the back of her horse, her suit of lights torn open to reveal her breasts. Her assailant is the mighty bull, and in spite of the matador's sword piercing his neck, he carries off his victims in triumph. Compositionally, one is reminded of another mythological scene of death, the *Fall of Phaethon* (G./B. 146), which Picasso did for Ovid's *Metamorphoses*, in which the body of the naked youth is borne by the chariot horses in much the same manner as the bull takes the burden of the *rejoneadora* and her horse.

The subject of the death of the woman torero turns out to be prophetic, for, in 1935, one of the last drawings Picasso did at Boisgeloup, *Woman, Bull, Horse* (14 April 1935) (Fig. 4), signalled not only the end of his passion for Marie-Thérèse,[35] who had his child in that year, but the loss of the chateau itself. Picasso's marriage to Olga finally broke up and, as a result of their official separation, she was awarded the property at Boisgeloup. Just as the vengeful Juno had brought about the young, pregnant Semele's death when Jupiter was forced to reveal his true identity, so Olga's public fury and the imminent birth of a daughter destroyed the secrecy which, for nearly a decade, had heightened the excitement of Picasso's most carnal relationship. Picasso's art during these years was also characterized by a strong obsessive eroticism, for which the creative arena was the chateau of Boisgeloup from which he was now deposed, the studio that had been his Olympus.

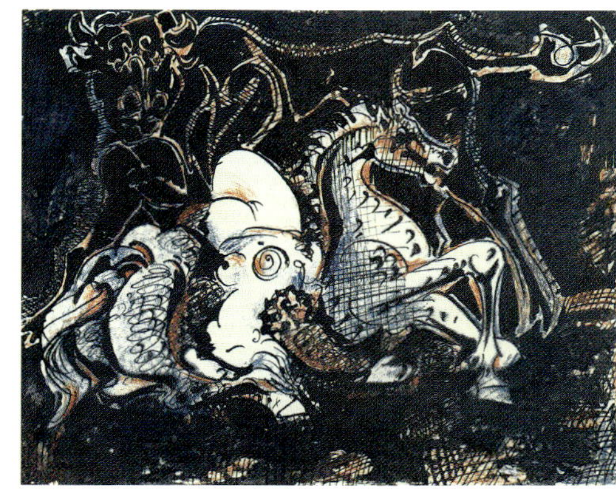

Fig. 4: *Woman, Bull, Horse*, 14 April 1935
Pen, India ink and coloured pencil on paper; 19 x 24
Paris, Private collection

The translations of excerpts from *The Metamorphoses of Ovid* are by Mary M. Innes (Harmondsworth: Penguin, 1955).

35 Picasso continued to see Marie-Thérèse and their daughter Maya and to provide for them but, according to Marie-Thérèse, he became bored with the affair (Gasman, p. 1189–90). He started a new relationship, with Dora Maar, in 1936. Marie-Thérèse appeared in Picasso's art until the end of the decade, but she no longer played the role of erotic muse.

CHRONOLOGICAL CATALOGUE
OF EXHIBITED WORKS

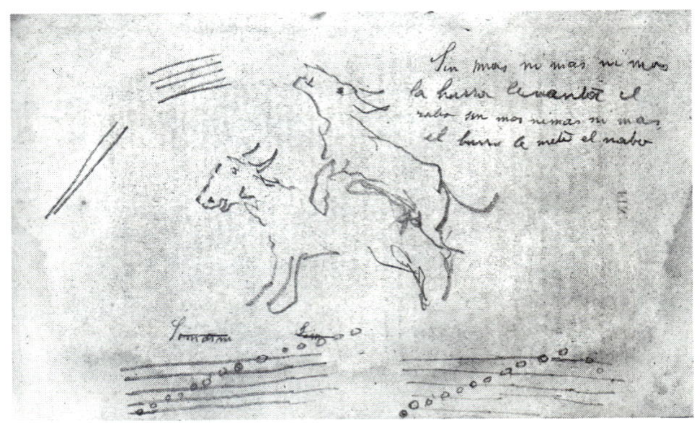

1 Donkey and She-Ass, circa 1894
Pencil on paper; 14.5 x 20.3
Barcelona, Museu Picasso, MPB 110.927

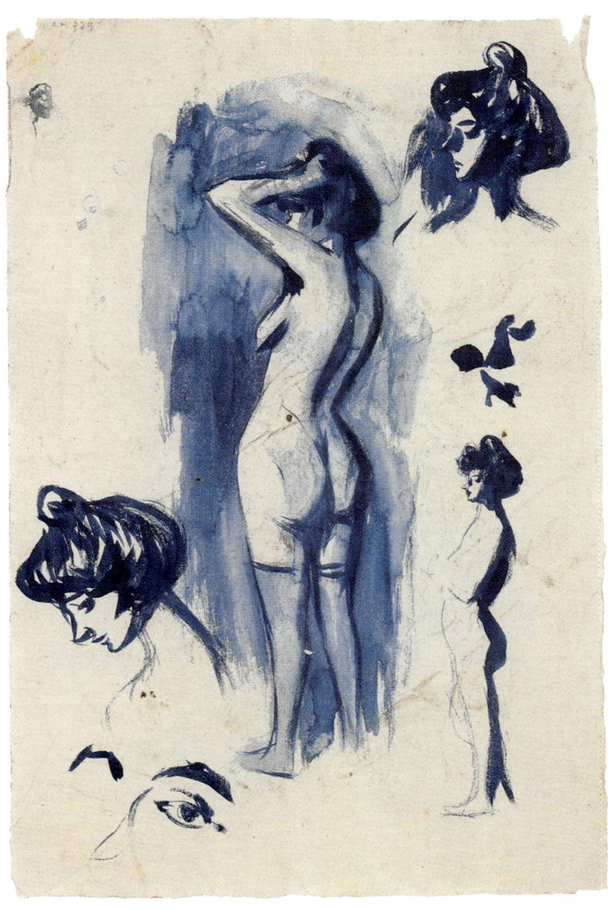

3 Nude, 1898–1899
Blue ink and charcoal on paper; 34 x 23
Paris, Private collection

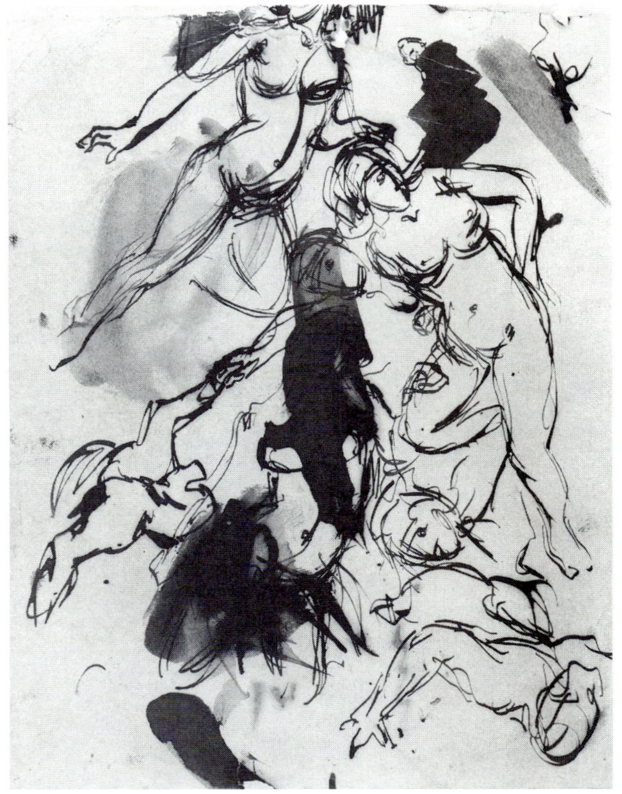

2 Sketch: Female Nudes, circa 1896
Ink on paper; 16.8 x 13.2
Barcelona, Museu Picasso, MPB 110.606

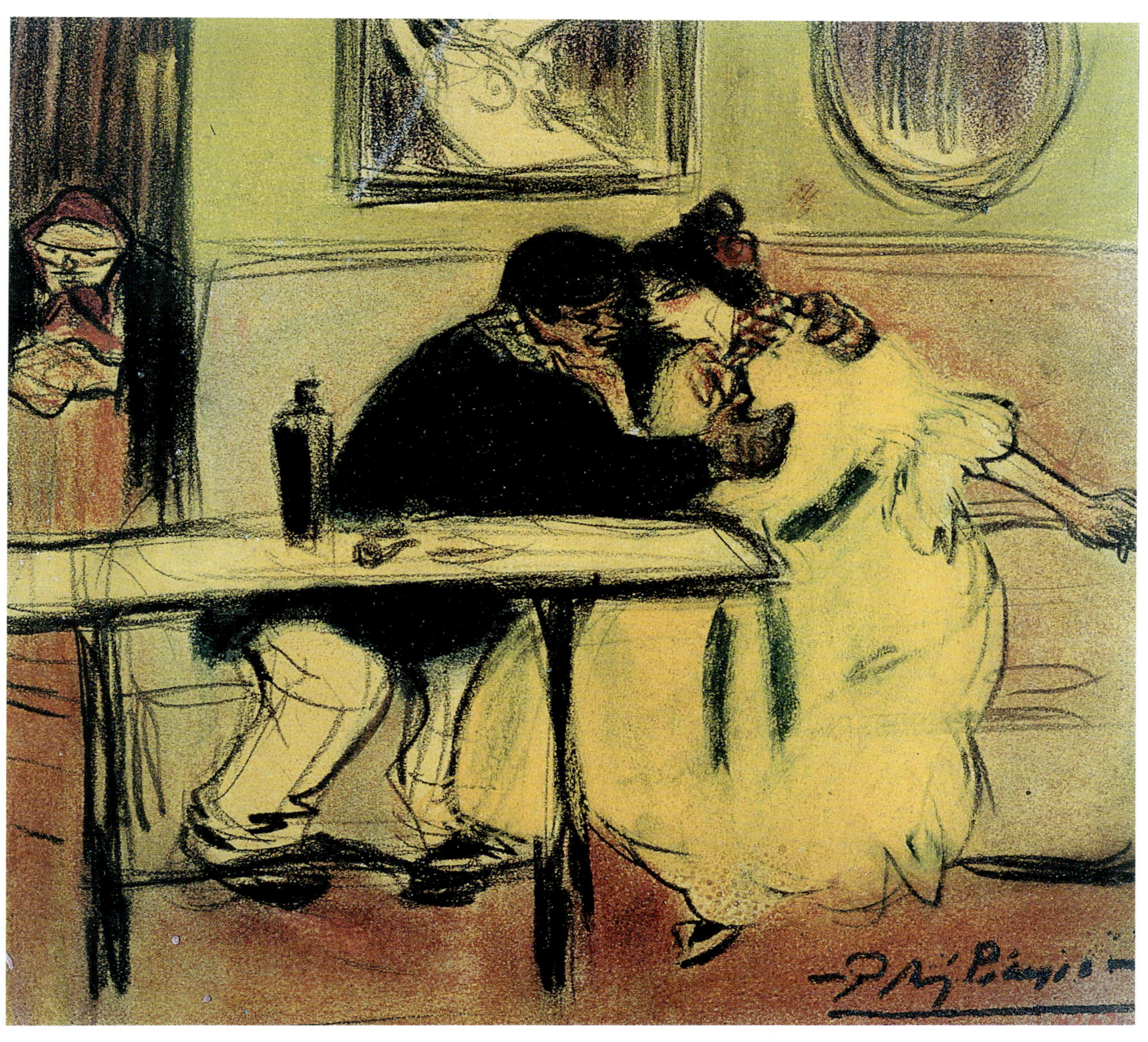

4 El Diván, circa 1899
  Charcoal, pastel and coloured pencil on paper ("fried" drawing); 26.2 x 29.7
  Barcelona, Museu Picasso, MPB 4.267

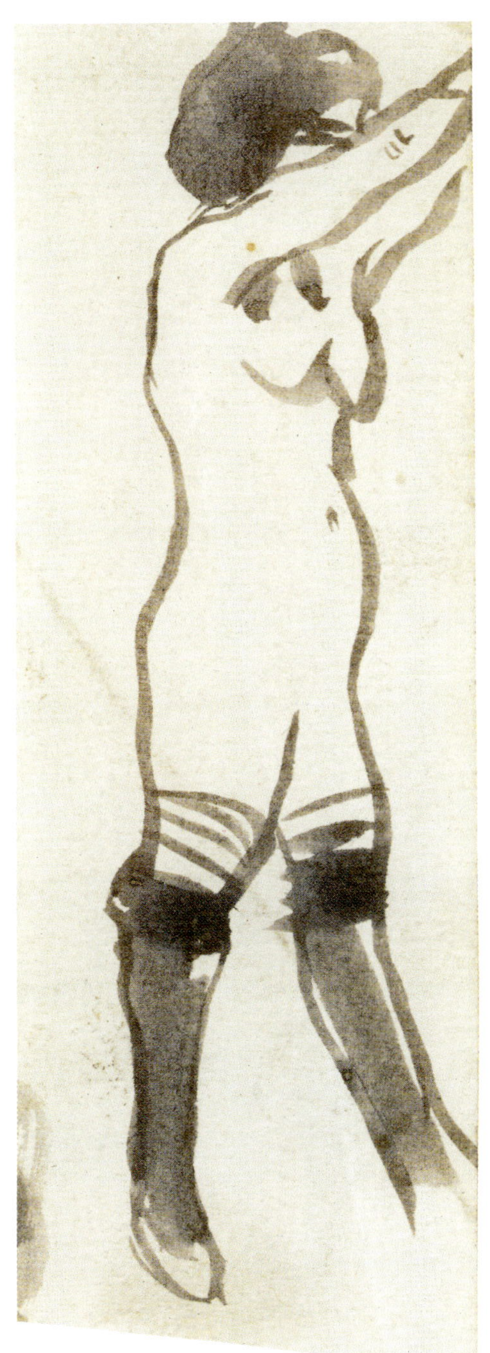

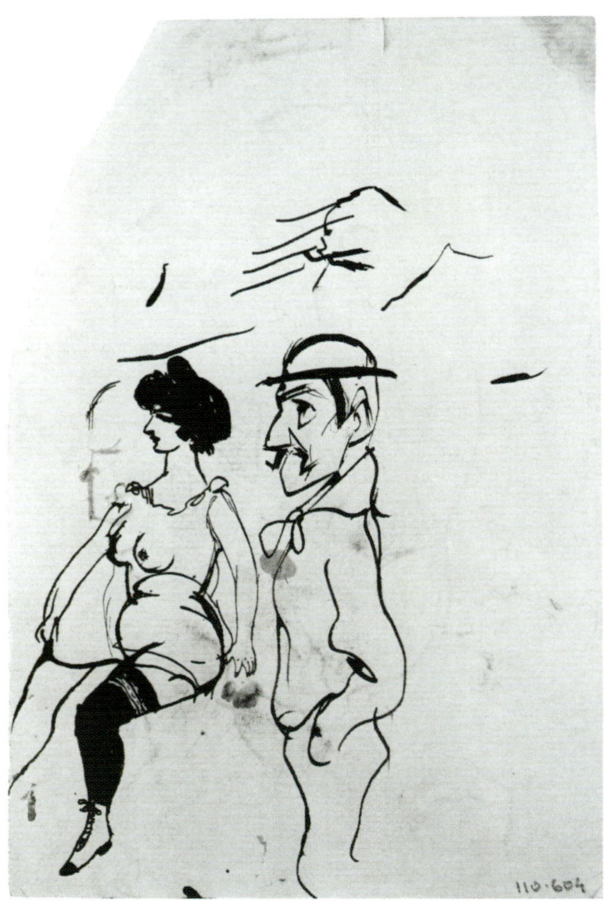

7 Sketch, circa 1900
Woman in Stockings and Boots and Man in Profile with Scarf around His Neck
Pen on paper; 17.5 x 11.7
Barcelona, Museu Picasso, MPB 110.604 r° [PB]

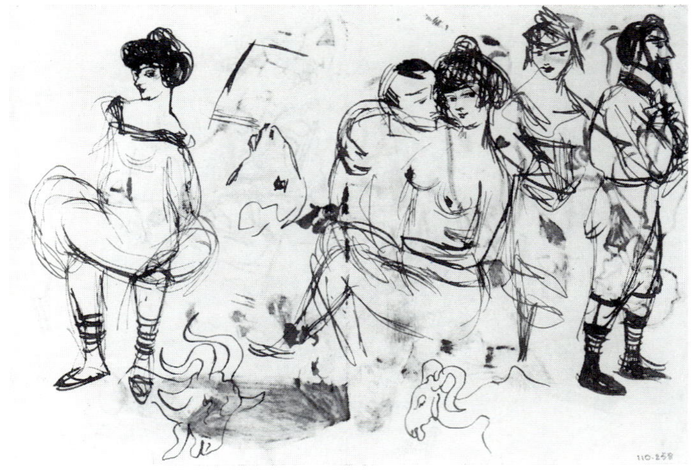

8 Brothel Scene, circa 1900
Pen on paper; 13.3 x 20.8
Barcelona, Museu Picasso, MPB 110.258 r° [PB]

5 Nude in Black Stockings, 1899–1900
India ink on paper; 11.5 x 4
Geneva, Marina Picasso collection (inv. 0220),
Courtesy Galerie Jan Krugier, Ditesheim & Cie

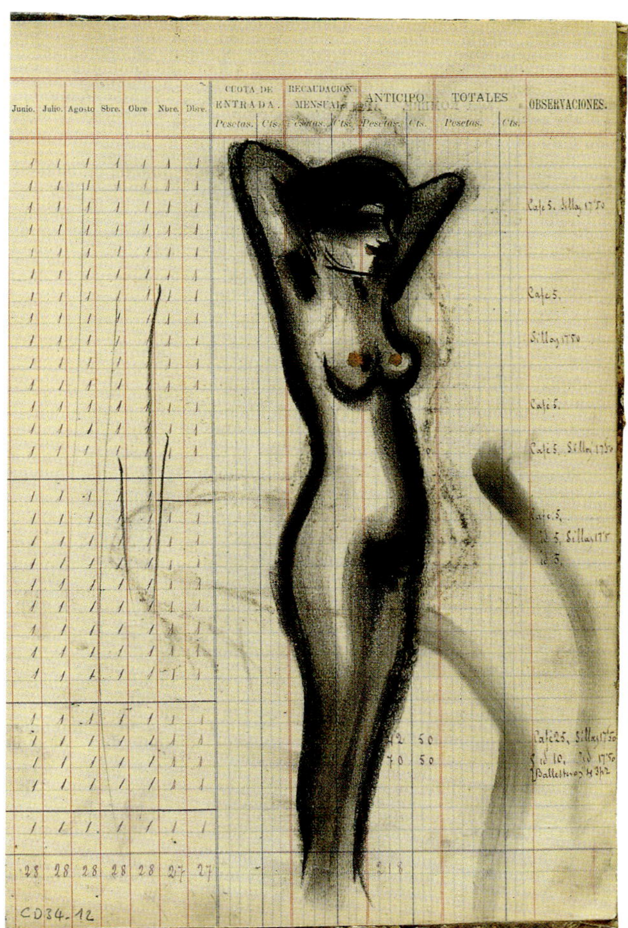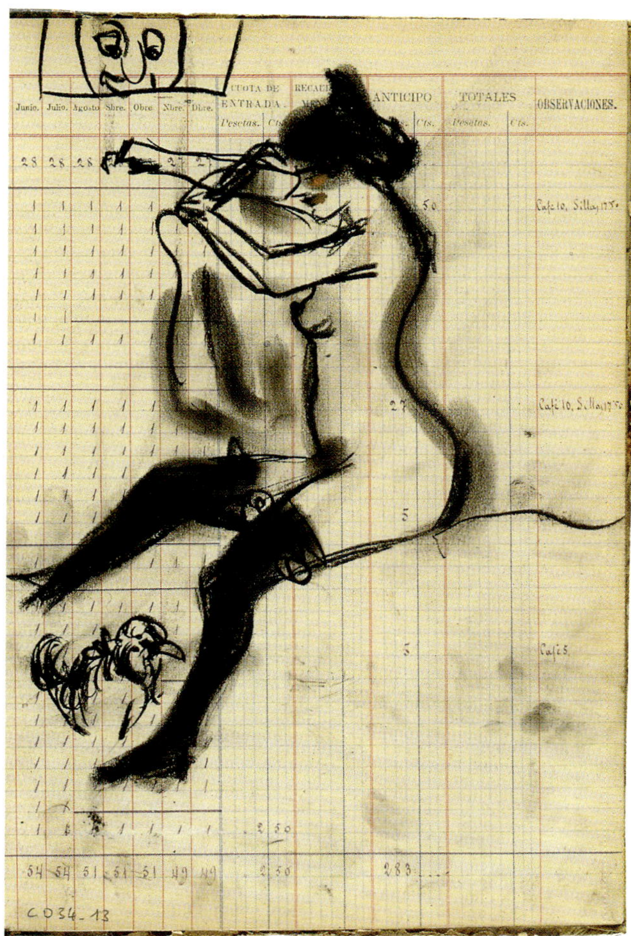

6 a and b Barcelona Sketchbook, Winter 1899–1900

Nude Standing with Arms Raised (f° 7 r°) and
Woman with Black Stockings Undressing (f° 8 r°)
Charcoal with oil highlights on paper; 31.5 x 22
Paris, Musée Picasso, MP 1990-93

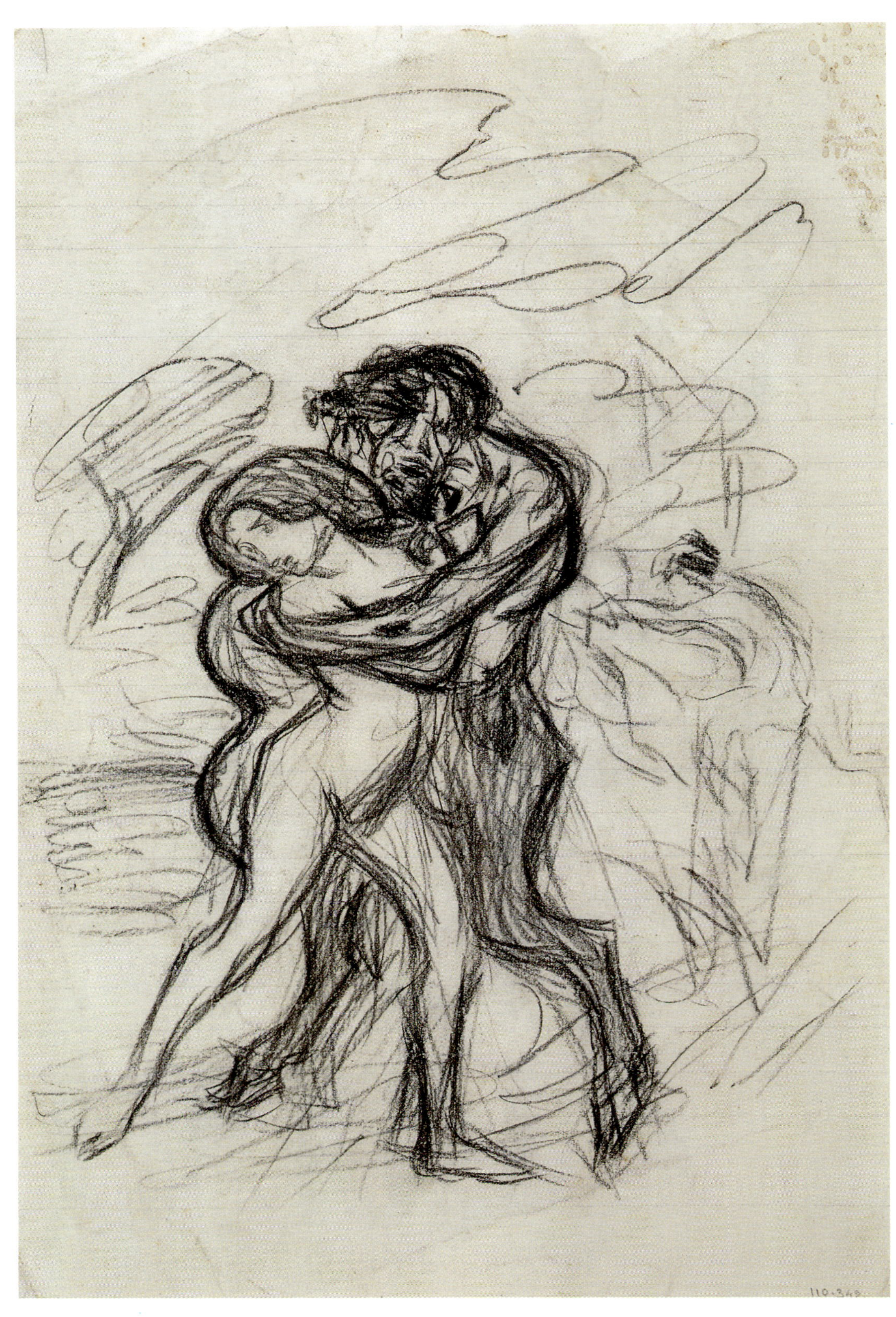

9 The Rape, circa 1900
Conté crayon on paper; 32 x 22.2
Barcelona, Museu Picasso, MPB 110.342 r°

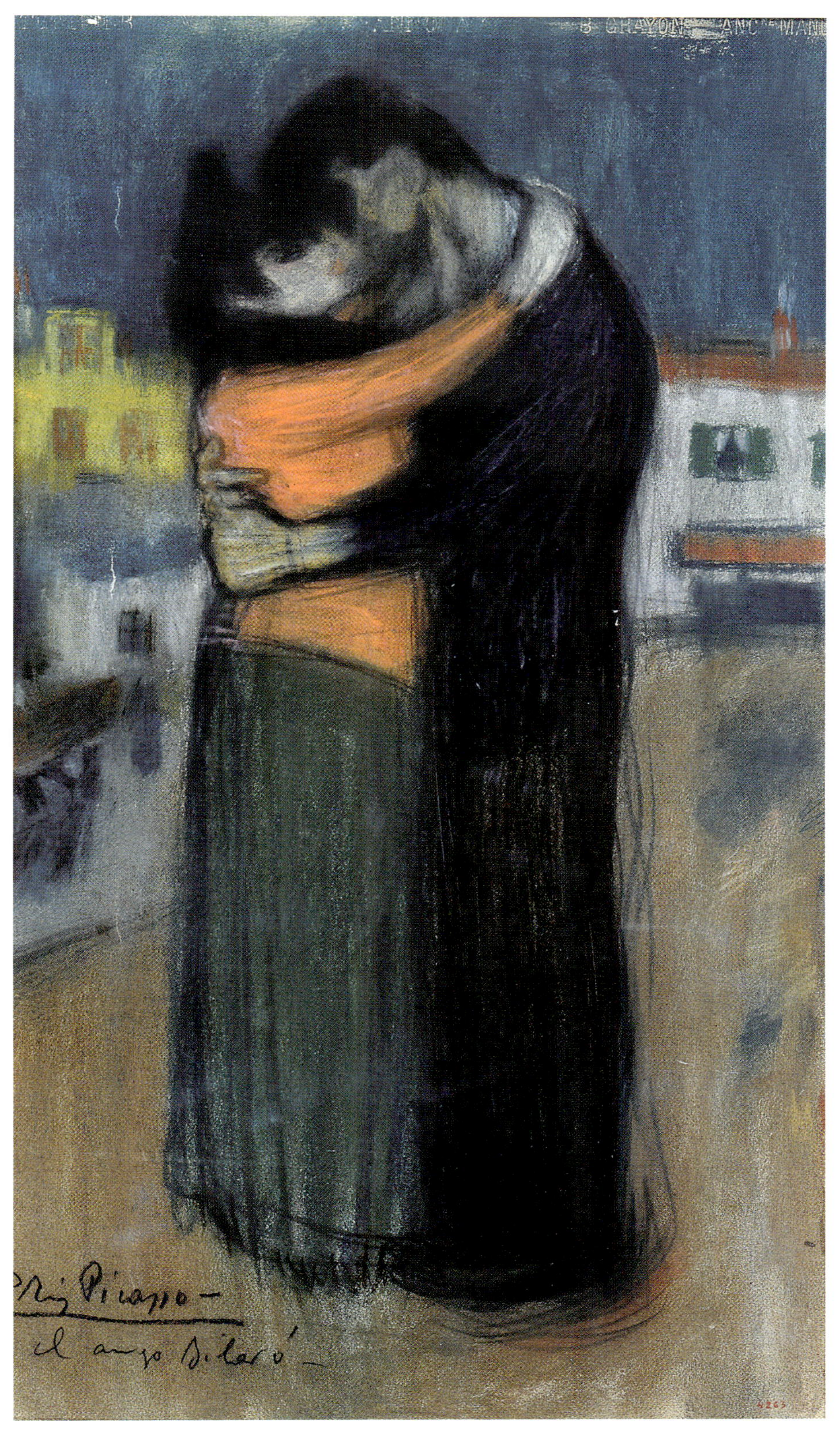

11 Embrace, 1900
Pastel on paper; 59 x 35
Barcelona, Museu Picasso, MPB 4.263 [PB]

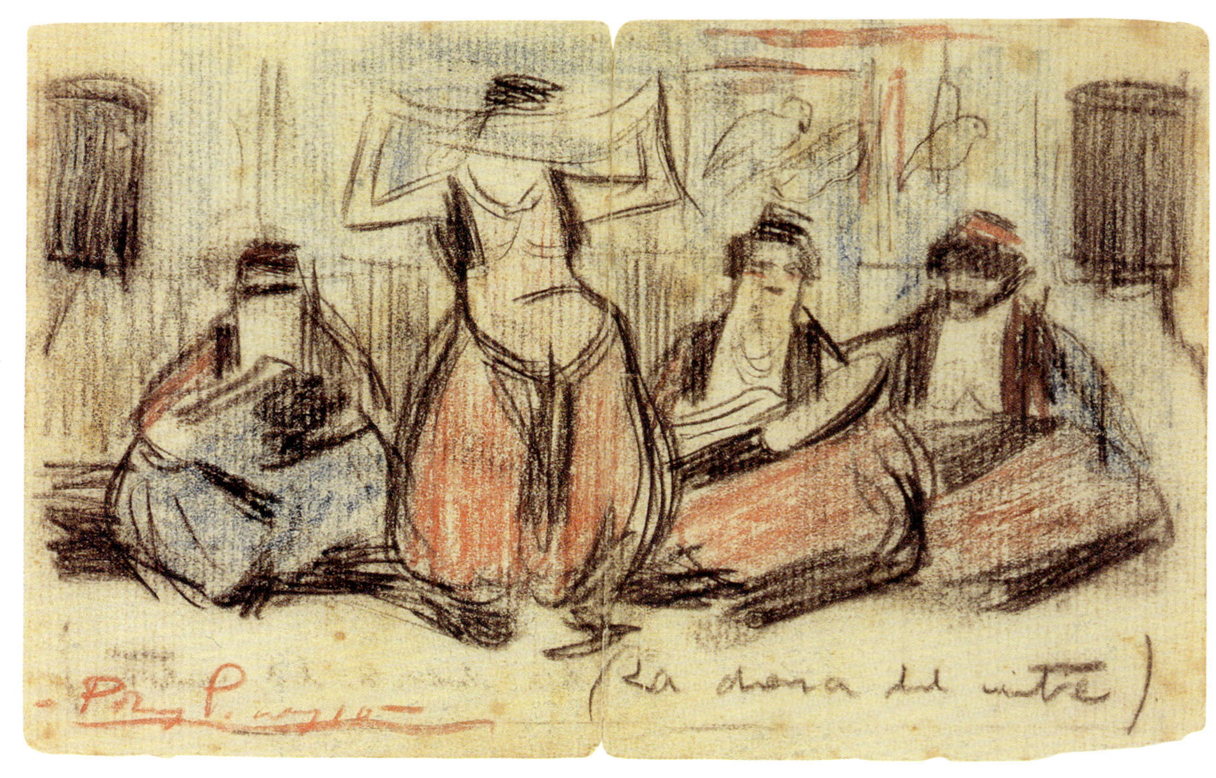

10 Belly Dance, 1900

Letter from Casagemas and Picasso to Cinto Reventós
Coloured pencil on paper; 10.8 x 17.4
Barcelona, Museu Picasso, MPB 113.026

13 La Celestina with a Couple, 1901

Graphite stick on paper; 33.1 x 24
Barcelona, Museu Picasso, MPB 110.356 [PB]

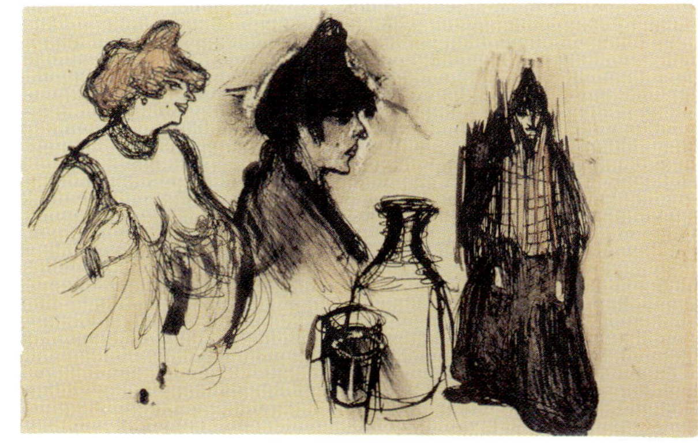

14 Three Busts of Women, 1901

India ink and coloured pencil on paper; 13 x 20.8
Barcelona, Museu Picasso, MPB 4.776 [PB]

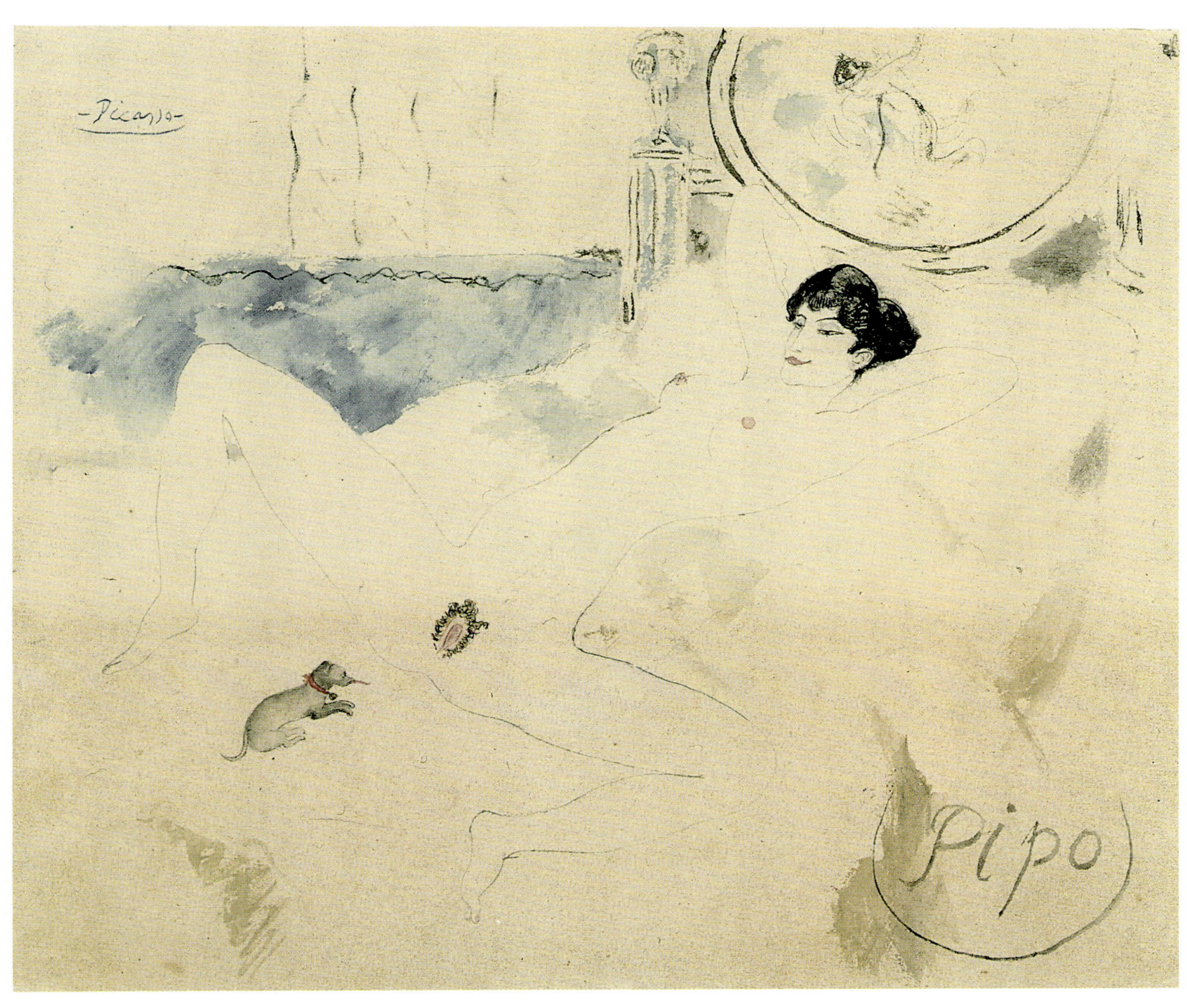

12 Pipo, 1901
   Ink, gold paint and watercolour on paper; 20.9 x 26
   London, Private collection, Courtesy James Roundell [P]

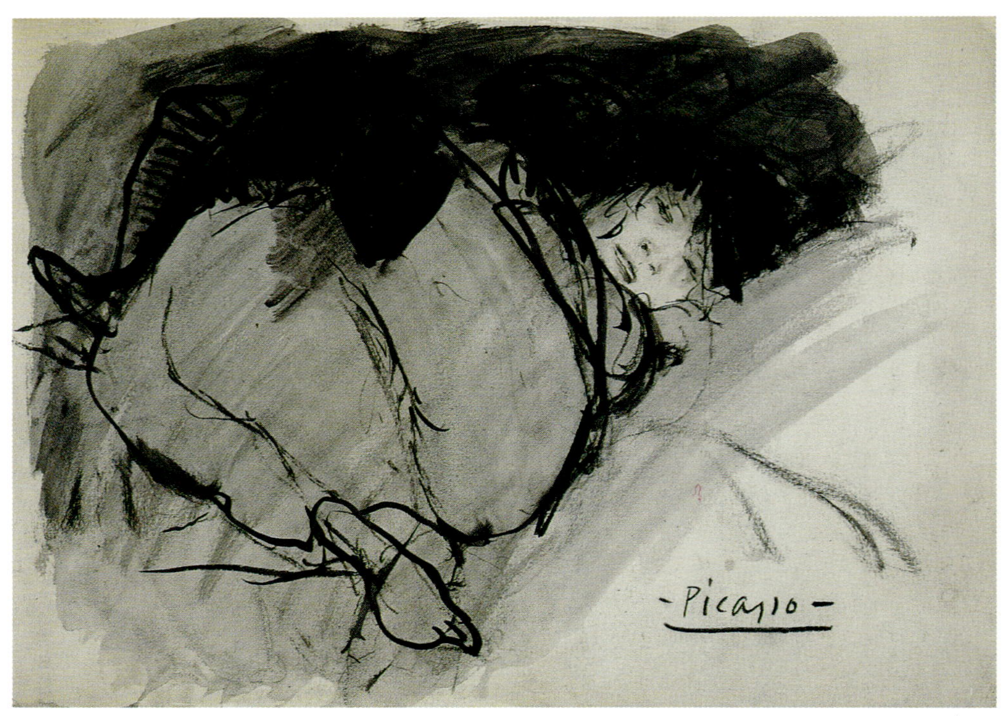

15 Entwined Couple, 1901
India ink and coloured wash on paper; 25.5 x 36.4
Paris, Musée Picasso, MP 437 [PB]

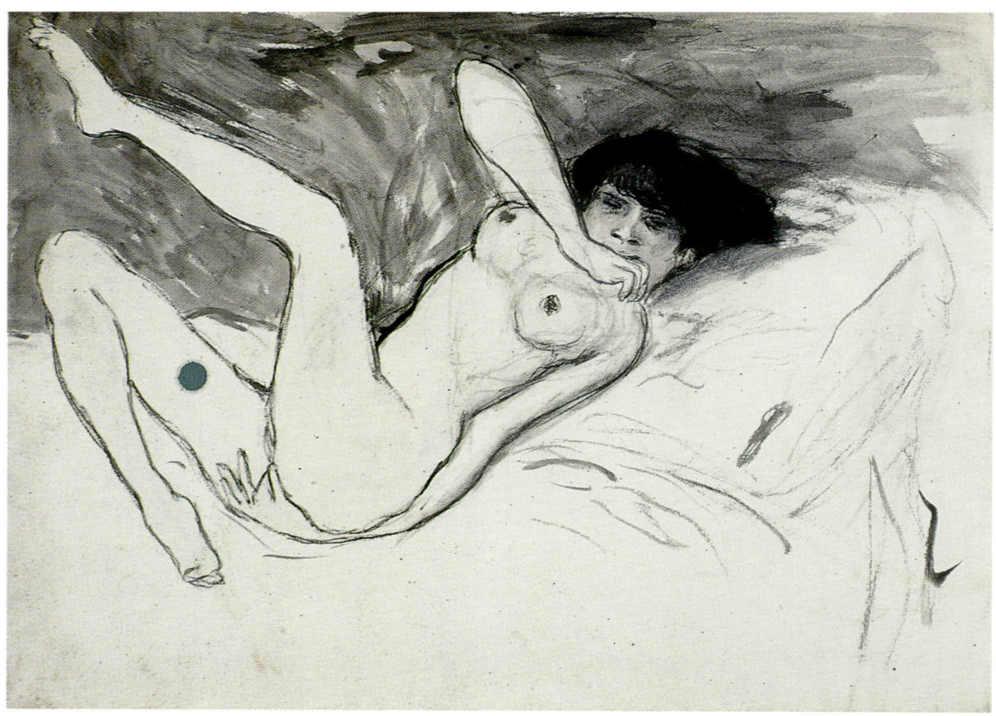

16 Reclining Nude, 1901
Gouache on paper; 25.5 x 36
Paris, Private collection

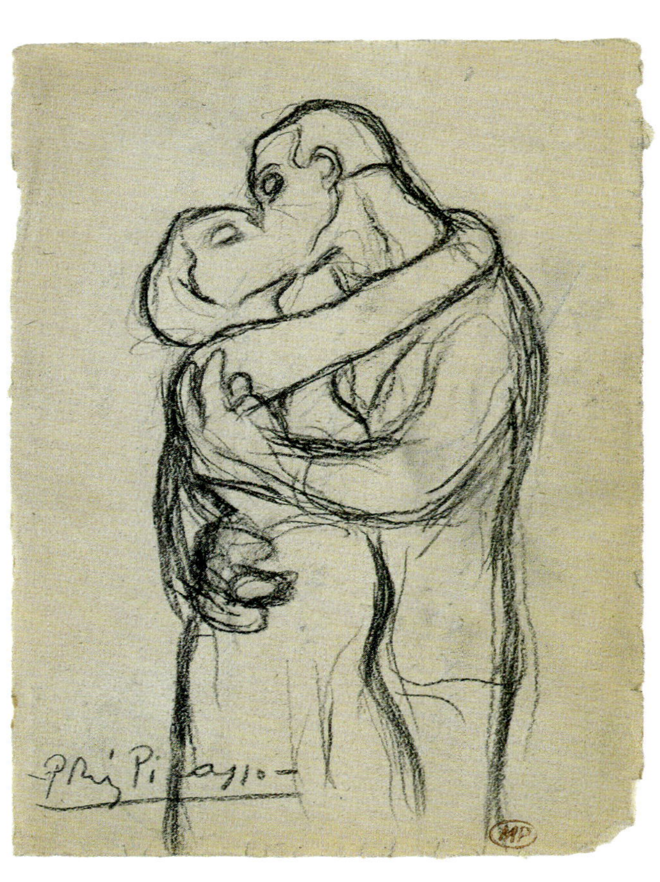

17 Embrace, Spring 1901
  Black crayon on the inside of an
  envelope mailed from Barcelona on
  19 March 1901; 14.1 x 11
  Paris, Musée Picasso, MP 433

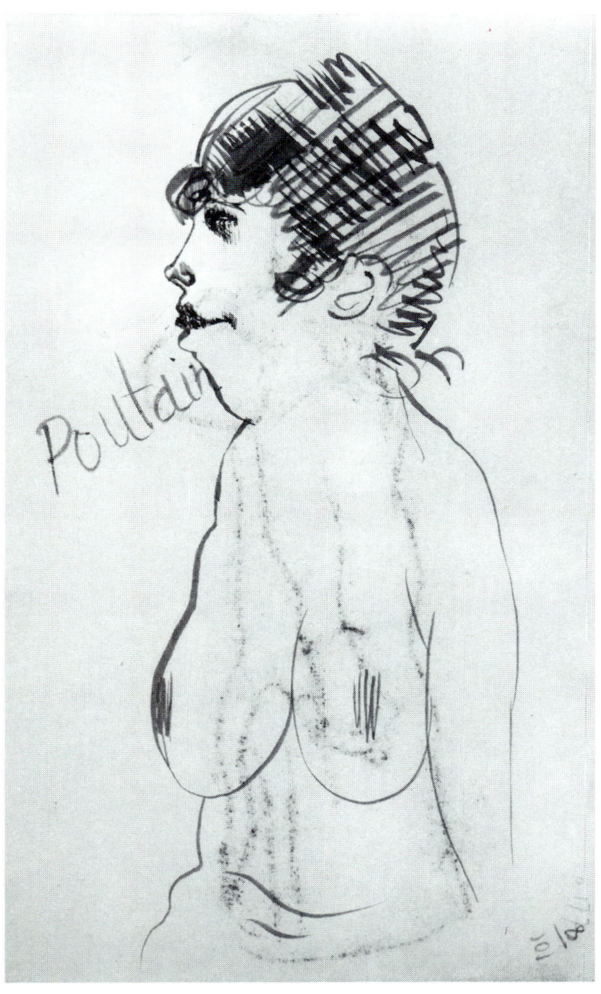

18 Paris Sketchbook, Spring 1901
  Portrait of a Prostitute (f° 8 v°)
  Oil stick and ink wash on paper; 19.6 x 12
  Paris, Musée Picasso, MP 1854

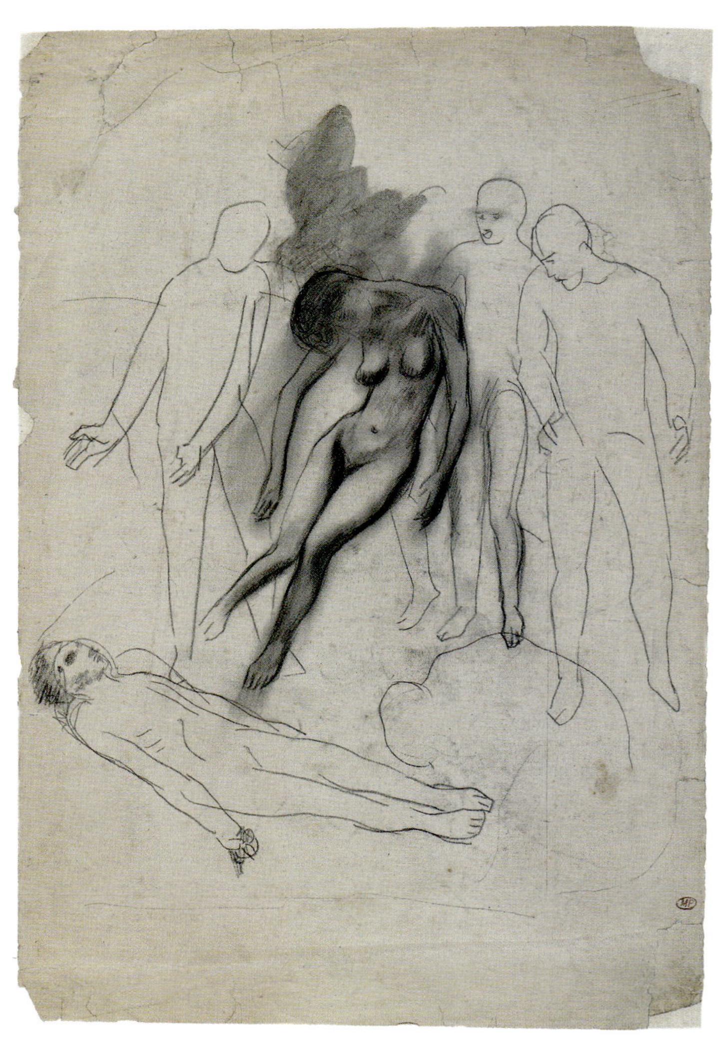

19 Study for *Evocation*, Spring-summer 1901

Black chalk on the reverse of a reproduction of
Regreso de la fiesta di Napoli (1885); 41.6 x 29
Paris, Musée Picasso, MP 442

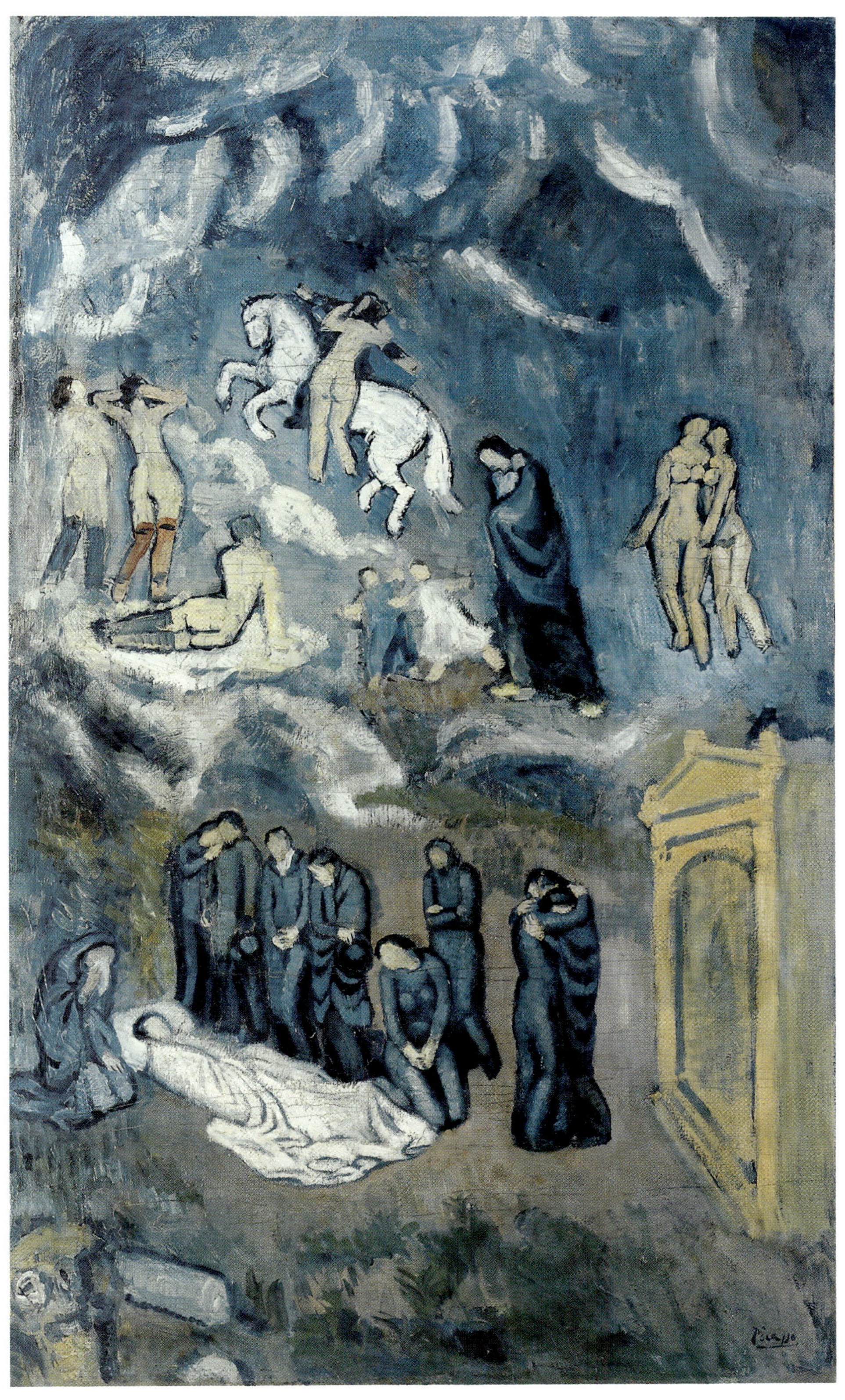

20 Evocation (The Burial of Casagemas), Summer 1901

Oil on canvas; 150 x 90

Paris, Musée d'Art moderne de la Ville de Paris [P]

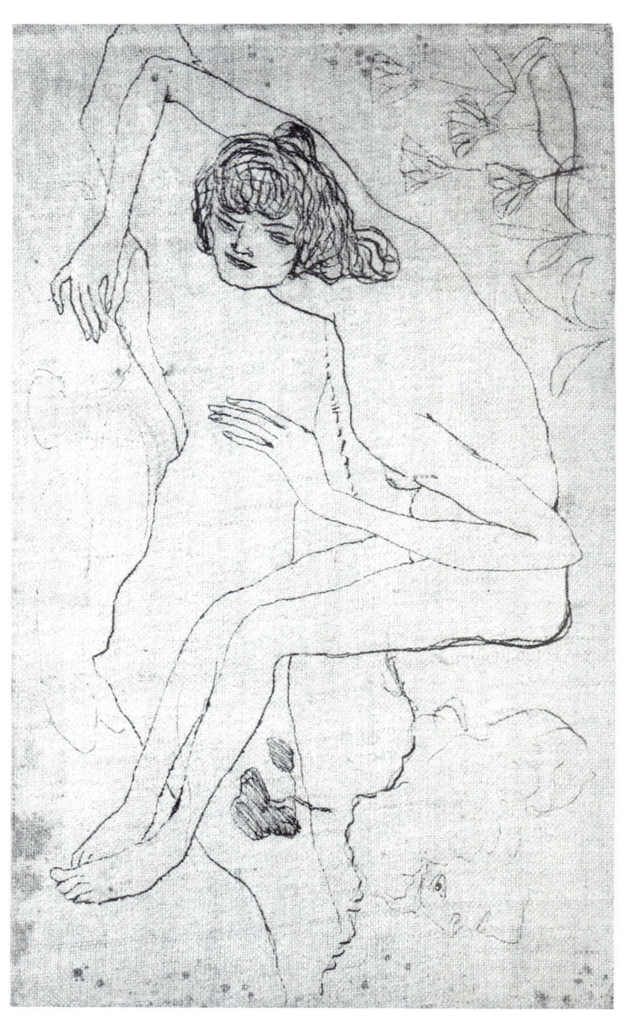

21 Paris Sketchbook, Fall 1901

Seated Nude and Profile of Woman in a Landscape
(outside back cover)
Pen and black ink on cardboard; 21 x 13
Paris, Musée Picasso, MP 1990-94

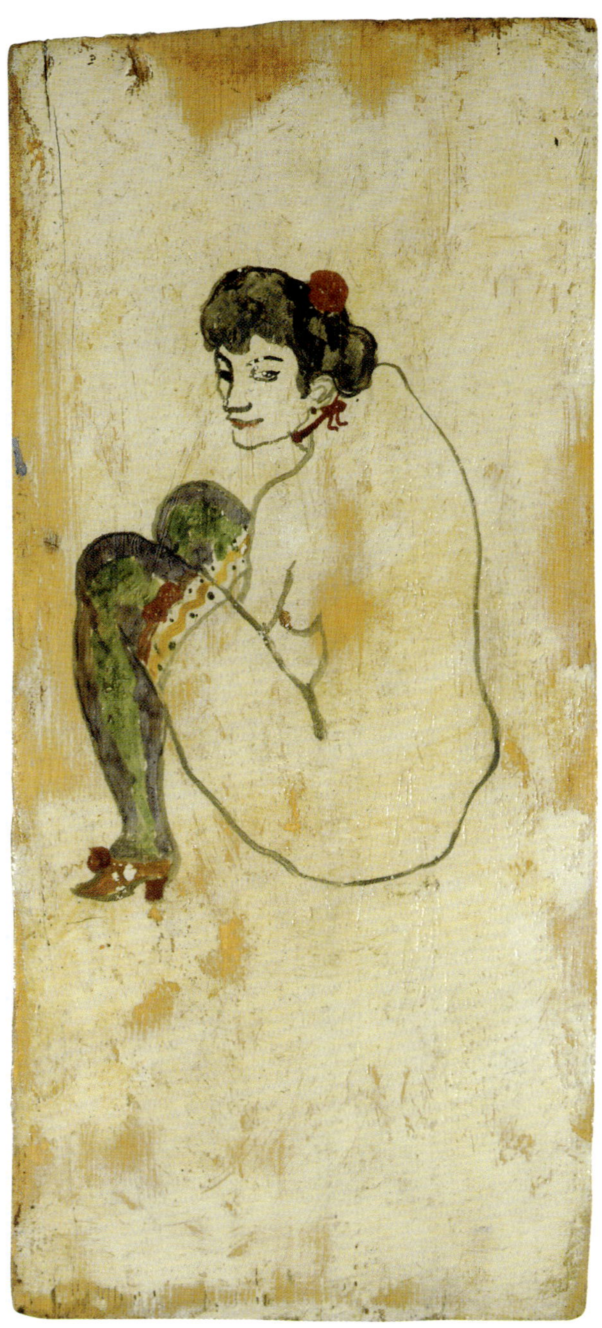

22 The Green Stockings, circa 1902

Oil on panel; 27.2 x 12.5
Barcelona, Museu Picasso, MPB 110.036

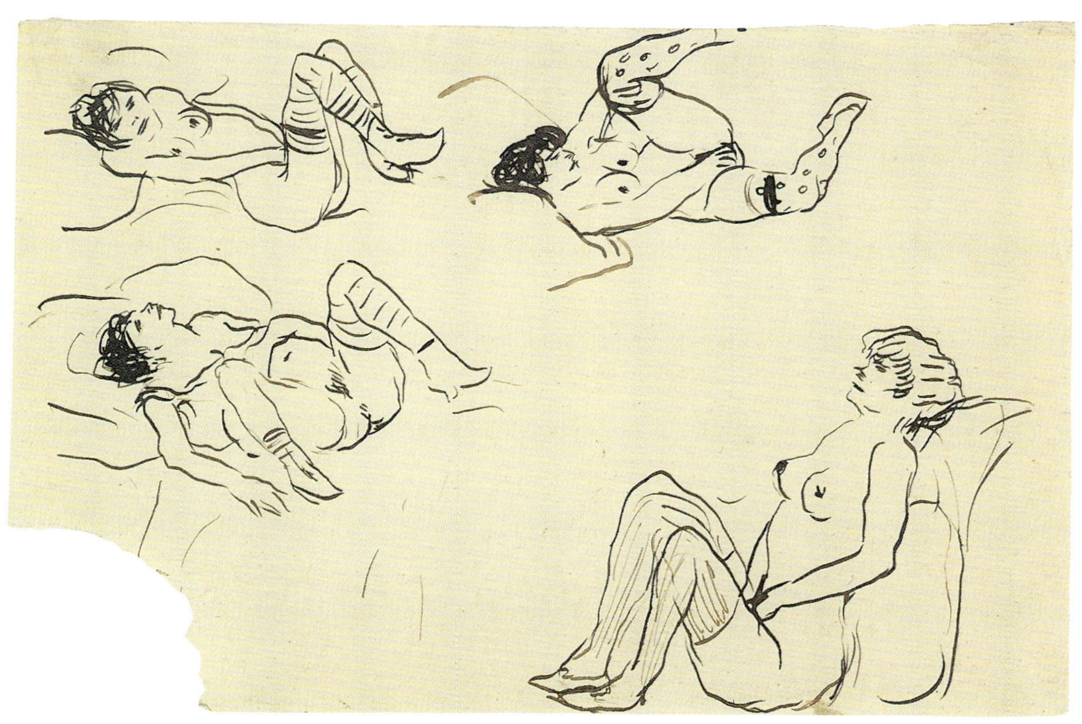

23 Women with Striped Socks, 1902
India ink on paper; 20 x 31
Paris, Private collection

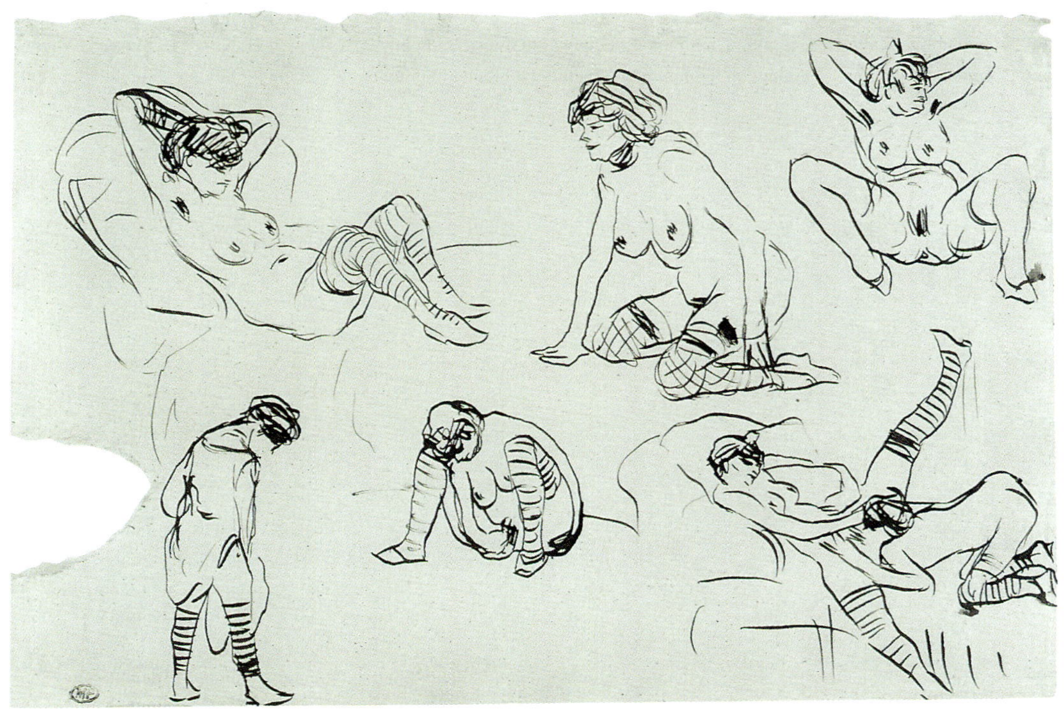

23 a Erotic Scenes, 1902
India ink on paper; 20 x 31.1
Paris, Musée Picasso, MP 452 [PM]

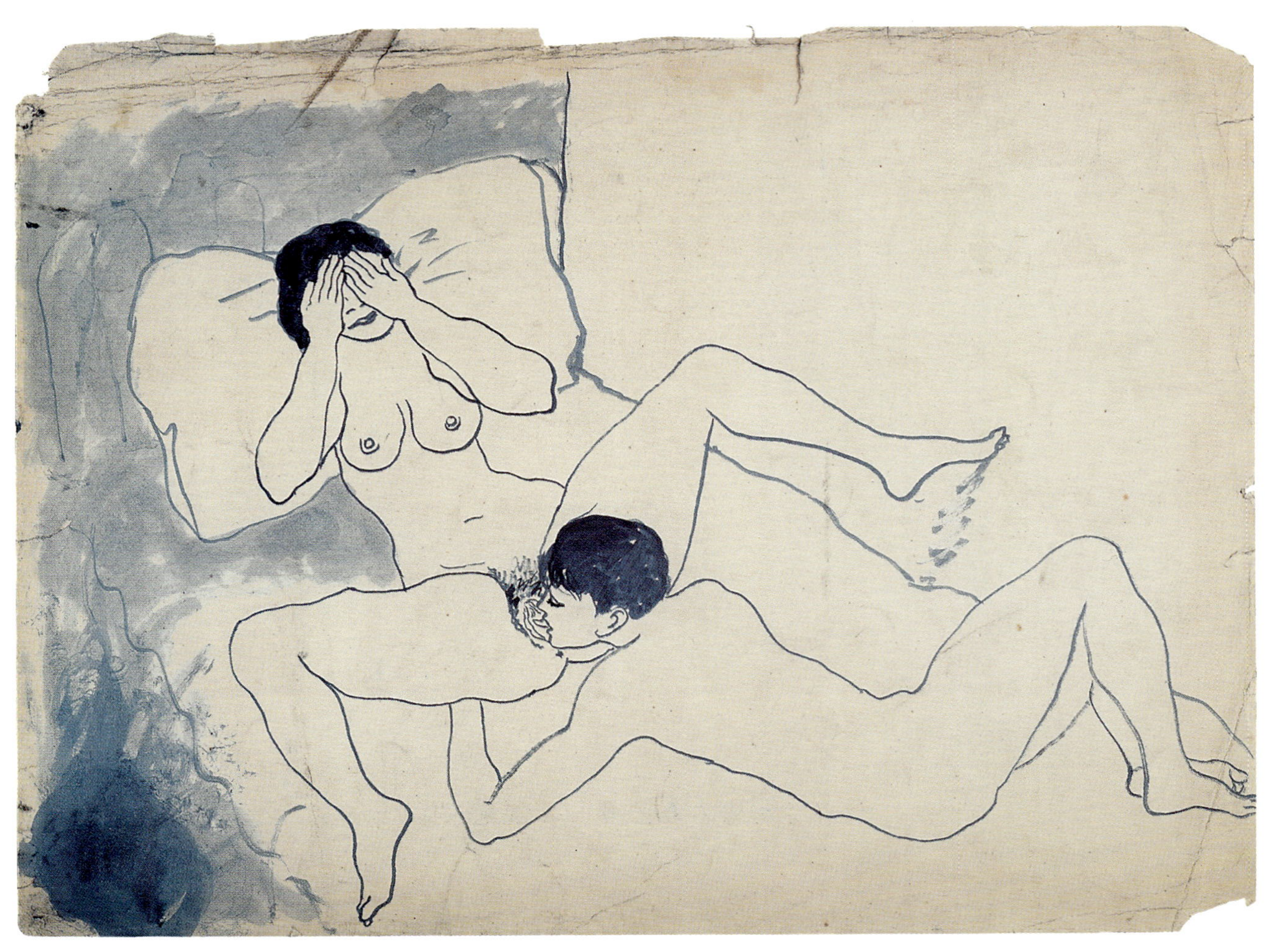

24 Erotic Scene, 1902

Ink and watercolour on paper; 32 x 44
Paris, Private collection

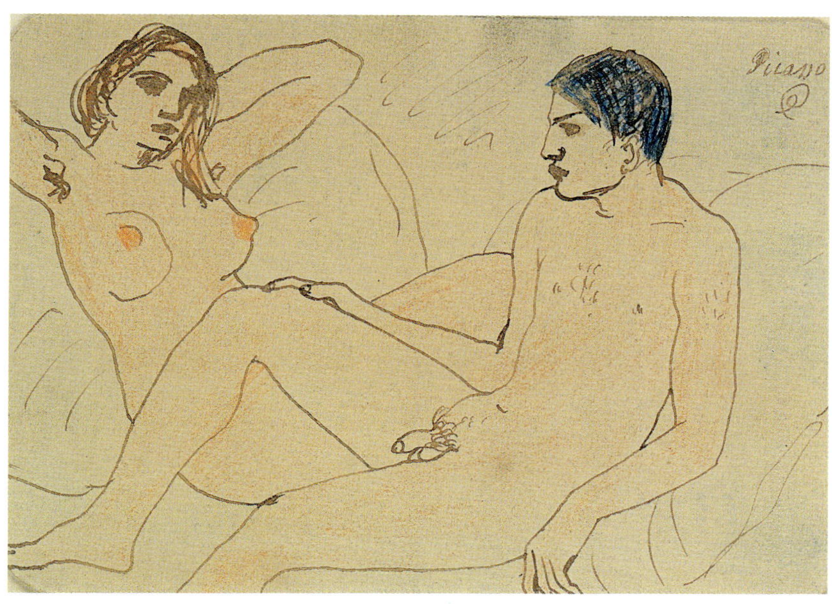

25 Self-Portrait with Nude, 1902

Coloured grease pencil, pencil and brown ink on trade card; 9 x 13.3
Private collection

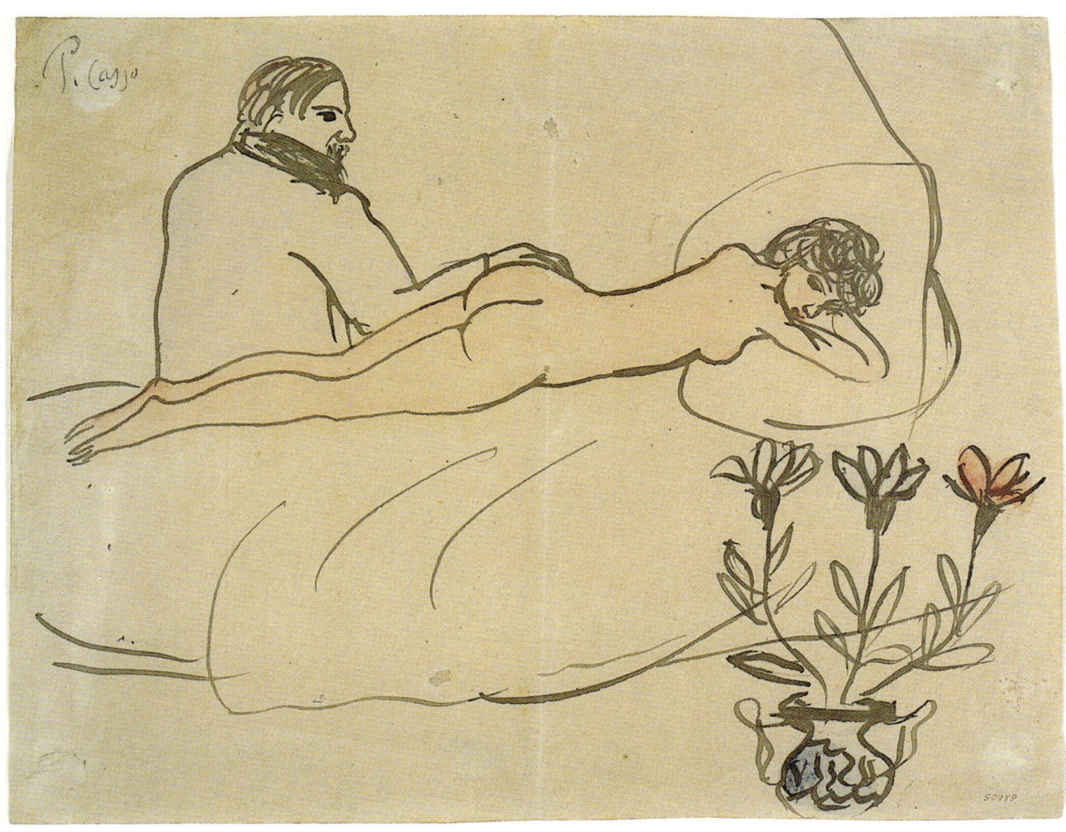

26 Reclining Nude, with Picasso at Her Feet, 1902–1903

Ink and watercolour on paper; 17.6 x 23.2
Barcelona, Museu Picasso, MPB 50.489

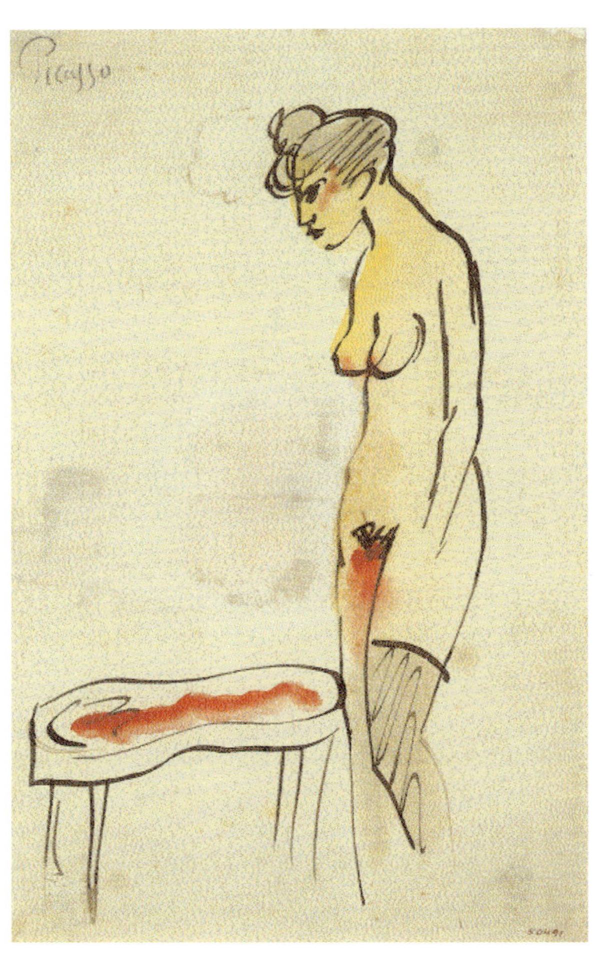

27 Woman at a Bidet, 1902–1903
    Pen and watercolour on paper; 19.8 x 13
    Barcelona, Museu Picasso, MPB 50.491

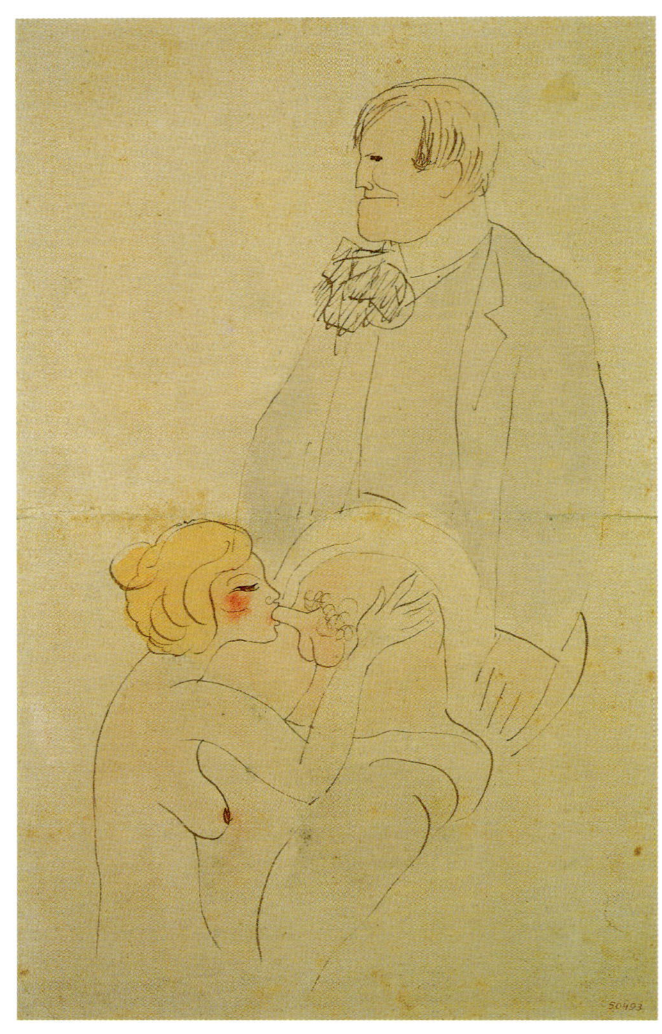

29 Isidro Nonell and a Female Figure, 1902–1903
    Ink and watercolour on paper; 24.8 x 16
    Barcelona, Museu Picasso, MPB 50.493

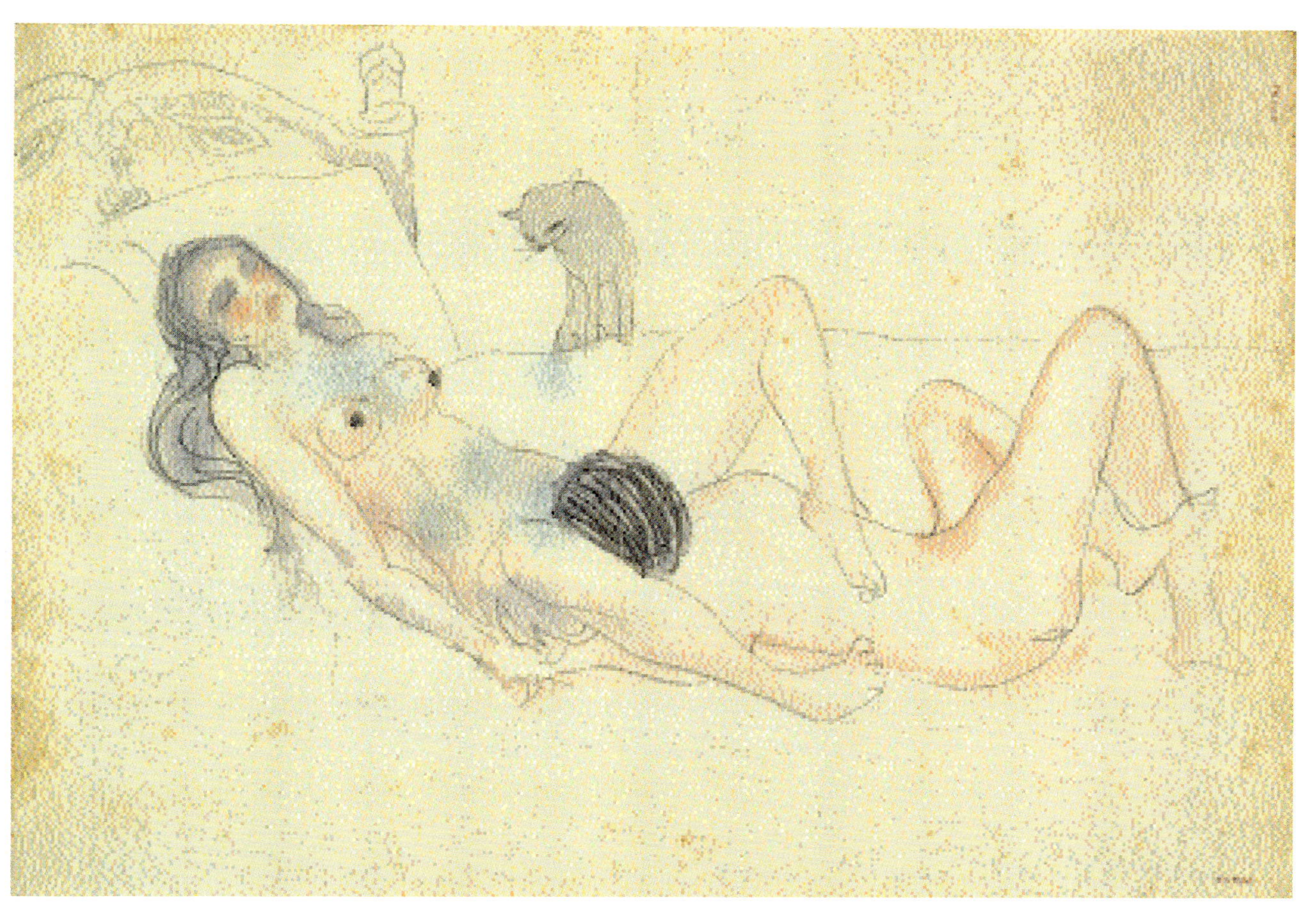

28 Two Figures and a Cat, 1902–1903

Pencil, watercolour and coloured pencil on paper; 18 x 26.5
Barcelona, Museu Picasso, MPB 50.492

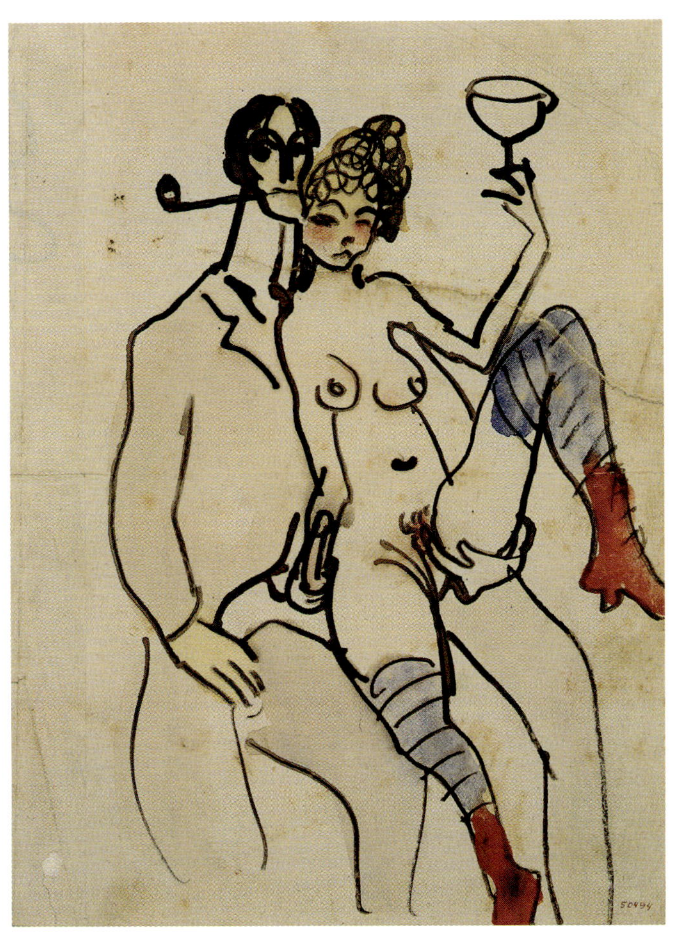

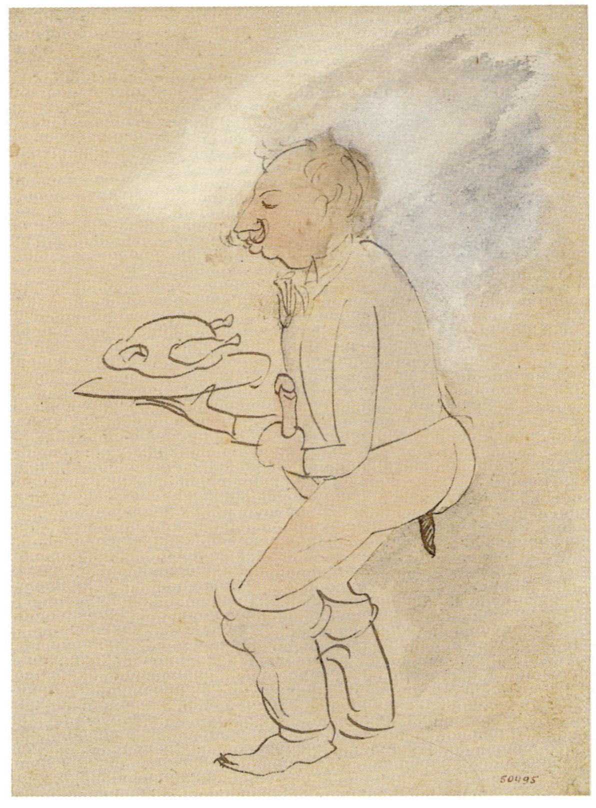

30 Ángel Fernández de Soto with a Woman, 1902–1903
Ink and watercolour on paper; 21 x 15.2
Barcelona, Museu Picasso, MPB 50.494

31 The Painter Joan Ossó, 1902–1903
Ink and watercolour on paper; 16.4 x 12
Barcelona, Museu Picasso, MPB 50.495 [MB]

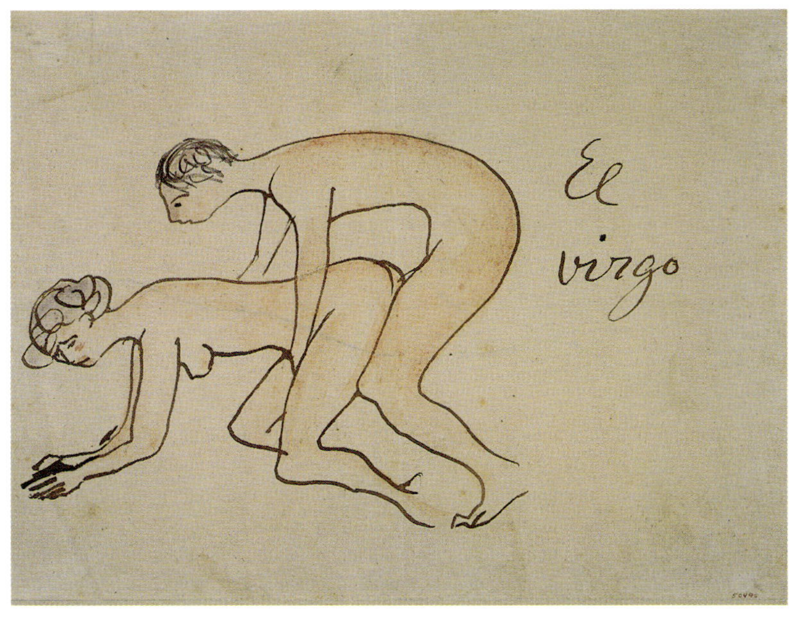

32 The Virgin (El Virgo), 1902–1903
Ink and watercolour on paper; 17.8 x 23.8
Barcelona, Museu Picasso, MPB 50.496

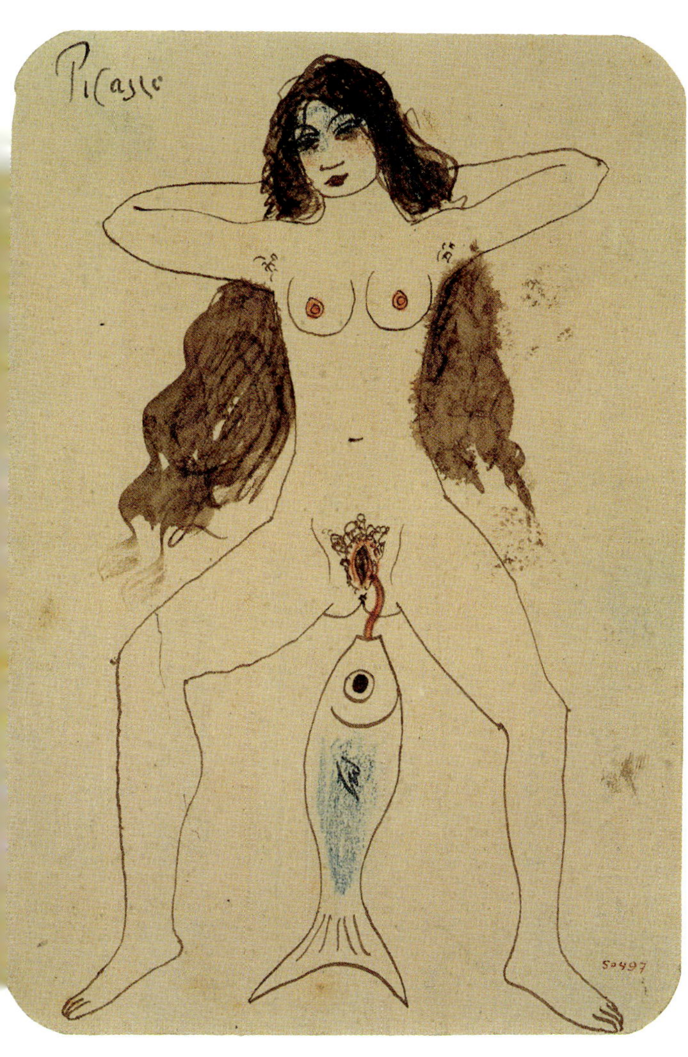

33 The Mackerel (Allegorical Composition), 1902–1903

Ink and coloured pencil on a postcard; 13.9 x 9
Barcelona, Museu Picasso, MPB 50.497

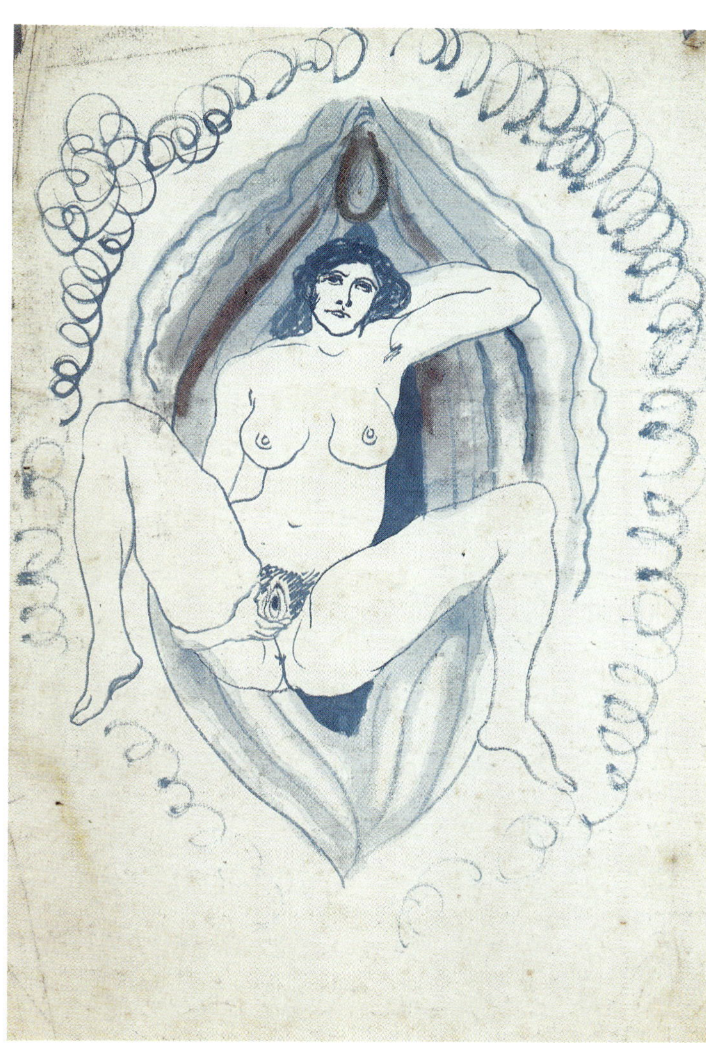

33 a Vaginal Environment, 1902–1903

Ink and watercolour on paper; 23 x 16
Private collection [B]

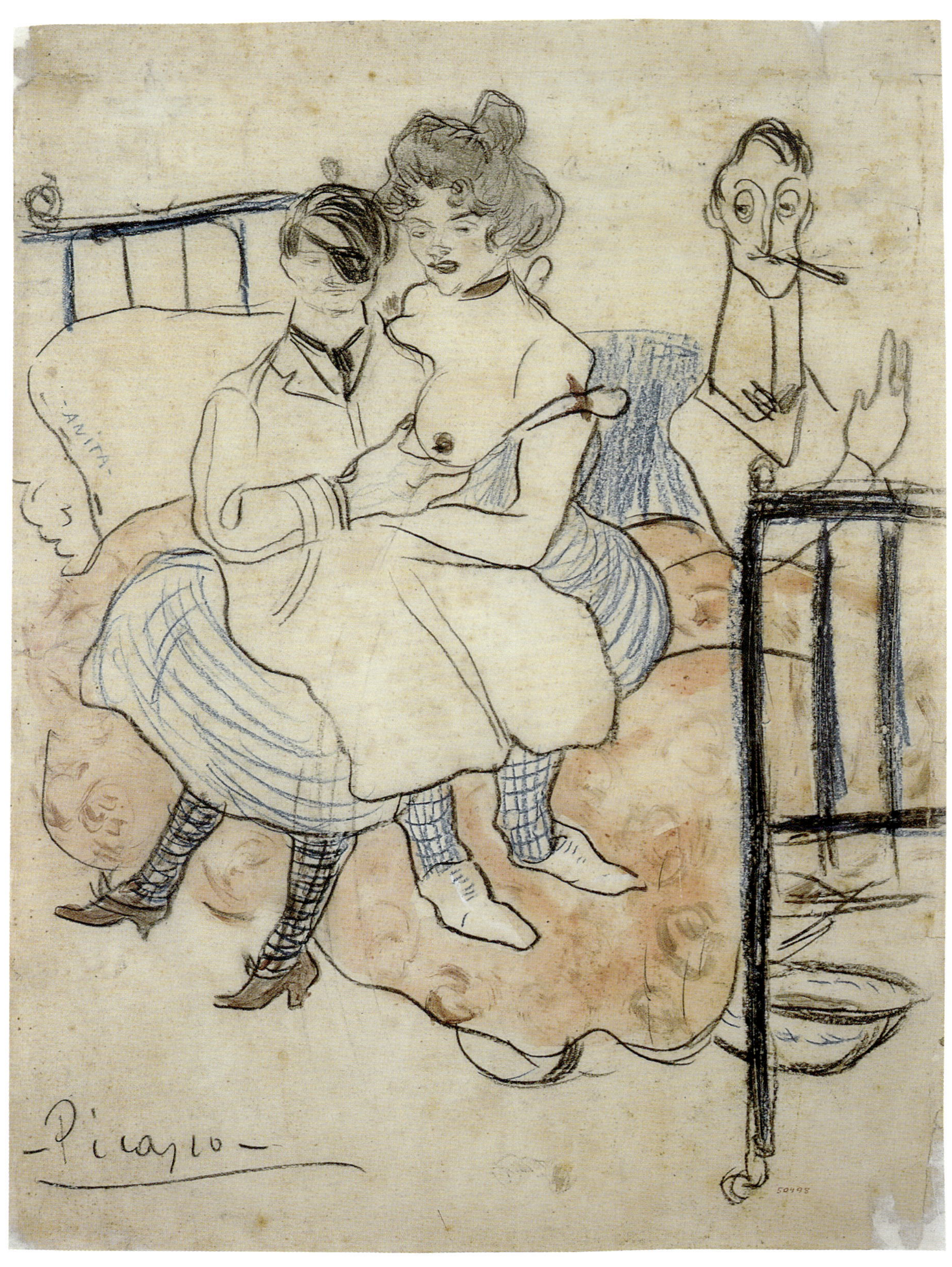

34 The Brothers Mateu and Ángel Fernández de Soto, with Anita, 1902–1903
Conté crayon, coloured pencil and watercolour on paper; 31 x 23.7
Barcelona, Museu Picasso, MPB 50.498

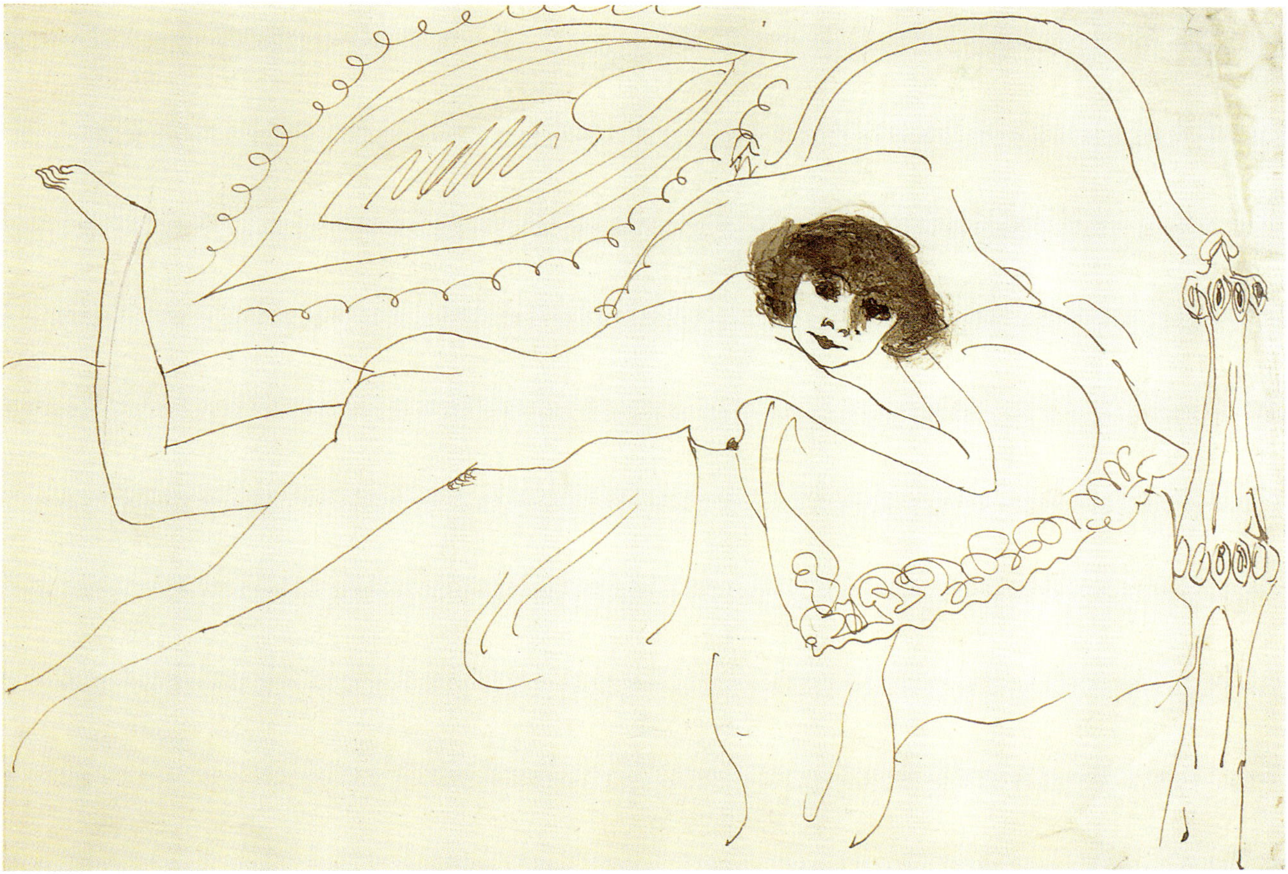

35 Nude on a Bed, Face-On, 1902–1903
Pen on paper; 23.1 x 33.8
Barcelona, Museu Picasso, MPB 110.534 [PB]

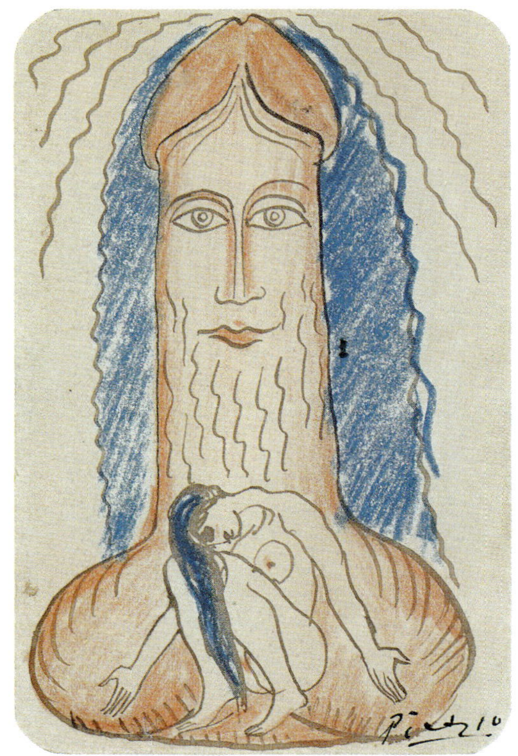

36 The Phallus, circa 1903
Ink and coloured wax crayon on paper; 13 x 9
Cologne, Private collection, Courtesy Galerie
Gmurzynska

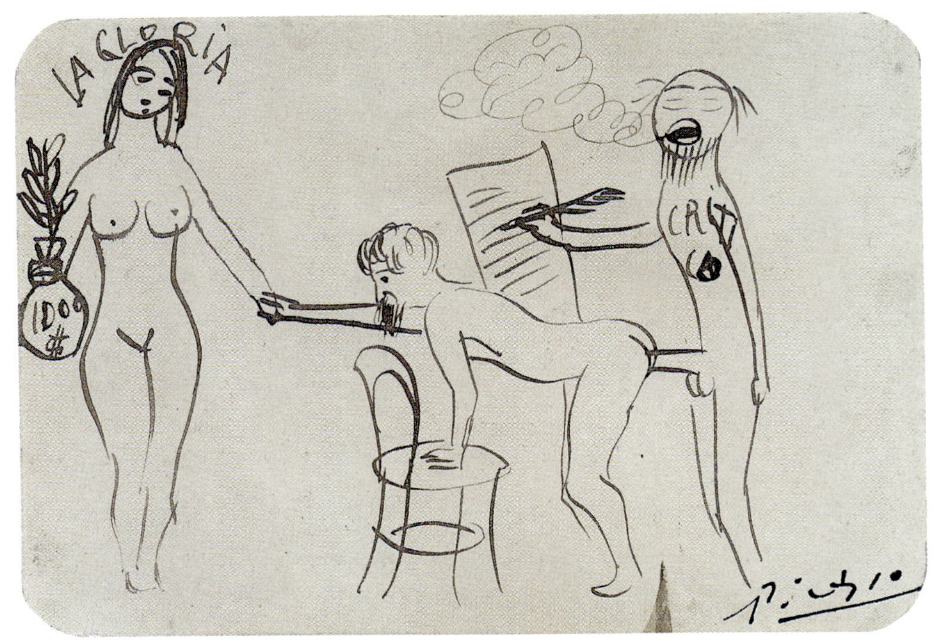

37 La Gloria-Criti, circa 1903
Brown ink on paper; 9 x 13.5
Cologne, Private collection,
Courtesy Galerie Gmurzynska

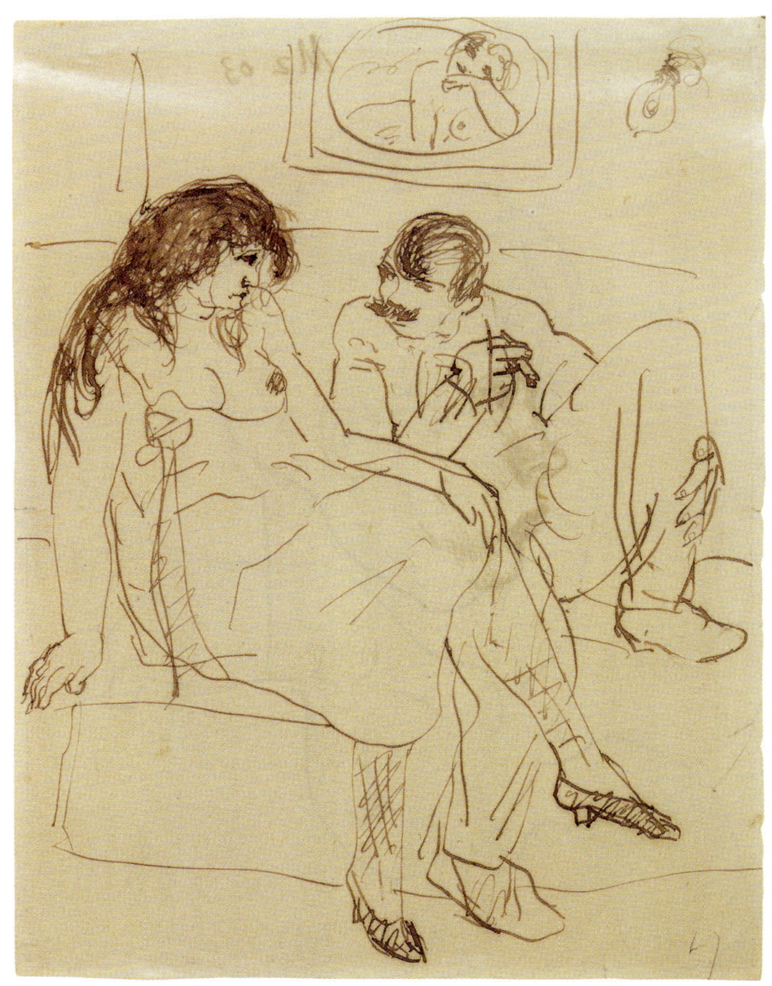

38 The Couple, 1903
Pen on paper; 23 x 18
Barcelona, Museu Picasso, MPB 110.499 [PB]

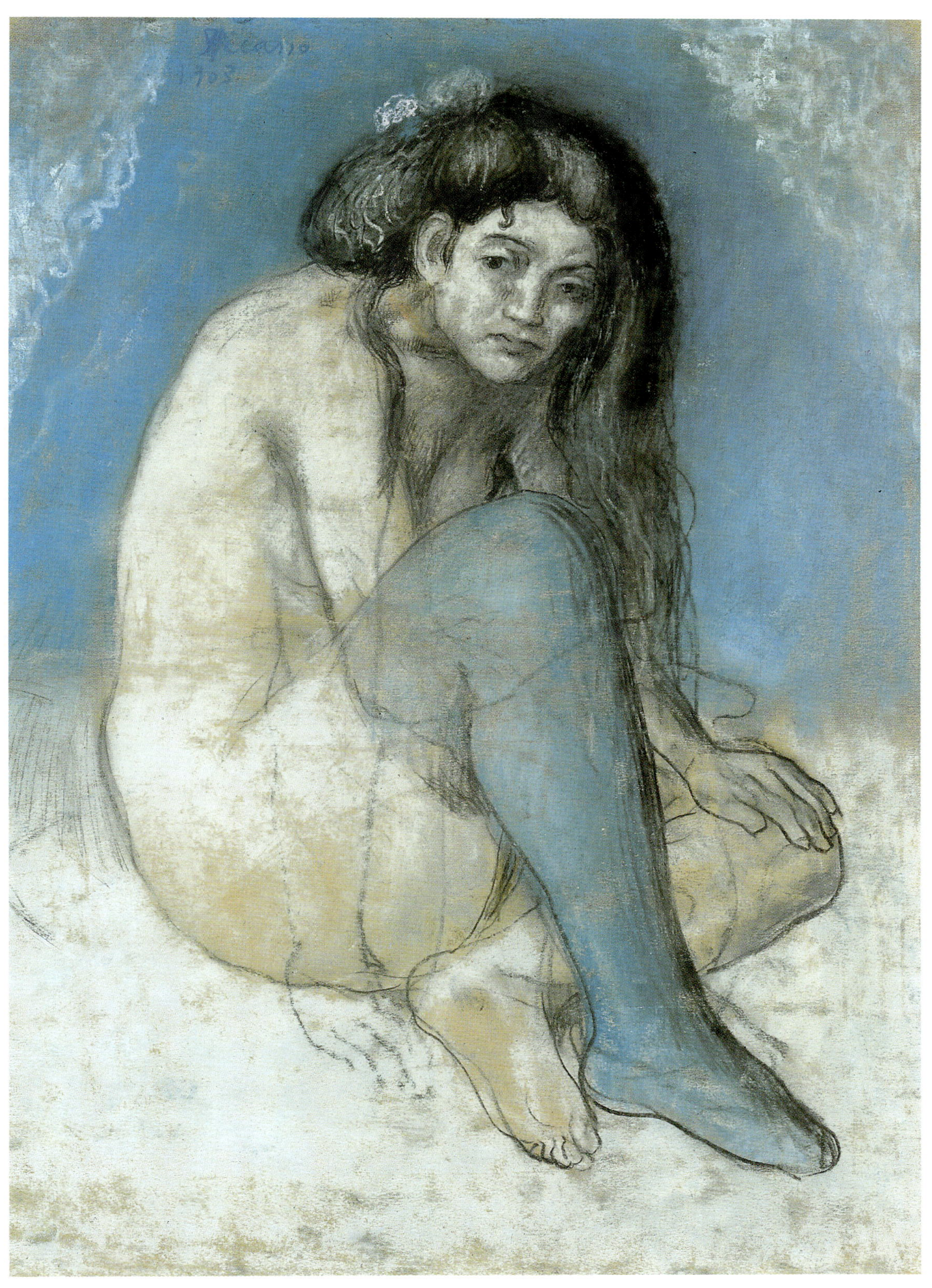

39 Nude with Legs Crossed, 1903
Pastel on paper mounted on canvas; 57 x 43
Martigny, Fondation Socindec, Courtesy Fondation Pierre Gianadda [P]

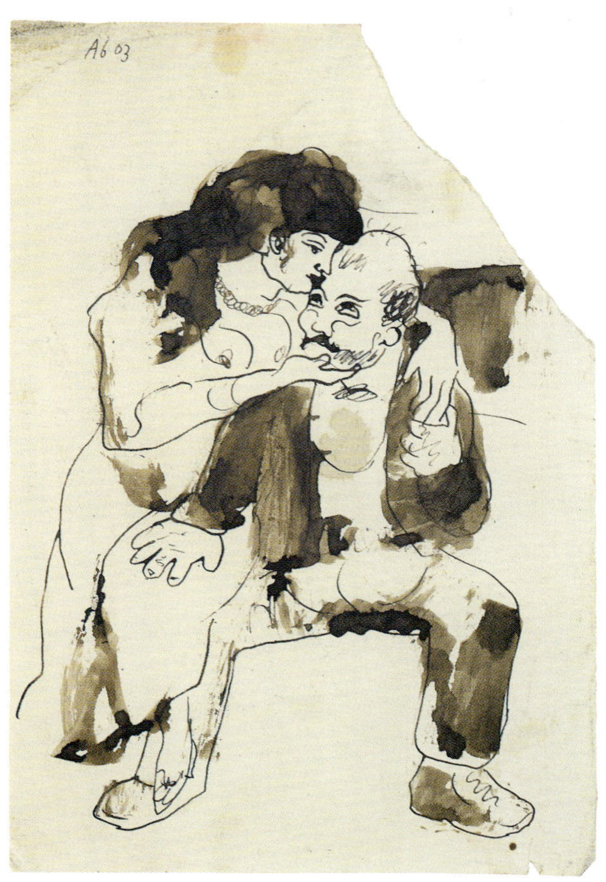

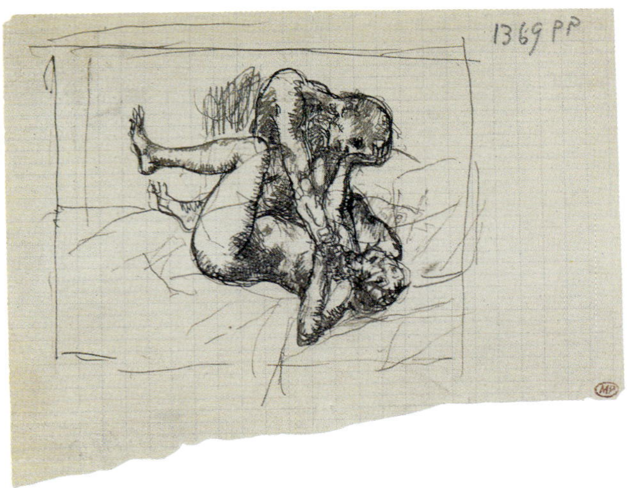

42 **The Woman Strangled**, circa 1904
Pen and brown ink on quadrille paper; 16 x 21
Paris, Musée Picasso, MP 462

41 **The Prostitute and Her Client**, April 1903
India ink on paper; 31.5 x 22
Paris, Private collection

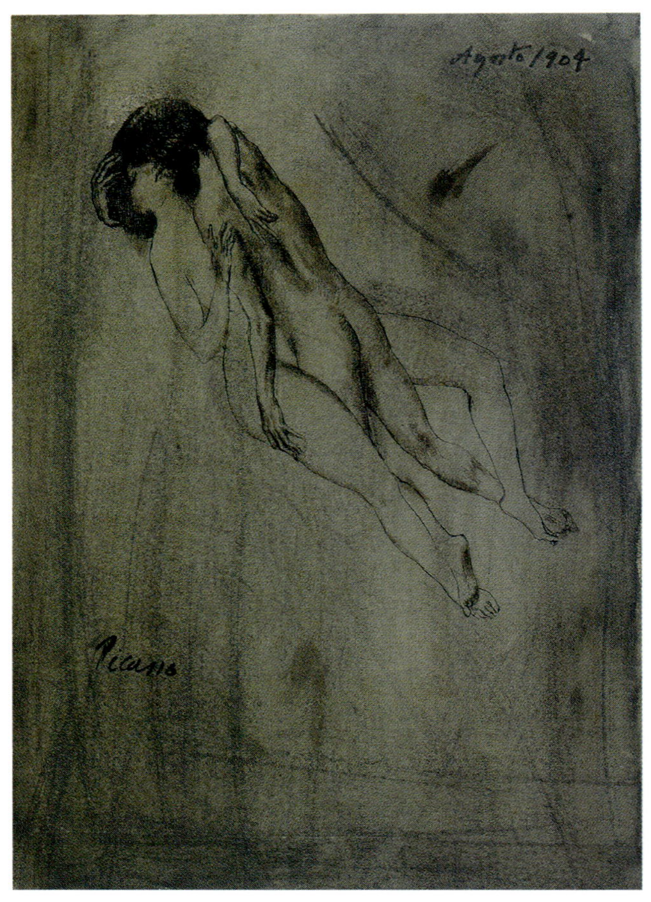

43 **The Lovers**, August 1904
Ink, watercolour and charcoal on paper; 37.2 x 26.9
Paris, Musée Picasso, MP 483

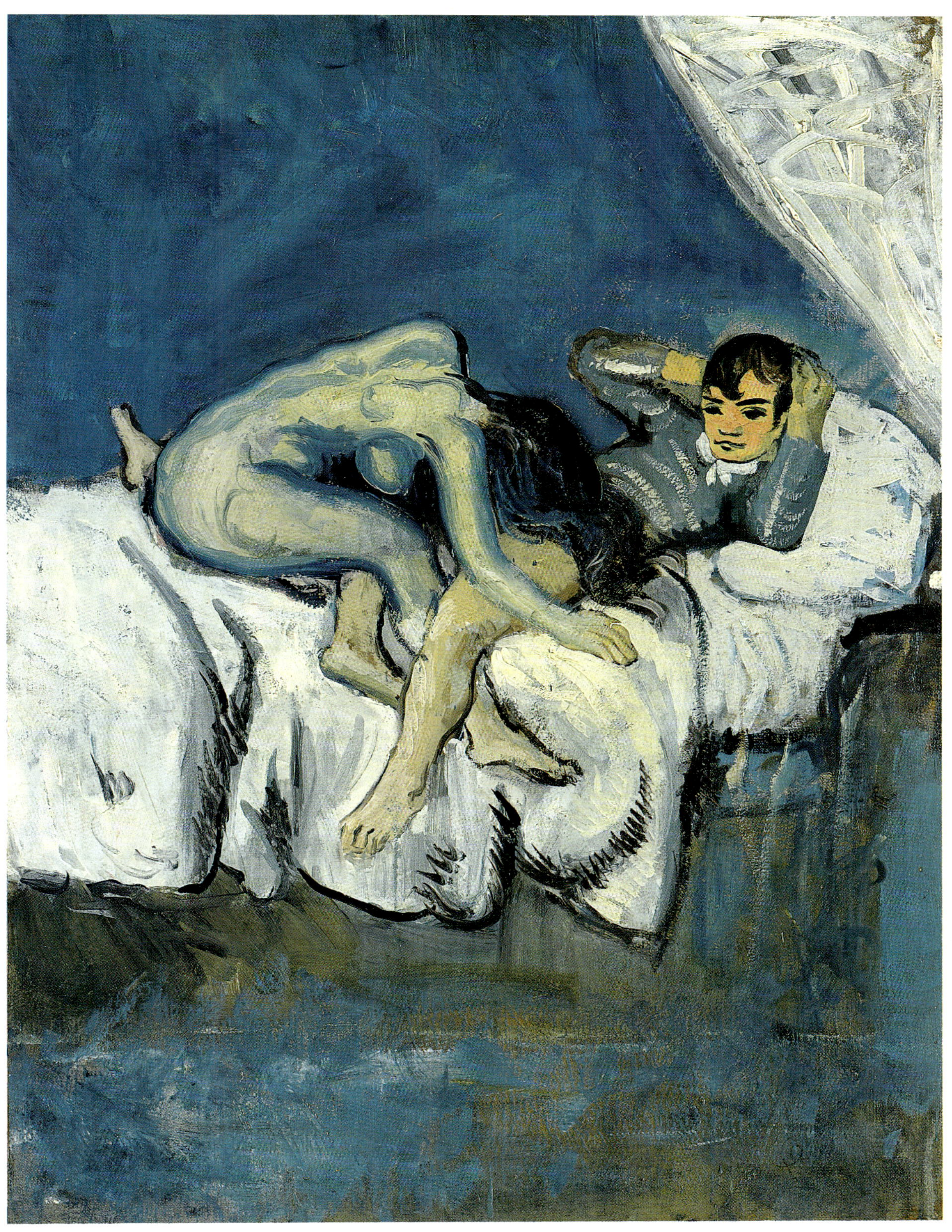

40 Portrait of the Artist Making Love, 1903

Oil on canvas; 53.3 x 37.3
New York, The Metropolitan Museum of Art, Bequest of Scofield Thayer, 1984 [PM]

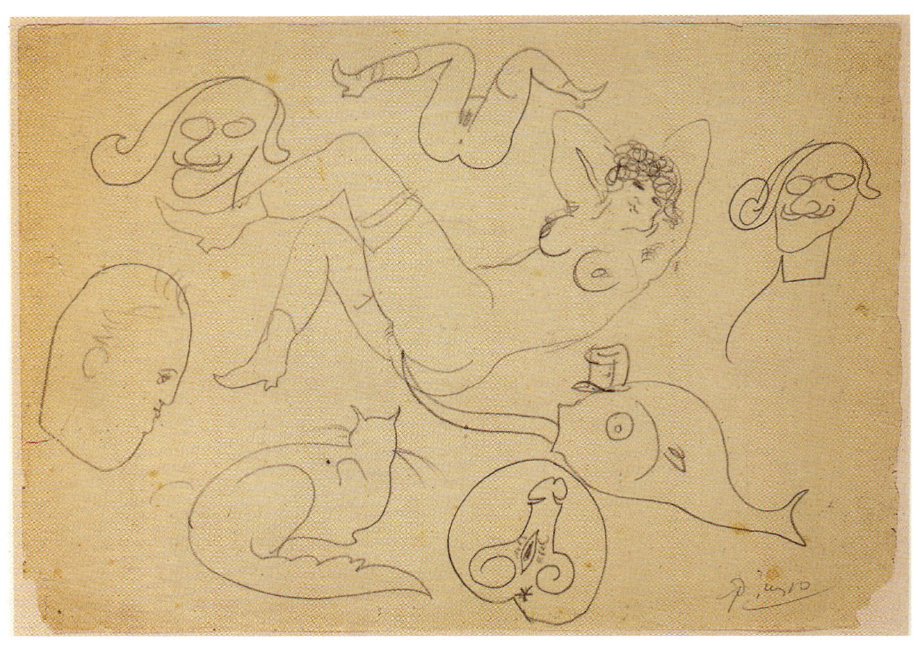

45 Woman Tickled by a Fish, circa 1905
Pencil on paper; 17 x 24.5
Paris, Private collection

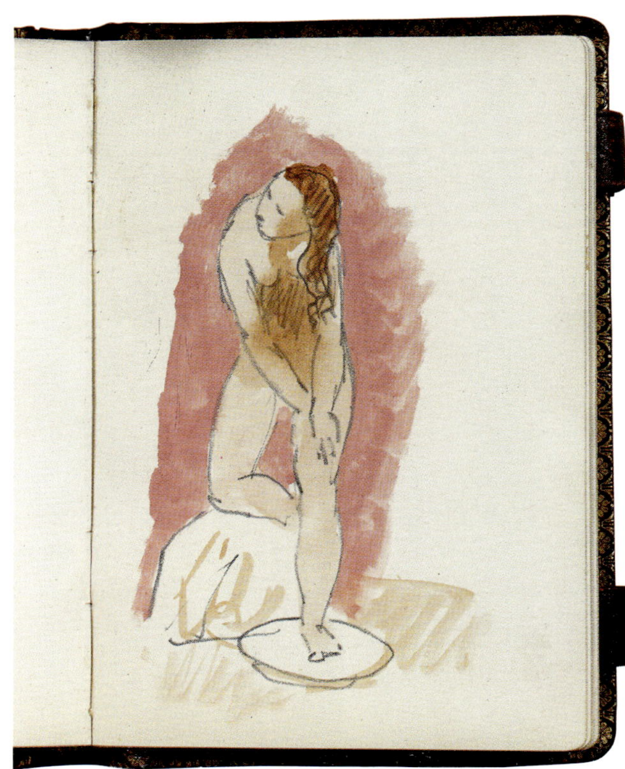

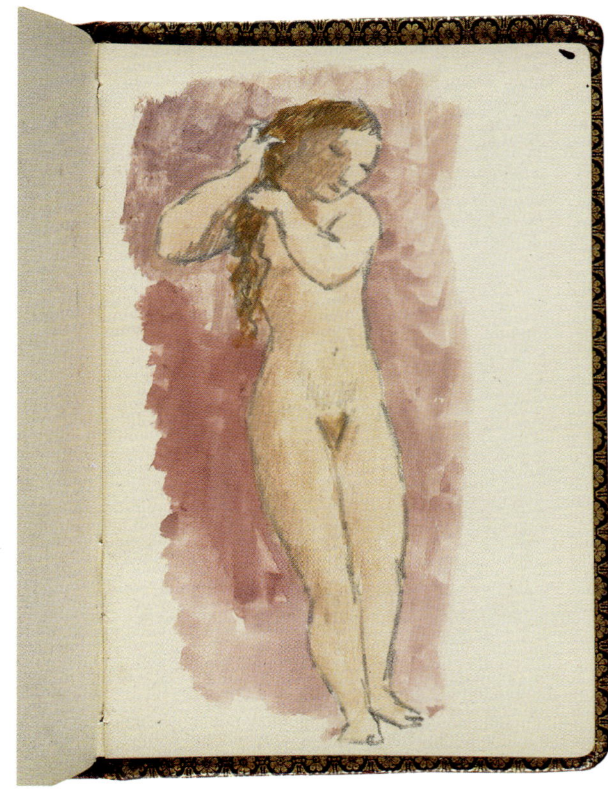

46 a and b Paris-Gosol Sketchbook, 1905 and spring-summer 1906
Study for The Harem: The Bath (f° 52 r°) and Study for The Harem: Nude Dressing Her Hair (f° 64 r°)
Graphite stick and gouache on paper; 17.5 x 12
Paris, Musée Picasso, MP 1857

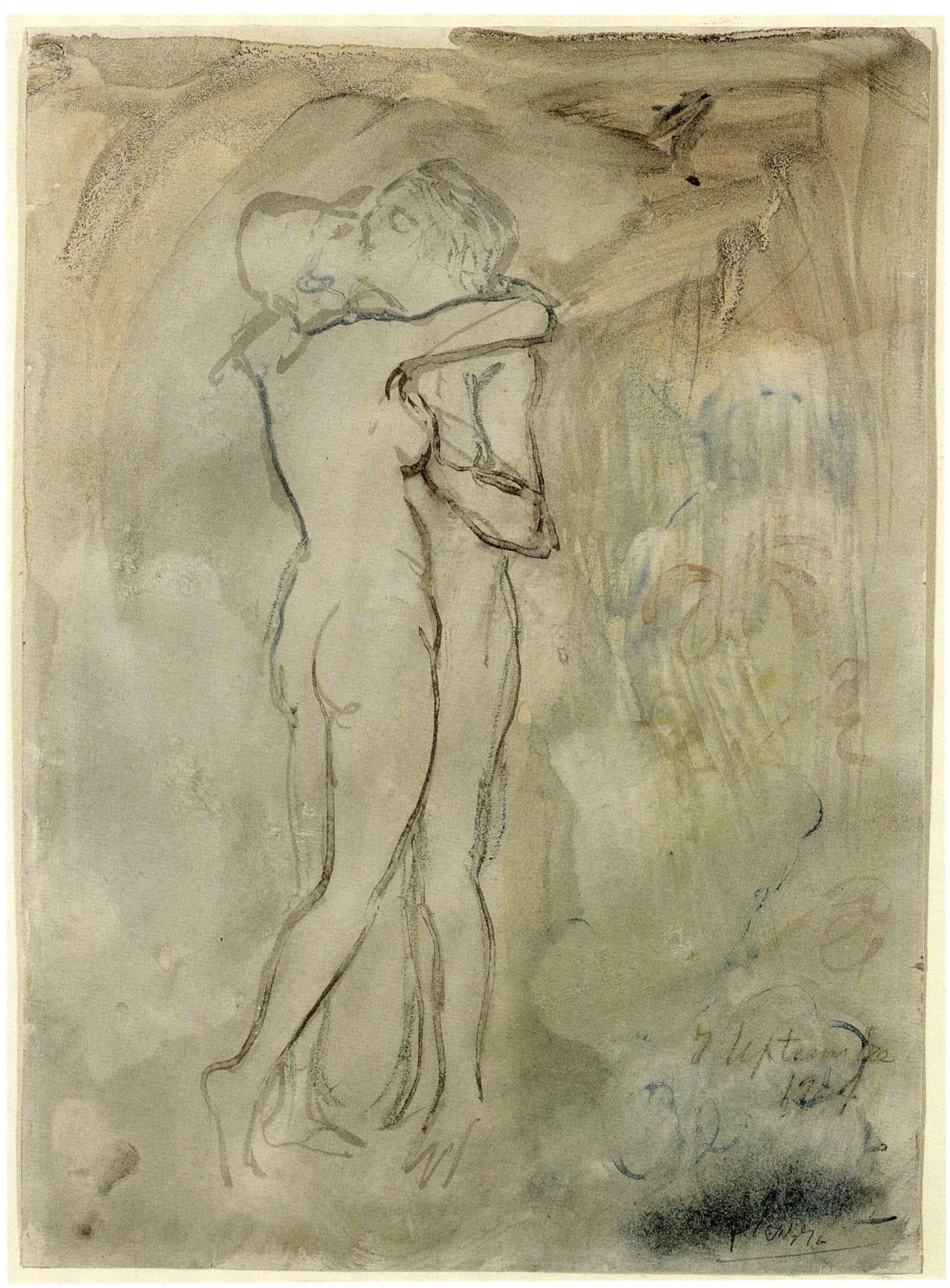

44 The Kiss, 7 September 1904

Watercolour on paper; 36.5 x 26.5
Göteborg, Göteborgs Konstmuseum [M]

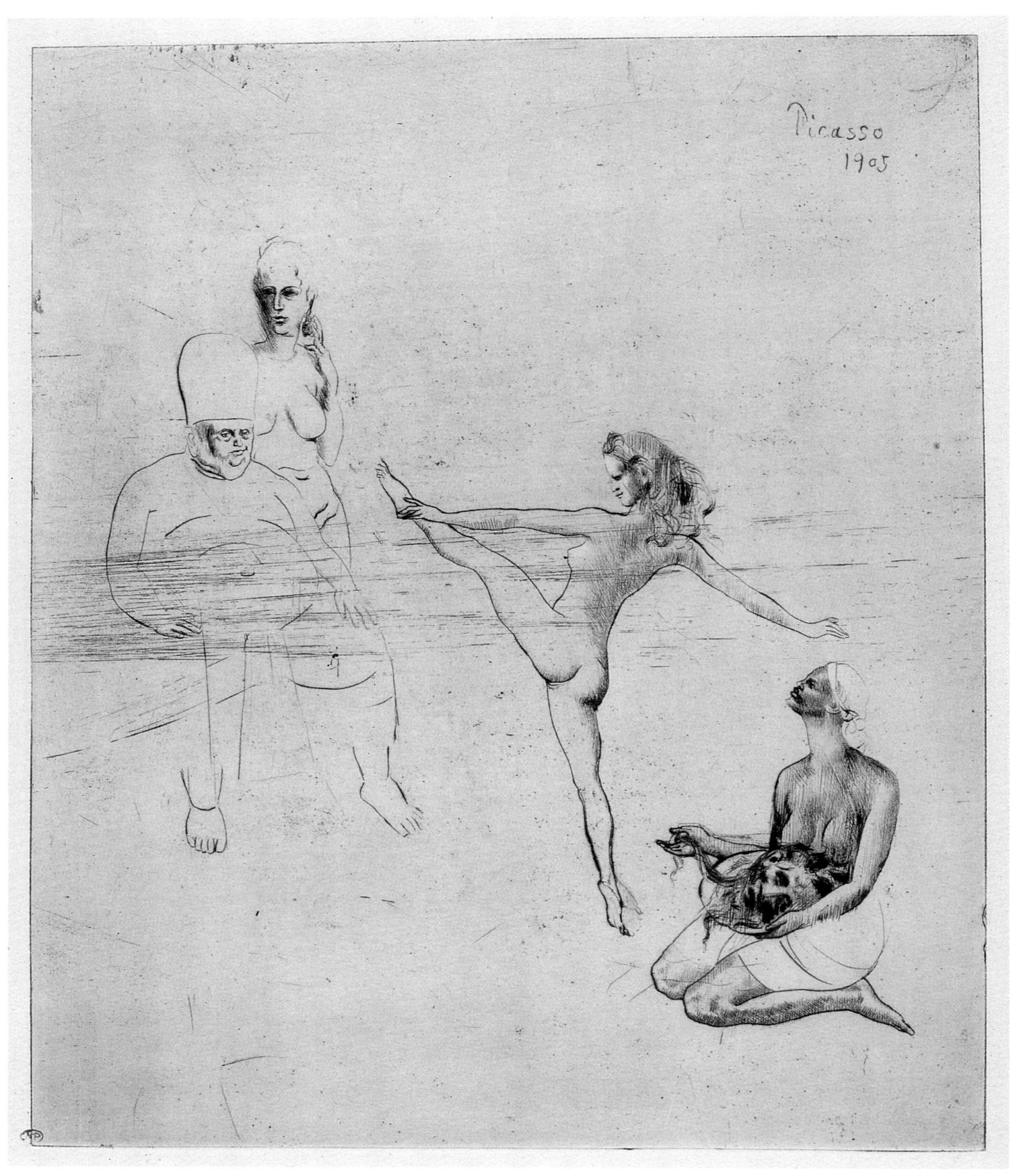

47 Salome, 1905

Drypoint on copper; 40 x 34.8
Paris, Musée Picasso, MP 1903

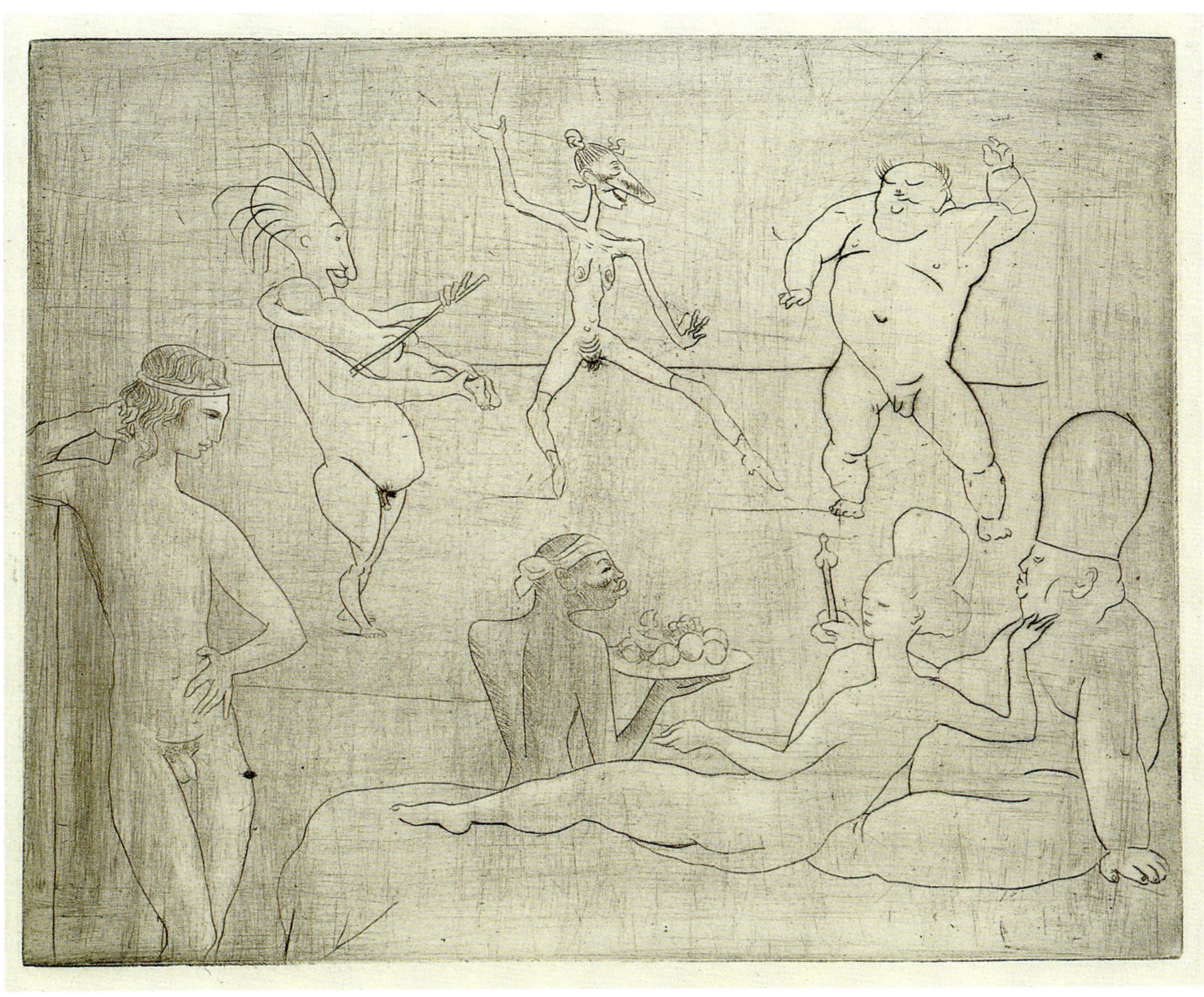

48 The Danse Barbare (before Salome and Herod), 1905
Drypoint on copper; State III; 40 x 34.8
Paris, Musée Picasso, MP 1904

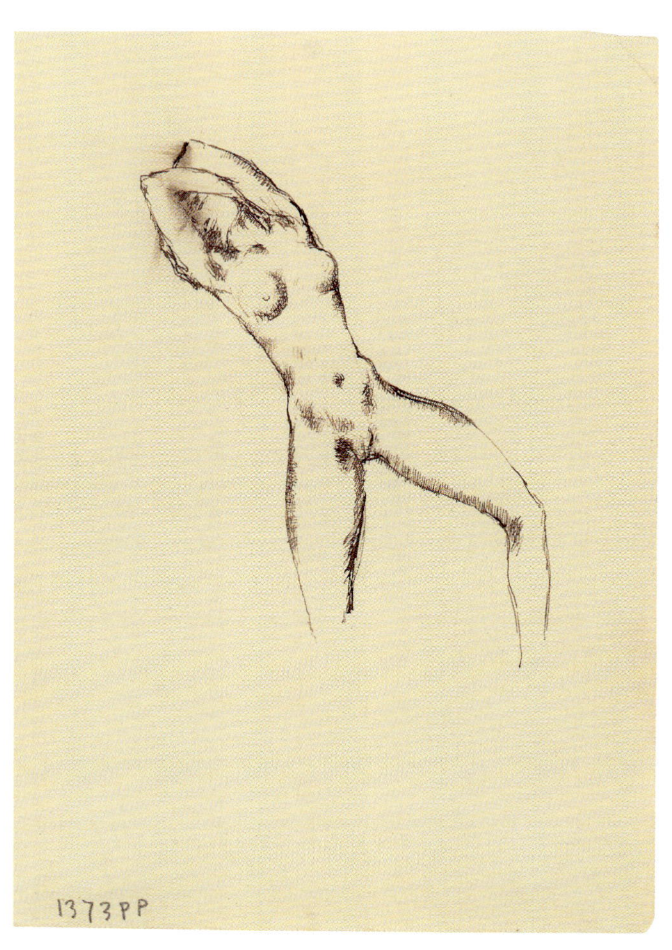

49 Reclining Nude, 1905
India ink on paper; 37.5 x 27
Geneva, Marina Picasso collection, inv. 0467
Courtesy Galerie Jan Krugier, Ditesheim & Cie

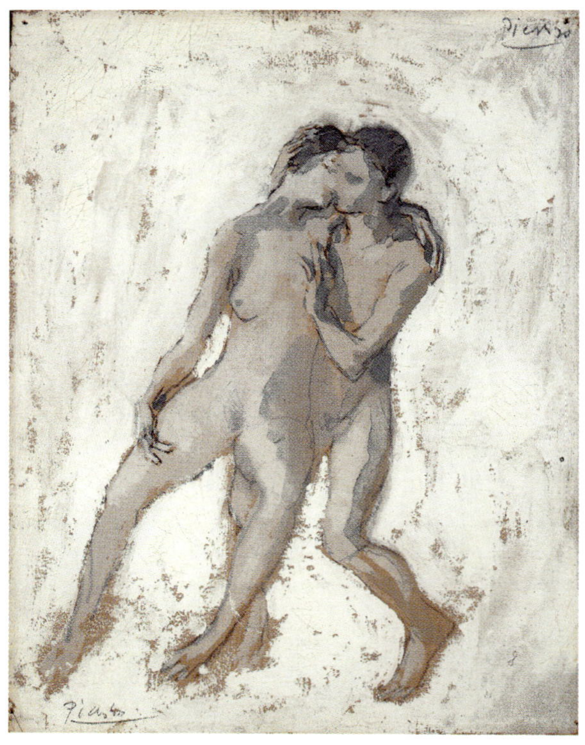

50 Entwined Nudes, 1905
Gouache and watercolour on paper; 26.5 x 21
Copenhagen, Statens Museum for Kunst, KMSr 175

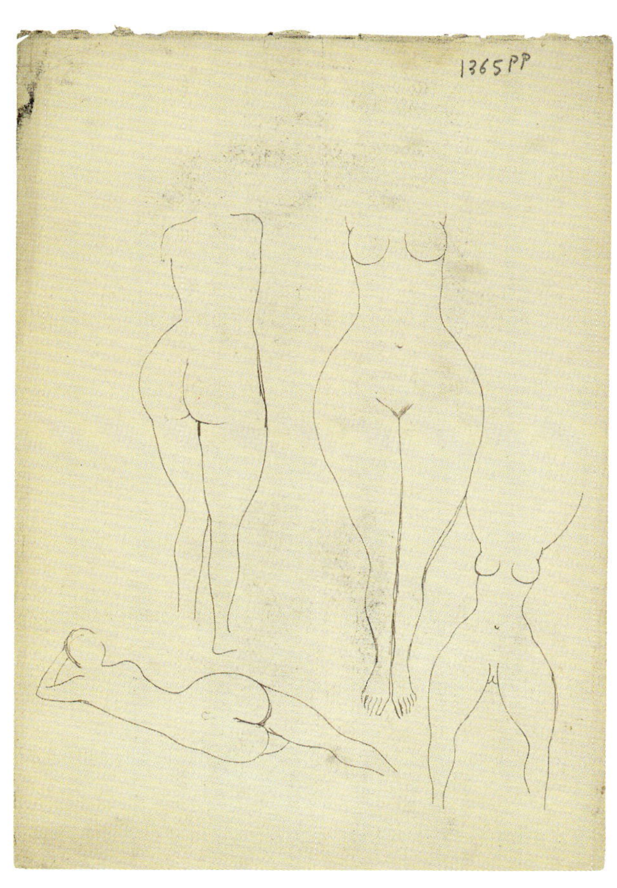

51 Reclined Nude, 1905
India ink on paper; 37.5 x 27
Paris, Private collection

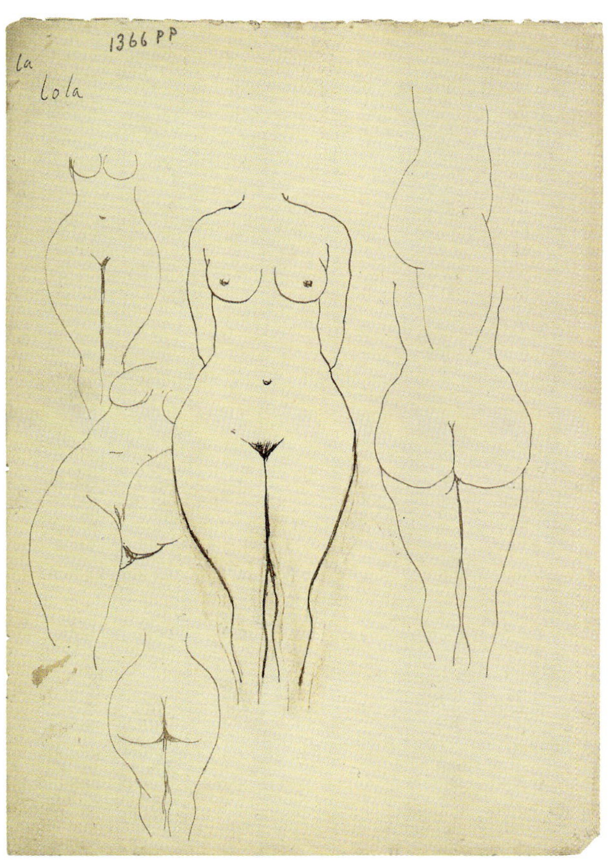

52 Nude from Behind and Face-On, 1905
India ink on paper; 37.5 x 27
Paris, Private collection

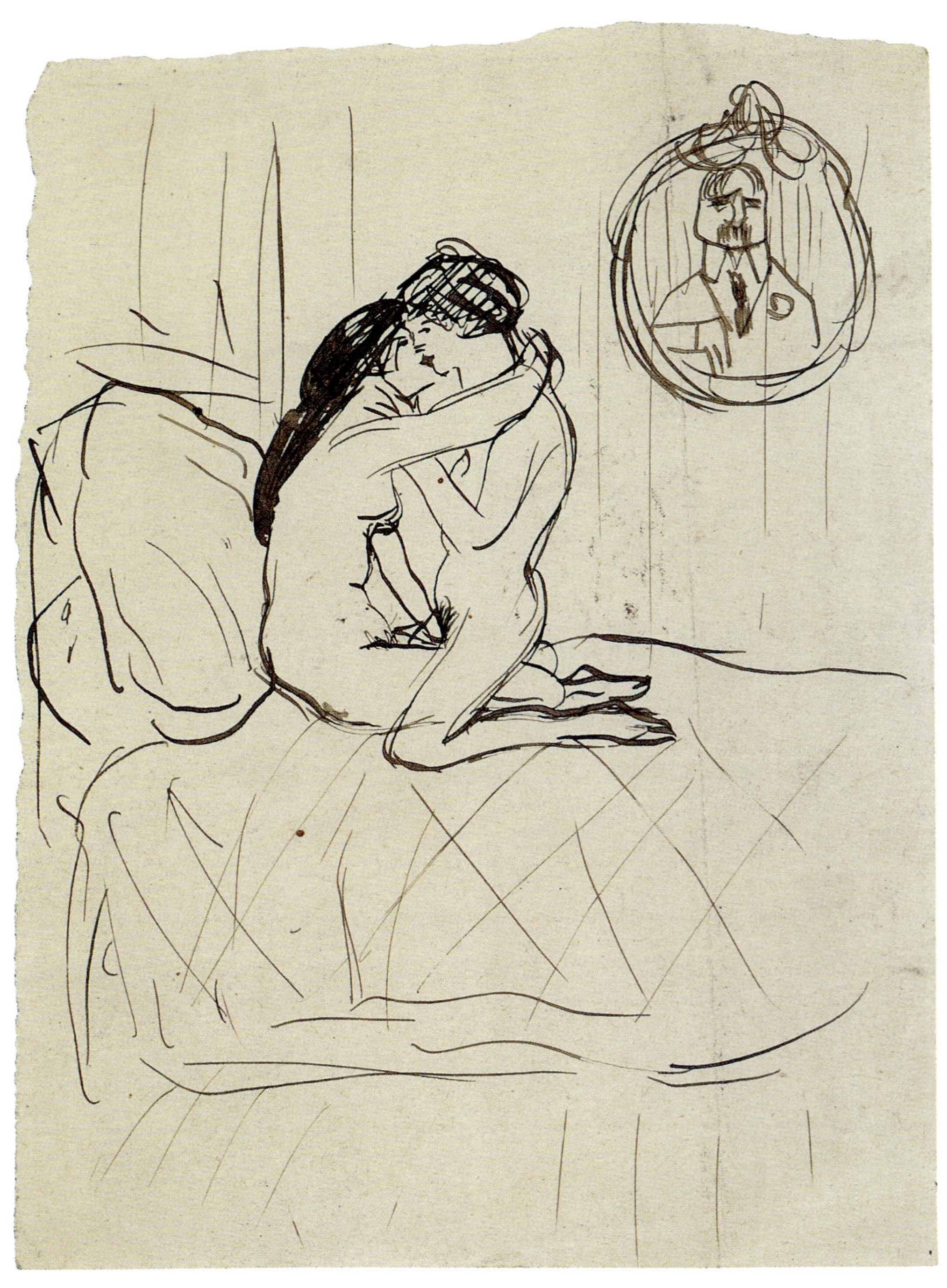

53 Two Women on a Bed, 1905
India ink on paper; 21 x 15.5
Paris, Private collection

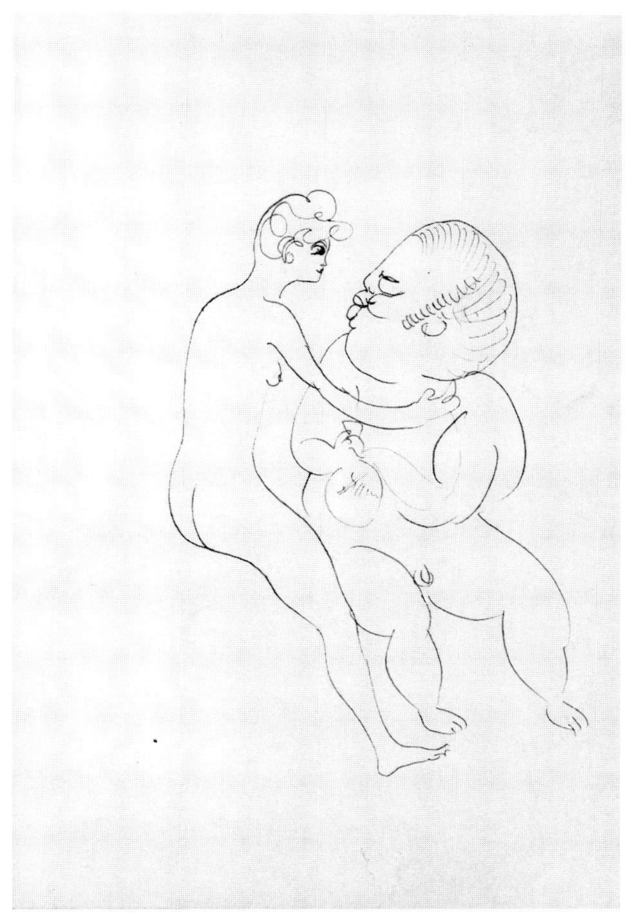

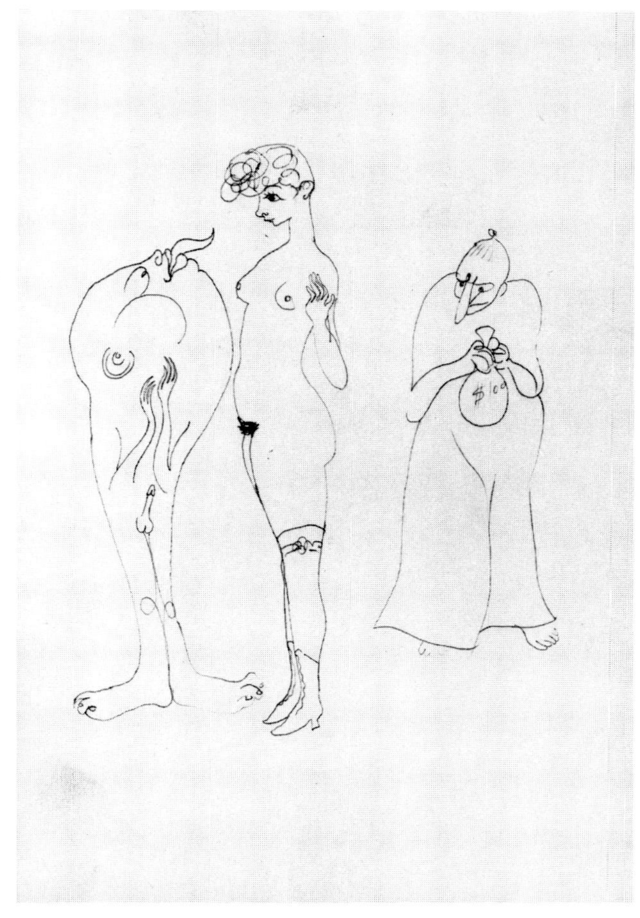

54 a and b Holland Sketchbook, June–July 1905

Caricature: Nude and Large Man (f° 21 r°) and *Caricature: Nude Woman, Old Woman and Grotesque Man* (f° 28 r°)
Pen and black ink on paper; 12.5 x 18.5
Paris, Musée Picasso, MP 1856

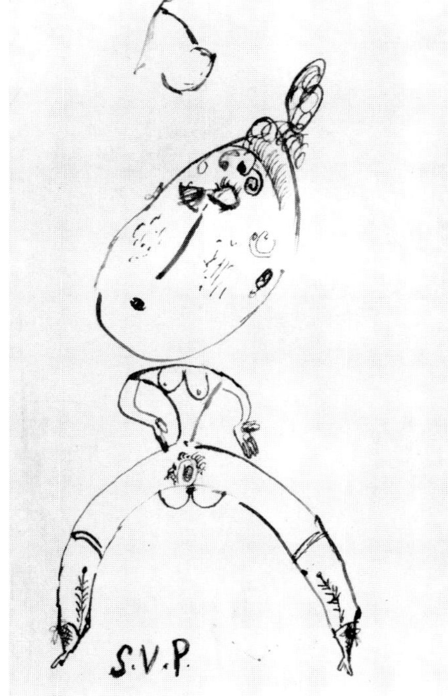

55 S.V.P., Winter 1905–1906

Pen and brown ink on paper; 21.7 x 13.5
Paris, Musée Picasso, MP 487 r°

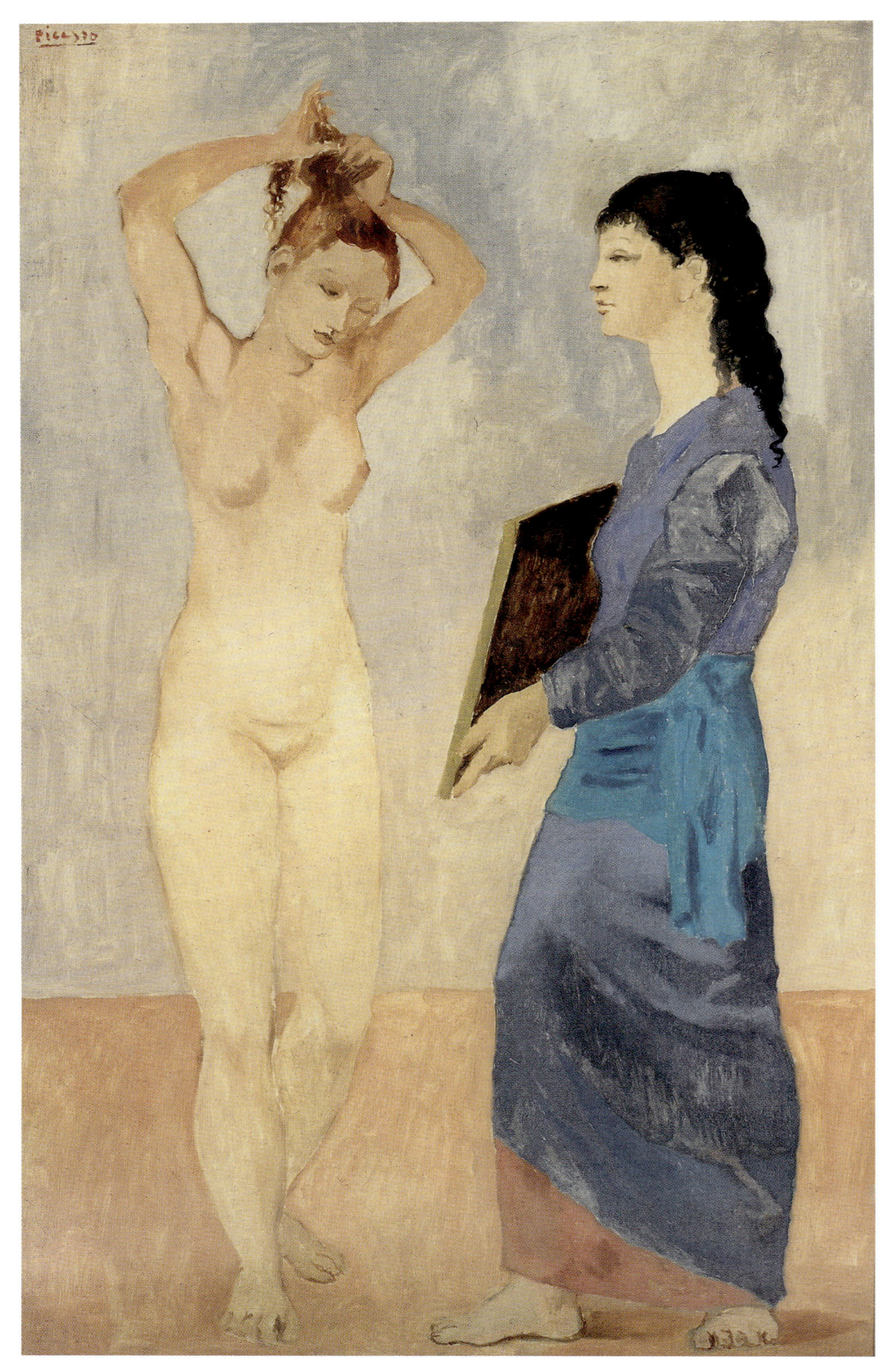

56 La Toilette, Summer 1906

Oil on canvas; 99.1 x 51.1
Buffalo, Albright-Knox Art Gallery, Fellows for Life Fund, 1926 [PM]

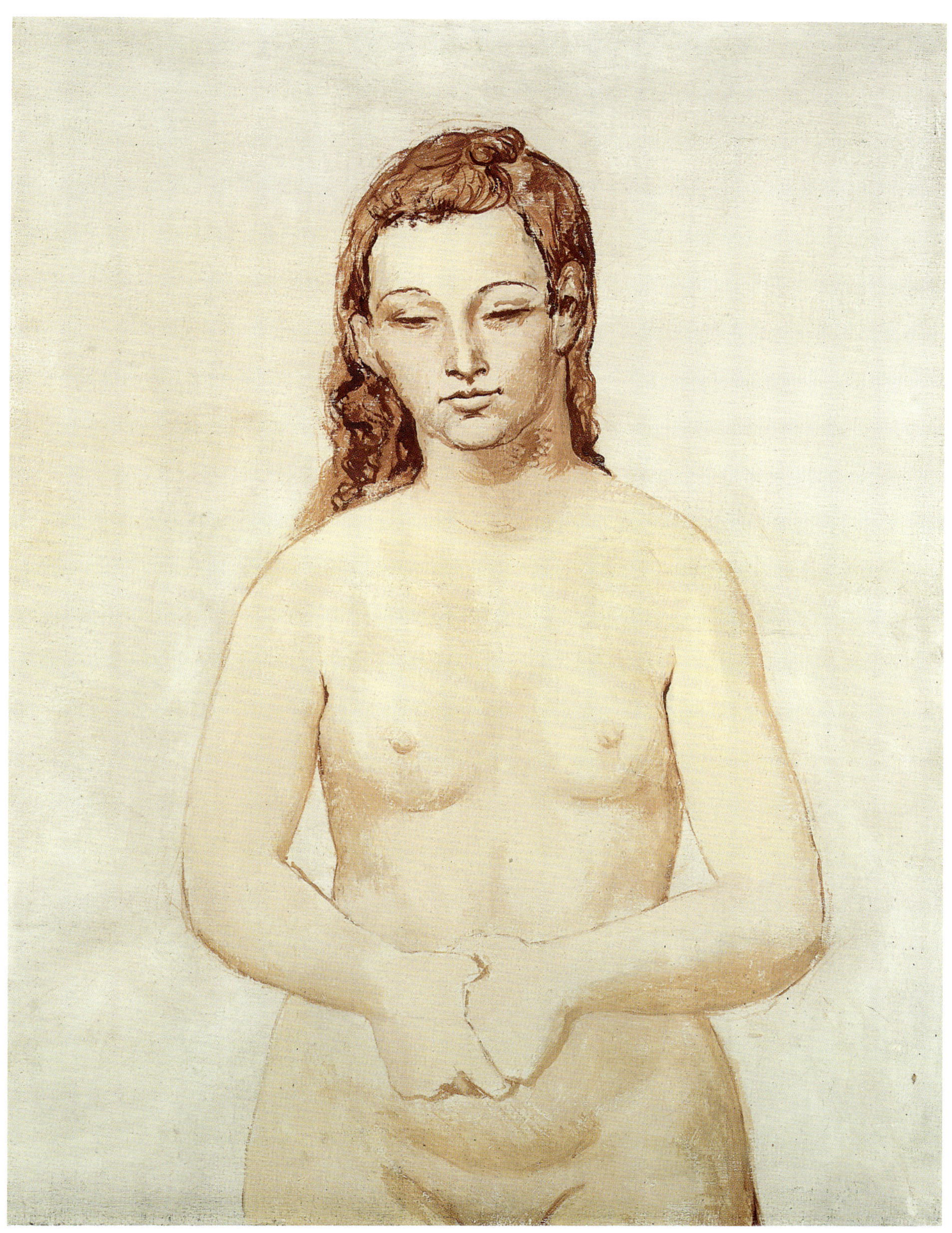

57 Nude with Clasped Hands, Summer 1906
Gouache on canvas; 96.5 x 75.6
Toronto, Art Gallery of Ontario, Gift of Sam and Ayala Zacks, 1970, inv. 71/297 [B]

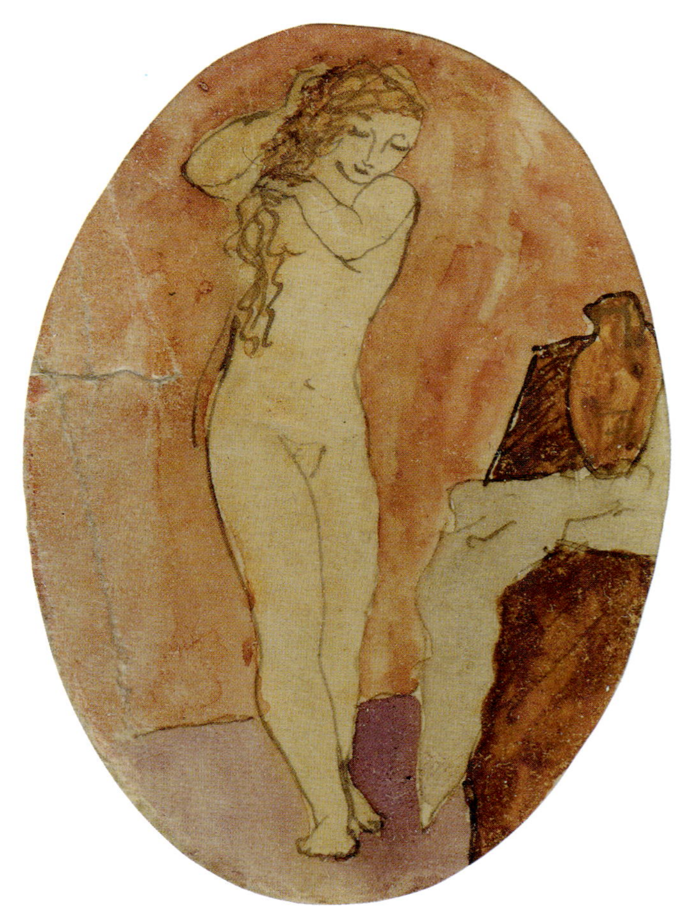

58 Study for *The Harem*: Woman Bathing, Spring-summer 1906
Pen, ink and watercolour on the reverse of an oval-shaped advertising label for "Crème Simon"; 7 x 5
Paris, Musée Picasso, MP 514

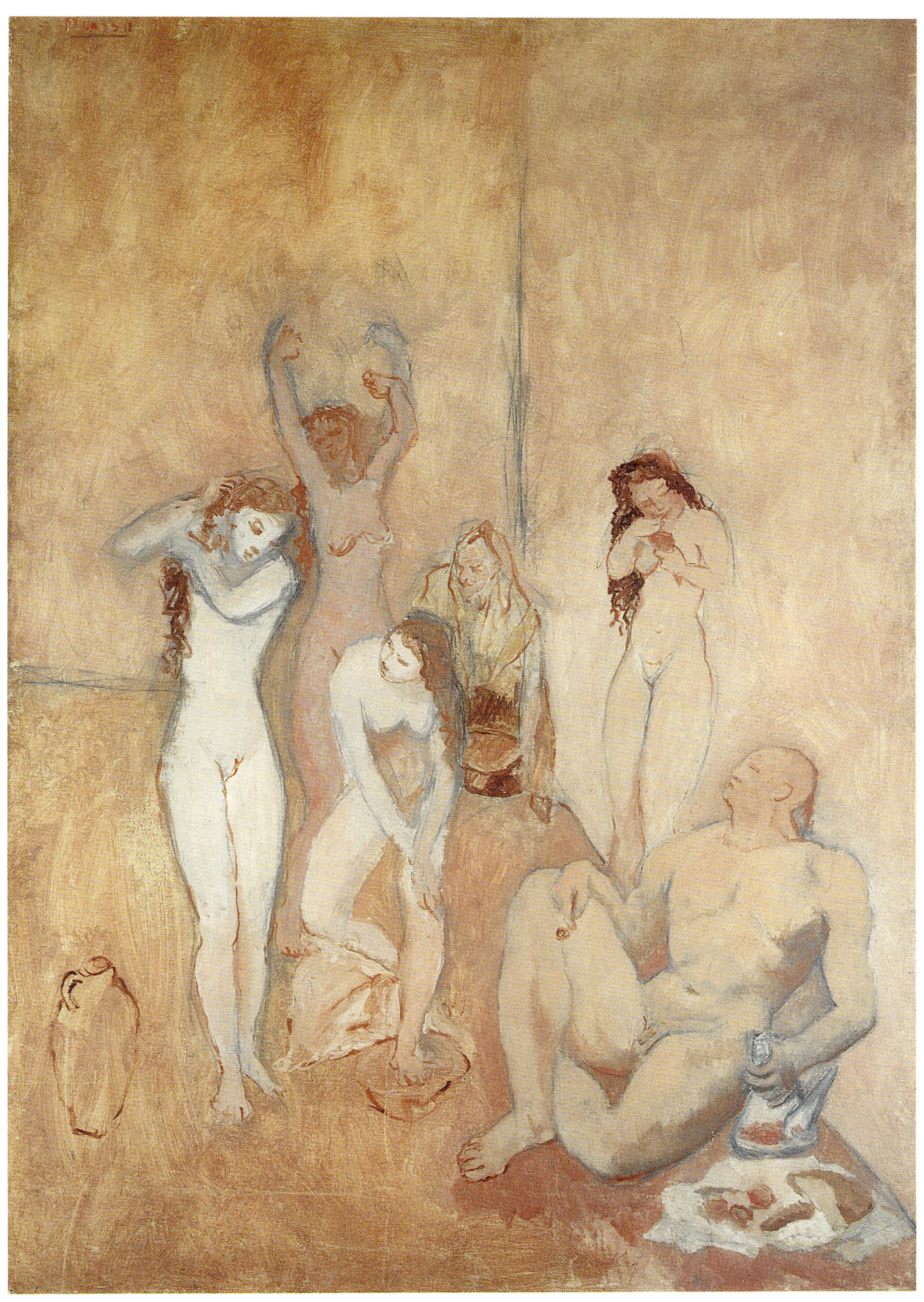

59 The Harem, Summer 1906

Oil on canvas; 154.3 x 109.5
Cleveland, The Cleveland Museum of Art, Bequest of Leonard C. Hanna Jr.

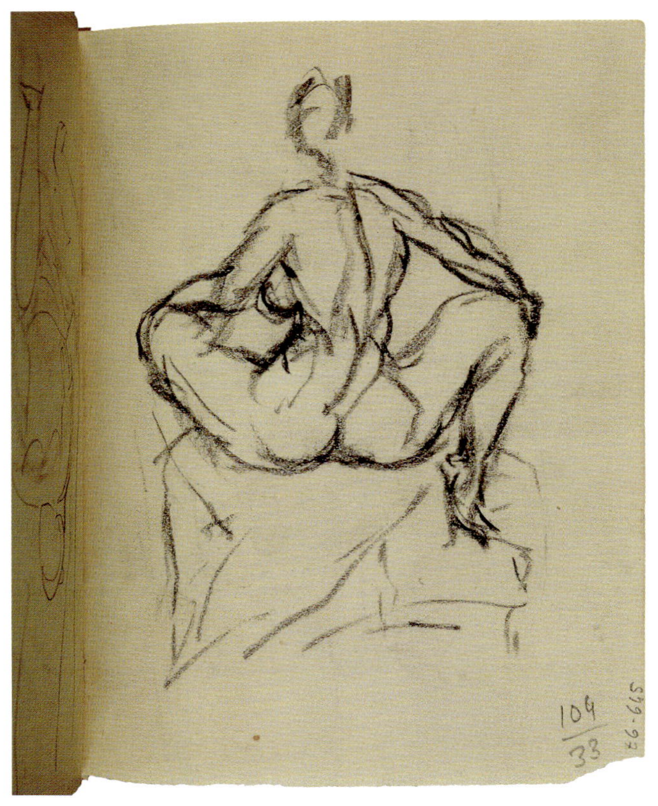

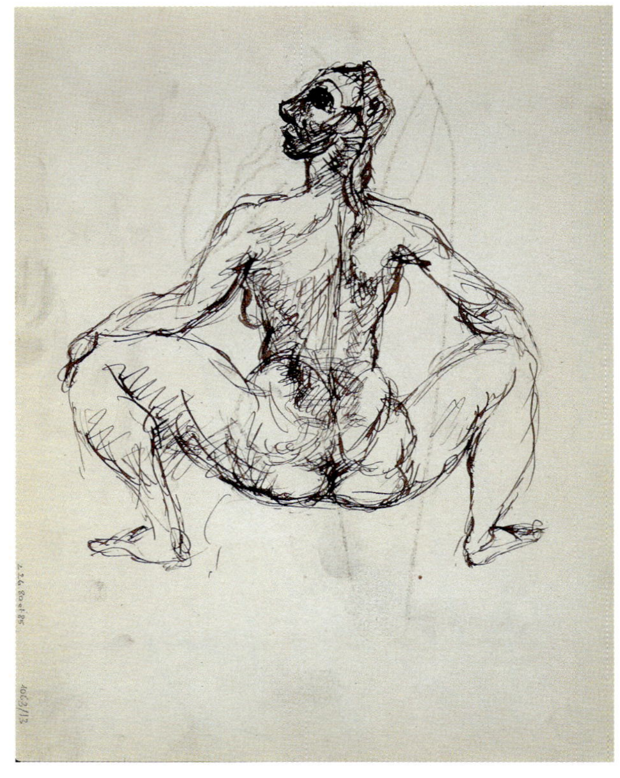

63 Sketchbook, March–July 1907

Study for the demoiselle squatting and seen from behind, at right: seated nude, legs spread (f° 13 r°)
Black crayon, black ink, coloured pencil, pastel, and charcoal on Ingres paper; 24.3 x 19.5
Paris, Musée Picasso, MP 1861

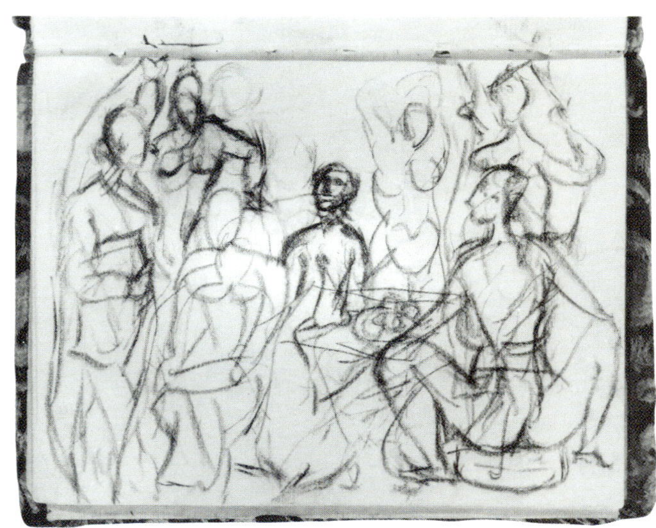

60 a and b Sketchbook, Winter 1906–1907

Group study with seven figures. Left to right: the medical student; the demoiselle standing behind the demoiselle seated face-on; the sailor; the demoiselle with arms raised; the demoiselle standing at right; and the demoiselle squatting and seen from behind, at right (f° 32 r°); *and Study for the demoiselle squatting and seen from behind, at right: seated nude, legs spread* (f° 33 r°)
Graphite stick (f° 32 r°); black crayon on paper (f° 33 r°); 13.5 x 10.5
Paris, Musée Picasso, MP 1859

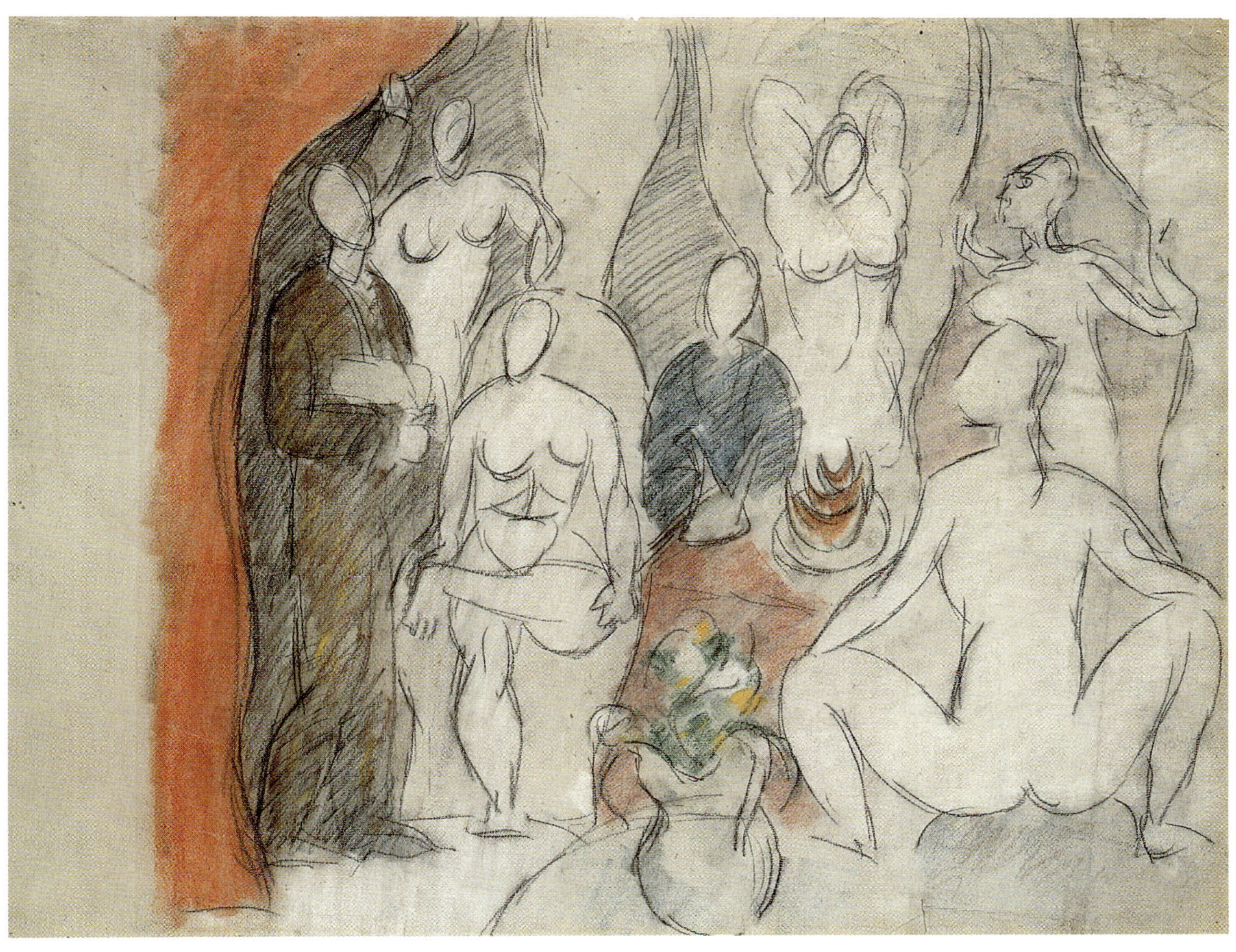

62 Study for *Les Demoiselles d'Avignon*, March–April 1907

Black crayon and pastel on paper ; 47.7 x 63.5
Basel, Öffentliche Kunstsammlung, Kupferstichkabinett, inv. 1967.106

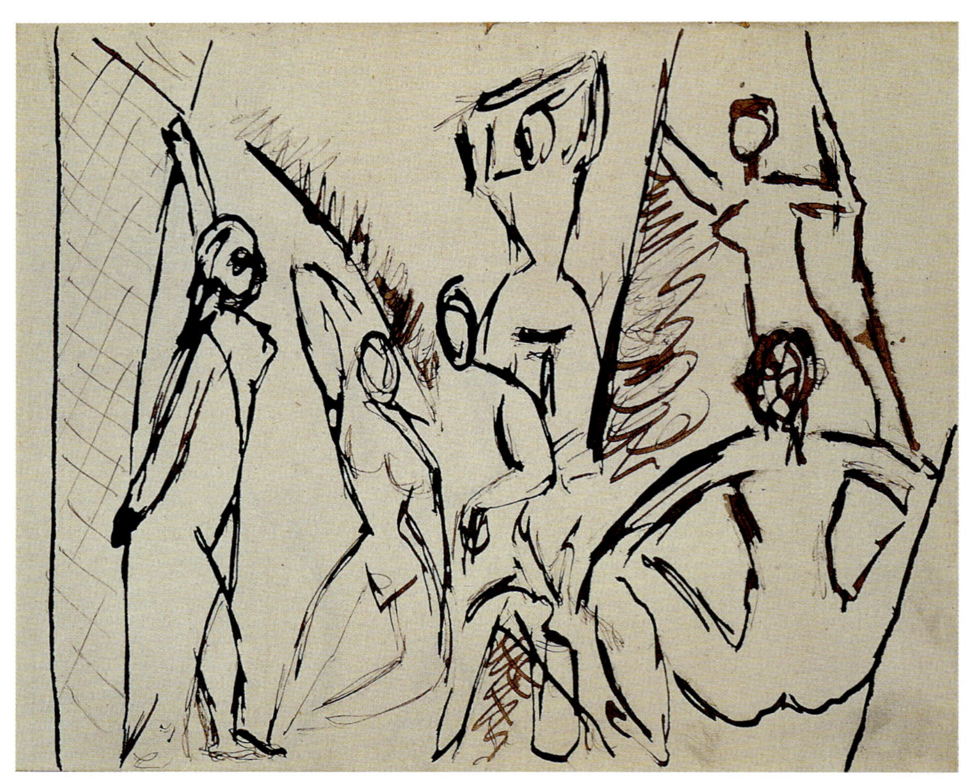

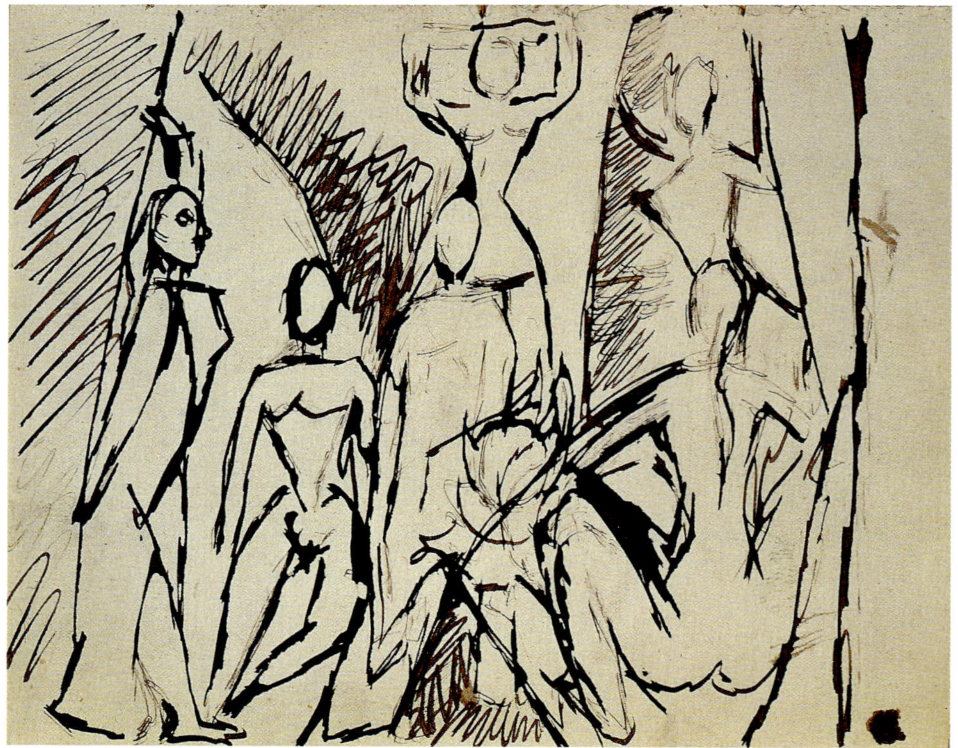

64 a and b Sketchbook, May–June 1907

Five Demoiselles and the Sailor (f° 11 r°; f° 18 r°)
Pen and India ink on beige paper; 10.5 x 13.5
Paris, Musée Picasso, MP 1862

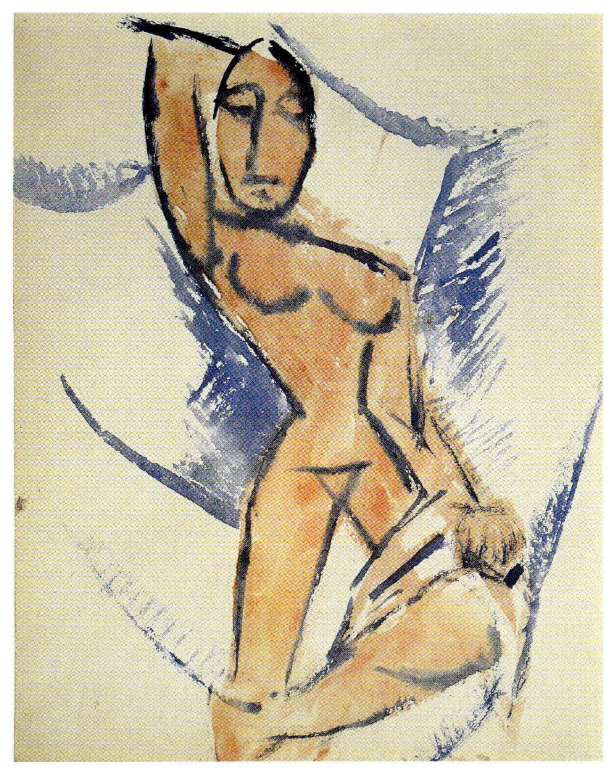

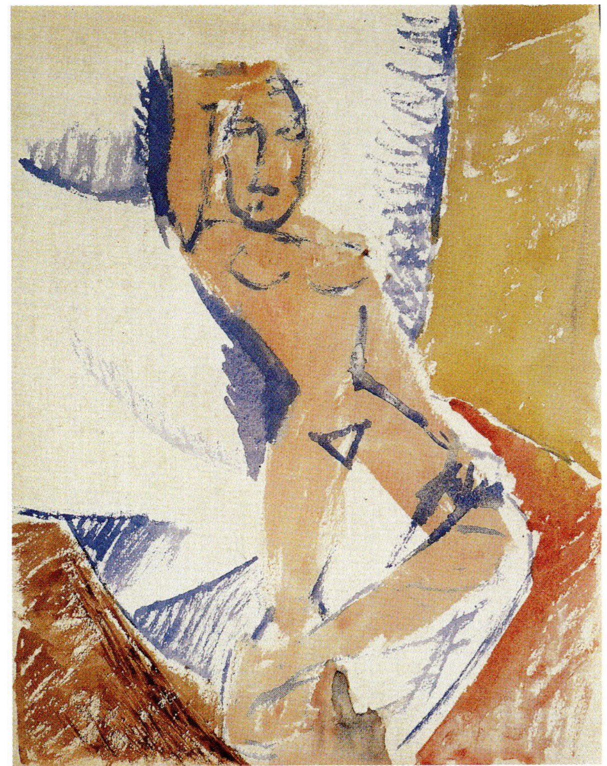

65 a and b Sketchbook, May–early July 1907

Nude with Drapery: Study for the Seated Demoiselle (f° 10 r°; f° 11 r°)
Watercolour on cream laid paper; 22.4 x 17.5
Paris, Musée Picasso, MP 1990-95

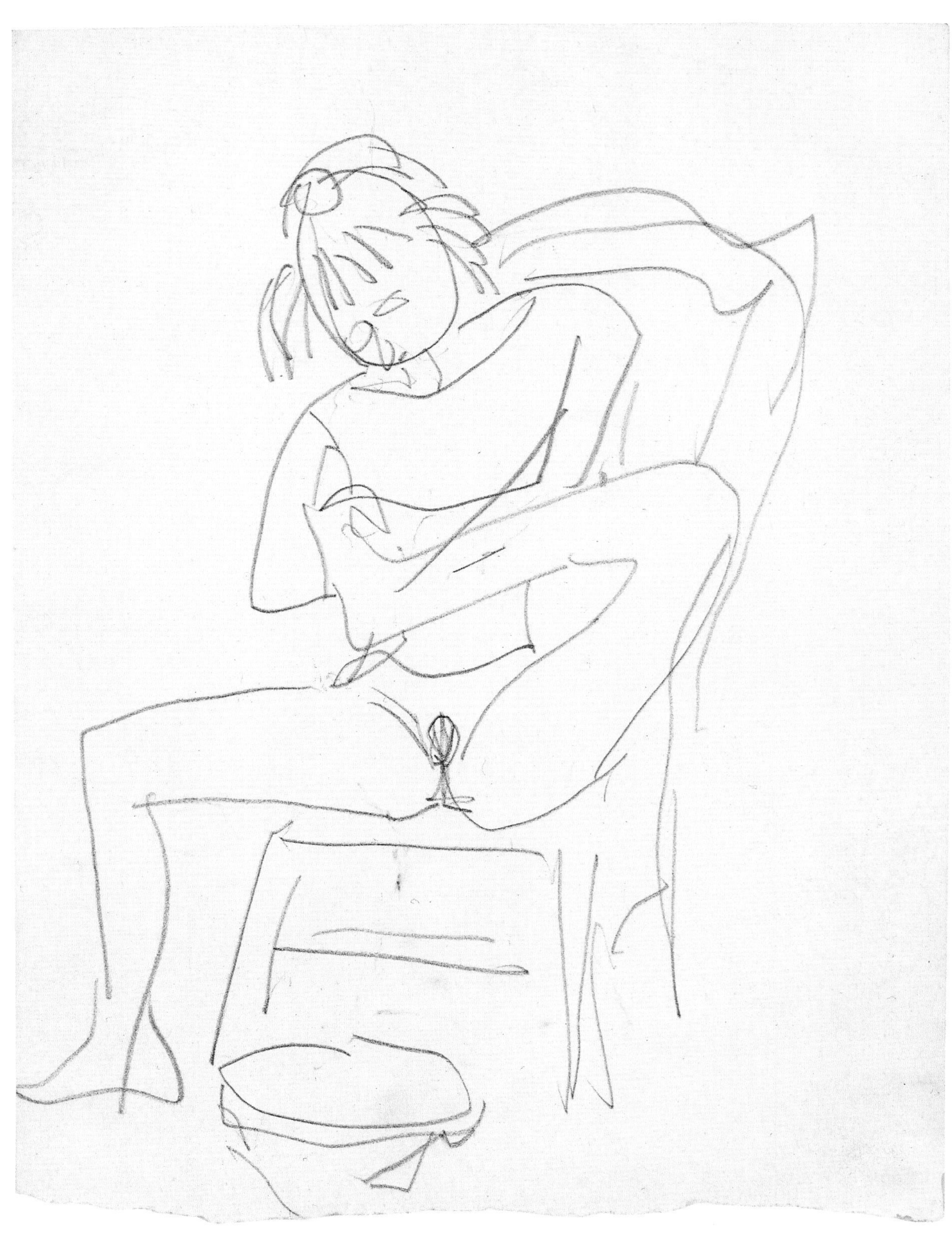

61 Woman Wiping Her Feet (Raymonde), 1907
Pencil on paper; 22 x 17
London, Private collection

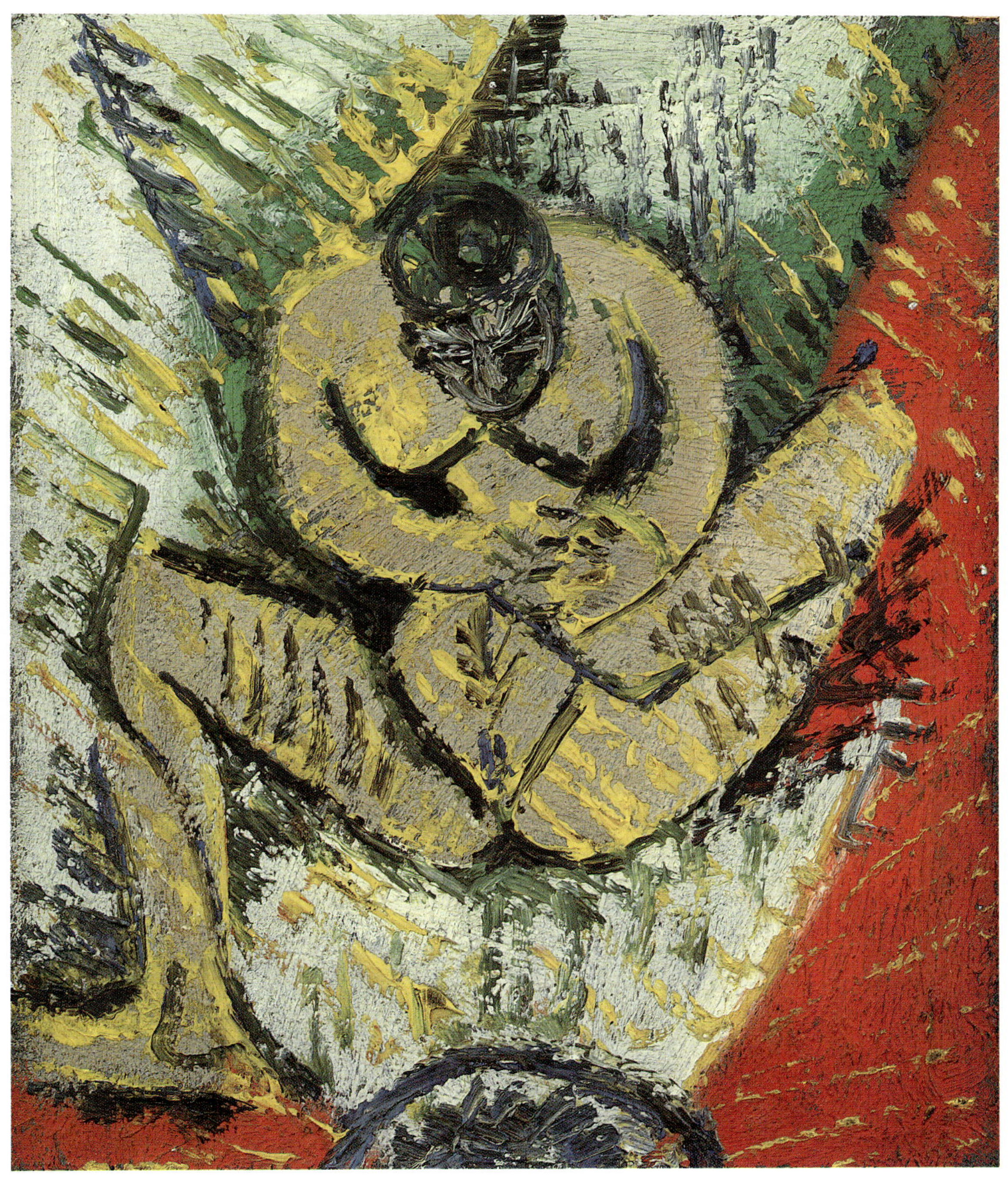

67 Small Seated Nude, Summer 1907
  Oil on panel; 17.6 x 15
  Paris, Musée Picasso, MP 20

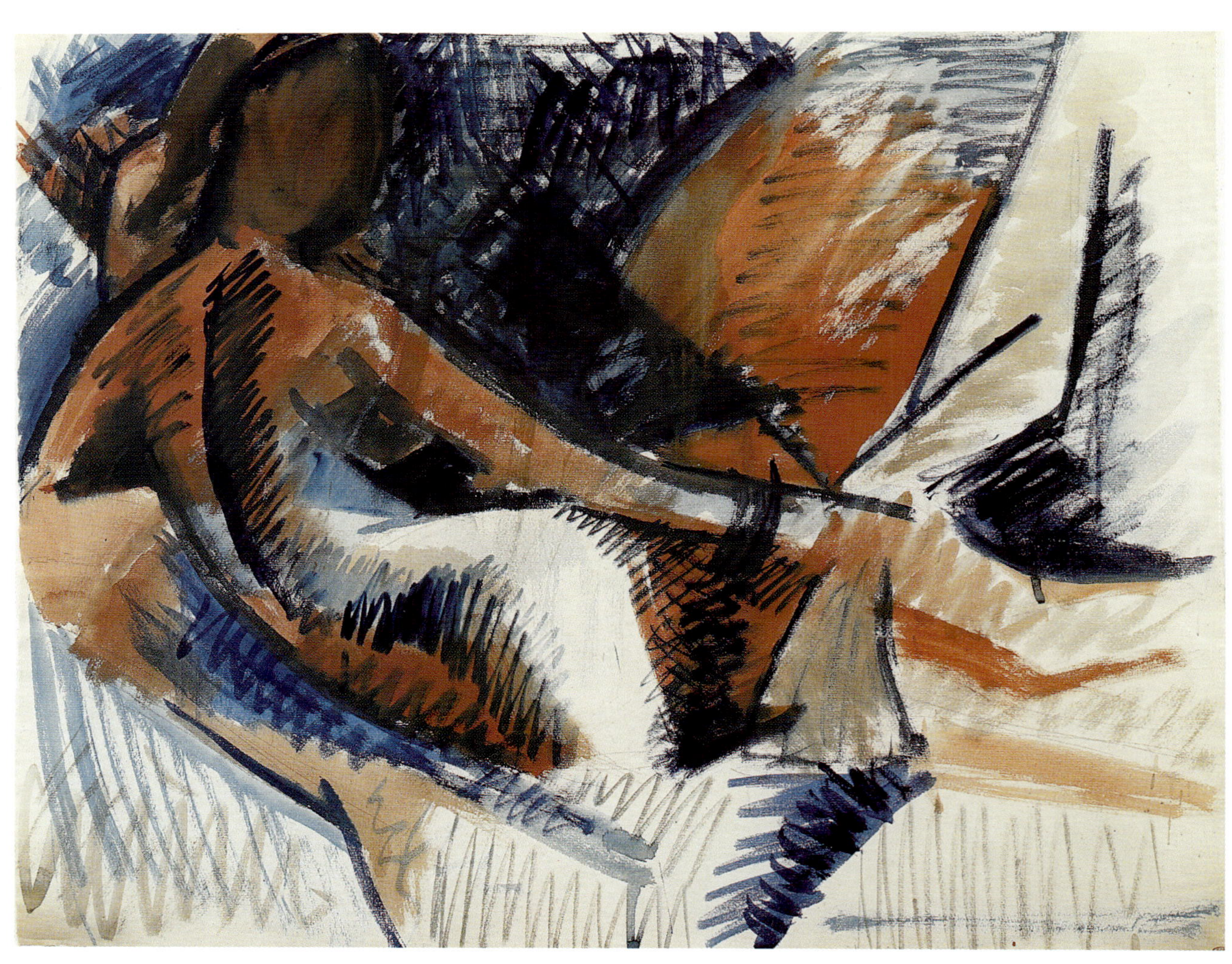

66 Odalisque, after Ingres, Summer 1907
Blue ink and gouache over pencil; 47.7 x 62.5
Paris, Musée Picasso, MP 545

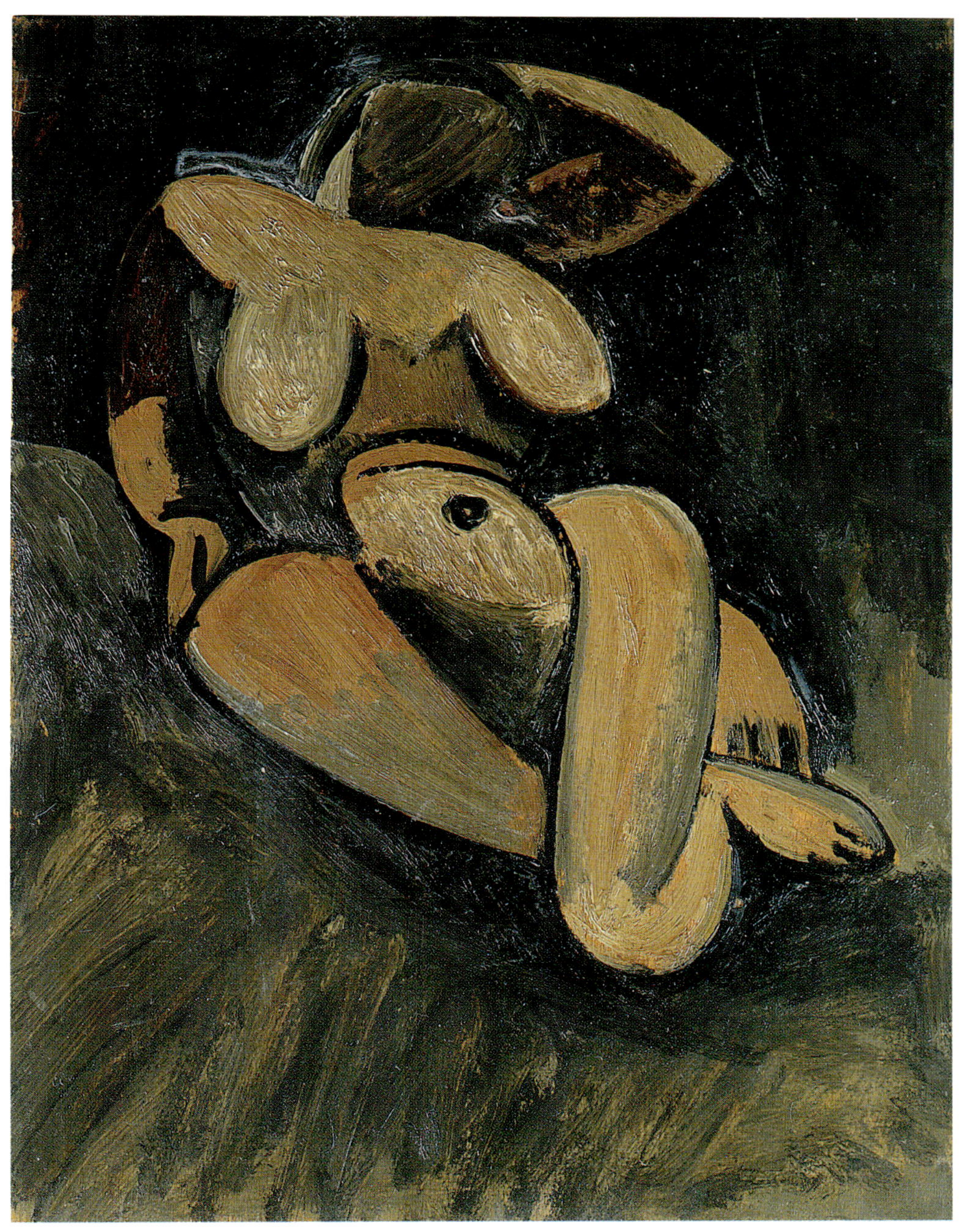

68 Reclining Nude, Spring 1908
Oil on panel; 27 x 21
Paris, Musée Picasso, MP 22

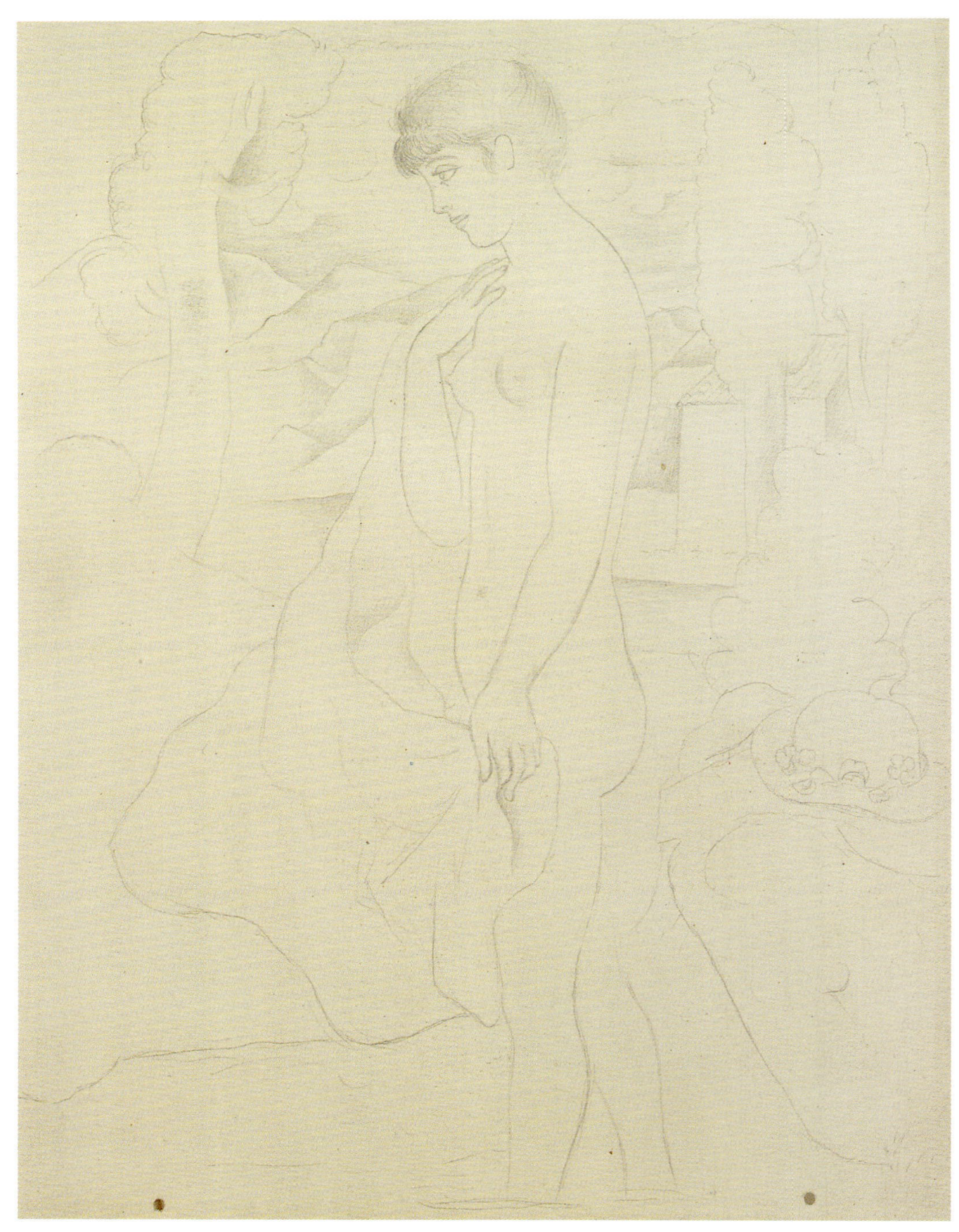

70 Bather: Left Profile, 1915
Graphite stick on paper; 29 x 23
Paris, Private collection

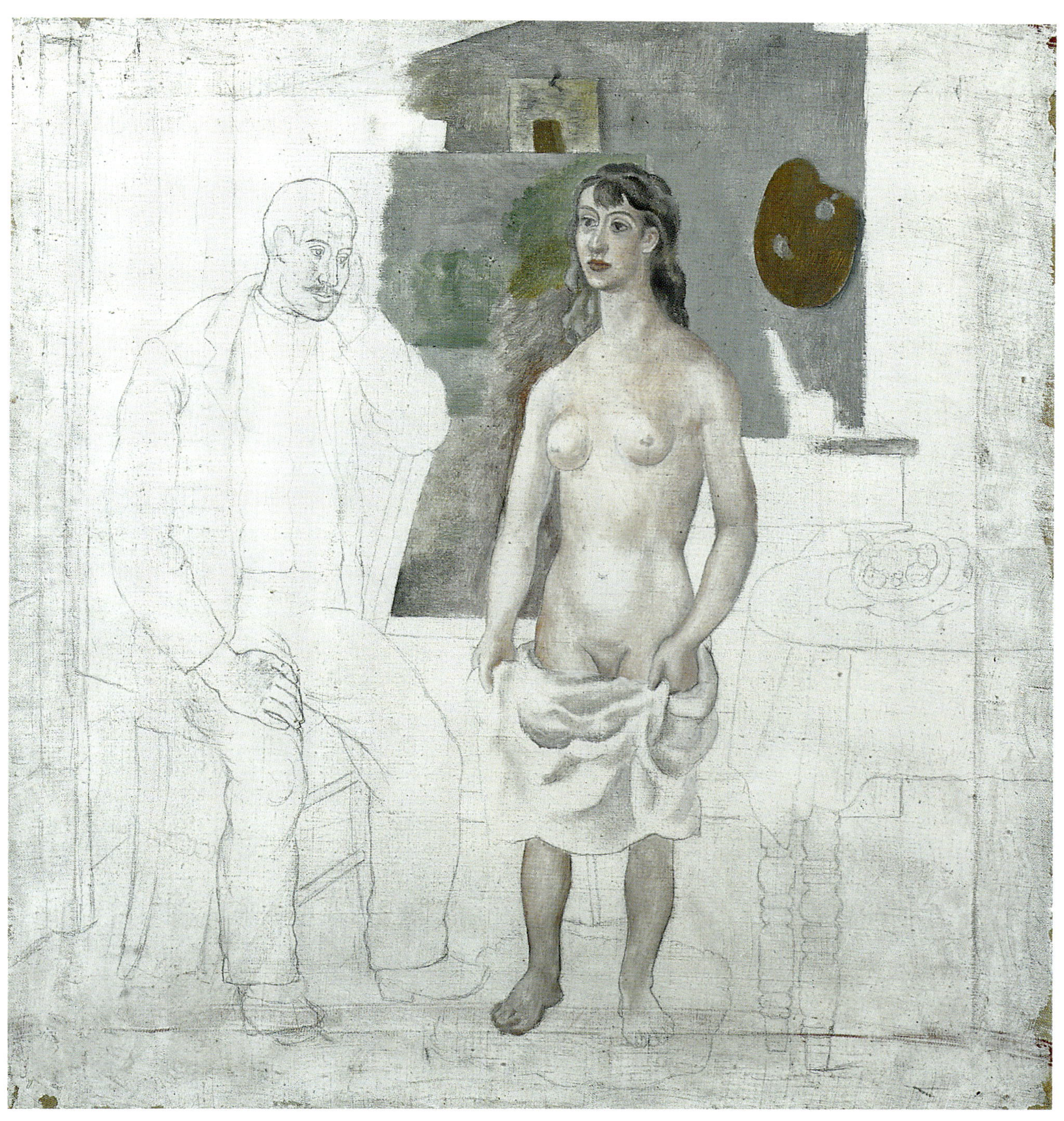

69 The Artist and His Model, Summer 1914

Oil and pencil on canvas; 58 x 55.9
Paris, Musée Picasso, MP 53

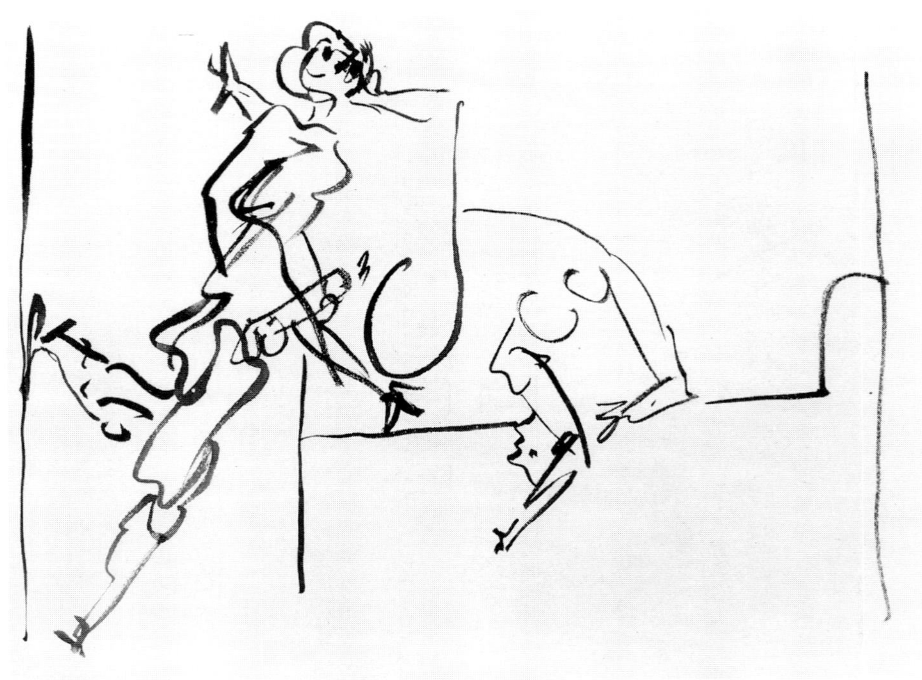

72 Erotic Scene, 1917
Brown watercolour on paper; 20.5 x 28
London, Private collection

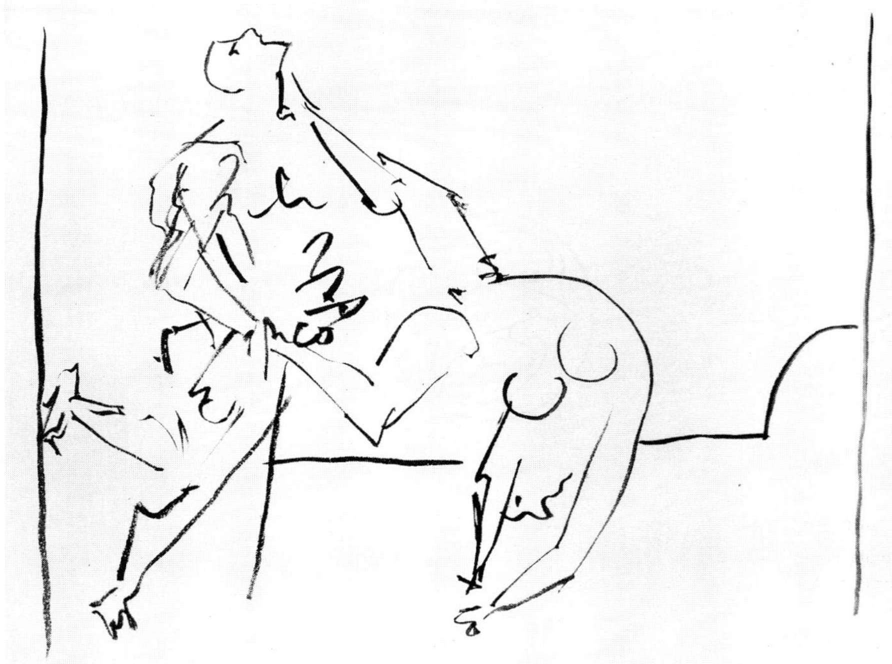

73 Erotic Scene, 1917
Brown watercolour on paper; 20.5 x 28
London, Private collection

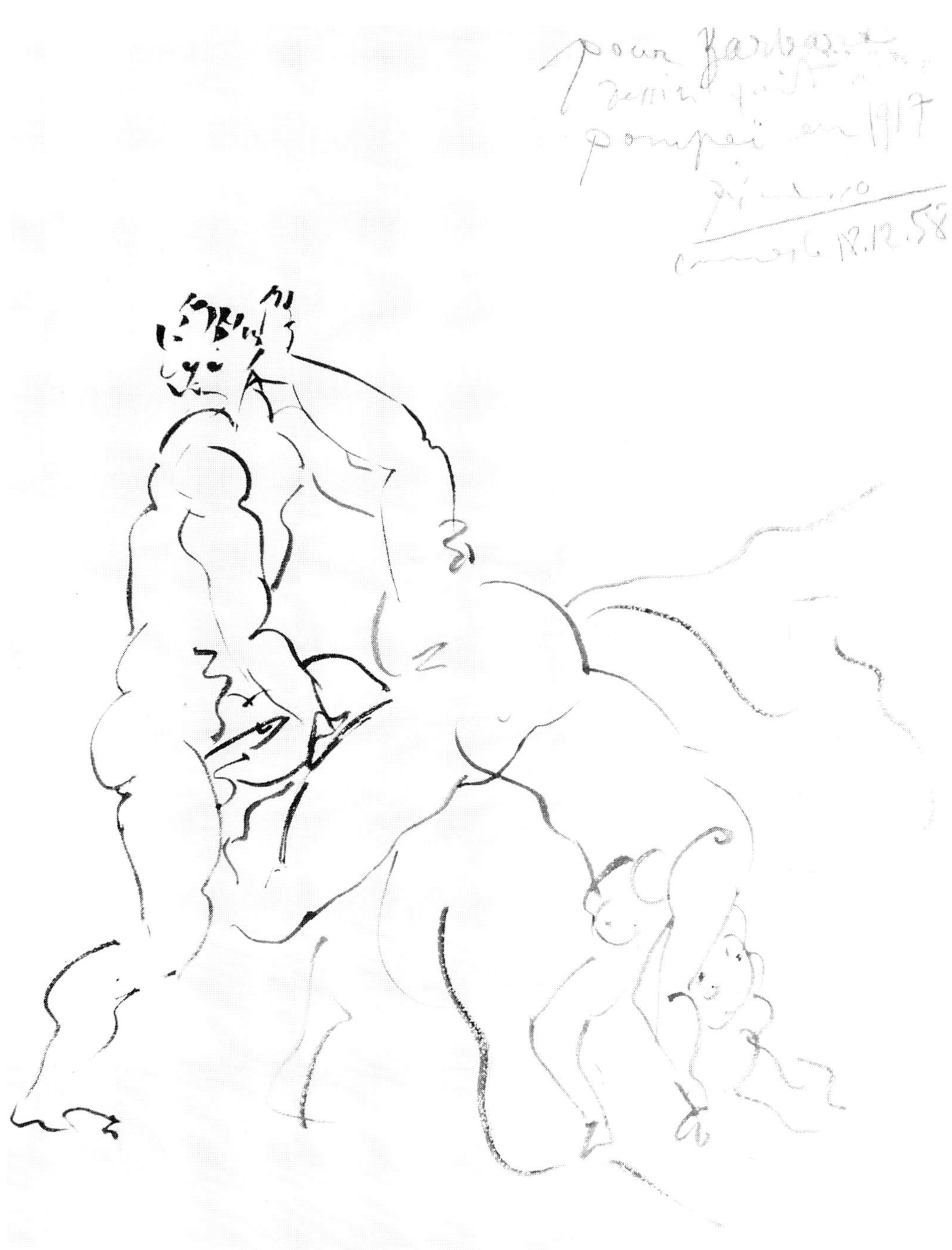

71 Erotic Scene ("for Barbara"), 1917
  Pen and India ink on paper; 26 x 20
  Paris, Private collection, Courtesy Galerie Vallois

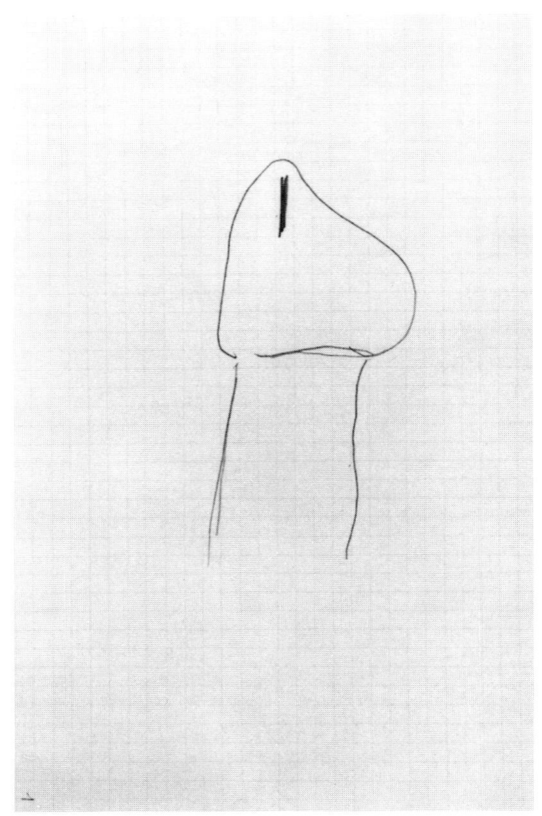

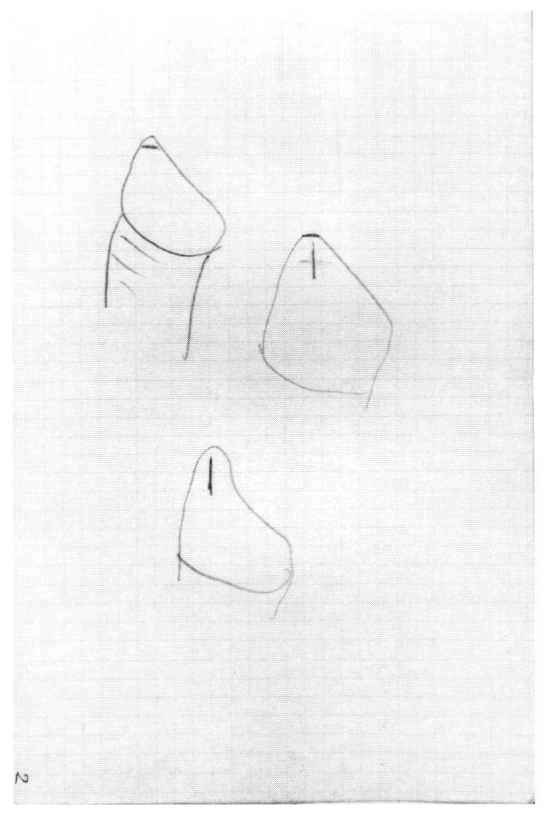

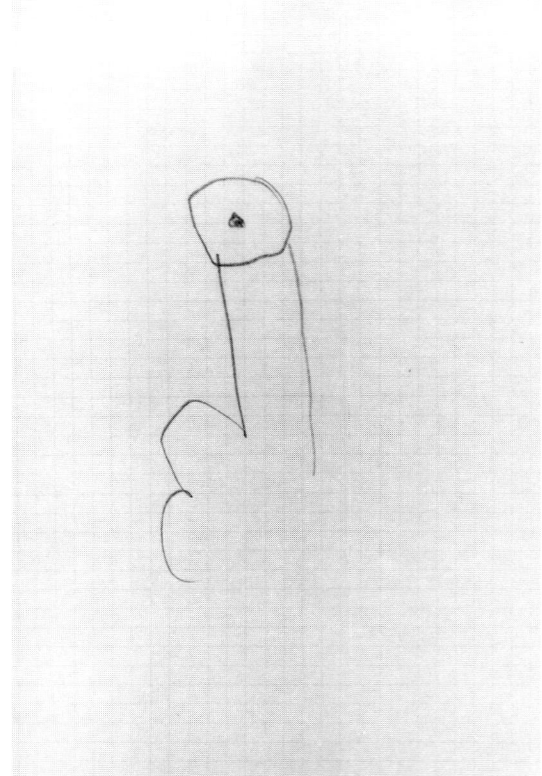

75 a, b and c **Italian Sketchbook**, Winter–spring 1917
Erotic Study (f° 4 r°); *Erotic Studies* (f° 51 v°)
and *Erotic Study* (f° 11 r°)
Graphite stick on quadrille paper; 11.4 x 17.2
Paris, Musée Picasso, MP 1867

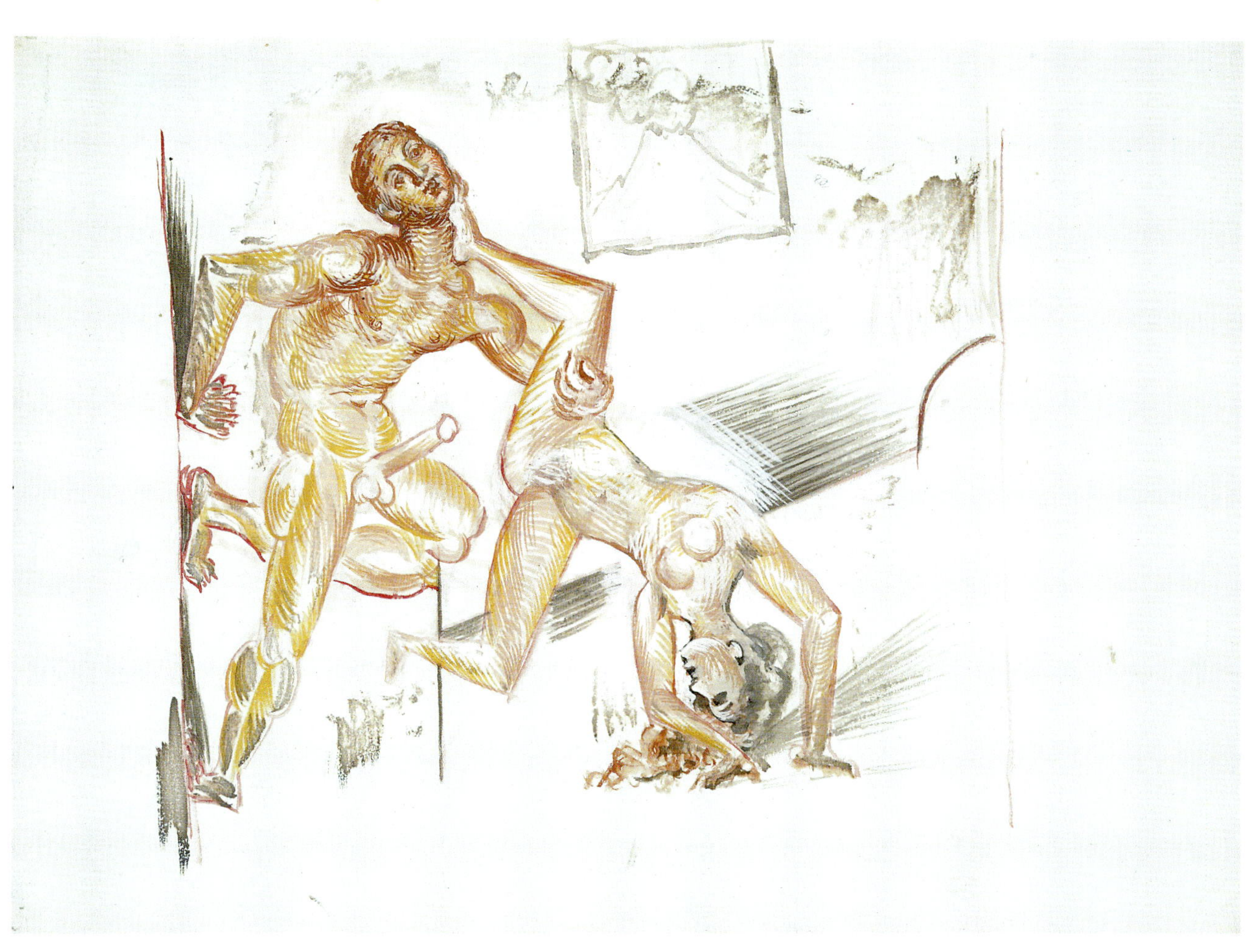

74 The Couple, 1917
Gouache on paper; 20 x 28
London, Private collection

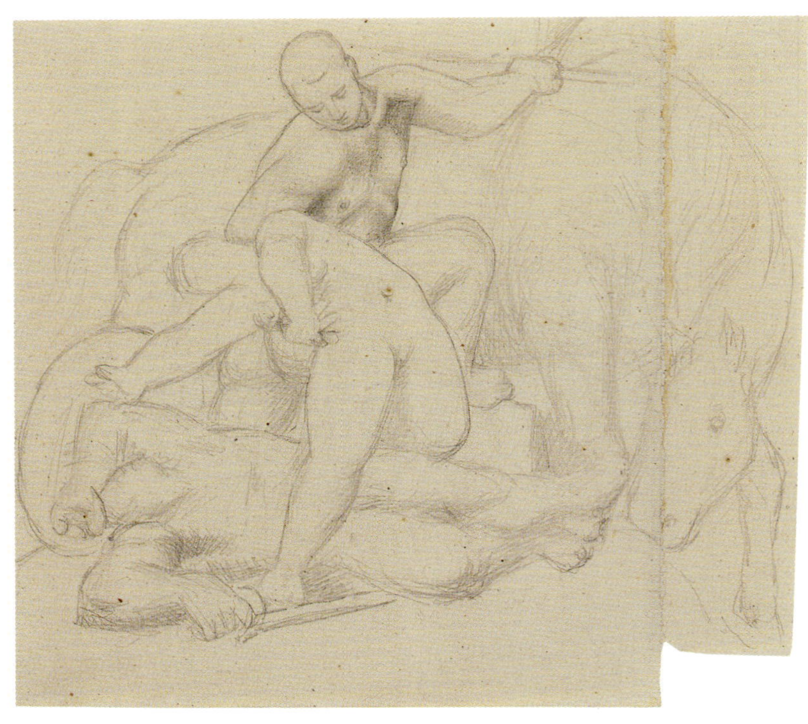

76 The Ravishment, 1920
Pencil on paper, cut and assembled; 22.5 x 23.5
Geneva, Private collection, Courtesy Galerie Jan Krugier, Ditesheim & Co.

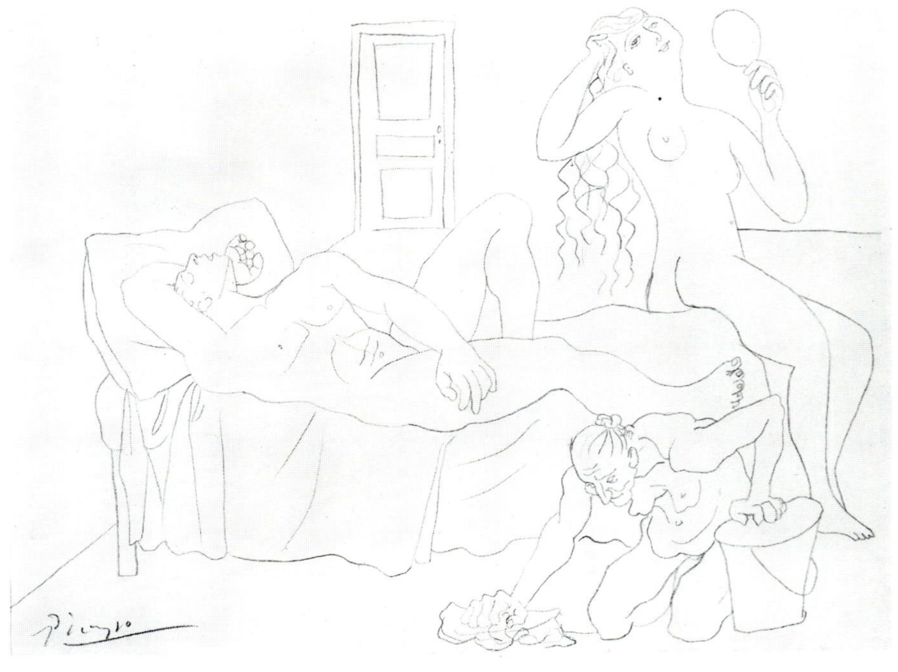

77 Nude Couple and Old Woman, 28 May 1920
Pencil on paper; 24 x 34.5
Jerusalem, The Israel Museum [B]

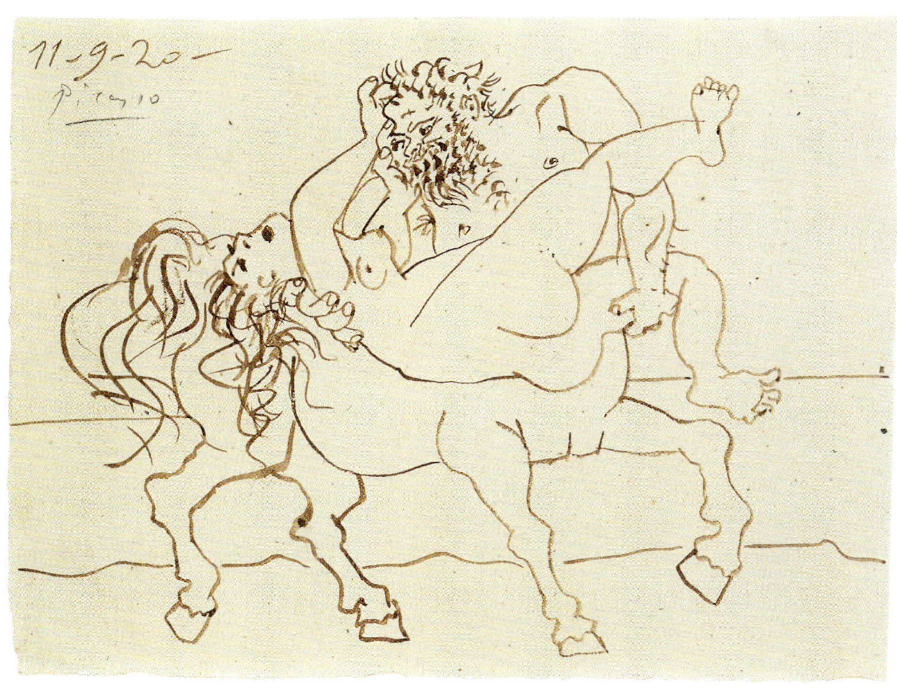

79 The Ravishment, 11 September 1920
India ink on paper; 20 x 27
Private collection

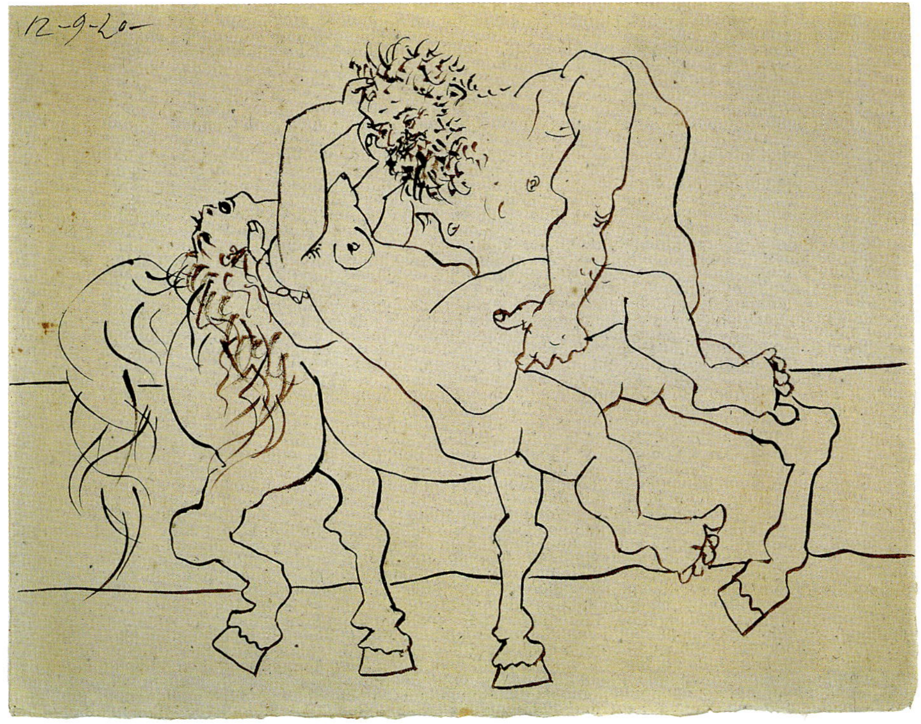

80 Nessus and Dejanira, 12 September 1920
Brown ink on paper, folded in two; 21.3 x 27.3
Paris, Musée Picasso, MP 935 [PM]

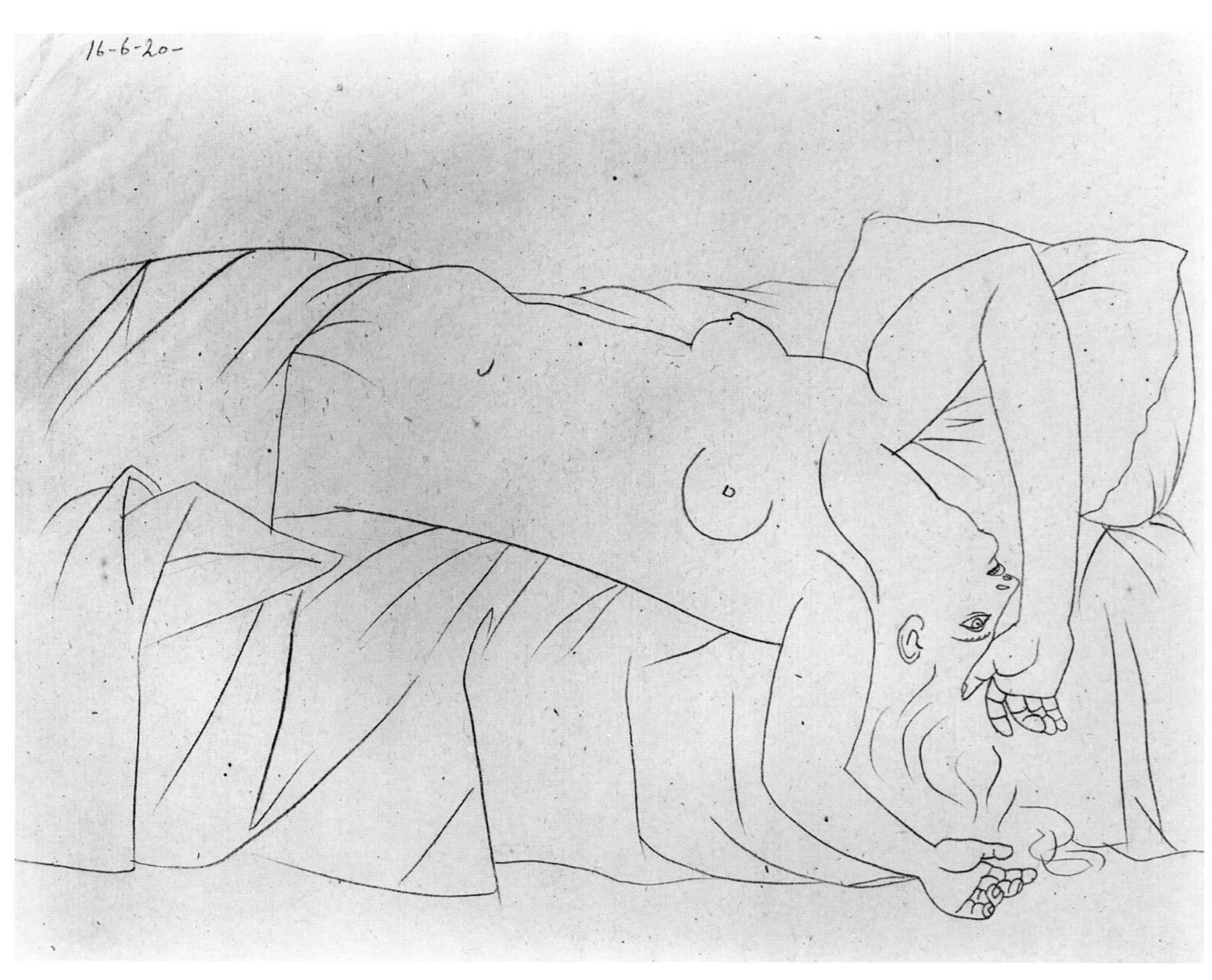

78 Nude Reclining on a Bed, 16 June 1920
Pencil on paper; 21.5 x 27.1
Paris, Musée Picasso, MP 920 [PM]

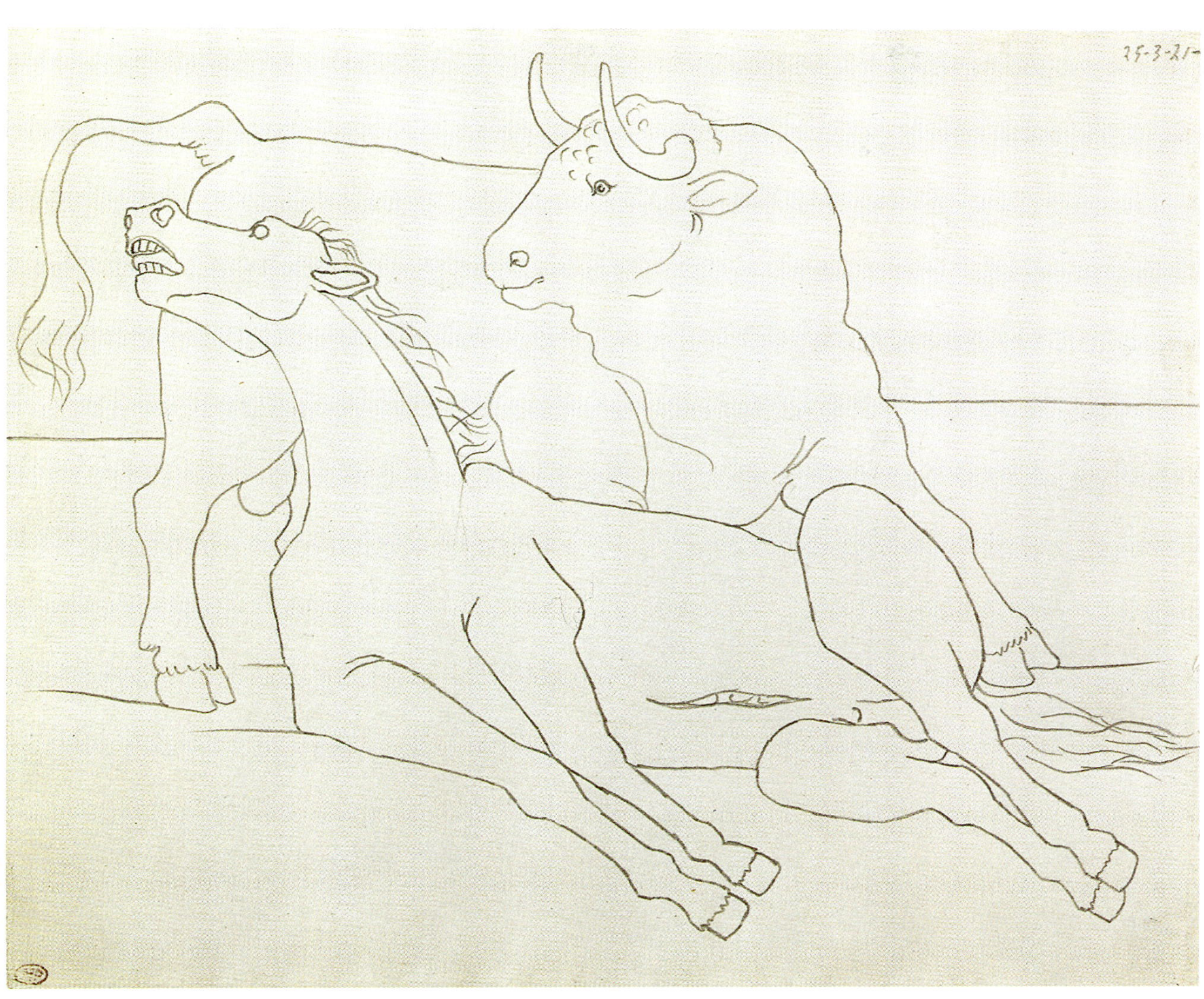

81 Bull and Wounded Horse, 25 March 1921

Pencil on paper; 24.5 x 30.5
Paris, Musée Picasso, MP 958 [P]

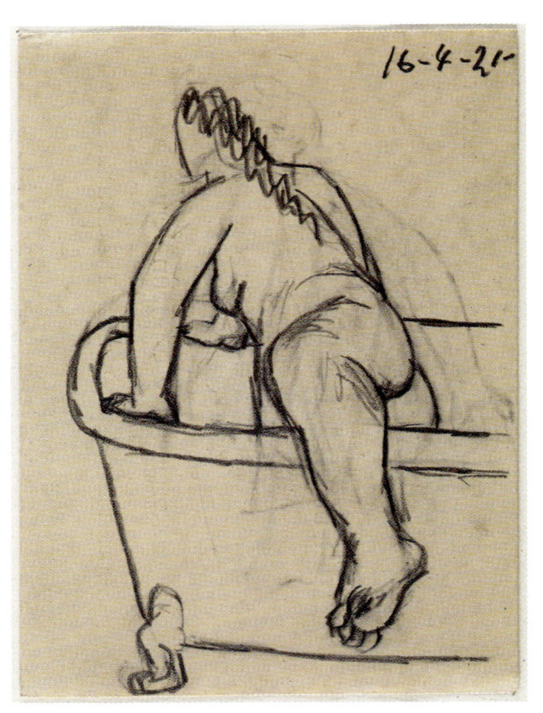

82 Woman in the Bath, 16 April 1921

Pencil on cardboard; 20 x 16
Paris, Musée Picasso, MP 959 [P]

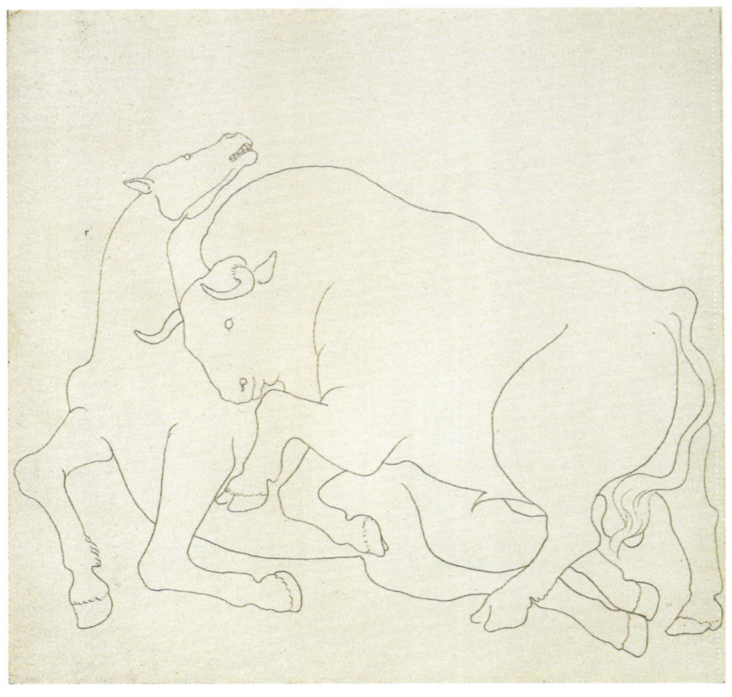

85 Corrida: Bull and Horse, 1923

Pencil on paper; 24.1 x 25
Paris, Musée Picasso, MP 998 [P]

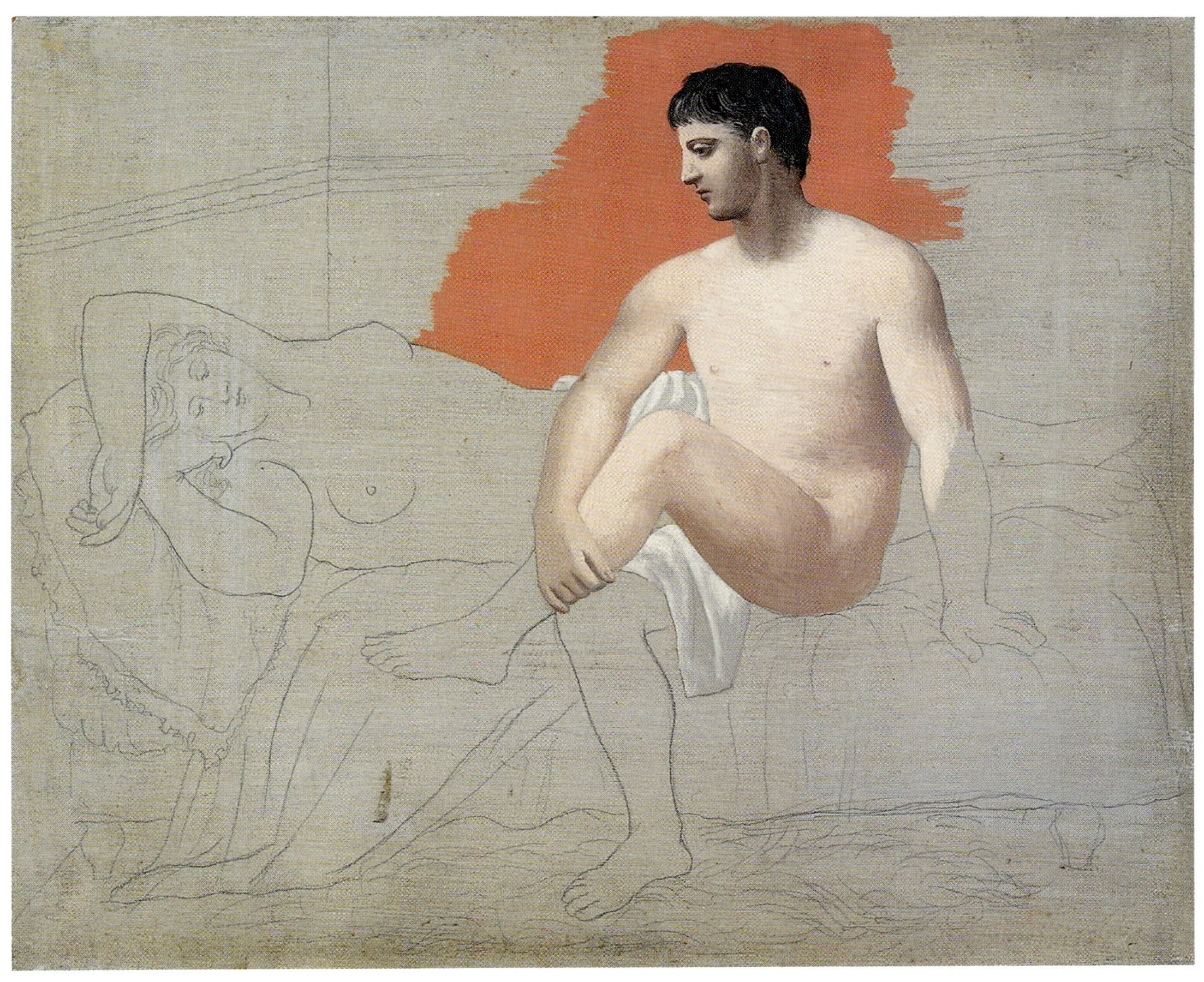

83 Nude Man Observing a Sleeping Woman, 1922
Pencil and oil on panel; 19 x 24
Private collection

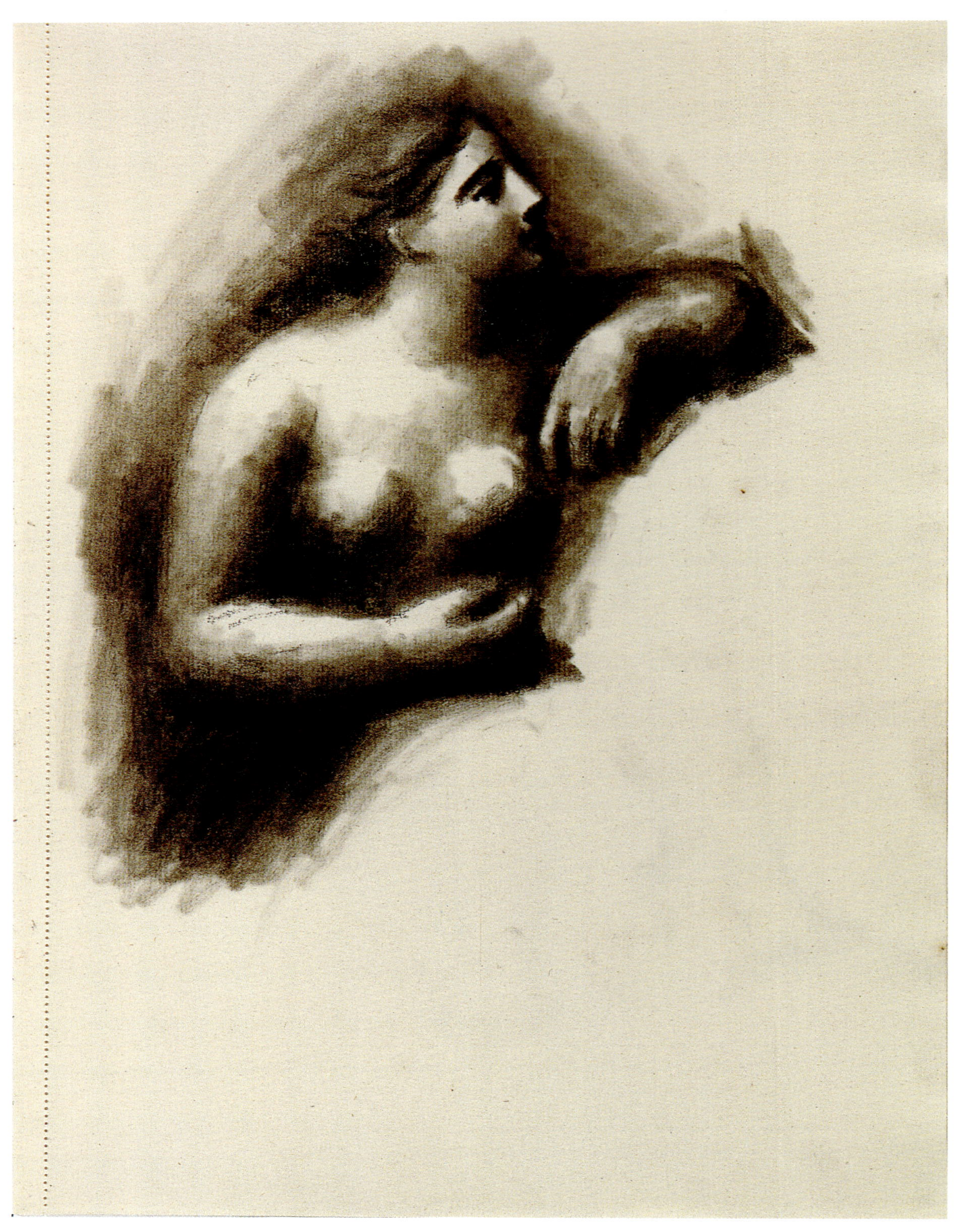

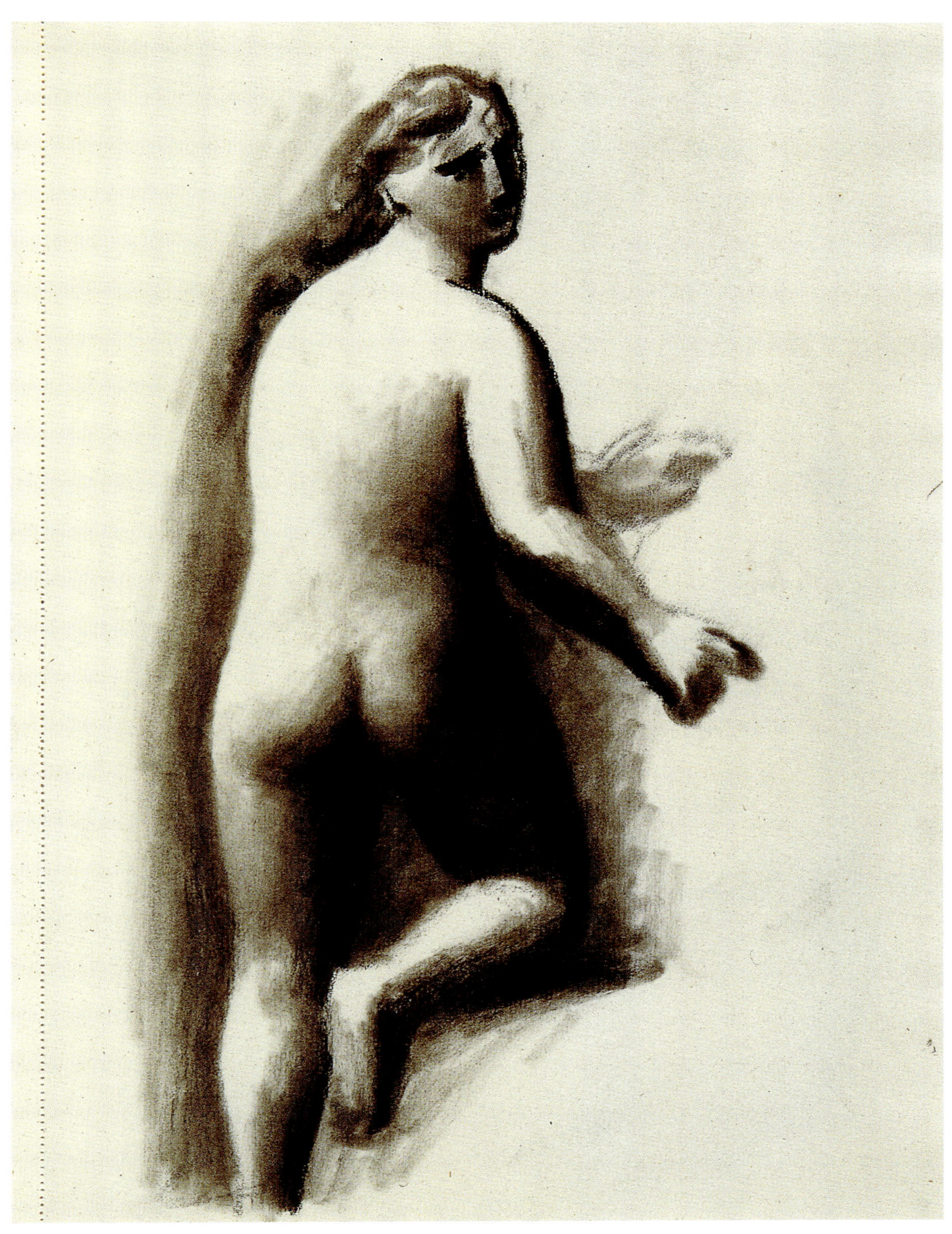

84 a and b Sketchbook, 1922

Bust of Woman Leaning on Her Elbow (f° 9 r°) and *Nude from Behind* (f° 11 r°)
Charcoal on paper; 29.5 x 23.2
Paris, Musée Picasso, MP 1868

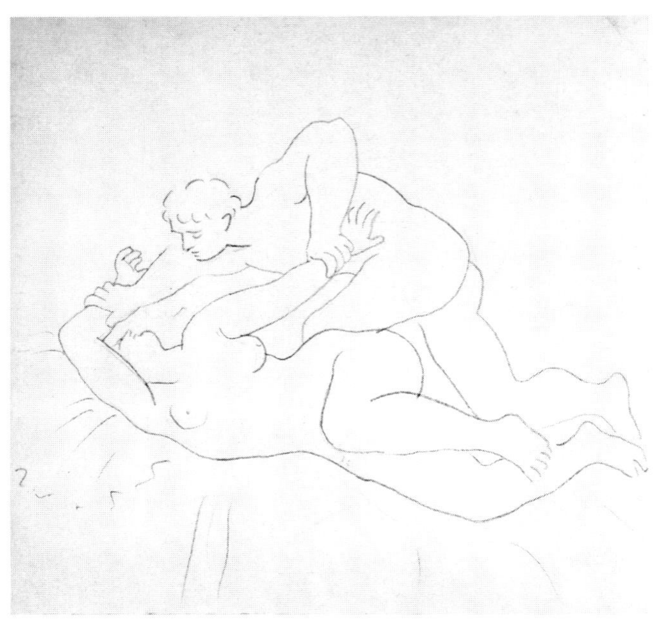

86 Embrace, circa 1925
Graphite stick on paper; 10.9 x 11.5
Paris, Musée Picasso, MP 1008

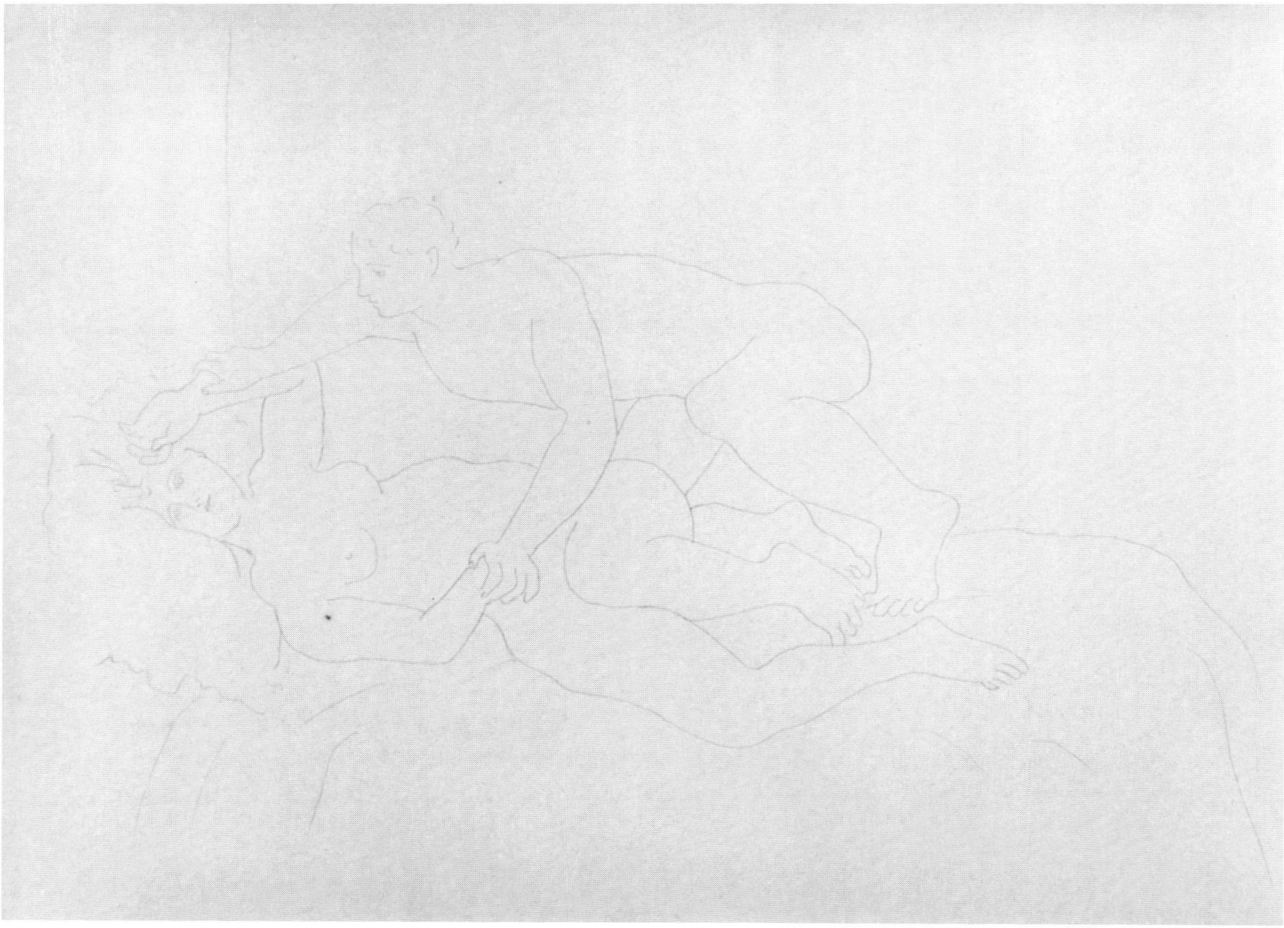

87 Embrace, circa 1925
Graphite stick on paper; 25.5 x 35.6
Paris, Musée Picasso, MP 1009 [P]

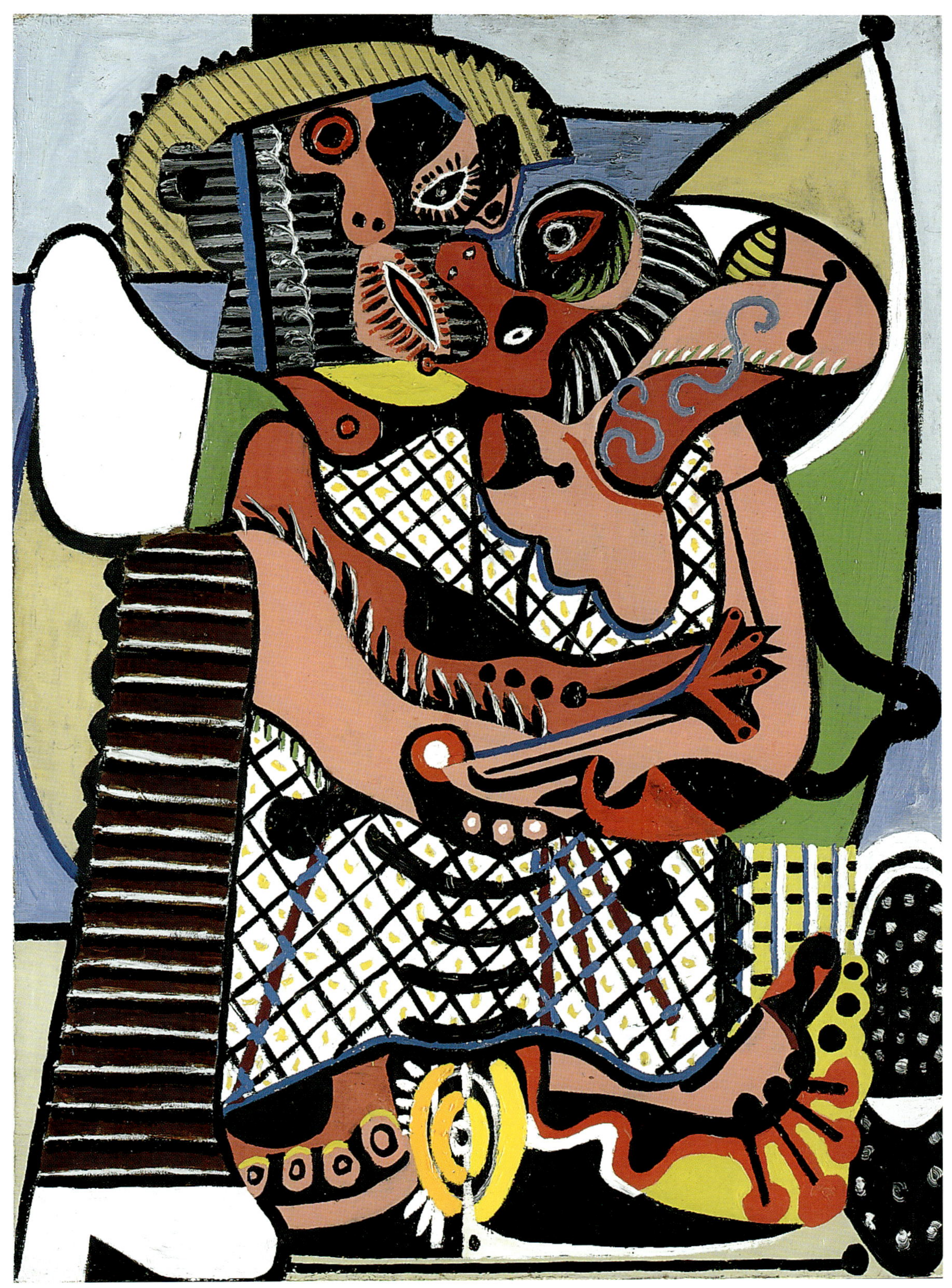

88 The Kiss, Summer 1925
Oil on canvas; 130.5 x 97.7
Paris, Musée Picasso, MP 85

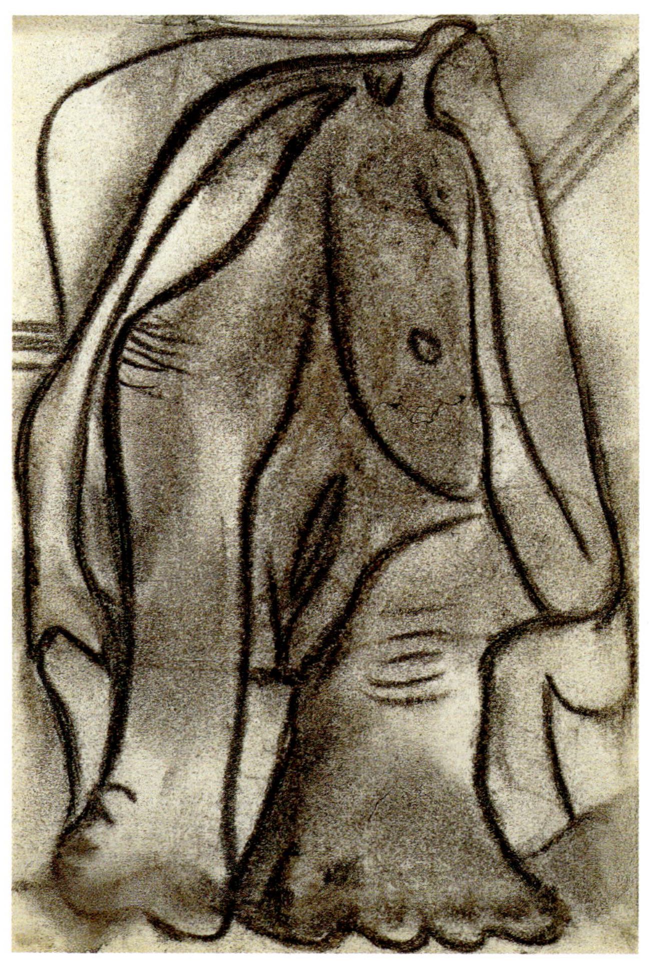

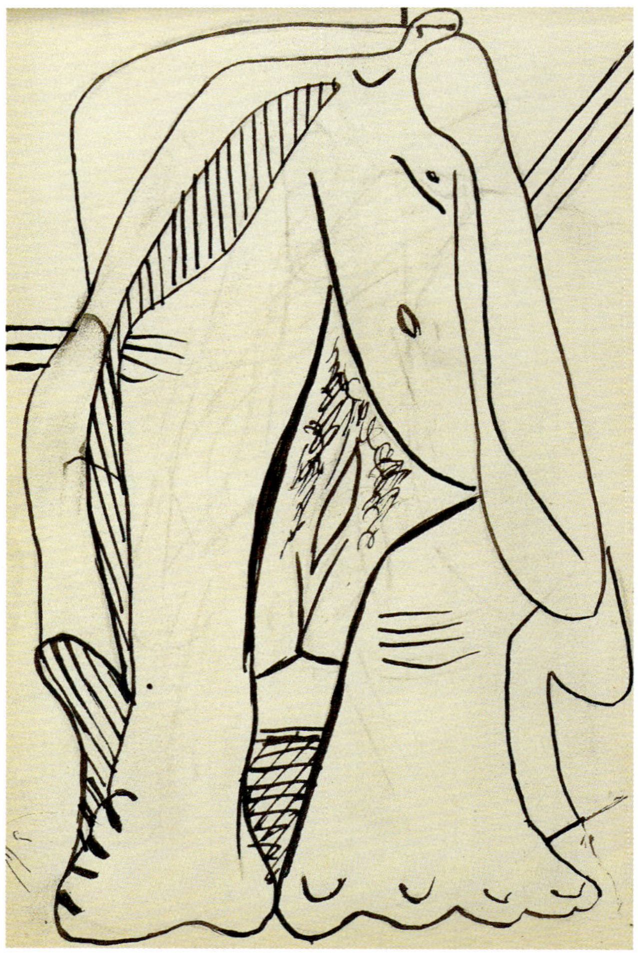

89 a and b **Sketchbook**, December 1926–8 May 1927
Nude Seated in an Armchair (f° 4 r°; f° 5 r)
Charcoal on Ingres paper (f° 4 r°); charcoal, pen and India
ink on Ingres paper (f° 5 r°); 26 x 17.5
Paris, Musée Picasso, MP 1873

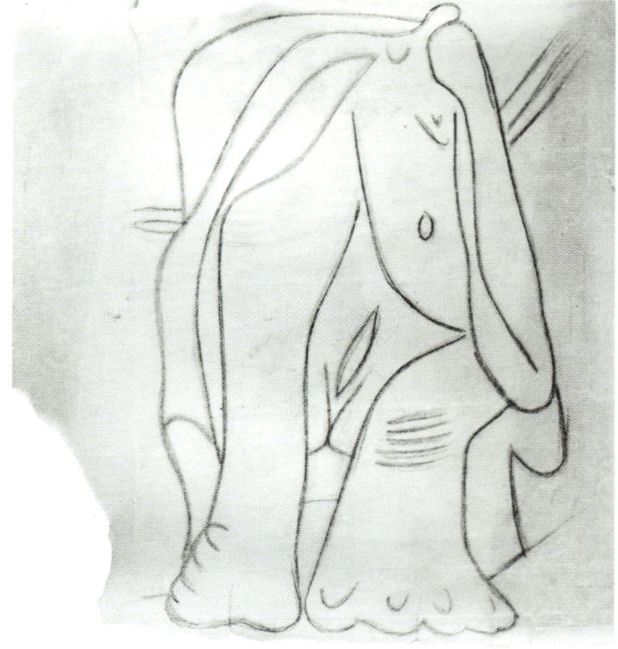

91 **Woman Seated in an Armchair**, January 1927
Graphite stick on tracing paper; 26 x 24.7
Paris, Musée Picasso, MP 1022

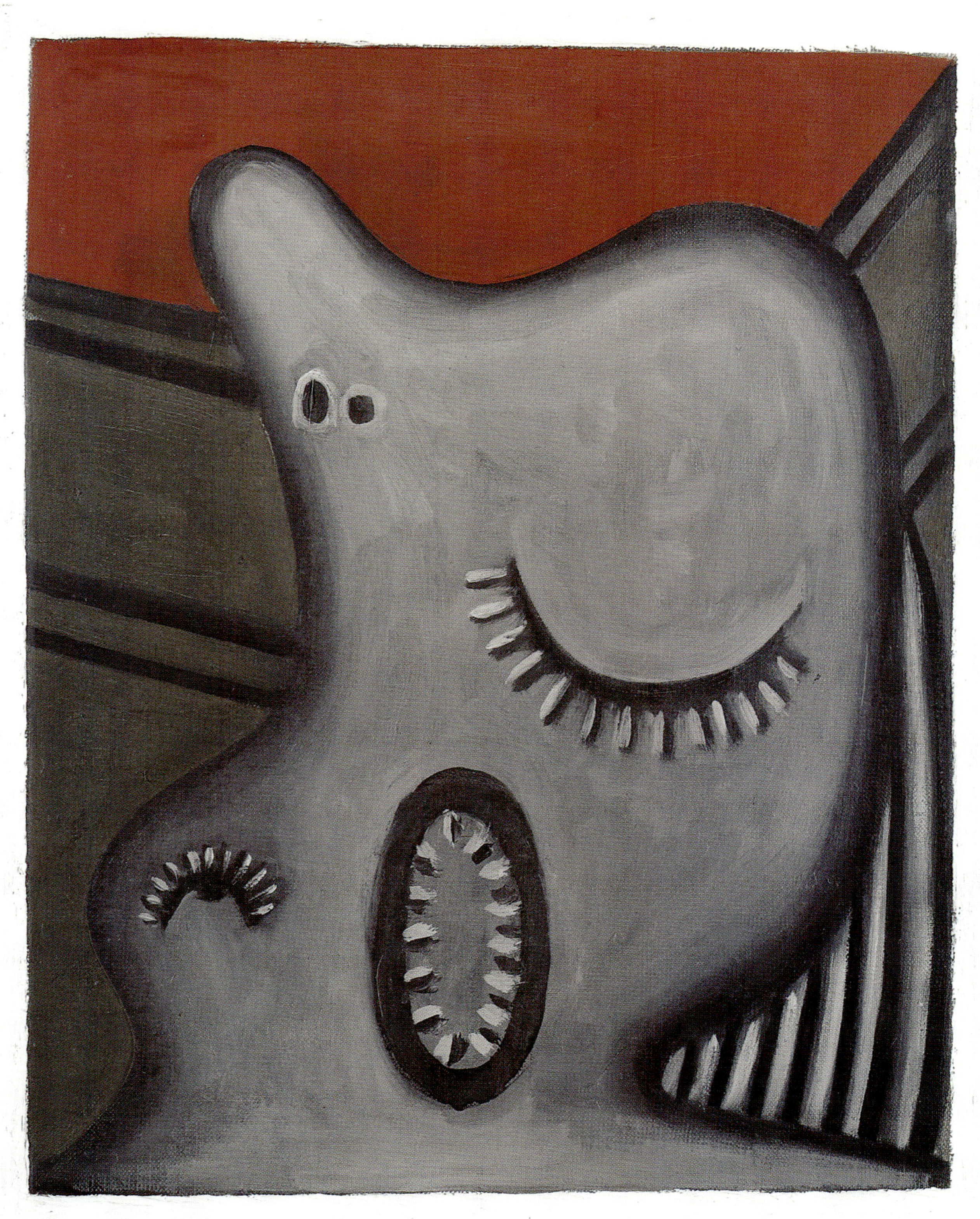

90 The Sleeper, 1927
   Oil on canvas; 46 x 38
   Paris, Musée Picasso, MP 98

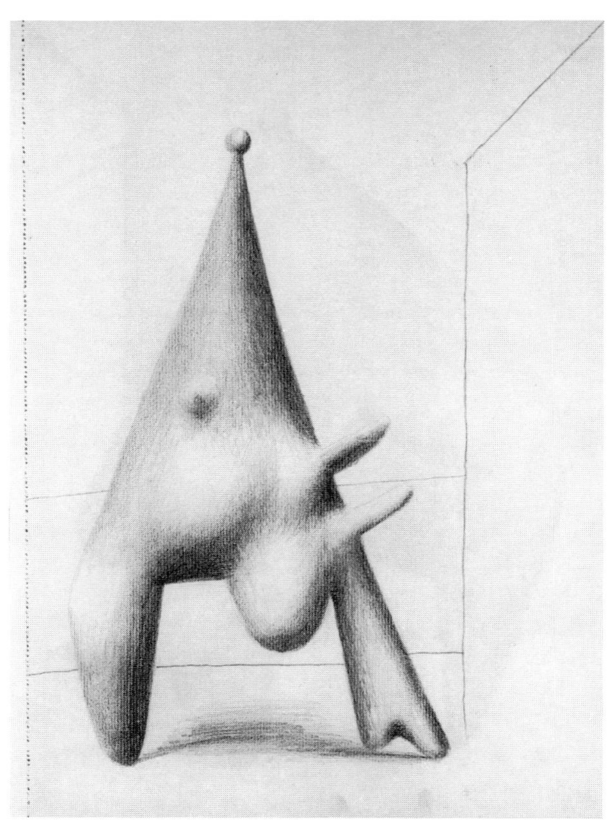

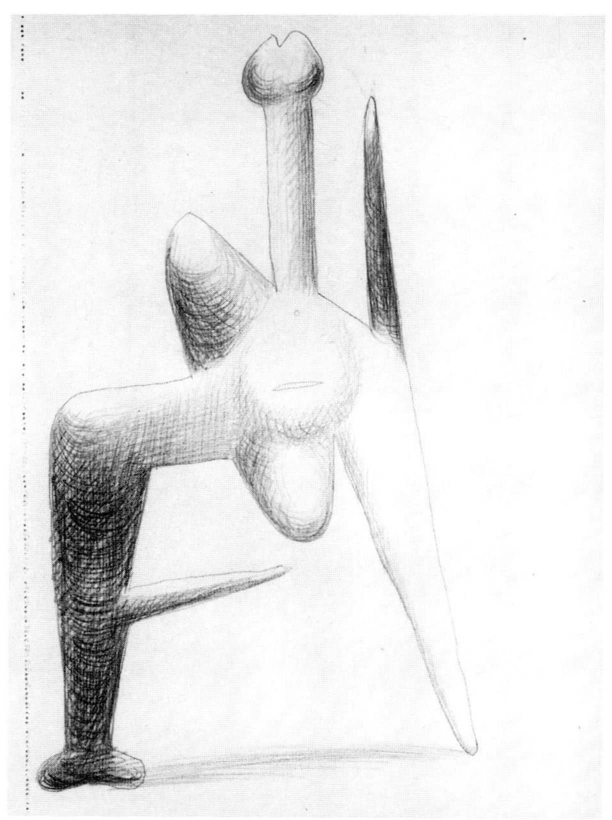

92 a, b and c **Sketchbook**, 17 July–11 September 1927
Bather and Cabana (f° 9 r°; f° 28 r°) and *Bather* (f° 19 r°)
Graphite stick on Ingres paper; 30 x 23
Paris, Musée Picasso, MP 1874

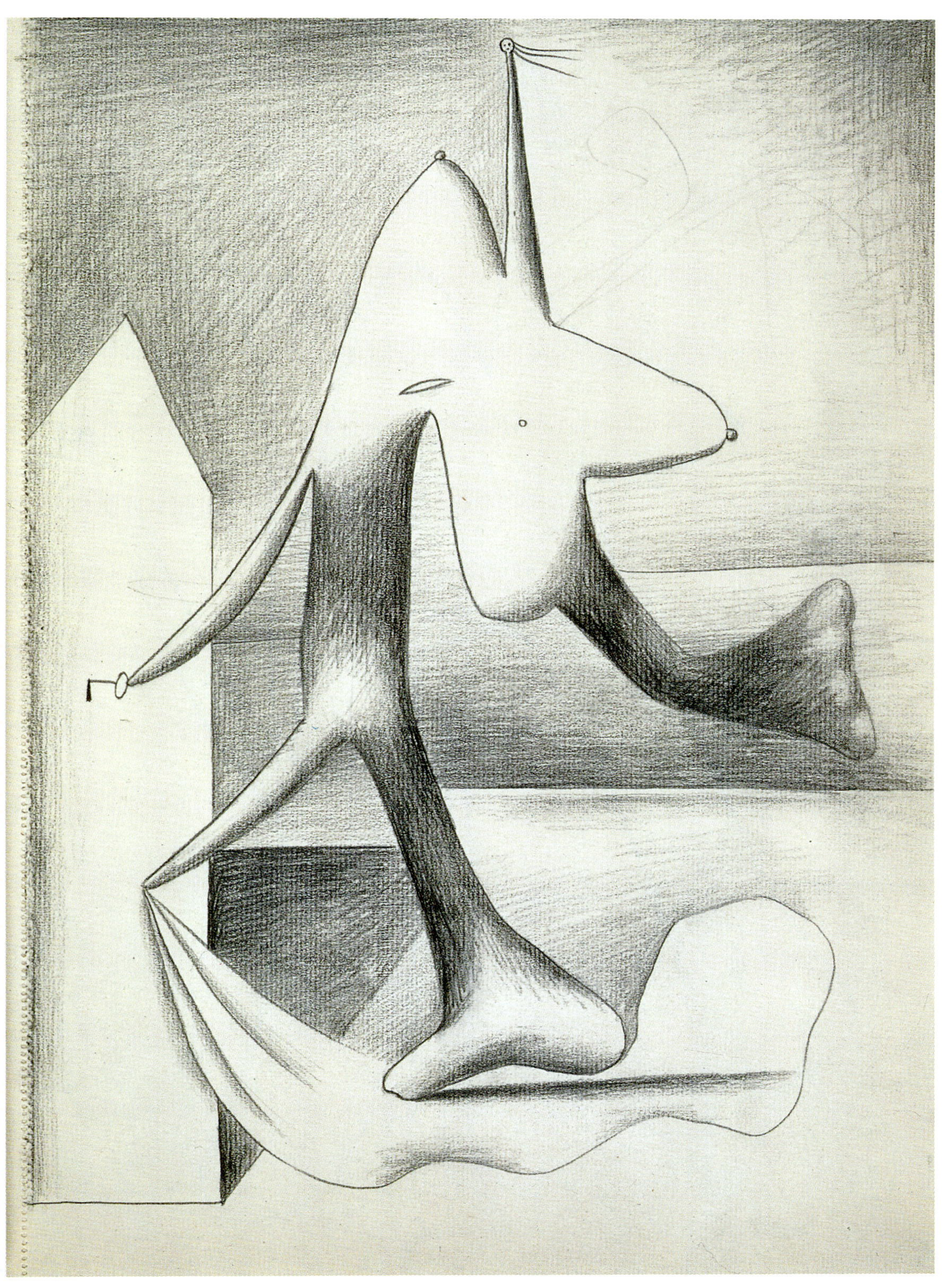

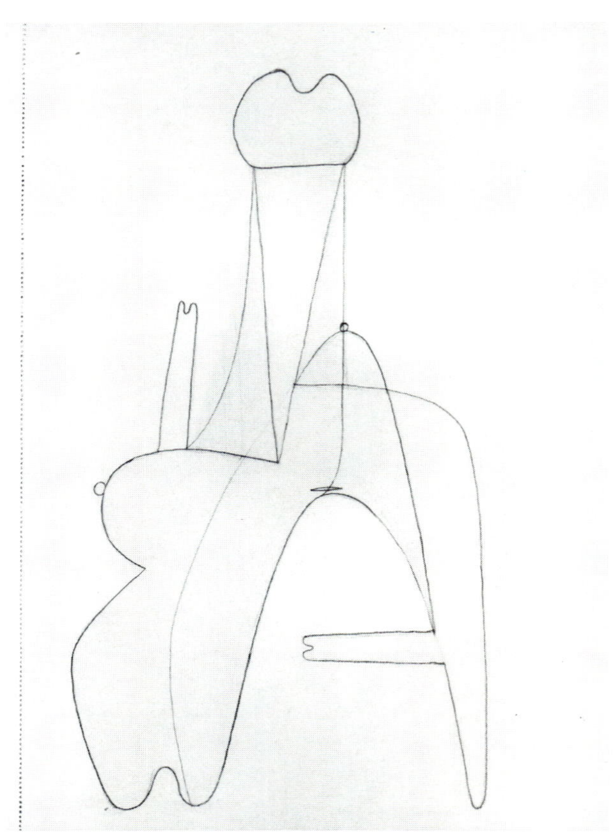

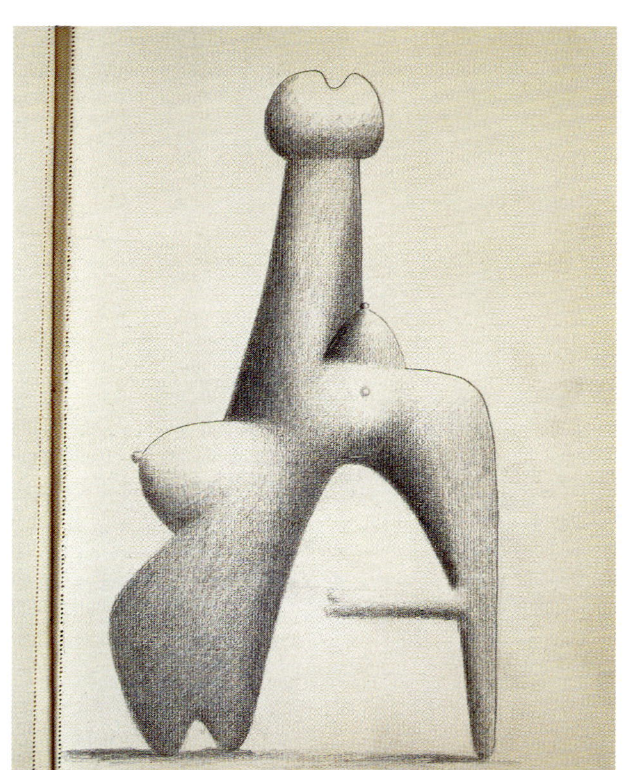

93 a and b Sketchbook, 11–24 September 1927
Bather (f° 13 r°; f° 14 r°)
Graphite stick on Ingres paper; 30.5 x 23.2
Paris, Musée Picasso, MP 1990-107

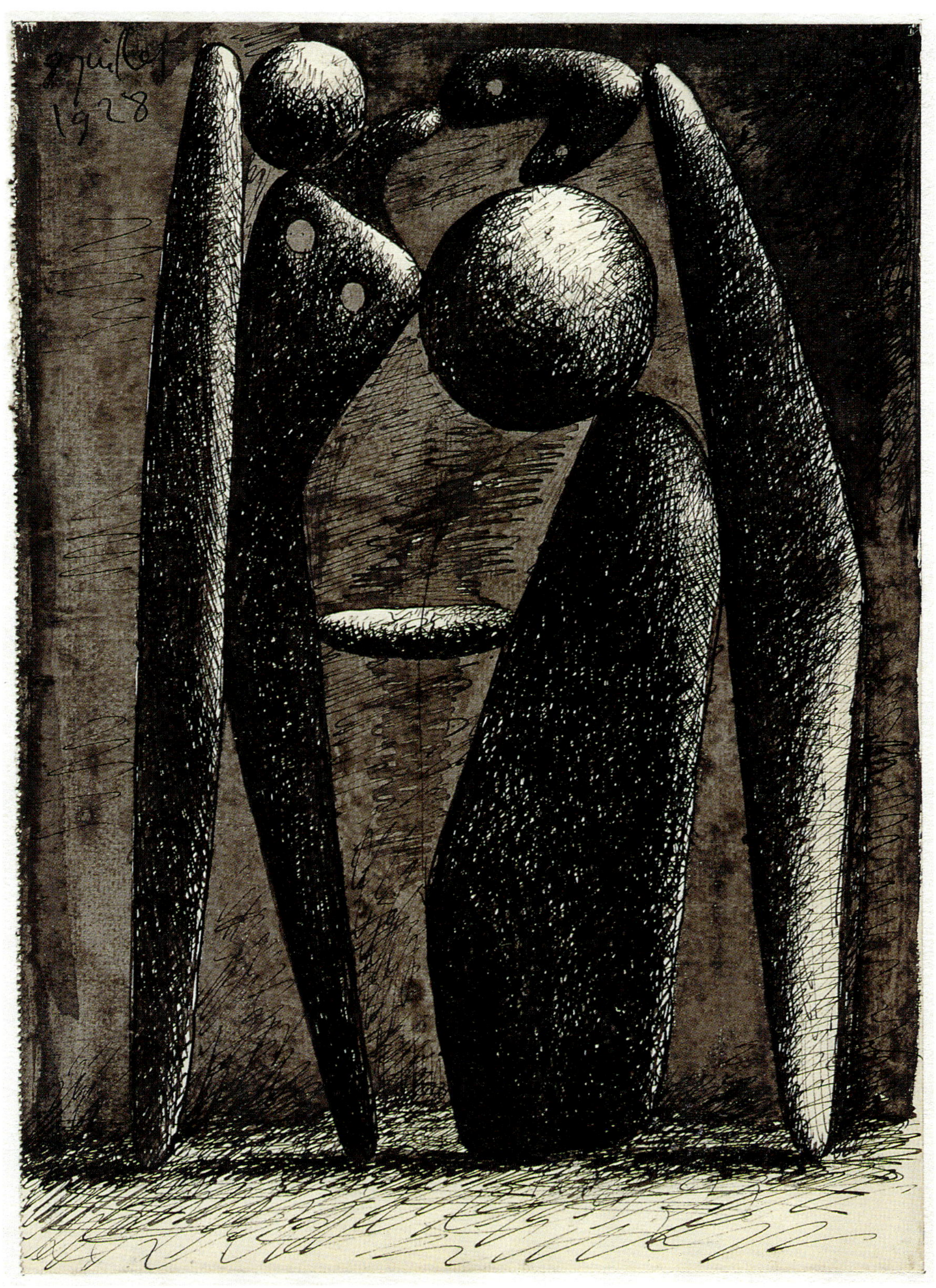

96 Bathers (Study for a Monument), 8 July 1928
India ink and wash on sketchbook page; 30.2 x 22
Paris, Musée Picasso, MP 1030

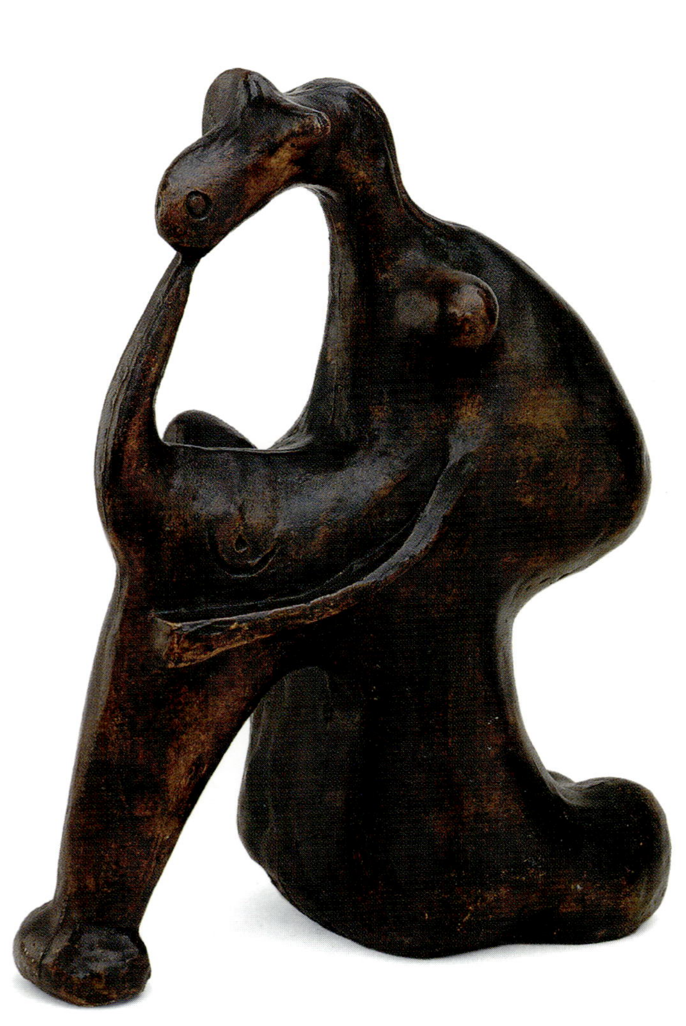

94 Metamorphosis I, 1928
Bronze; 22.8 x 18.3 x 11
Paris, Musée Picasso, MP 261 [MB]

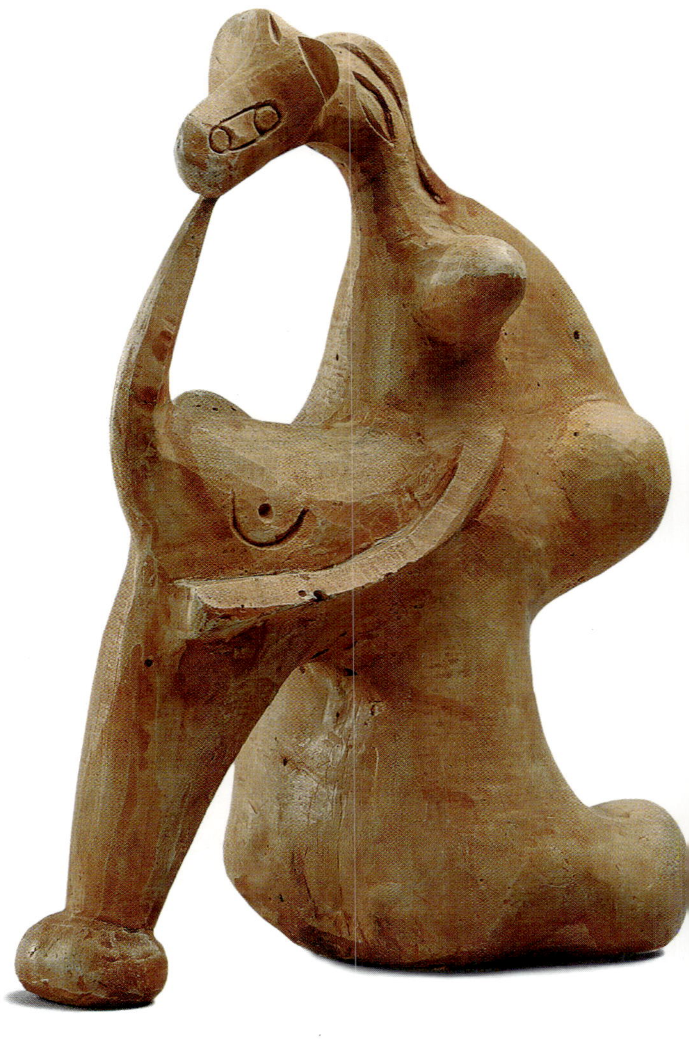

95 Metamorphosis II, 1928
Original plaster; 23 x 18 x 11
Paris, Musée Picasso, MP 262 [P]

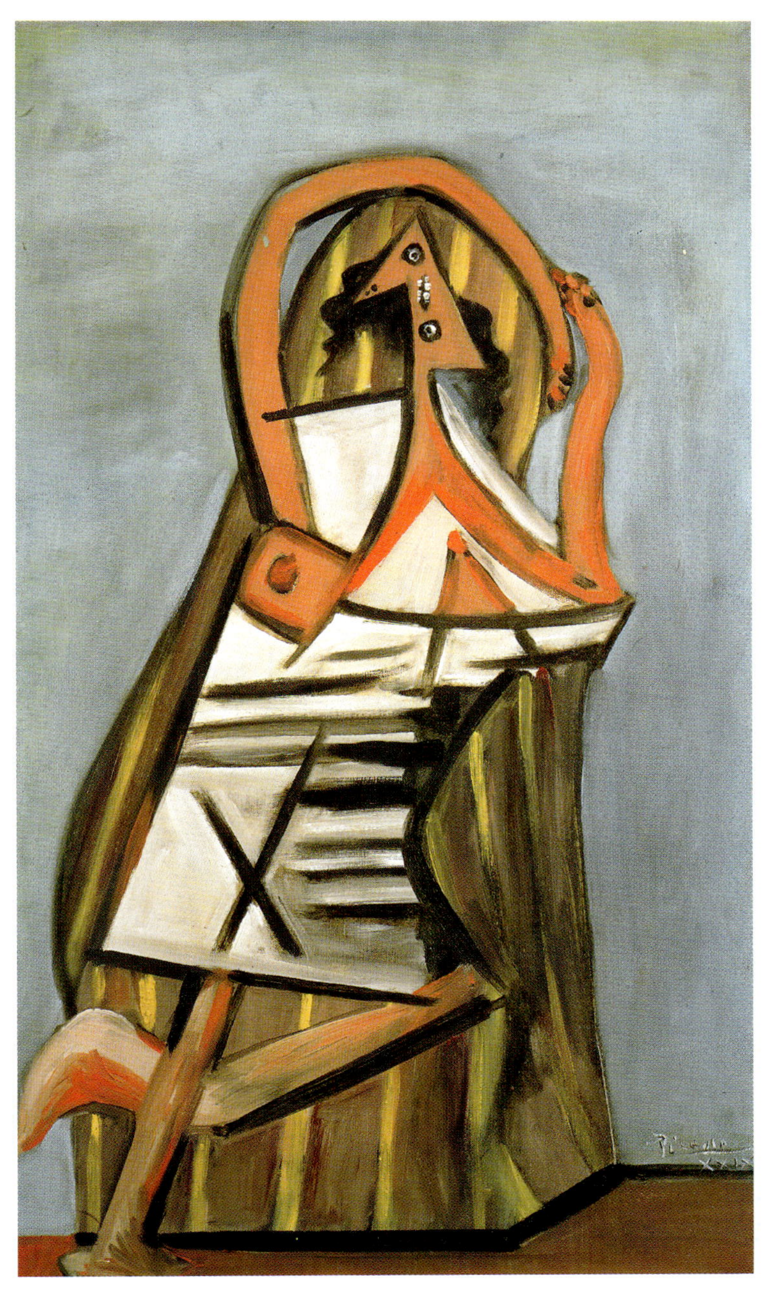

97 Woman in an Armchair, 2 March 1929
Oil on canvas; 81.2 x 50.4
Madrid, Private collection

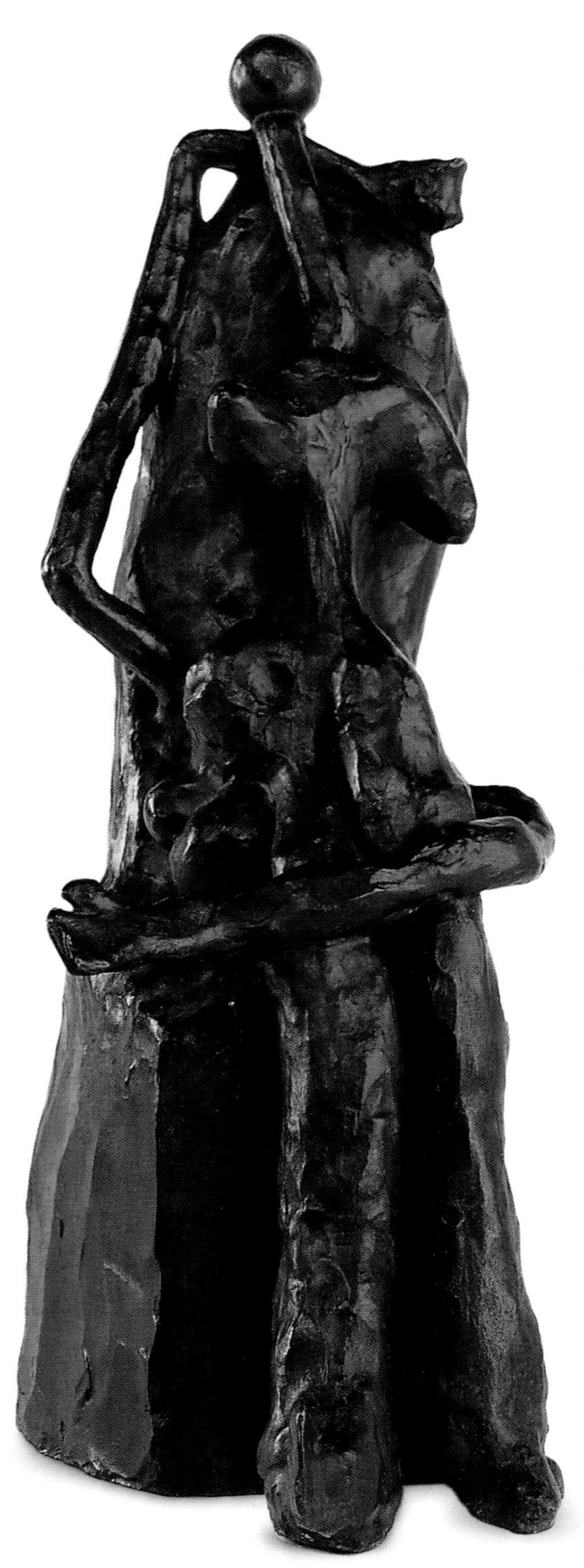

98 Seated Woman, Spring 1929

Bronze; 42.5 x 16.5 x 25
Paris, Musée Picasso, MP 287

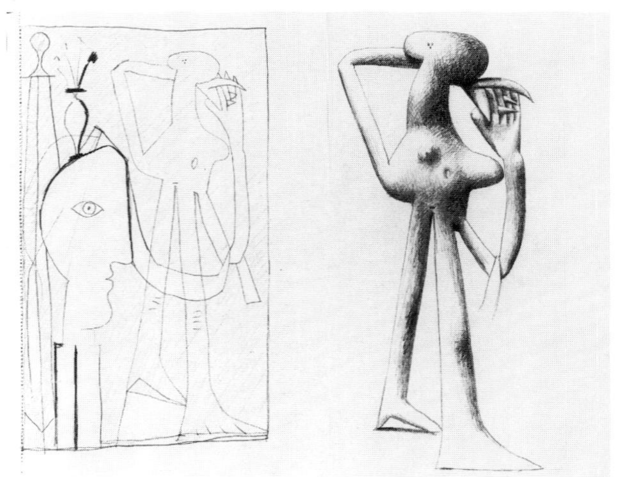

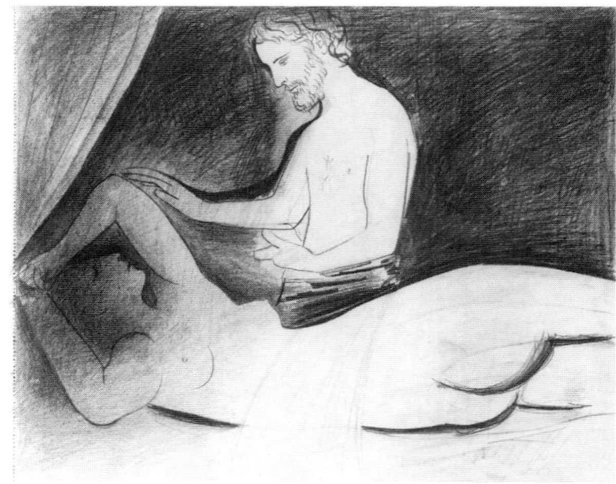

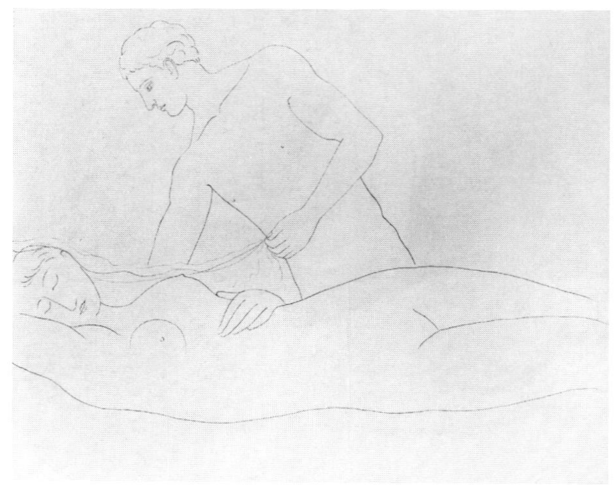

100 a, b and c Sketchbook, 25 February 1929–12 January 1930

Study of Woman, Sculpture and Vase of Flowers (f° 26 r°),
Bearded Man Watching Over a Sleeping Woman (f° 35 r°) and
Man Covering a Sleeping Woman (f° 36 r°)
Graphite stick on paper; 23.5 x 30.5
Paris, Musée Picasso, MP 1875

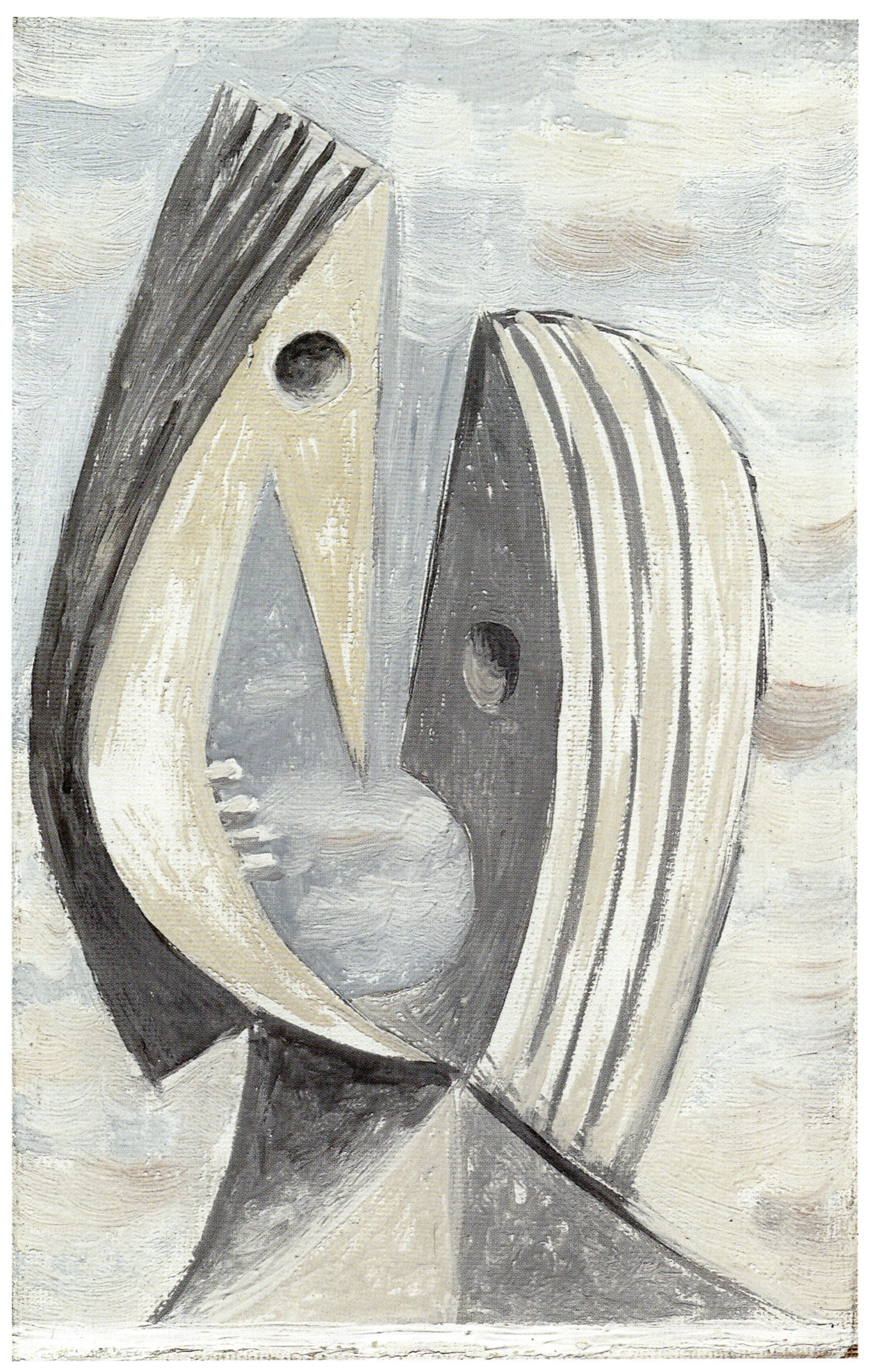

99 The Kiss, 25 August 1929
Oil on canvas; 22 x 14
Paris, Musée Picasso, MP 117

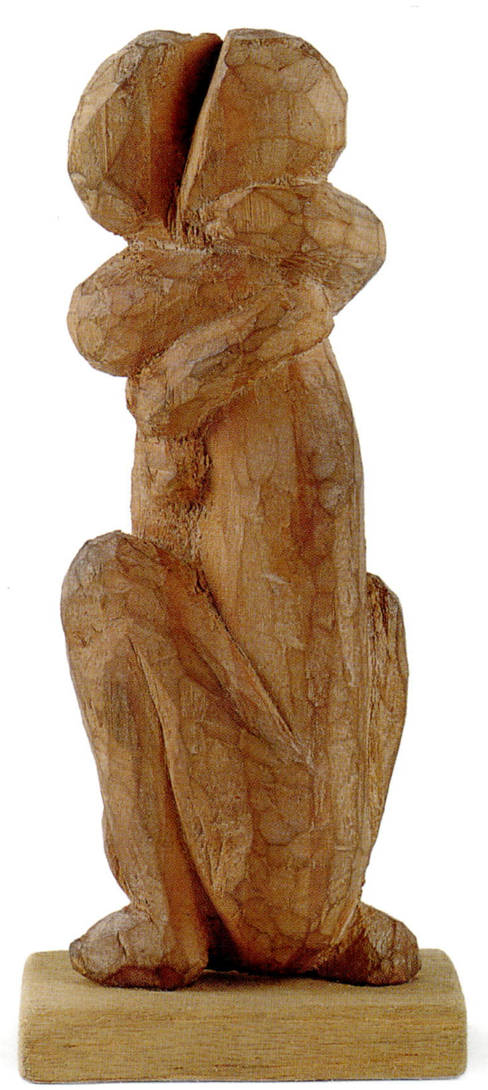

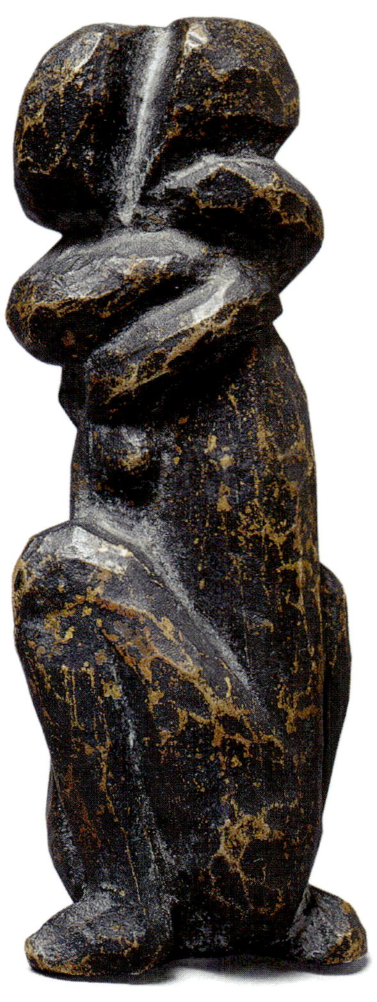

101 Couple, 1930
Sculpted linden; 10.5 x 3.5 x 2.2
Paris, Musée Picasso, MP 285 [P]

102 The Couple, 1930
Bronze; 10.5 x 3.5 x 2.2
London, Private collection [MB]

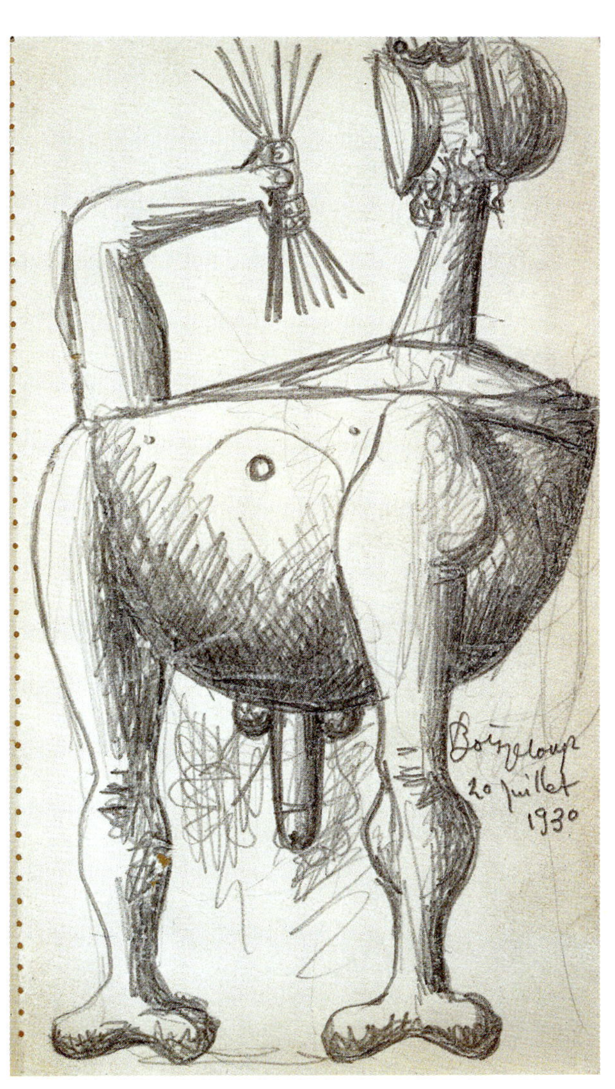
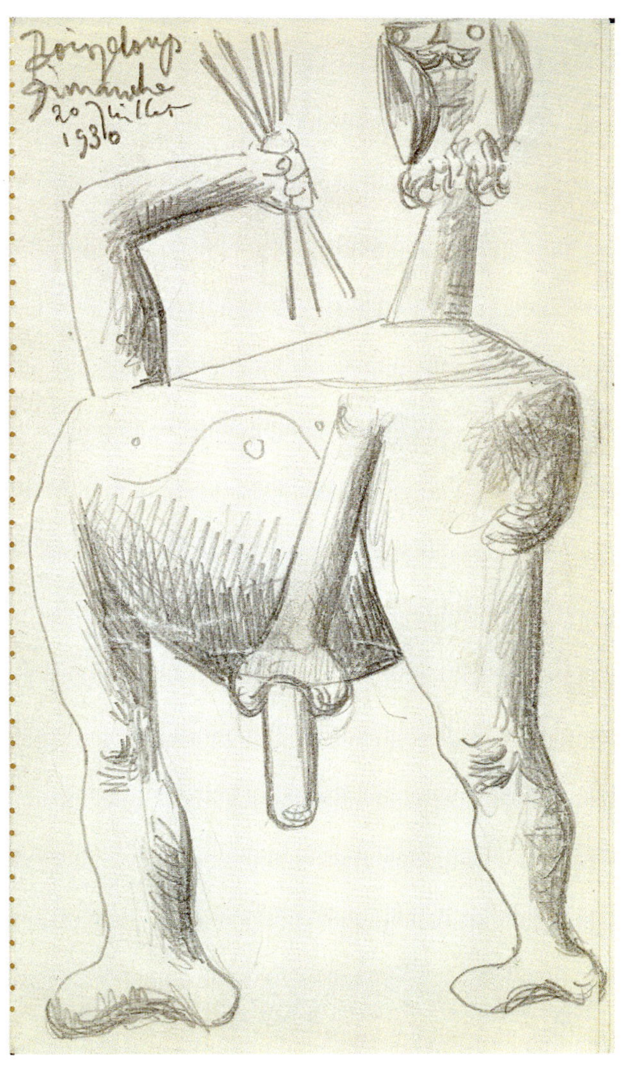

103 a and b Sketchbook, 20 July 1930

Figure of Man's Head Brandishing Rods (f° 46 r°; f° 47 r°)
Graphite stick on paper; 17 x 10.5
Paris, Musée Picasso, MP 1990-109

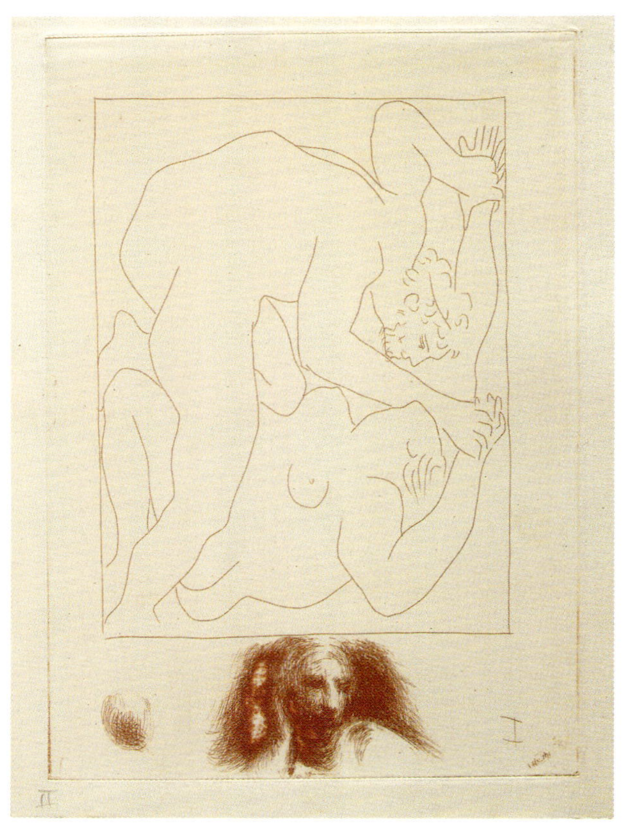 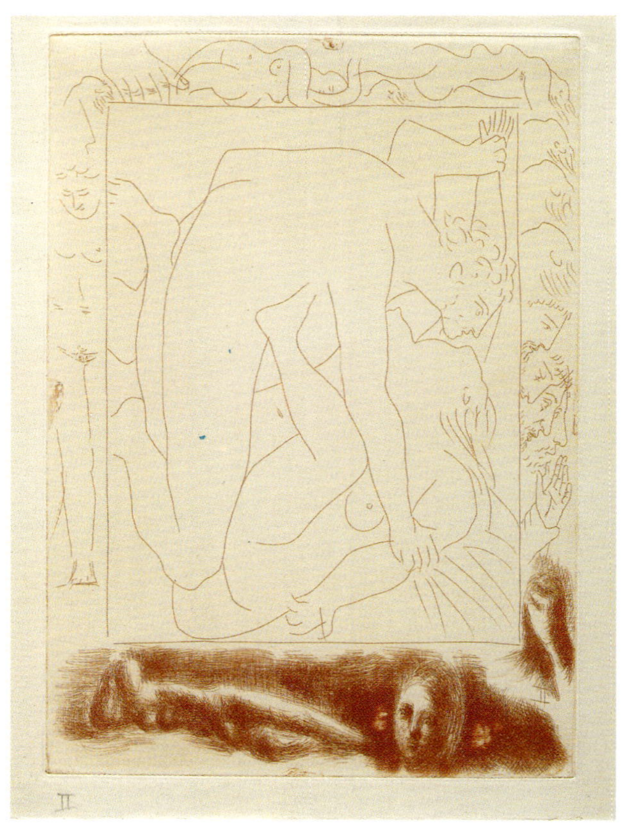

104 Struggle between Tereus and His Sister-in-Law
Philomela (Plate I), 18 October 1930

Etching on copper; 31 x 22.3
Paris, Musée Picasso, MP 2155 [M]

105 Struggle between Tereus and His Sister-in-Law
Philomela (Plate II), 18 October 1930

Etching on copper; 31 x 22.3
Paris, Musée Picasso, MP 2156 [B]

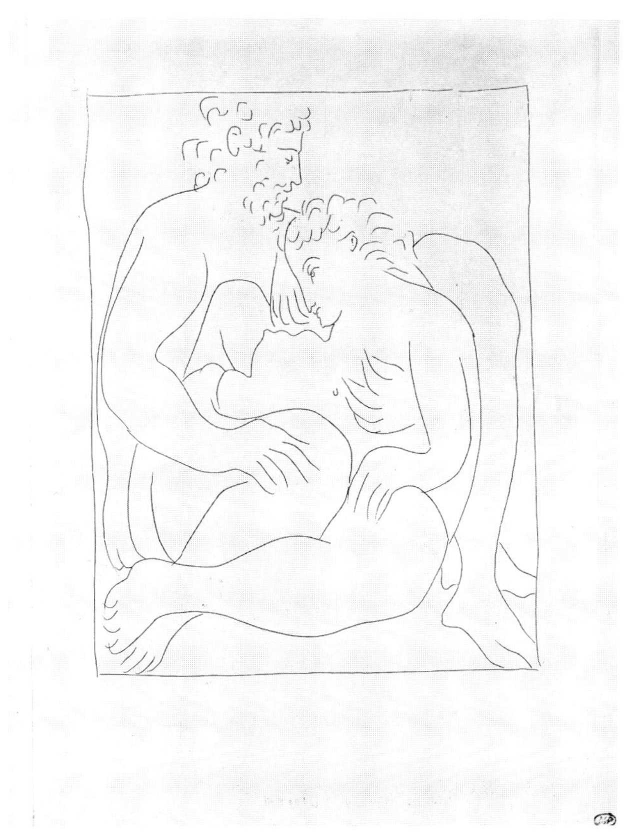

106 Jupiter and Semele (Plate IV), 25 October 1930
Etching on copper; 31.3 x 22.3
Paris, Musée Picasso, MP 2160 [M]

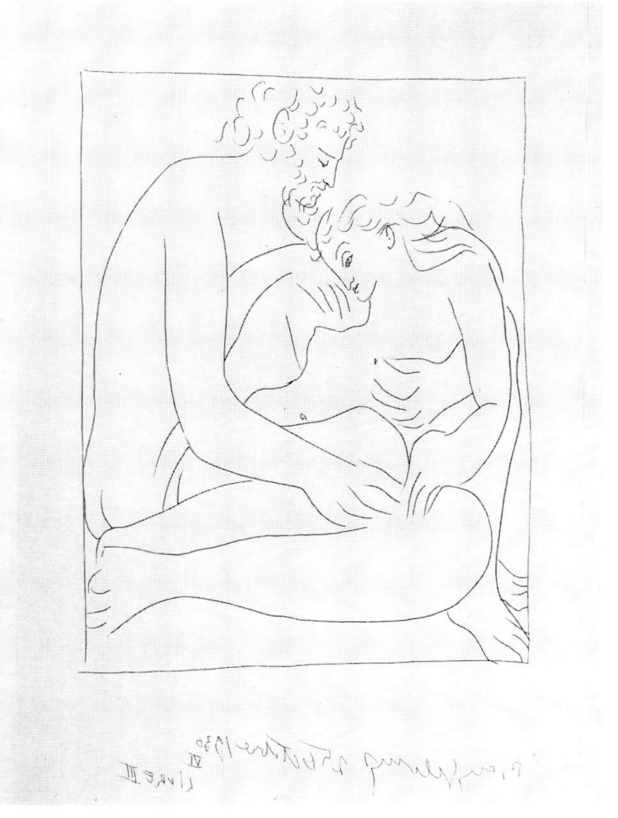

107 Jupiter and Semele (Plate VI), 25 October 1930
Etching on copper; 31.3 x 22.2
Paris, Musée Picasso, MP 2162 [B]

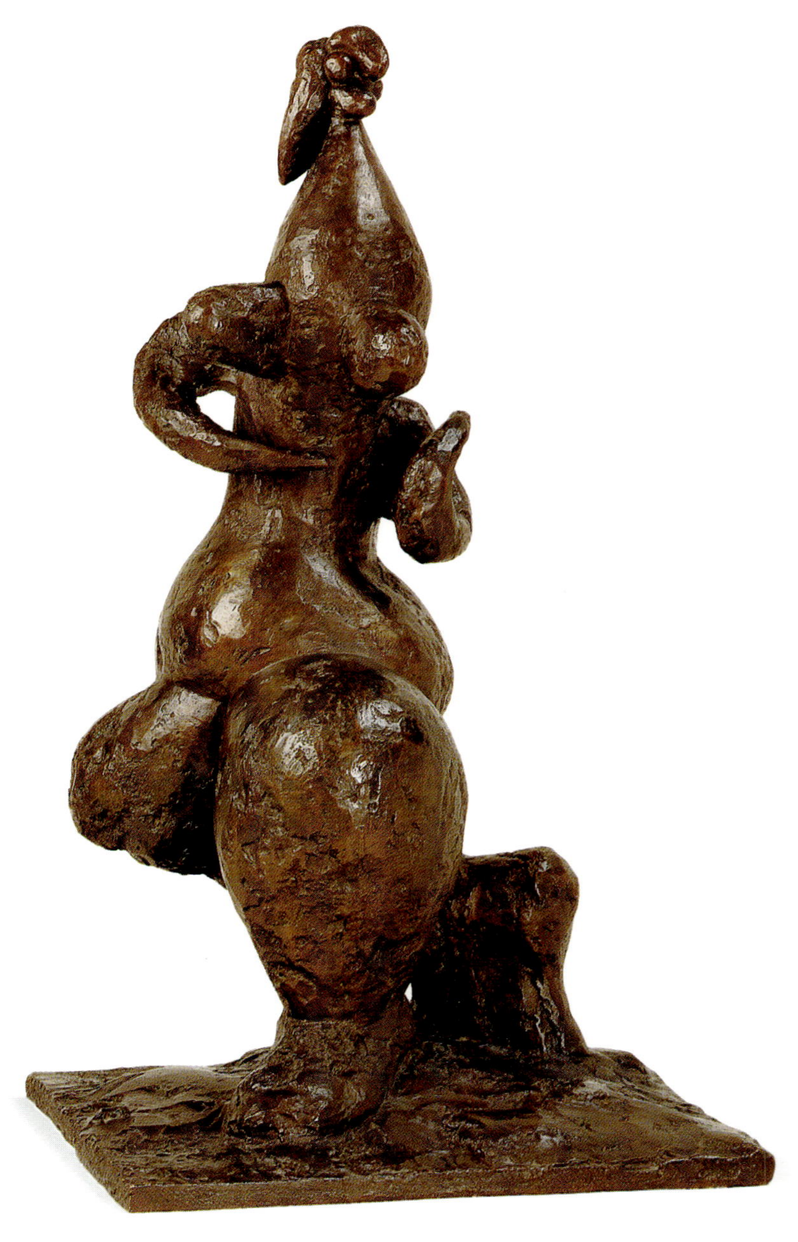

108 Bather, 1931
Bronze; 70 x 40.2 x 31.5
Paris, Musée Picasso, MP 289 [P]

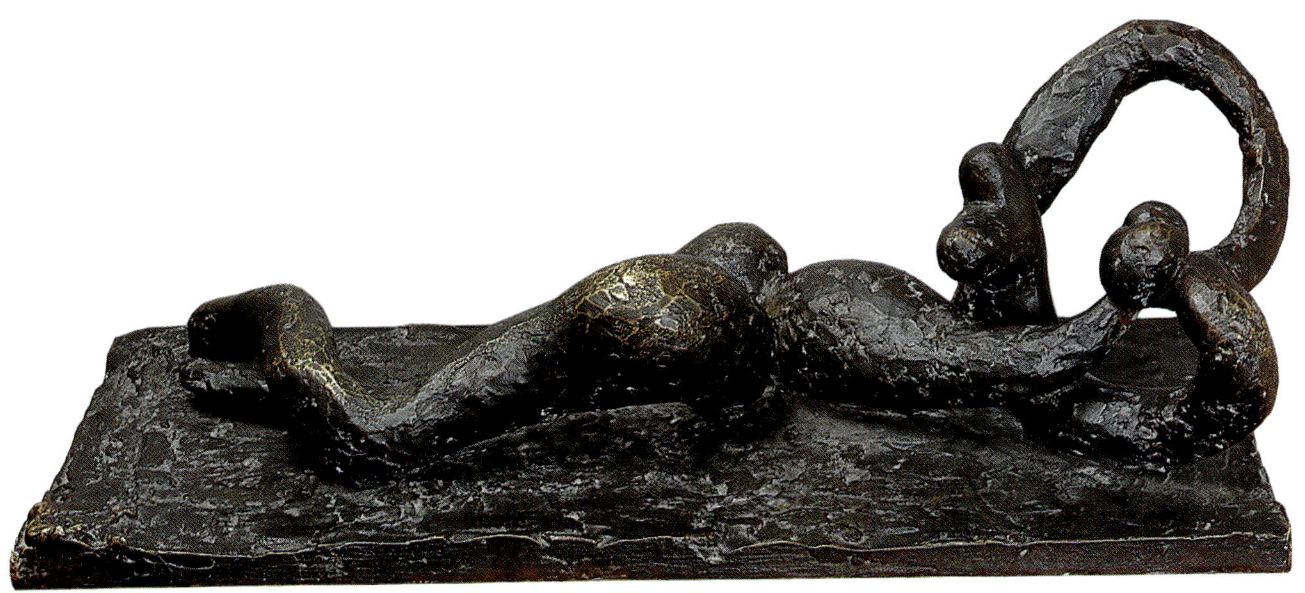

110 Reclining Bather, 1931
Bronze; 23 x 72 x 31
Paris, Musée Picasso, MP 290

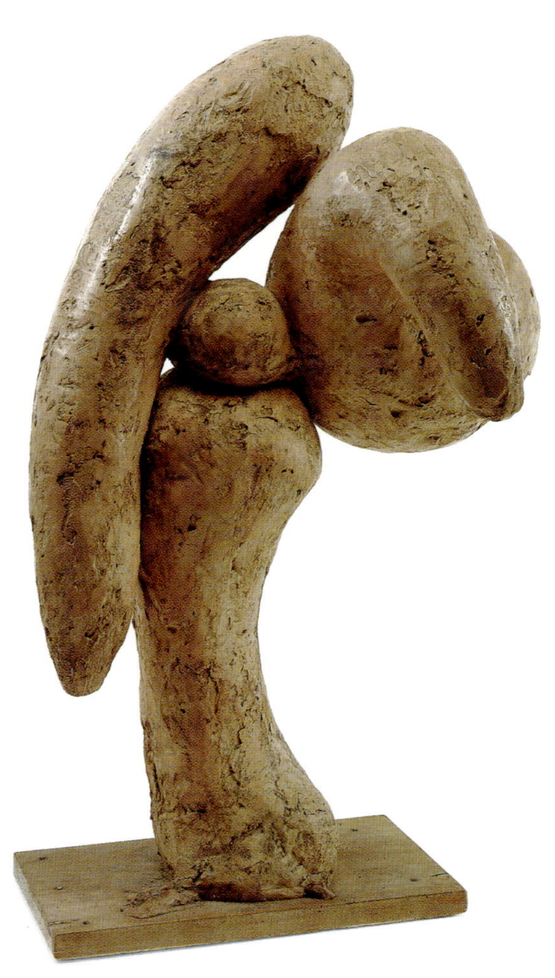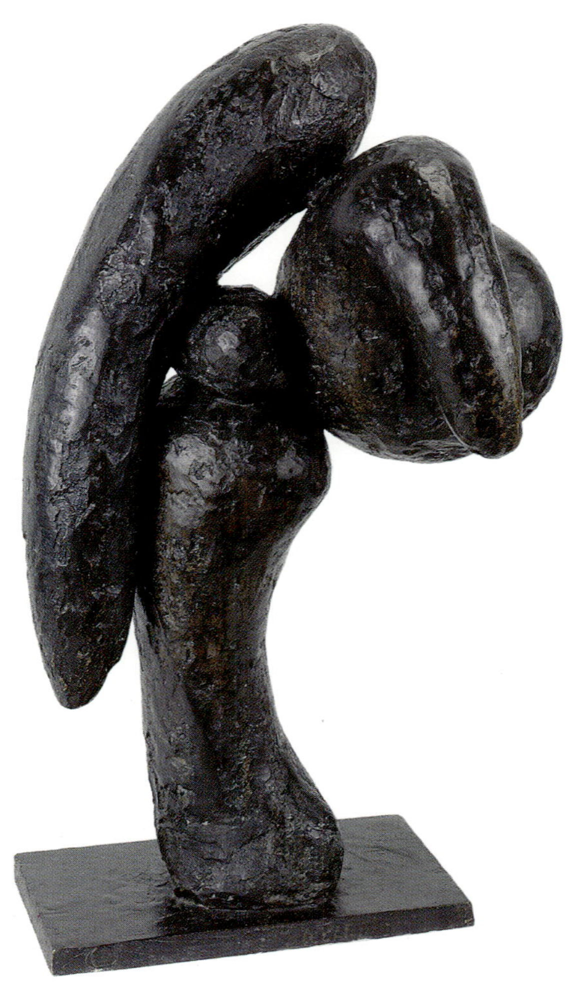

111 Head of a Woman, 1931
Original plaster; 71.5 x 41 x 33
Paris, Musée Picasso, MP 291 [P]

114 Head of a Woman, 1931
Bronze; 71.5 x 41 x 33
Paris, Musée Picasso, MP 292 [MB]

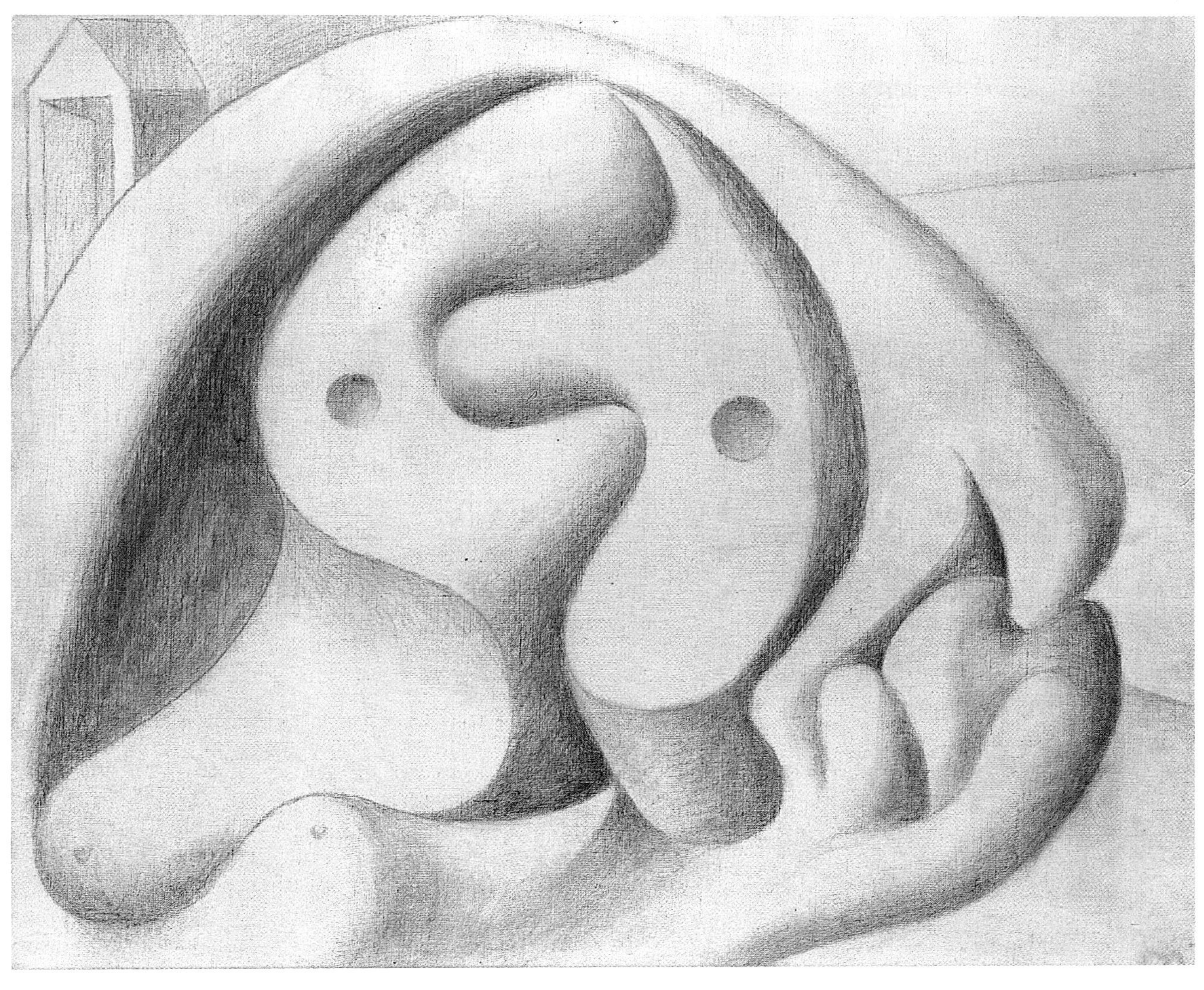

109 Bather on the Beach, 1931
Charcoal on canvas; 65 x 81
New York, Marina Picasso collection (inv. 12553), Courtesy Jan Krugier Gallery, Ditesheim & Co.

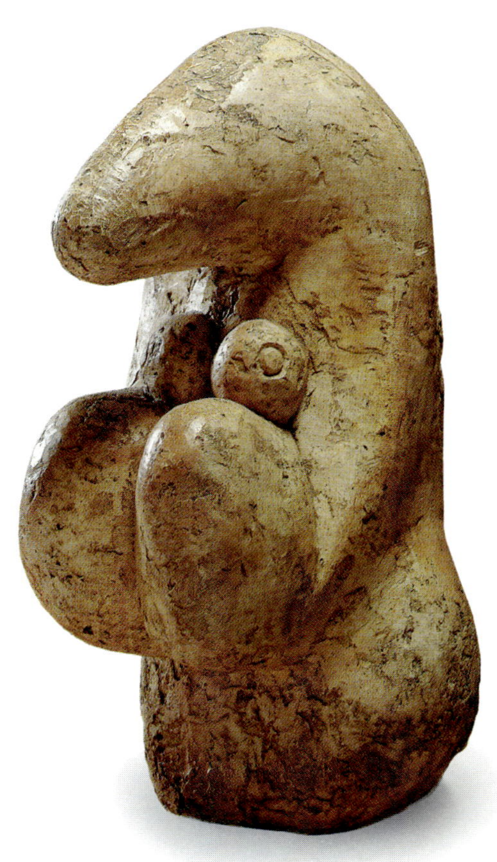

112 Head of a Woman, 1931
Original plaster; 62.5 x 28 x 41.5
Paris, Musée Picasso, MP 293 [P]

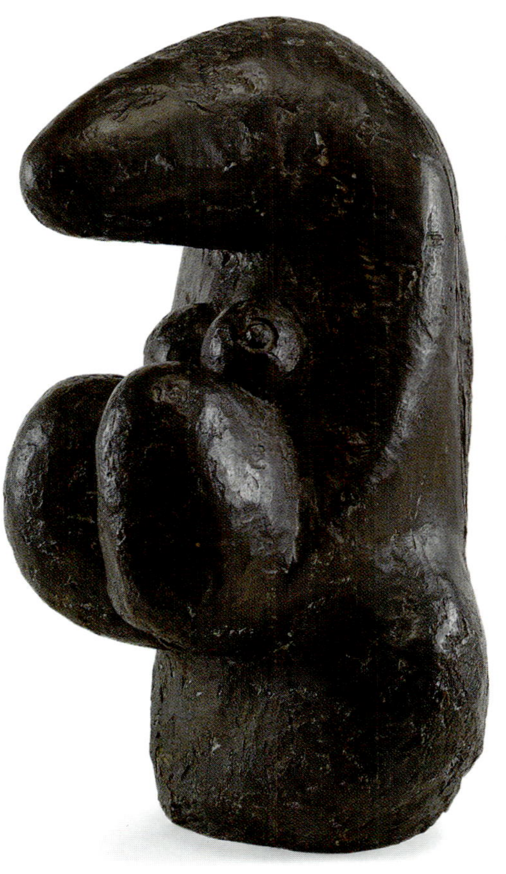

115 Bust of a Woman, 1931
Bronze; 62.5 x 28 x 41.5
Paris, Musée Picasso, MP 294 [MB]

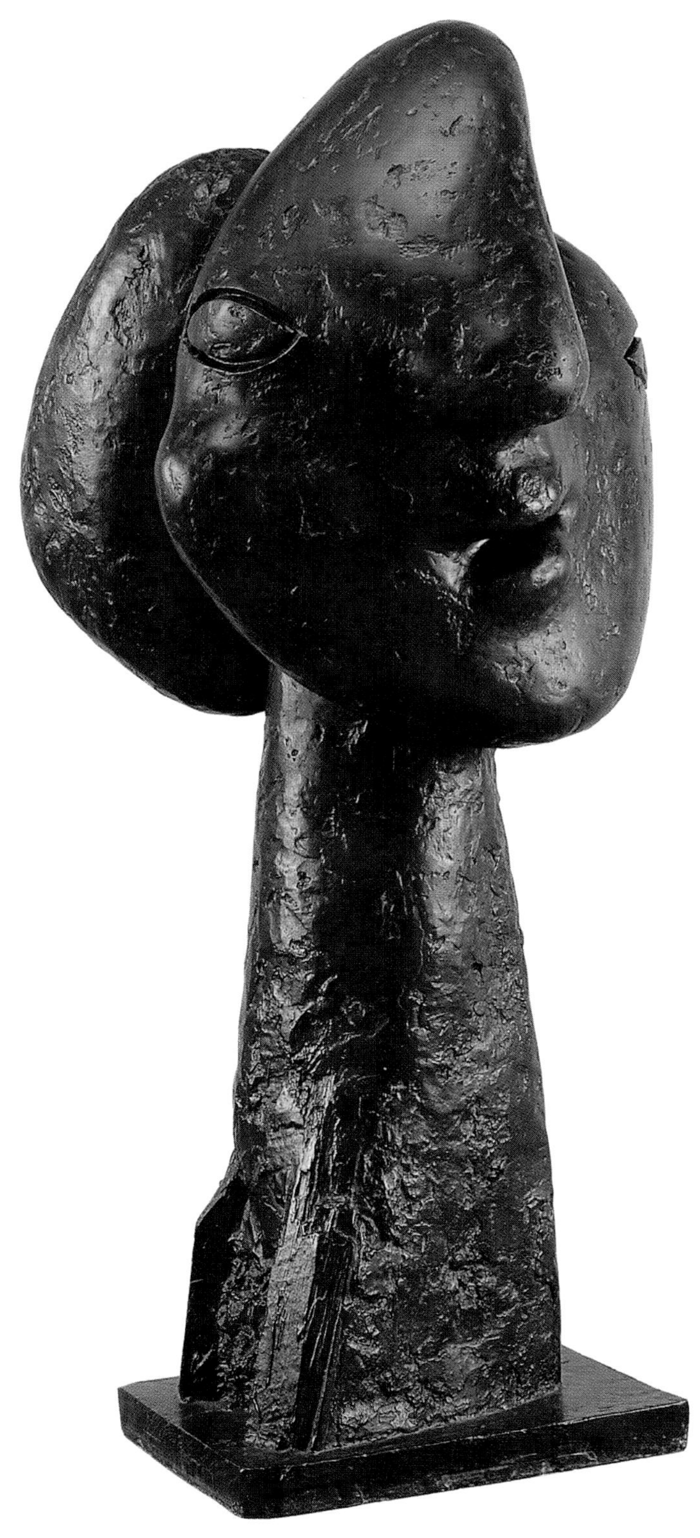

113 Head of a Woman, 1931
Bronze; 128.5 x 54.5 x 62.5
Paris, Musée Picasso, MP 302

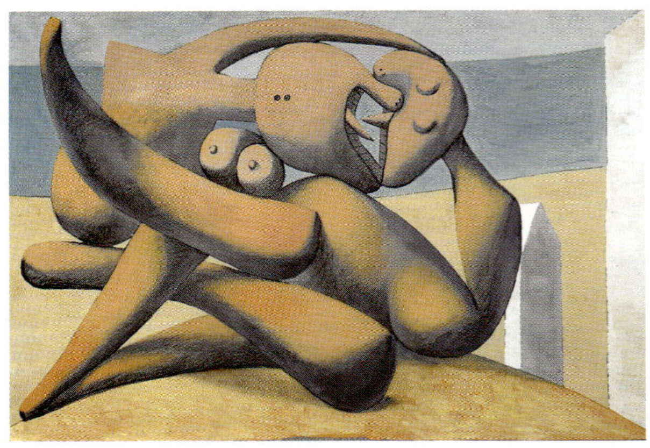

116 Figures at the Seashore, 12 January 1931
Oil on canvas; 130 x 195
Paris, Musée Picasso, MP 131

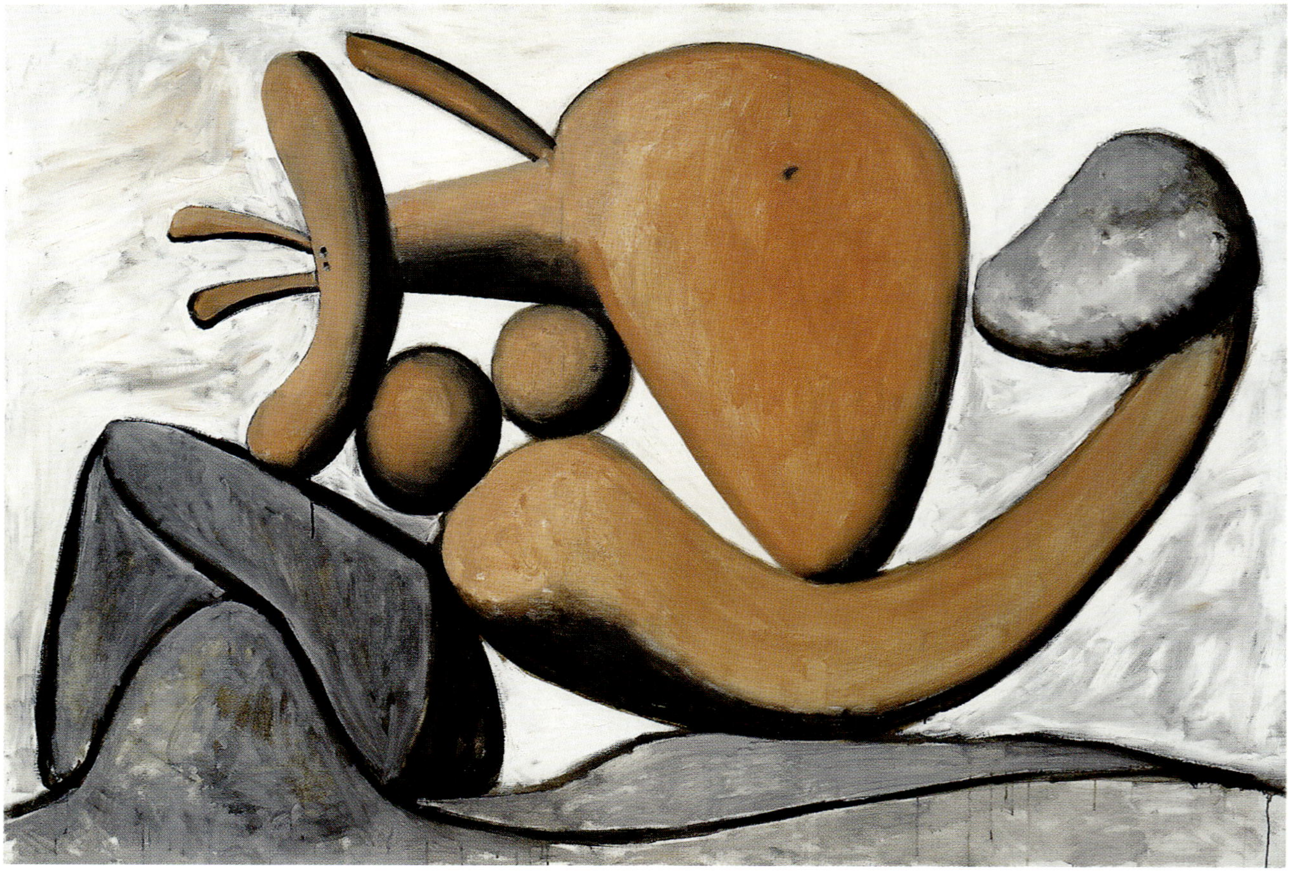

118 Woman Throwing a Stone, 8 March 1931
Oil on canvas; 130.5 x 195.5
Paris, Musée Picasso, MP 133

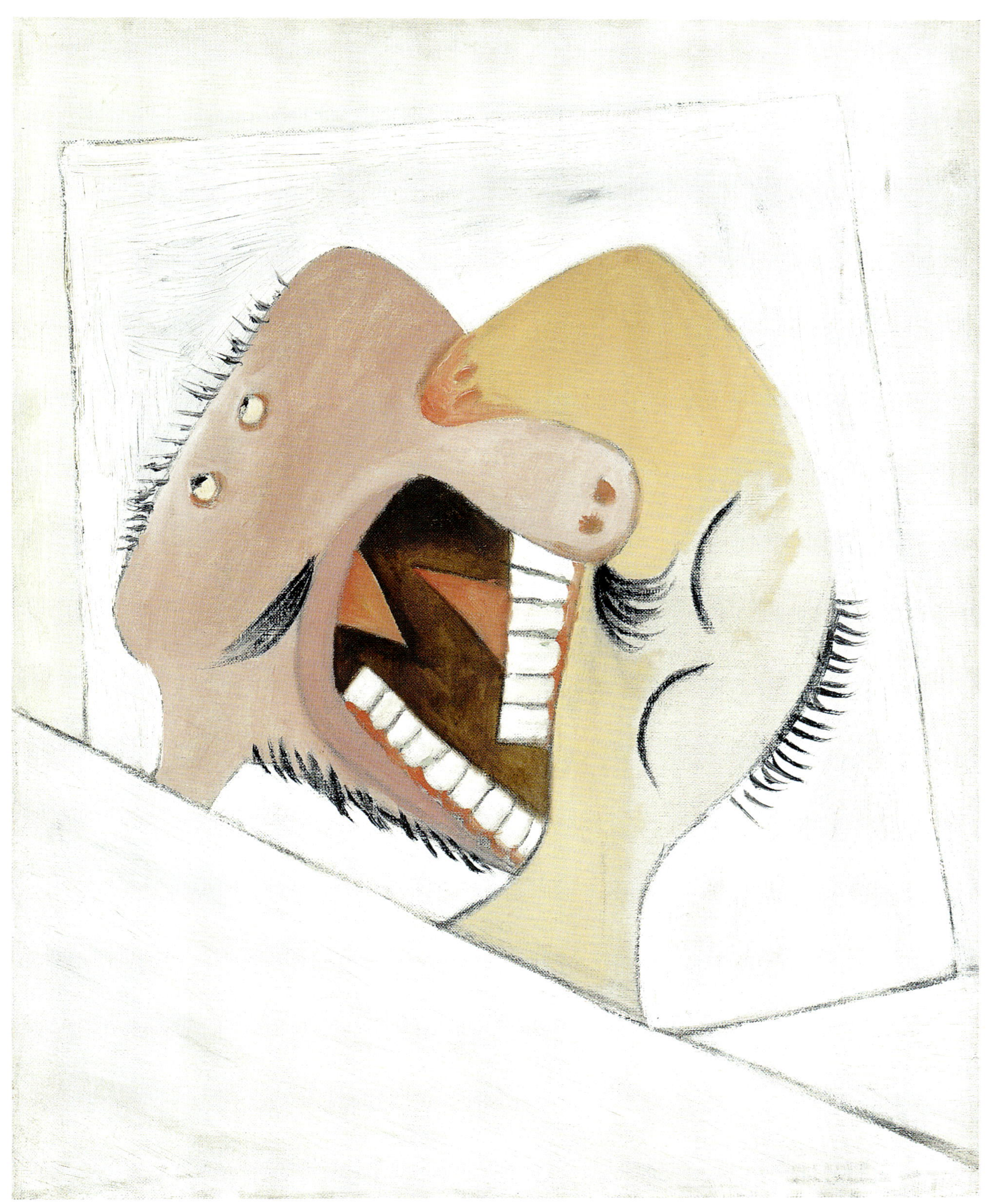

117 The Kiss, 12 January 1931
Oil on canvas; 61 x 50.5
Paris, Musée Picasso, MP 132

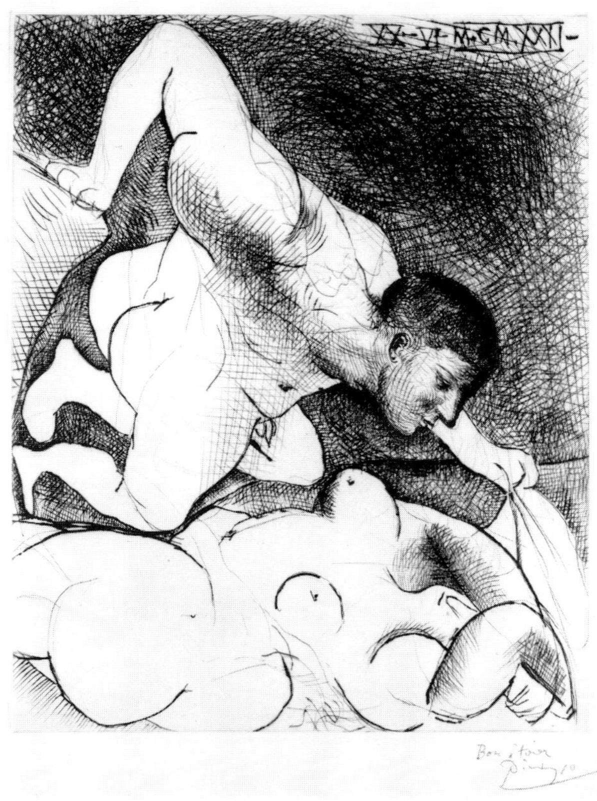

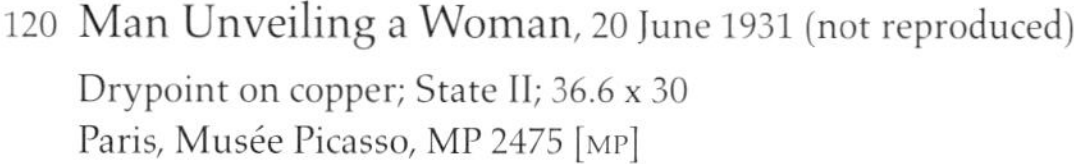

121 Man Unveiling a Woman, 20 June 1931
     Drypoint on copper; trial proof; 36.6 x 30
     Paris, Musée Picasso, MP 1982-64 [B]

120 Man Unveiling a Woman, 20 June 1931 (not reproduced)
     Drypoint on copper; State II; 36.6 x 30
     Paris, Musée Picasso, MP 2475 [MP]

123 The Rape, 9 July 1931 (not reproduced)
     Etching on copper; trial proof; 22.3 x 31.2
     Paris, Musée Picasso, MP 1982-68 [MB]

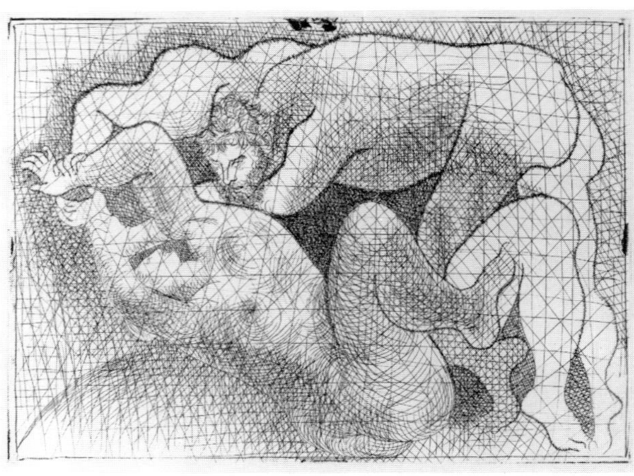

122 The Rape, 9 July 1931
     Etching on copper; 22.3 x 31.2
     Paris, Musée Picasso, MP 2479 [P]

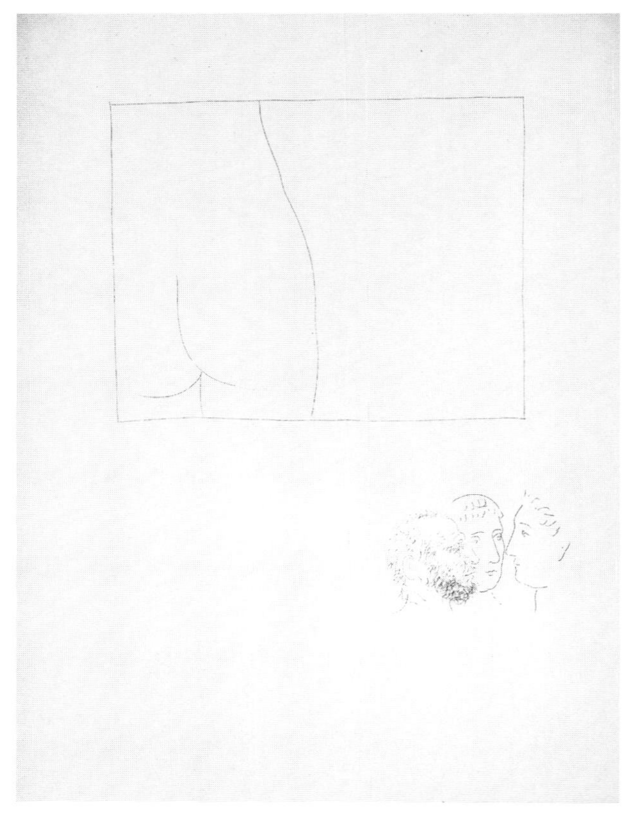

119 Fragment of a Female Body, April 1931
     Etching on copper; 38.1 x 29.9
     Paris, Musée Picasso, MP 2144

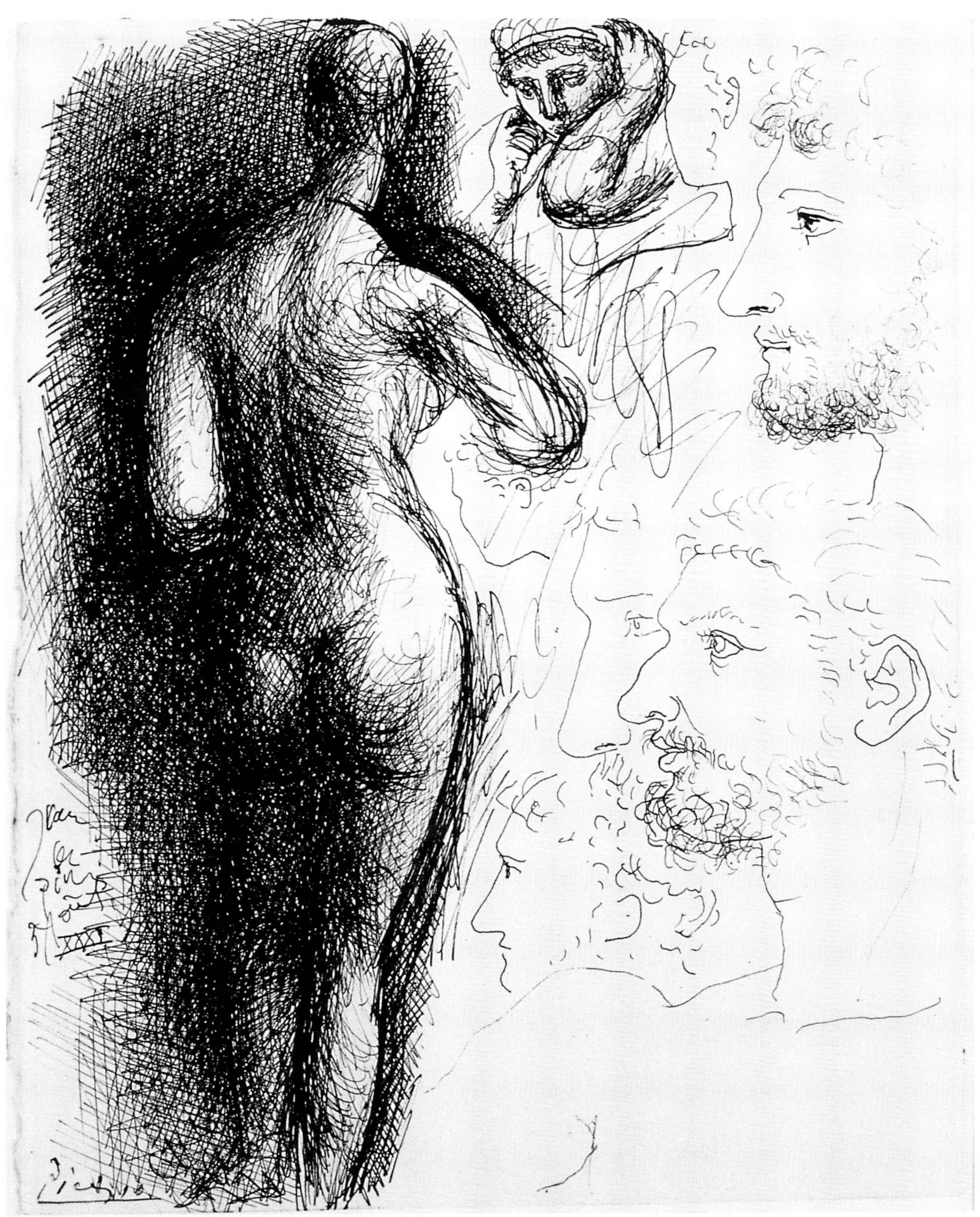

124 Nude. Sketchbook Page, 31 August 1931

Pencil and ink on paper; 32.3 x 25.4
Boston, The Museum of Fine Arts, Arthur Mason Knopp Fund [M]

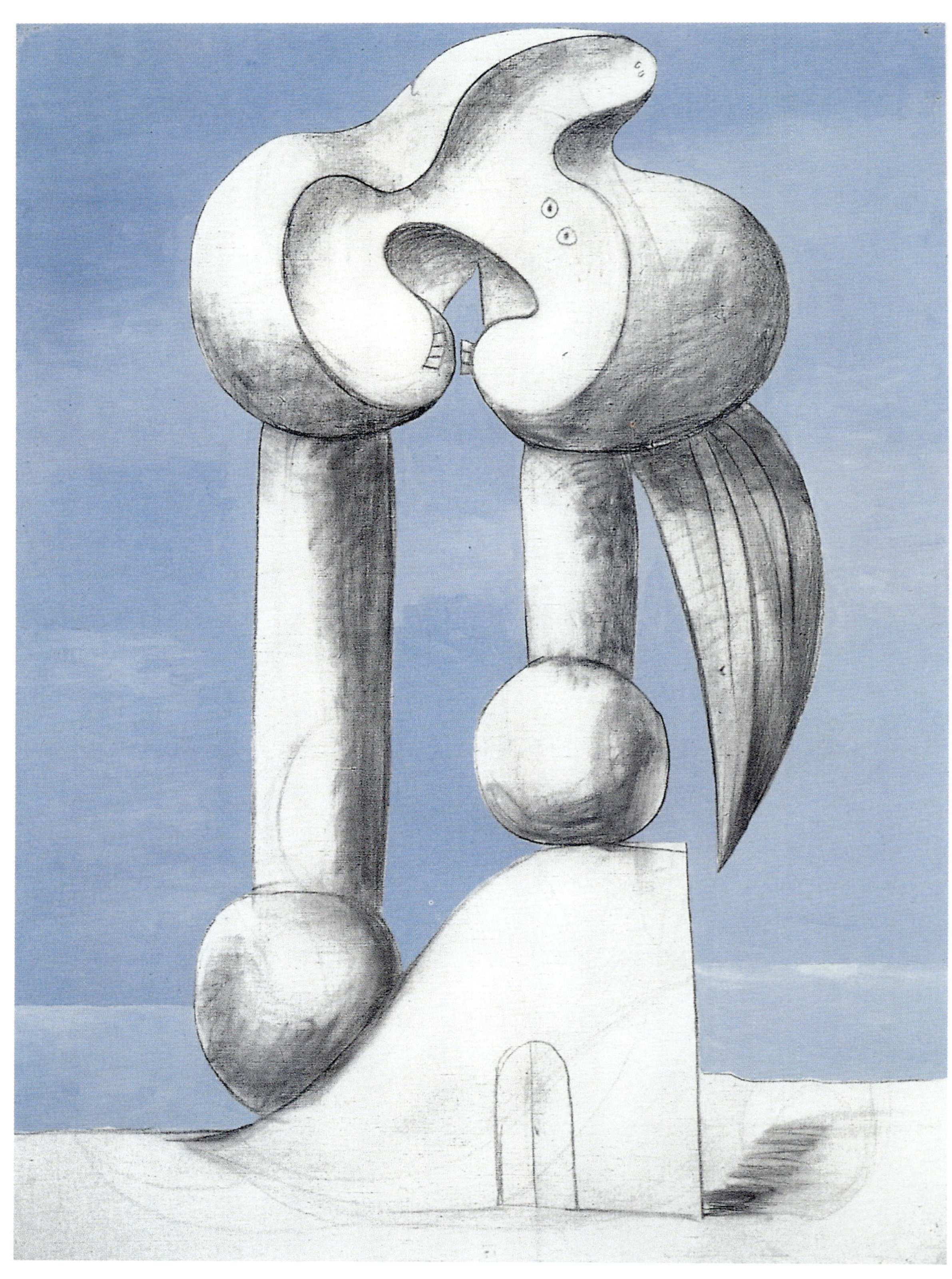

125 Figures at the Seashore, 1932
Oil and charcoal on canvas; 130 x 97
Madrid, Museo Nacional, Centro de Arte Reina Sofía

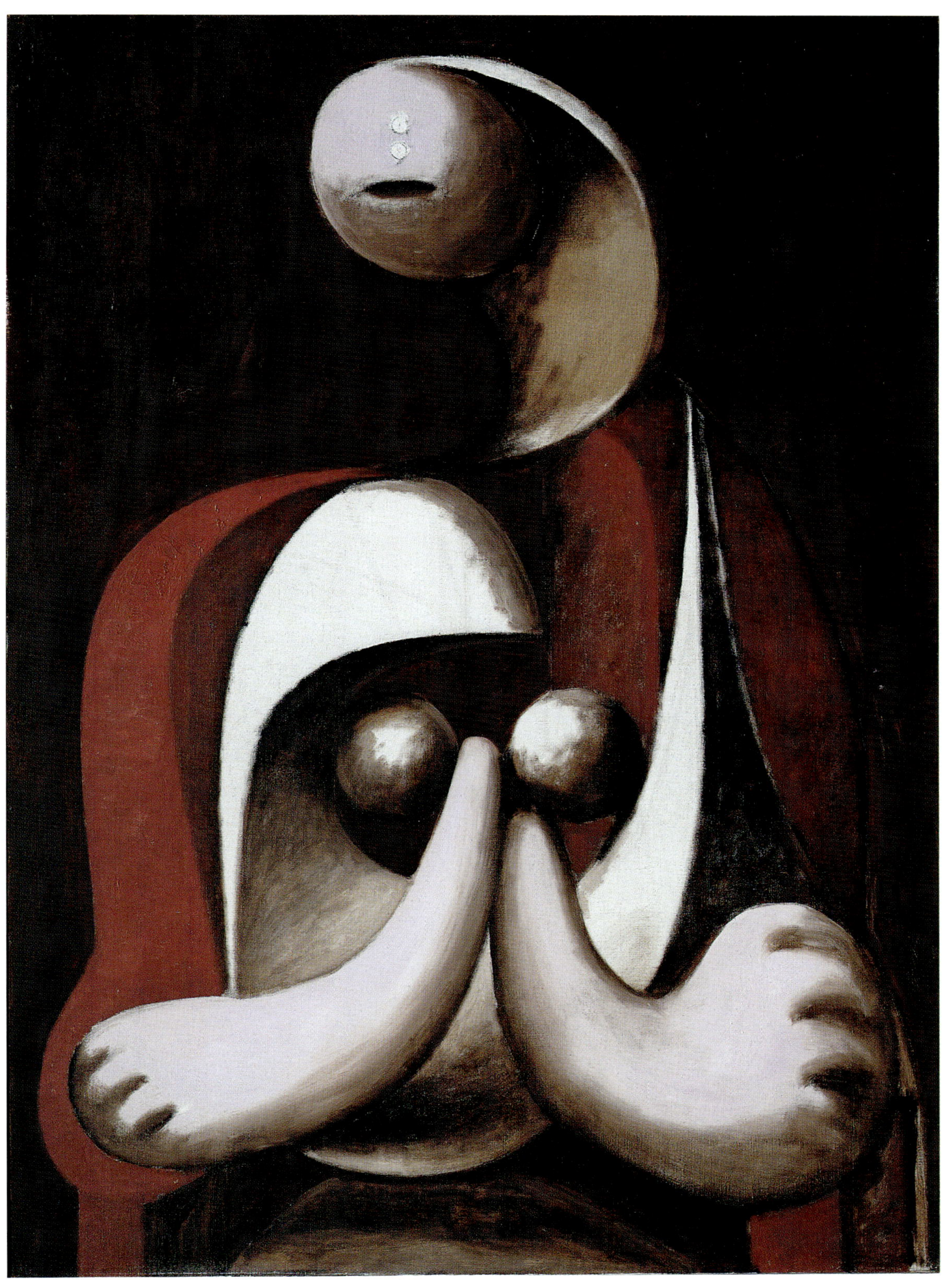

126 Woman in a Red Armchair, 1932
  Oil on canvas; 130 x 97
  Paris, Musée Picasso, MP 139

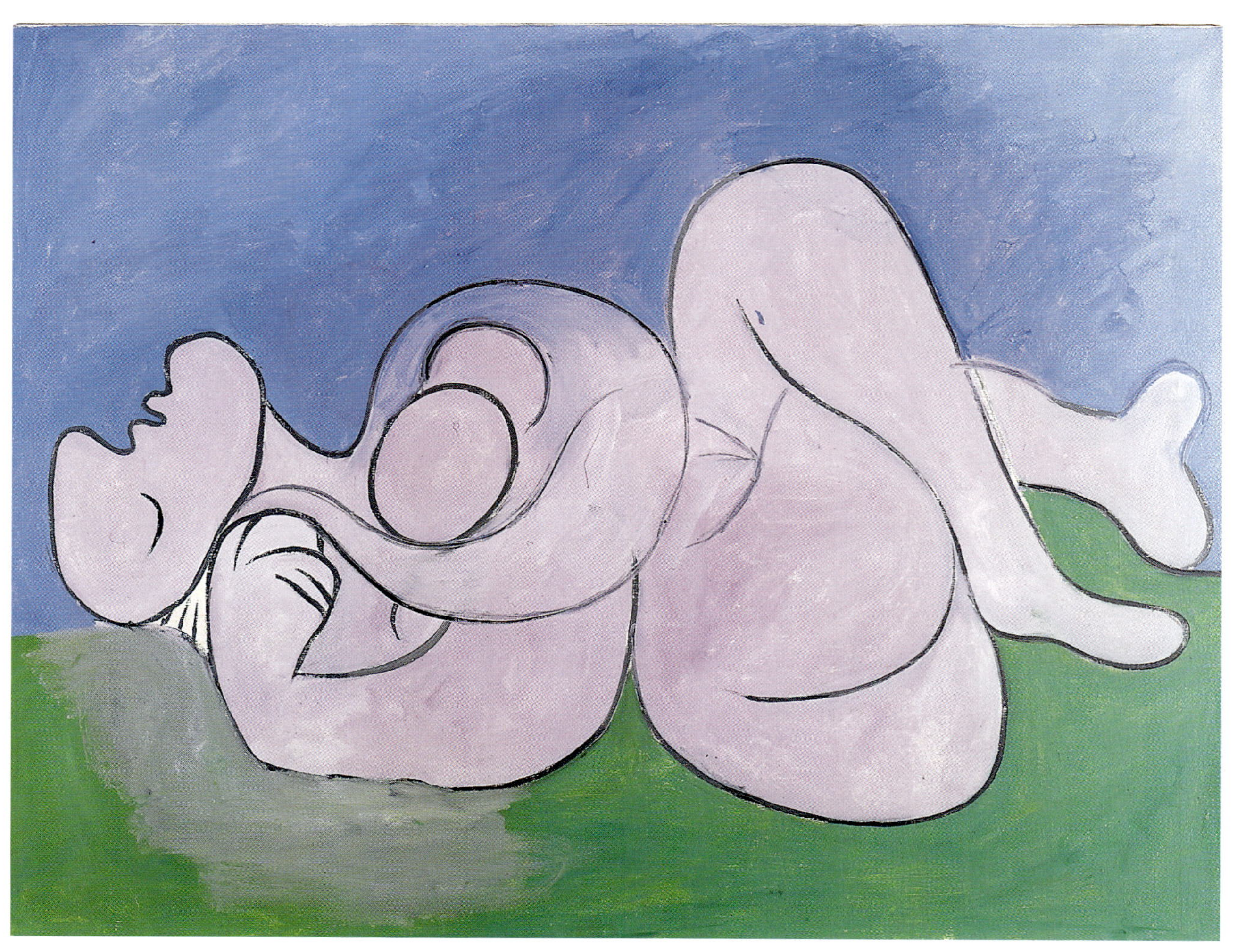

127 Siesta, 1932
Oil on canvas; 97 x 130
Paris, Private collection [P]

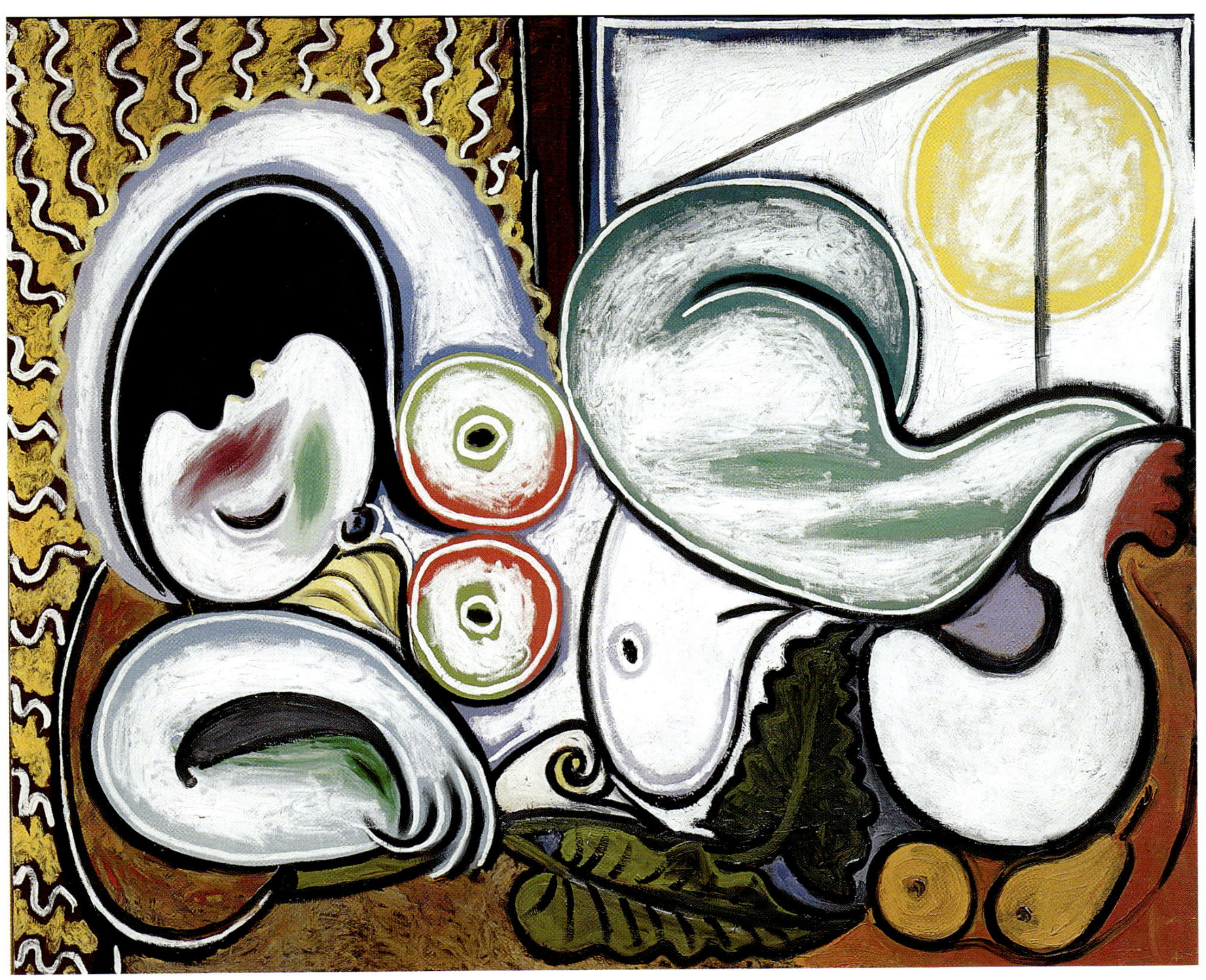

128 Recumbent Woman, 4 April 1932
    Oil on canvas; 130 x 161.7
    Paris, Musée Picasso, MP 142

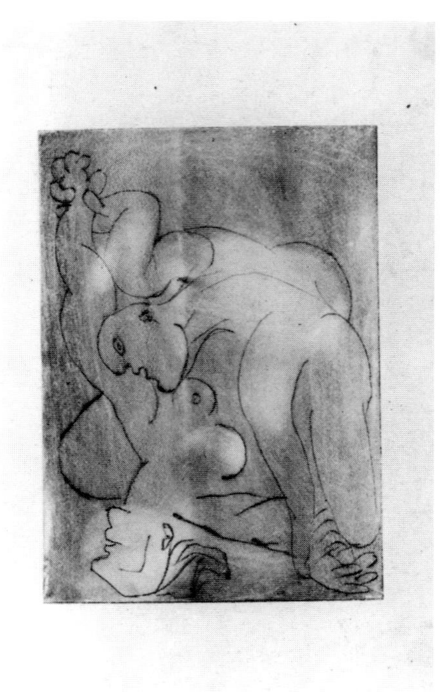

129 The Rape, 21 November 1932

Drypoint on copper; 12.3 x 9.1
Paris, Musée Picasso, MP 2202 [P],
MP 2203* [M] and MP 2204 [B]

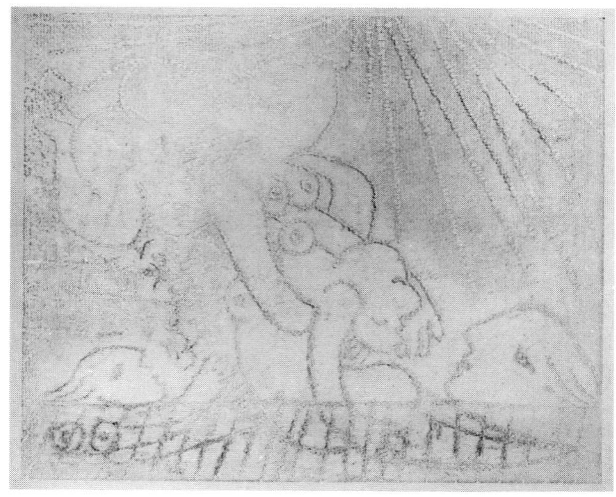

131 The Rescue of the Drowning Woman II, 18 December 1932

Etching on copper; 15.8 x 19.9
Paris, Musée Picasso, MP 2233 [M] and MP 2234* [B]

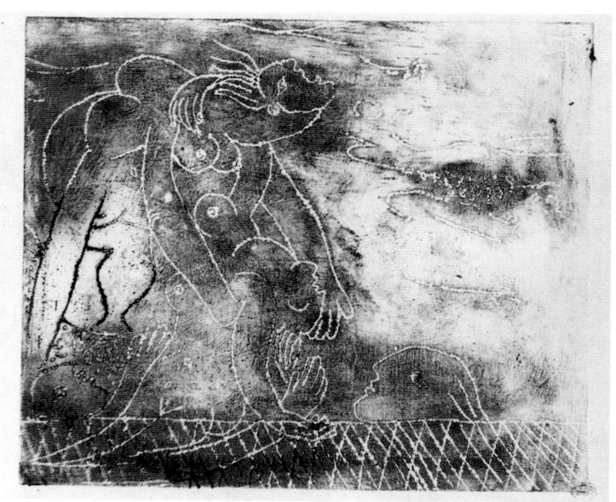

130 The Rescue of the Drowning Woman I, 17 December 1932

Etching on copper; 15.8 x 19.4
Paris, Musée Picasso, MP 2228* [M] and MP 2229 [B]

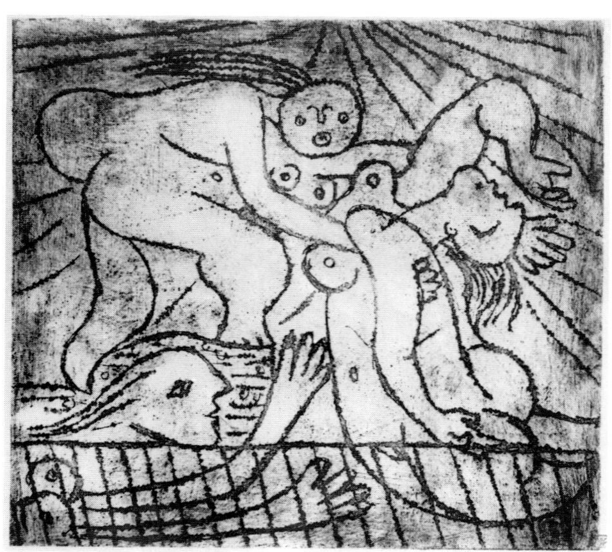

132 The Rescue of the Drowning Woman III, 18 December 1932

Etching on copper; 20.4 x 22.8
Paris, Musée Picasso, MP 2238* [M] and MP 2239 [B]

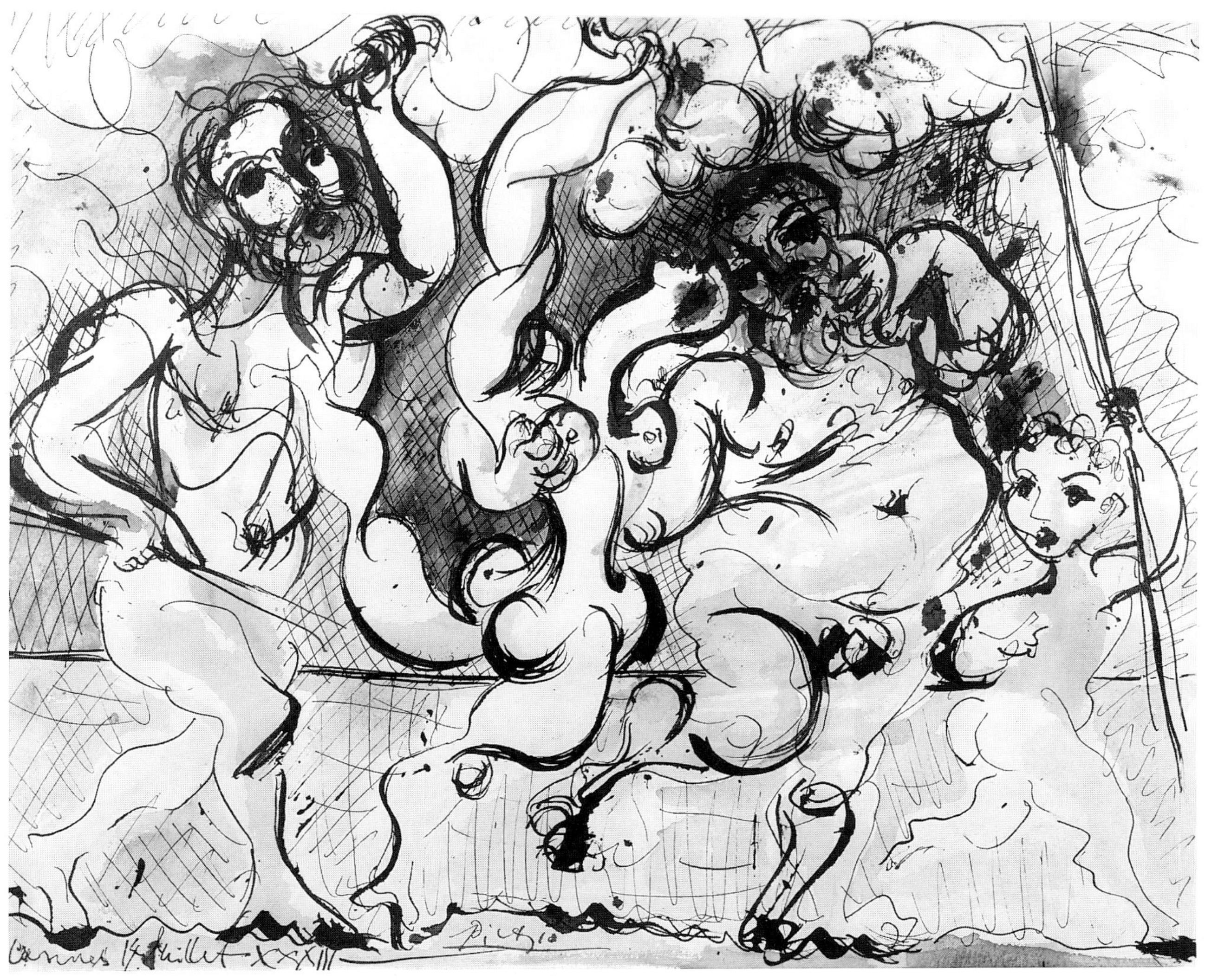

133 Le Cortège, 1933
   Watercolour, ink and coloured pencil on paper; 40.5 x 50.7
   Buffalo, Albright-Knox Art Gallery, Gift of the ACG Trust, 1970 [P]

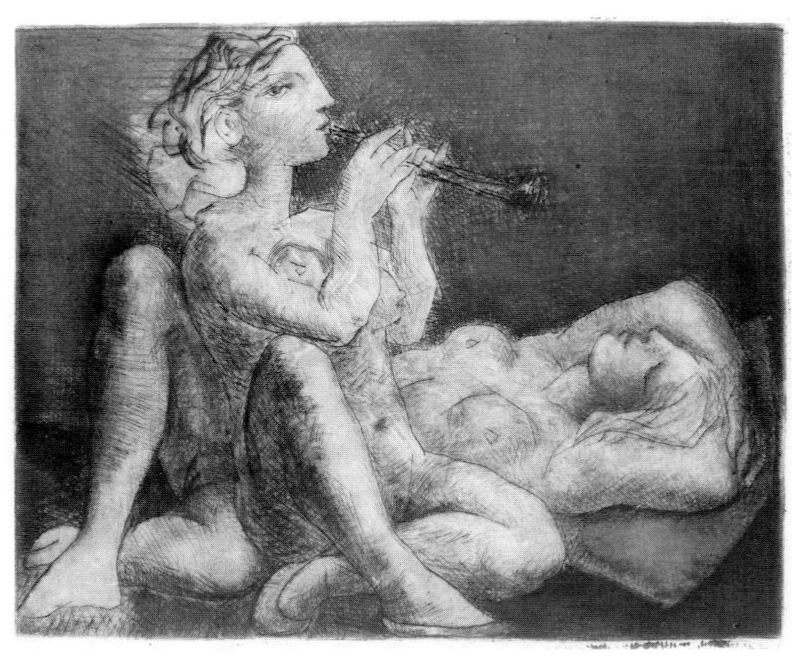

134 Flute Player and Sleeping Woman, 24 January 1933
Drypoint and scraper on copper; State XXXI; colour proof;
15 x 18.7
Paris, Musée Picasso, MP 2331

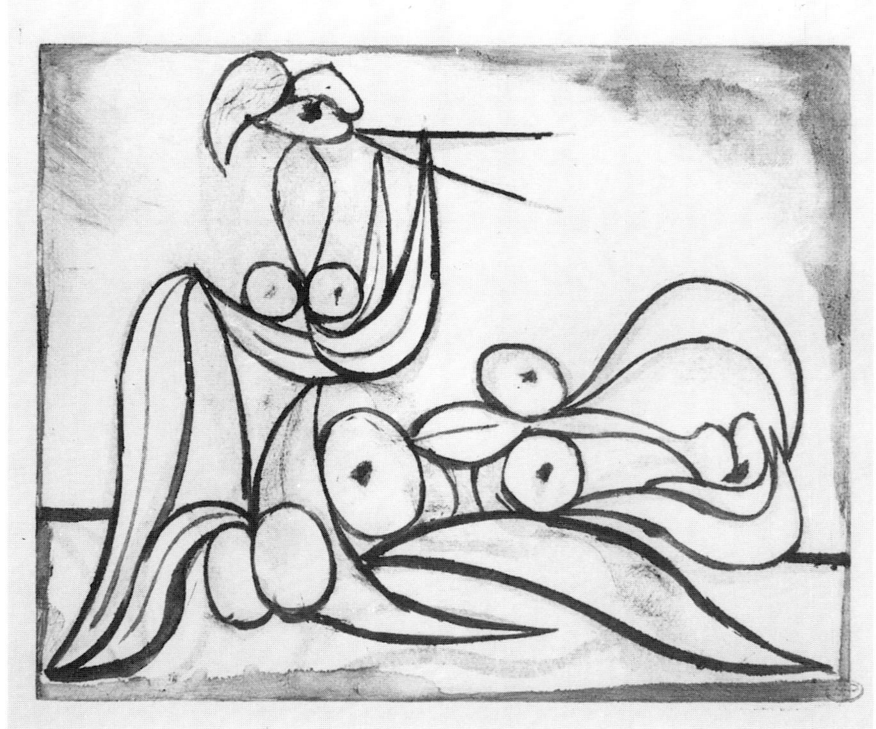

135 Flute Player and Sleeping Woman, February 1933
Monotype on copper; State XXXVII; 14.9 x 18.7
Paris, Musée Picasso, MP 3205

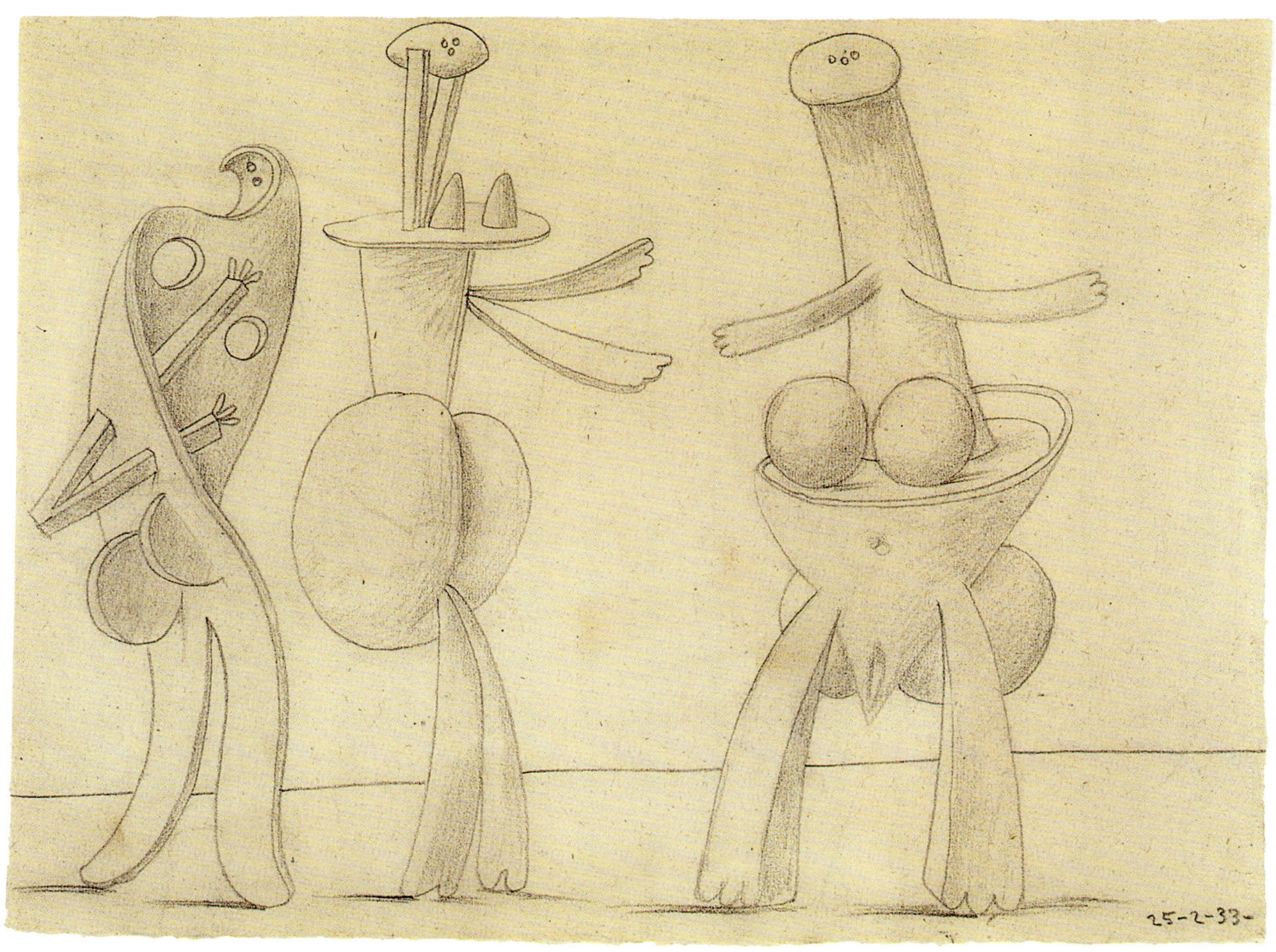

136 An Anatomy: Three Women, 25 February 1933
Graphite stick on paper; 20 x 27
Paris, Musée Picasso, MP 1090 [PM]

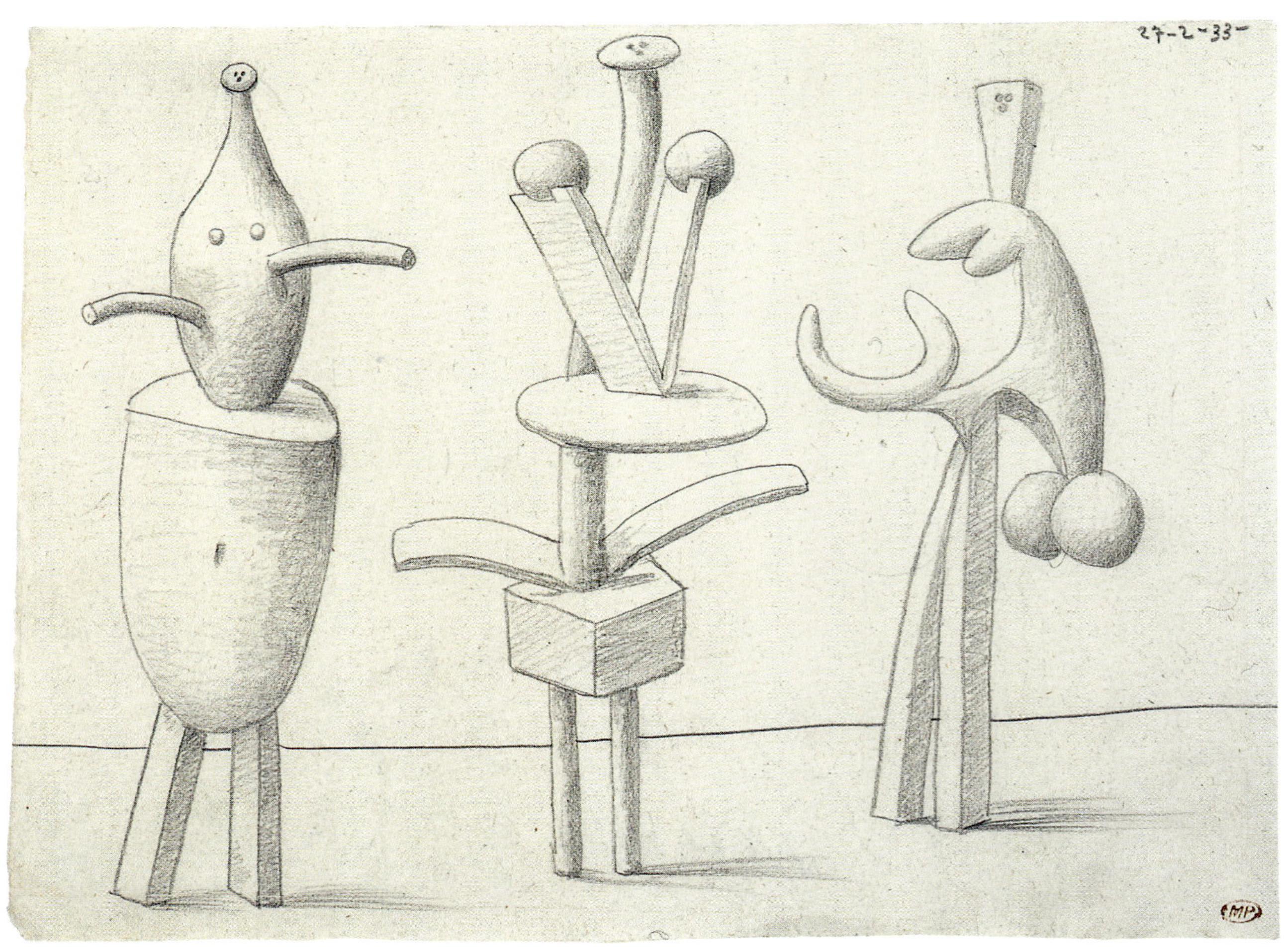

137 **An Anatomy: Three Women**, 27 February 1933
   Graphite stick on paper; 19.8 x 27.4
   Paris, Musée Picasso, MP 1095 [PB]

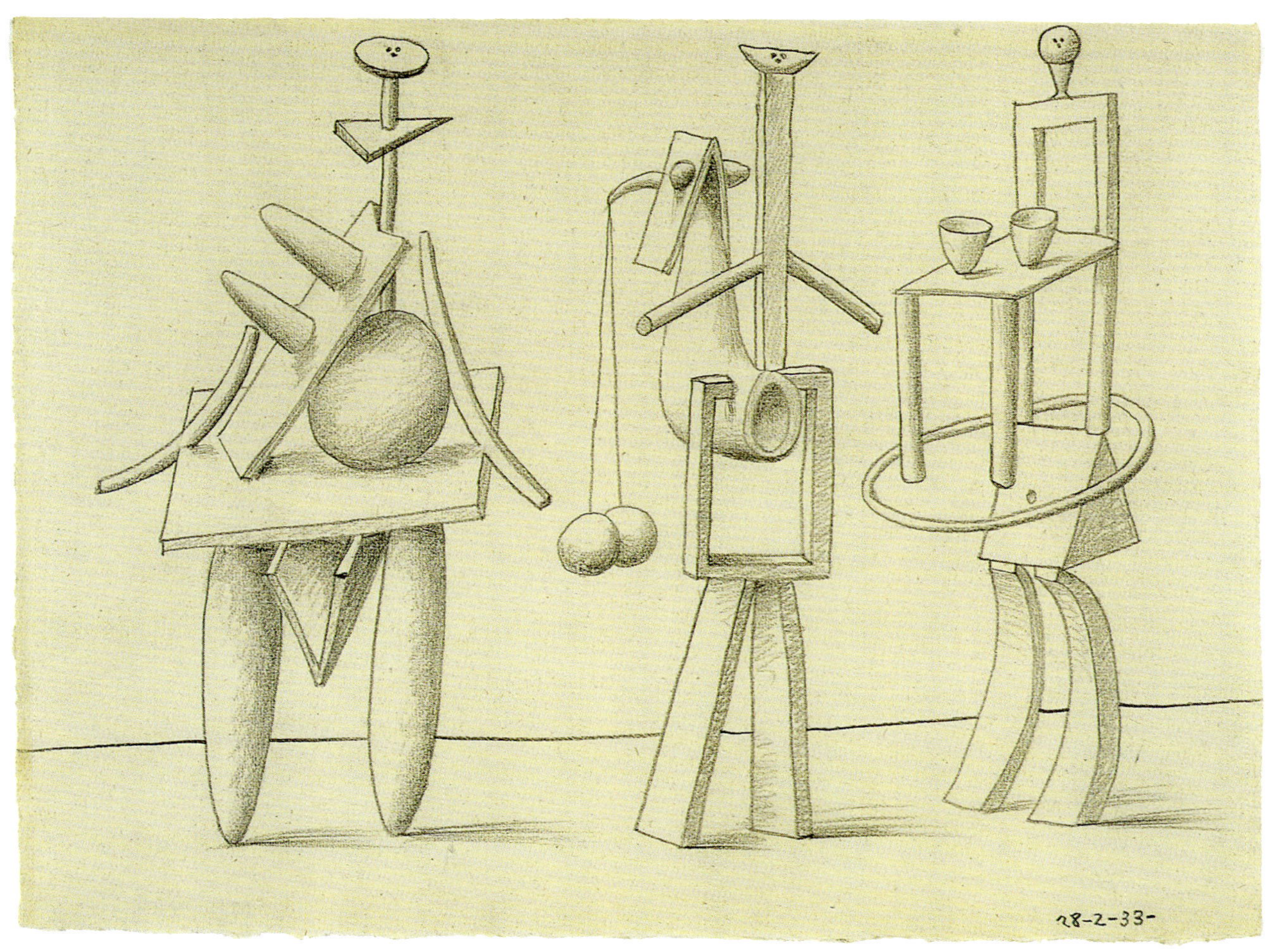

138 An Anatomy: Three Women, 28 February 1933
Graphite stick on paper; 19.7 x 27
Paris, Musée Picasso, MP 1096

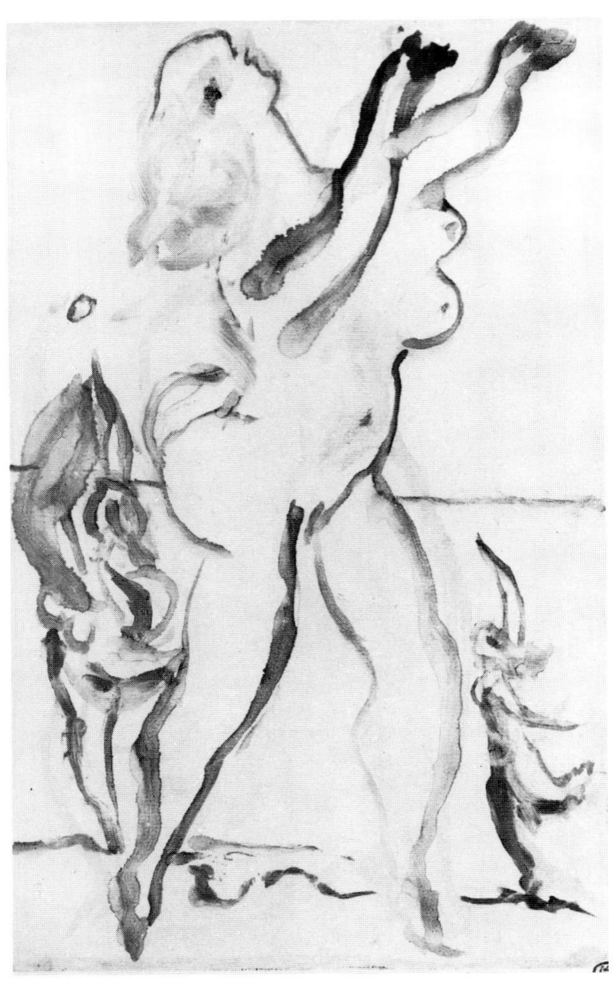

139 Bathers and Ball III, February–March 1933
Monotype; 27.8 x 17.7
Paris, Musée Picasso, MP 3239 [M]

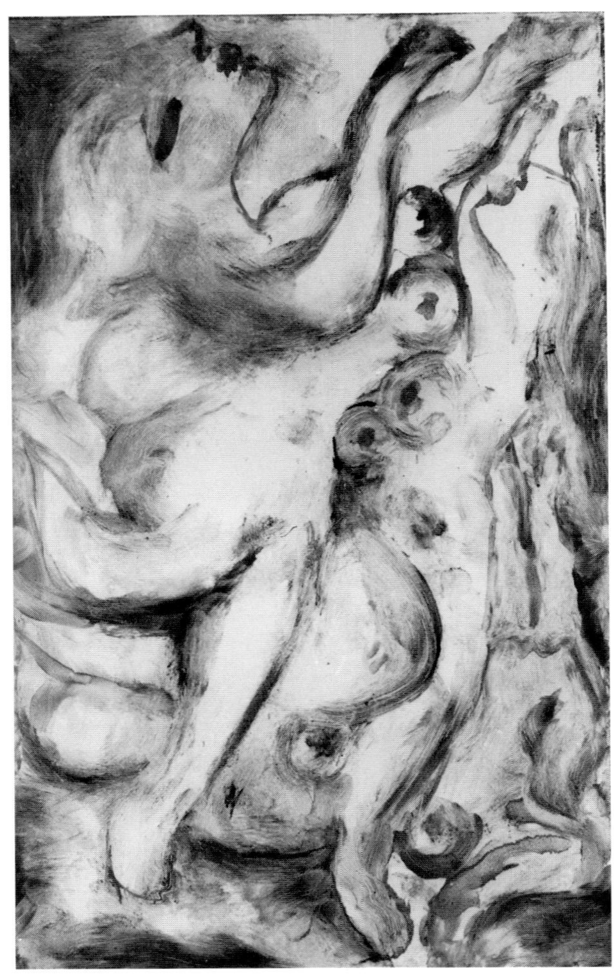

140 Bathers and Ball IV, February–March 1933
Monotype; 27.8 x 17.7
Paris, Musée Picasso, MP 3240 [B]

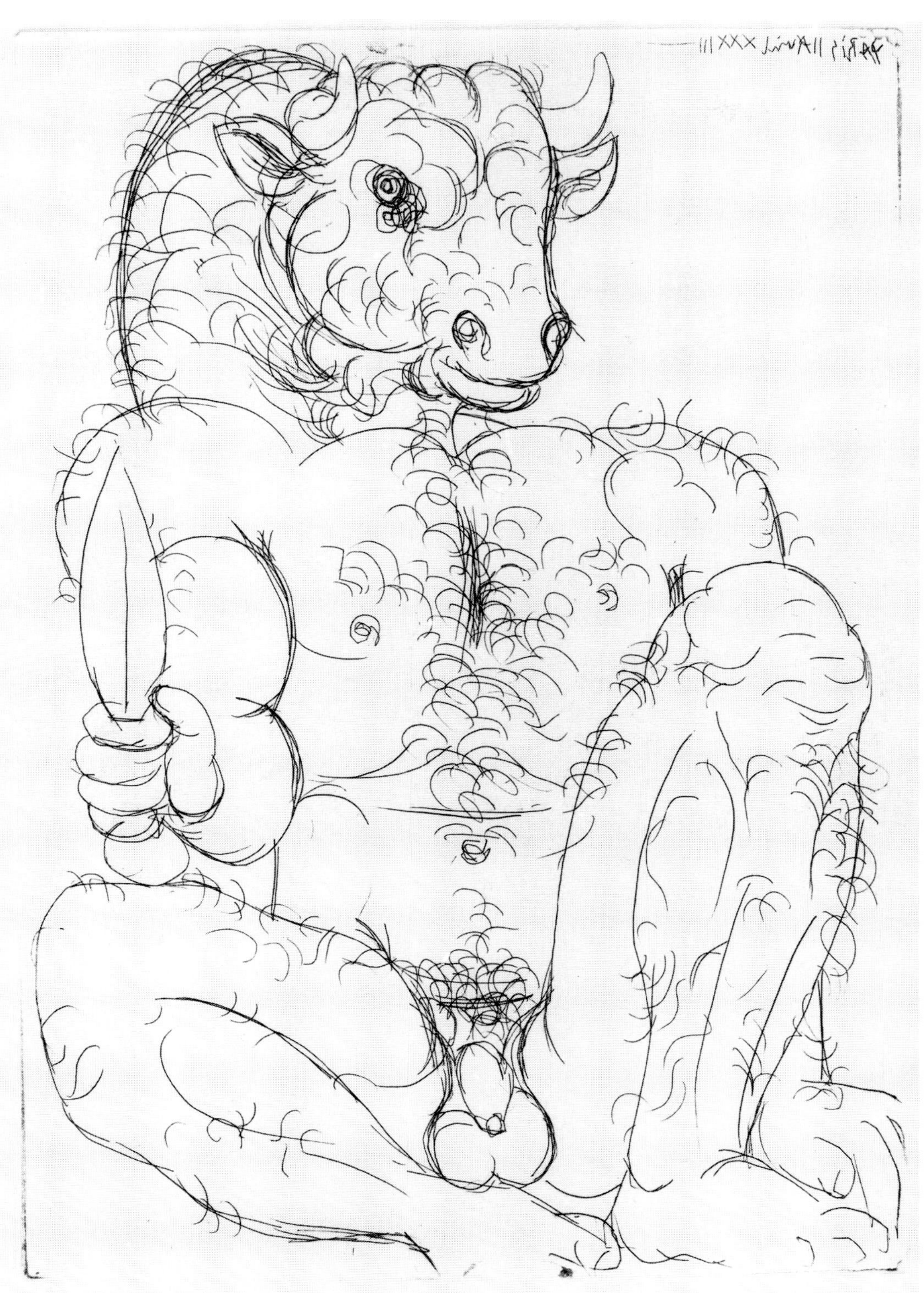

142 Seated Minotaur with Dagger, 11 April 1933
     Etching on copper; 26.9 x 19.4
     Paris, Musée Picasso, MP 2388

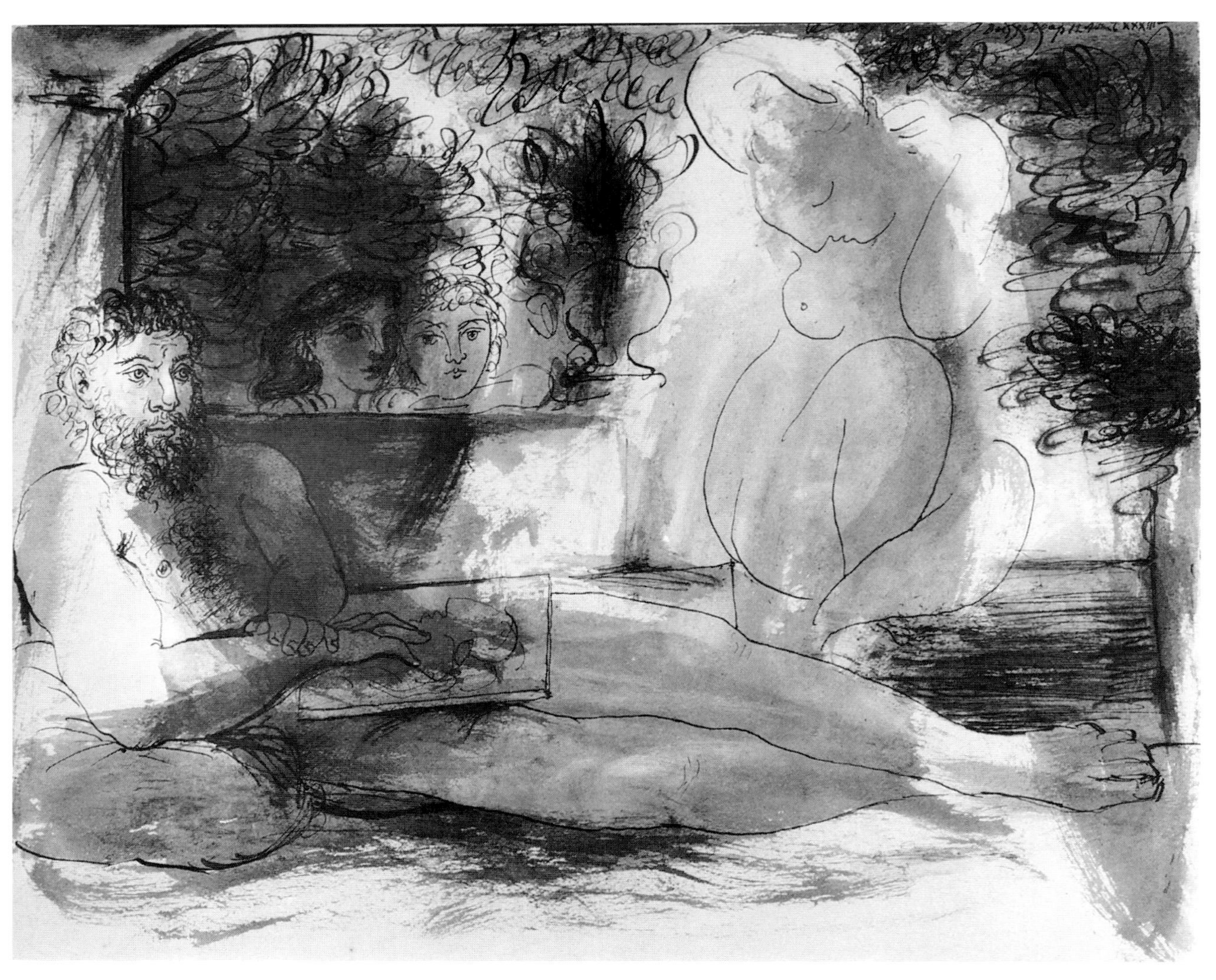

143 The Artist and His Model, 12 April 1933
Pen, India ink and wash on paper; 23 x 29
Paris, Musée Picasso, MP 1099

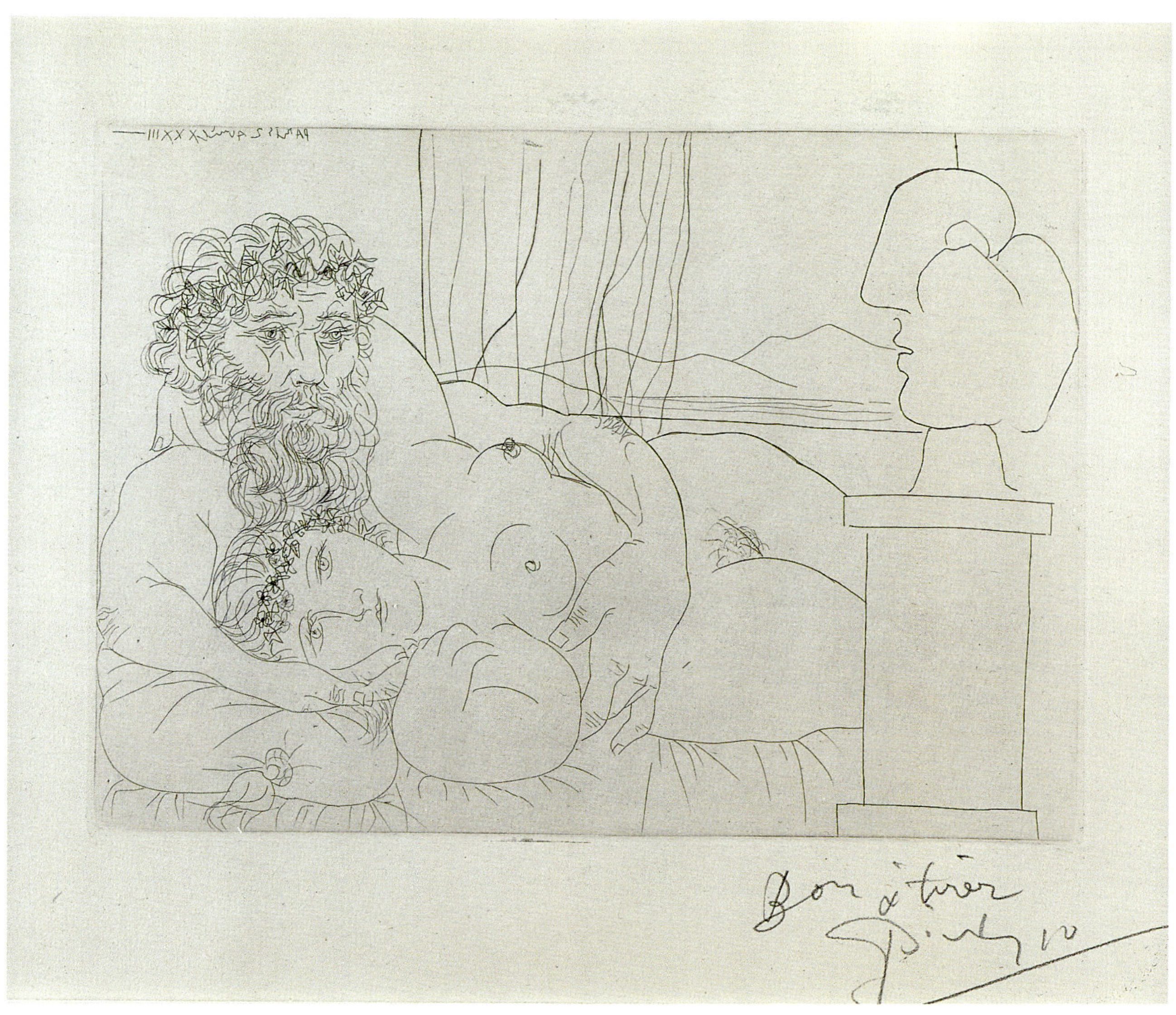

141 Sculptor and His Model with Sculpted Head of the Model, 2 April 1933

Etching on copper; trial proof; 19.3 x 26.8
Paris, Musée Picasso, MP 1982-121 [B]

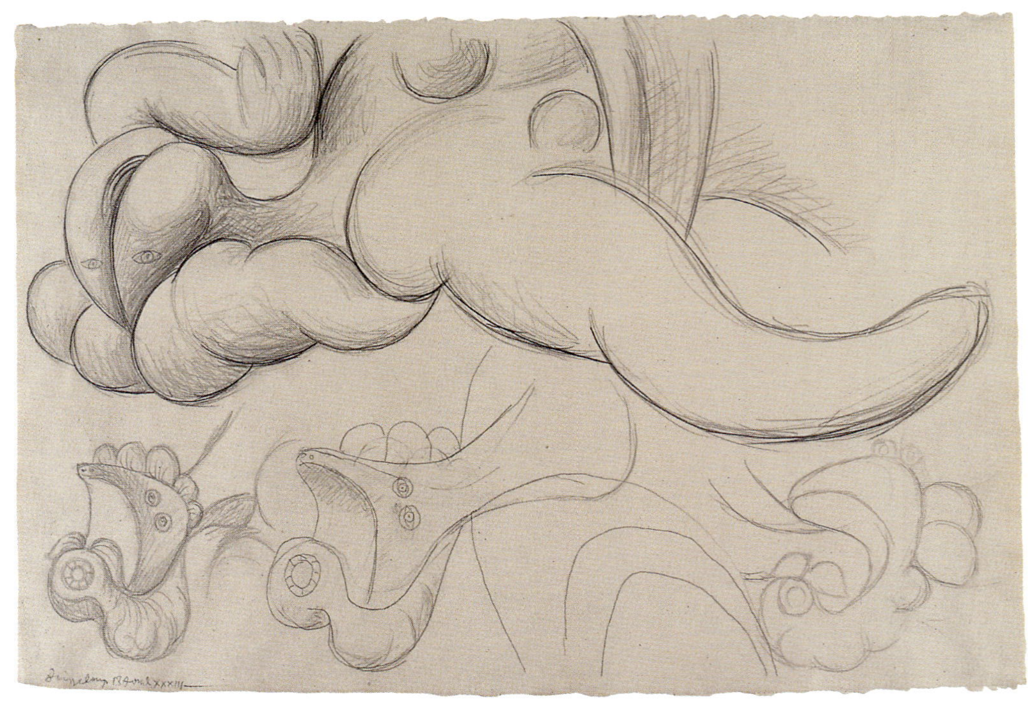

144 Study for *Coupling*: Nude Woman and Head, 18 April 1933
   Graphite stick on paper; 34 x 51.5
   Paris, Musée Picasso, MP 1102

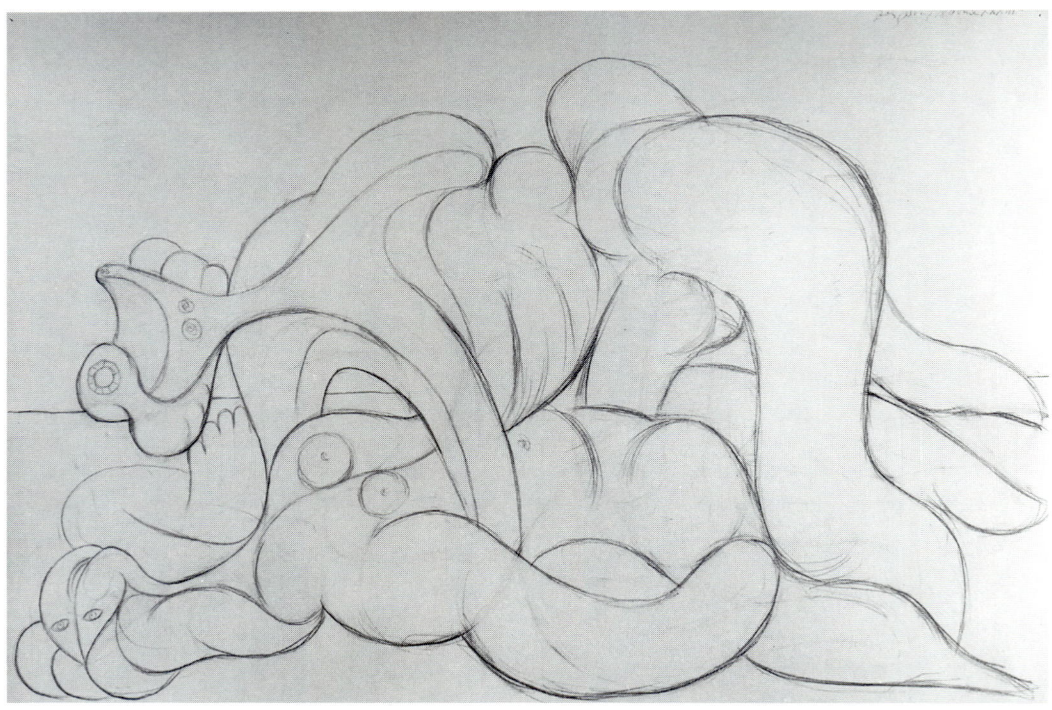

145 Coupling, 18 April 1933
   Graphite stick on paper; 34.4 x 51.5
   Paris, Musée Picasso, MP 1103

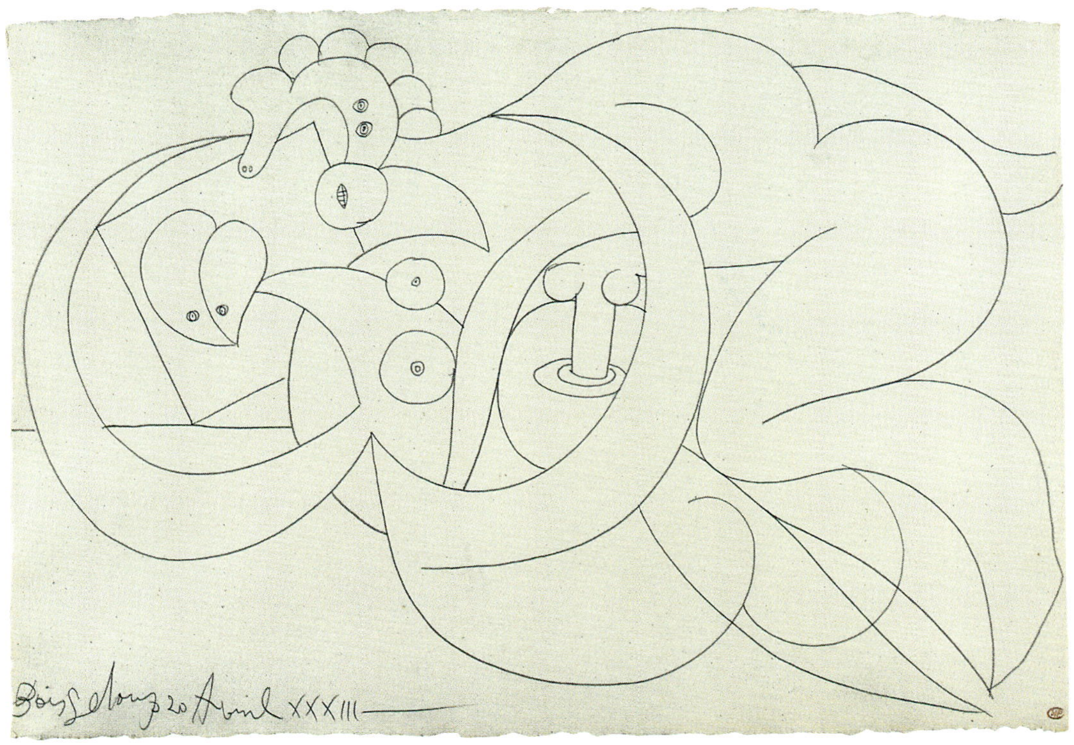

146 Coupling, 20 April 1933
   Graphite stick on paper; 34.5 x 51
   Paris, Musée Picasso, MP 1106

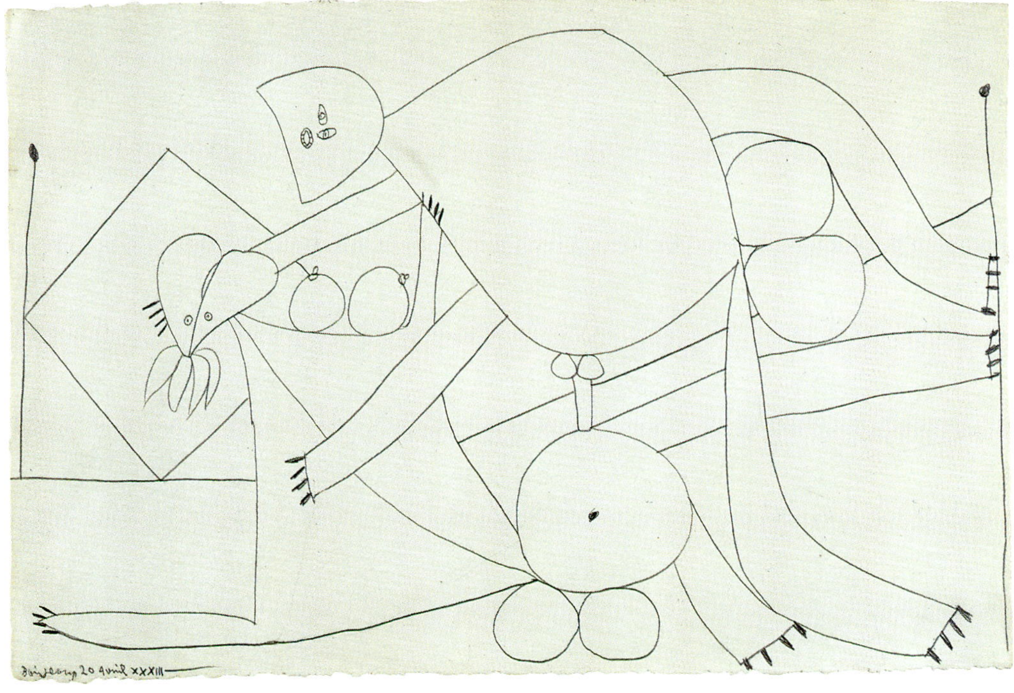

147 Coupling, 20 April 1933
   Graphite stick on paper; 34 x 25
   Paris, Musée Picasso, MP 1105

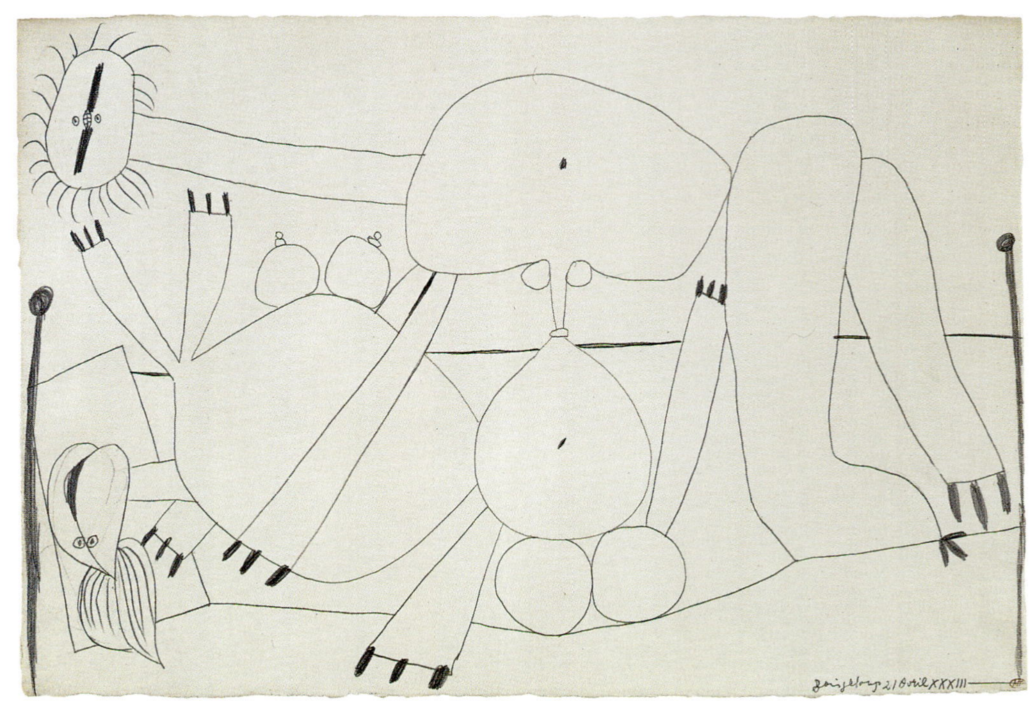

148 Coupling, 21 April 1933
Graphite stick on paper; 34.1 x 51.5
Paris, Musée Picasso, MP 1112

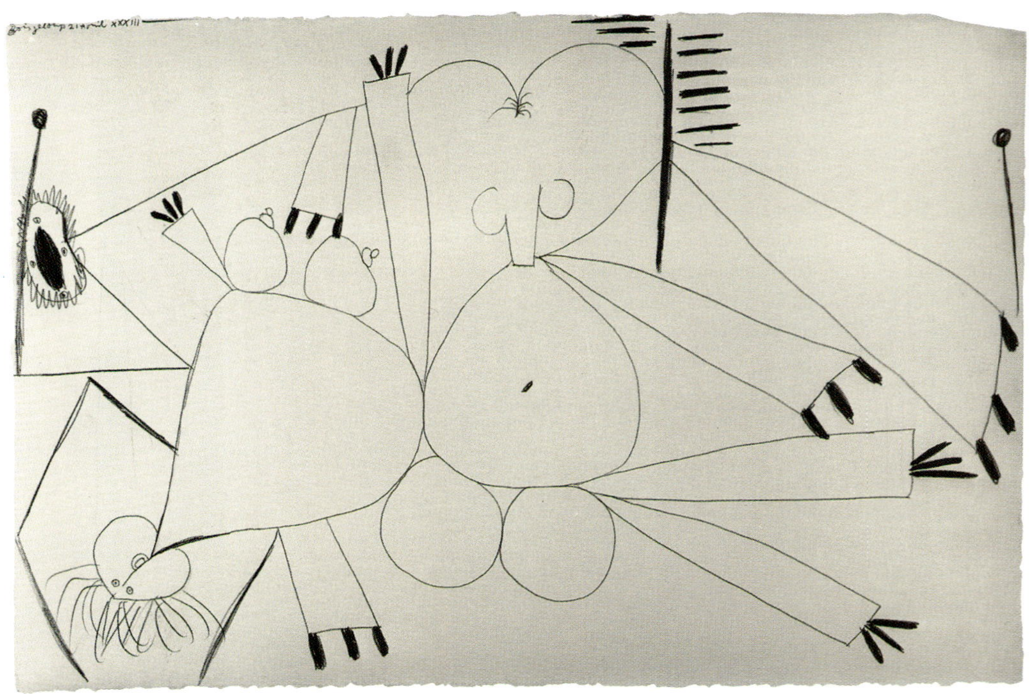

149 Coupling, 21 April 1933
Graphite stick on paper; 34 x 51.5
Paris, Musée Picasso, MP 1111

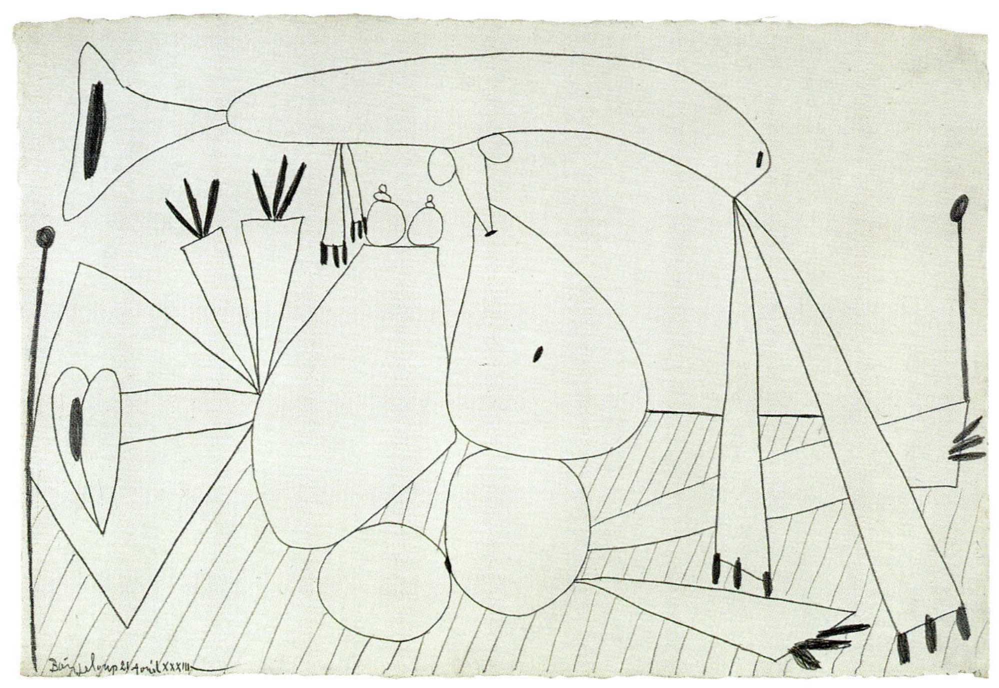

150 Coupling, 21 April 1933
     Graphite stick on paper; 34 x 51
     Paris, Musée Picasso, MP 1109

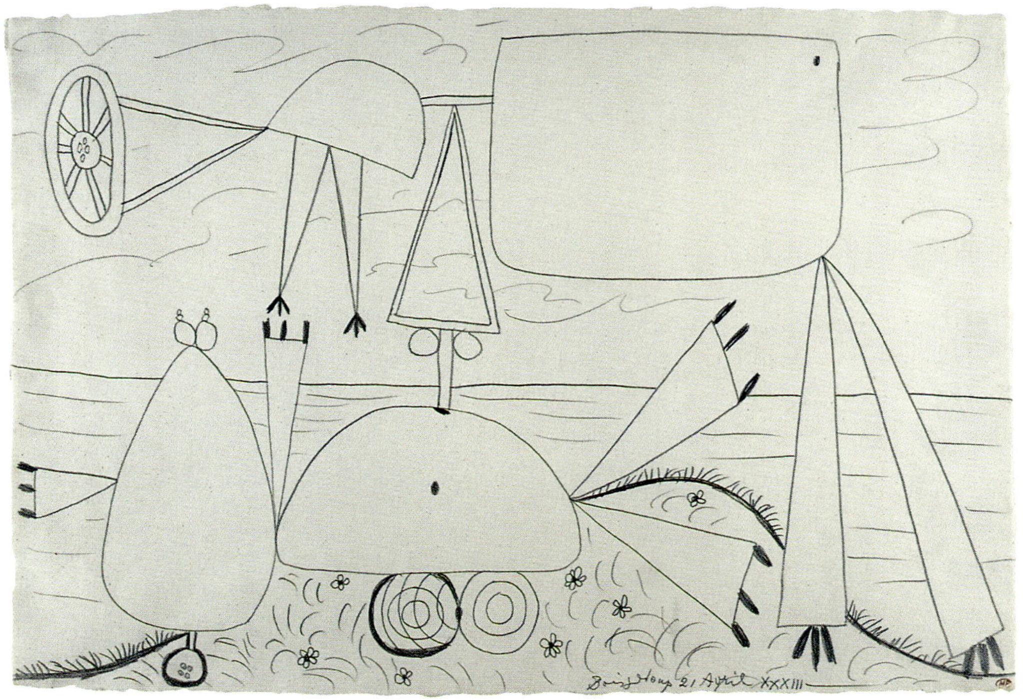

151 Coupling, 21 April 1933
     Graphite stick on paper; 34 x 51.4
     Paris, Musée Picasso, MP 1107

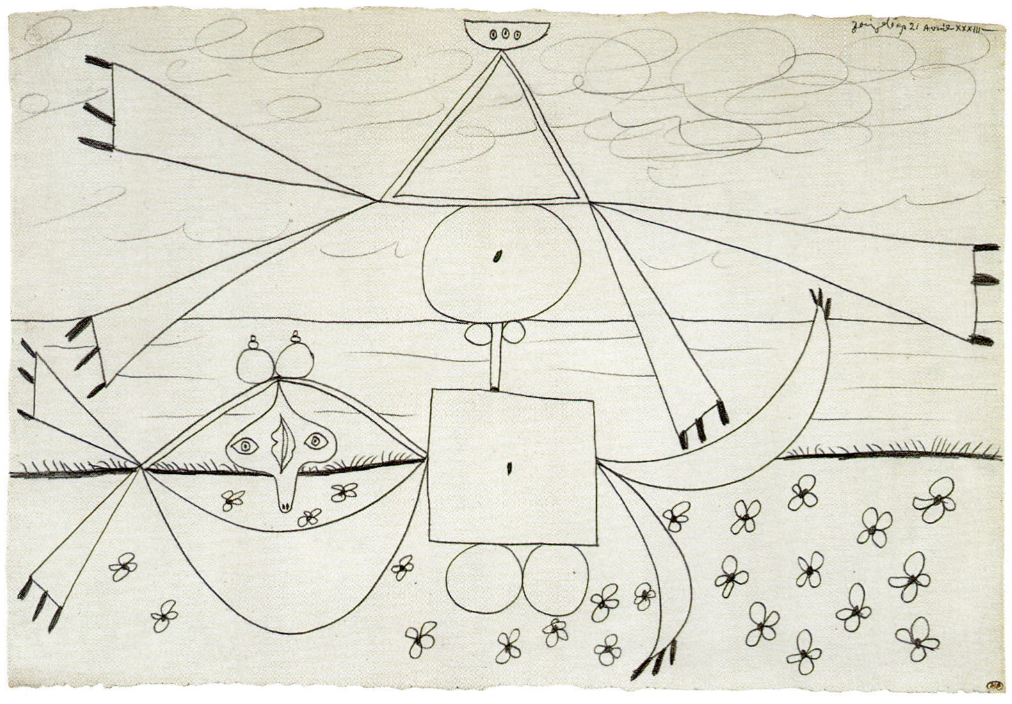

152 Coupling, 21 April 1933
Graphite stick on paper; 34.5 x 51.5
Paris, Musée Picasso, MP 1108

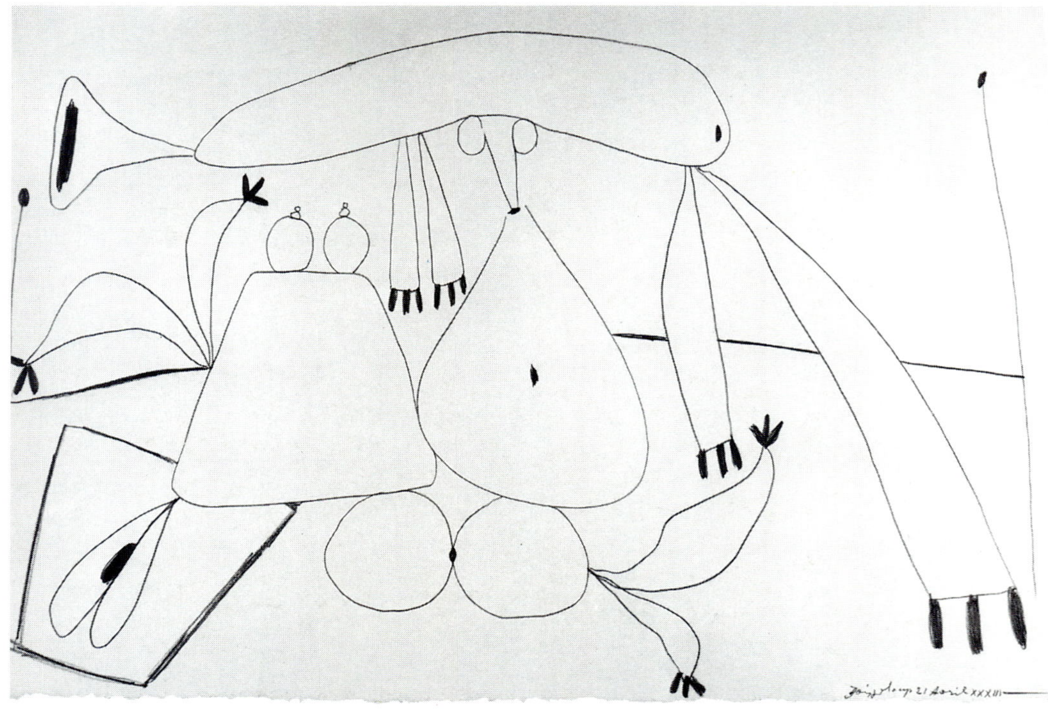

153 Coupling, 21 April 1933
Graphite stick on paper; 34.2 x 51.4
Paris, Musée Picasso, MP 1110

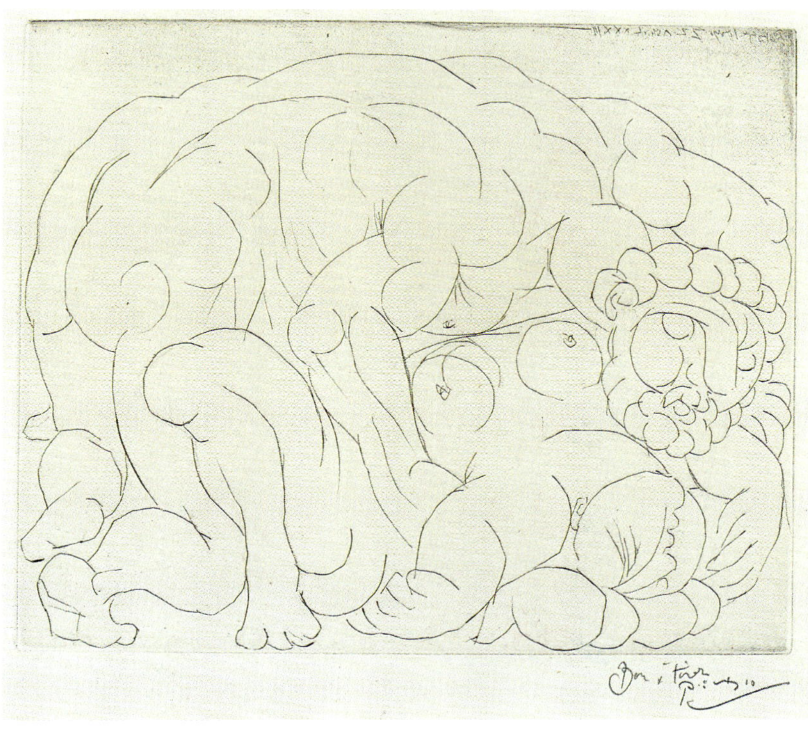

154 The Embrace I, 23 April 1933

Drypoint on copper; trial proof; 30 x 36.5
Paris, Musée Picasso, MP 1982-89 [MB]

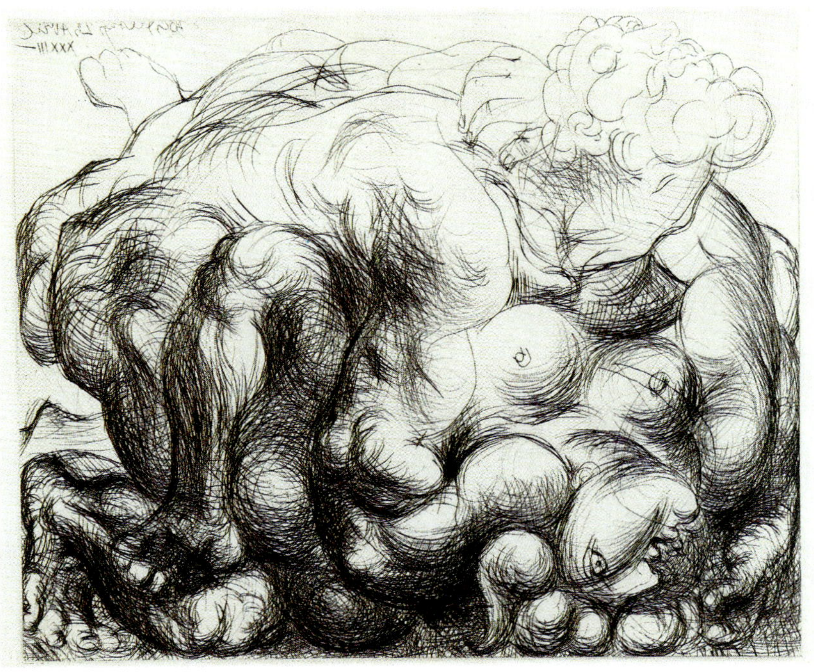

155 The Embrace III, 23 April 1933

Drypoint on copper; 29.9 x 36.7
Paris, Musée Picasso, MP 2551 [P] and MP 1982-90* (trial proof) [MB]

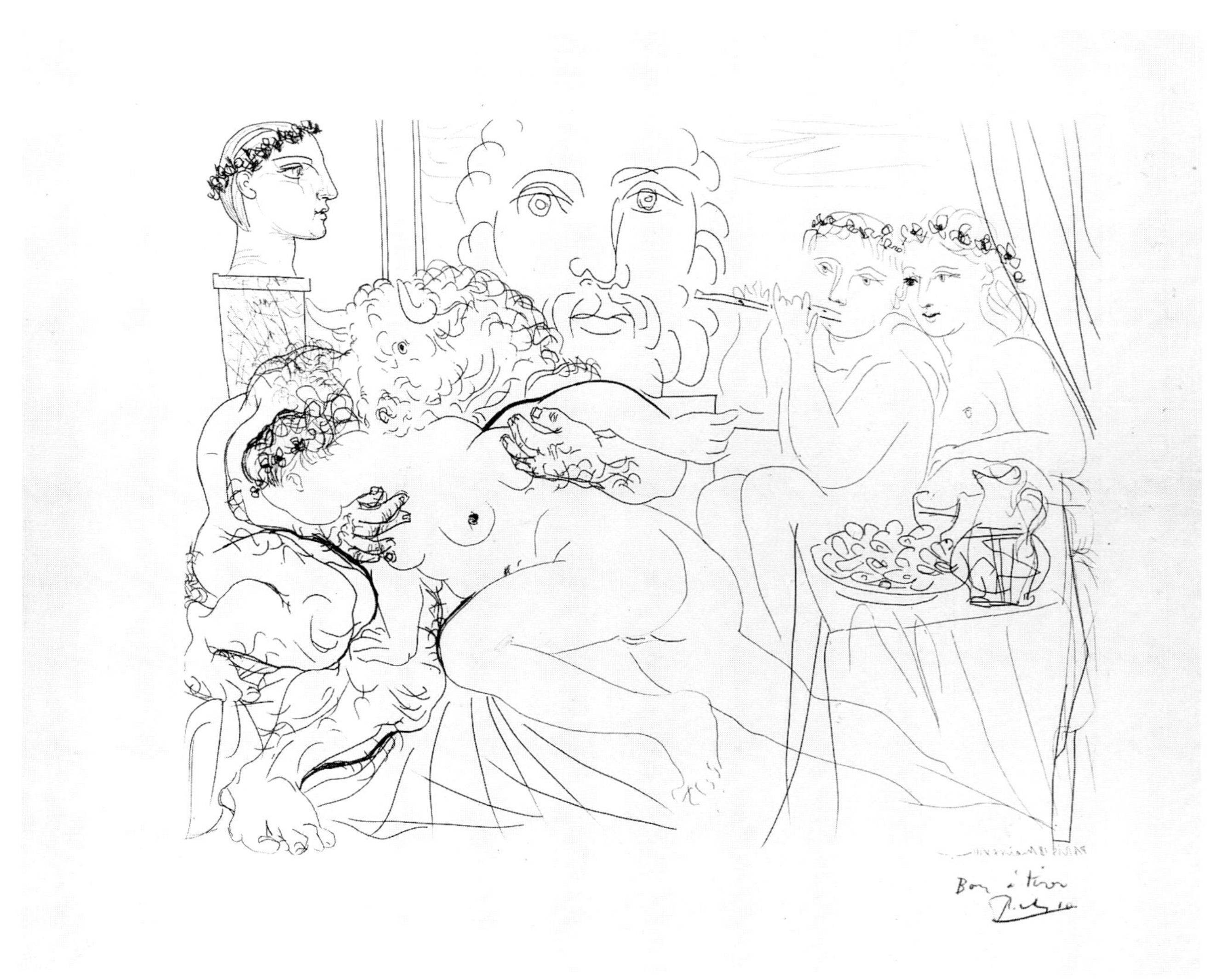

156 Self-Portrait, Three Forms: Crowned Painter, Bust of Sculptor and Amorous Minotaur, 18 May 1933
Etching on copper; trial proof; 30 x 36.7
Paris, Musée Picasso, MP 1982-143 [MB]

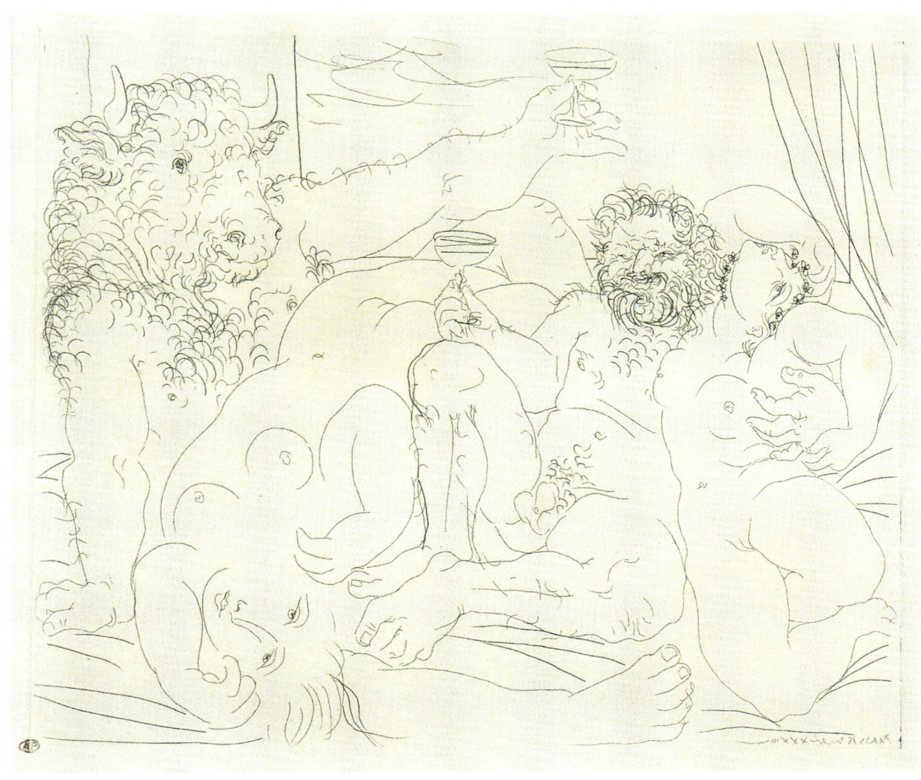

157 Bacchanal with Minotaur, 18 May 1933

Etching on copper; States I, II and III; 29.9 x 36.5
Paris, Musée Picasso, MP 2655* [P], MP 2656 [M] and MP 2657 [B]

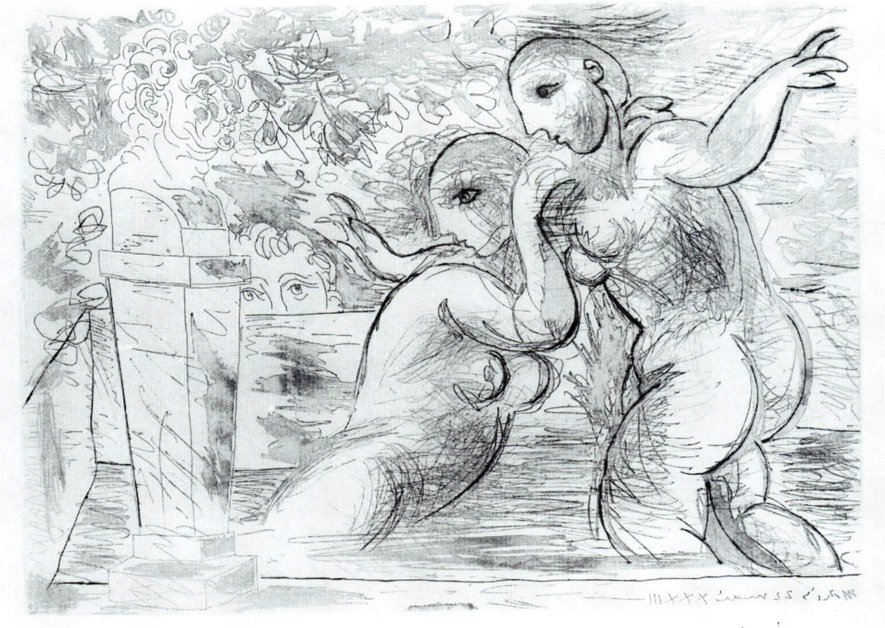

158 The Bathers Caught Unawares, 22 May 1933

Etching and drypoint on copper; State II and trial proof; 19.4 x 26.8
Paris, Musée Picasso, MP 2485 [PM] and MP 1982-73* [B]

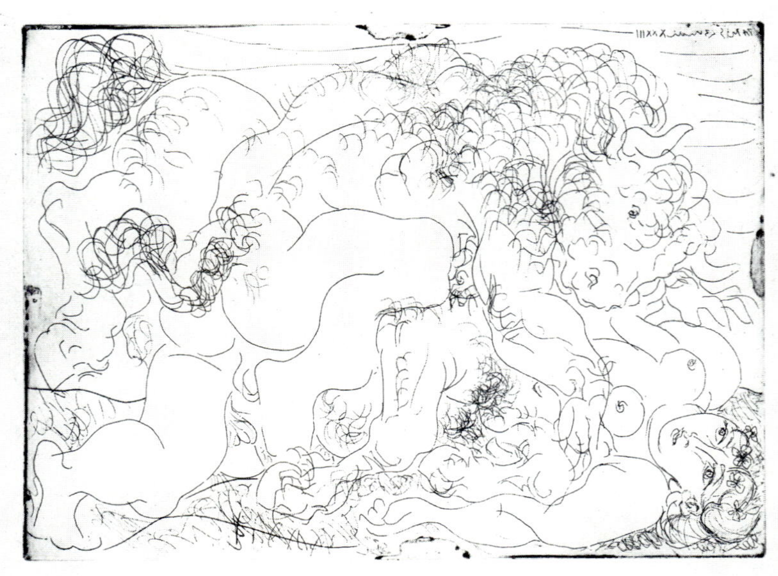

159 Minotaur in Love with a Centaur-Woman, 23 May 1933
   Etching on copper; States I, II and III; 19.4 x 26.8
   Paris, Musée Picasso, MP 2662* [P], MP 2663 [M] and MP 2664 [B]

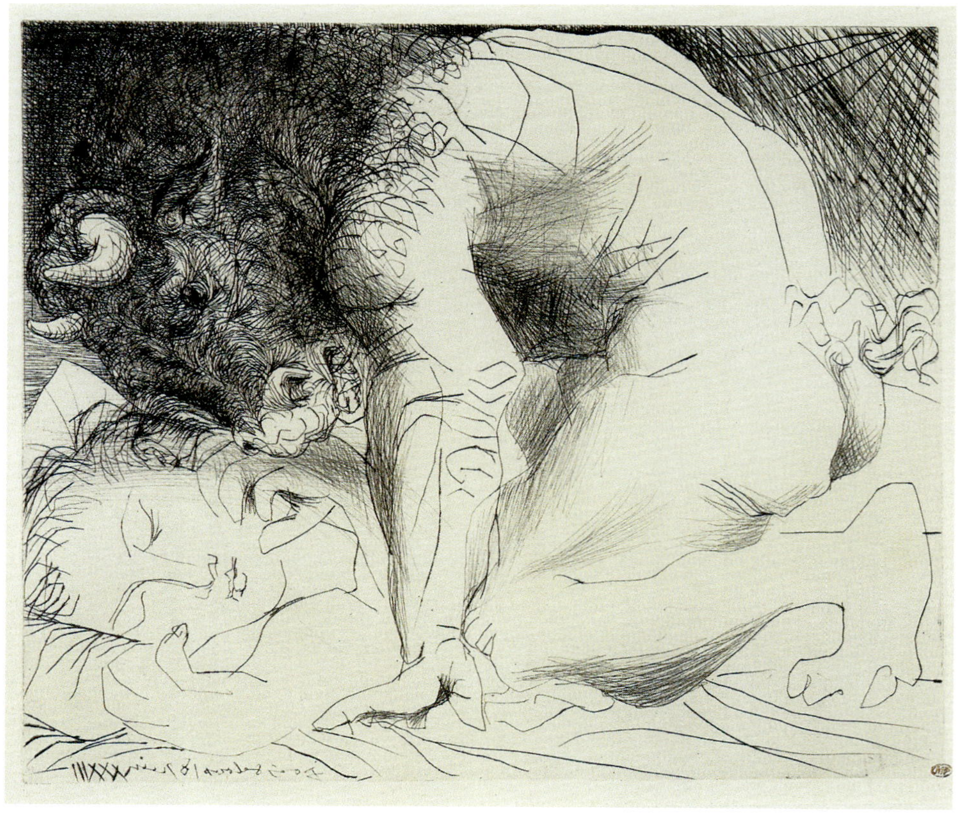

160 Minotaur Caressing the Hand of a Sleeping Woman with His Muzzle, 18 June 1933
   Drypoint on copper; States I and II; 29.9 x 36.5
   Paris, Musée Picasso, MP 2673 [P] and MP 2674* [M]

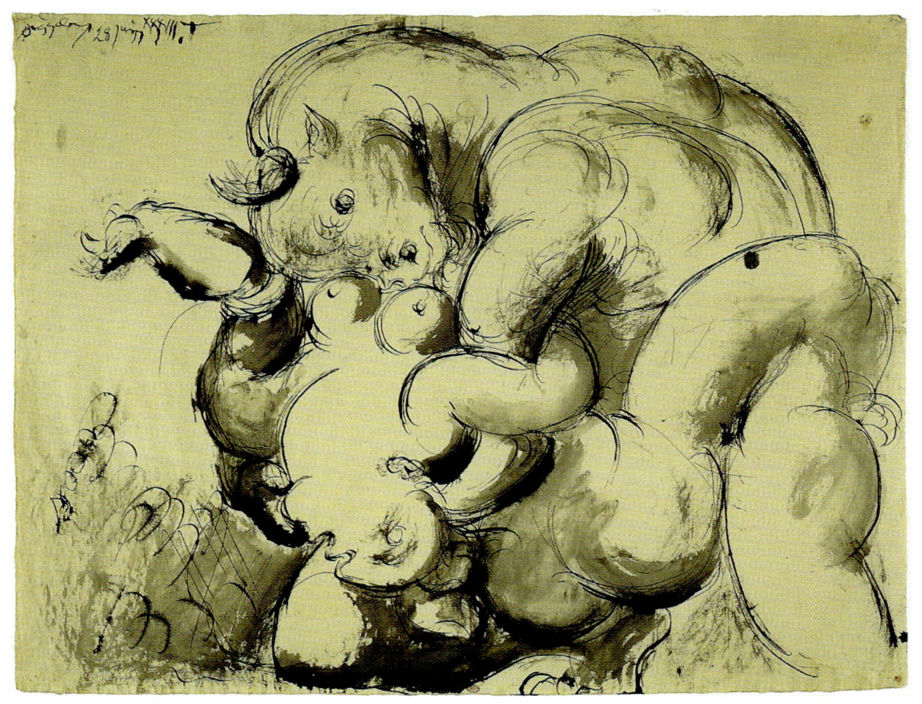

161 Minotaur Raping a Woman, 28 June 1933
       Pen, India ink and wash on paper; 47 x 62
       Paris, Musée Picasso, MP 1115

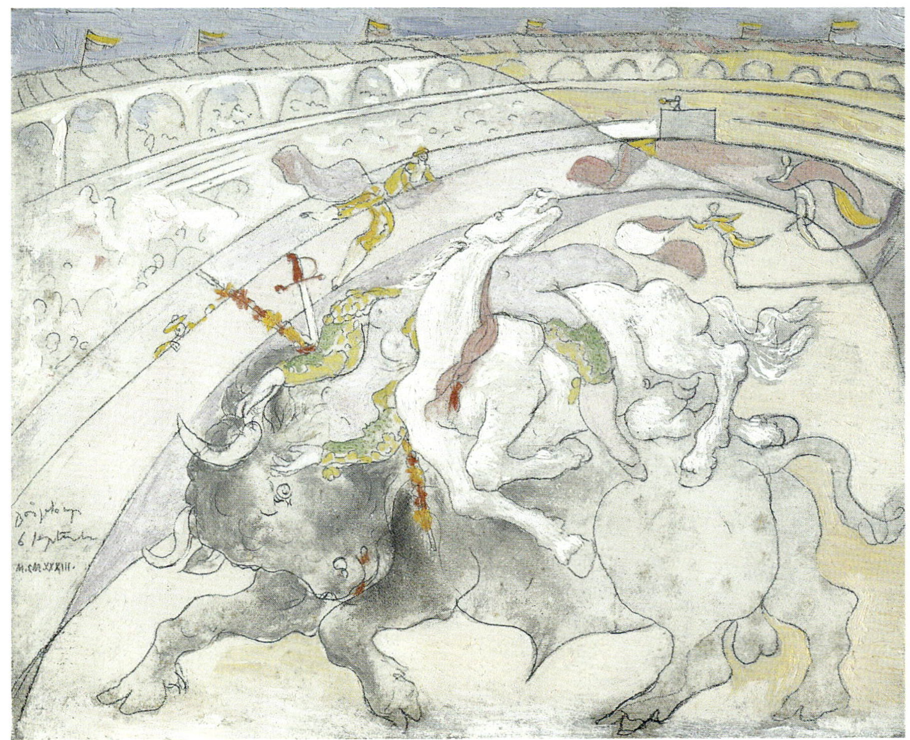

162 Bullfight: Death of the Female Toreador, 6 September 1933
       Oil and pencil on panel; 21.7 x 27
       Paris, Musée Picasso, MP 144

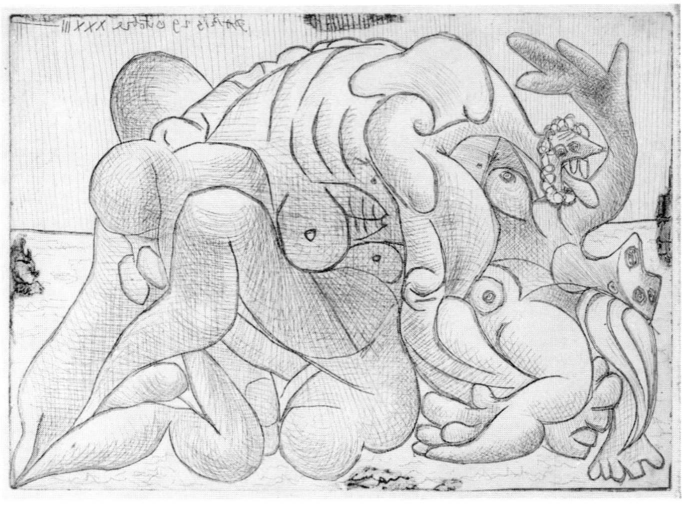

163 Embrace on the Beach, 29 October 1933

Etching on copper; State II; 19.3 x 26.6
Paris, Musée Picasso, MP 2409 [P]

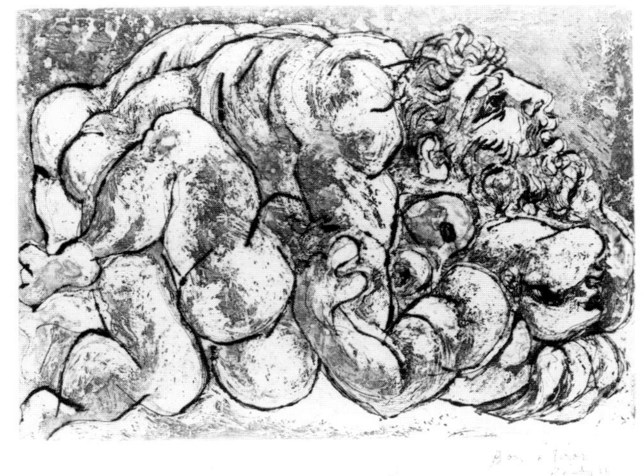

165 Coupling I, 2 November 1933

Etching and drypoint on copper; State II; 20 x 27.7
Paris, Musée Picasso, MP 2548 [P], MP 2549 [M] and
MP 1982-88* (trial proof) [B]

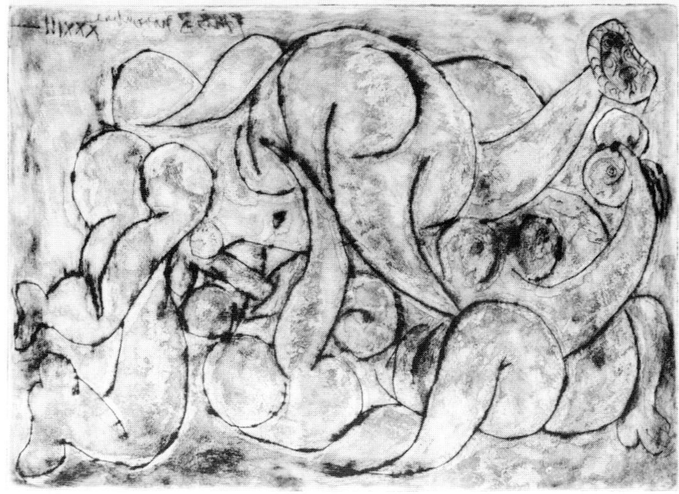

166 Coupling II, 3 November 1933

Etching and drypoint on copper; States II, III and IV;
19.9 x 27.8
Paris, Musée Picasso, MP 2413* [P], MP 2412 [M] and
MP 2414 [B]

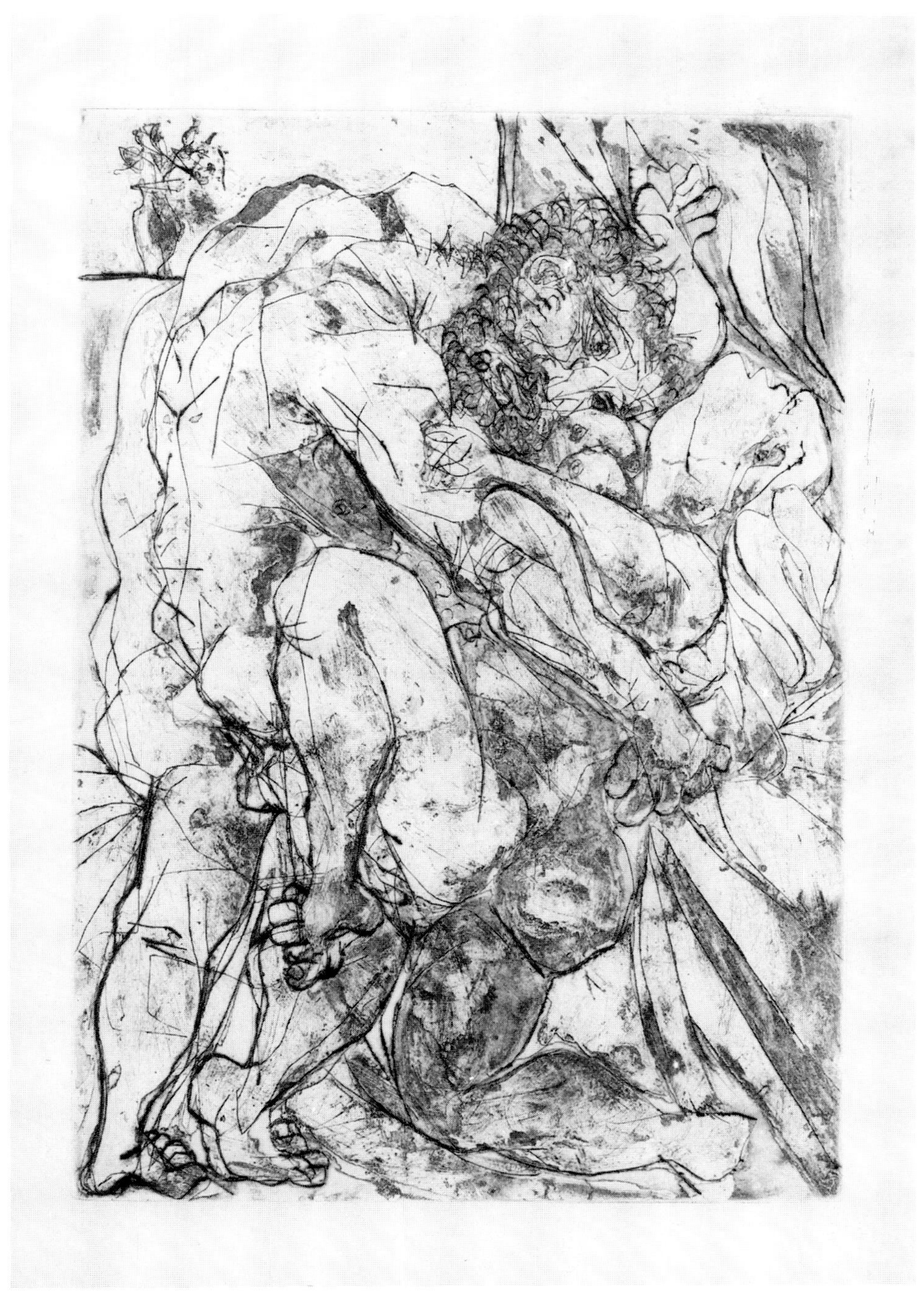

164 The Rape beneath the Window, Early November 1933
   Etching and drypoint on copper; State XIV; 27.8 x 19.9
   Paris, Musée Picasso, MP 2545 [M] and MP 2546* [B]

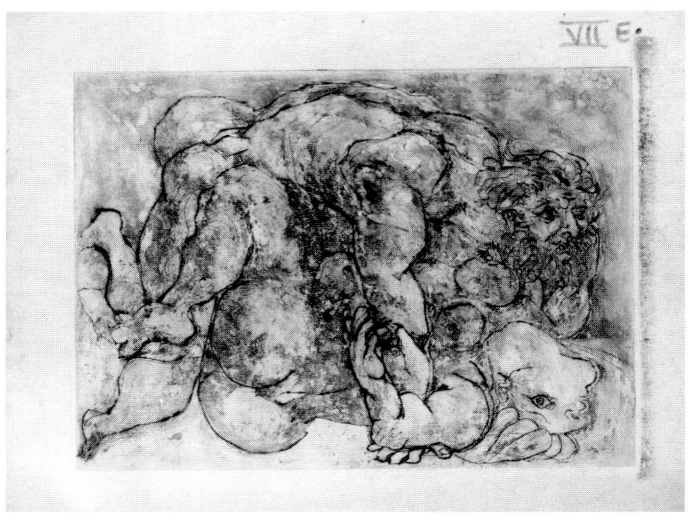

167 Couple Making Love, 2 November 1933
   Etching, scraper and drypoint on copper; State VII;
   19.8 x 27.9
   Paris, Musée Picasso, MP 2559 [P]

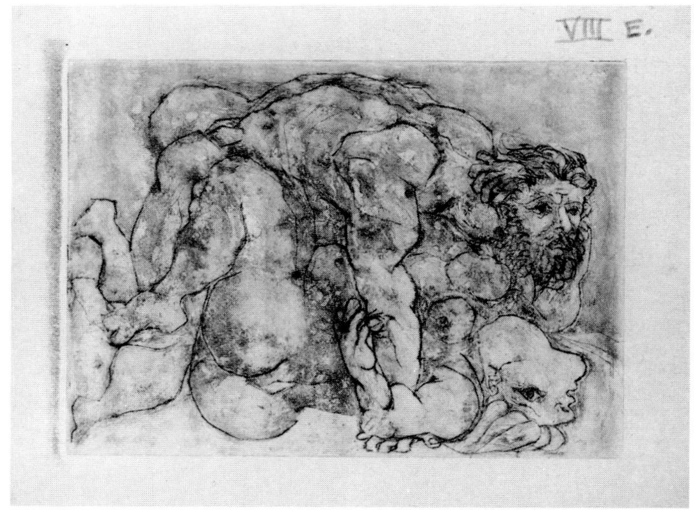

168 Couple Making Love, 3 November 1933
   Etching, scraper and drypoint on copper; State VIII;
   19.8 x 27.9
   Paris, Musée Picasso, MP 2561 [M]

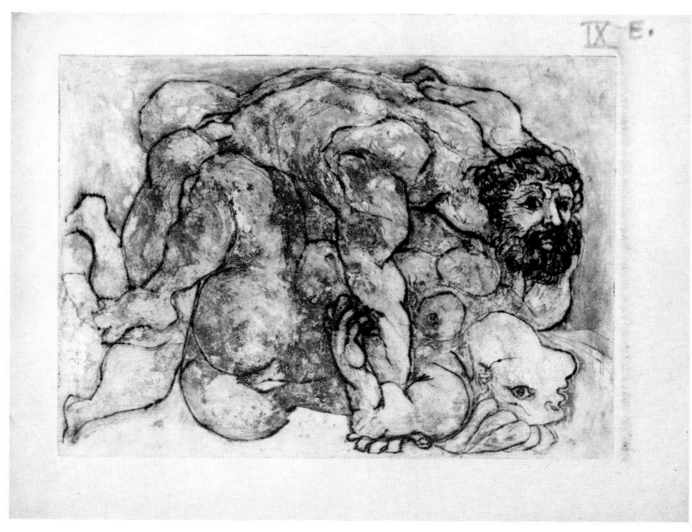

169 Couple Making Love, 4 November 1933
   Etching, scraper and drypoint on copper; State IX;
   19.8 x 27.9
   Paris, Musée Picasso, MP 2563 [B]

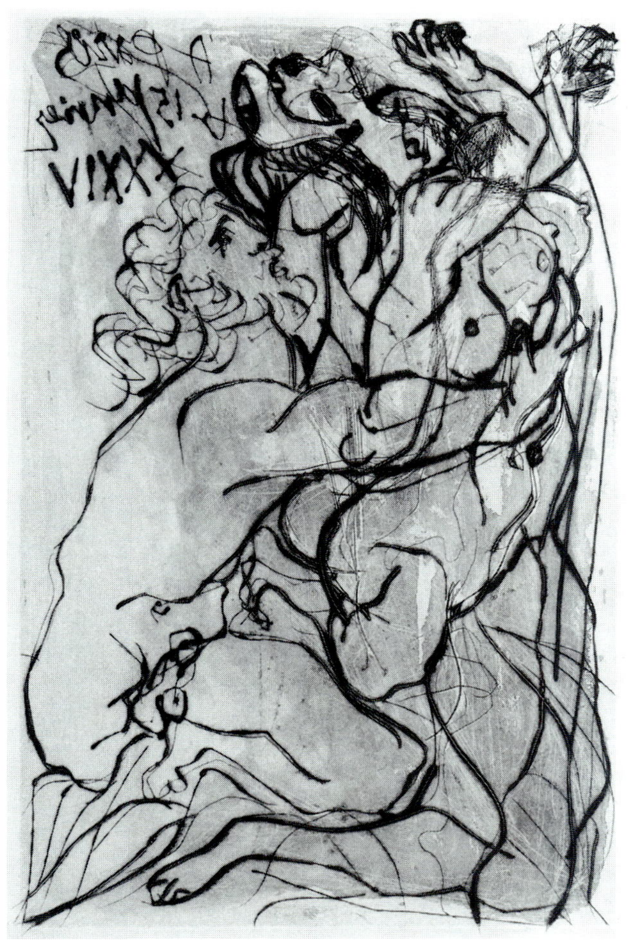

172 Kinesias Pursuing Myrrhina, 15 January 1934
Drypoint on copper; State III; 20.8 x 13.9
Paris, Musée Picasso, MP 2431 [M]

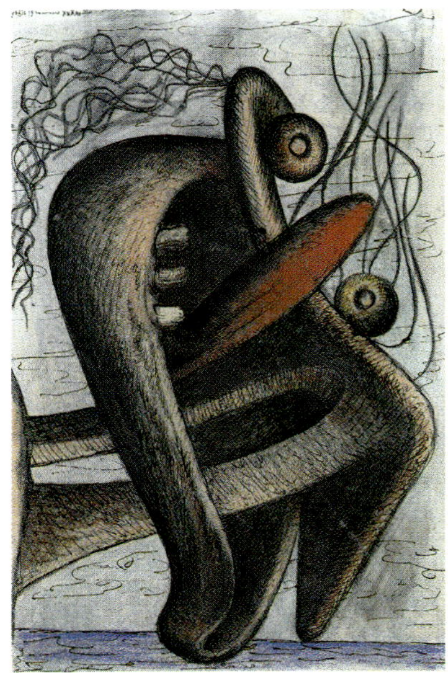

171 Figure at the Seashore,
19 November 1933
Pastel, India ink and charcoal on paper;
51 x 34.2
Paris, Musée Picasso, MP 1116

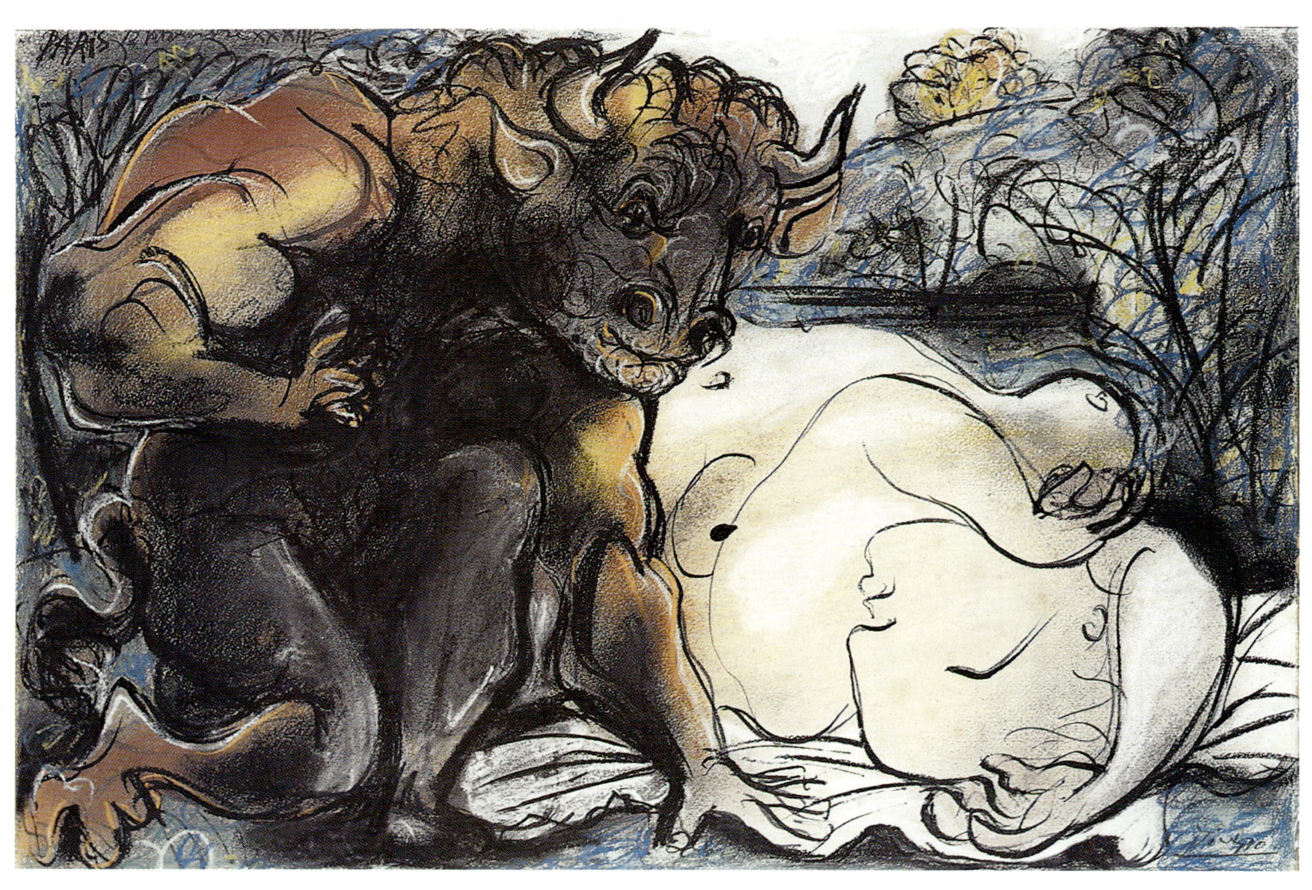

170 The Minotaur, 12 November 1933

Gouache, pastel, coloured pencil,
pen and India ink on paper; 34 x 51.4
Dijon, Musée des Beaux-Arts, inv. D G44 [P]

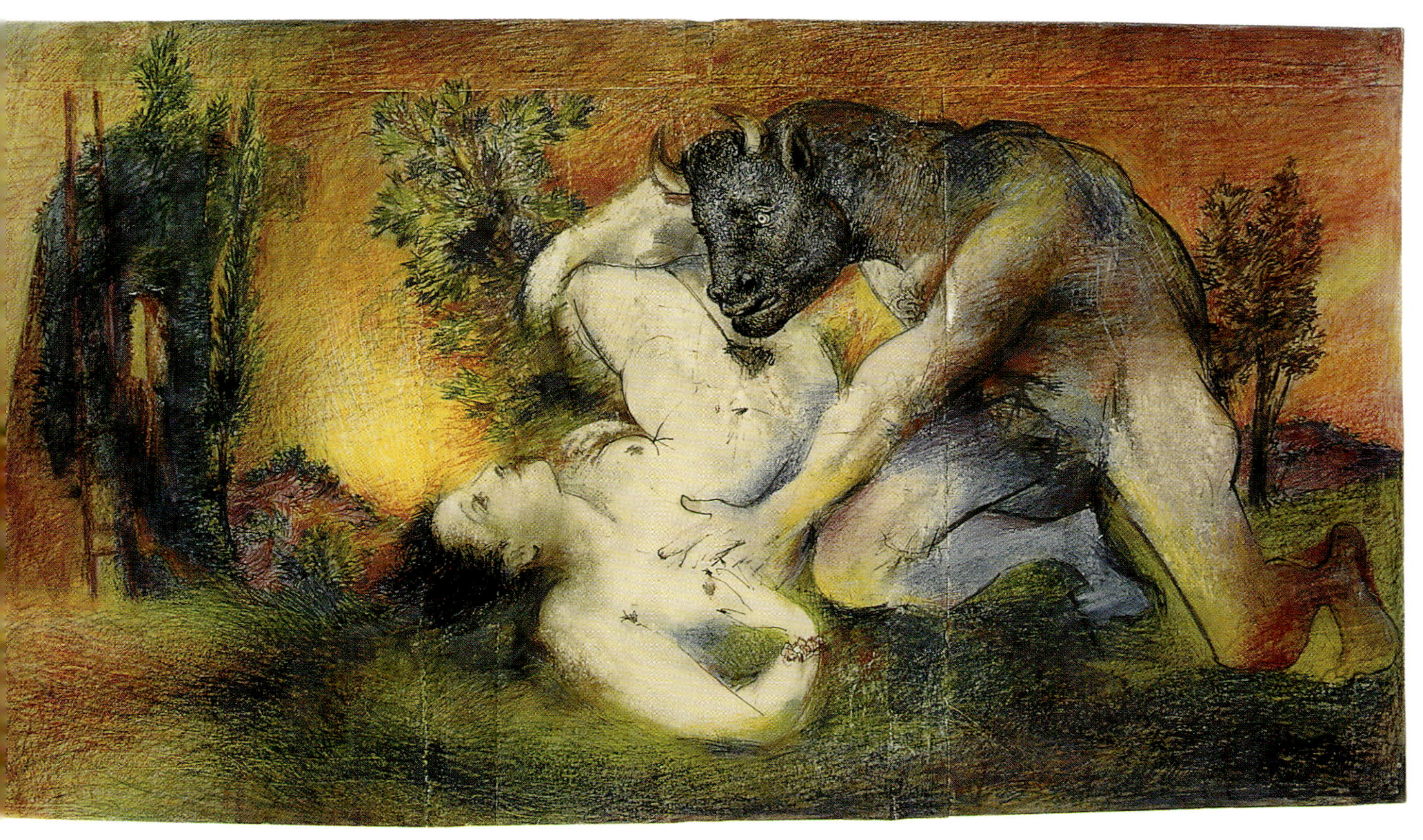

187 Dora and the Minotaur, 5 September 1936
India ink, coloured pencil and grattage on paper; 40.5 x 72
Paris, Musée Picasso, MP 1998-308

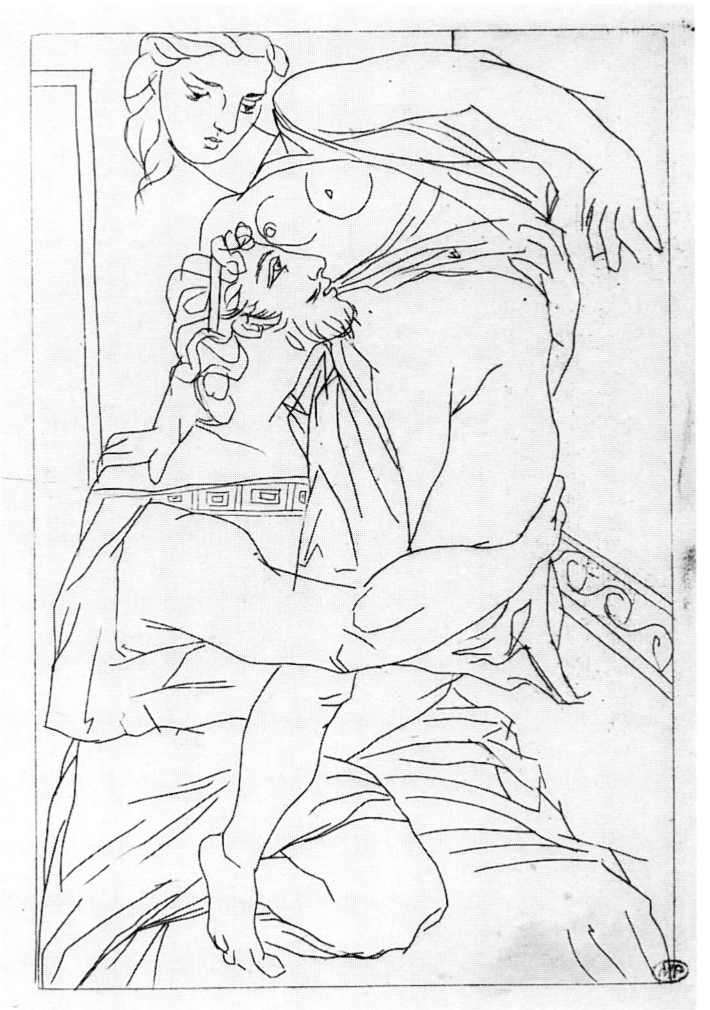

173 **Kinesias and Myrrhina**, 17 January 1934
Etching on copper; State I; 22 x 15.2
Paris, Musée Picasso, MP 2419 [PB]

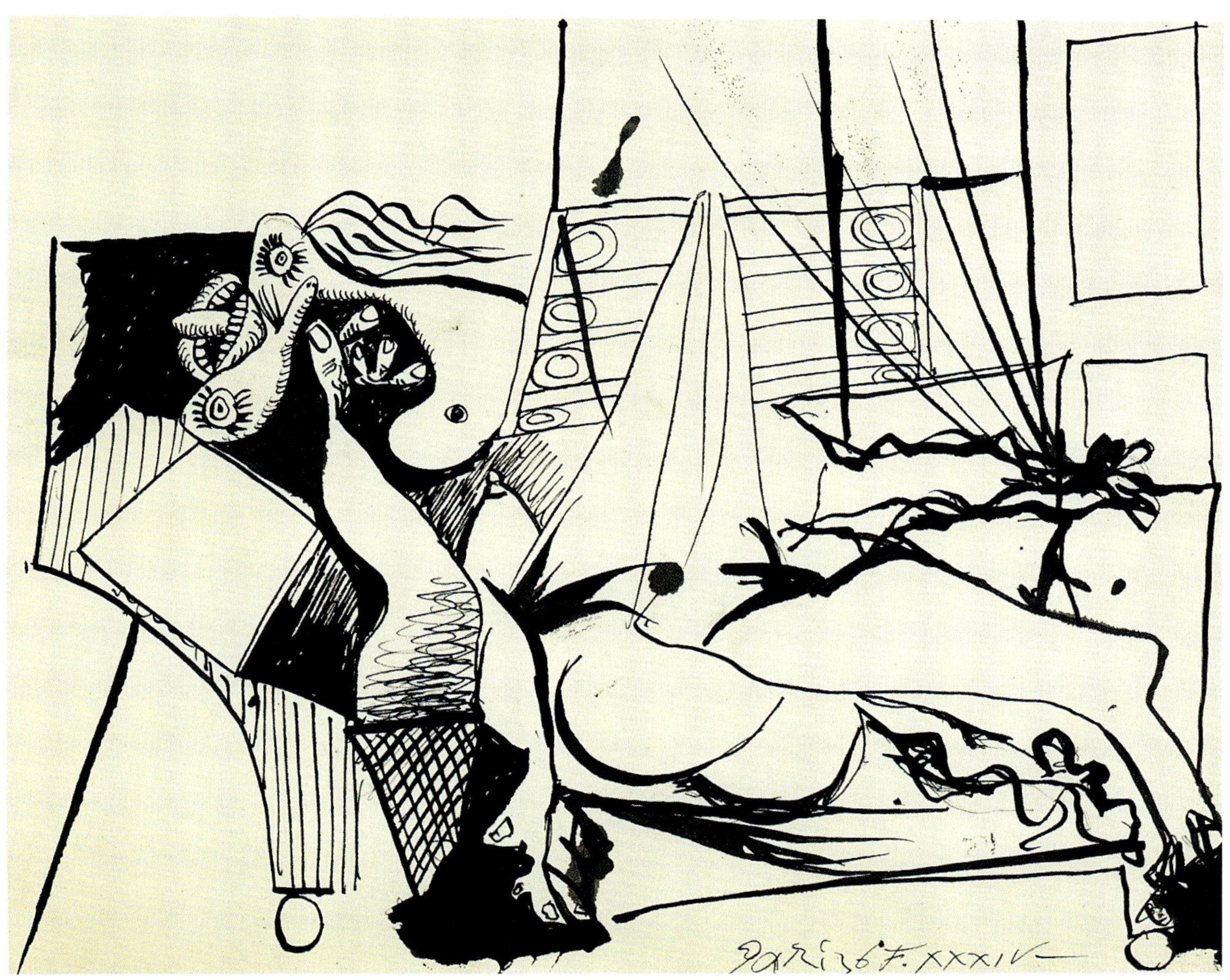

174 Composition, 6 February 1934
India ink on paper; 26 x 32.5
Paris, Private collection

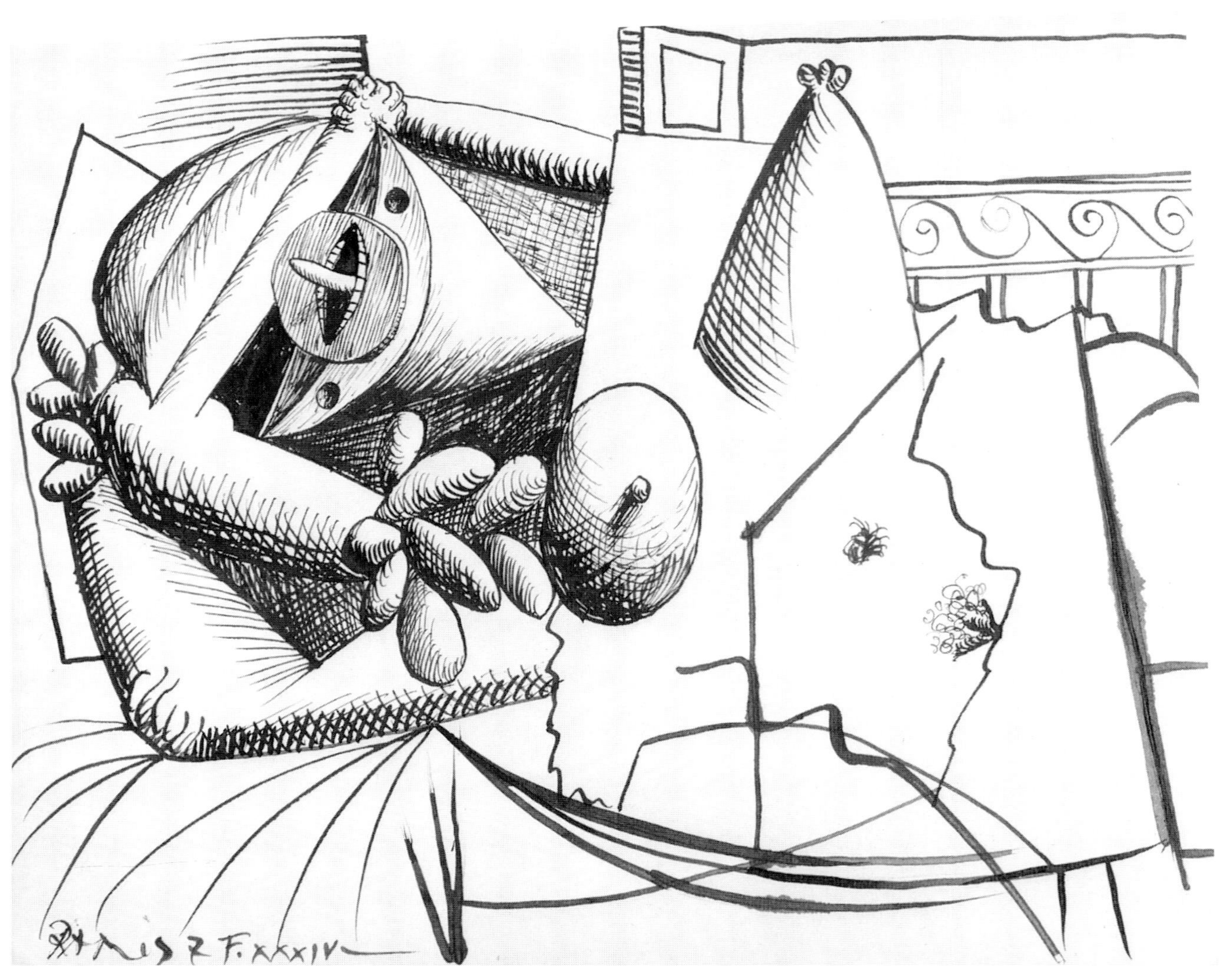

175 Reclining Nude by the Window, 7 February 1934
Pen and India ink on paper; 26.2 x 32.7
Paris, Musée Picasso, MP 1131

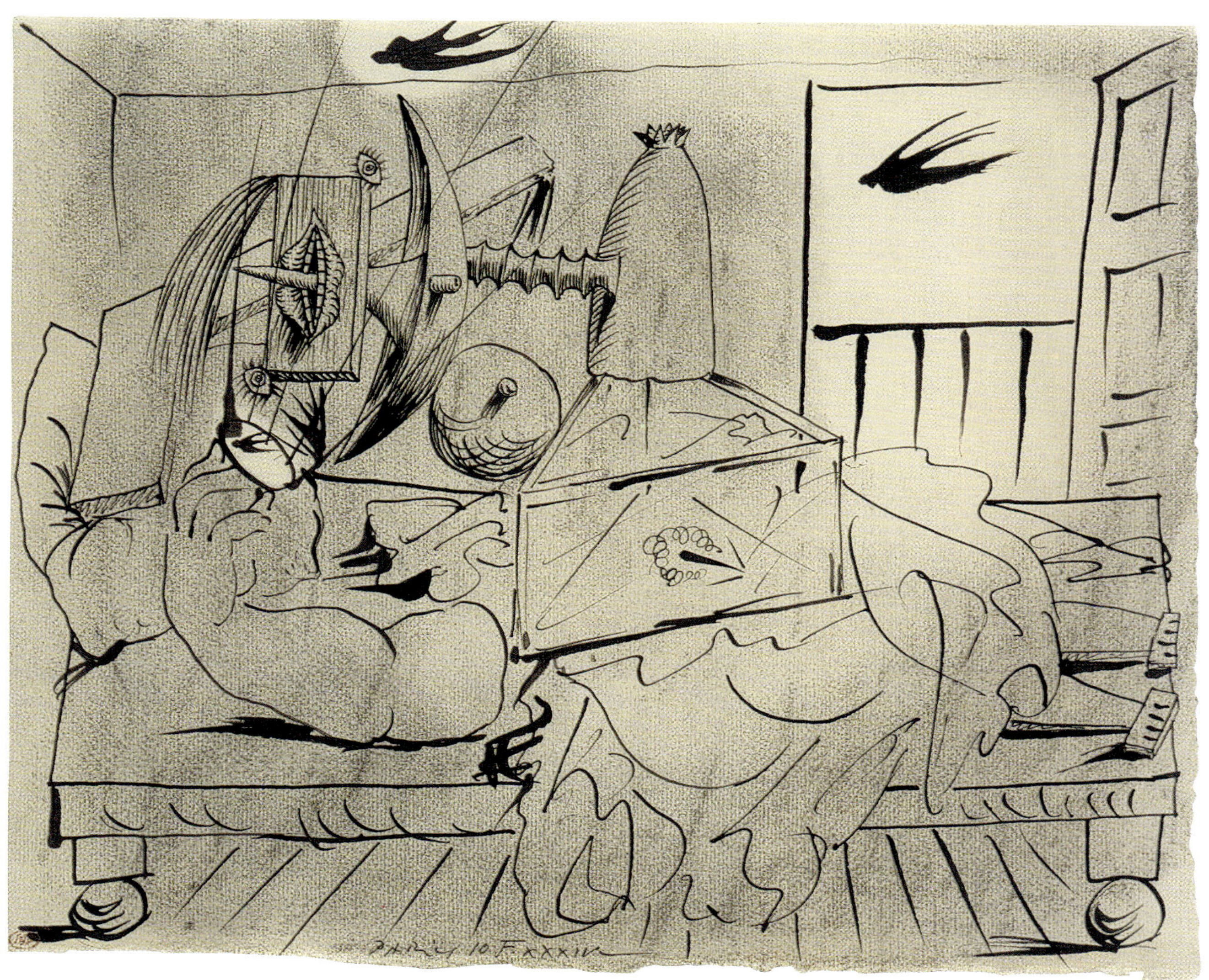

176 Interior with Swallows I, 10 February 1934
India ink and charcoal on paper; 25.7 x 32.5
Paris, Musée Picasso, MP 1133

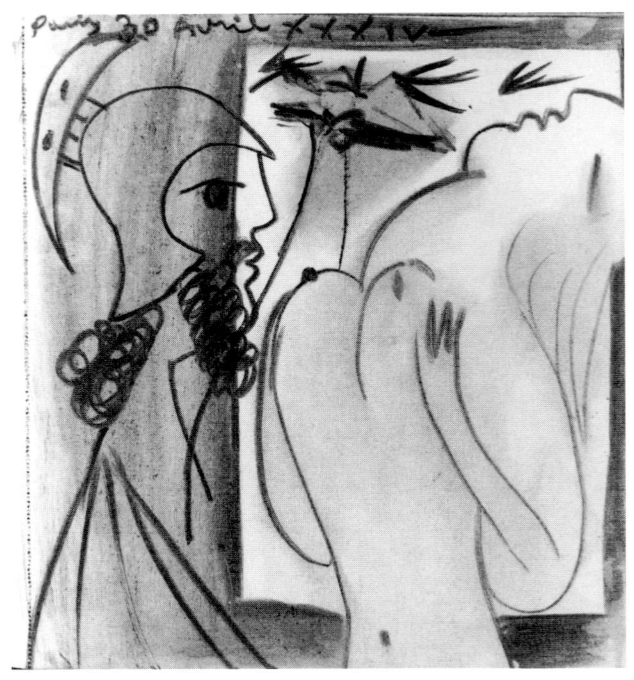

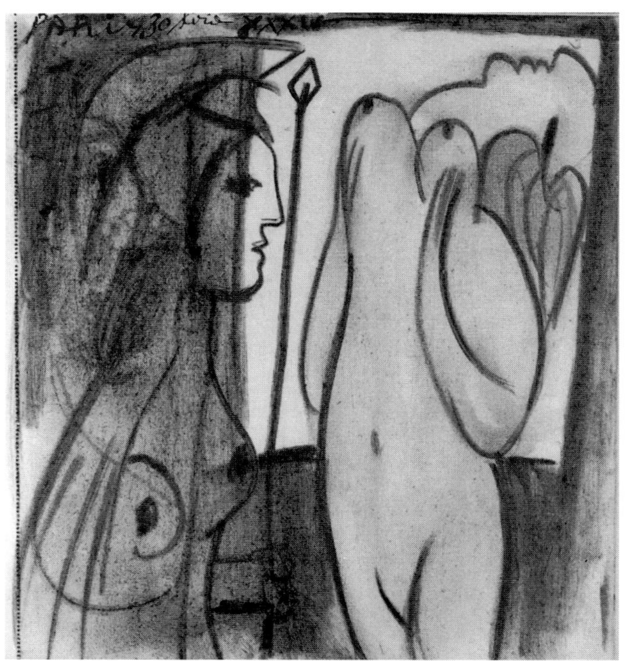

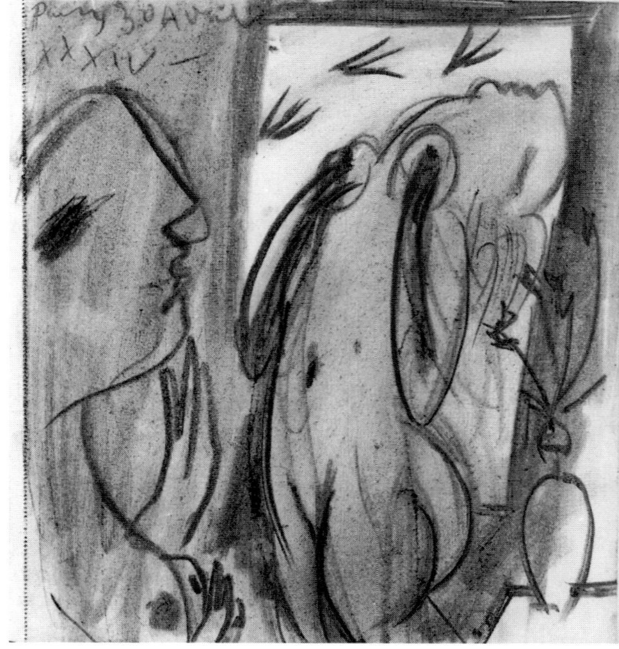

177 a, b and c Sketchbook, 25 January 1932–1 May 1934

Warrior with Javelin and Backward Nude (f° 33 r°), *Nude and Woman Warrior with Javelin* (f° 34 r°)
and *Nude and Woman in Profile* (f° 36 r°)
Charcoal on Vergé paper; 28 x 26.5
Paris, Musée Picasso, MP 1990-110

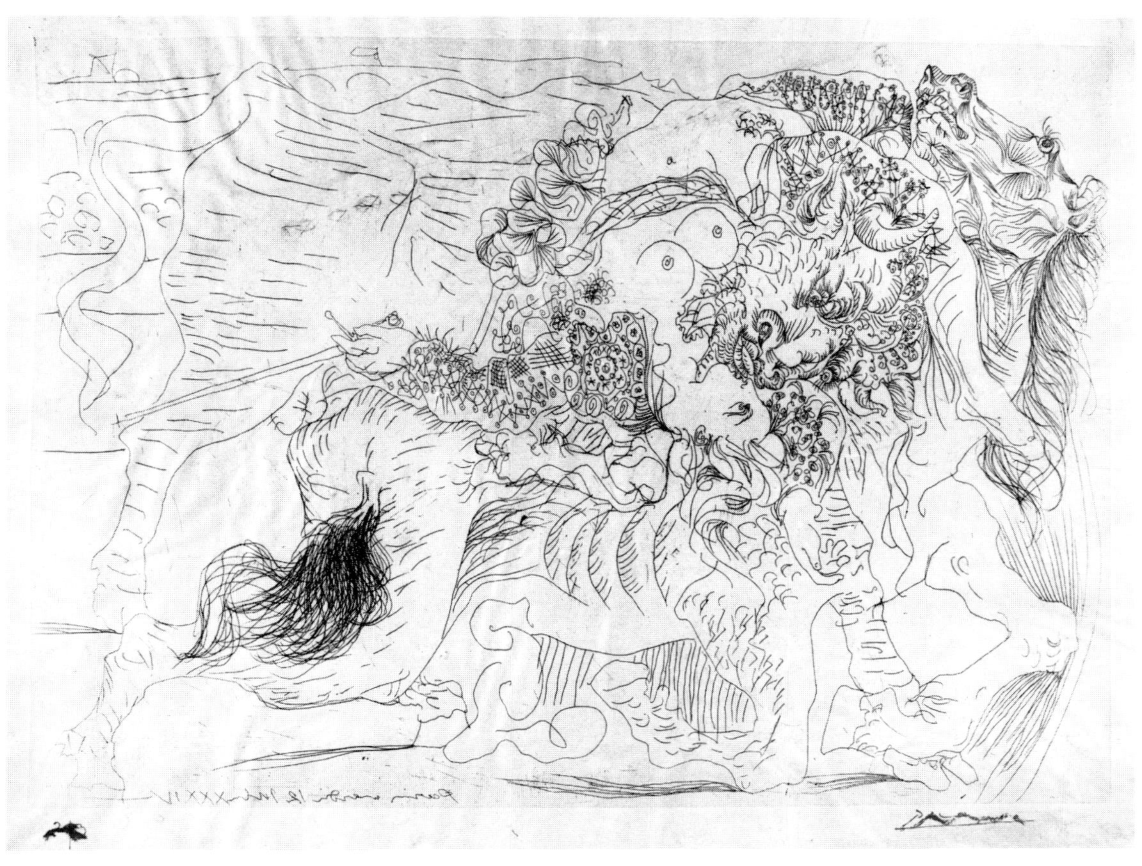

178 Female Toreador. Last Kiss? 12 June 1934

Etching on copper; 49.7 x 69.7
Paris, Musée Picasso, MP 2447* [B]
New York, The Museum of Modern Art [M]

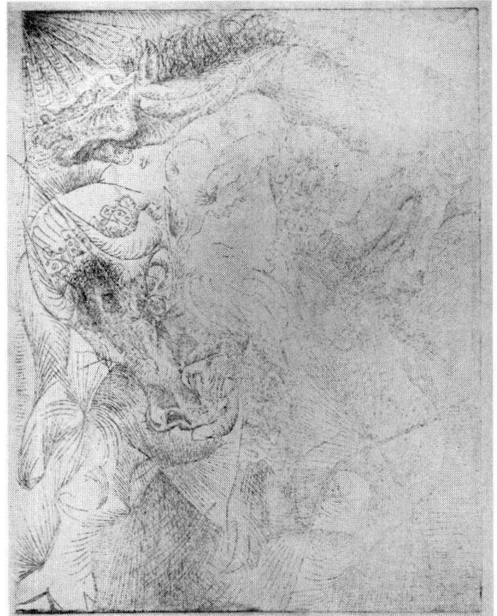

179 Marie-Thérèse as a Female Toreador, 20 June 1934

Etching on copper; 29.7 x 23.7
Paris, Musée Picasso, MP 2510* [M] and MP 1982-81 (trial proof) [B]

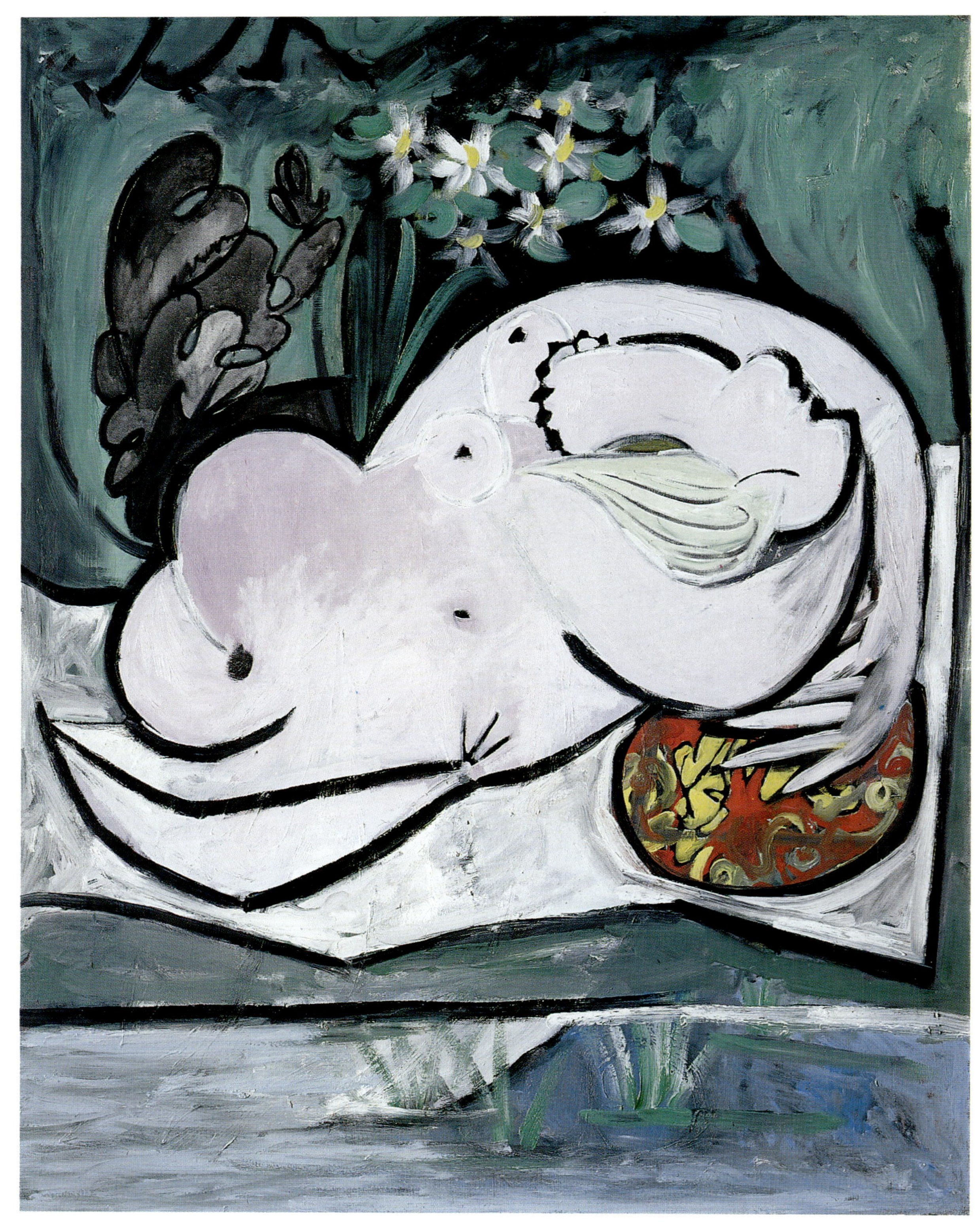

180 Nude in a Garden, 4 August 1934
Oil on canvas; 162 x 130
Paris, Musée Picasso, MP 148 [MB]

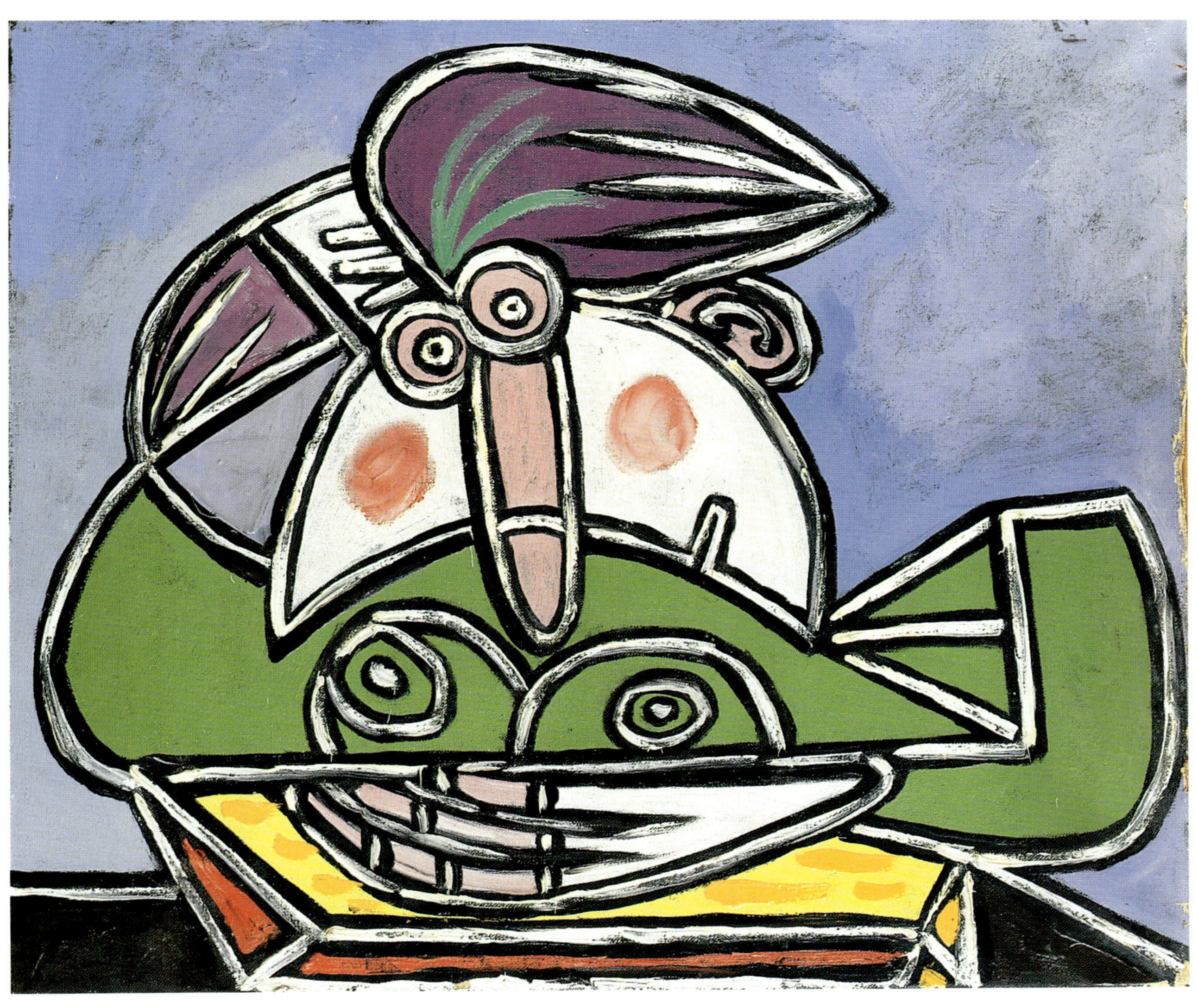

181 Woman Leaning on Her Elbow, 10 March 1935
Oil on canvas; 50.2 x 61
Private collection [P]

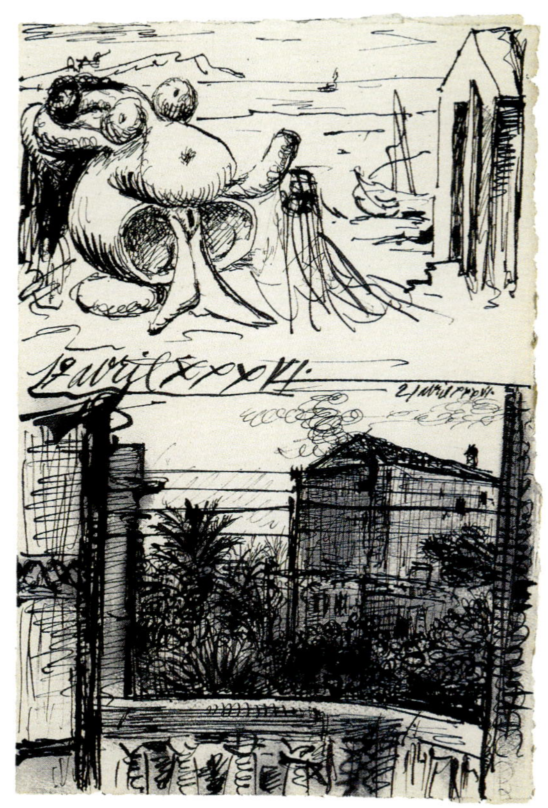

183 Bather with Cabana; Landscape at Juan-les-Pins,
12 April 1936

India ink and wash on paper; 26 x 17.3
Paris, Musée Picasso, MP 1157 [P]

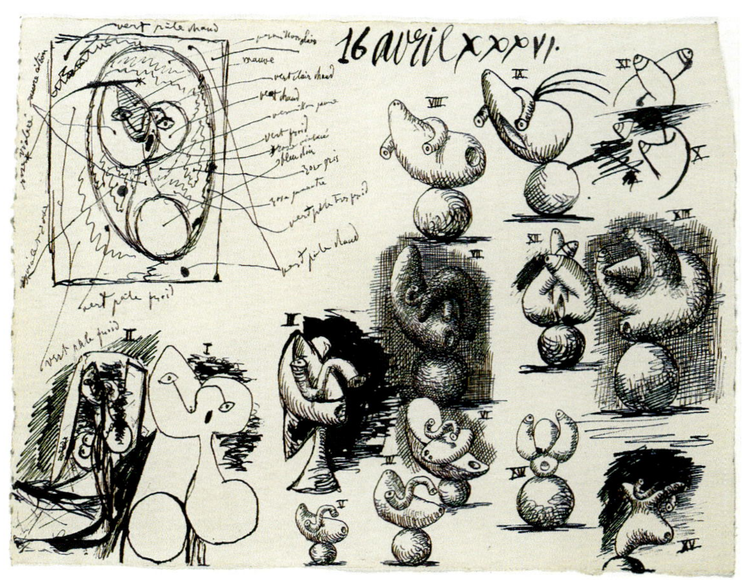

184 Sheet of Studies: Head of a Woman, 16 April 1936

Pen and India ink on paper, with coloured handwritten annotations; 26 x 34
Paris, Musée Picasso, MP 1155

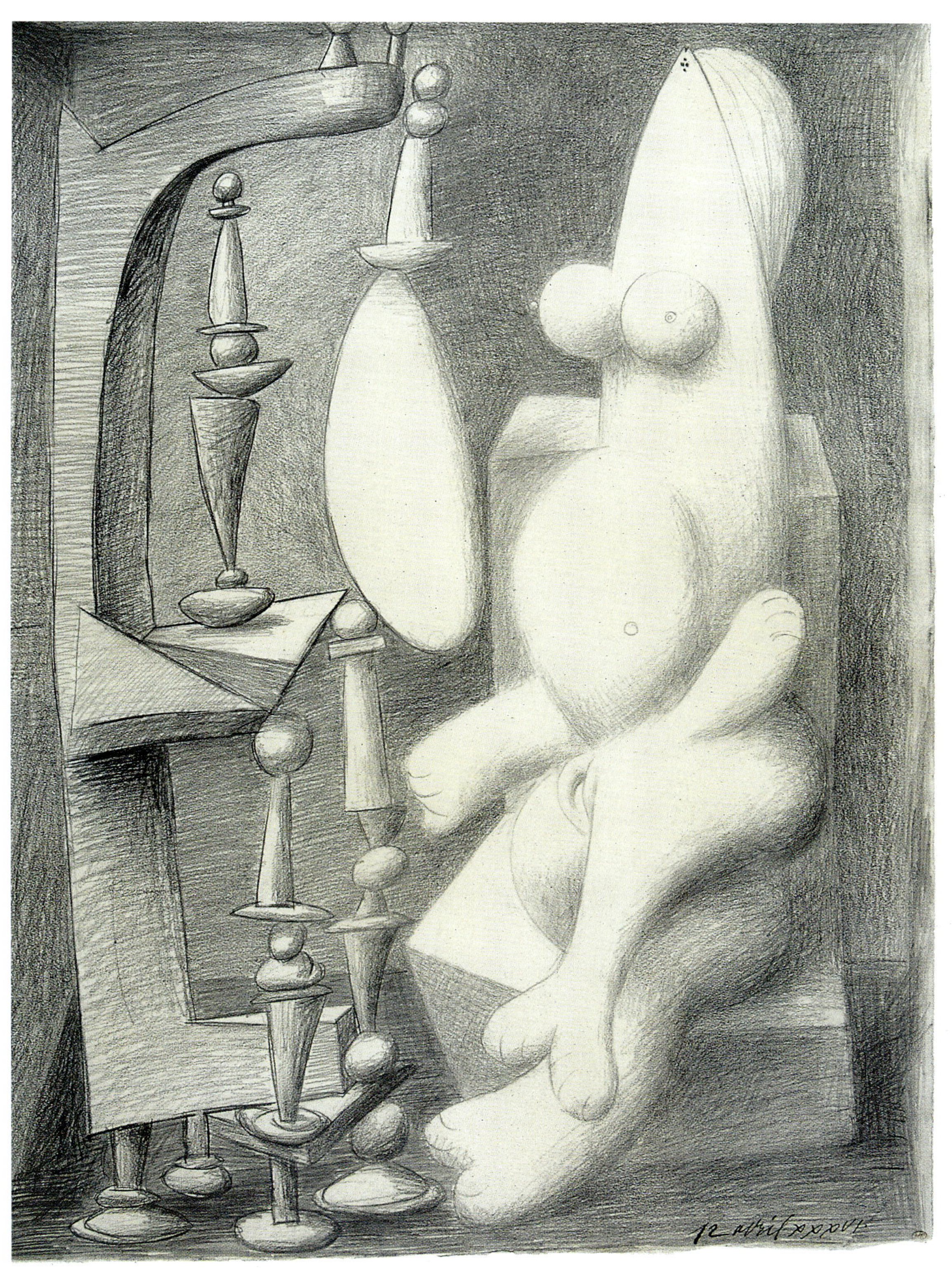

182 Nude before a Dresser, 12 April 1936

Graphite stick on paper; 65 x 50
Paris, Musée Picasso, MP 1153 [P]

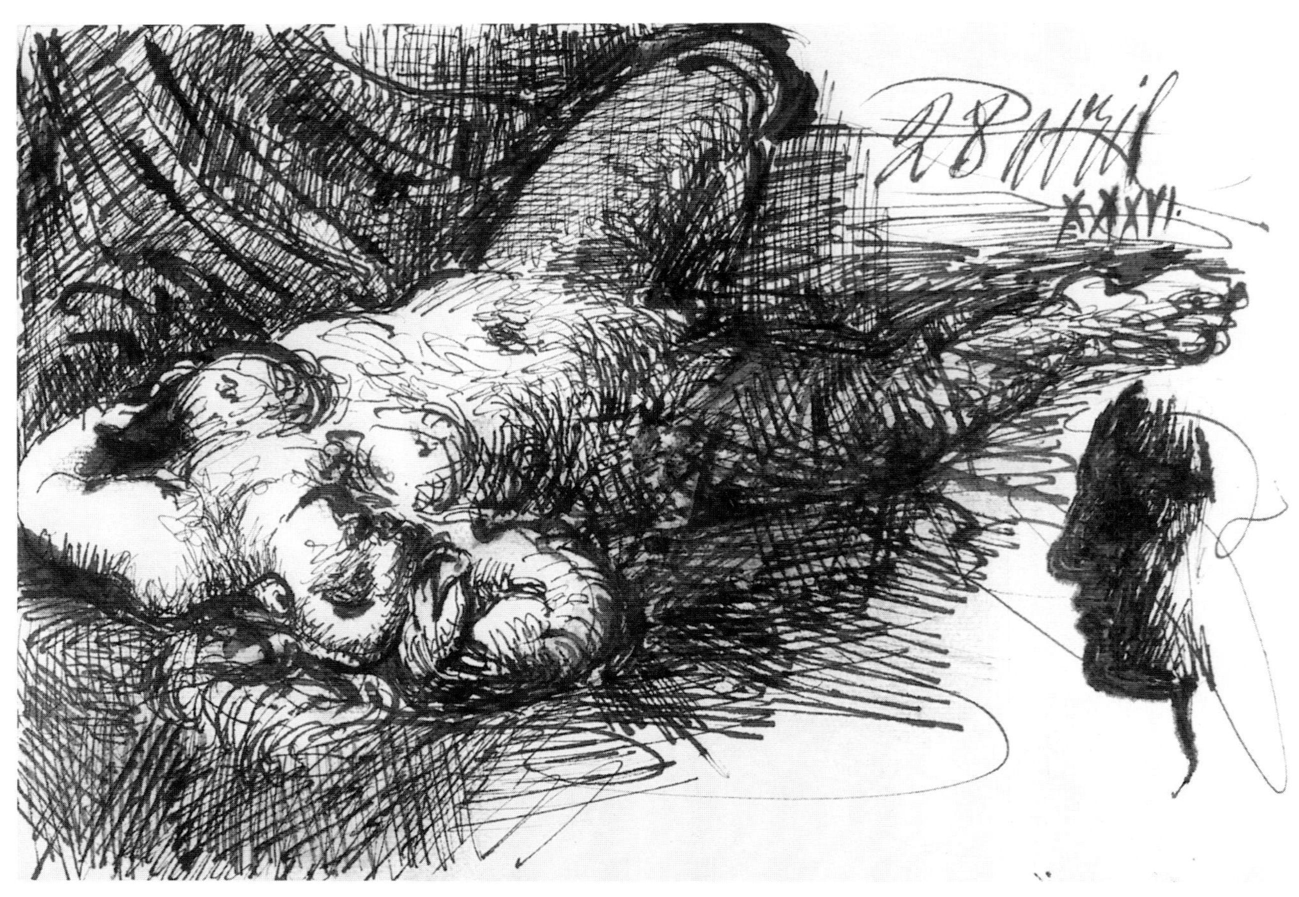

185 Reclining Nude and Profile, 28 April 1936
India ink on paper; 17.2 x 25.5
Paris, Musée Picasso, MP 1161 [PB]

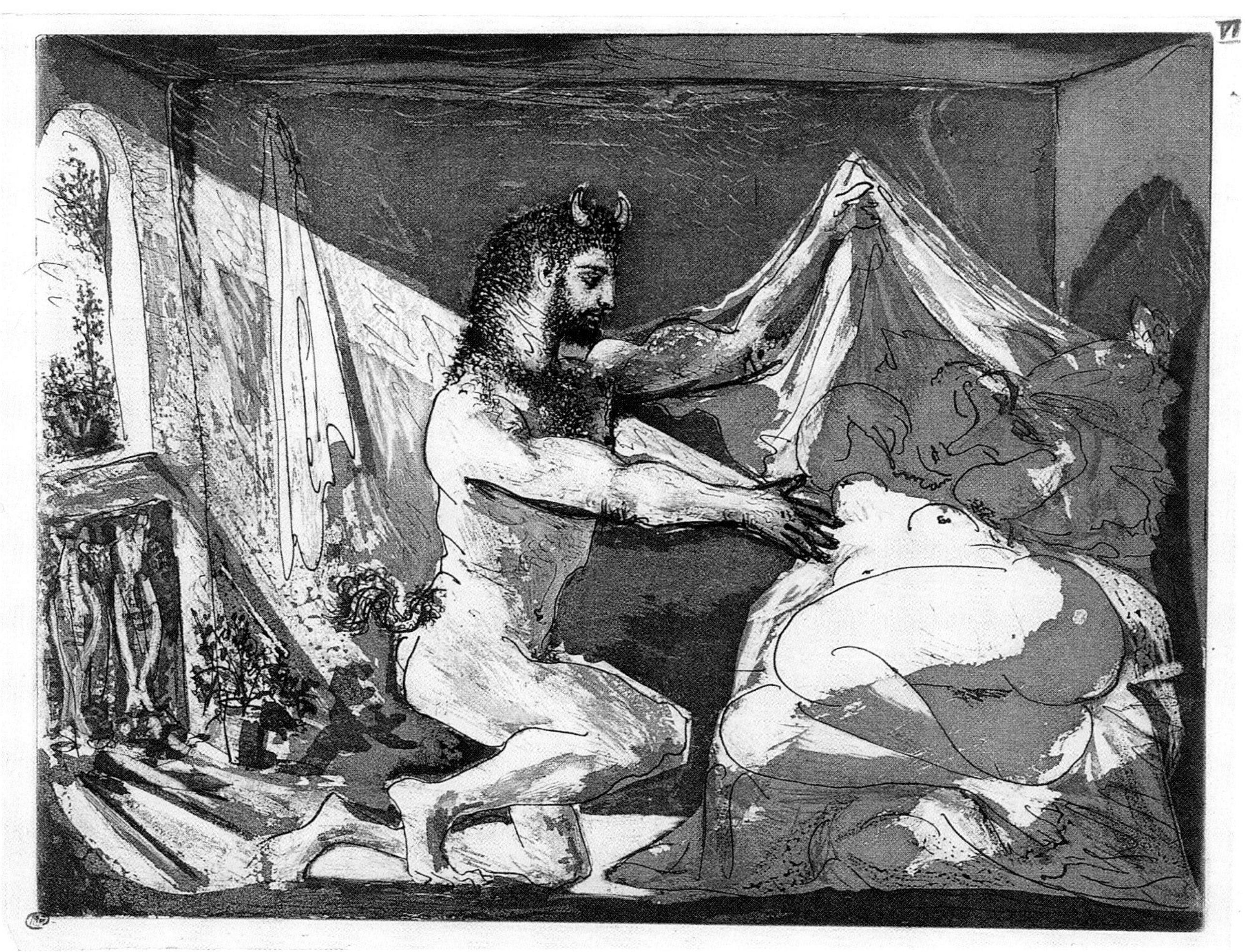

186 Faun Unveiling a Woman, 12 June 1936

Sugar-lift aquatint, scraper and burin on copper; States IV, V and VI; 31.6 x 41.7
Paris, Musée Picasso, MP 2529 [P], MP 2530 [M] and MP 2531* [B]

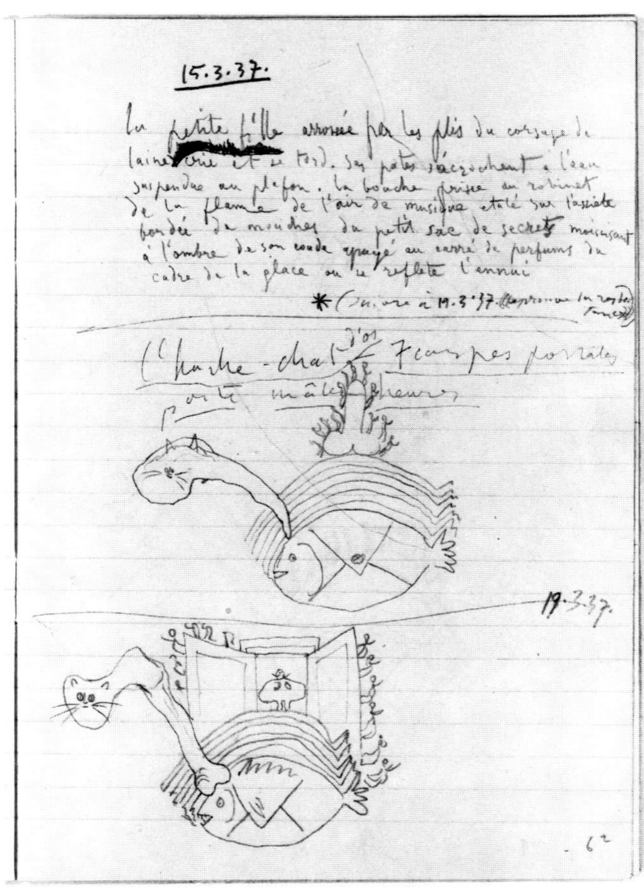

188 Sketchbook Page, 13 February–9 March 1937

Two studies of the hache-chat d'os (f° 6 r°)
Graphite stick on lined paper; 21 x 15
Handwritten text, in graphite stick:
15.3.37.
La petite fille arrossée par les plis du corsage de/laine crie et se tord. Ses pates s'acrochent à l'eau/suspendue au plafon. La bouche prisse au robinet/de la flame de l'air de musique étalé sur l'assiete/bordée de mouches du petit sac de secrets moisissont/à l'ombre de son coude apuyé au carré de parfums du/cadre de la glace ou se reflète l'ennui/ (Suivre à 19.3.37 (eprouve la resist/ance))*
L'hache-chat d'os. 7 carpes postales/
Porte mâle heures.
19.3.37.
[*15.3.37. The little girl sploshed by the folds of the corsage in/wool cries and twists. Her paws get stuck in the/water/hanging from the ceeling. The mouth stock on the tap/of the flaim of the musical air spread across the/plait/bounded by flies from the small sack of secrets going moldi/in the shadow of her elbow leening on the square/of perfumes of/the frame of the mirror whence ennui is reflected/**
(Continue on 19.3.37 (experience the resist/ance))
Th'axe-cat o' bone. 7 post cards/
brings male diction.
19.3.37.]
Paris, Musée Picasso, MP 1887

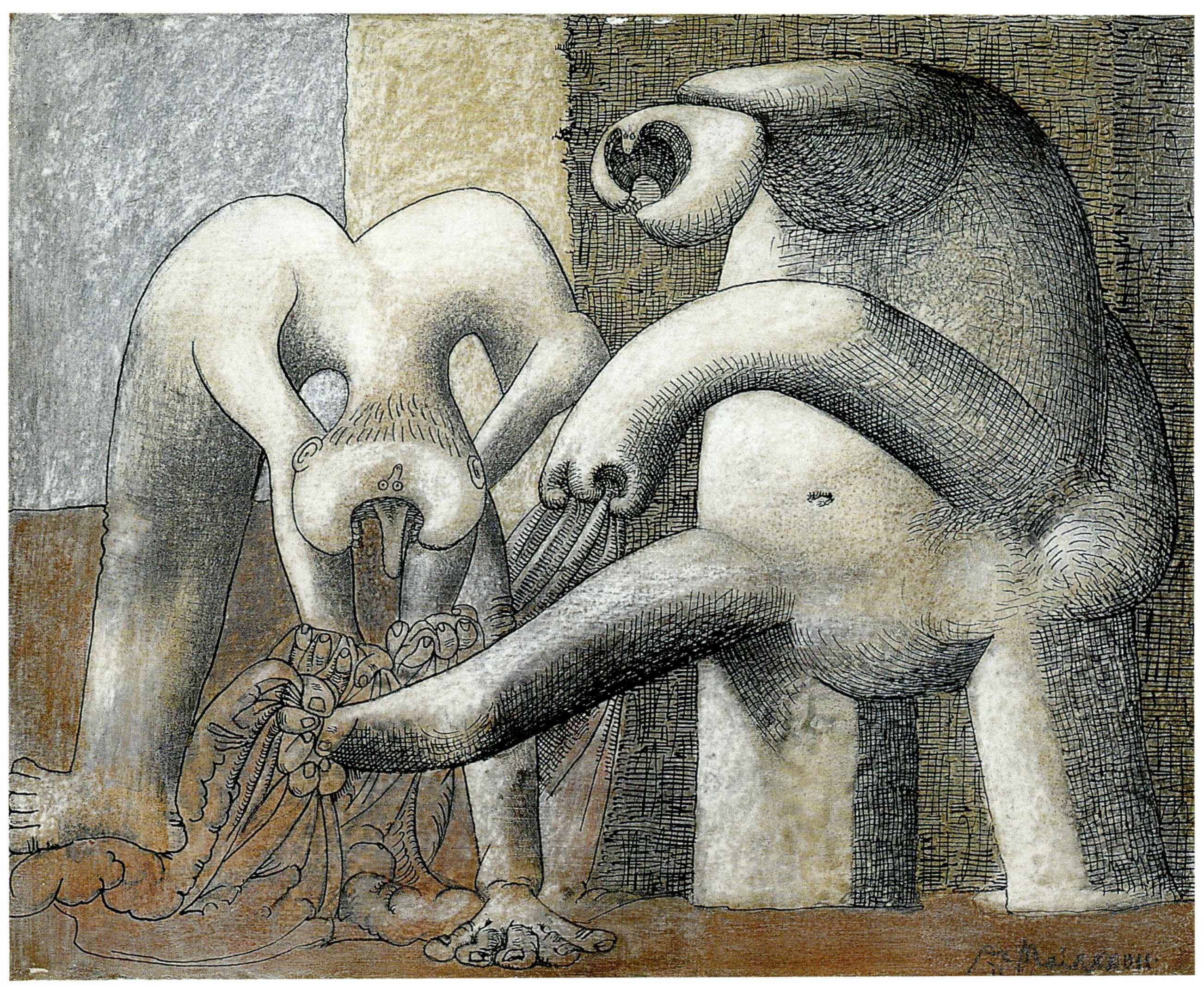

189 Two Nude Women on the Beach, 1 May 1937

India ink and gouache on panel; 22 x 27
Paris, Musée Picasso, MP 163

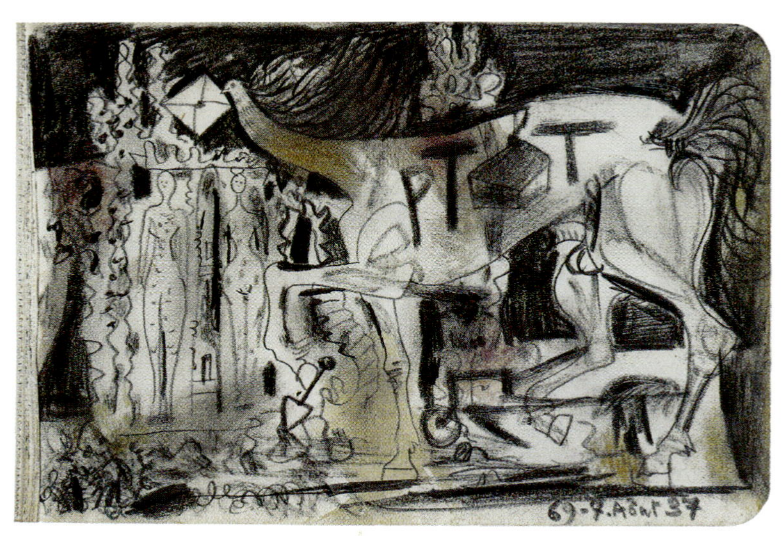

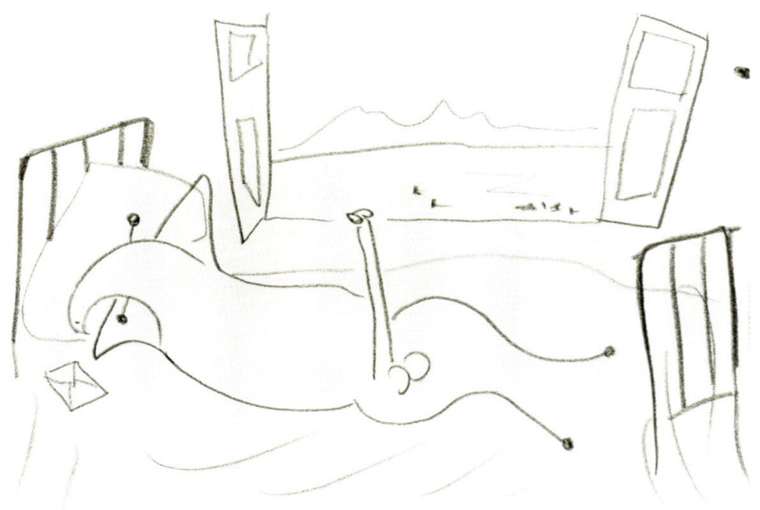

190 a, b, c, d and e The Horse Brings the Mail, 7 August 1937
Black and coloured pencil on sketchbook pages; 14 x 22
Geneva, Private collection, Courtesy LS Art

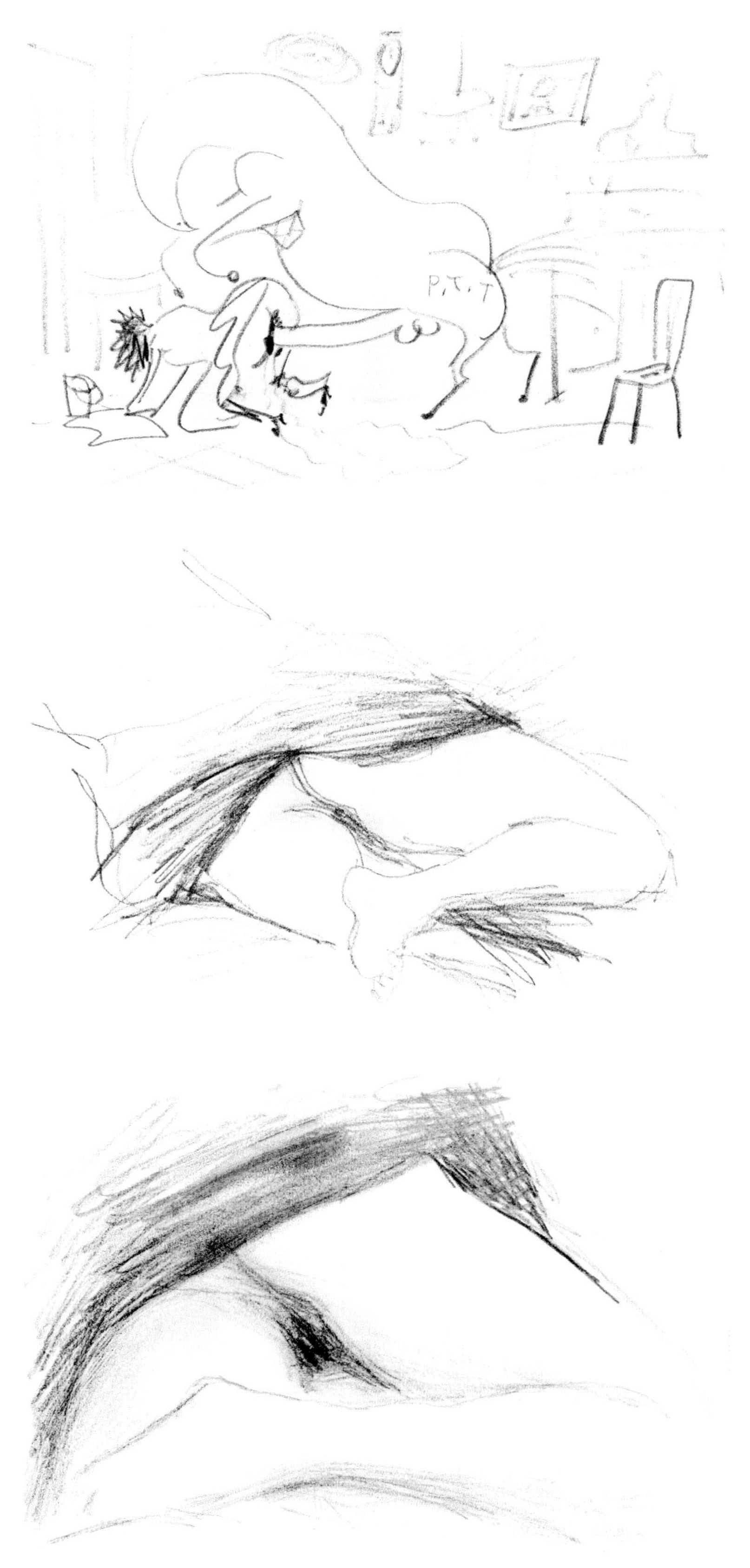

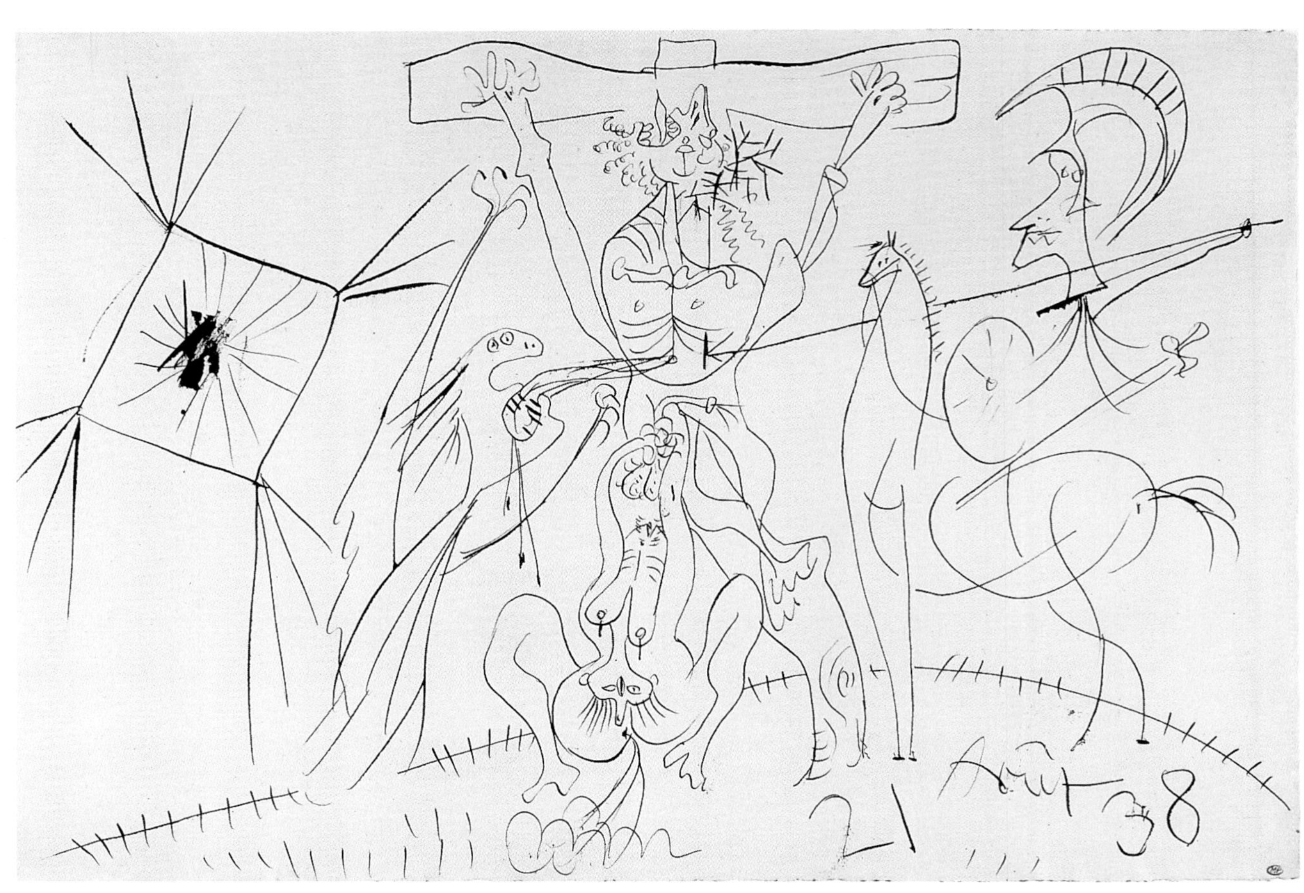

191 The Crucifixion, 21 August 1938

Pen and India ink on paper; 44.5 x 67
Paris, Musée Picasso, MP 1210

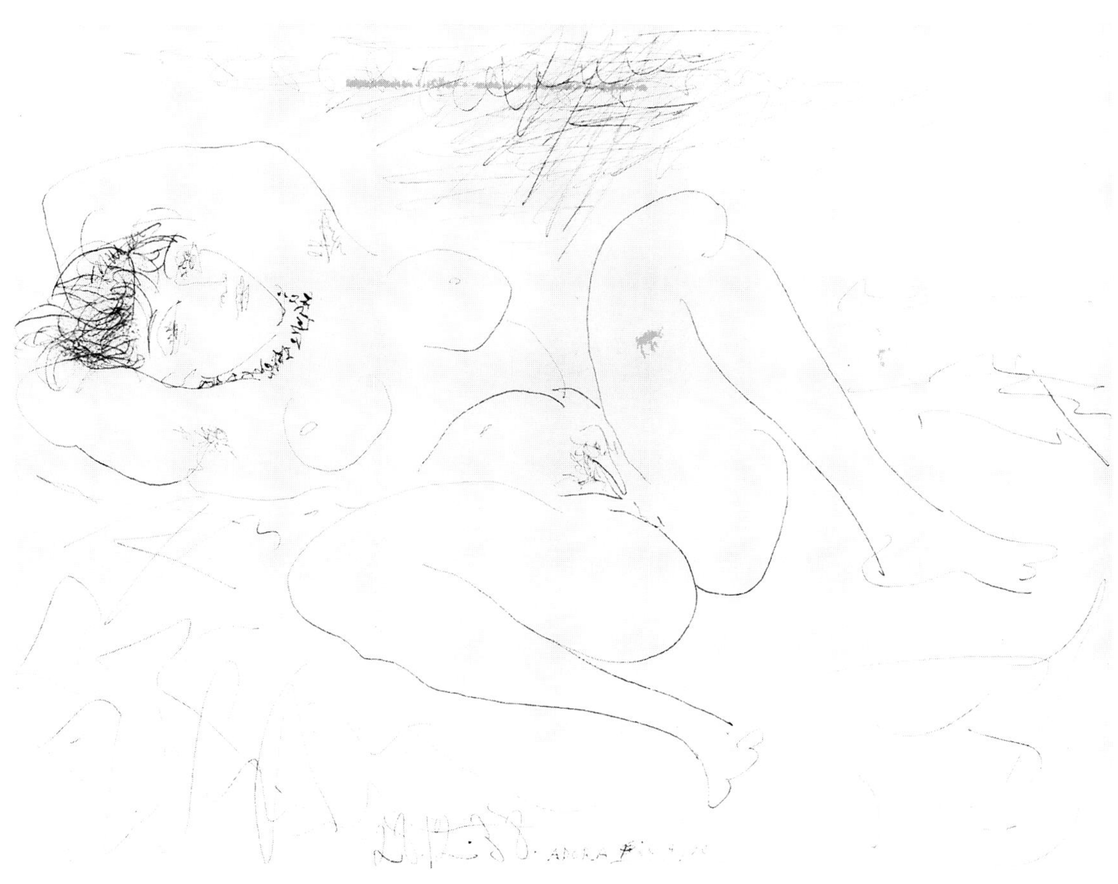

192 ADORA, 28 December 1938

India ink on paper; 27 x 35
Zurich, Courtesy Galerie Pels-Leusden A.G.

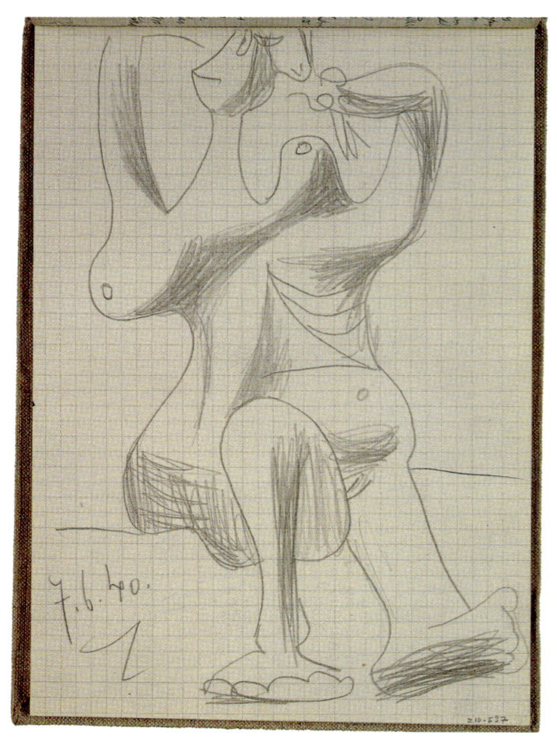

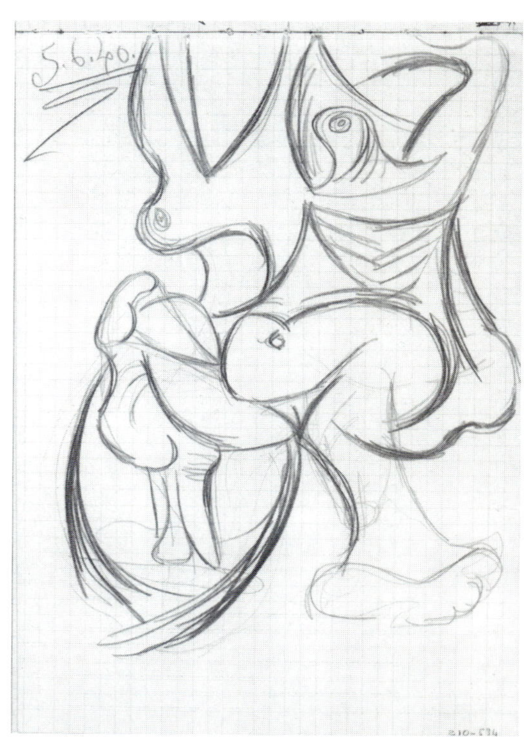

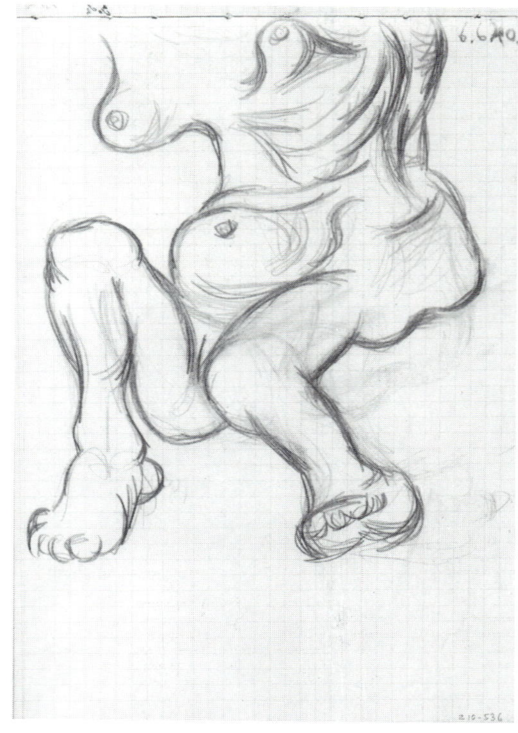

193 a, b and c Royan Sketchbook, 26 October 1939–19 September 1940
Study for Woman Dressing Her Hair (f° 33 r°; f° 35 r°; f° 39 r°)
Graphite stick on quadrille paper; 22.3 x 16.3
Paris, Musée Picasso, MP 1877

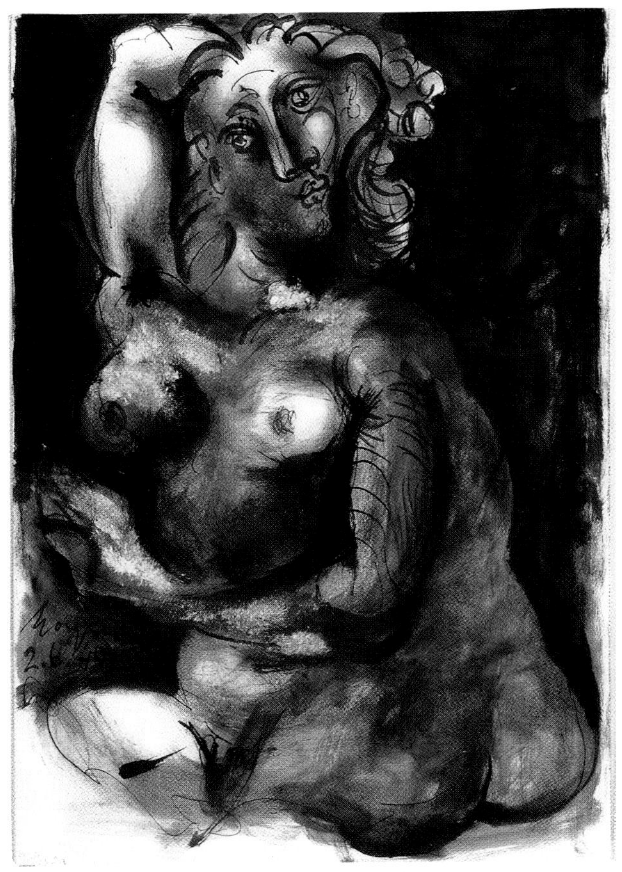 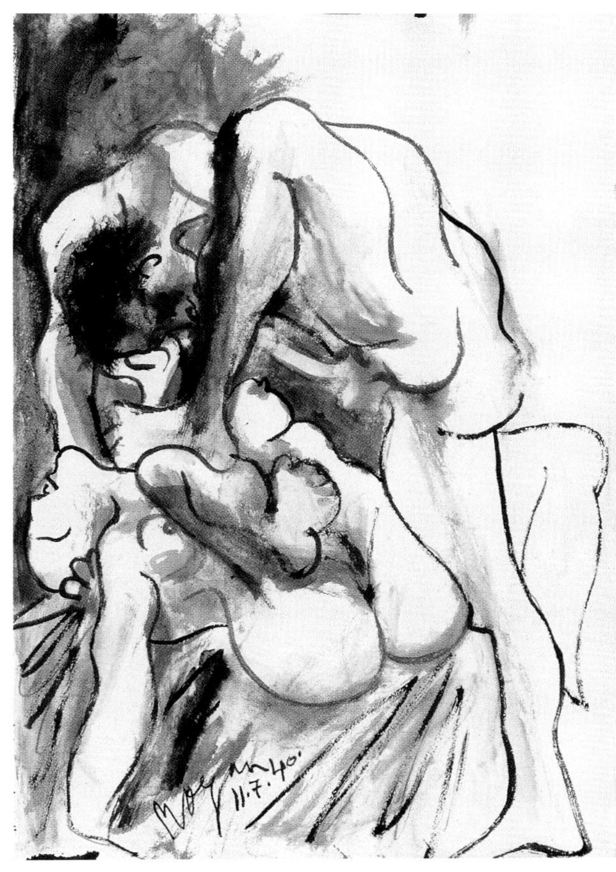

194 a and b Royan Sketchbook, 30 May 1940–19 February 1942
Seated Nude (f° 5 v°) and *Embrace* (f° 17 r°)
Pen and India ink wash on Ingres paper; 41.3 x 30
Paris, Musée Picasso, MP 1880

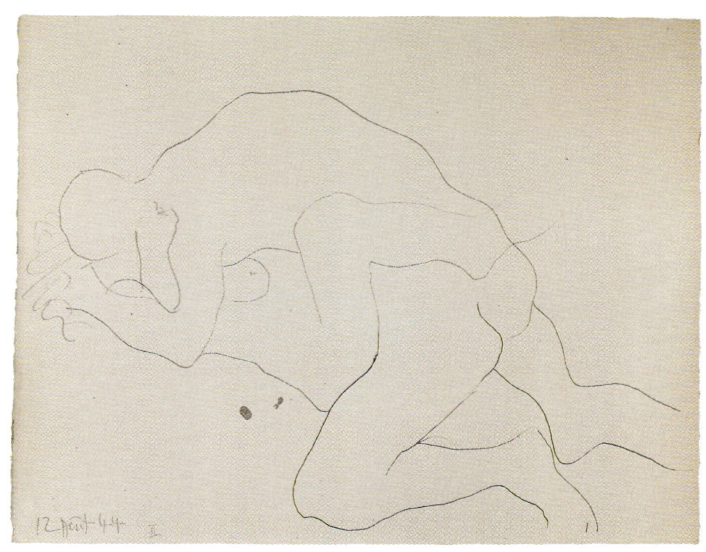

195 The Embrace, 12 August 1944
India ink on paper; 50.5 x 66
Paris, Private collection

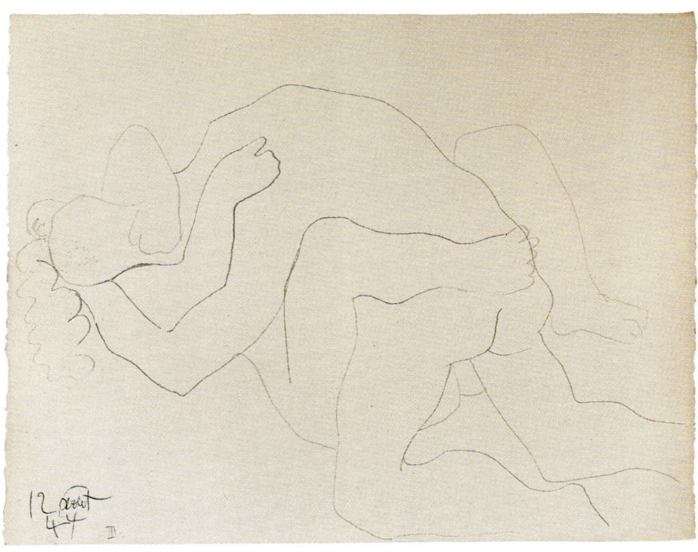

196 The Embrace, 12 August 1944
India ink on paper; 50.5 x 66
Paris, Private collection

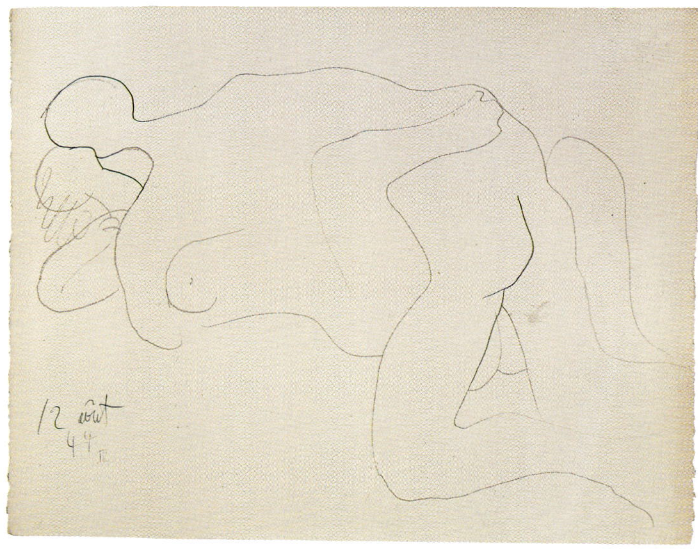

197 The Embrace, 12 August 1944
India ink on paper; 50.5 x 66
Paris, Private collection

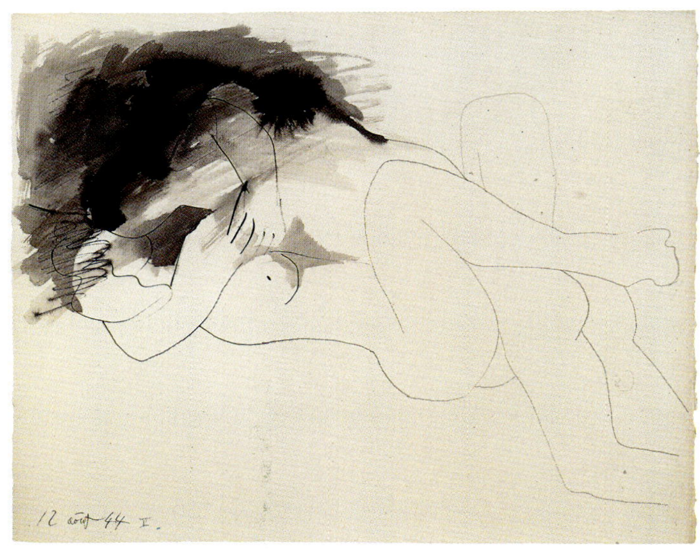

198 **The Embrace**, 12 August 1944
India ink on paper; 50.5 x 66
Paris, Private collection

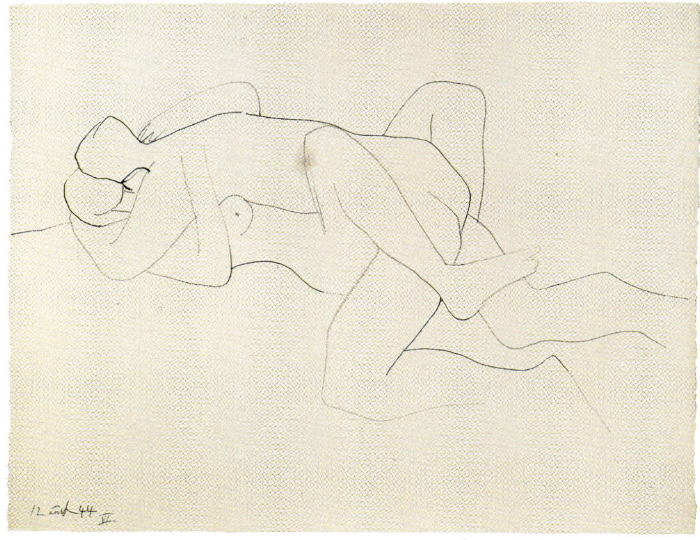

199 **The Embrace**, 12 August 1944
India ink on paper; 50.5 x 66
Paris, Private collection

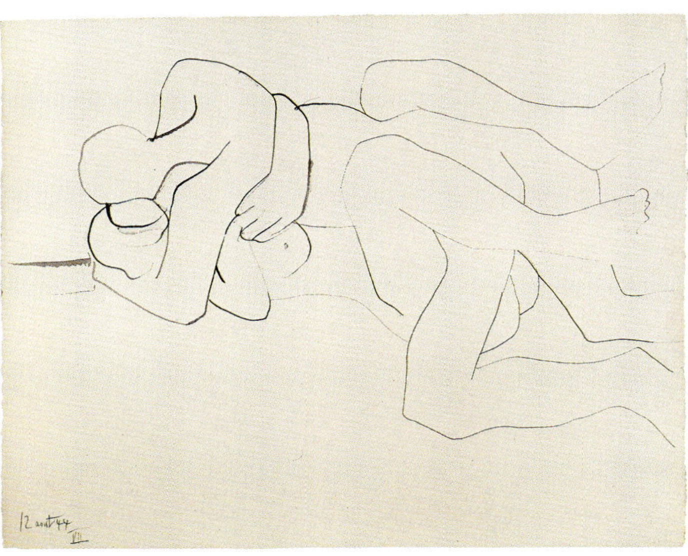

199 a **The Embrace**, 12 August 1944
India ink on paper; 50.5 x 66
Paris, Private collection

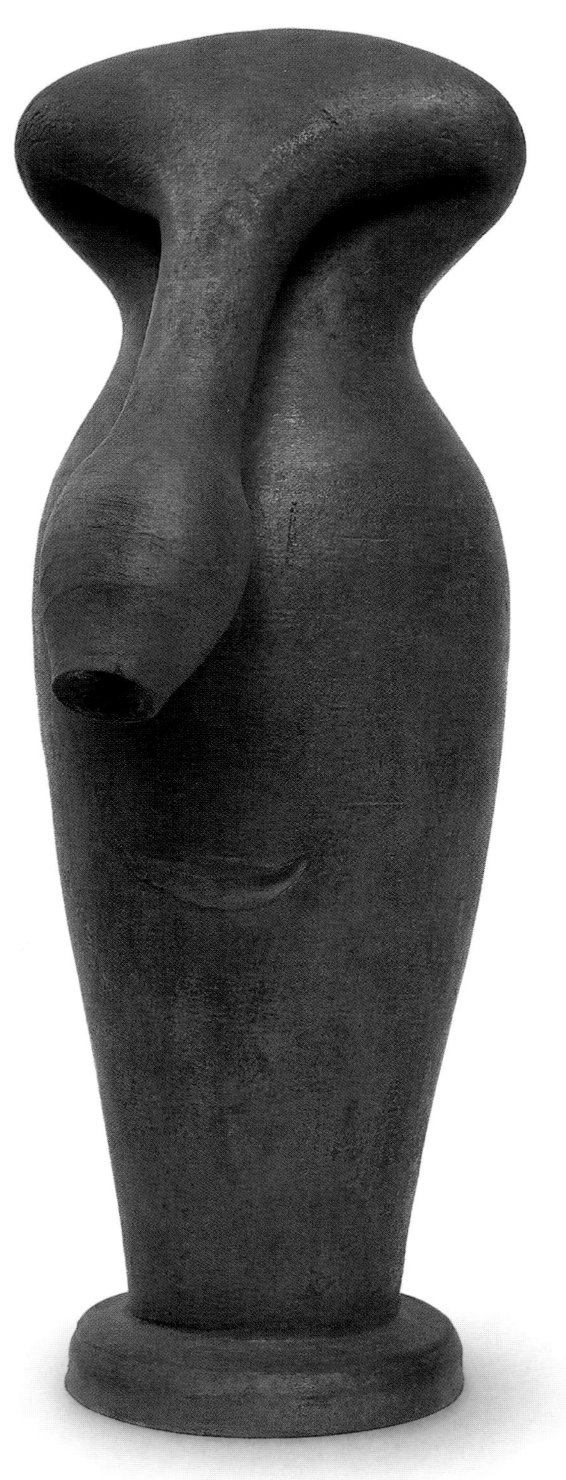

200 Vase-Face, 1948
Bronze; 28 x 10 x 14
Paris, Private collection

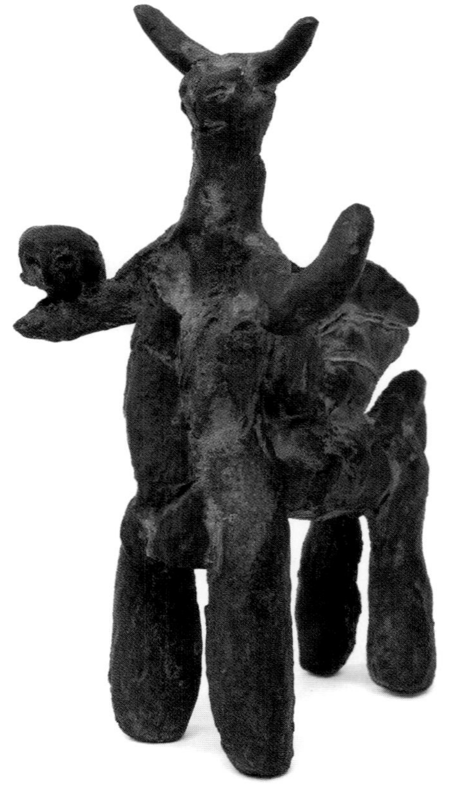

200 a Winged Centaur Holding an Owl, 1950
Bronze; 14 x 11
Paris, Private collection

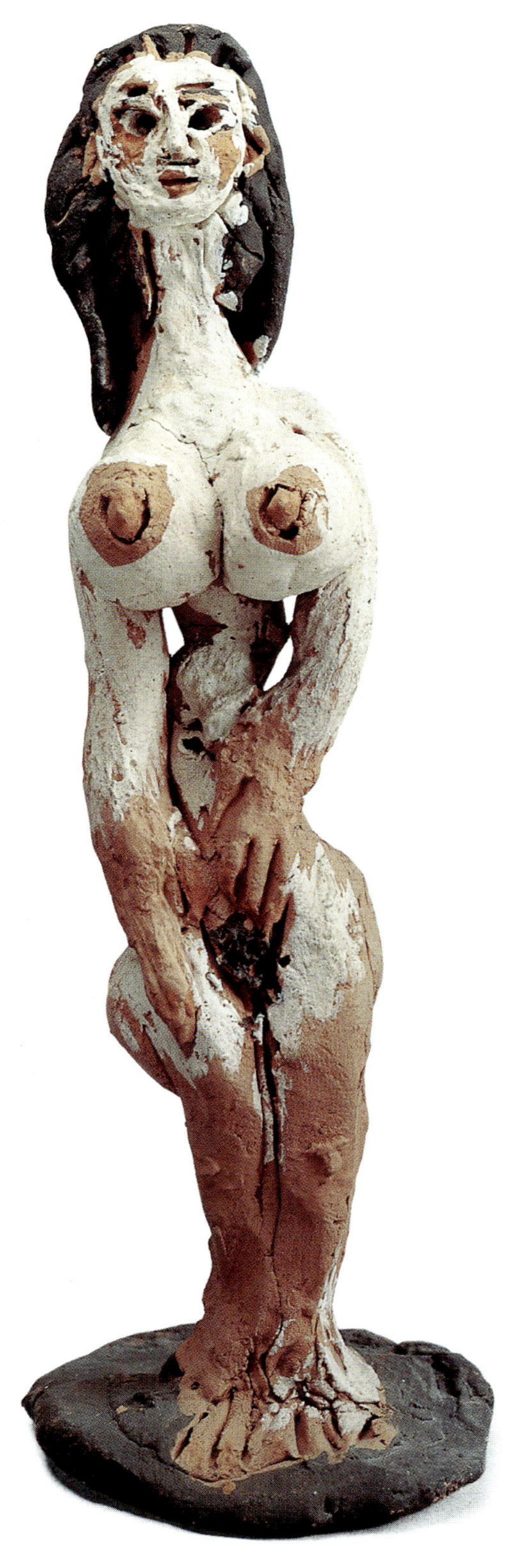

201 **Standing Nude Woman**, 20 July 1950
Modelled red clay; slip decoration; incision; 17 x 5.8 x 6.2
Paris, Musée Picasso, MP 3696

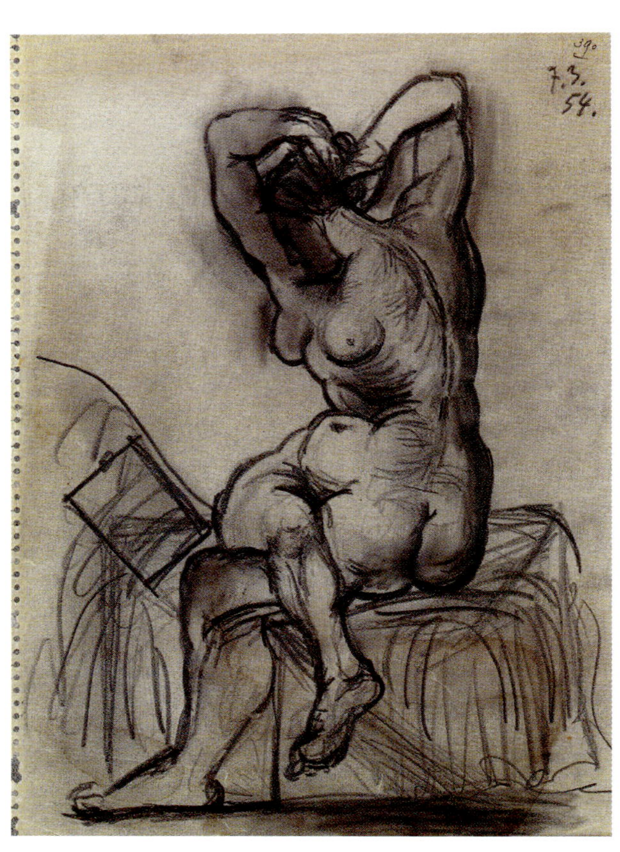

203 Seated Nude Dressing Her Hair, 7 March 1954
Graphite stick and stump on sketchbook page; 31.5 x 23.5
Paris, Musée Picasso, MP 1423 [P]

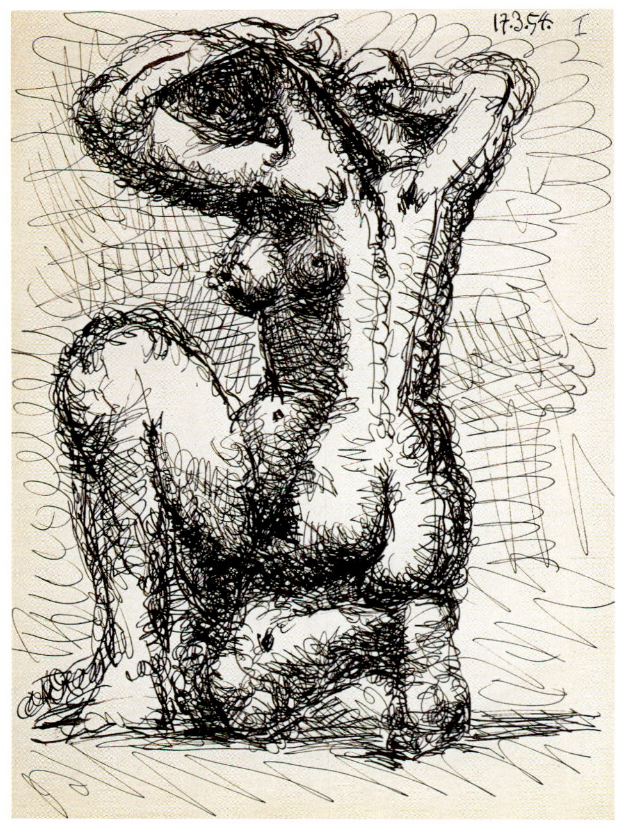

204 Seated Nude Dressing Her Hair, 17 March 1954
Graphite stick on sketchbook page; 31.5 x 23.5
Paris, Musée Picasso, MP 1427 [P]

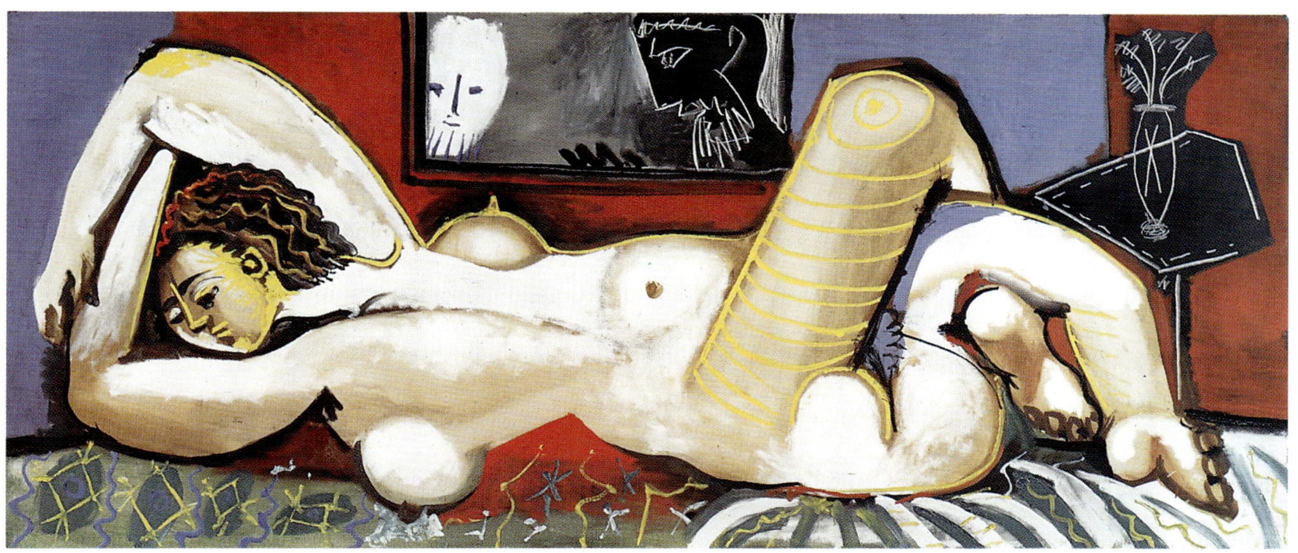

207 Susanna and the Elders, 1955
Oil on canvas; 80 x 190
Paris, Private collection [P]

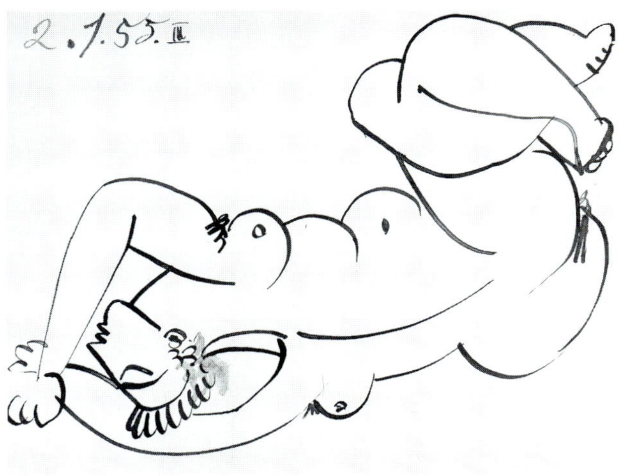

205 Study for *Women of Algiers*, after Delacroix,
2 January 1955 (III)

Pen and India ink on quadrille paper; 21 x 27
Paris, Musée Picasso, MP 1474 [M]

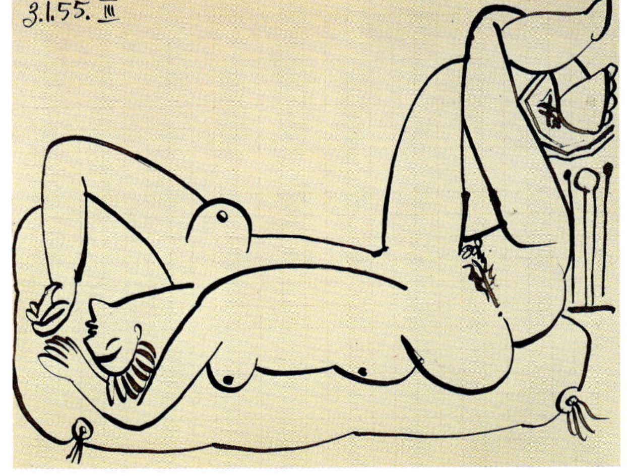

206 Study for *Women of Algiers*, after Delacroix,
3 January 1955 (III)

Pen and India ink on quadrille paper; 21 x 27
Paris, Musée Picasso, MP 1477 [B]

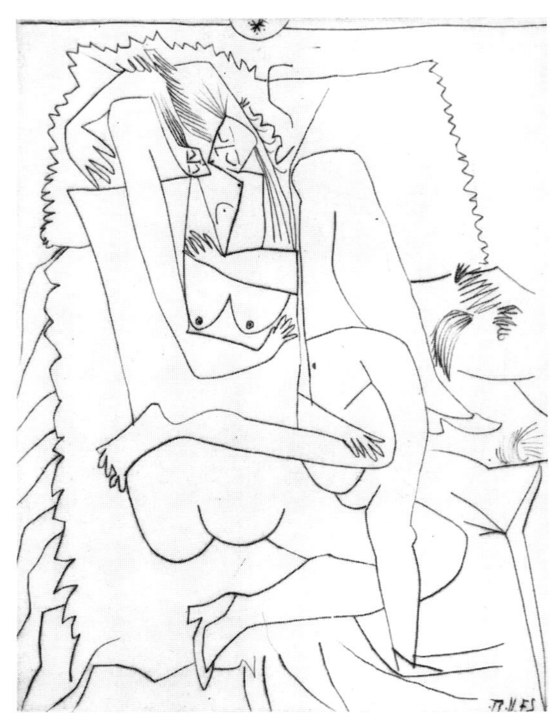

202 Feminine Lovemaking (The Couple), 27 November 1951
Drypoint on copper; 21.7 x 16.8
Paris, Musée Picasso, MP 2987

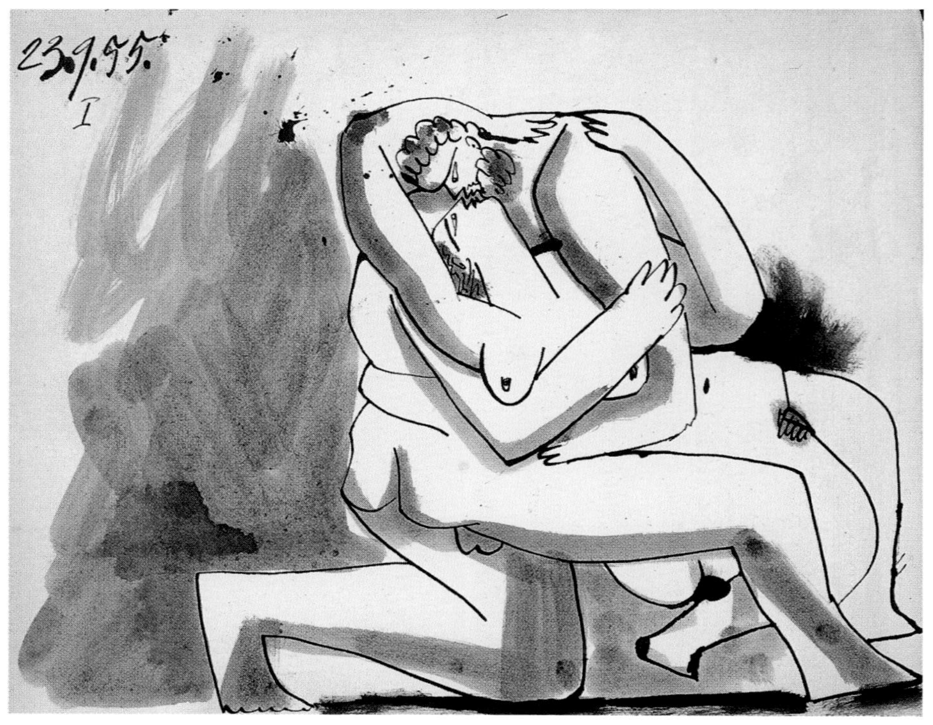

209 The Embrace, 23 September 1955
India ink wash on paper; 25.5 x 33
Paris, Private collection

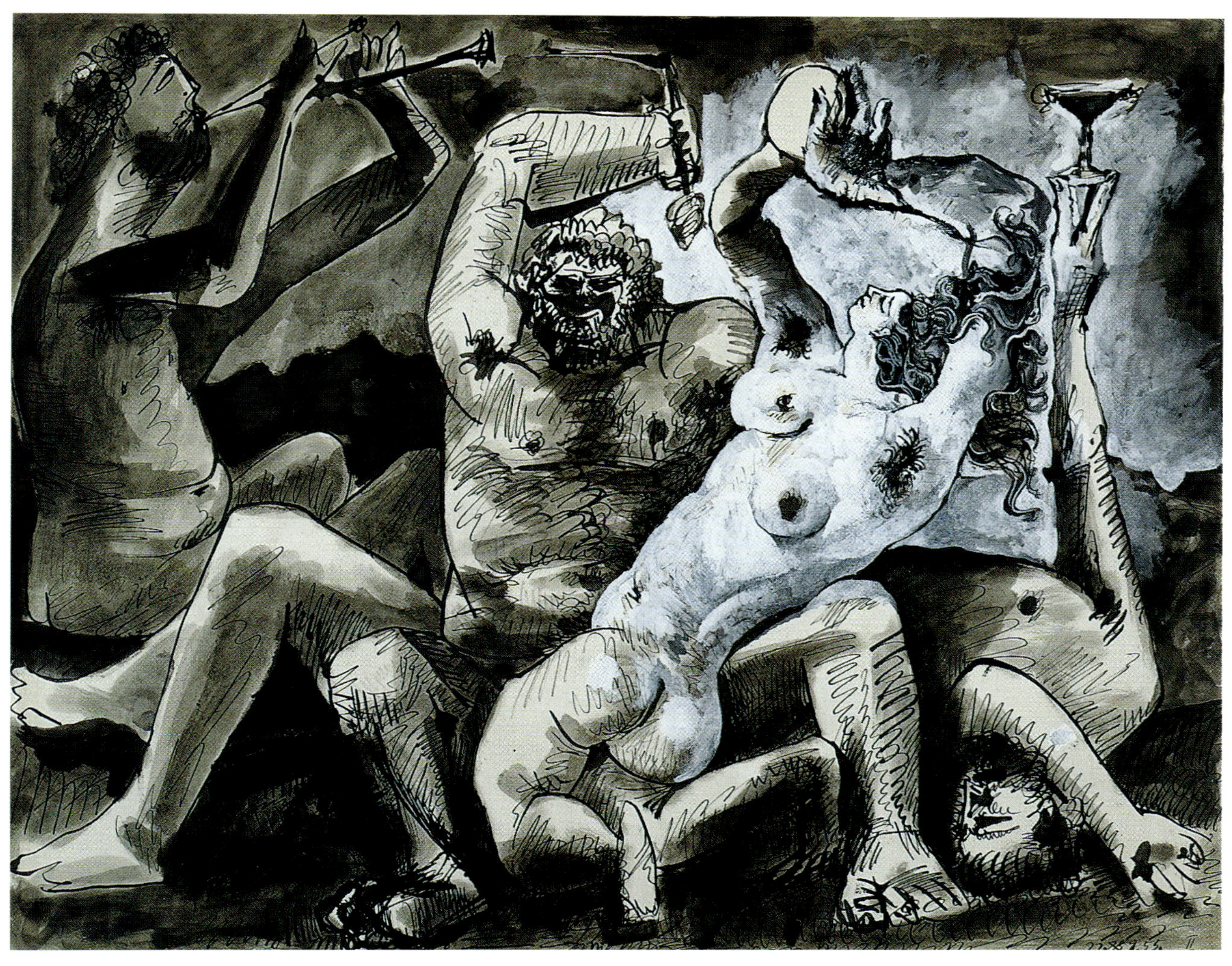

208 Bacchanal, 22 and 23 September 1955
India ink and wash with white gouache highlights on paper; 50 x 65.5
Paris, Musée Picasso, MP 1990-92

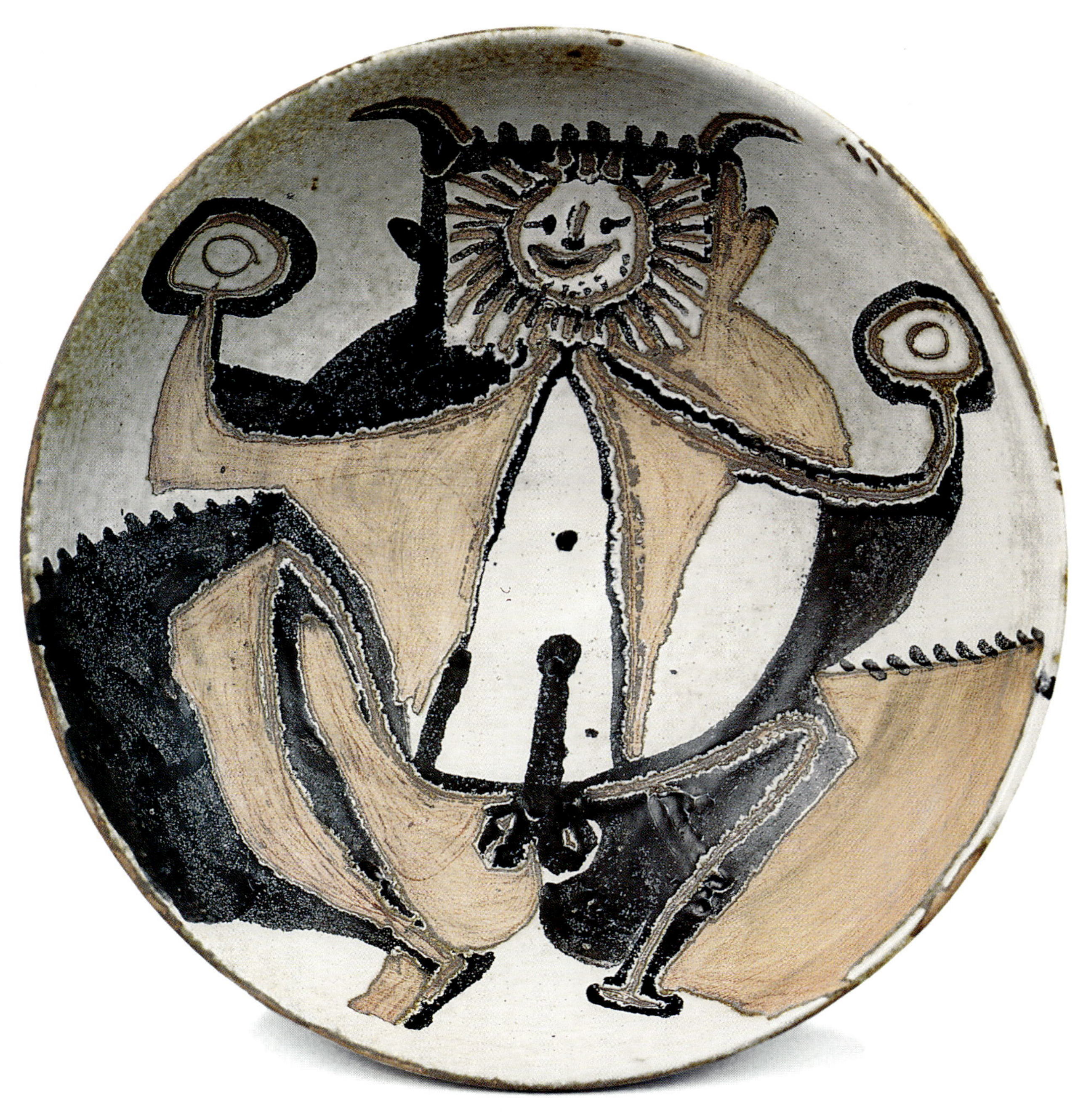

210 Decorated Cup: Faun with Cymbals, 10 May 1957
White clay; turned piece, iron oxide veil covered with matte enamel overglaze; 29 (diam.) x 8 (depth)
Paris, Musée Picasso, MP 3740 [PB]

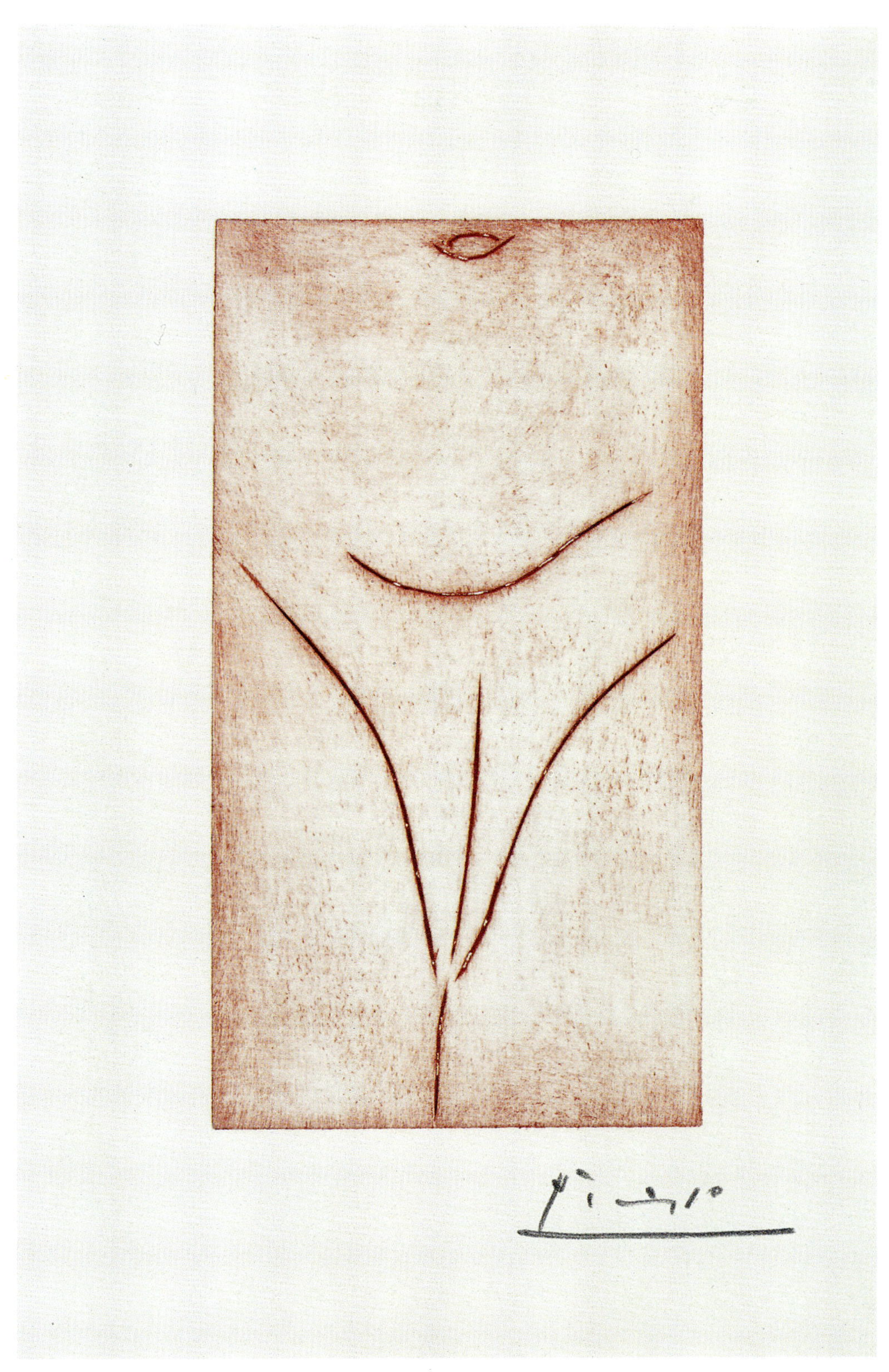

215 Fragment of a Female Body, 28 December 1960

Illustration for P. A. Benoit, *Les Livres de Picasso réalisés par PAB*, May 1966
Burin on plastic matter; 16.5 x 9
Paris, Musée Picasso, MP 3578

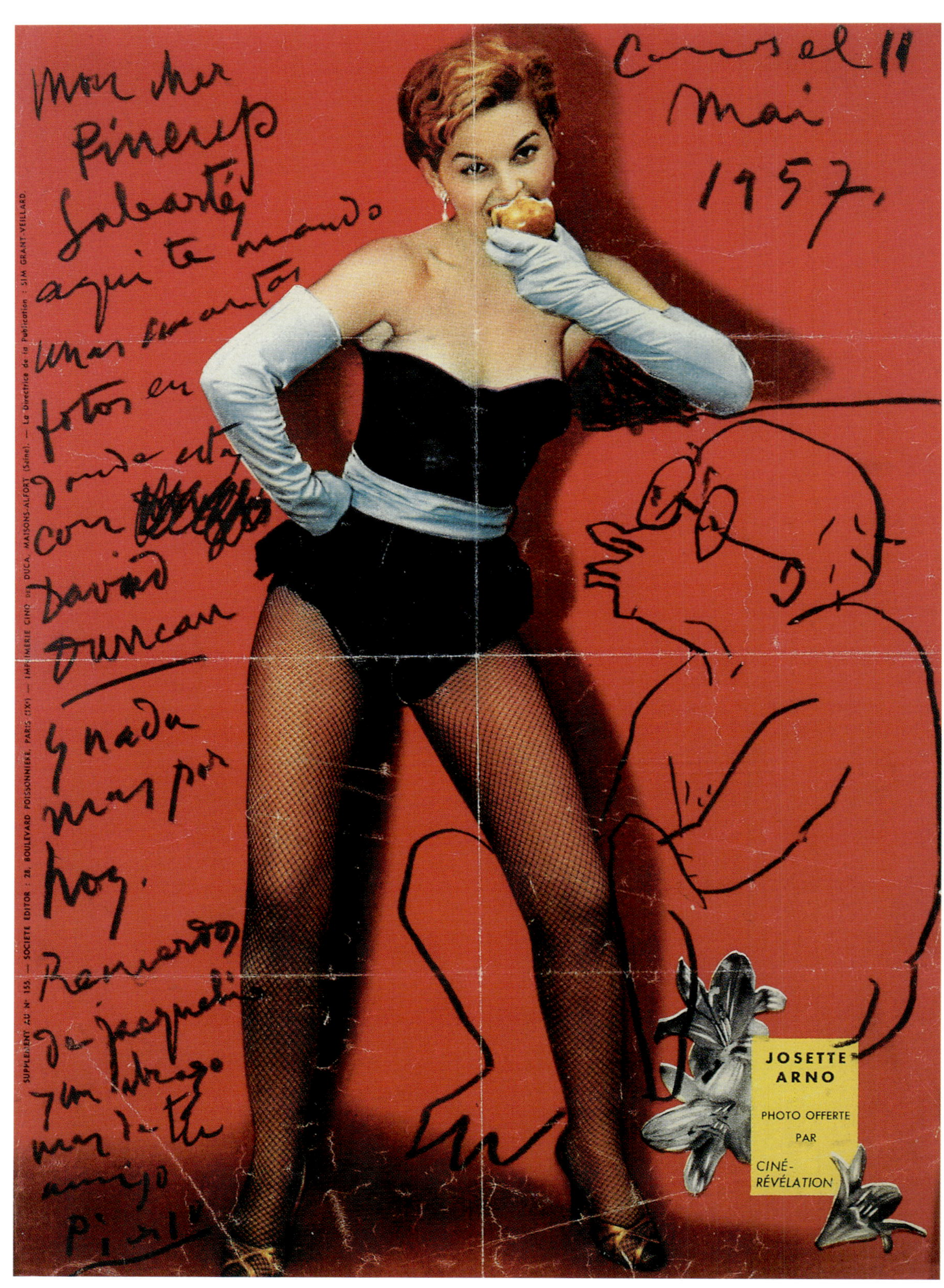

211 Humorous Composition, 11 May 1957
Coloured heliograph with India ink; 35 x 26.5
Barcelona, Museu Picasso, MPB 70.671

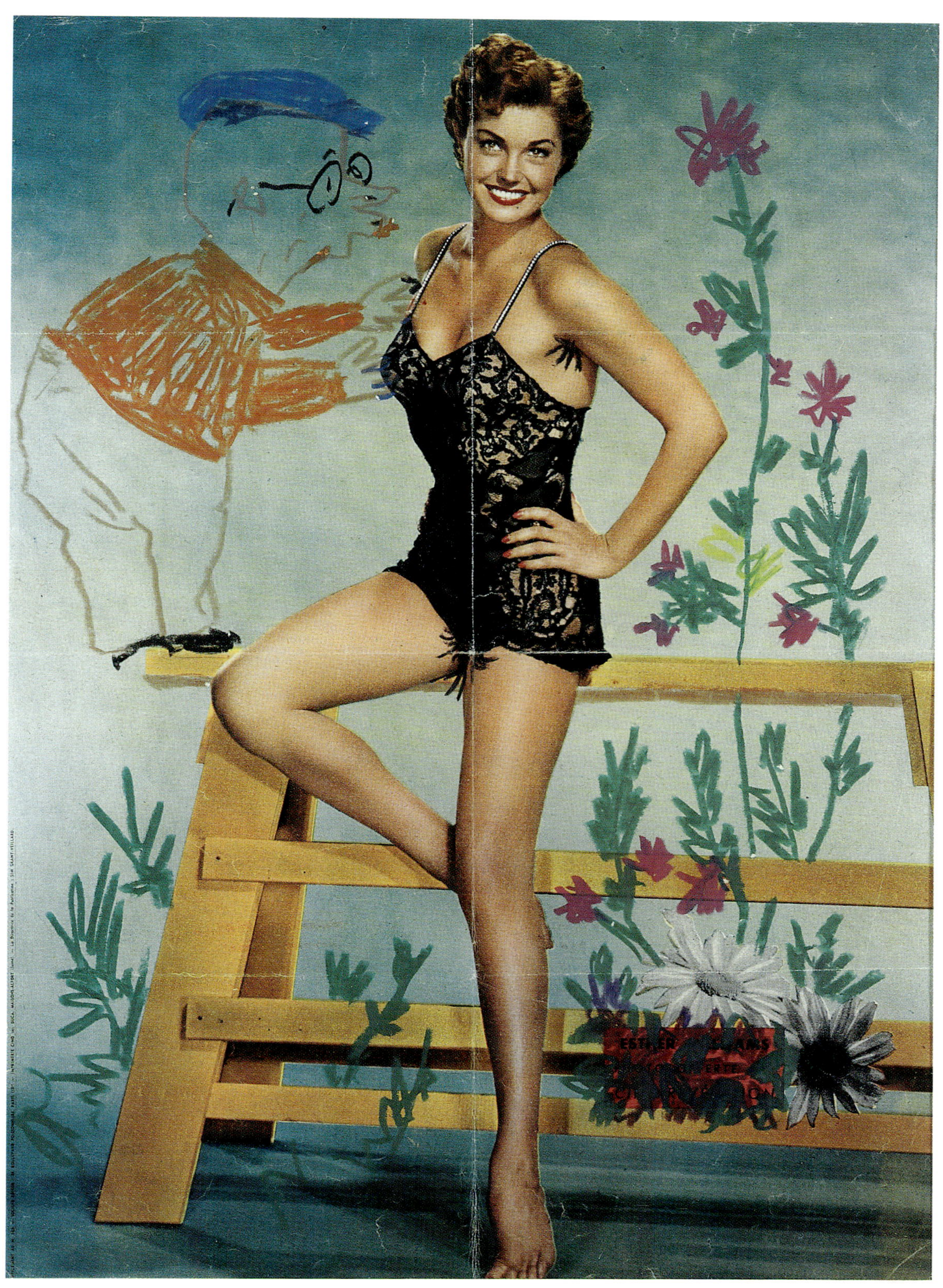

212 Humorous Composition, 23 May 1957
  Coloured heliograph with India ink; 35.6 x 26.5
  Barcelona, Museu Picasso, MPB 70.675 [M]

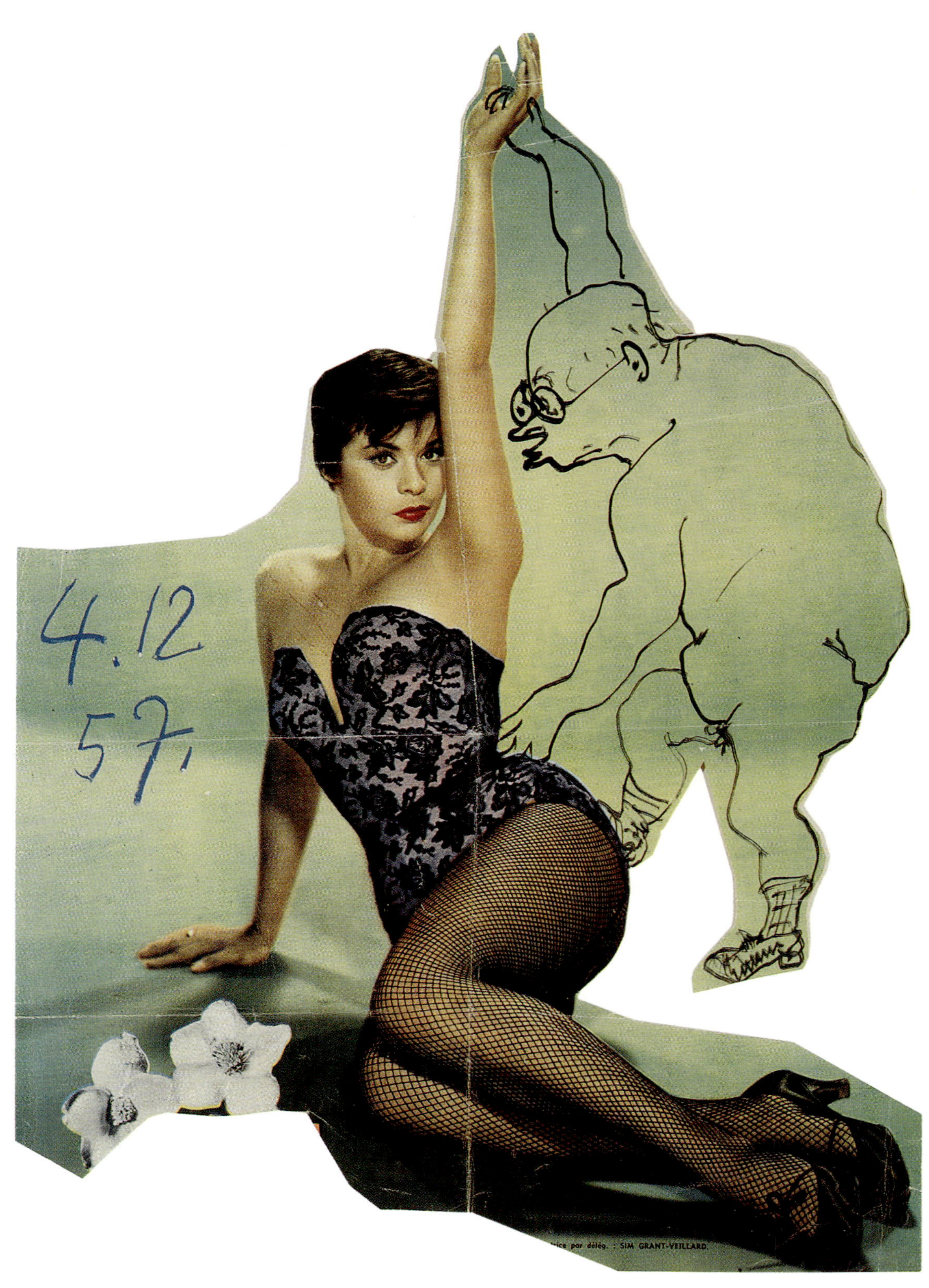

214 Humorous Composition, 4 December 1957
Coloured heliograph with India ink; 35.6 x 26
Barcelona, Museu Picasso, MPB 70.674

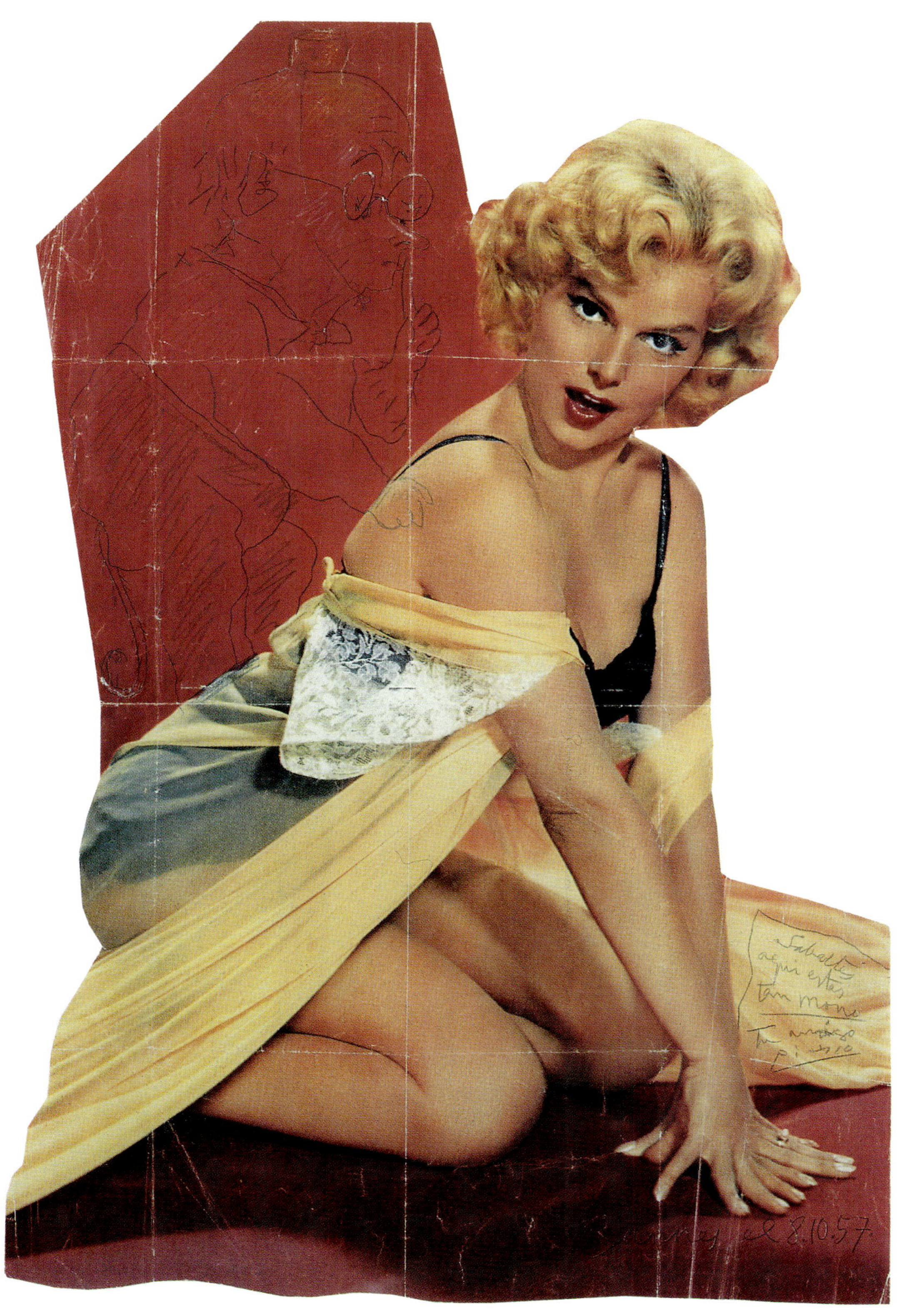

213 Humorous Composition, 8 October 1957
Coloured heliograph with India ink; 43.6 x 30.6
Barcelona, Museu Picasso, MPB 70.679 [M]

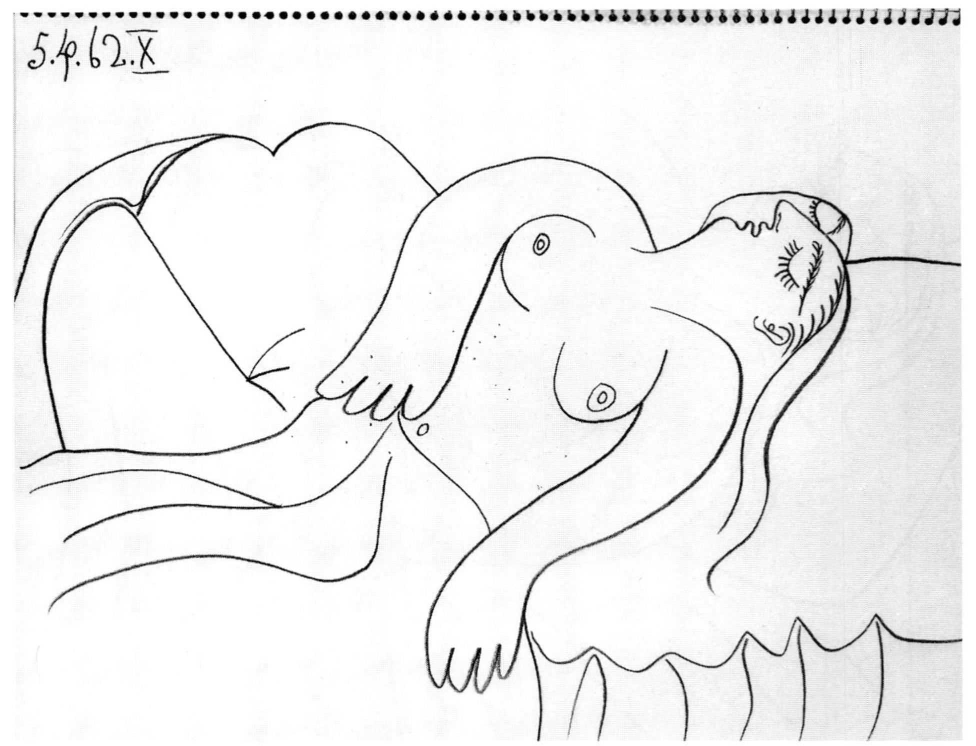

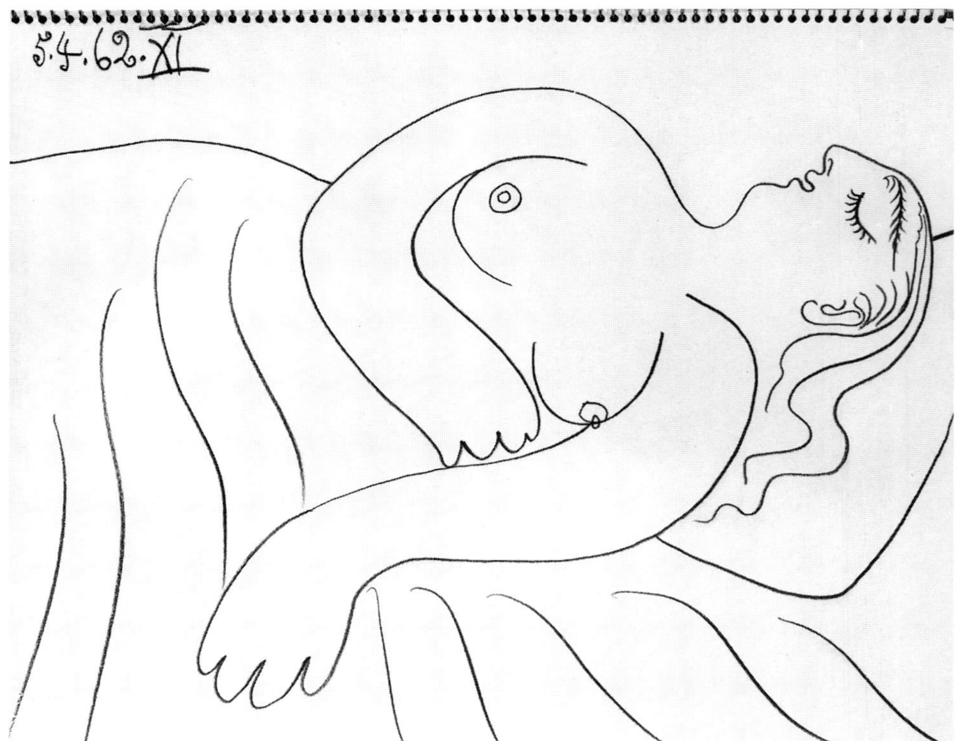

216 a and b Sketchbook, 12 January–5 April 1962

Reclining Nude (f° 10 r°; f° 11 r°)
Graphite stick on Ingres paper; 35 x 27
Paris, Musée Picasso, MP 1990-114

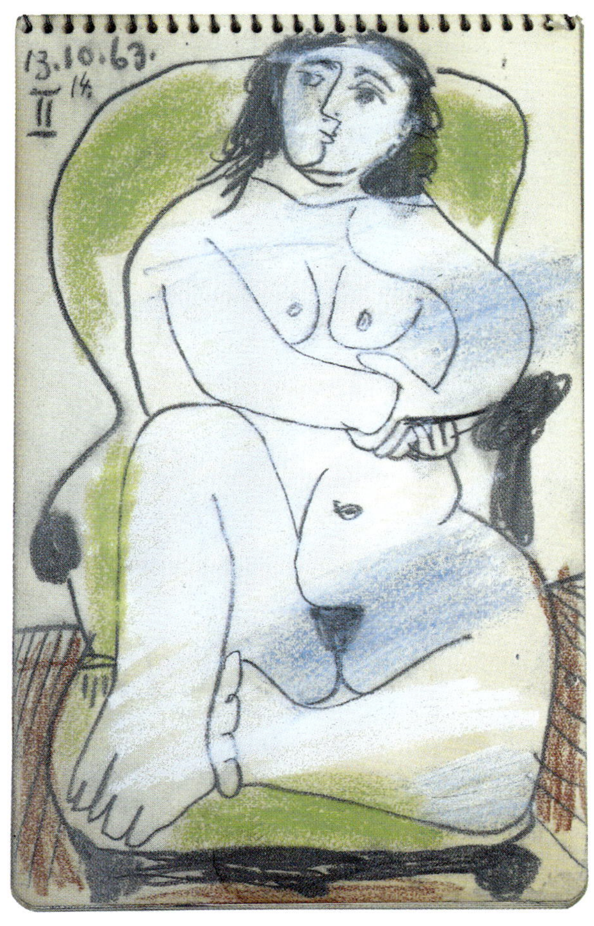
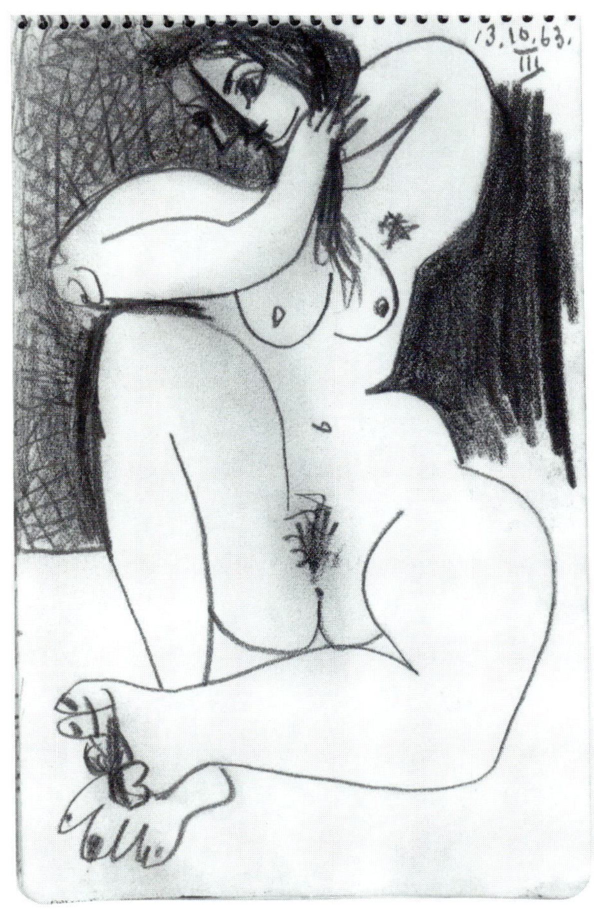

221 a, b and c Sketchbook, 13 October–28 November 1963

Nude Seated in an Armchair (f° 2 r°), *Seated Nude* (f° 3 r°) and *Reclining Nude* (f° 5 r°)
Black crayon, graphite stick, coloured pencil and wax crayon on Ingres paper; 20.5 x 13.5
Paris, Musée Picasso, MP 1990-115

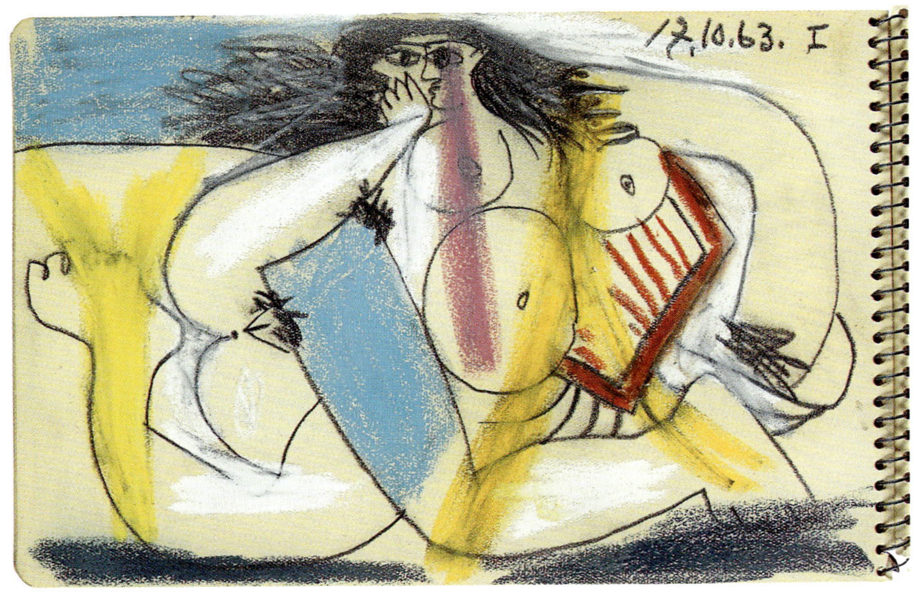

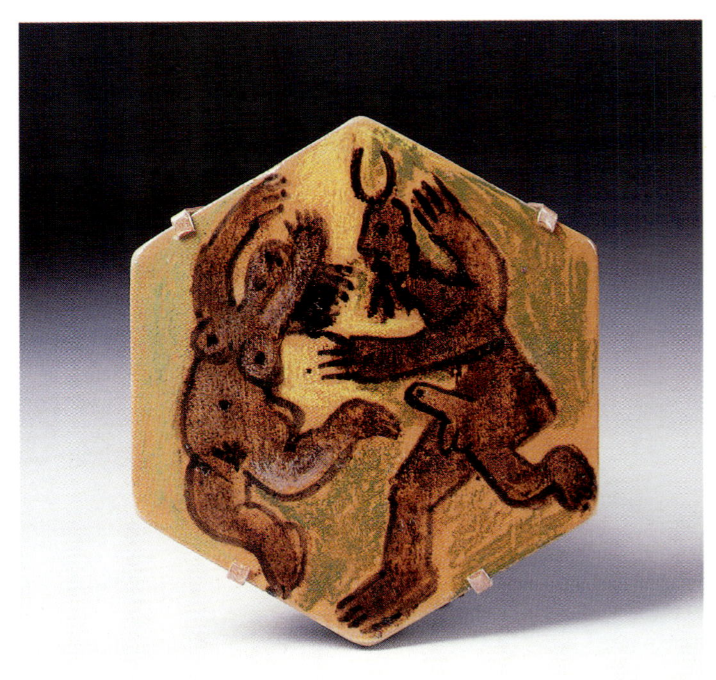

217 Erotic Scene, 1962
    Tomette (Salerne tile) in red ball clay; 16.5 x 16.5
    Cologne, Museum Ludwig, inv. C 570 [P]

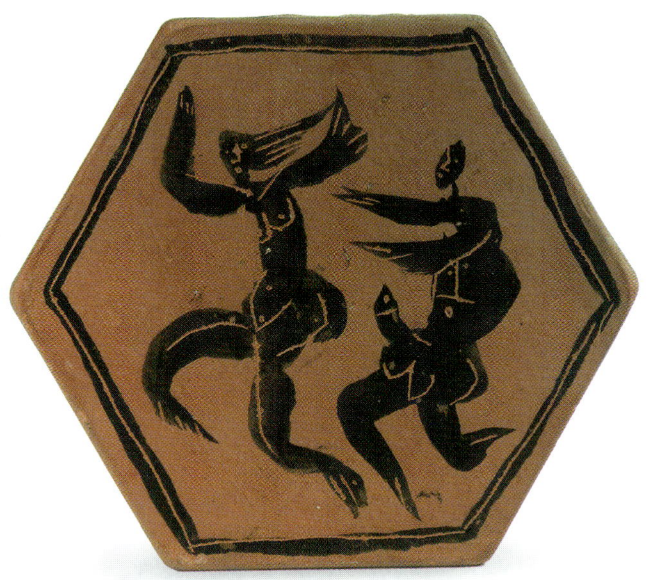

218 Erotic Scene, 7 August 1962
Ceramic Tomette; 16.5 x 16.5
Basel, Galerie Beyeler

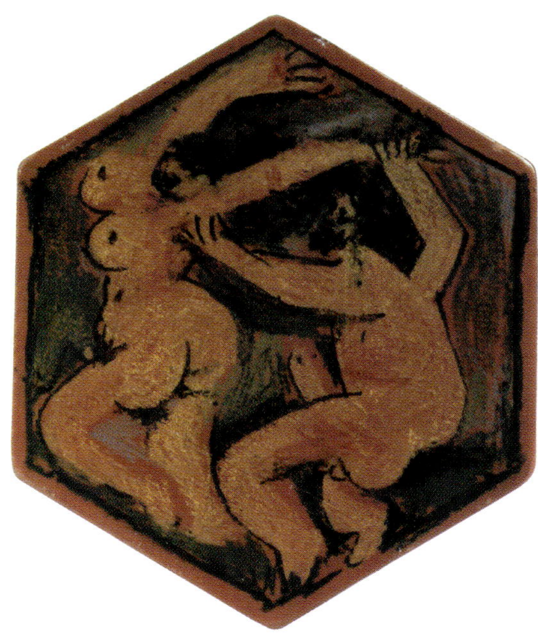

219 Erotic Scene, 12 August 1962
Tomette in red ball clay; 16.5 x 18.7
Cologne, Private collection, Courtesy Galerie Gmurzynska

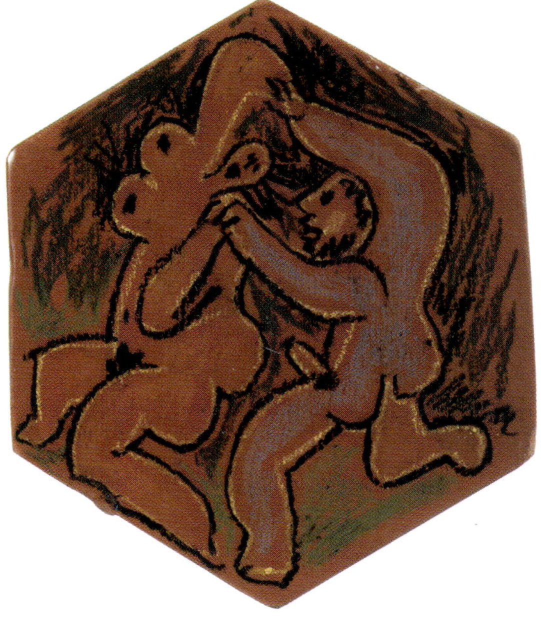

220 Erotic Scene, 14 August 1962
Tomette in red ball clay; 16.5 x 19
Cologne, Private collection, Courtesy Galerie Gmurzynska

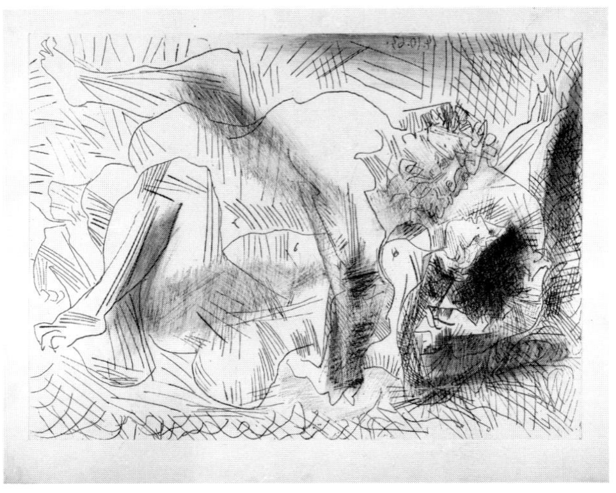

222 Embrace I, 14 October 1963
Etching, glasspaper, scraper, drypoint and burin on copper;
States III and IV; 42.3 x 57.5
Paris, Musée Picasso, MP 2711* [M] and MP 2712 [B]

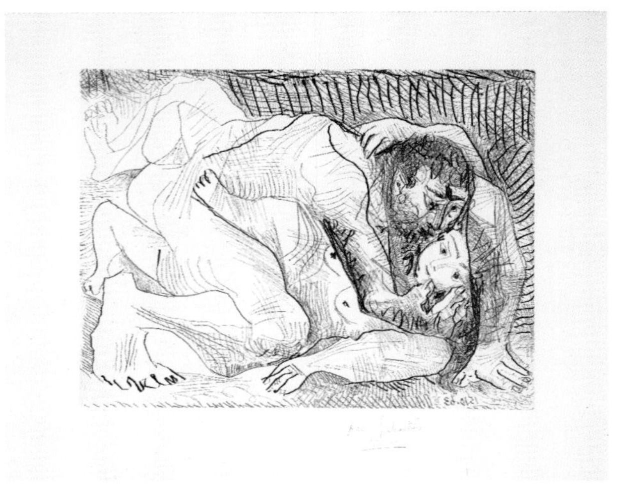

223 Embrace II, 15 October 1963
Etching, drypoint and scraper on copper; 42.5 x 57.2
Barcelona, Museu Picasso, MPB 70.415 [B]

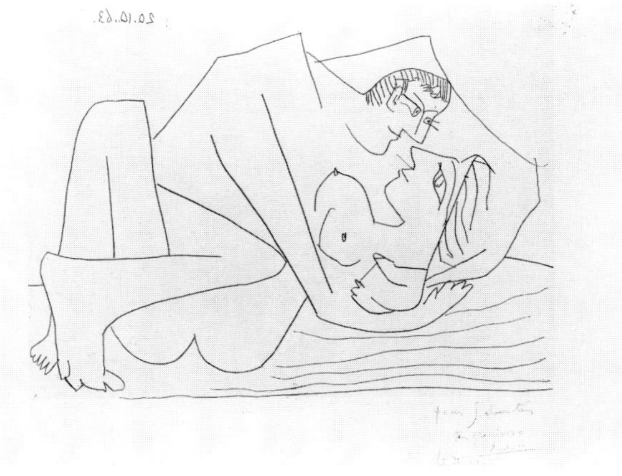

224 Embrace III, 20 October 1963
Etching on copper; 42.3 x 47.3
Barcelona, Museu Picasso, MPB 70.423 [M]

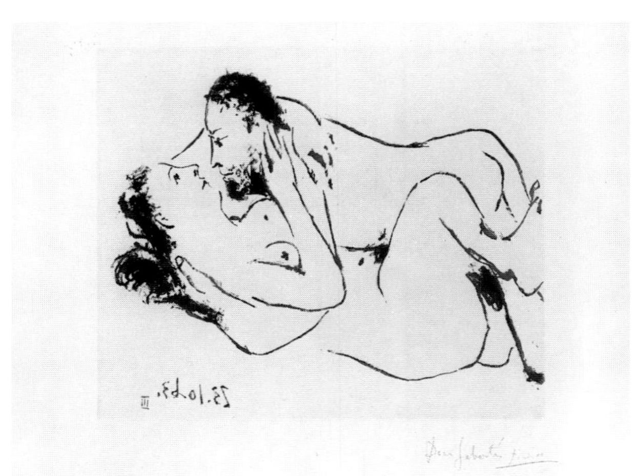

225 Embrace VIII, 23 October 1963
Etching on copper; 34.6 x 42.3
Barcelona, Museu Picasso, MPB 70.421 [B]

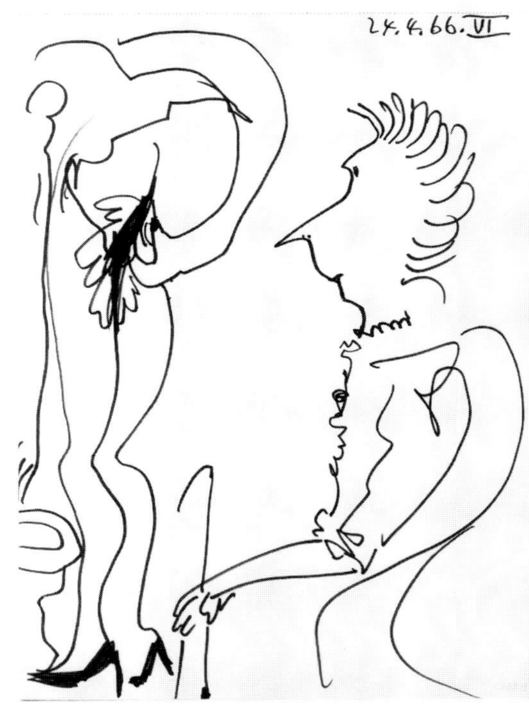

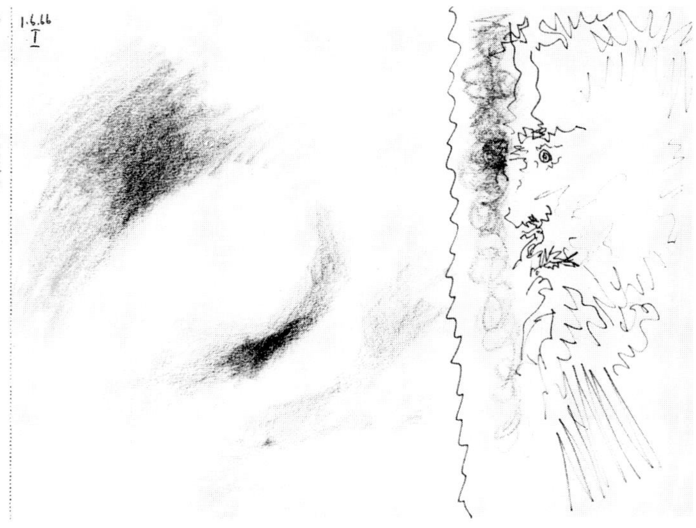

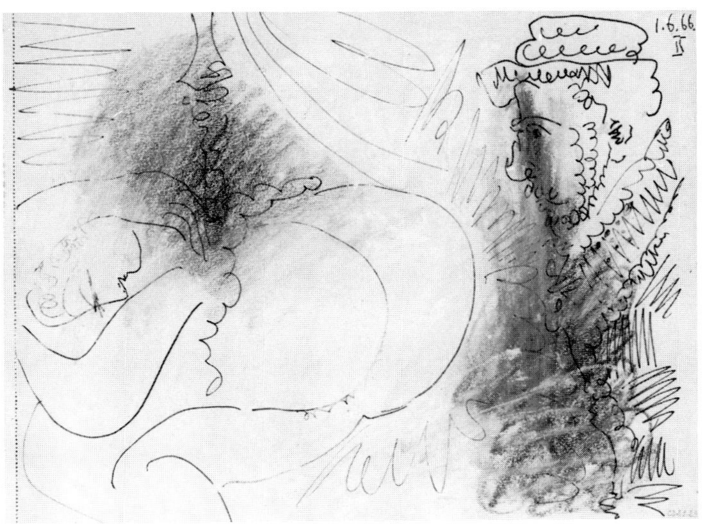

227 a, b and c Sketchbook, 14 April–24 July 1966

Caricature: Woman with Cane and Nude Bathing (f° 7 r°) and *Nude Watched by an Old Man* (f° 19 r°; f° 20 r°)
Black felt marker, coloured pencil, grease pencil and wax crayon on Ingres paper; 27 x 37
Paris, Musée Picasso, MP 1990-116

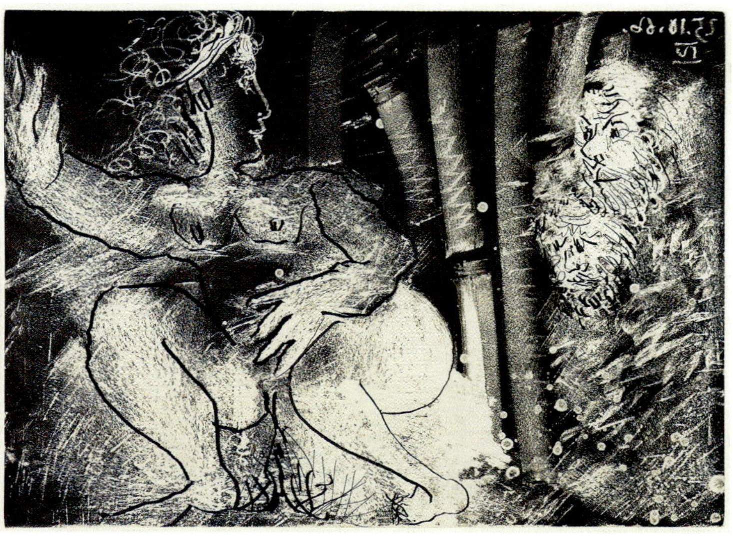

228 Woman Pissing Surprised by Two Old Men, 25 October 1966

Aquatint and etching on copper; 27.2 x 37.6
Paris, Bibliothèque nationale de France, Département des Estampes et de la Photographie
Paris, Private collection* [M]
Barcelona, Museu Picasso, MPB 70.510

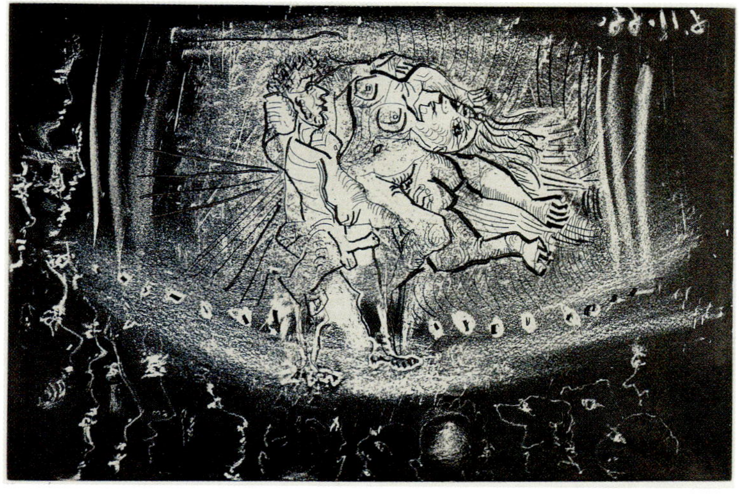

229 At the Theatre: The Ravishment, 6 November 1966

Aquatint and etching on copper; 24.8 x 37.9
Paris, Bibliothèque nationale de France, Département des Estampes et de la Photographie
Paris, Private collection* [M]
Barcelona, Museu Picasso, MPB 112.596 [B]

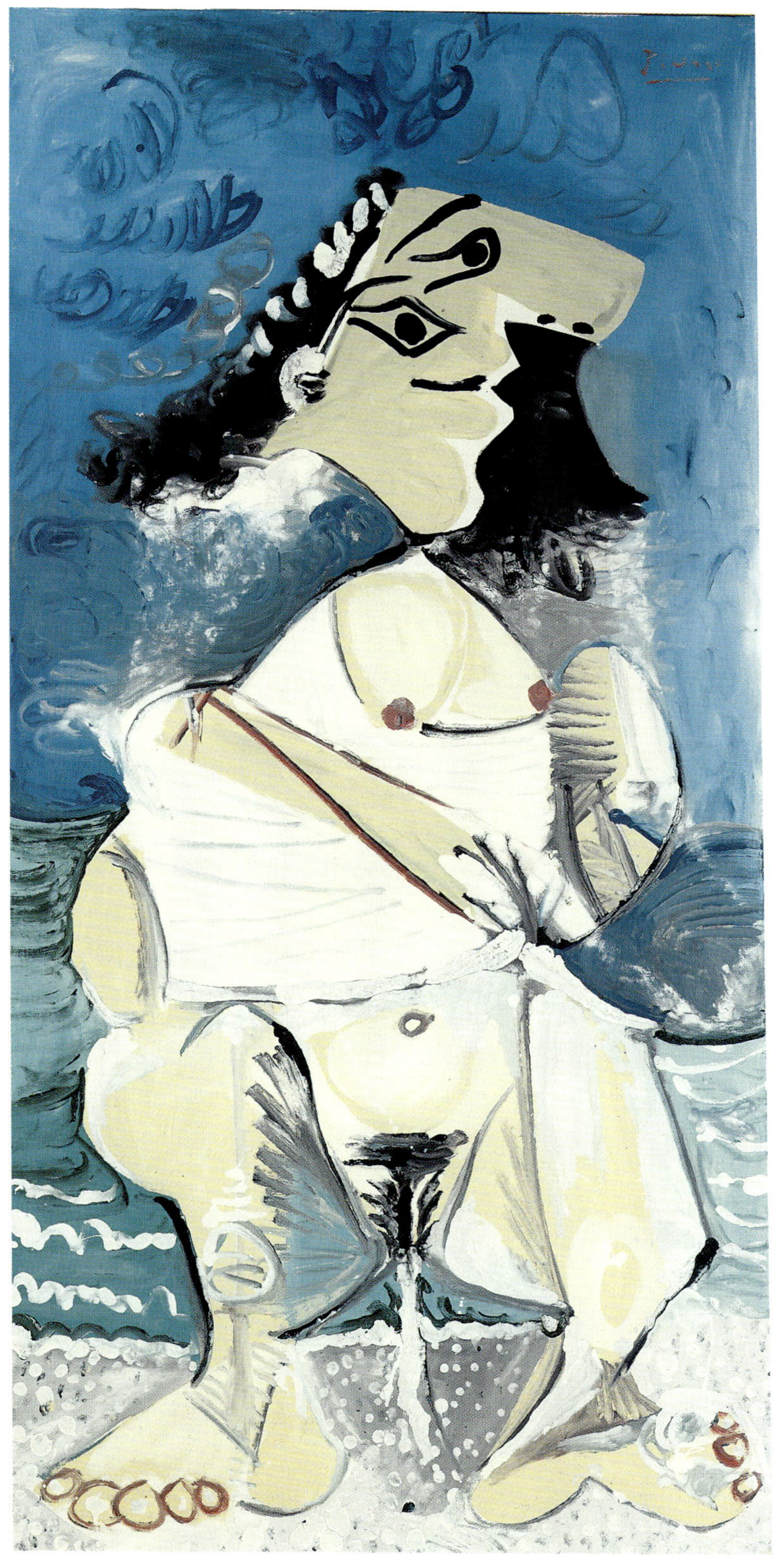

226 **Woman Pissing**, 16 April 1965
Oil on canvas; 195 x 97
Paris, Centre Georges-Pompidou, Musée national d'Art moderne, AM 1984-641

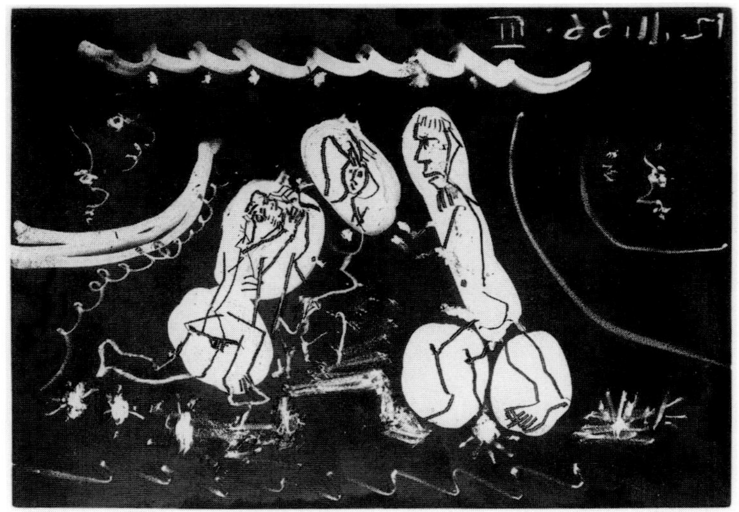

230 Under the Footlights: Nude Woman between
Two Men, 12 November 1966

Aquatint and etching on copper; 22.3 x 32
Paris, Musée Picasso, on deposit at the
Musée de Strasbourg, MP 1990-162* [PM]
Barcelona, Museu Picasso, MPB 112.608 [B]

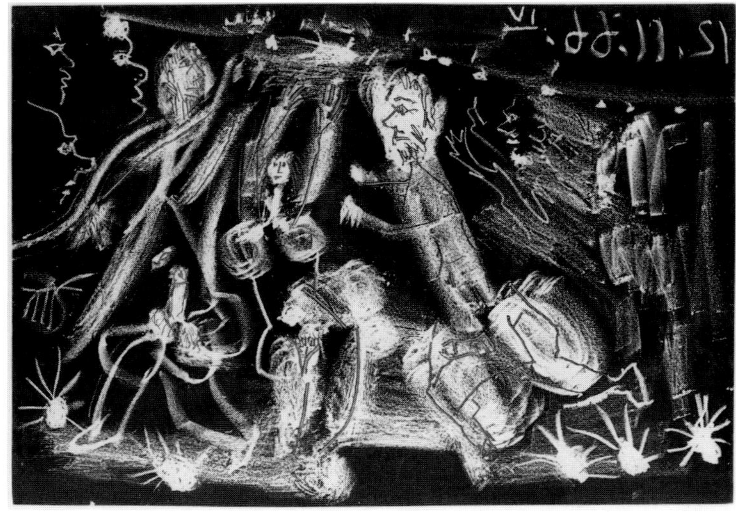

231 Under the Footlights: "Rape!" 12 November 1966

Aquatint and etching on copper; 22.4 x 32.2
Paris, Musée Picasso, on deposit at the Musée de Strasbourg,
MP 1990-163* [PM]
Barcelona, Museu Picasso, MPB 112.610 [B]

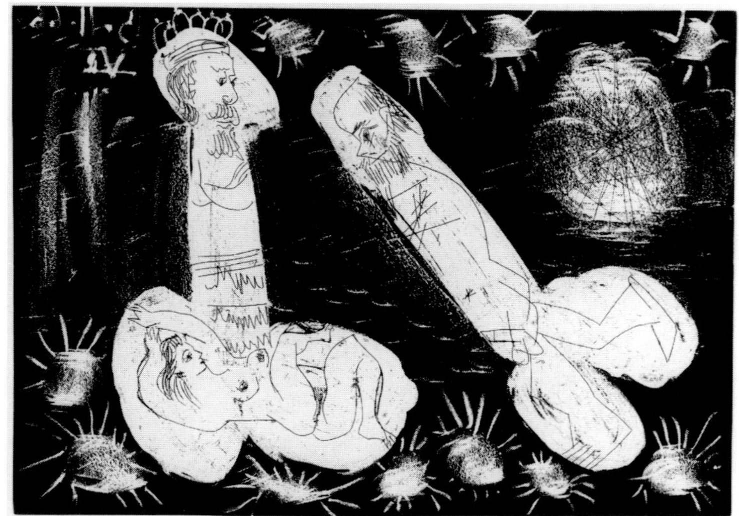

232 Under the Footlights: Young Girl with
Two Bearded Phalluses, 15 November 1966

Aquatint, litho chalk resists and etching on copper;
22.3 x 32.1
Paris, Musée Picasso, on deposit at the
Musée de Strasbourg, MP 1990-166* [P]
Paris, Bibliothèque nationale de France, Département des
Estampes et de la Photographie [M]
Barcelona, Museu Picasso, MPB 112.612 [B]

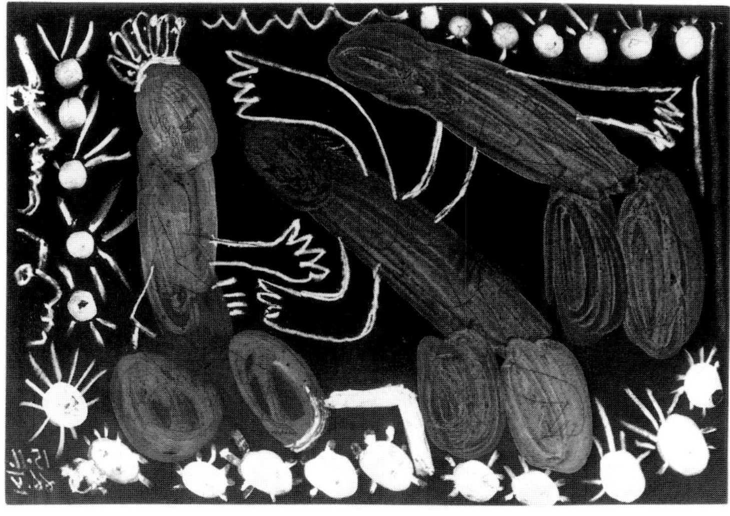

233 On Stage: King and Phallus-Couple,
15 November 1966

Aquatint, litho chalk resists and etching on copper;
22.3 x 32.1
Paris, Musée Picasso, on deposit at the
Musée de Strasbourg, MP 1990-165* [P]
Paris, Bibliothèque nationale de France, Département des
Estampes et de la Photographie [M]
Barcelona, Museu Picasso, MPB 112.611 [B]

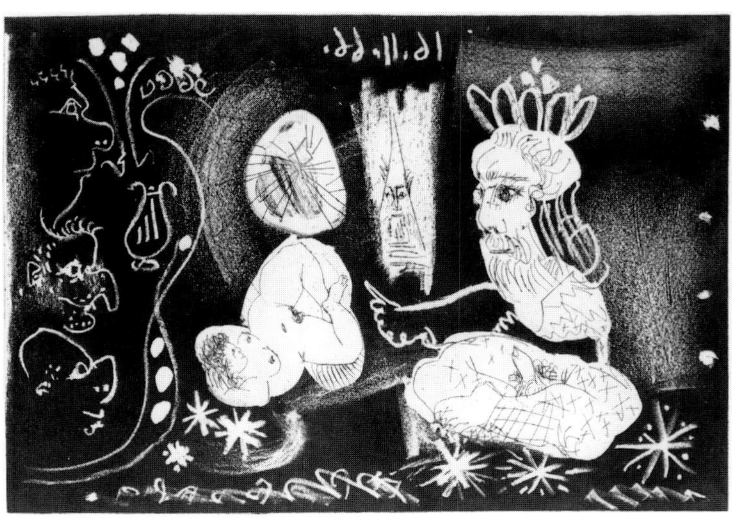

234 At the Theatre: Scene in the Style of the
Thousand and One Nights, 16 November 1966

Aquatint and etching on copper; 22.1 x 32.2
Paris, Bibliothèque nationale de France, Département des
Estampes et de la Photographie
Paris, Musée Picasso, MP 1990-143* [PM]

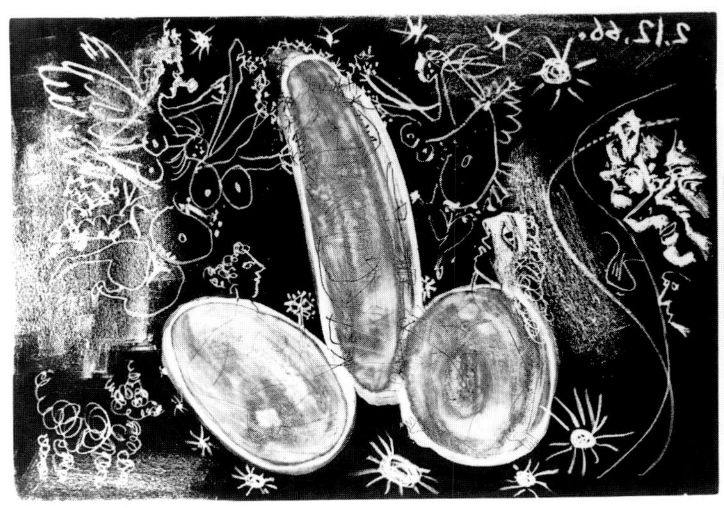

235 At the Theatre: Old Man Crowned with Flowers
by Women and Fairies, 2 December 1966

Aquatint and etching on copper; 31.9 x 46.8
Paris, Musée Picasso, on deposit at the
Musée de Strasbourg, MP 1990-177* [PM]
Barcelona, Museu Picasso, MPB 112.579 [B]

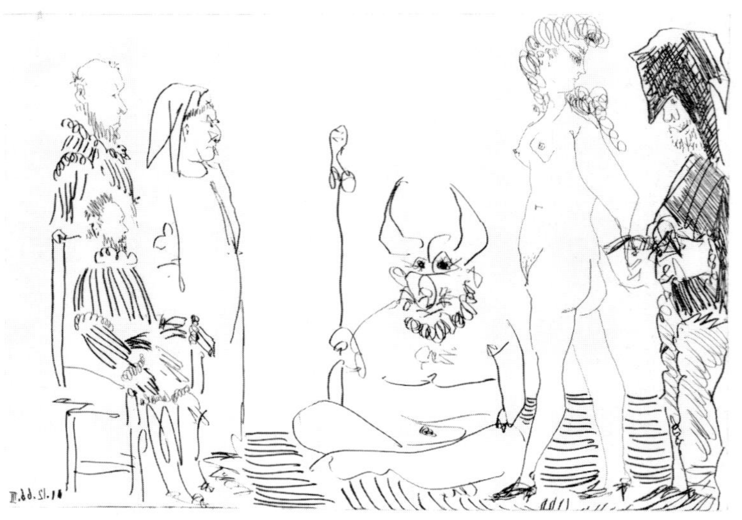

236 The Cuckolded Man Attending the Testimony,
before the Inquisition, of a Naked Woman
Chained by an Executioner, 11 December 1966
Etching on copper; 22.1 x 32.2
Paris, Musée Picasso, MP 1990-144* [MB]

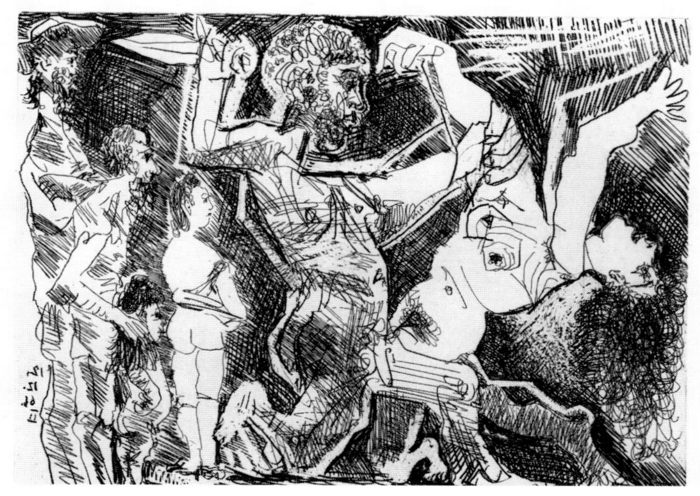

237 At the Theatre: The Clyster, 12 December 1966
Aquatint and etching ; 22.4 x 32.2
Paris, Musée Picasso, on deposit at the
Musée de Strasbourg, MP 1990-141* [PM]
Barcelona, Museu Picasso, MPB 112.628 [B]

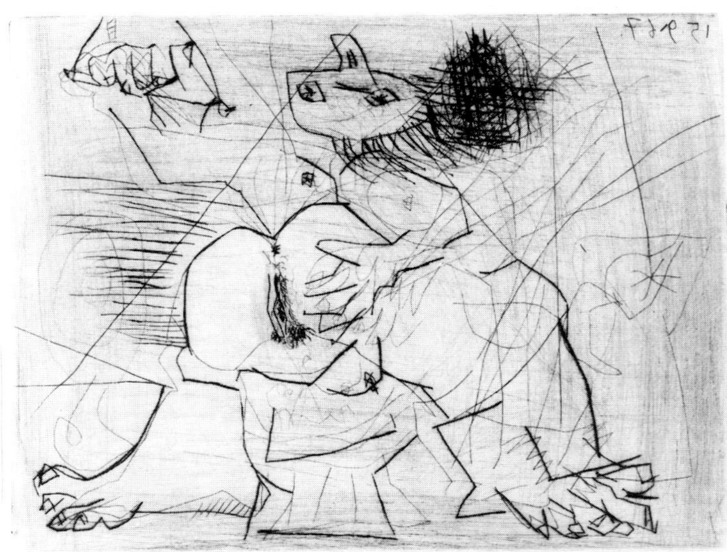

239 Two Women, 15 September 1967
Drypoint and glasspaper on copper; 16.1 x 22.7
Illustration for Iliazd, *Rogero Lacourière, pêcheur de
cuivre* (Paris: Le degré quarante et un, 1968)
Paris, Musée Picasso, MP 3038*

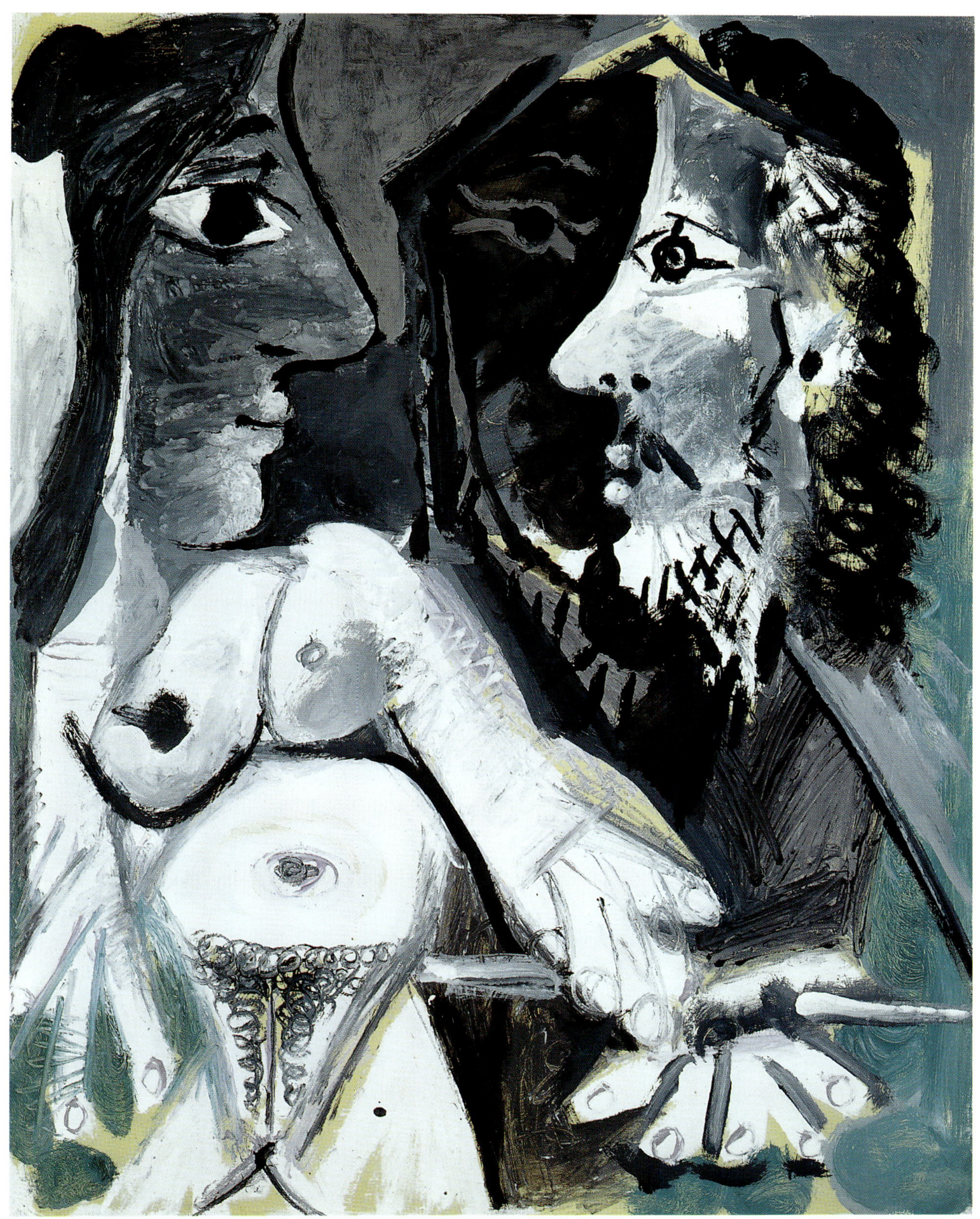

238 The Artist and His Model, 10 April 1967
Oil on canvas; 100 x 80.5
Paris, Musée Picasso, on deposit at the Musée de Picardie, Amiens, MP 1990-32

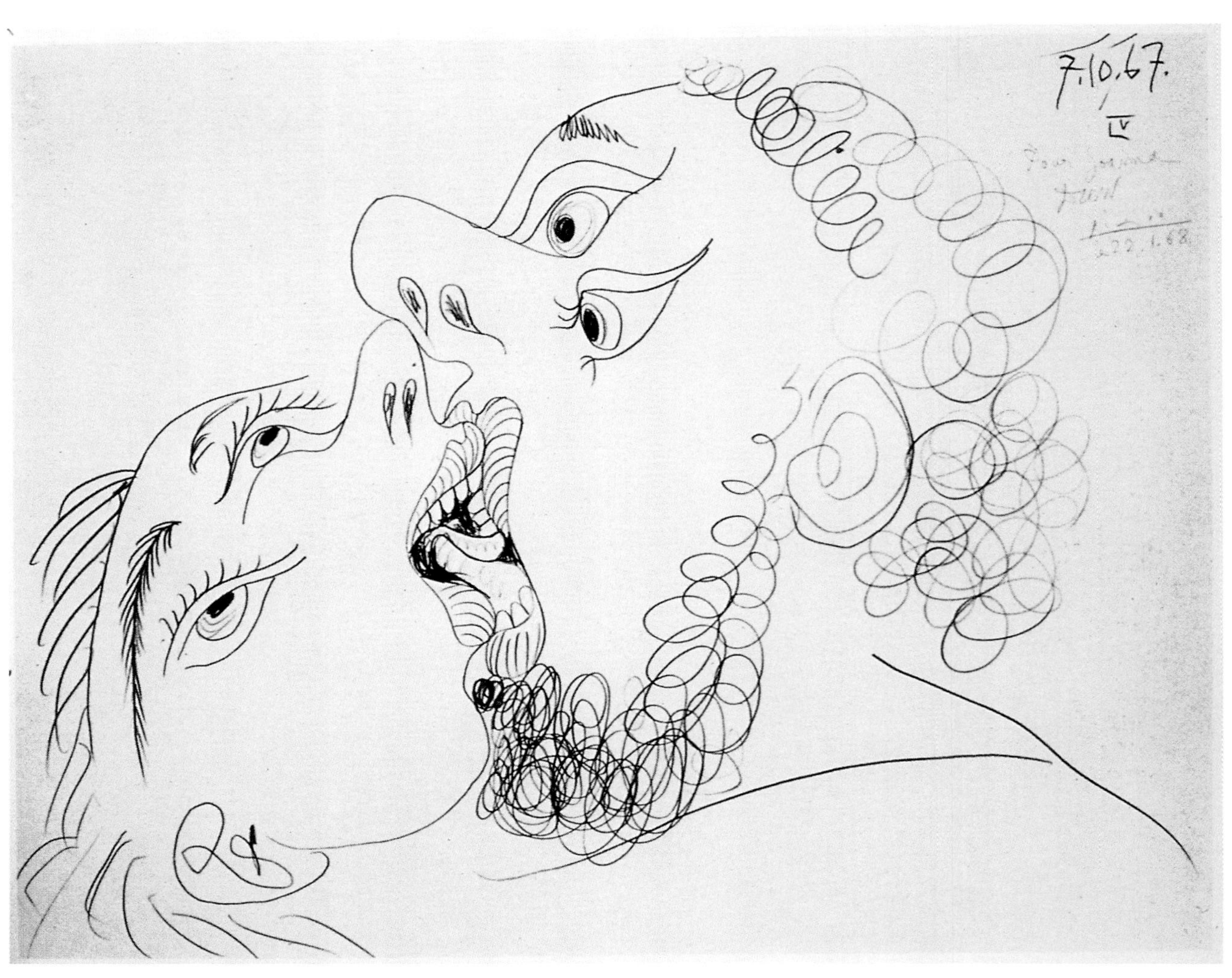

240 The Kiss, 7 October 1967 (IV)

Pencil on paper; 50.5 x 64.5
Basel, Beyeler Foundation

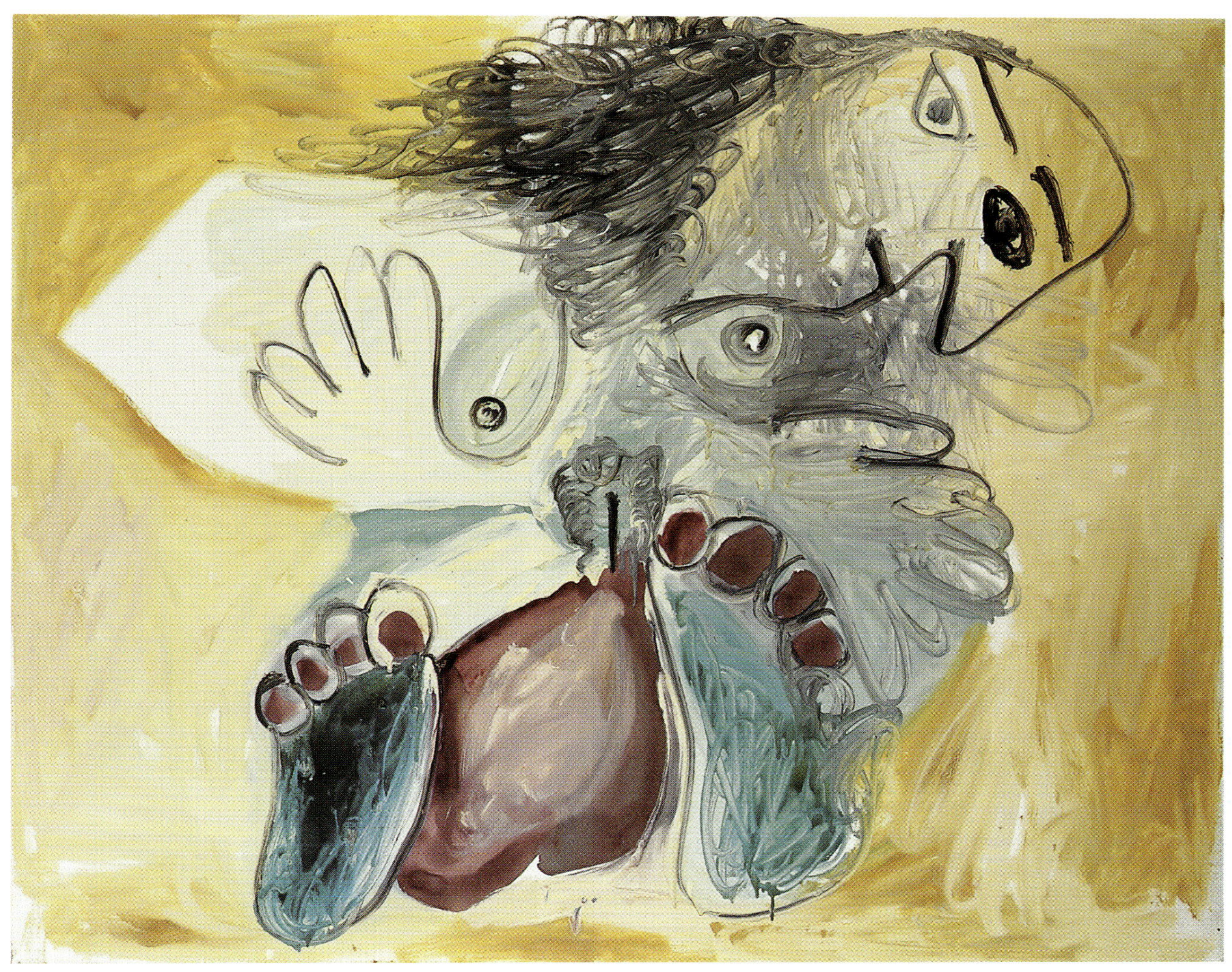

241 Nude with Yellow Background, 9 October 1967
  Oil on canvas; 114 x 146
  Paris, Private collection

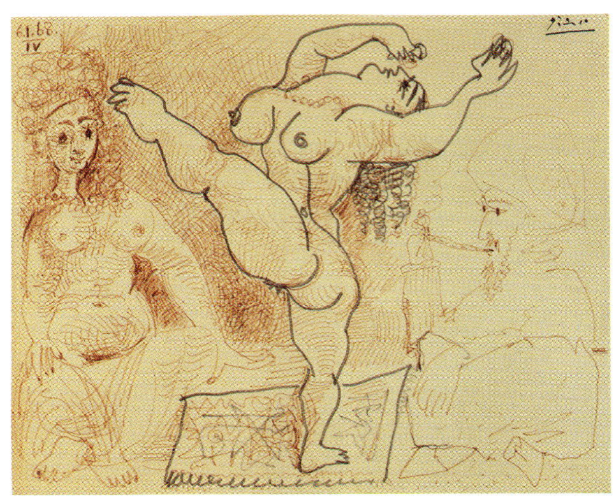

243 The Oriental Dancer, 6 January 1968

Pen, sepia and black ink on bristol board; 22 x 27.5
Barcelona, Museu Picasso, MPB 112.752* [PB]

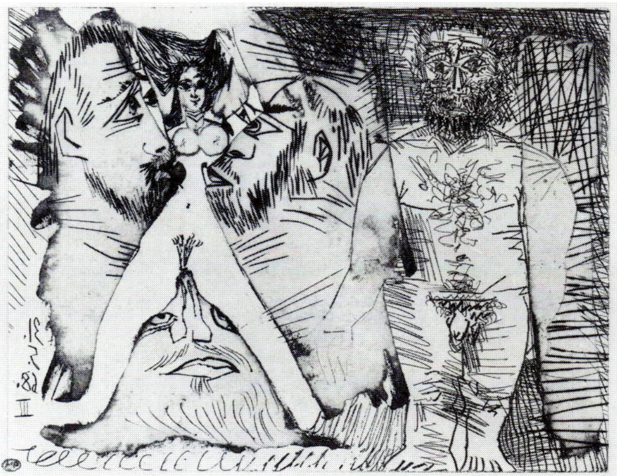

244 About the How-to Guide to a Young Woman, 31 May 1968

Etching, scraper, drypoint and burin on copper; State III; 19.8 x 25.7
Paris, Musée Picasso, MP 3061* [P]
Paris, Bibliothèque nationale de France, Département des Estampes et
de la Photographie [M]

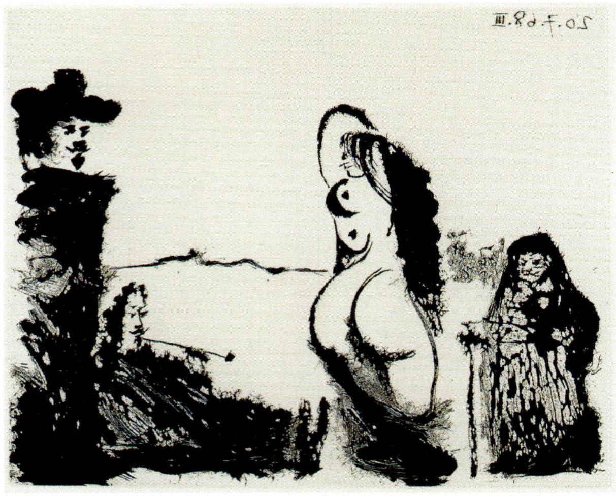

245 A Rembrantesque Luncheon on the Grass, with
Maja and Celestina, 20 July 1968

Sugar-lift aquatint on copper; 17.7 x 22.3
Paris, Bibliothèque nationale de France, Département des Estampes et
de la Photographie [P]
Paris, Private collection* [M]
Barcelona, Museu Picasso, MPB 111.874 [B]

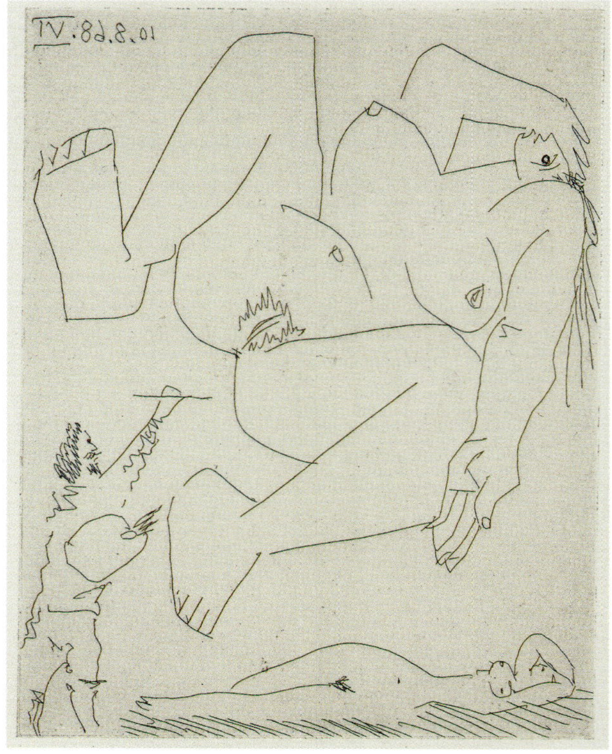

246 The Painter's Excess, 10 August 1968

Etching on copper; 13.8 x 11
Paris, Bibliothèque nationale de France, Département des Estampes et
de la Photographie [P]
Paris, Private collection* [M]
Barcelona, Museu Picasso, MPB 111.933 [B]

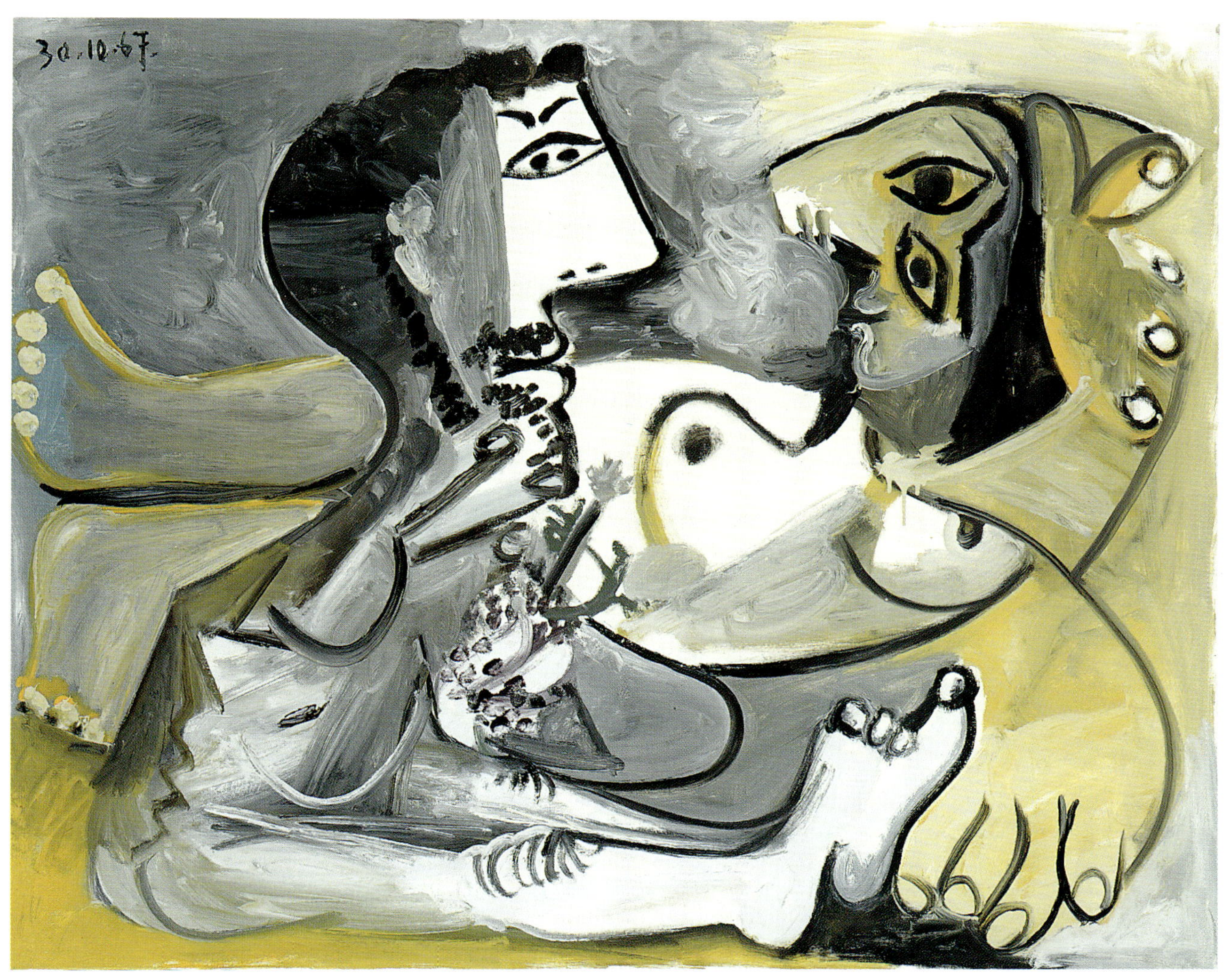

242 The Couple, 30 October 1967
Oil on canvas; 113.5 x 145.5
Paris, Musée Picasso, on deposit at the Musée des Beaux-Arts, Nantes, MP 1990-33

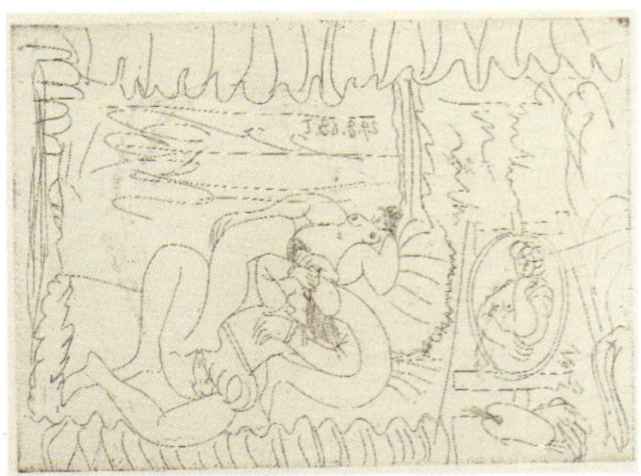

247 Raphael and La Fornarina I, 29 August 1968

Etching on copper; 27.9 x 38.9
Paris, Bibliothèque nationale de France,
Département des Estampes et de la Photographie [P]
Paris, Private collection* [M]
Barcelona, Museu Picasso, MPB 70.593 [B]

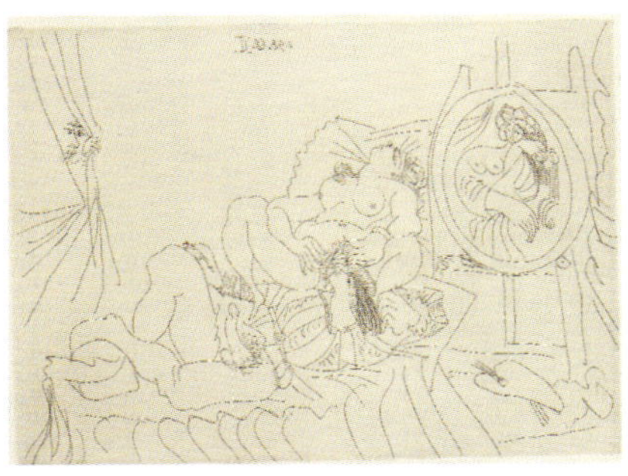

248 Raphael and La Fornarina II, with a Hidden Voyeur,
29 August 1968

Etching on copper; 27.9 x 38.9
Paris, Bibliothèque nationale de France,
Département des Estampes et de la Photographie [P]
Paris, Private collection* [M]
Barcelona, Museu Picasso, MPB 70.594 [B]

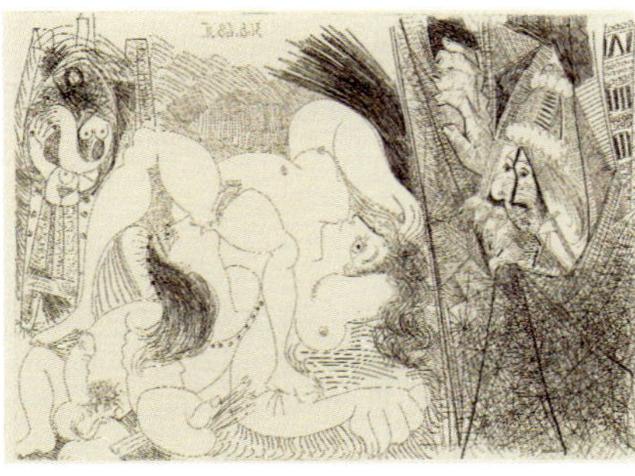

250 Raphael and La Fornarina IV, with the Pope Drawing
the Curtain, 31 August 1968

Etching on copper; 23.2 x 33.1
Paris, Bibliothèque nationale de France,
Département des Estampes et de la Photographie [P]
Paris, Private collection* [M]
Barcelona, Museu Picasso, MPB 70.599 [B]

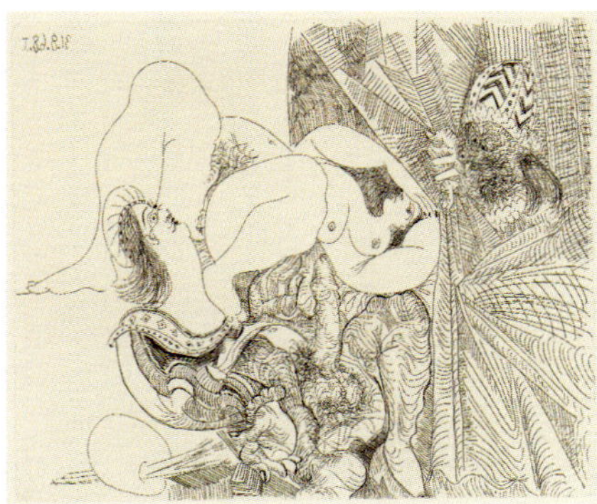

249 Raphael and La Fornarina III, with the Pope as
Hidden Voyeur, 31 August 1968

Etching on copper; 16.7 x 20.8
Paris, Bibliothèque nationale de France,
Département des Estampes et de la Photographie [P]
Paris, Private collection* [M]
Barcelona, Museu Picasso, MPB 111.886 [B]

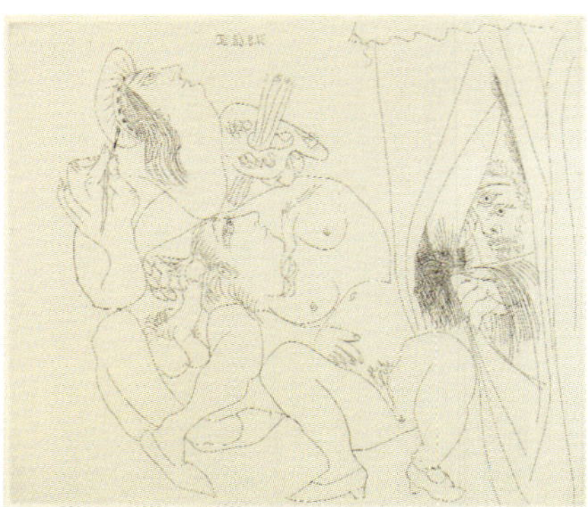

251 Raphael and La Fornarina V, with Voyeur Parting
the Curtain, 31 August 1968

Etching on copper; 41.4 x 49.5
Paris, Bibliothèque nationale de France,
Département des Estampes et de la Photographie [P]
Paris, Private collection* [M]
Barcelona, Museu Picasso, MPB 70.634 [B]

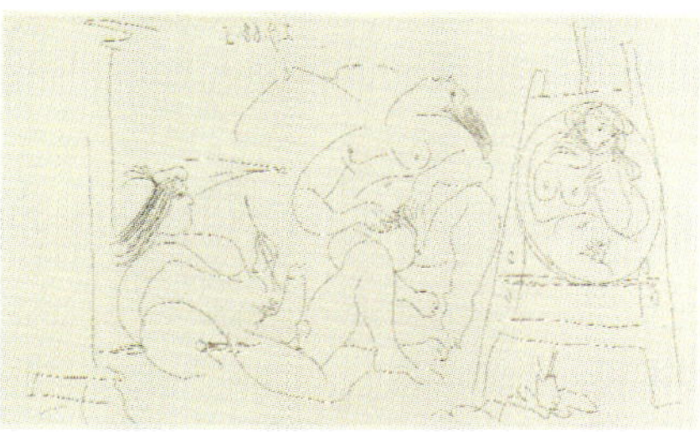

252 Raphael and La Fornarina VI: Alone at Last!
1 September 1968

Etching on copper; 29.6 x 51.4
Paris, Bibliothèque nationale de France,
Département des Estampes et de la Photographie [P]
Paris, Private collection* [M]
Barcelona, Museu Picasso, MPB 70.635 [B]

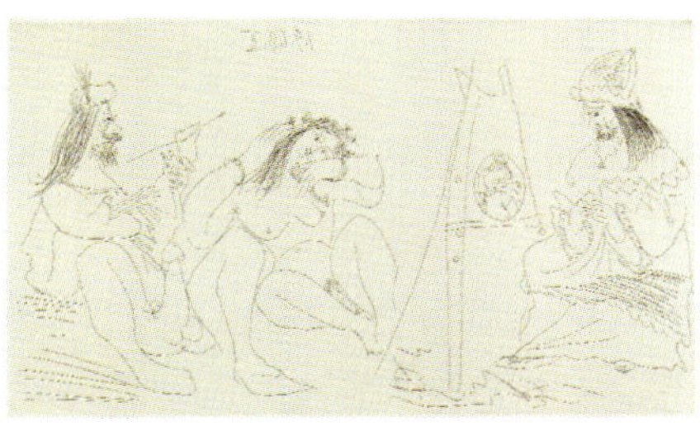

253 Raphael and La Fornarina VII: The Pope Is There, Sitting,
1 September 1968

Etching on copper; 29.7 x 51.4
Paris, Bibliothèque nationale de France,
Département des Estampes et de la Photographie [P]
Paris, Private collection* [M]
Barcelona, Museu Picasso, MPB 70.636 [B]

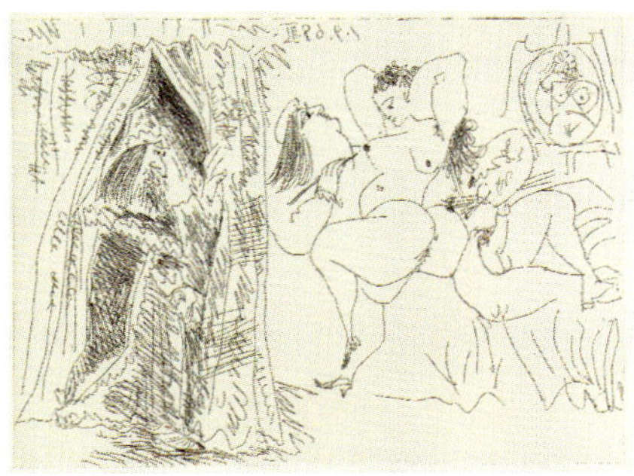

254 Raphael and La Fornarina VIII: The Pope Enters,
with a Slick Smile, 1 September 1968

Etching on copper; 14.8 x 20.9
Paris, Bibliothèque nationale de France,
Département des Estampes et de la Photographie [P]
Paris, Private collection* [M]
Barcelona, Museu Picasso, MPB 111.940 [B]

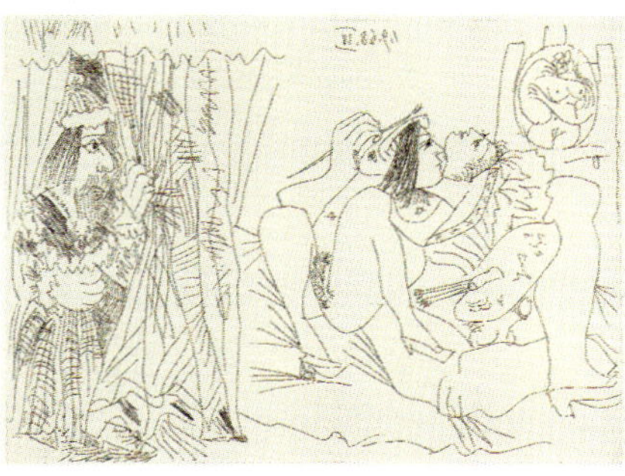

255 Raphael and La Fornarina IX: The Pope Arrives,
1 September 1968

Etching on copper; 14.8 x 20.9
Paris, Bibliothèque nationale de France, Département des Estampes et
de la Photographie [P]
Paris, Private collection* [M]
Barcelona, Museu Picasso, MPB 111.941 [M]

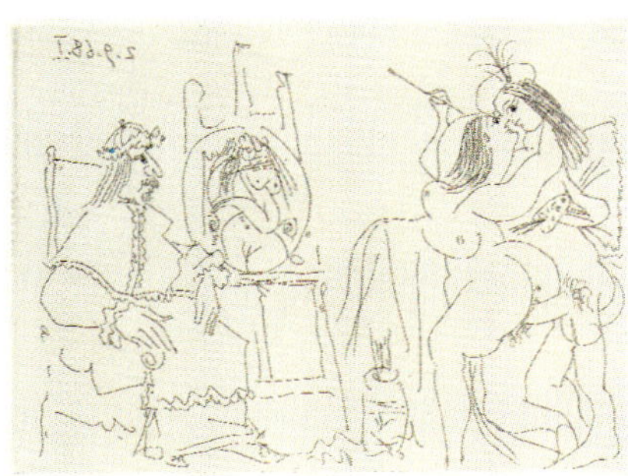

256 Raphael and La Fornarina X: The Pope Has Had
His Armchair Brought, 2 September 1968

Etching on copper; 14.8 x 20.9
Paris, Bibliothèque nationale de France,
Département des Estampes et de la Photographie [P]
Paris, Private collection* [M]
Barcelona, Museu Picasso, MPB 111.942 [B]

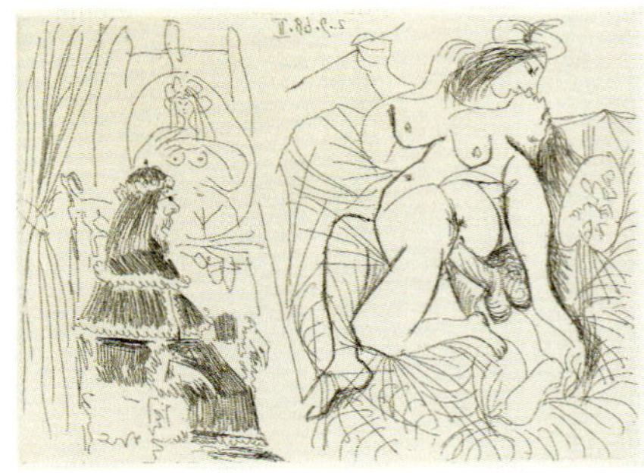

257 Raphael and La Fornarina XI: The Pope Is Open-Mouthed
in His Armchair, 2 September 1968

Etching on copper; 14.8 x 20.9
Paris, Bibliothèque nationale de France,
Département des Estampes et de la Photographie [P]
Paris, Private collection* [M]
Barcelona, Museu Picasso, MPB 111.943 [B]

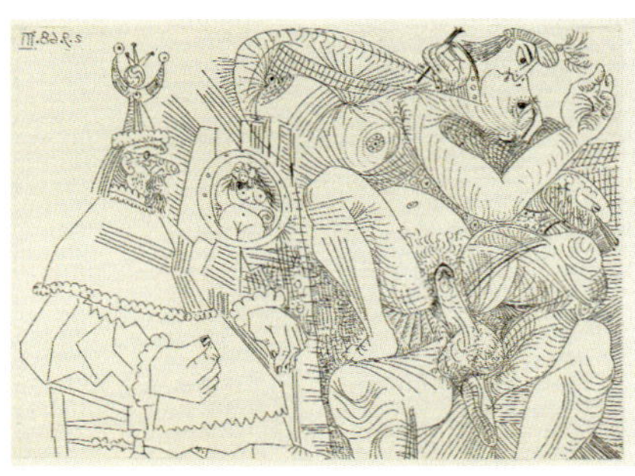

258 Raphael and La Fornarina XII: In His Armchair,
the Pope Feels Cuckolded, 2 September 1968

Etching on copper; 14.8 x 20.9
Paris, Bibliothèque nationale de France,
Département des Estampes et de la Photographie [P]
Paris, Private collection* [M]
Barcelona, Museu Picasso, MPB 111.944 [B]

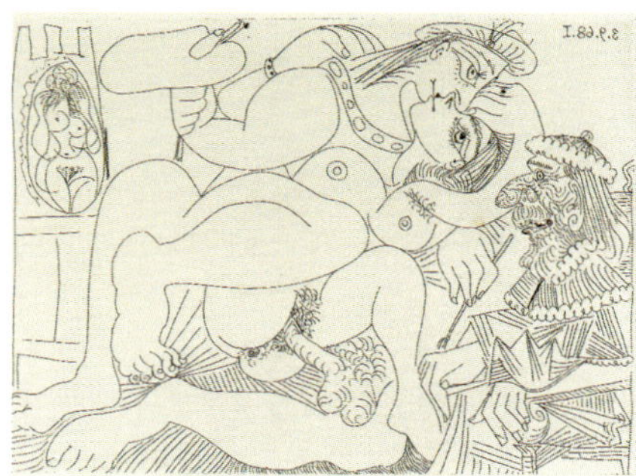

259 Raphael and La Fornarina XIII: The Pope Sticks Out
His Tongue at the Whole Thing, 3 September 1968

Etching on copper; 14.8 x 20.9
Paris, Bibliothèque nationale de France,
Département des Estampes et de la Photographie [P]
Paris, Private collection* [M]
Barcelona, Museu Picasso, MPB 111.945 [B]

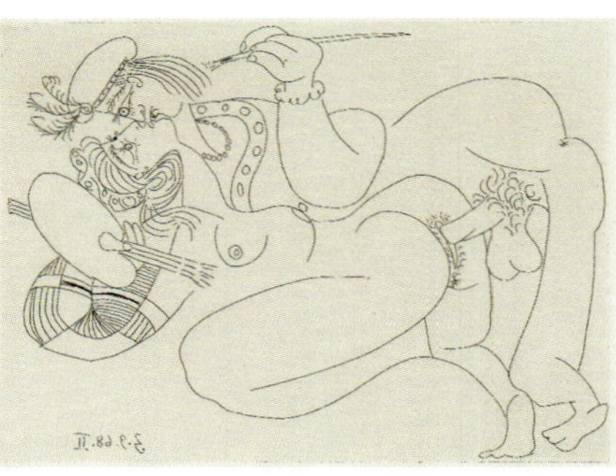

260 Raphael and La Fornarina XIV: The Pope
Has Slipped Away, 3 September 1968

Etching on copper; 14.8 x 20.9
Paris, Bibliothèque nationale de France,
Département des Estampes et de la Photographie [P]
Paris, Private collection* [M]
Barcelona, Museu Picasso, MPB 111.946 [B]

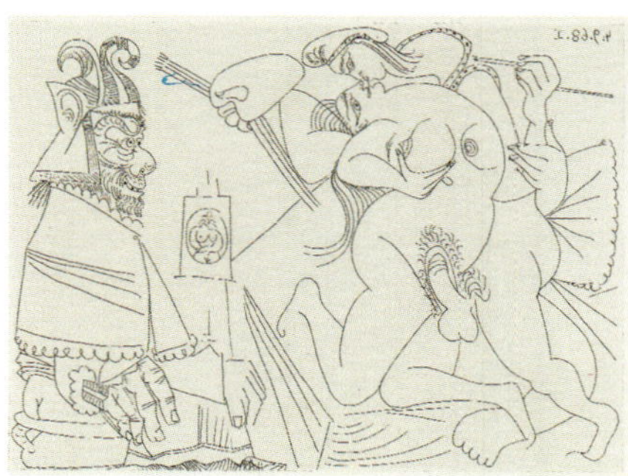

261 Raphael and La Fornarina XV: The Pope Is Back,
on His Chamberpot, 4 September 1968

Etching on copper; 14.8 x 20.9
Paris, Bibliothèque nationale de France,
Département des Estampes et de la Photographie [P]
Paris, Private collection* [M]
Barcelona, Museu Picasso, MPB 111.947 [B]

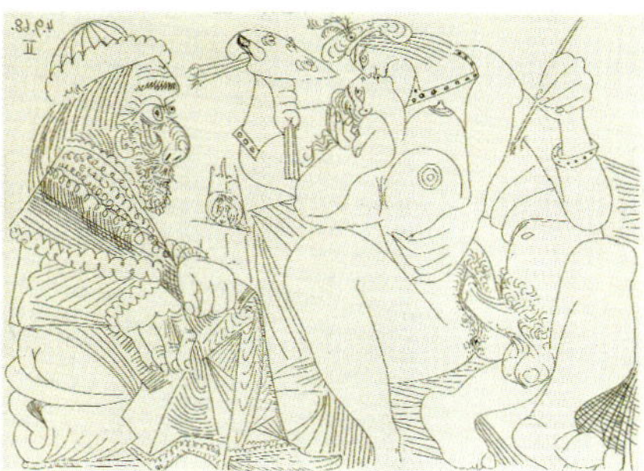

262 Raphael and La Fornarina XVI: The Pope Is Still
on His Chamberpot, Pondering, 4 September 1968

Etching on copper; 14.8 x 20.9
Paris, Bibliothèque nationale de France,
Département des Estampes et de la Photographie [P]
Paris, Private collection* [M]
Barcelona, Museu Picasso, MPB 111.948 [B]

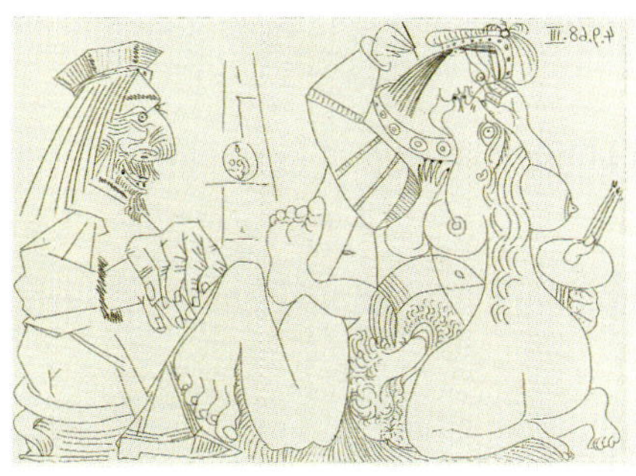

263 Raphael and La Fornarina. XVII: On His Chamberpot,
a Cardinal, Tickled, Laughs, 4 September 1968

Etching on copper; 14.8 x 209
Paris, Bibliothèque nationale de France,
Département des Estampes et de la Photographie [P]
Paris, Private collection* [M]
Barcelona, Museu Picasso, MPB 111.949 [B]

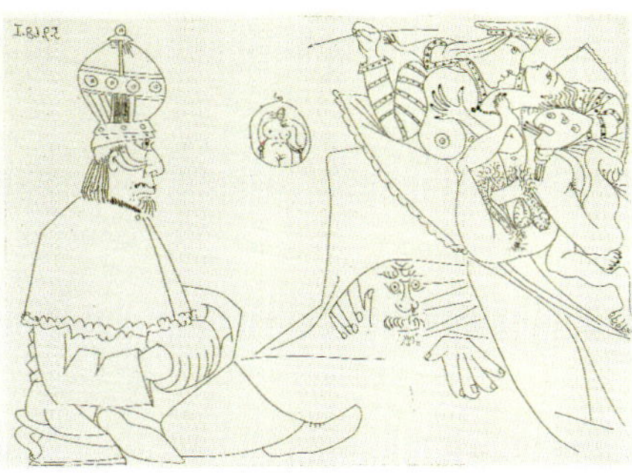

265 Raphael and La Fornarina XIX:
Pope on His Chamberpot, with Tiara and Muff;
Michelangelo Is Hiding under the Bed, 5 September 1968

Etching on copper; 14.8 x 20.9
Paris, Bibliothèque nationale de France,
Département des Estampes et de la Photographie [P]
Paris, Private collection [M]
Barcelona, Museu Picasso, MPB 111.951 [B]

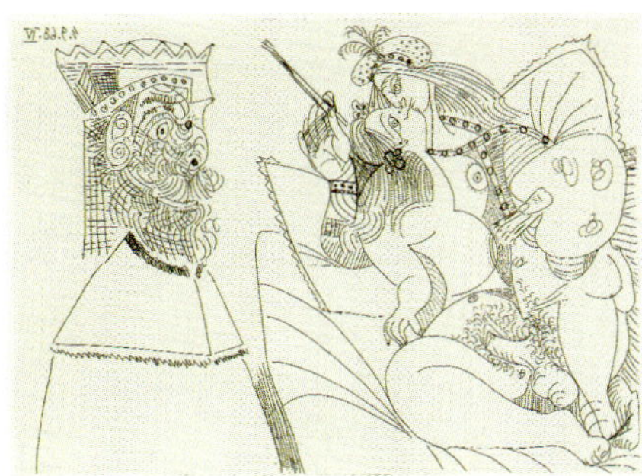

264 Raphael and La Fornarina XVIII: The Pope Is Oddly
Coiffed, 4 September 1968

Etching on copper; 14.8 x 20.9
Paris, Bibliothèque nationale de France,
Département des Estampes et de la Photographie [P]
Paris, Private collection* [M]
Barcelona, Museu Picasso, MPB 111.950 [B]

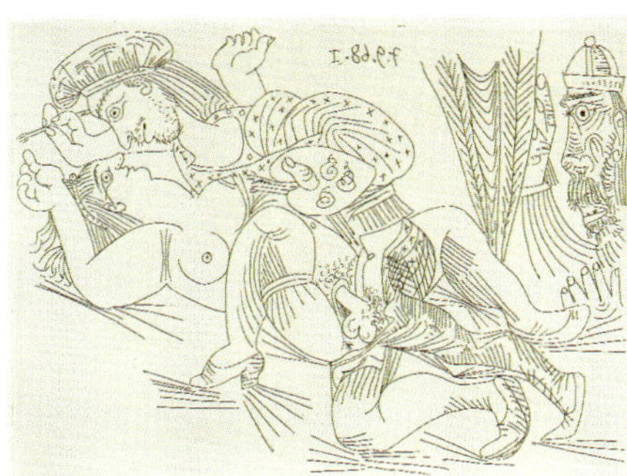

266 Raphael and La Fornarina XX: Exit the Pope,
7 September 1968

Etching on copper; 14.8 x 20.9
Paris, Bibliothèque nationale de France,
Département des Estampes et de la Photographie [P]
Paris, Private collection* [M]
Barcelona, Museu Picasso, MPB 111.952 [B]

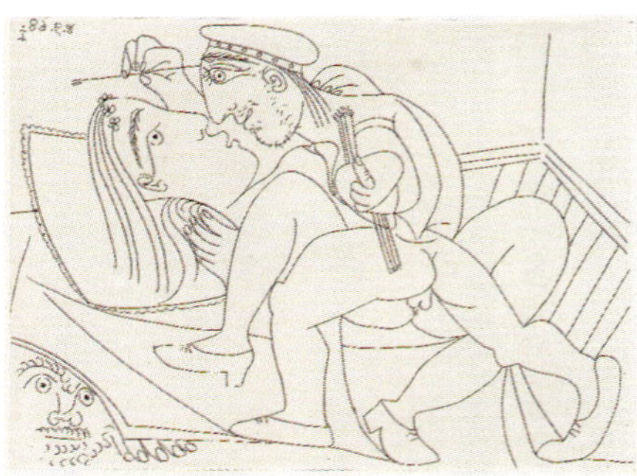

267 Raphael and La Fornarina XXI: Michelangelo Is
Hiding under the Bed, 8 September 1968

Etching on copper; 14.8 x 20.9
Paris, Bibliothèque nationale de France,
Département des Estampes et de la Photographie [P]
Paris, Private collection* [M]
Barcelona, Museu Picasso, MPB 111.953 [B]

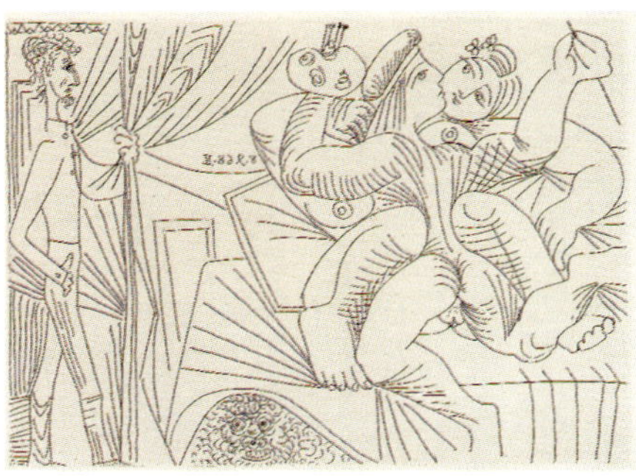

268 Raphael and La Fornarina XXII: Michelangelo under
the Bed; Enter Piero Crommelynck, 8 September 1968

Etching on copper; 14.8 x 20.9
Paris, Bibliothèque nationale de France,
Département des Estampes et de la Photographie [P]
Paris, Private collection* [M]
Barcelona, Museu Picasso, MPB 111.954 [B]

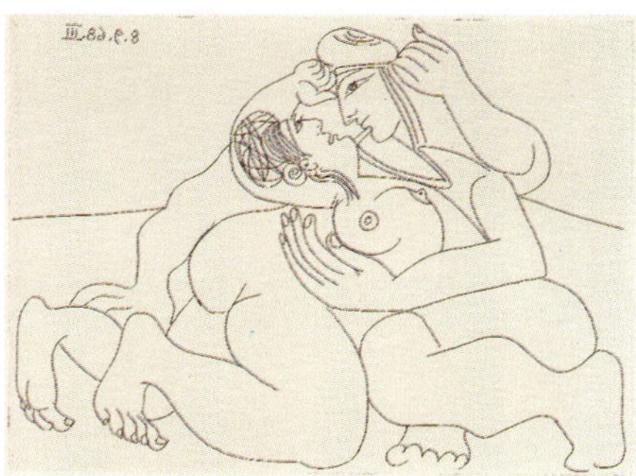

269 Raphael and La Fornarina XXIII: Alone, Embracing
on the Ground, 8 September 1968

Etching on copper; 14.8 x 20.9
Paris, Bibliothèque nationale de France,
Département des Estampes et de la Photographie [P]
Paris, Private collection* [M]
Barcelona, Museu Picasso, MPB 112.022 [B]

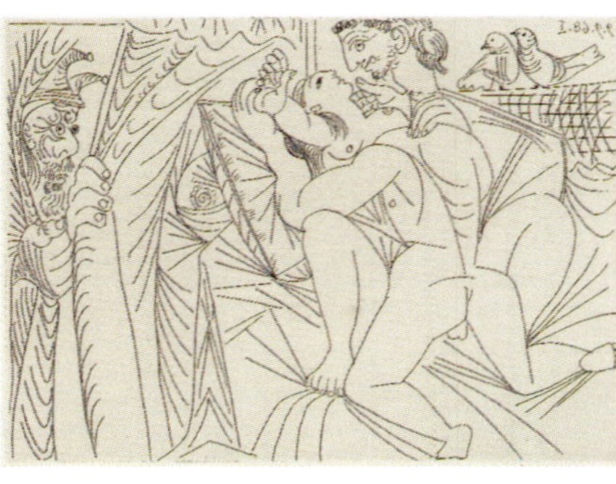

270 Raphael and La Fornarina XXIV: With Voyeur Wearing
a Two-Horned Hat, and Two Pigeons, 9 September 1968

Etching on copper; 14.8 x 20.9
Paris, Bibliothèque nationale de France,
Département des Estampes et de la Photographie [P]
Paris, Private collection* [M]
Barcelona, Museu Picasso, MPB 111.955 [B]

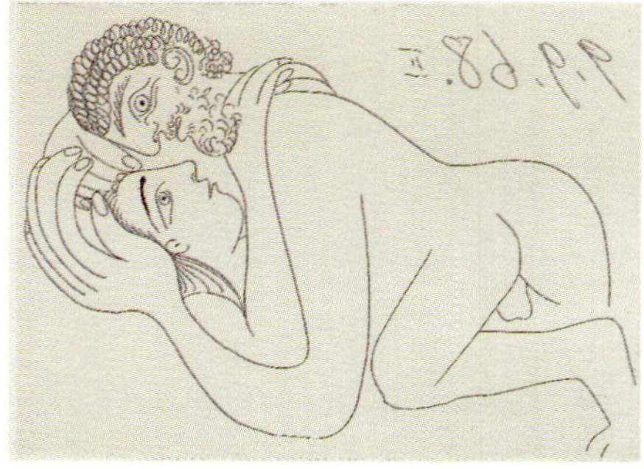

271 Amorous Couple (Raphael and La Fornarina:
The End), 9 September 1968

Etching on copper; 14.8 x 20.9
Paris, Bibliothèque nationale de France,
Département des Estampes et de la Photographie [P]
Paris, Private collection* [M]
Barcelona, Museu Picasso, MPB 111.956 [B]

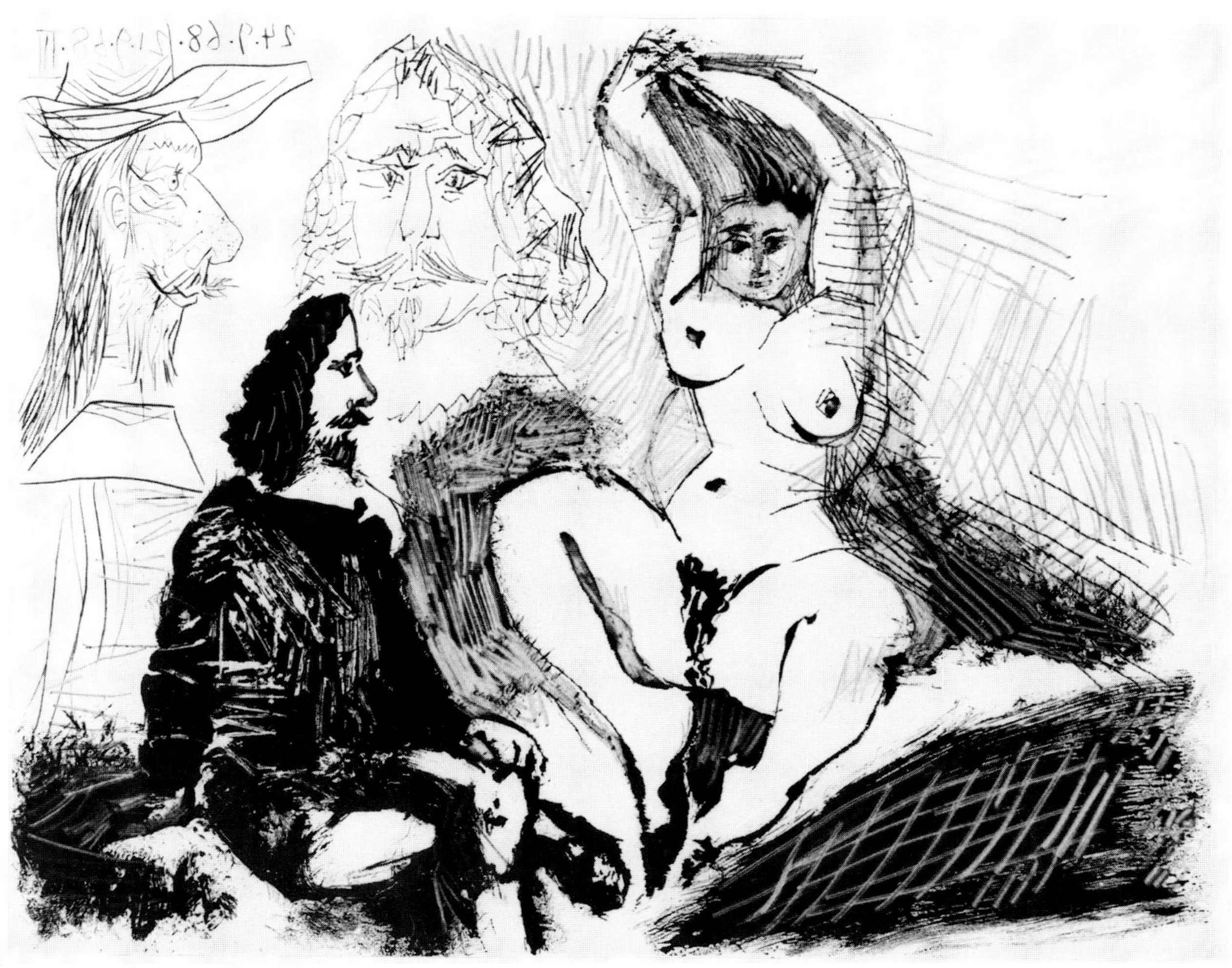

272 Man Seated beside a Woman Dressing Her Hair and, behind, Two Painters, 24 September 1968

Sugar-lift aquatint, direct scraper and drypoint on copper; State II; 20.8 x 26.6
Paris, Musée Picasso MP 3065* [M]
Barcelona, Museu Picasso, MPB 111.906 [B]

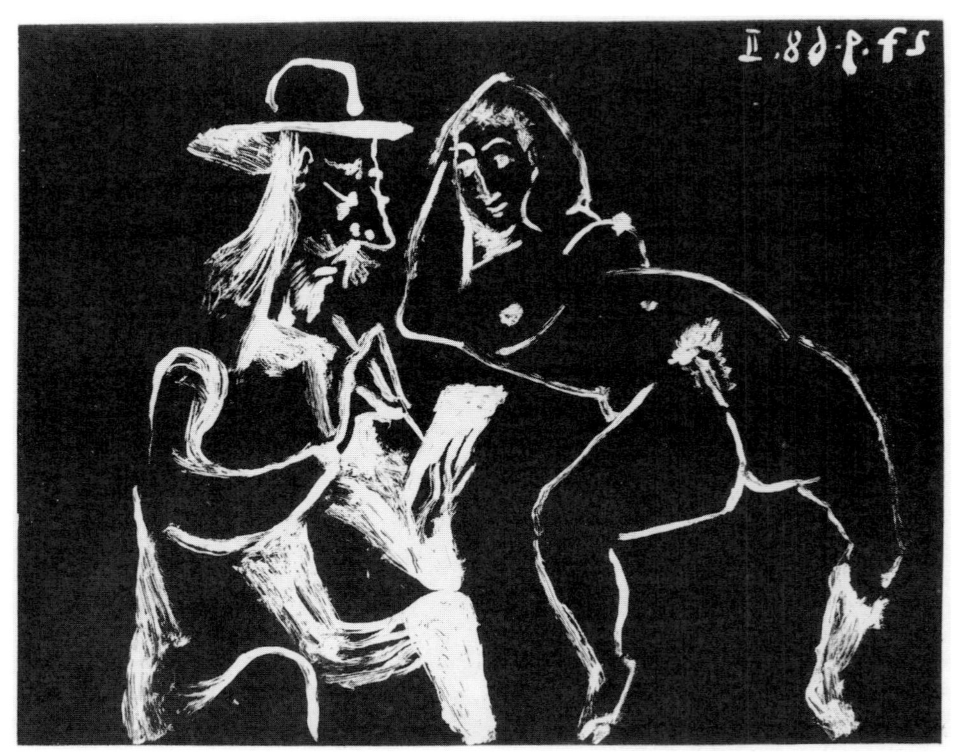

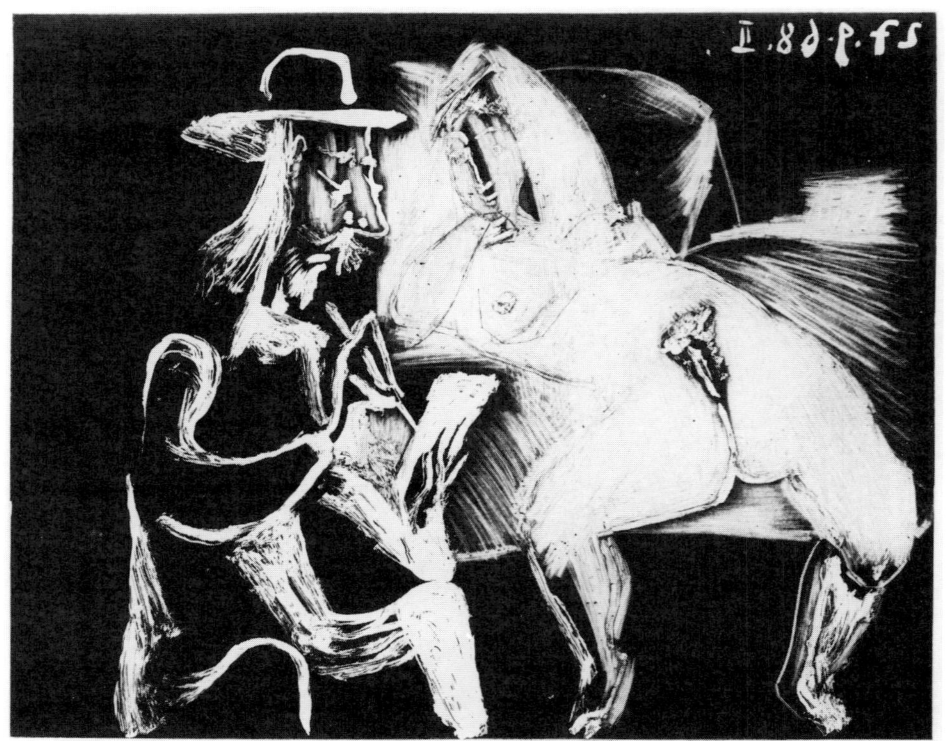

273 a and b **Man in Hat Drawing beside a Woman Offering Herself,** 27 September 1968

Sugar-lift aquatint, direct scraper and drypoint on copper; States I and II; 20.7 x 26.7
Paris, Musée Picasso, MP 3066* [M] and MP 3067* [P]
Barcelona, Museu Picasso, MPB 111.914 [B]

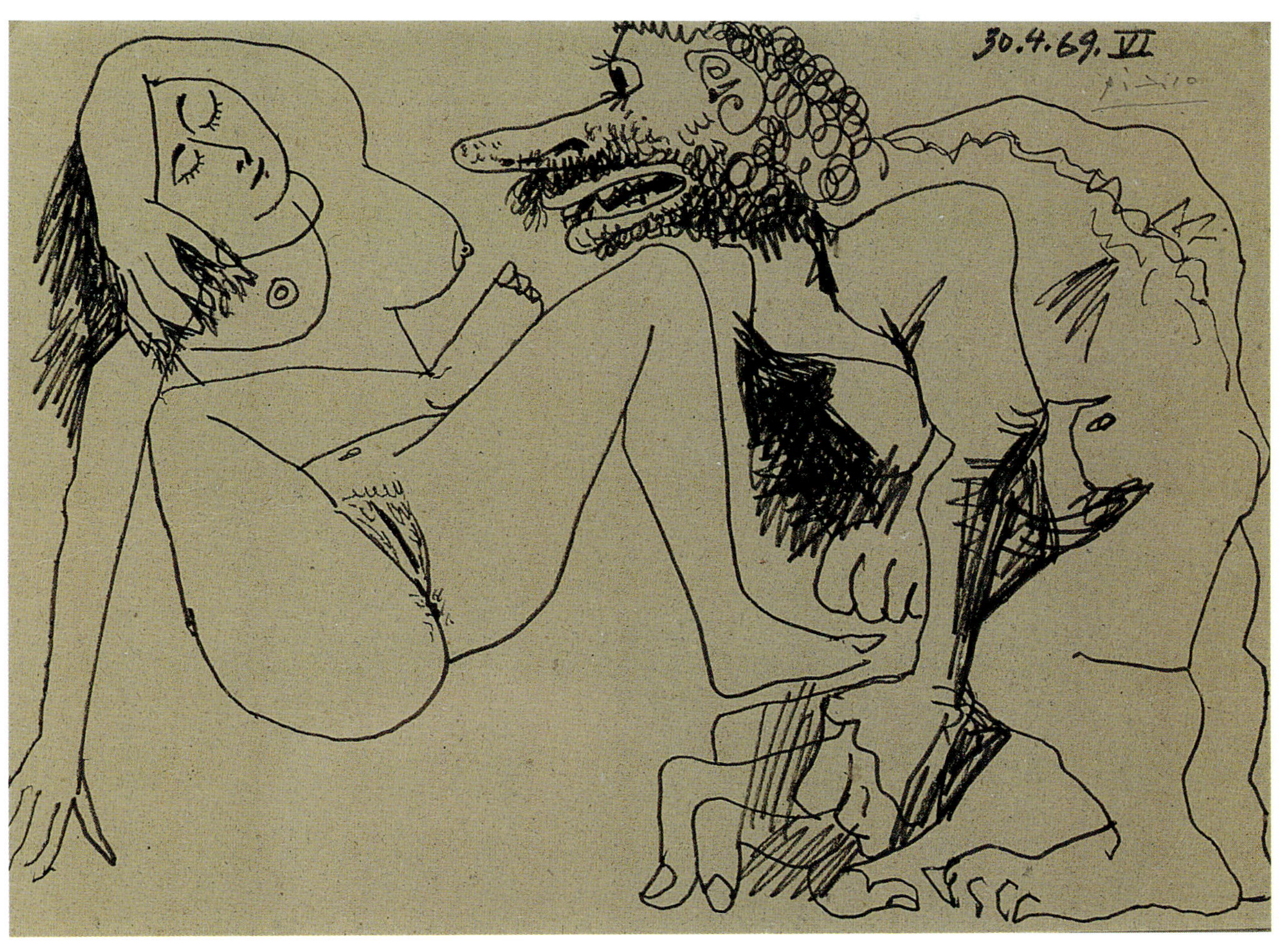

273 c Nude Man and Woman (Embrace), 30 April 1969
India ink on grey board; 22 x 31
Private collection; Courtesy Leslee and David Rogath

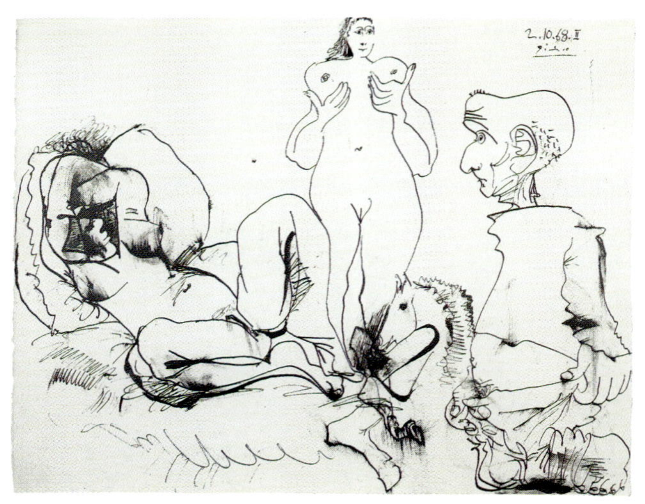

274 Man with Nude Women, 2 October 1968

Ink on paper; 50.5 x 65
Paris, Galerie Louise Leiris [PB]

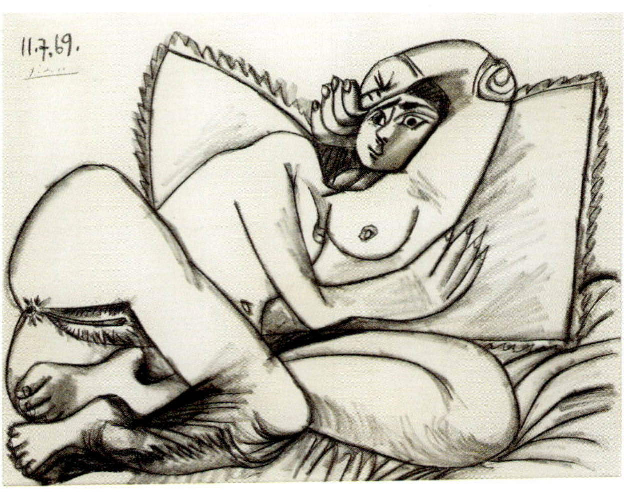

275 Nude Leaning on Her Elbow, 11 July 1969

Black crayon on paper; 50.5 x 65.5
Berlin, Staatliche Museen, Nationalgalerie

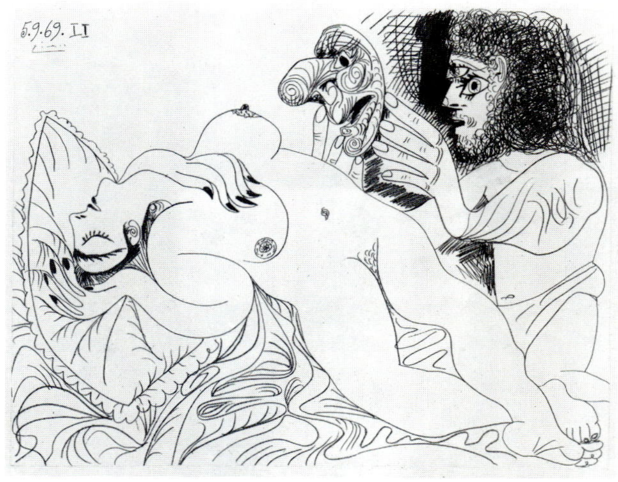

277 Reclining Nude and Man with Mask, 5 September 1969 (II)

Pencil on paper; 50 x 65.5
Basel, Beyeler Foundation [PB]

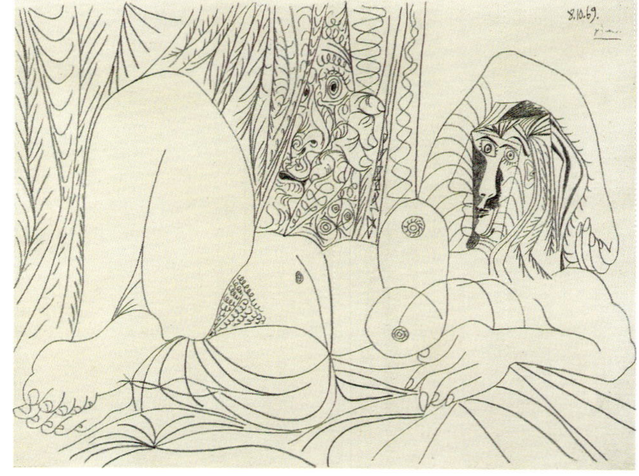

278 Characters, 8 October 1969

Pencil on paper; 54 x 70.5
Paris, Galerie Louise Leiris [PB]

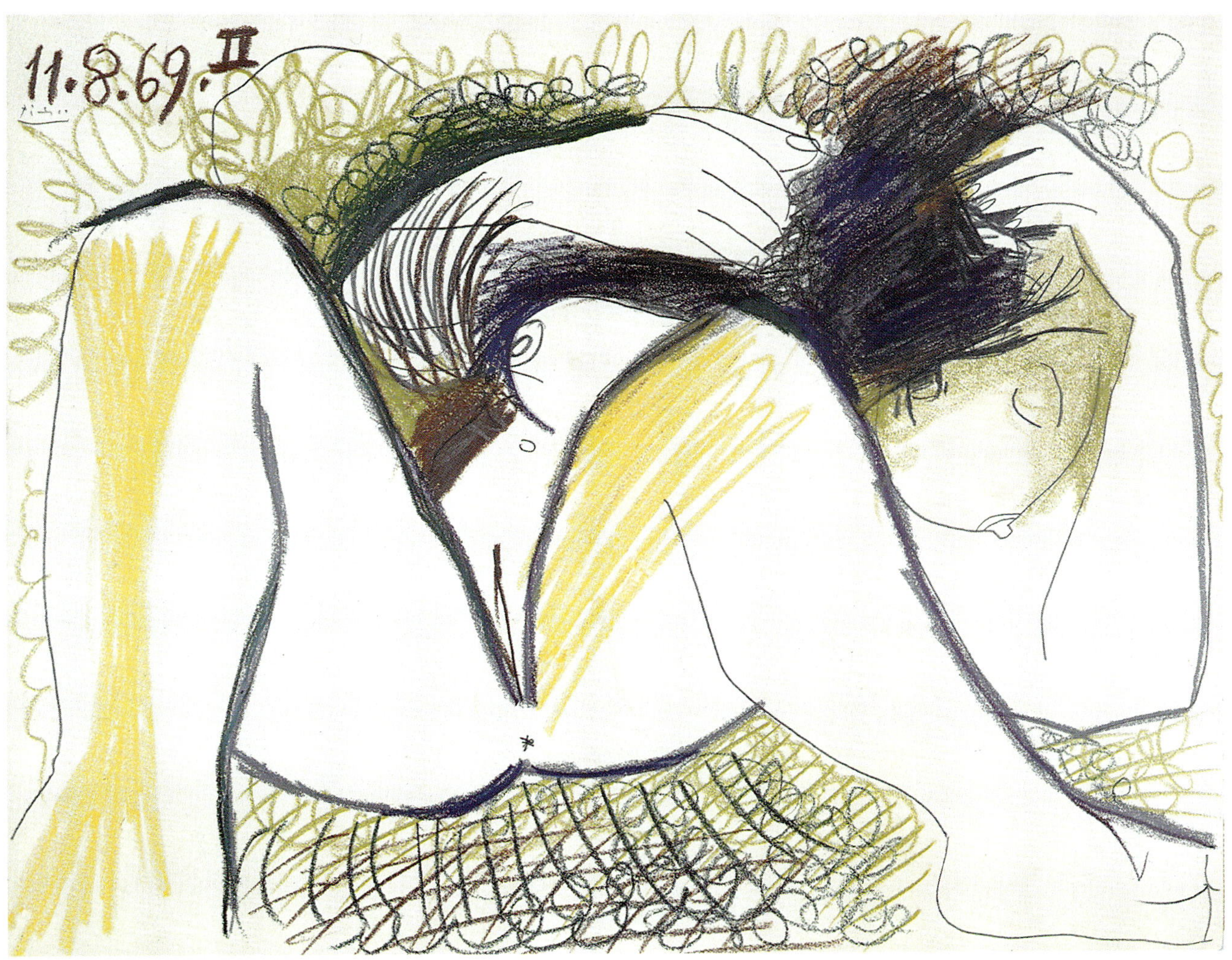

276 Reclining Woman, 11 August 1969
Coloured pencil on paper; 50.5 x 65.5
Paris, Galerie Louise Leiris [PB]

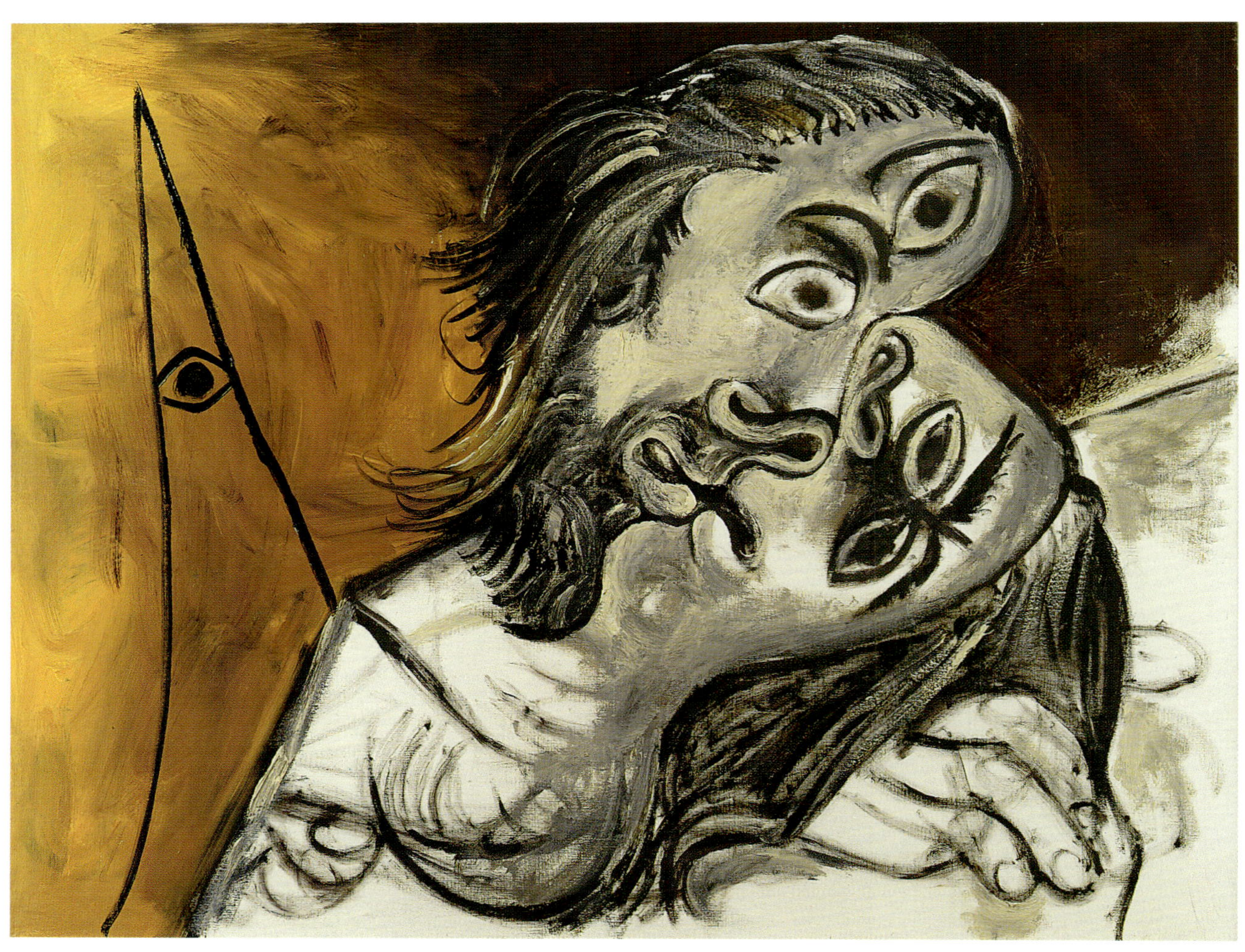

279 **The Kiss**, 24 October 1969
Oil on canvas; 97 x 130
Bermuda, Private collection

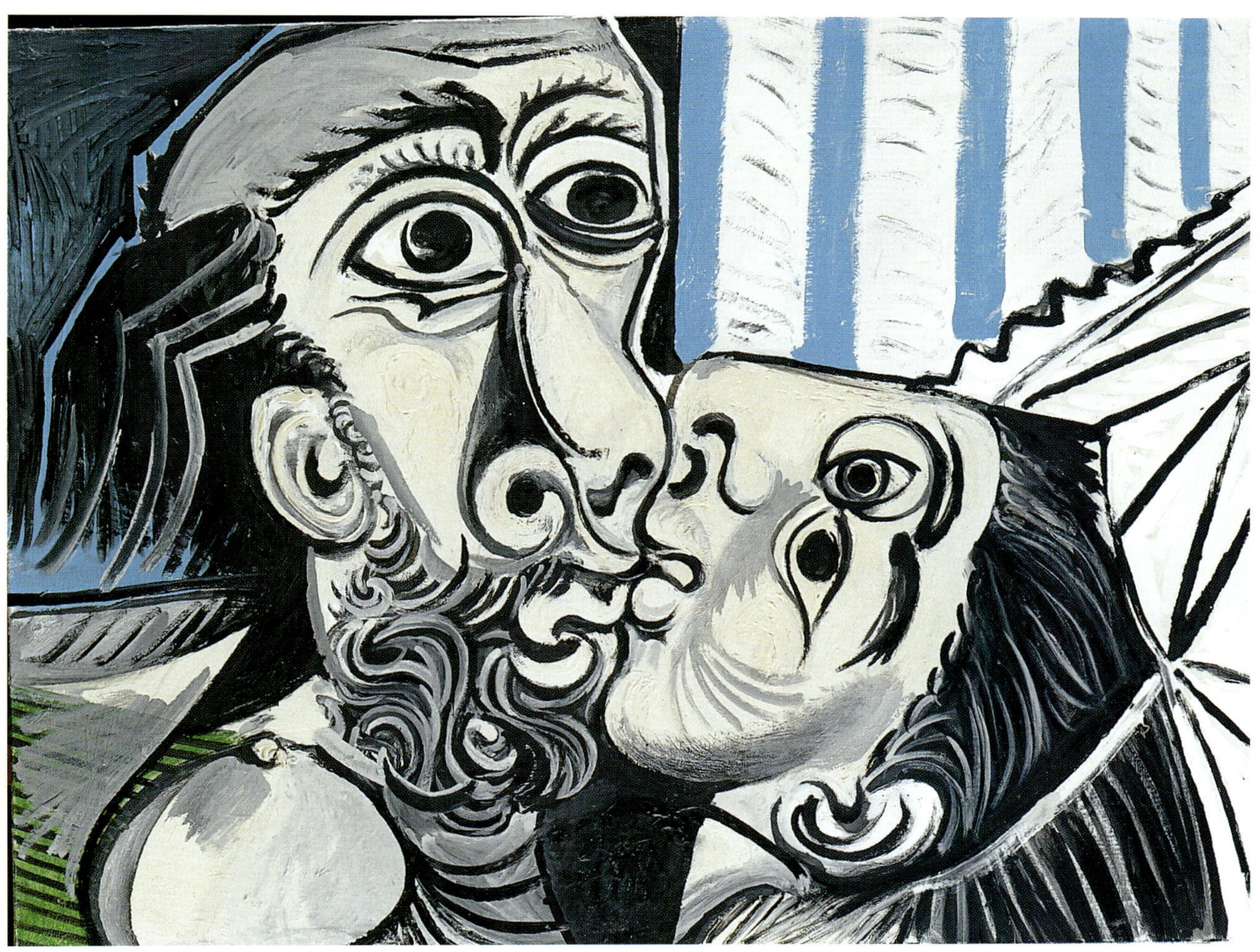

280 The Kiss, 26 October 1969

Oil on canvas; 97 x 130
Paris, Musée Picasso, MP 220

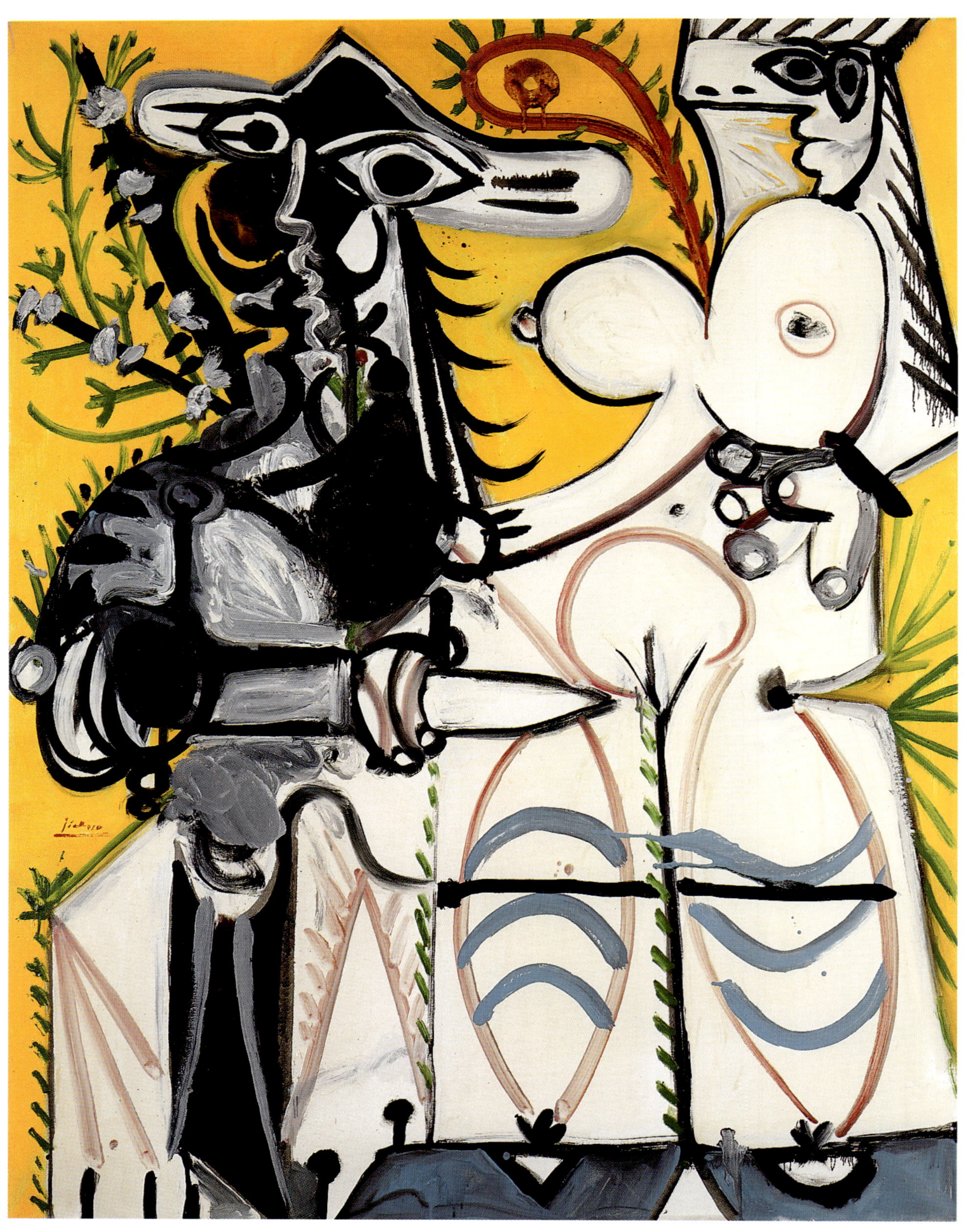

281 Man and Woman, 17 December 1969
Oil on canvas; 162 x 130
Zurich, Galerie Art Focus

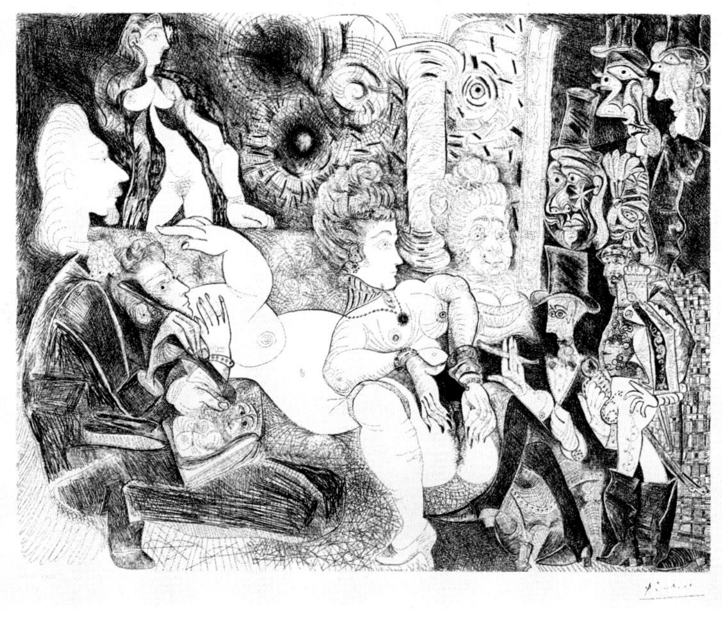

282 Painter with a Lavallière Drawing His Model within the Maison Tellier, 19 February 1970

Etching on copper; 50.6 x 63
Paris, Musée Picasso, on deposit at the Musée d'Art moderne, Saint-Étienne, MP 1990-222* [P]
Paris, Bibliothèque nationale de France, Département des Estampes et de la Photographie [M]
Barcelona, Museu Picasso, MPB 112.181 [B]

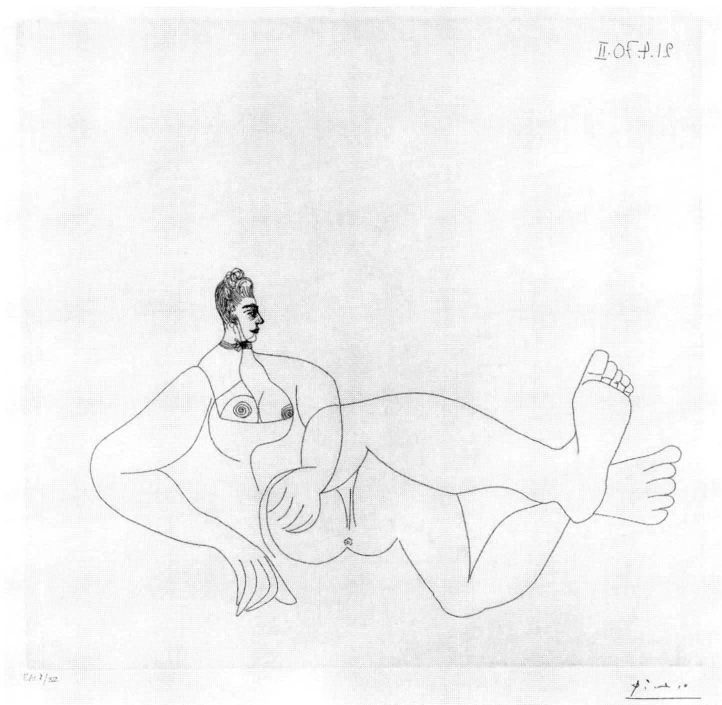

283 Odalisque with Dog Collar, 21 April 1970

Etching on copper; 50.6 x 53.2
Barcelona, Museu Picasso, MPB 112.173 [B]

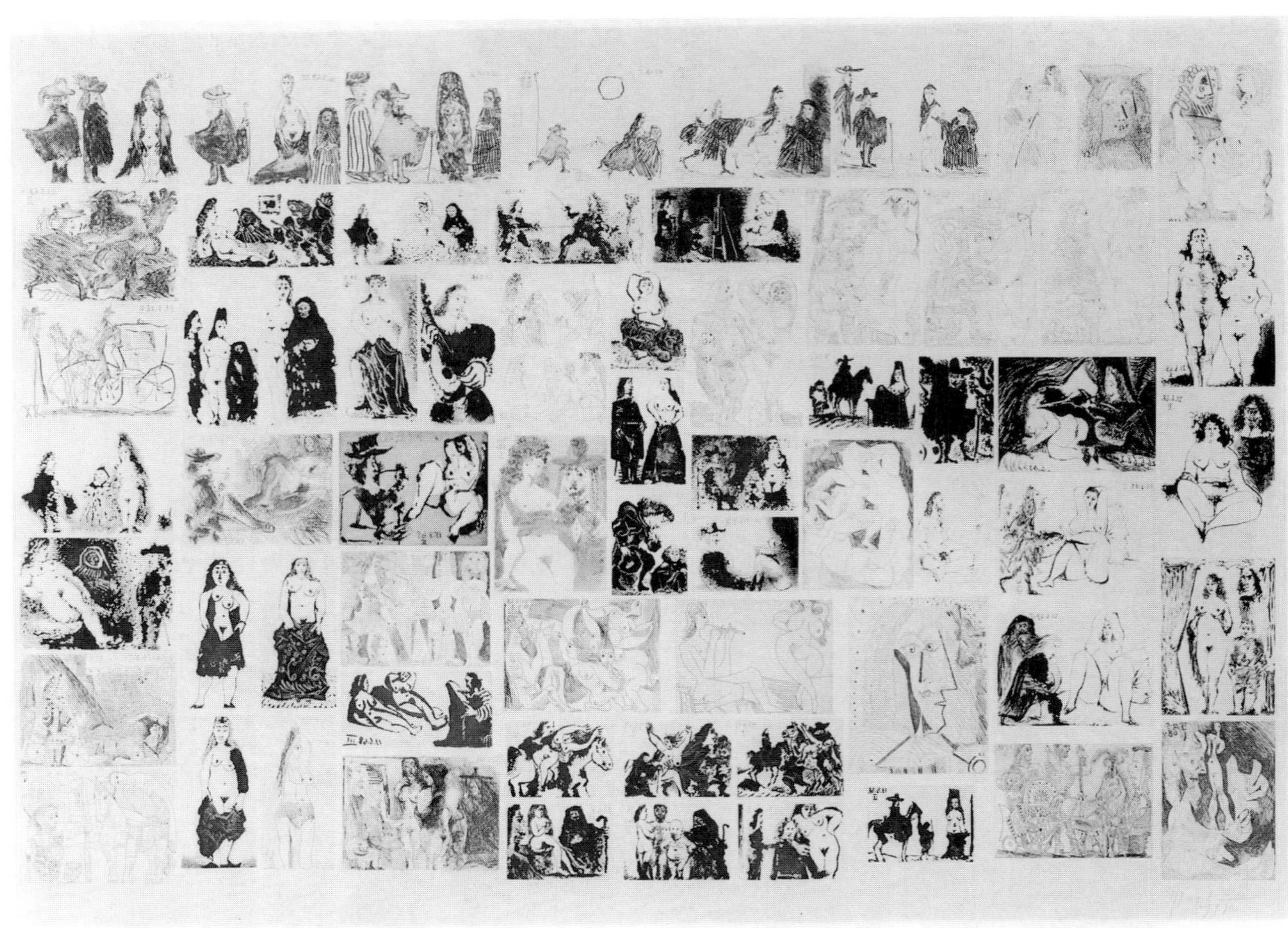

285 La Celestina, 9 September 1970

Print pulled from the 66 copper plates; 74.8 x 105
Paris, Musée Picasso, MP 3053

284 La Celestina, 1968 (not reproduced)

66 copper plates
Paris, Musée Picasso, MP 1985-6 to MP 1985-71 [P]

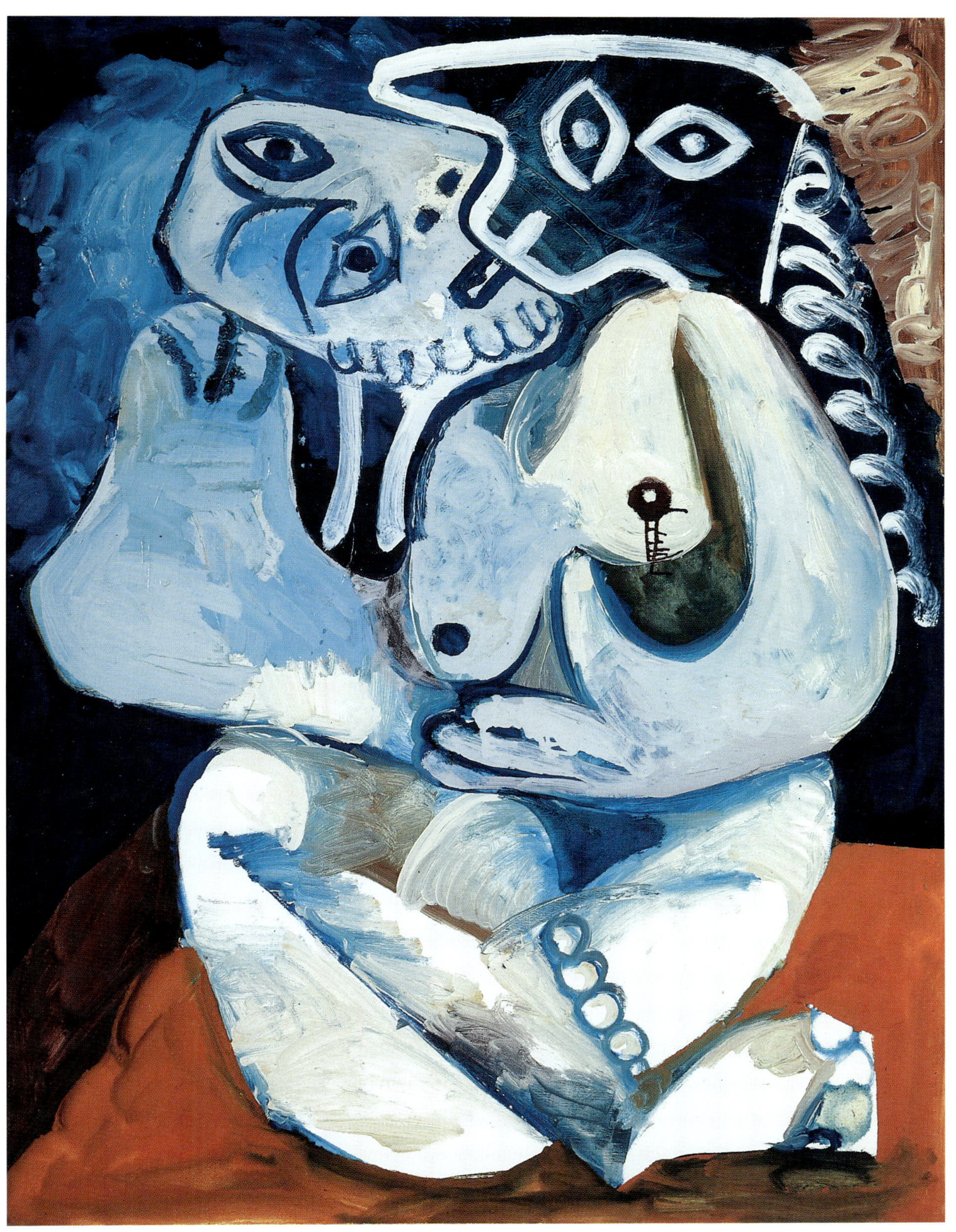

286 The Embrace, 26 September 1970
Oil on canvas; 146 x 114
Paris, Musée Picasso, MP 1990-39

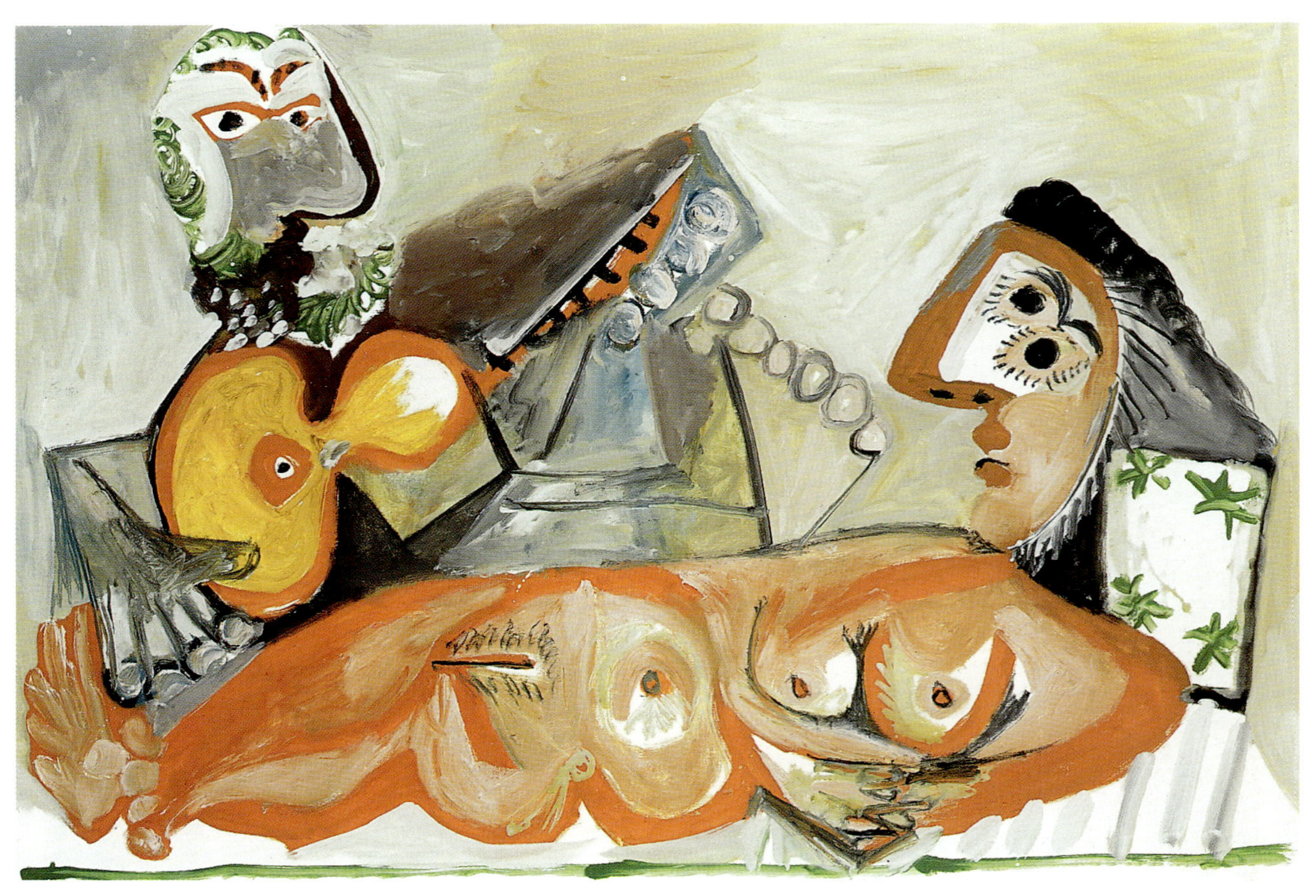

287 Reclining Nude and Man Playing Guitar, 27 October 1970
Oil on canvas; 130 x 195
Paris, Musée Picasso, MP 224 [P]

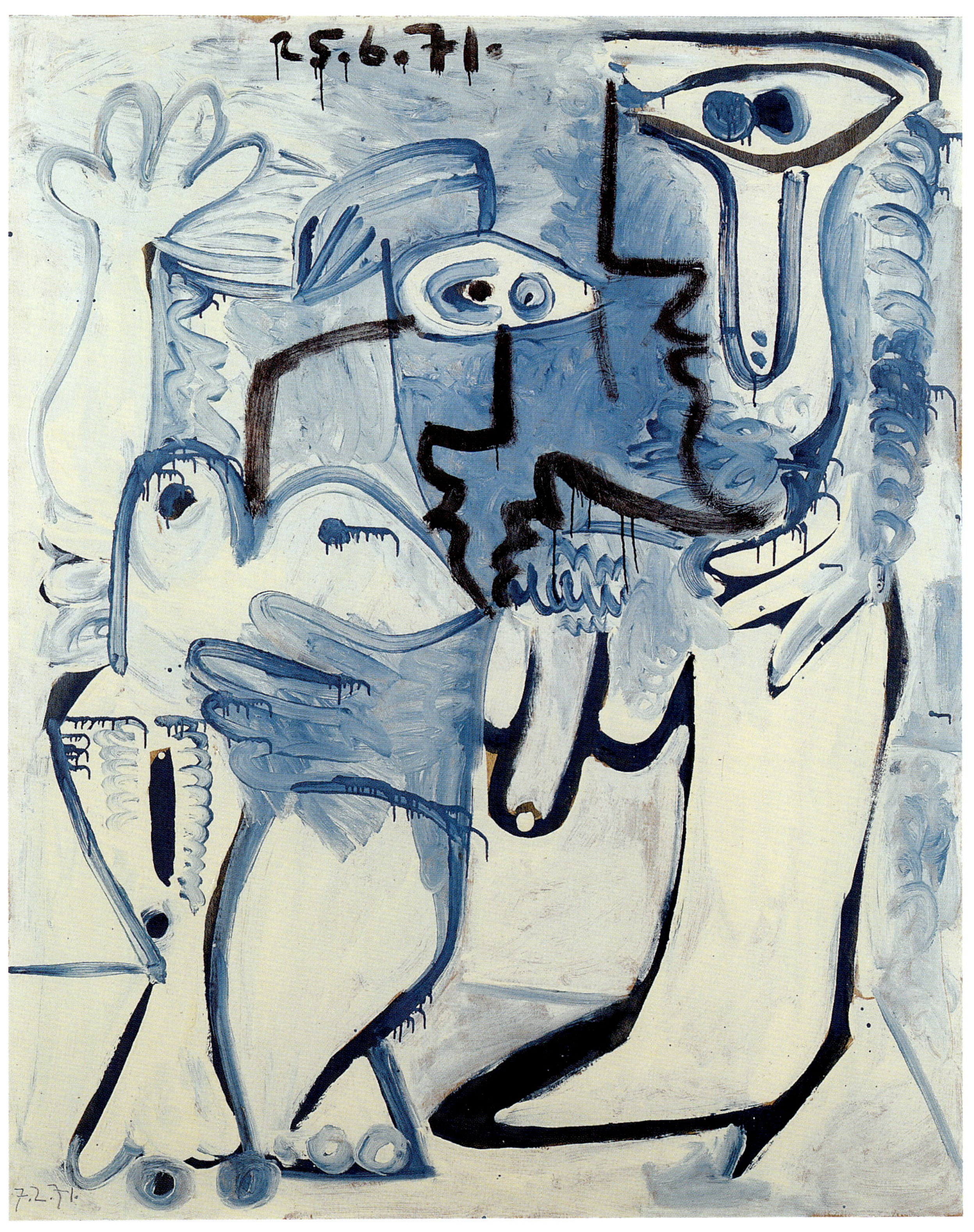

288 Couple, 1970–1971

Oil on canvas; 163.3 x 131.5
Paris, Musée Picasso, on deposit at Centre Georges-Pompidou, Musée national d'Art moderne, MP 1990-41

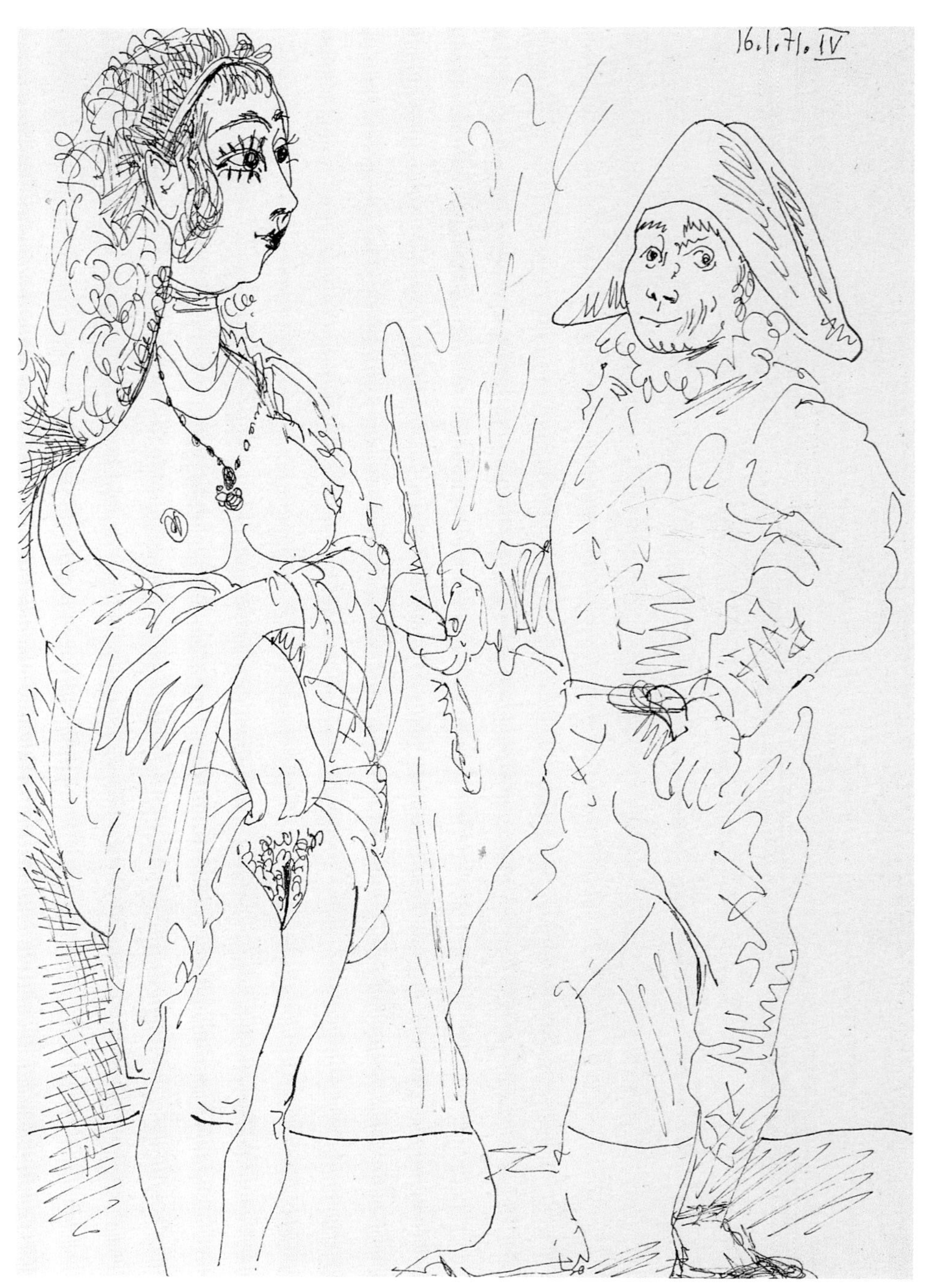

290 Harlequin with Wooden Sword and Young Woman, 16 January 1971 (IV)
India ink on white bristol board; 21.8 x 15.7
Arles, Musée Réattu, inv. 72-2-14

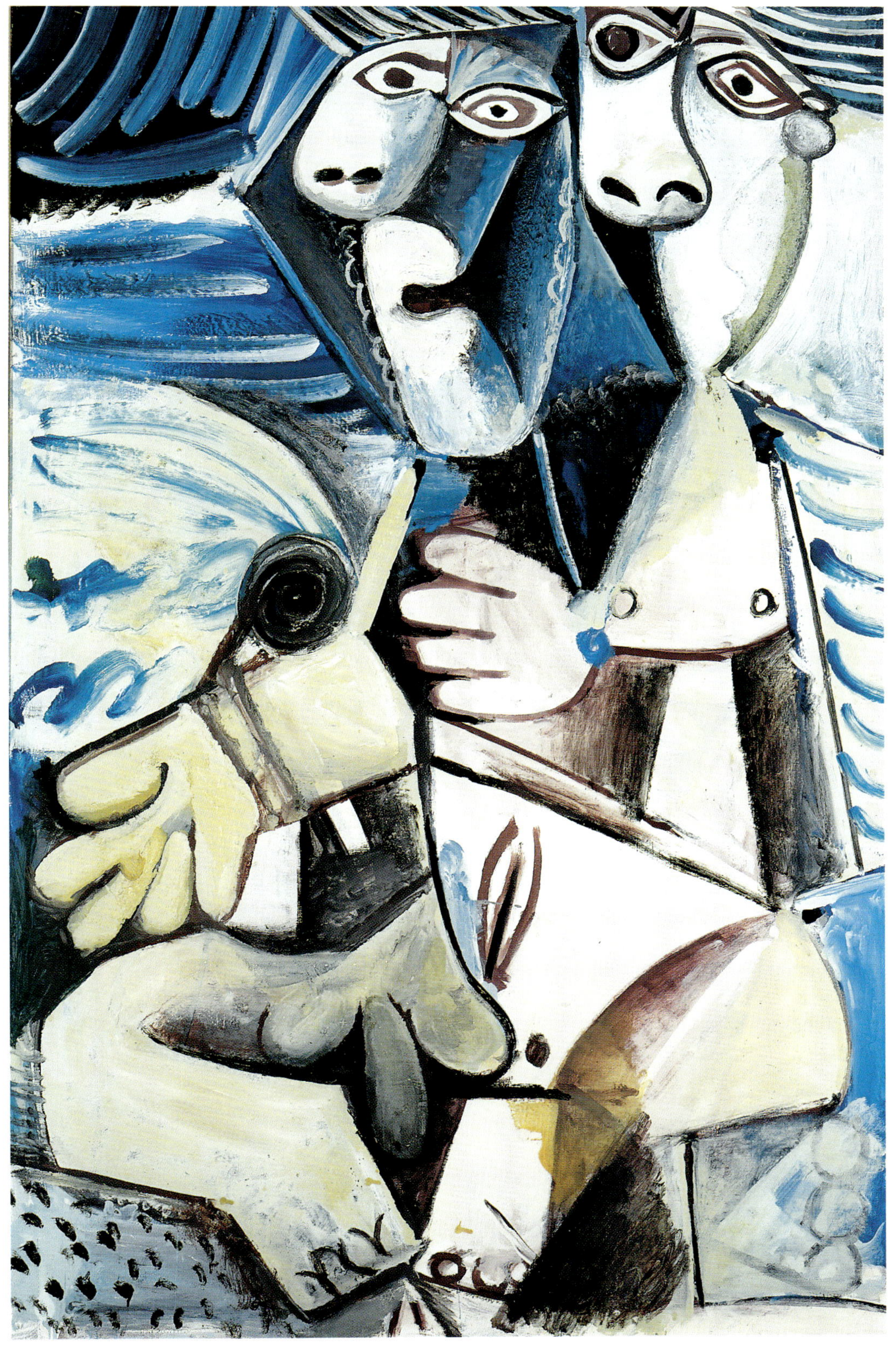

289 The Embrace, 1971

Oil on canvas; 195 x 130
The Montreal Museum of Fine Arts, Gift of Jacqueline Picasso

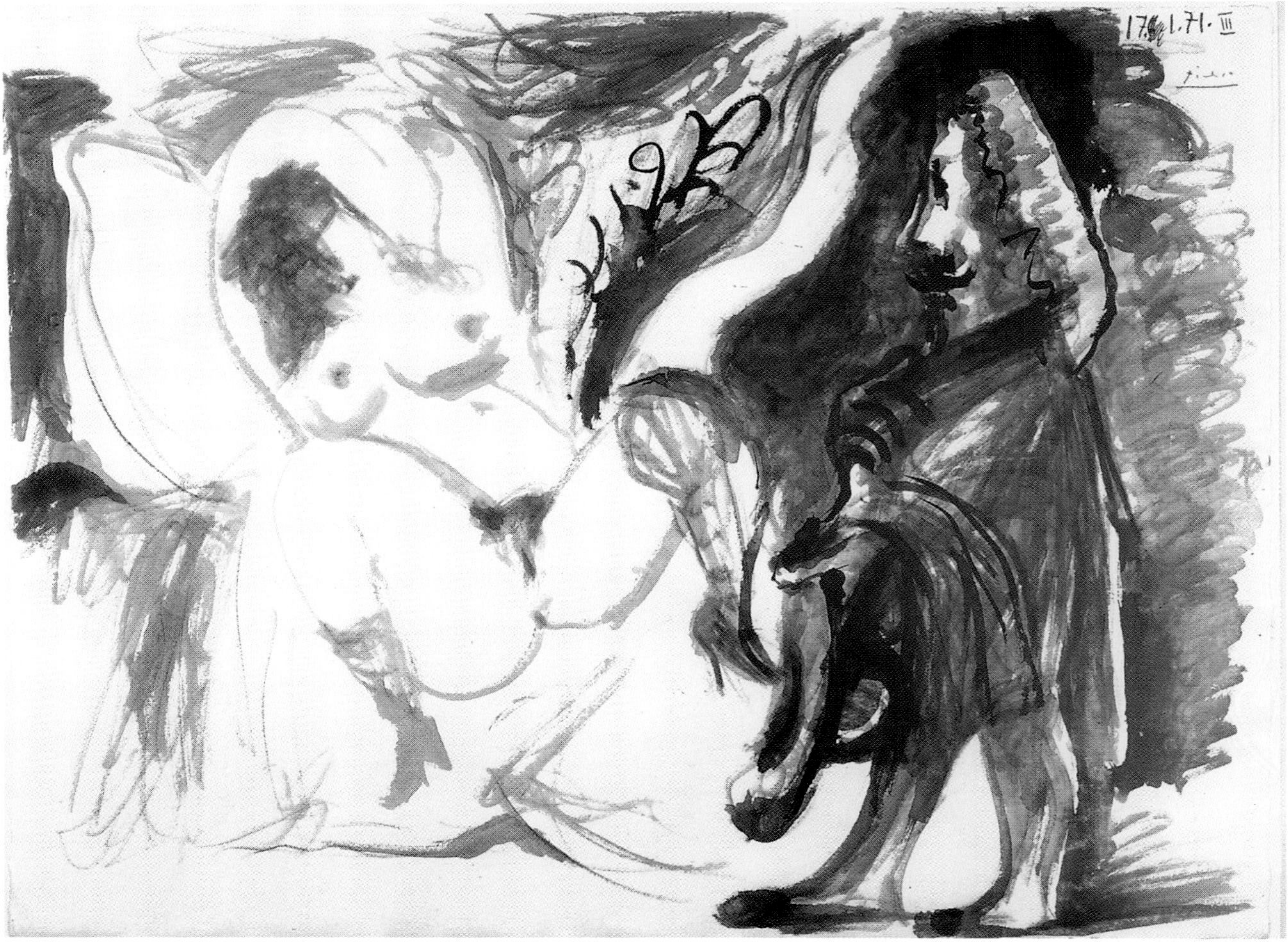

291 Man and Woman, 17 January 1971
Ink wash on paper; 58.4 x 79
Paris, Galerie Louise Leiris [PB]

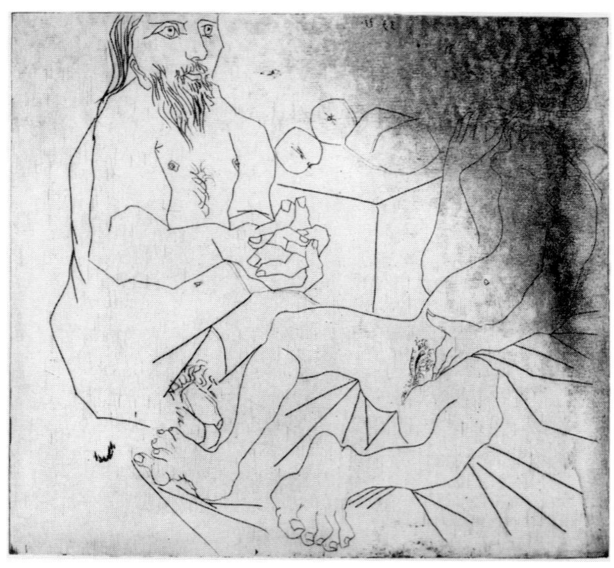

292 Couple with Bread and Apples, 3 March 1971
Drypoint on hard plastic matter; 49.7 x 55
Paris, Musée Picasso, MP 3154

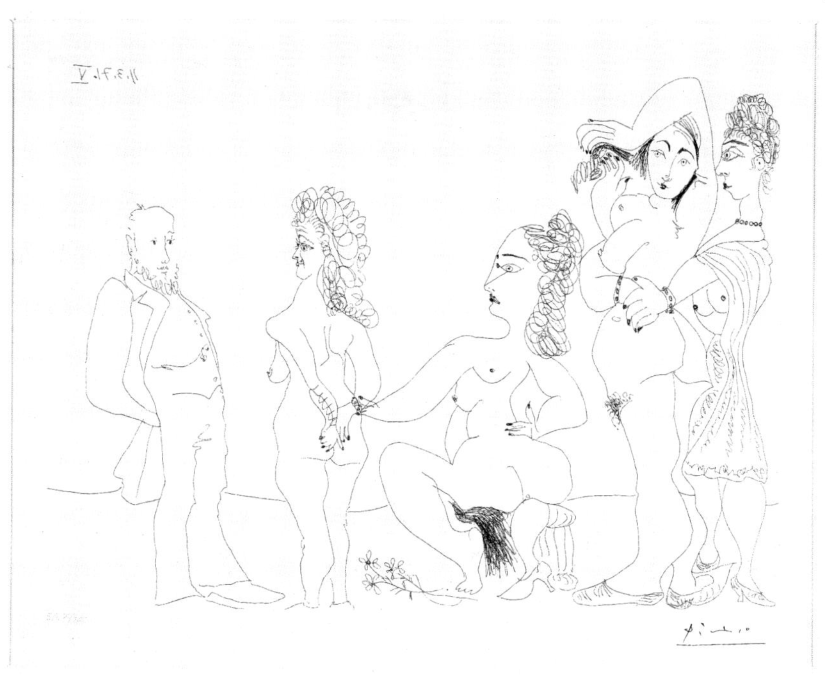

293 Degas at the Girls'. Degas First Appears, 11 March 1971

Etching on copper; 36.6 x 48.8
Paris, Musée Picasso, on deposit at the Musée d'Art moderne, Saint-Étienne, MP 1990-281* [PM]
Barcelona, Museu Picasso, MPB 112.231 [B]

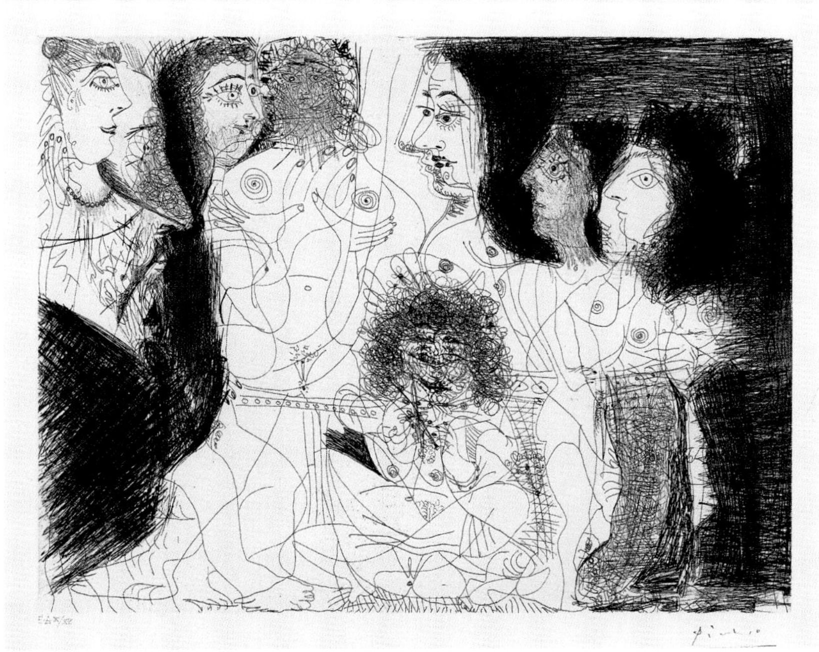

294 Degas at the Girls'. Rest and Intimacy, 11, 17 and 28 March 1971

Etching, drypoint, glasspaper and scraper on copper; State IV; 36.7 x 48.7
Paris, Bibliothèque nationale de France, Département des Estampes et de la Photographie [M]
Paris, Musée Picasso, on deposit at the Musée d'Art moderne, Saint-Étienne, MP 1990-282* [P]
Barcelona, Museu Picasso, MPB 112.216 [B]

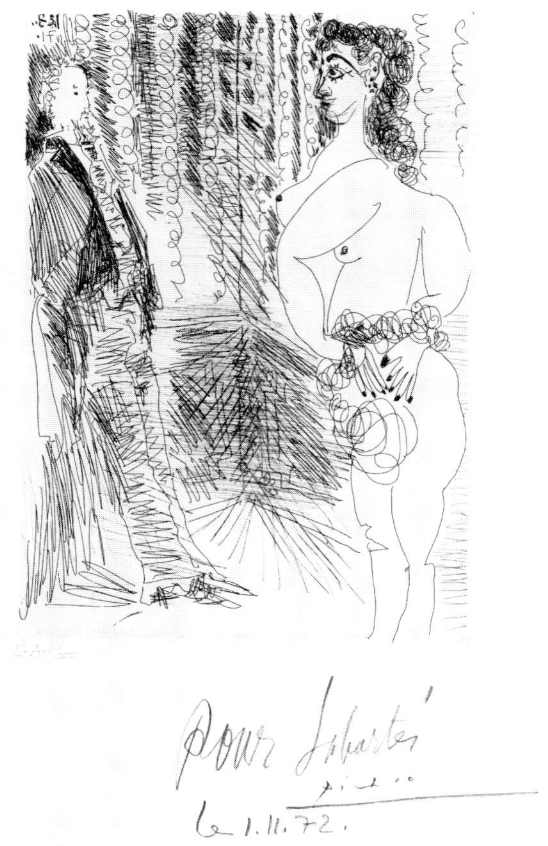

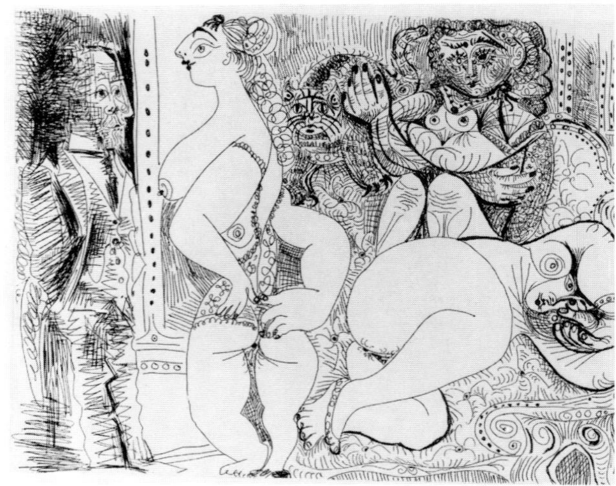

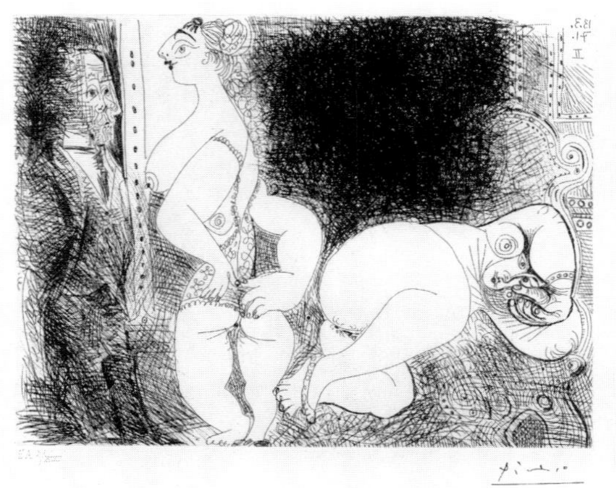

295 The Private Study. Degas and a Girl, 12 March 1971
   Etching, scraper and drypoint on copper; States I and II; 20.8 x 14.7
   Paris, Musée Picasso, MP 3129 [PM]
   Barcelona, Museu Picasso, MPB 112.289* [B]

296 a and b Girls at Rest with Degas Pondering, 13 March 1971
   Etching and drypoint on copper; States I and II; 22.9 x 30.6
   Paris, Musée Picasso, MP 3130 [PM]
   Barcelona, Museu Picasso, MPB 112.270 [B]

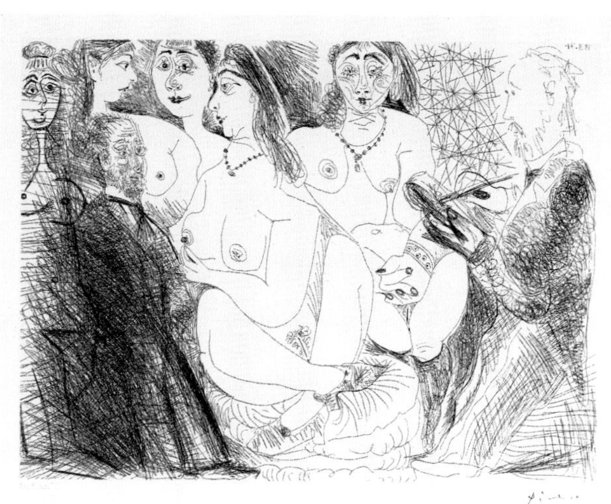

297 Degas, Jacketed, Drawing Himself in Tails, at the Girls',
   13 March 1971
   Etching on copper; 36.7 x 48.9
   Paris, Musée Picasso, on deposit at the Musée d'Art moderne,
   Saint-Étienne, MP 1990-283* [P]
   Paris, Bibliothèque nationale de France, Département des Estampes et de
   la Photographie [M]
   Barcelona, Museu Picasso, MPB 112.228 [B]

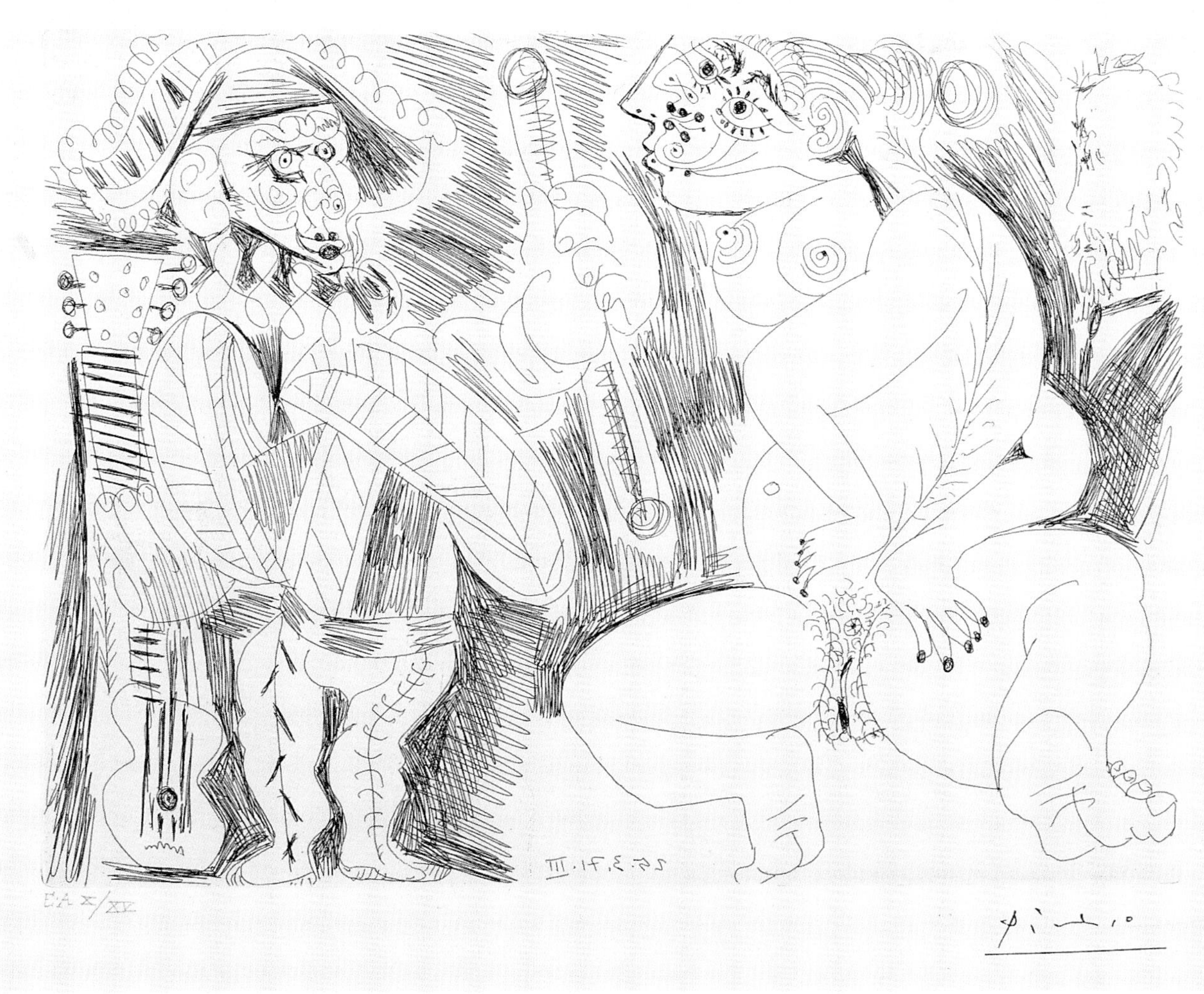

298 Seduction Scene between Polichinelle and a Girl with Degas as Voyeur, 25 March 1971

Etching on copper; 22.9 x 30.7
Paris, Musée Picasso, on deposit at the Musée d'Art moderne, Saint-Étienne, MP 1990-294* [P]
Paris, Bibliothèque nationale de France, Département des Estampes et de la Photographie [M]
Barcelona, Museu Picasso, MPB 112.271 [B]

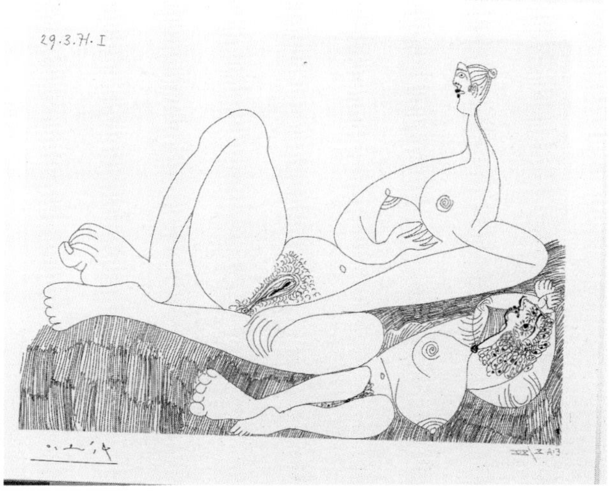

299 Rest. Two Nude Girls, 29 March 1971
Etching on copper; 22.9 x 30.5
Paris, Musée Picasso, on deposit at the Musée d'Art moderne,
Saint-Étienne, MP 1990-298* [PM]
Barcelona, Museu Picasso, MPB 112.280 [B]

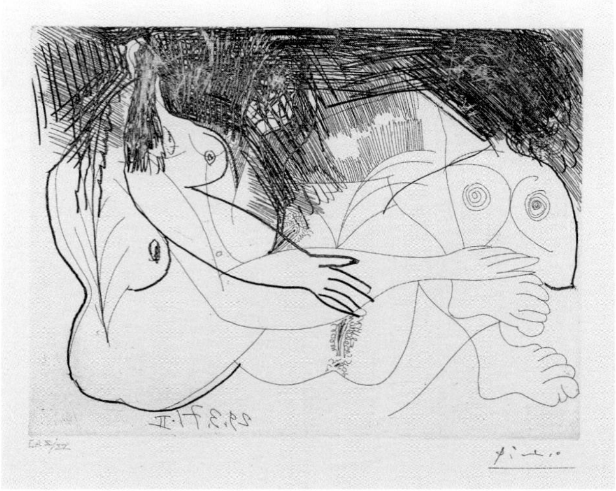

300 Two Girls at Rest, 29 March 1971
Etching on copper; 22.9 x 30.7
Paris, Musée Picasso, on deposit at the Musée d'Art moderne,
Saint-Étienne, MP 1990-299* [PM]
Barcelona, Museu Picasso, MPB 112.268 [B]

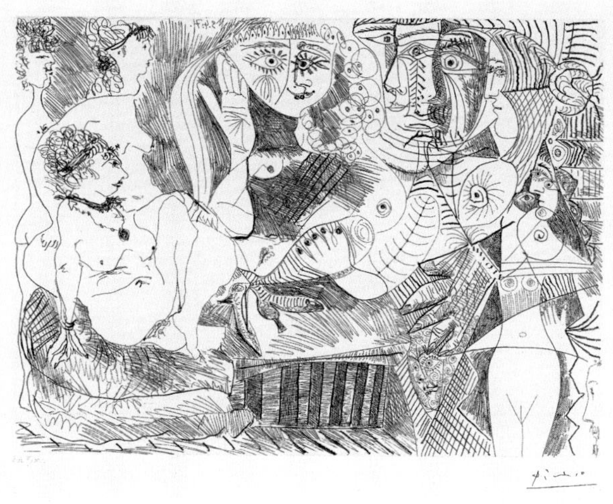

301 Degas the Visionary. Girl Listening to Her Girlfriends'
Stories at Rest, 3 April 1971
Etching on copper; 36.7 x 49.4
Paris, Musée Picasso, on deposit at the Musée d'Art moderne,
Saint-Étienne, MP 1990-308* [PM]
Barcelona, Museu Picasso, MPB 112.207 [B]

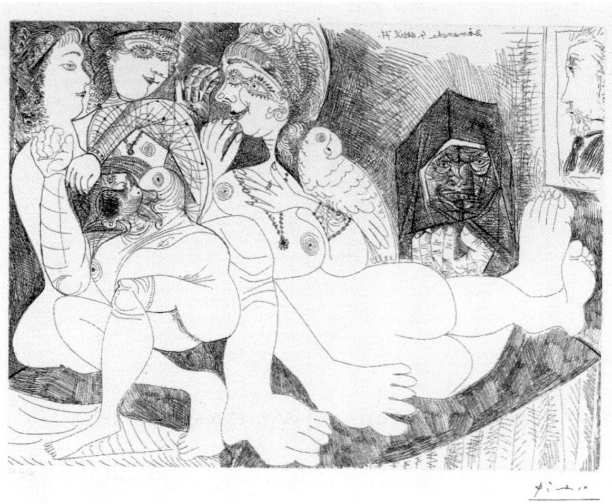

302 Maison Close. Prattlings, with Parrot, Celestina and
Degas' Portrait, 4 April 1971
Etching on copper; 36.7 x 49.4
Paris, Musée Picasso, on deposit at the Musée d'Art moderne,
Saint-Étienne, MP 1990-309* [P]
Paris, Bibliothèque nationale de France, Département des Estampes et
de la Photographie [M]
Barcelona, Museu Picasso, MPB 112.184 [B]

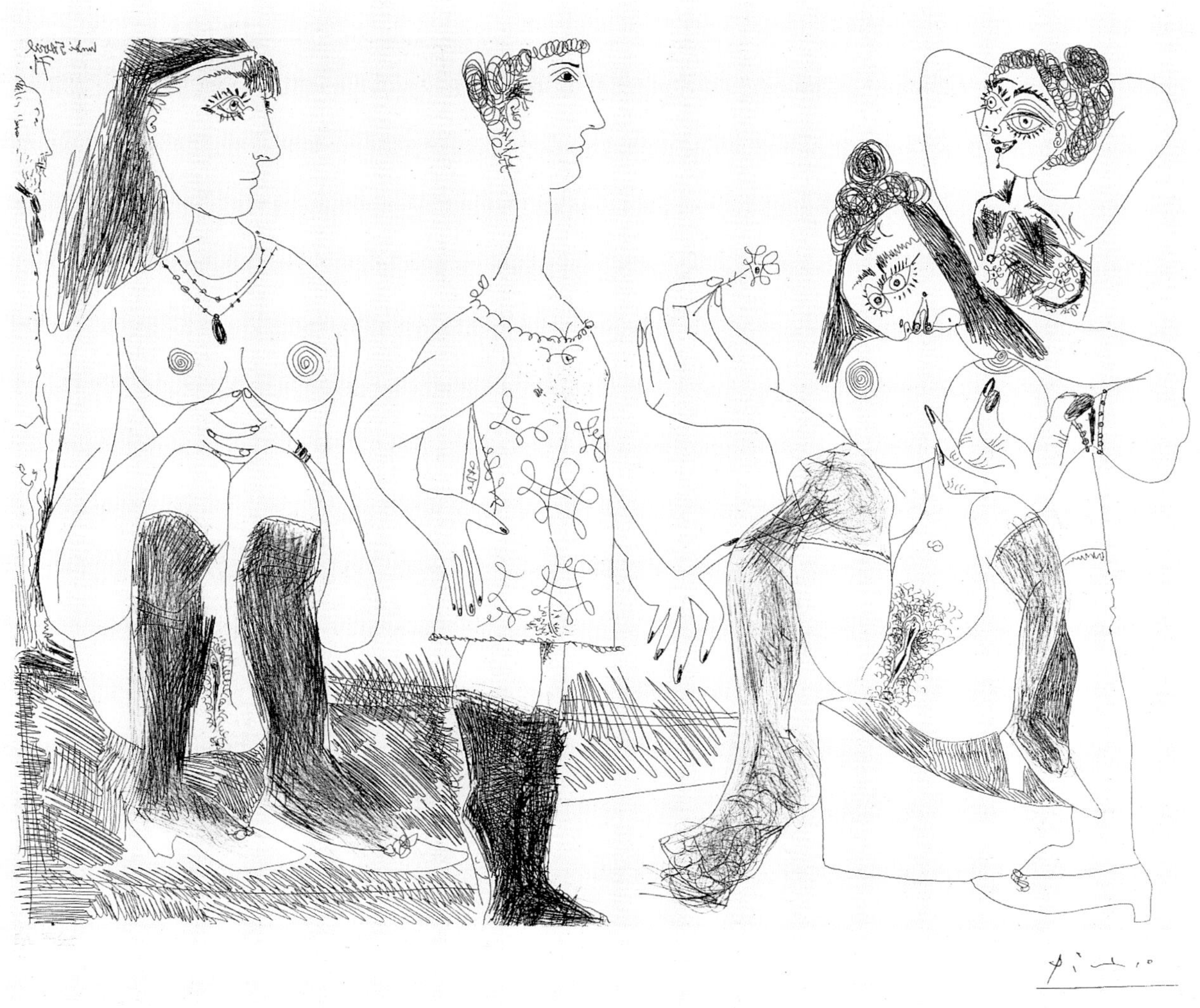

303 Degas Pondering. Girls to Themselves, 5 April 1971

Etching and glasspaper on copper; State II; 36.7 x 49.4
Paris, Musée Picasso, on deposit at the Musée d'Art moderne, Saint-Étienne, MP 1990-310* [P]
Paris, Bibliothèque nationale de France, Département des Estampes et de la Photographie [M]
Barcelona, Museu Picasso, MPB 112.185 [B]

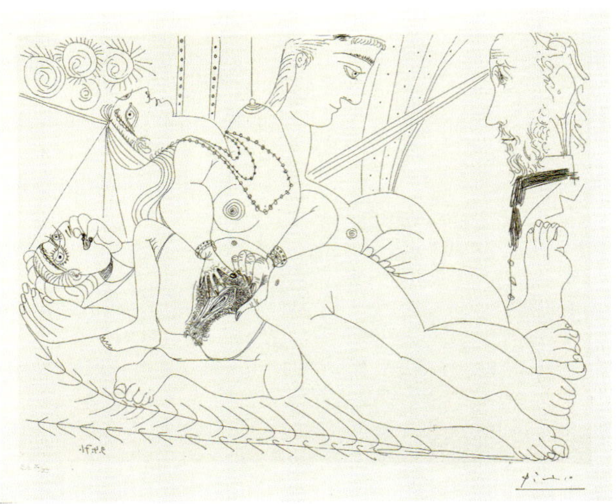

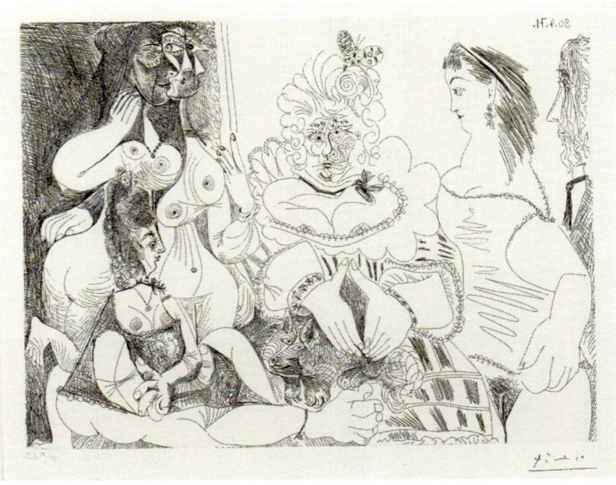

304 The Maison Tellier. Girls to Themselves.
Degas Flabbergasted, 9 April 1971

Etching on copper; 36.7 x 49.4
Paris, Musée Picasso, on deposit at the Musée d'Art moderne,
Saint-Étienne, MP 1990-311* [P]
Paris, Bibliothèque nationale de France, Département des Estampes et
de la Photographie [M]
Barcelona, Museu Picasso, MPB 112.225 [B]

306 The Proprietress's Party, with a Little Dog.
Degas with a Double Gaze, 30 April 1971

Etching on copper; 36.6 x 49.4
Paris, Musée Picasso, on deposit at the Musée d'Art moderne,
Saint-Étienne, MP 1990-316* [PM]
Barcelona, Museu Picasso, MPB 112.221 [B]

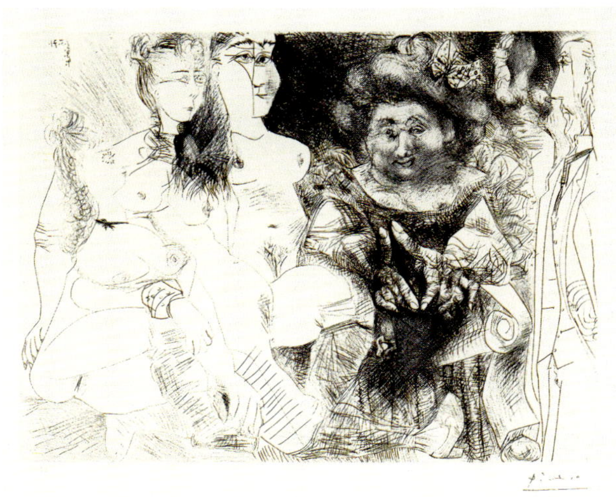

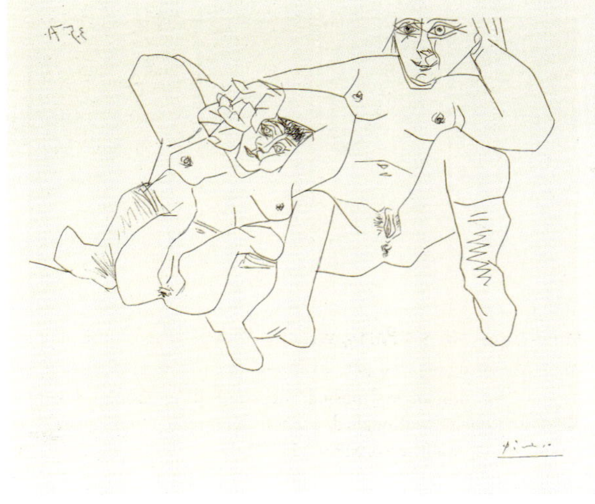

307 The Proprietress as Amateur Abortionist.
With Three Girls. Degas with Hands behind His Back,
1, 2, 3 and 4 May 1971

Drypoint and scraper on copper; 36.7 x 49.5
Paris, Musée Picasso, on deposit at the Musée d'Art moderne,
Saint-Étienne, MP 1990-317* [PM]
Paris, Bibliothèque nationale de France, Département des Estampes et
de la Photographie
Barcelona, Museu Picasso, MPB 112.234 [B]

308 Two Women Wearing Socks, 3 May 1971

Drypoint on copper; 36.5 x 49.3
Paris, Musée Picasso, on deposit at the Musée d'Art moderne,
Saint-Étienne, MP 1990-318* [P]
Barcelona, Museu Picasso, MPB 112.222 [B]

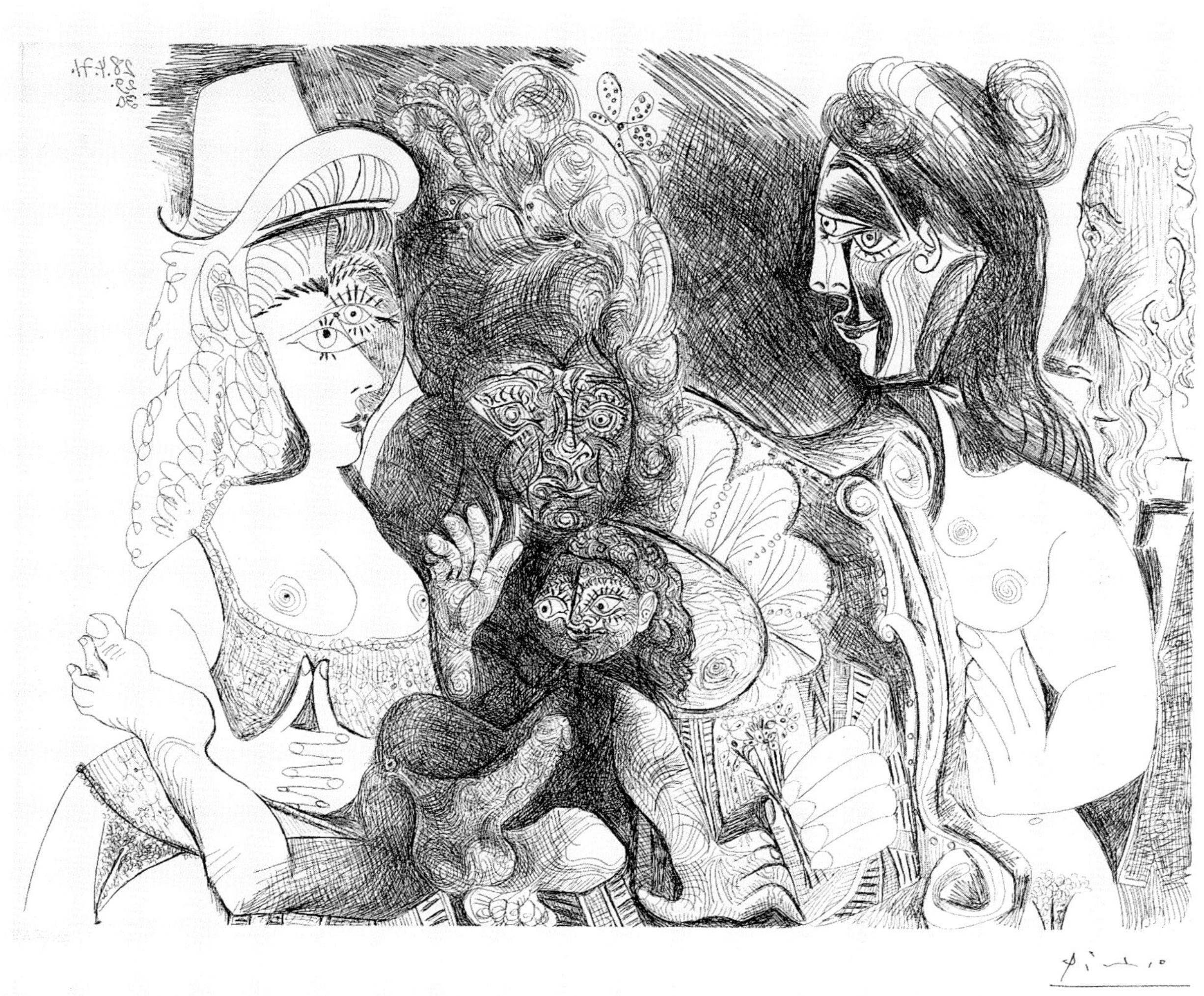

305 The Proprietress's Party, with an Ithyphallic Cupid. Degas Red-nosed, 28, 29 and 30 April 1971

Etching on copper; 36.7 x 49.2
Paris, Musée Picasso, on deposit at the Musée d'Art moderne, Saint-Étienne, MP 1990-315* [P]
Paris, Bibliothèque nationale de France, Département des Estampes et de la Photographie [M]
Barcelona, Museu Picasso, MPB 112.197 [B]

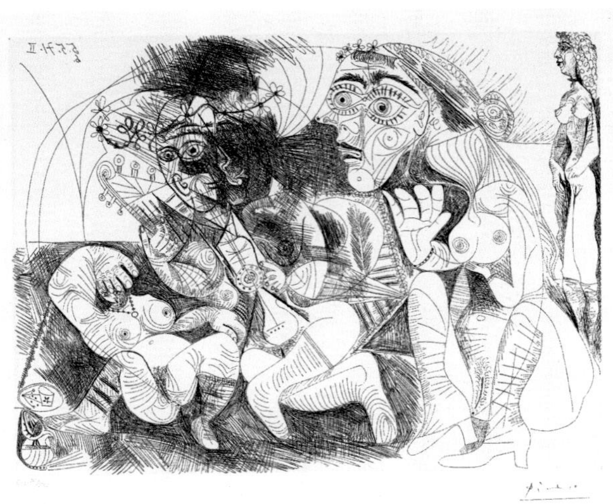

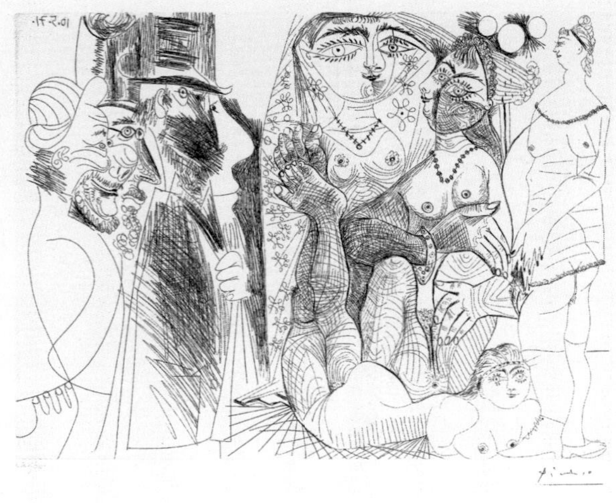

309 **Girls to Themselves. Musical Recreation,** 5 and 6 May 1971

Etching on copper; 36.6 x 49.2
Paris, Musée Picasso, on deposit at the Musée d'Art moderne,
Saint-Étienne, MP 1990-320* [PM]
Barcelona, Museu Picasso, MPB 112.209 [B]

310 **The Maison Tellier. Arrival of the Clients,** 10 May 1971

Etching on copper; 36.7 x 49.4
Paris, Musée Picasso, on deposit at the Musée d'Art moderne,
Saint-Étienne, MP 1990-321* [P]
Paris, Bibliothèque nationale de France, Département des Estampes et
de la Photographie [M]
Barcelona, Museu Picasso, MPB 112.201 [B]

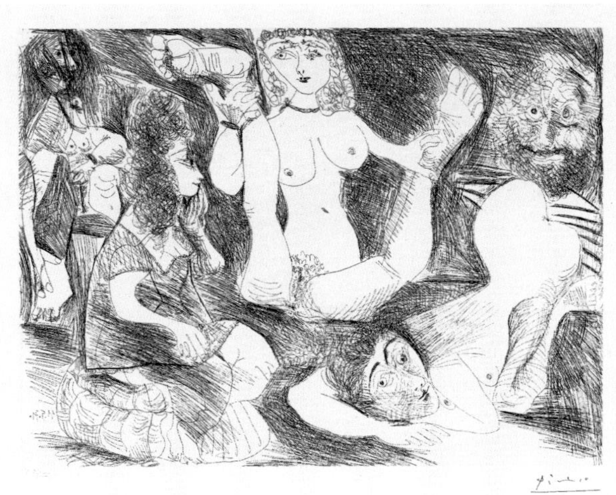

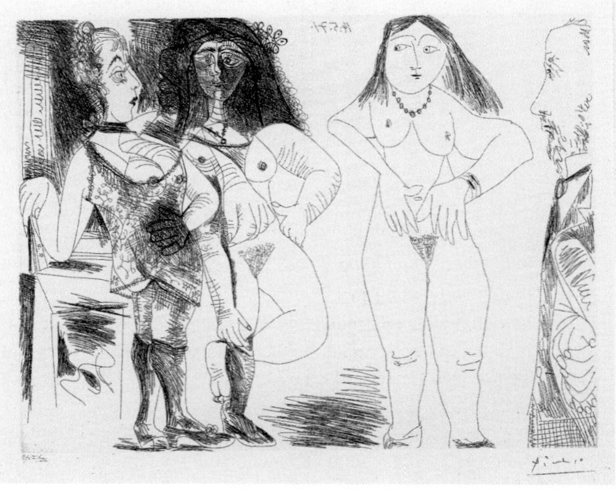

311 **Midnight Bath. Women Surprised by a Beaming Sailor,**
11 May 1971

Etching on copper; 36.6 x 49.4
Paris, Musée Picasso, on deposit at the Musée d'Art moderne,
Saint-Étienne, MP 1990-323* [P]
Paris, Bibliothèque nationale de France, Département des Estampes et
de la Photographie [M]
Barcelona, Museu Picasso, MPB 112.196

312 **Degas at the Girls'. The Bill,** 14 May 1971

Etching on copper; 36.7 x 49.1
Paris, Musée Picasso, on deposit at the Musée d'Art moderne,
Saint-Étienne, MP 1990-326* [PM]
Barcelona, Museu Picasso, MPB 112.250 [B]

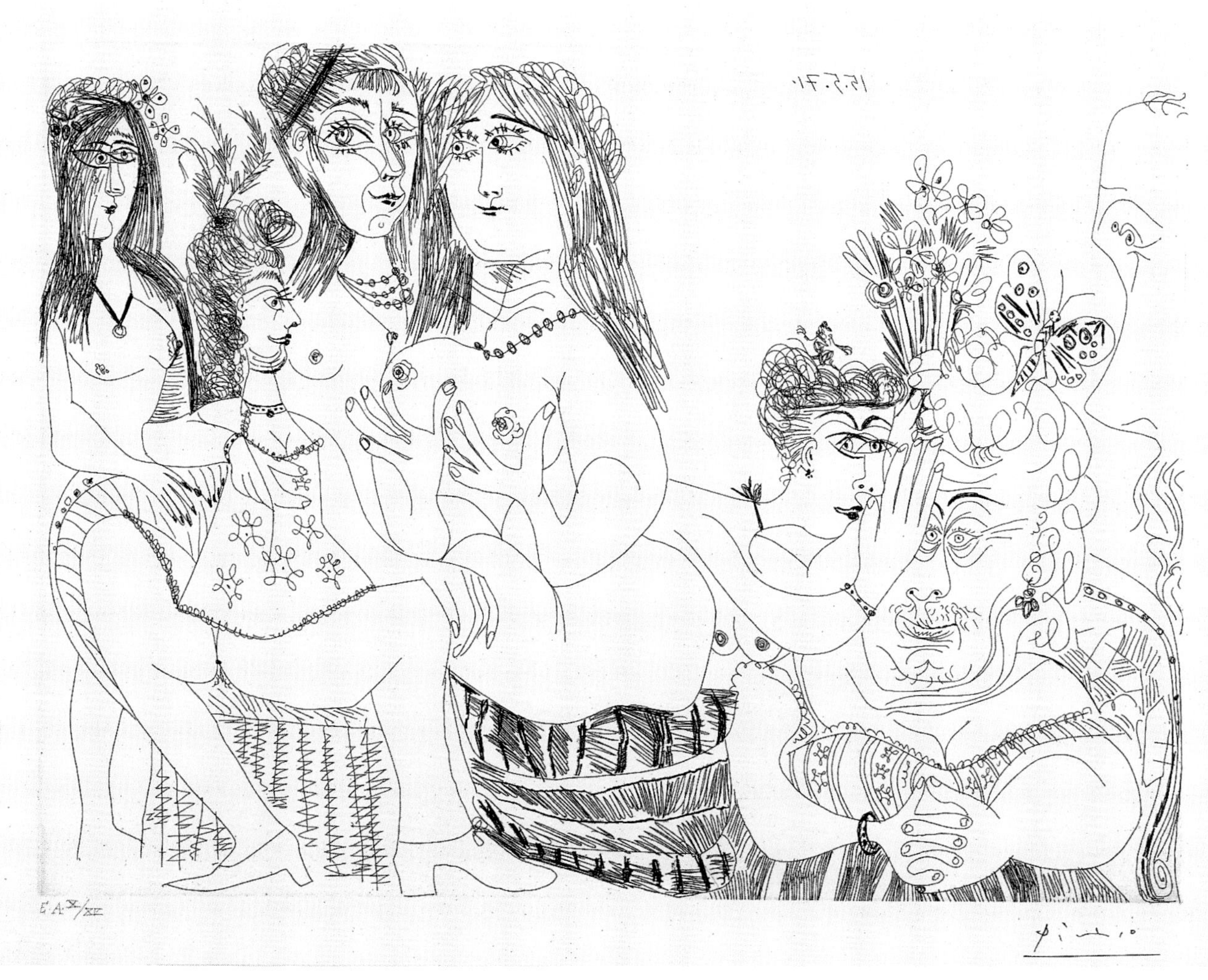

313 The Proprietress's Party. The Women Slander Degas, Reduced to One-Third Profile, 15 May 1971

Etching on copper; 36.6 x 49.3
Paris, Musée Picasso, on deposit at the Musée d'Art moderne, Saint-Étienne, MP 1990-327* [p]
Paris, Bibliothèque nationale de France, Département des Estampes et de la Photographie [M]
Barcelona, Museu Picasso, MPB 112.223 [B]

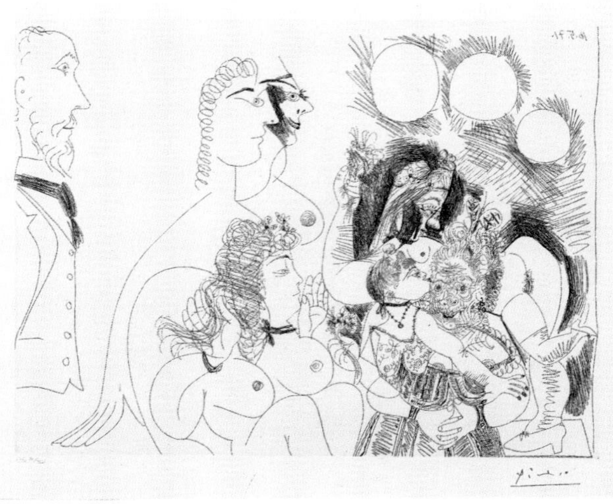

314 The Proprietress's Party. Flowers and Kisses.
Degas Enjoys Himself, 16 May 1971

Etching on copper; 36.6 x 49.2
Paris, Musée Picasso, on deposit at the Musée d'Art moderne,
Saint-Étienne, MP 1990-328* [PM]
Barcelona, Museu Picasso, MPB 112.211 [B]

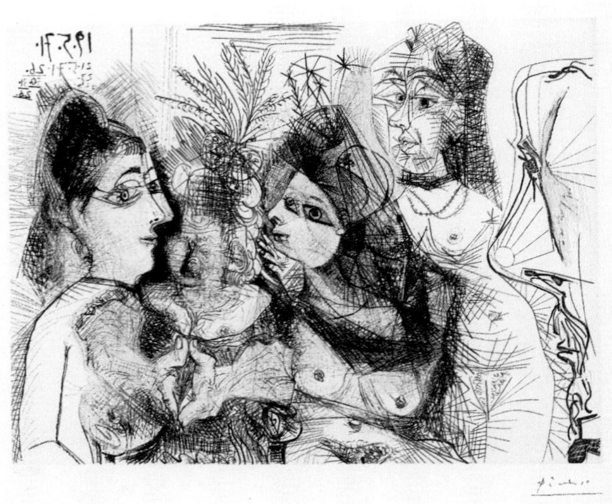

316 Maison Close. Slanderings. With Profile of Degas,
Nose Wrinkled, 19, 21, 23, 24, 26, 30, 31 May and 2 June 1971

Sugar-lift aquatint, scraper and drypoint on copper; States VI and VII;
36.7 x 49.6
Paris, Musée Picasso, on deposit at the Musée d'Art moderne,
Saint-Étienne, MP 1990-330 [PM]
Barcelona, Museu Picasso, MPB 112.208 [B]
Paris, Musée Picasso, MP 3140* [P]

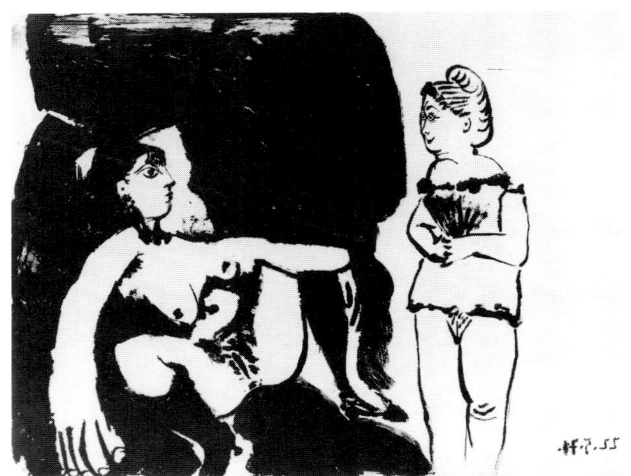

317 Girls to Themselves. The Madam, 22 May 1971

Sugar-lift aquatint; State I; 36.6 x 49.3
Paris, Musée Picasso, MP 3143 [P]

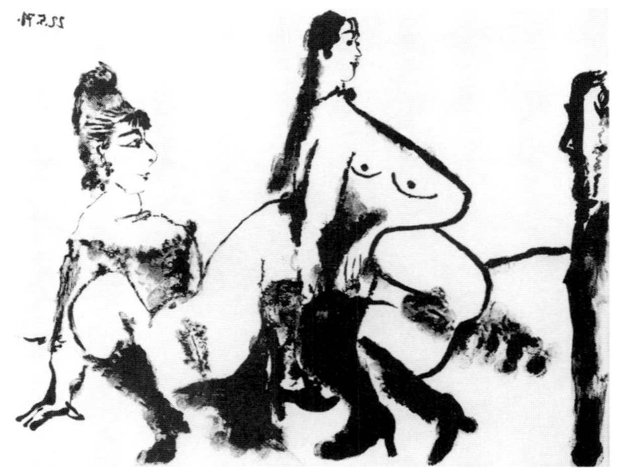

318 Degas Pays and Leaves. The Girls Are Not Kind,
22 May 1971

Sugar-lift aquatint, scraper and drypoint on copper; State I; 36.6 x 49.3
Paris, Musée Picasso, MP 3141 [P]

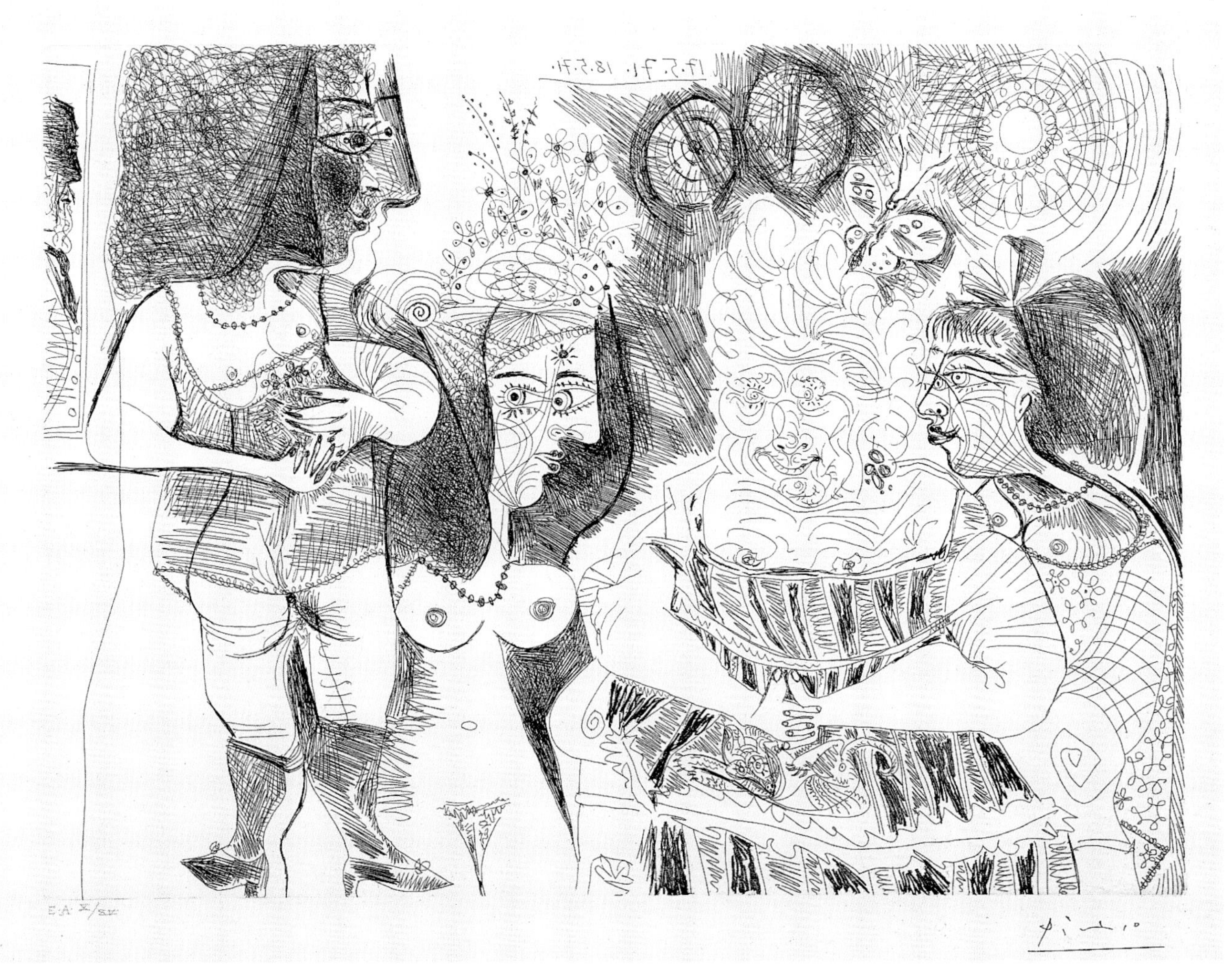

315 The Proprietress's Party. Little Dog, Flowers and Gossip. Portrait of Degas on the Wall, 17 and 18 May 1971

Etching on copper; 36.5 x 49.1
Paris, Musée Picasso, on deposit at the Musée d'Art moderne, Saint-Étienne, MP 1990-329* [PM]
Barcelona, Museu Picasso, MPB 112.212 [B]

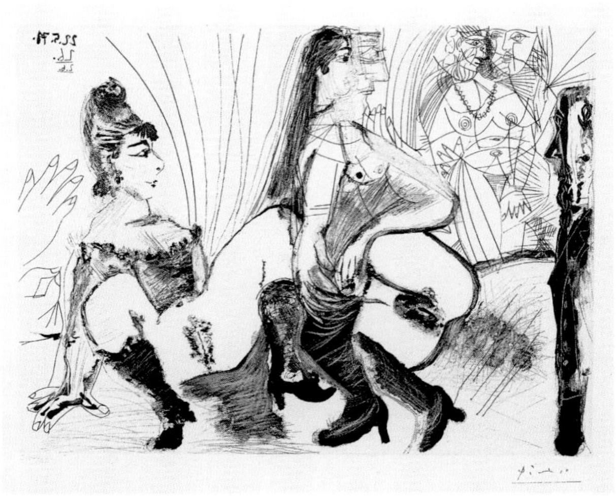

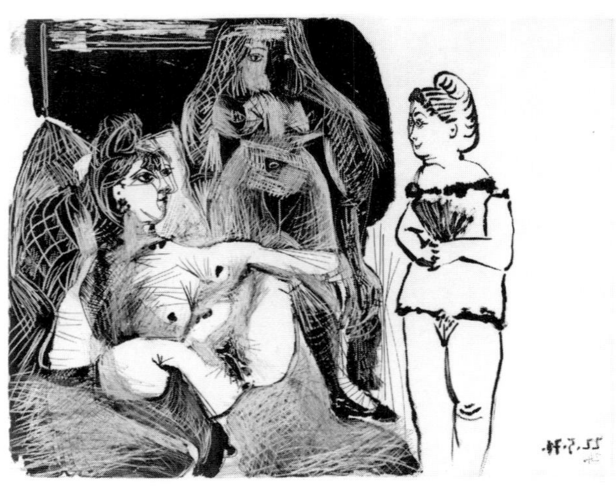

319 Degas Pays and Leaves. The Girls Are Not Kind,
22 and 26 May and 2 June 1971
Sugar-lift aquatint, scraper and drypoint on copper; State III;
36.6 x 49.2
Paris, Musée Picasso, on deposit at the Musée d'Art moderne,
Saint-Étienne, MP 1990-333* [P]
Paris, Bibliothèque nationale de France,
Département des Estampes et de la Photographie [M]
Barcelona, Museu Picasso, MPB 112.210 [B]

320 Girls to Themselves. The Madam, 24 May 1971
Sugar-lift aquatint, scraper and drypoint on copper; State II;
36.6 x 49.3
Paris, Musée Picasso, MP 3144 [M]

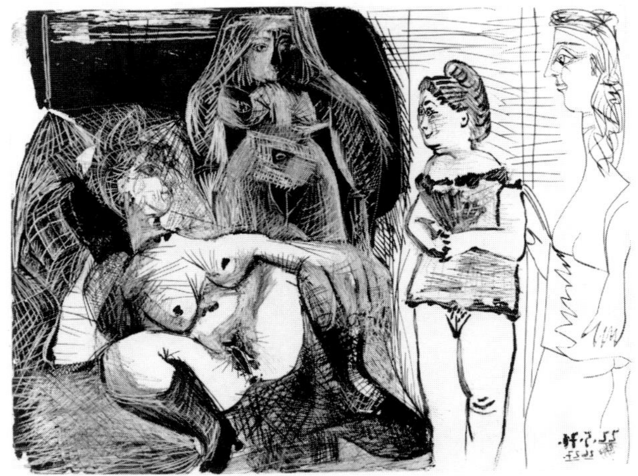

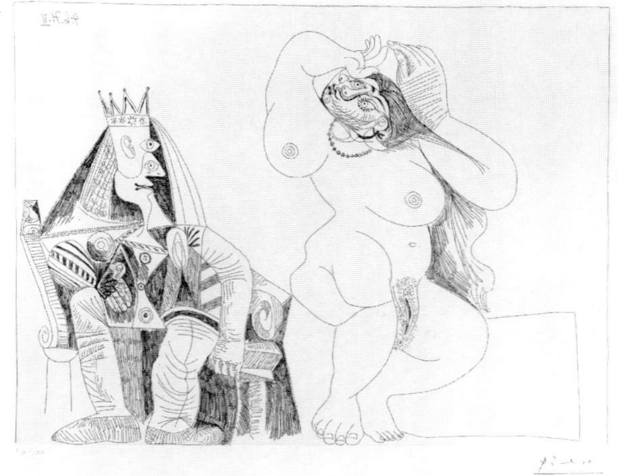

321 Girls to Themselves. The Madam, 26 and 27 May 1971
Sugar-lift aquatint, scraper and drypoint on copper;
State III; 36.6 x 49.3
Paris, Musée Picasso, MP 3145 [B]

323 Salome Dancing for Herod, 4 June 1971
Etching on copper; 36.6 x 49.3
Barcelona, Museu Picasso, MPB 112.218 [B]

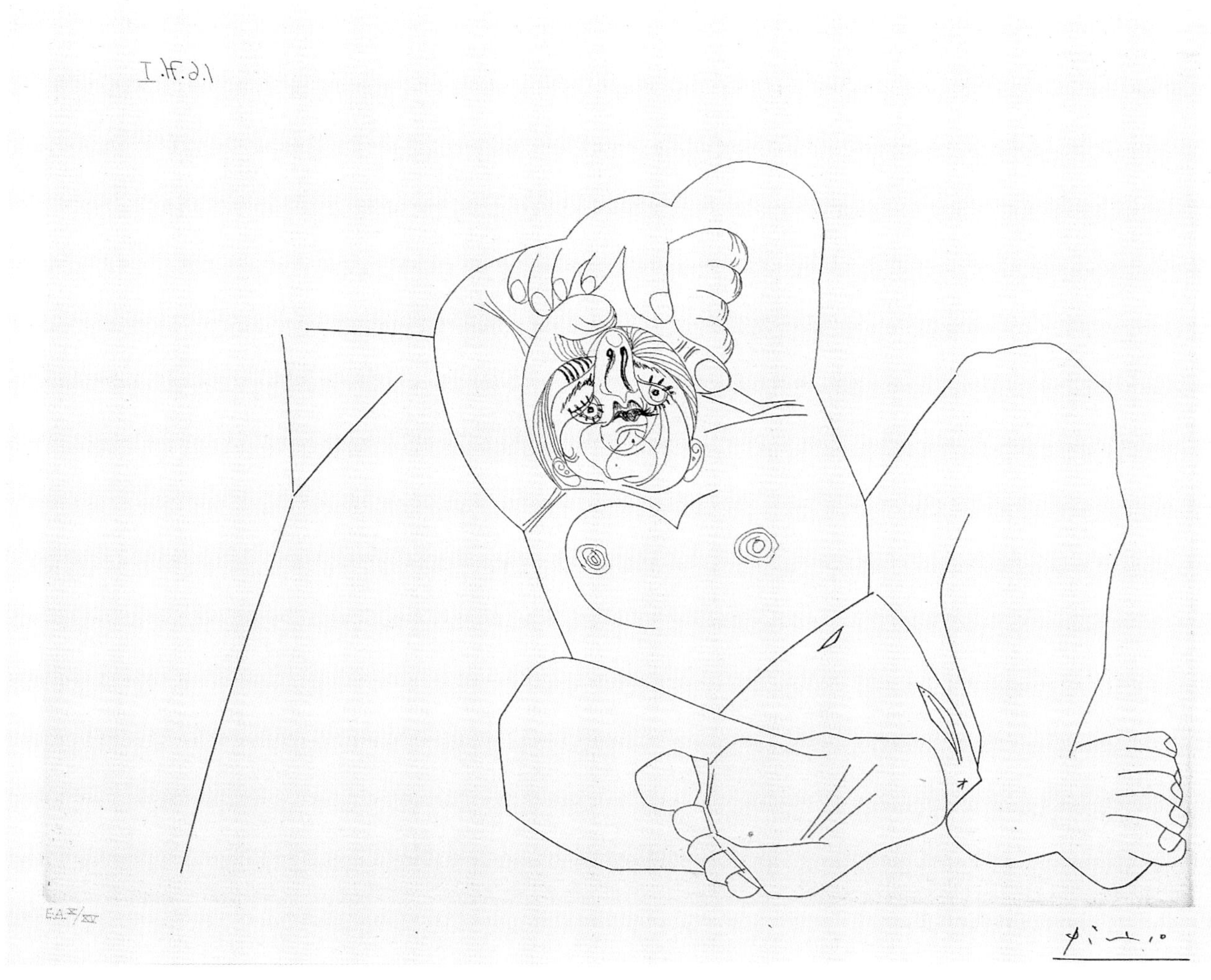

322 Woman with a Big Nose, Foreshortened, on a Bed, 1 June 1971

Etching on copper; 36.8 x 49.6
Paris, Musée Picasso, on deposit at the Musée d'Art moderne, Saint-Étienne, MP 1990-338* [PM]
Barcelona, Museu Picasso, MPB 112.202 [B]

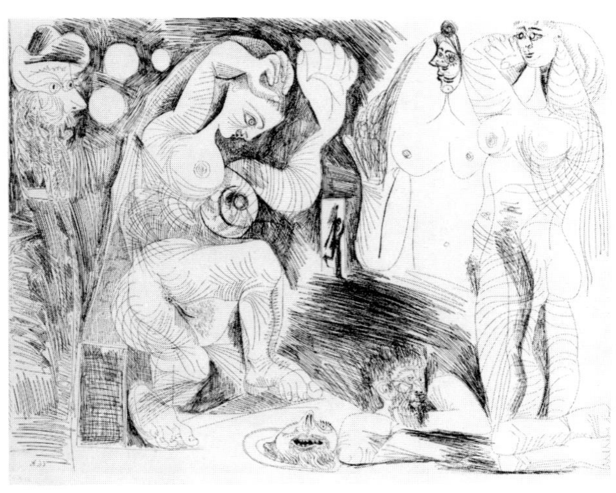

325 The Maison Tellier. Two Girls Fantasizing: Salome
Dancing Her Love for the Head of Saint John the Baptist,
6 June 1971

Etching on copper; 36.4 x 49.4
Paris, Musée Picasso, MP 1990-343* [P]
Paris, Bibliothèque nationale de France,
Département des Estampes et de la Photographie [M]
Barcelona, Museu Picasso, MPB 112.193 [B]

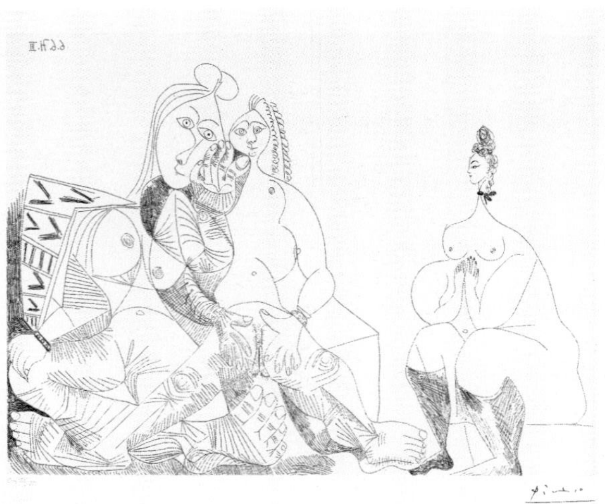

326 Maison Close. Rest and Prattlings, 6 June 1971

Etching on copper; 36.8 x 49.5
Paris, Musée Picasso, on deposit at the Musée d'Art moderne,
Saint-Étienne, MP 1990-344* [PM]
Barcelona, Museu Picasso, MPB 112.229 [B]

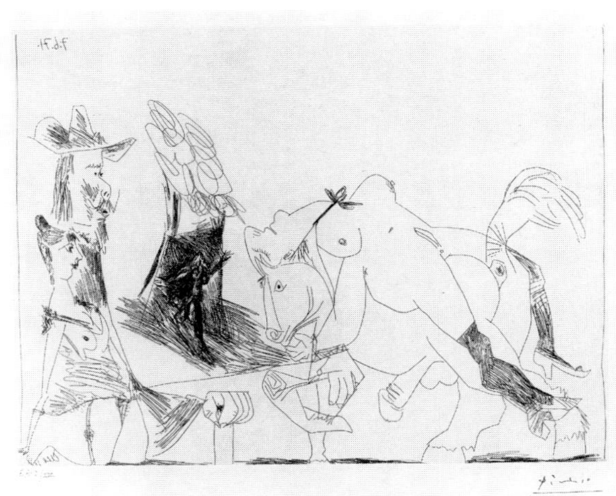

327 Remembrances. Spain. With Woman Swooning on
an Amorous Horse, 17 June 1971

Etching on copper; 36.6 x 49.4
Paris, Bibliothèque nationale de France,
Département des Estampes et de la Photographie [M]
Barcelona, Museu Picasso, MPB 112.183* [B]

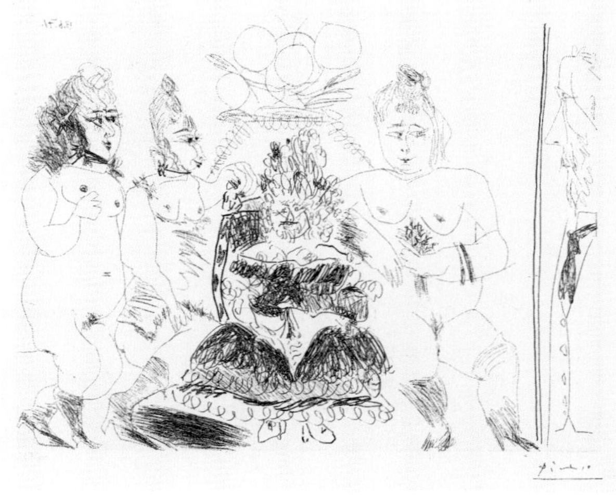

328 The Maison Tellier. The Proprietress's Party.
Degas behind a Window, 13 June 1971

Etching on copper; 36.7 x 49.5
Paris, Musée Picasso, on deposit at the Musée d'Art moderne,
Saint-Étienne, MP 1990-349* [P]
Paris, Bibliothèque nationale de France,
Département des Estampes et de la Photographie [M]
Barcelona, Museu Picasso, MPB 112.235 [B]

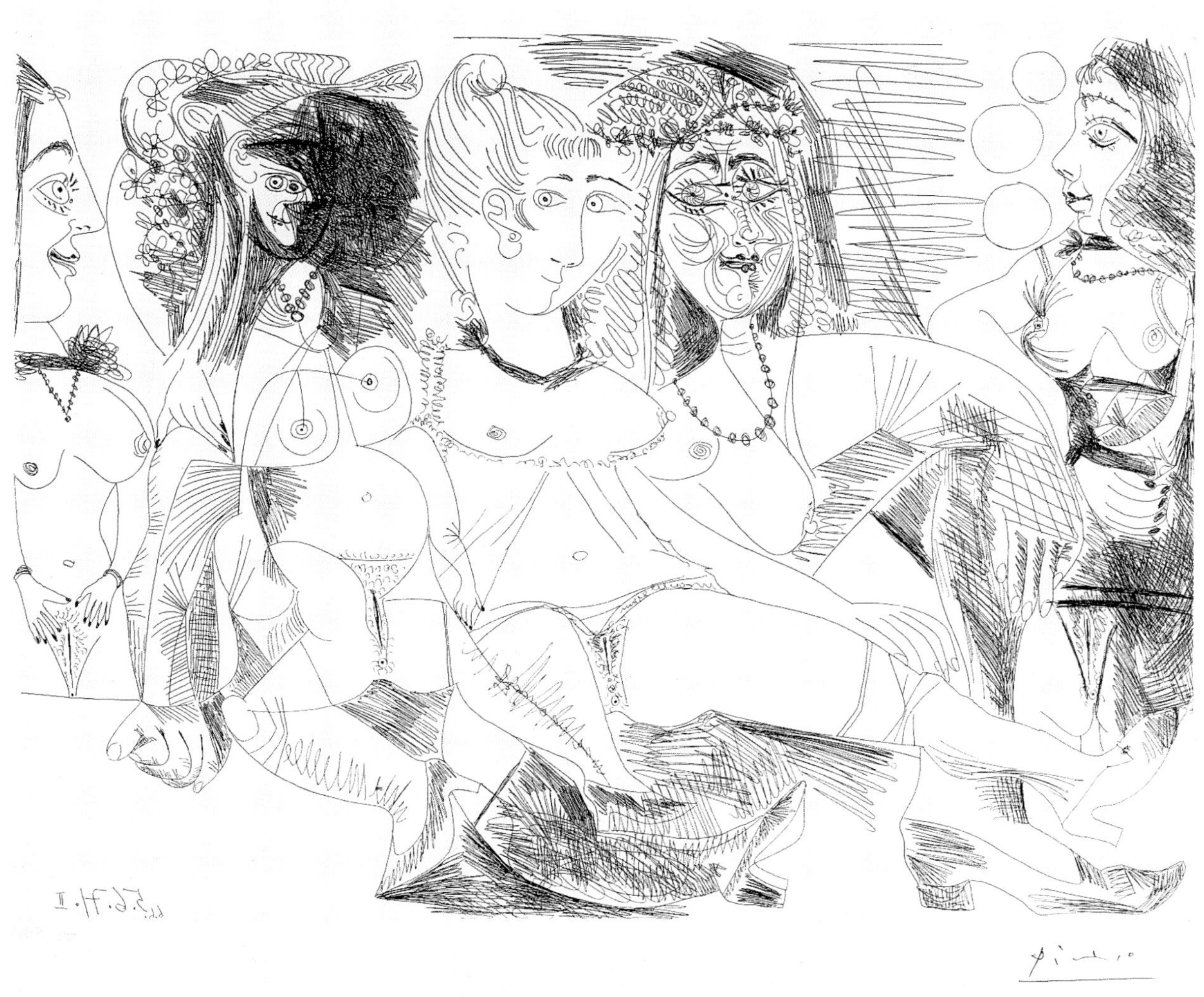

324 The Maison Tellier: Girls to Themselves, 5 and 6 June 1971

Etching on copper; 36.6 x 49.3
Paris, Musée Picasso, on deposit at the Musée d'Art moderne, Saint-Étienne, MP 1990-342* [PM]
Barcelona, Museu Picasso, MPB 112.219 [B]

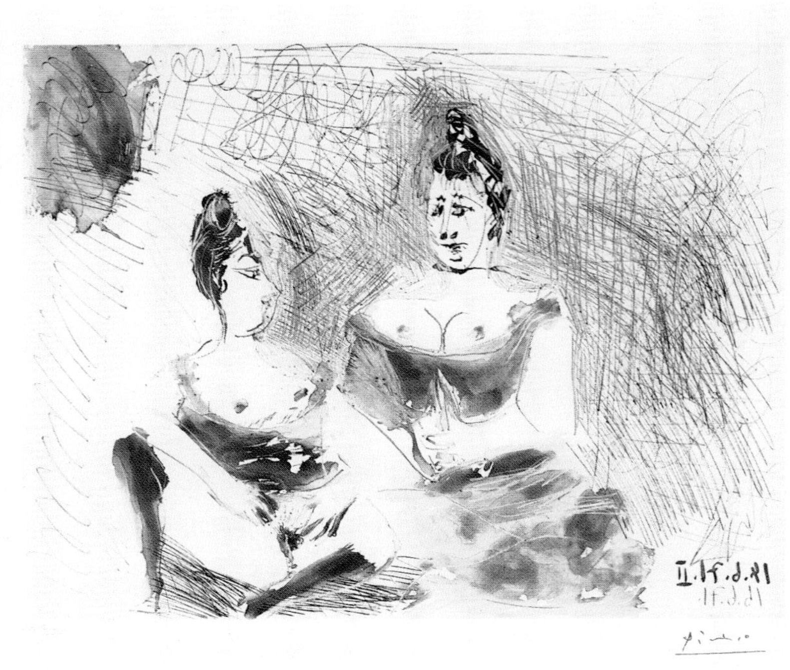

329 Rest. Two Girls, 14 and 16 June 1971

Aquatint, drypoint and direct scraper on copper; 31.6 x 41.8
Paris, Musée Picasso, on deposit at the Musée d'Art moderne, Saint-Étienne, MP 1990-351* [PM]
Barcelona, Museu Picasso, MPB 112.250 [B]

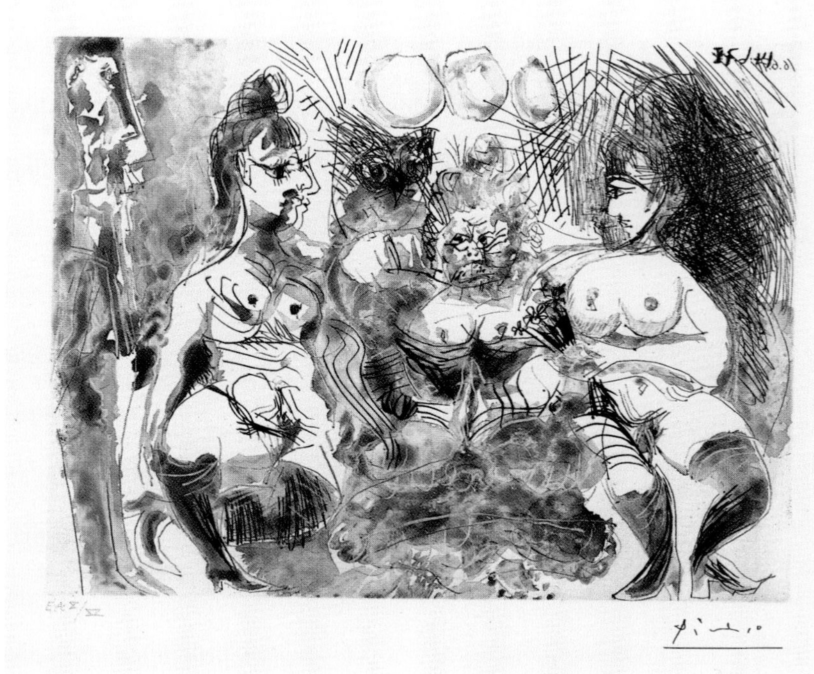

330 The Maison Tellier. The Proprietress's Party. Owl. Degas Leaning against the Wall, 14 and 16 June 1971

Aquatint, drypoint and scraper on copper; 22.9 x 30.7
Paris, Musée Picasso, on deposit at the Musée d'Art moderne, Saint-Étienne, MP 1990-350* [PM]
Barcelona, Museu Picasso, MPB 112.269 [B]

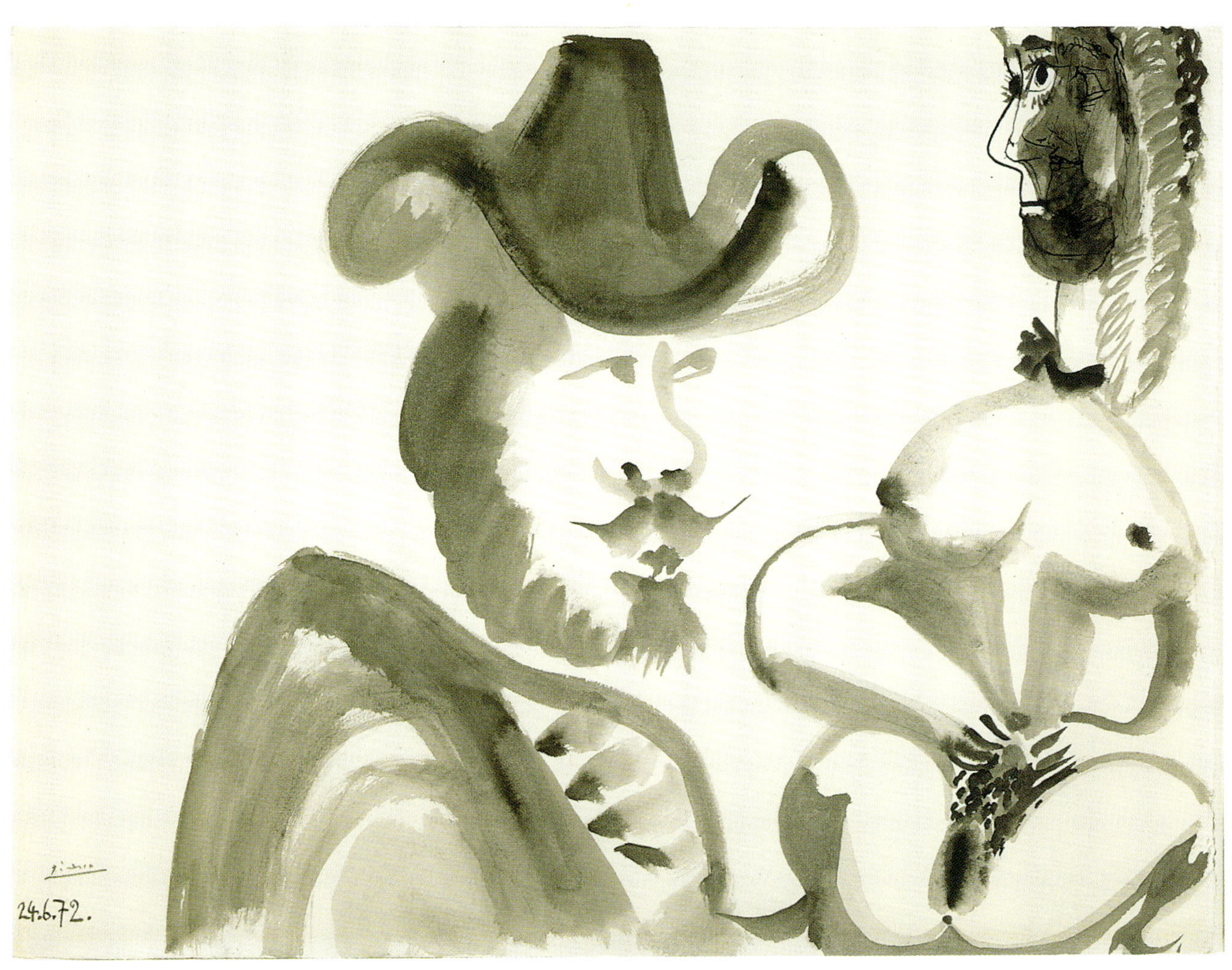

332 Seated Nude and Bust of Man with Hat, 1972

Ink on paper; 50 x 75.5
Montreal, Landau Fine Art

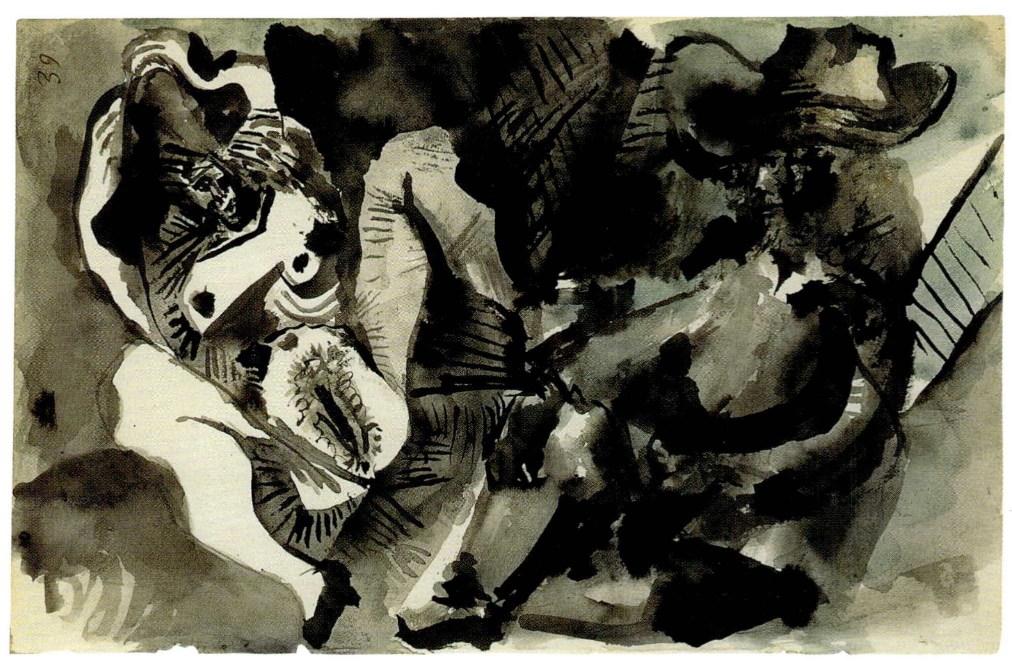

331 Musketeer and Nude Woman, 1972
India ink, wash and watercolour on paper; 22.5 x 35.2
Paris, Musée Picasso, MP 1540

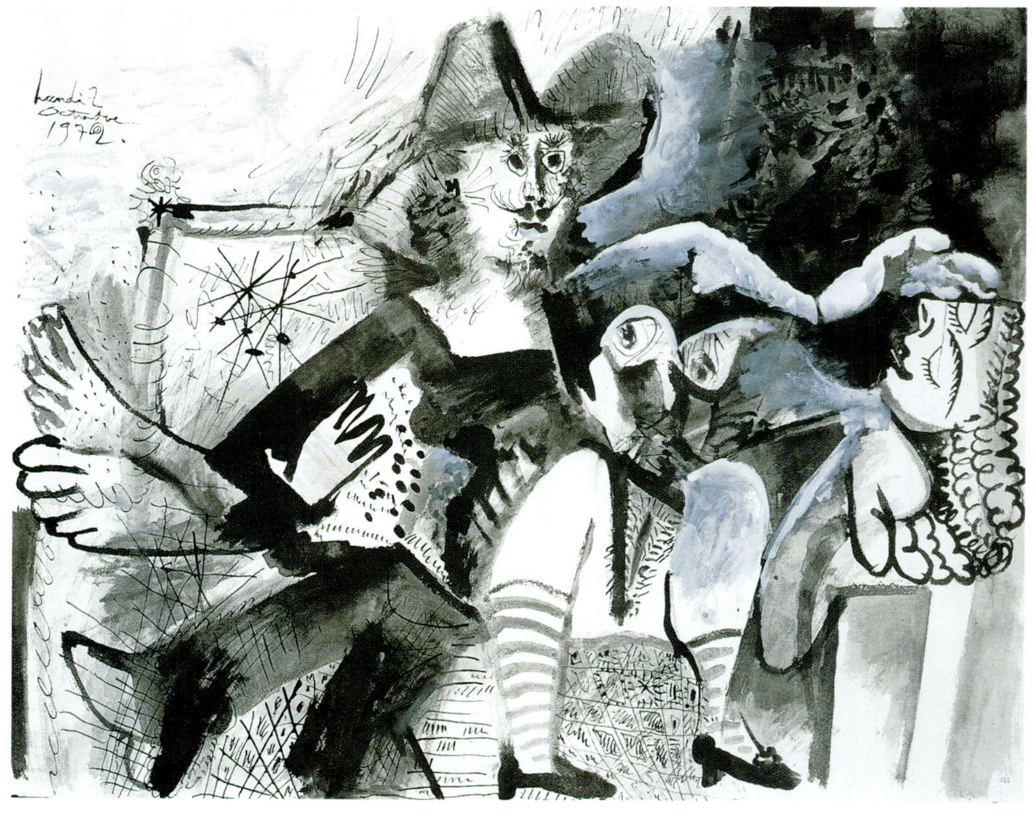

331 a Musketeer and Nude Woman, Interior, 2 October 1972
Pen, India ink and wash with gouache highlights on paper; 58 x 75.8
Geneva, Courtesy Galerie Jan Krugier, Ditesheim & Co. [B]

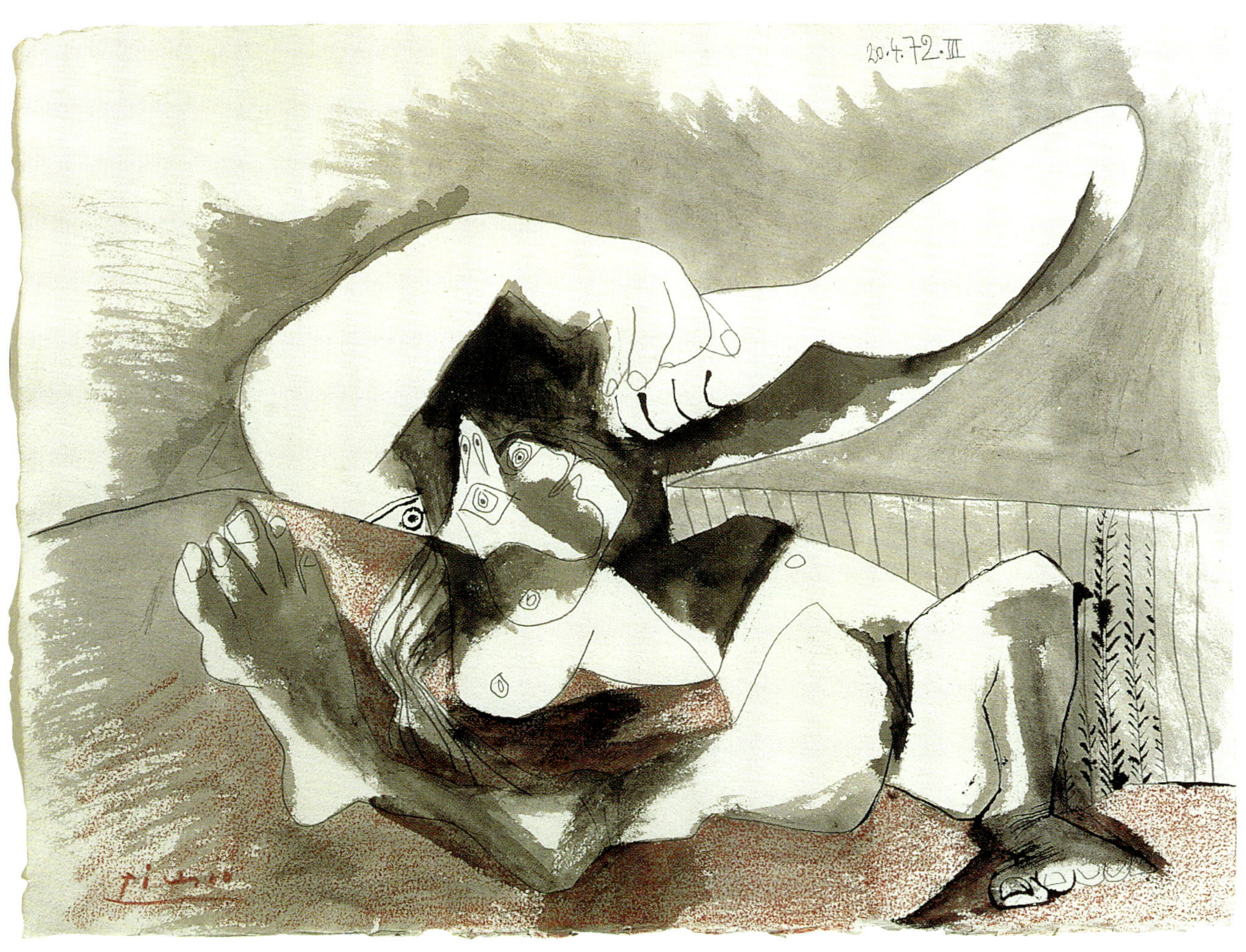

333 Reclining Nude, 20 April 1972 (III)

India ink wash, gouache and coloured pencil on paper; 56.5 x 75
Belfort, Musée d'Art et d'Histoire, Gift of Maurice Jardot

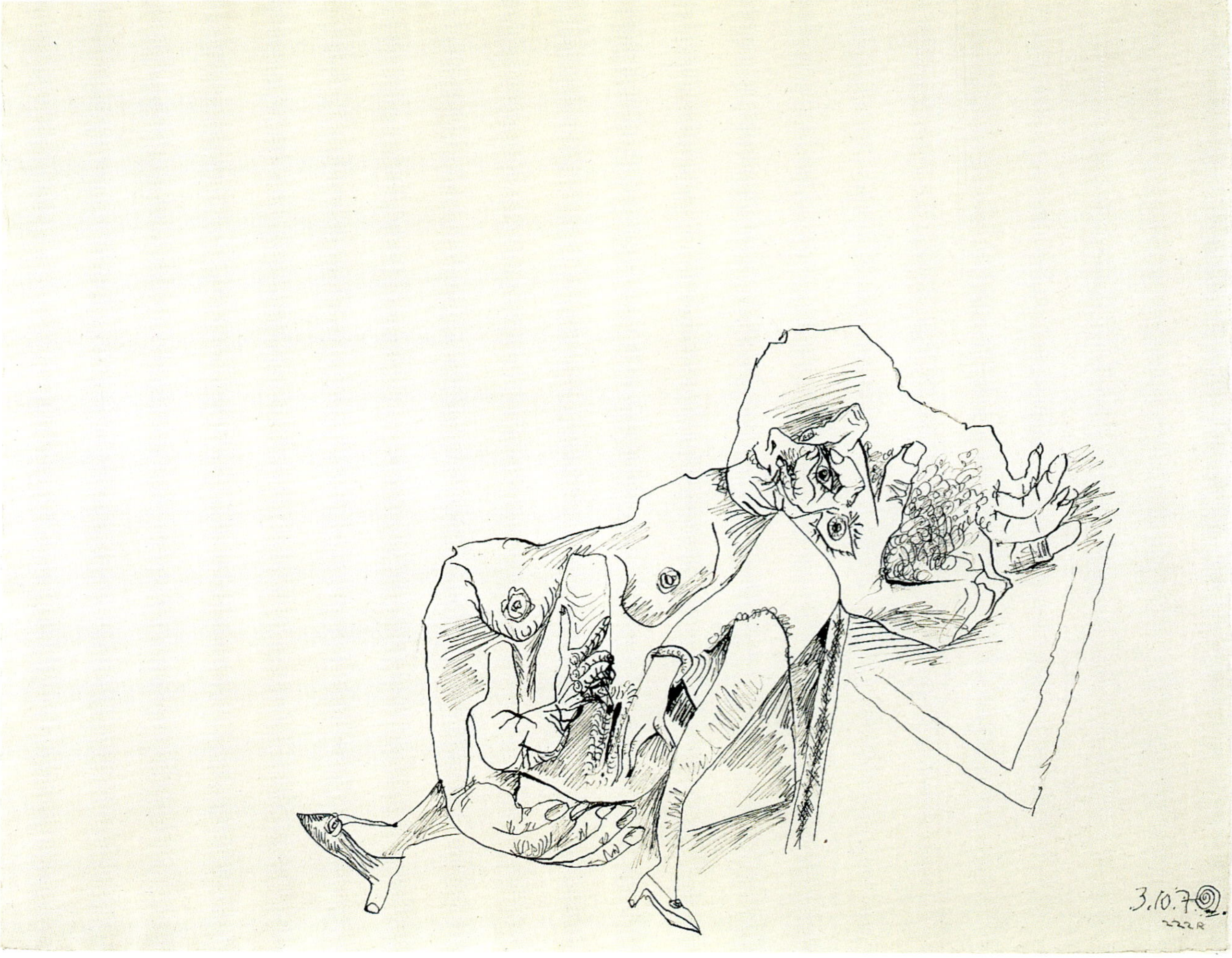

334 Nude in an Armchair, 3 October 1972
Pen and India ink on paper; 59 x 75.5
Paris, Musée Picasso, MP 1544

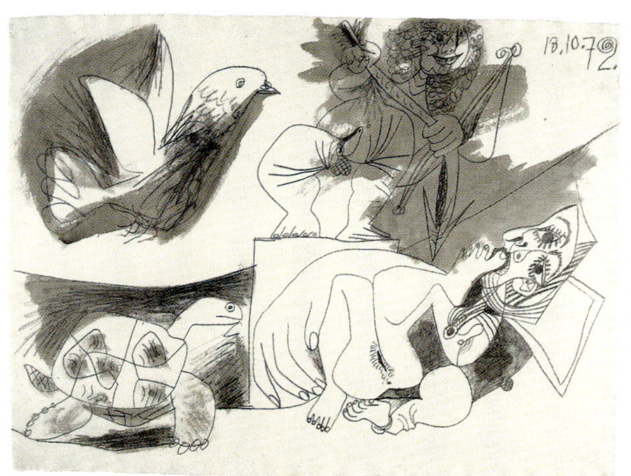

336 Dove, Cupid, Tortoise and Reclining Nude, 13 October 1972
Pencil, black crayon and India ink wash on paper; 57 x 77.5
Paris, Musée Picasso, MP 1541

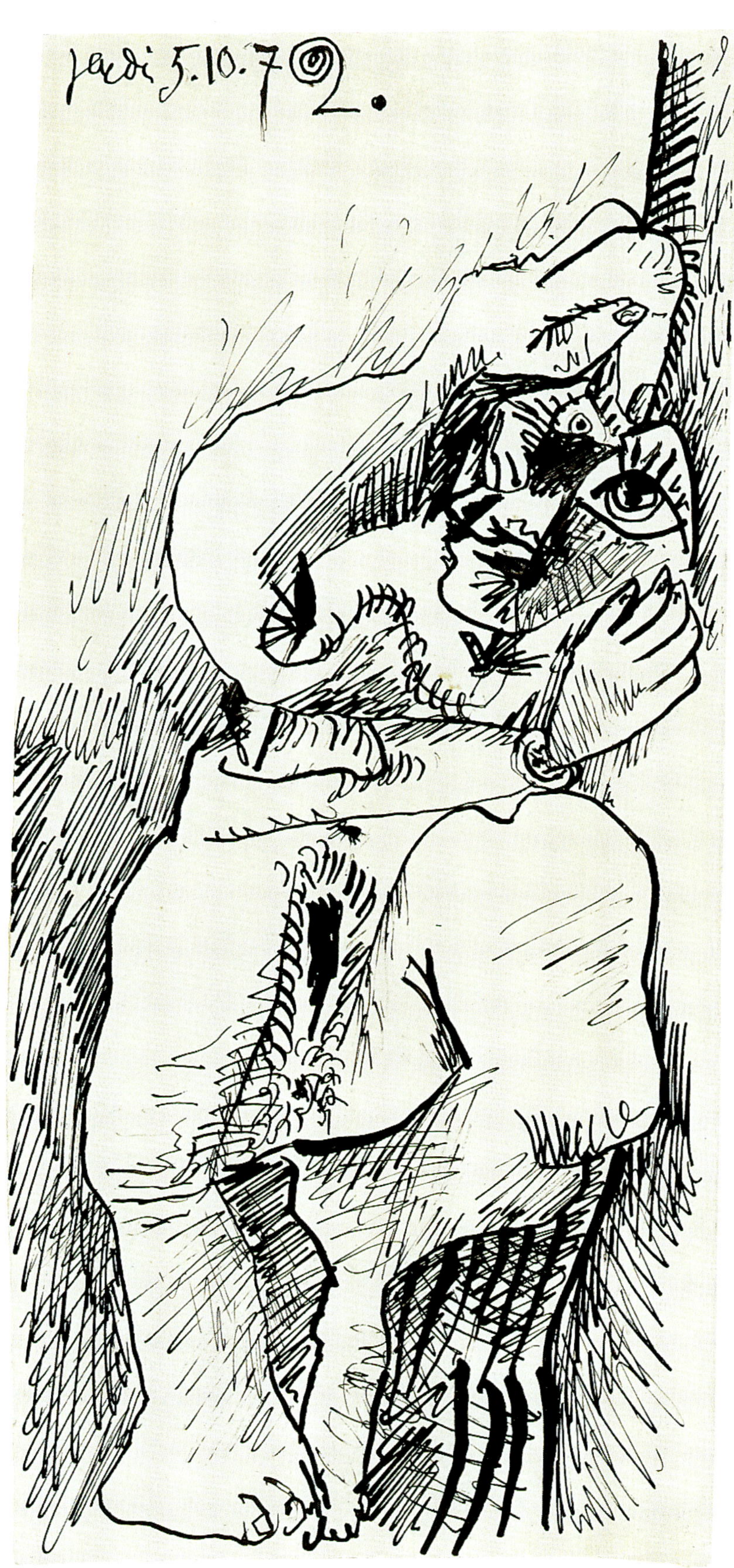

335 Nude, 5 October 1972
India ink and felt pen on cardboard; 34 x 16
Paris, Musée Picasso, MP 1542 r°

SELECTED BIBLIOGRAPHY

Baer, Brigitte,
Picasso peintre-graveur. Bern: Kornfeld, 1990–1996, 7 vols.
(vols. I and II: Bernhard Geiser; corrections, revision and
supplement by Brigitte Baer):
Vol. I: 1899-1931, nos. 1–257 bis, 1990 (G./B.).
Vol. II: 1932-1934, nos. 258–572 bis, 1992 (G./B.).
Vol. III: 1935-1945, nos. 573–730, 1986 (Baer).
Vol. IV: 1946-1958, nos. 731–1058, 1988 (Baer).
Vol. V: 1959-1965, nos. 1059–1369, 1989 (Baer).
Vol. VI: 1966-1968, nos. 1370–1860, 1994 (Baer).
Vol. VII: Addendum, 1996.

Barr-Sharrar, Beryl,
"Some aspects of early autobiographical imagery in Picasso's
Suite 347," *Art Bulletin*, Vol. LIV, No. 4 (Dec. 1972), p. 516–39.

Bataille, Georges,
L'Érotisme. Paris: Minuit, 1957. (English ed.:
Erotism: Death and Sensuality, trans. Mary Dalwood.
San Francisco: City Lights Books, 1986.)

Bayl, Friedrich,
"L'art obscène et la provocation hédoniste,"
Opus, 1970, p. 4–9.

Clair, Jean,
Picasso et l'abîme. Éros, Nomos et Thanatos.
Paris: L'Échoppe, 2000.

Diehl, Gaston, Roger Passeron, Osvaldo Patani
and Pierre Restany,
Vienne, Picasso. Die verborgene Sammlung.
Munich: Metamorphosis Verlag, 1996.
(French ed.: Picasso. La Collection secrète.
Paris: Somogy, 1996.)

Dupuis-Labbé, Dominique,
Picasso érotique. Paris: Gallimard, 2001.

Geiser, Bernhard,
see Baer, Brigitte.

Picasso, Pablo,
Propos sur l'art (edition established by Marie-Laure
Bernadac and Androula Michael).
Paris: Gallimard, coll. Art et Artistes, 1998, p. 53–58.

Picon, Gaétan,
"Picasso et l'érotisme," in Jean Cassou, *Pablo Picasso*.
Paris, Somogy, 1975, p. 253–72.

Pierre, José,
"Raphaël le bienheureux ou le peintre récompensé,"
Opus, 1970, p. 66–69.

Rosenblum, Robert,
"Picasso and the anatomy of eroticism," in Theodore Bowie
and Cornelia V. Christenson (eds.), *Studies in Erotic Art*.
New York: Basic Books, 1970, p. 337–50.

Schiff, Gert,
"Picasso's *Suite 347*, or Painting as an act of love,"
in Gert Schiff (ed.), *Picasso in Perspective*.
Englewood Cliffs, N.J.: Prentice-Hall, 1976, p. 163–67.

Spies, Werner,
Picasso, Das plastische Werk (catalogue raisonné
of the sculptures, in collaboration with Christine Piot).
Stuttgart: Gerd Hatje, 1983.

Steinberg, Leo,
"A working equation, or Picasso in the home stretch,"
The Print Collector's Newsletter, Vol. III, No. 5
(Nov.–Dec. 1972), p. 102–05.

Zervos, Christian,
Pablo Picasso. Paris: Cahiers d'art, 1932–1978
(Vols. I to XXXIII: 1895–1972).

EXHIBITIONS

1968–1969

16 March–5 October 1968, Paris, Galerie Louise Leiris;
18 December 1968–1 February 1969, Chicago,
The Art Institute of Chicago: *347 Gravures*.

1969

12 April–20 May, Zurich, Kunsthaus; 1–29 June, Berlin,
Akademie der Kunst; 11 July–10 August, Hamburg,
Hamburger Kunsthalle; 7 September–12 October, Cologne,
Kölnischer Kunstverein: *347 Graphische Blätter vom 16.3.
bis 5.10.1968*.

1970

16 March–5 October, London, The Institute of
Contemporary Arts: *347 Gravures*; 8 October–29 November,
Stuttgart, Würtembergischer Kunstverein: *347 X Picasso
graphische Blätter aus dem Jahre 1968*;
December, Barcelona, Sala Gaspar: *Picasso 347 Grabados*.

1971

April–June, Munich, Stuck-Villa:
347 Radierungen des Sommers 1968.

1972

13 September–17 October, London,
The Waddington Galleries: *Picasso, 347 Engravings*.

1979

27 February–18 March, Barcelona,
Museu Picasso: *Picasso erotic*.

1981

23 June–23 August, Høvikodden,
Henie-Onstad Kunstsenter: *Picasso 347*.

1982

November, Milan, Galleria Bergamini, Studio Marconi
and Galleria Seno: *Picasso, 347 immagini erotiche*.

1988

17 February–16 May, Paris, Centre Georges-Pompidou,
Musée national d'Art moderne, *Le dernier Picasso, 1953-1973*.

1989

9 June–25 July, Geneva, Galerie Jan Krugier: *Artistes
espagnols du XXᵉ siècle*.

1993–1994

30 November 1993–21 January 1994, Saragossa,
Patio de la Infanta, Centro de Exposiciones y Congresos:
Picasso íntimo.

1997–1998

23 June–31 August 1997, Tokyo, Odakyu Museum;
6 September–26 October 1997, Kawamura, Kawamura
Memorial Museum of Art; 1 November–7 December 1997,
Hokkaido, Hakodate Museum of Art; 10 January–1 February
1998, Kawaguchiko, Kawaguchiko Museum of Art;
4 February–1 March 1998, Kyoto, Kyoto Museum Eki;
7 March–12 April 1998, Marugame, Genichiro-Inokuma
Museum of Contemporary Art; 16 April–17 May 1998,
Sogo, Sogo Museum of Art: *Passion and Eroticism,
The Late Graphic Works by Pablo Picasso from the
Piero Crommelynck Collection*.

PHOTO CREDITS

Numbers in roman type correspond to the catalogue numbers, while page numbers, in italics, refer to the essay illustrations.

Private collections, all rights reserved: *p. 16* (bottom), *p. 41* (top), *p. 41* (bottom), *p. 43* (bottom), *p. 44*, *p. 47*, *p. 50* (bottom), *p. 51* (top: © ADAGP), *p. 51* (bottom), *p. 53*, *p. 55* (bottom), *p. 59*, *p. 60*, *p. 63* (bottom), *p. 66* (bottom), *p. 67*, *p. 70*, *p. 71*, *p. 82*, *p. 83* (top), *p. 84* (bottom), *p. 85*, *p. 88* (middle), *p. 98* (middle), *p. 99*, *p. 115*, *p. 122*, *p. 148*, *p. 153*, 12, 16, 24, 33 a, 36, 37, 45, 51, 52, 53, 61, 71, 72, 73, 97, 102, 174, 190 a, b, c, d and e, 192, 219, 220, 279; © Images Modernes, photos by E. Baudouin: 79, 83, 127, 181, 205, 207, 241; © Images Modernes, photo by M. Domage: 3, 23, 41, 70, 200, 200 a; © photos by Jacques Faujour: 228, 229, 245, 246, 247, 248, 249, 250, 251, 252, 253, 254, 255, 256, 257, 258, 259, 260, 261, 262, 263, 264, 265, 266, 267, 268, 269, 270, 271; © photos by Patrick Geotelen: 5, 49, 76, 109; © photo by Orlando Photo: 209; © photo by Christian Poite: 74; © Zurich, photo by Peter Schälchli: 281; © Succession Picasso, 2001;

© Angers, Musée des Beaux-Arts: *p. 120* (bottom);
© Arles, Musée Réattu, photo by Michel Lacanaud: 290;
© Balingen, Stadthalle: 25;
© Barcelona, Museu Picasso: *p. 63* (top), *p. 66* (top), *p. 74*, *p. 80*, *p. 83* (middle and bottom), *p. 88* (top), *p. 91* (top), 1, 2, 4, 7, 8, 9, 10, 11, 27, 28, 29, 31, 33, 35, 38, 212, 213, 223, 224, 225, 243, 283, 295, 296 b, 323, 327; photos by J. Calafell / R. Feliu: 11, 13, 14, 211, 214; photo by R. Feliu: 22; photos by J. Calafell: 26, 30, 32, 34;
© Basel, Fondation Beyeler: 240, 277;
© Basel, Galerie Beyeler: 218;
© Basel, Öffentliche Kunstsammlung, Kupferstichkabinett, photo by Martin Bühler: 62;
© Belfort, Gift of Maurice Jardot, photo by Galerie Leiris: 333;
© Berlin, Staatliche Museen, Nationalgalerie: 275;
© Boston, The Museum of Fine Arts: 124;
© Buffalo, Albright-Knox Art Gallery: 56, 133;
© Cambridge, Fogg Art Museum: *p. 120* (top);
© Chicago, The Art Institute: *p. 41* (middle);
© Cleveland, The Cleveland Museum of Art: *p. 91* (bottom), 59;
© Cologne, Museum Ludwig, Rheinisches Bildarchiv: 217;
© Copenhagen, Statens Museum for Kunst, photo by Hans Petersen: 50;
© Dijon, Musée des Beaux-Arts: 170;
© Geneva, Galerie Jan Krugier, Ditesheim & Co.: 331 a
© Göteborg, Göteborgs Konstmuseum, photo by Ebbe Carlsson: 44;
© Jerusalem, The Israel Museum, photo by David Harris: 77;
© Los Angeles, County Museum of Art: *p. 98* (top);
© Madrid, Centro de Arte Reina Sofía: 125;
© Malibu, The J. Paul Getty Museum: *p. 98* (bottom);
© Martigny, Fondation Pierre Gianadda: 39;
© Merion, Barnes Foundation: *p. 97* (bottom);
© Montpellier, Musée Fabre: *p. 96* (top);
© Montreal, Landau Fine Art: 332;
© Montreal, The Montreal Museum of Fine Arts: 289;
© New York, The Metropolitan Museum of Art: 40;
© New York, The Museum of Modern Art: *p. 95*, 178;
Strasbourg, Musée d'Art moderne et contemporain, cabinet d'Art Graphique, © RMN, photos by M. Coursaget: 230, 231, 232, 233, 235, 237;
Paris, © Bibliothèque nationale de France, Département des Estampes et de la Photographie: *p. 54*;
  © Centre Georges-Pompidou/Musée national d'Art moderne, photo courtesy of Centre collections photo library: 226, 288 (© RMN-G. Blot);
  © Galerie Louise Leiris: *p. 72*, 274, 278, 276, 291;
  © Photothèque des Musées de la Ville de Paris, photo by Ph. Joffre: 20;
  © Réunion des Musées nationaux: *p. 43* (top), *p. 50* (top), *p. 84* (bottom), *p. 96*, *p. 104* (bottom), *p. 105*, *p. 111*, *p. 113*, *p. 141*, 15, 17, 18, 21, 23 a, 42, 46 a, 54 a and b, 55, 58, 60 a, 65 a and b, 66, 75 a, b and c, 78, 86, 87, 91, 92 b and c, 93 a, 100 a, b and c, 106, 107, 119, 121, 129, 130, 131, 132, 134, 135, 139, 140, 142, 143, 144, 145, 146, 147, 149, 151, 153, 156, 158, 159, 163, 164, 165, 166, 167, 168, 169, 171, 172, 173, 175, 177 a, b and c, 179, 184, 185, 188, 195, 196, 197, 198, 199 a, 199 b, 202, 205, 216 a and b, 221 a and b, 222, 227 a, b and c, 234, 236, 239, 244, 272, 273 a and b, 285, 292, 296 a, 317, 318, 320, 321, 325, 331, 336; photos by D. Arnaudet: 182, 336; photo by D. Arnaudet / J. Schormans: *p. 97* (top); photos by M. Bellot: 19, 43, 48, 155, 157, 160, 186, 215; photos by M. Bellot/G. Blot: 84 a and b; photos by G. Blot: *p. 16* (top), *p. 96* (middle), 47, 154, 208, 210, 238, 242, 286; photo by G. Blot/C. Jean: *p. 97* (middle); photos by J. G. Berizzi: *p. 17*, 88, 117, 183, 187, 176, 189, 280, 287; photos by B. Hatala: *p. 88* (bottom); *p. 101*, 60 b, 63, 64 a and b, 80, 85, 89 a and b, 92 a, 93 b, 94, 95, 98, 101, 103 a and b, 108, 110, 111, 112, 113, 114, 115, 122, 136, 137, 138, 141, 148, 150, 152, 161, 193 a, b, and c, 201, 203, 204, 206, 334, 335; photos by C. Jean: *p. 107*, 67; photos by J. L'hoir: 6 a and b, 46 b, 194 a and b, 221 c; photos by H. Lewandowski: 81, 191; photos by R.G. Ojeda: 68, 69, 90, 99, 116, 118, 126, 128, 162, 180; photos by F. Raux: *p. 104* (top: © Brassaï Estate), 82, 96, 104, 105;
© Philadelphia, Museum of Art: *p. 65* (© ADAGP);
© Leslee and David Rogath: 273 c
© Rome, Galleria Nazionale d'Arte Antica, Palazzo Barberini: *p. 119*;
© Saint-Étienne, Musée d'Art moderne: 282, 293, 294, 297, 298, 299, 300, 301, 302, 303, 304, 305, 306, 307, 308, 309, 310, 311, 312, 313, 314, 315, 316, 319, 322, 326, 328, 324, 329, 330;
© Toronto, The Art Gallery of Ontario, photo by Larry Ostrom: 57;
© Vienna, Kunsthistorisches Museum: *p. 55* (top).

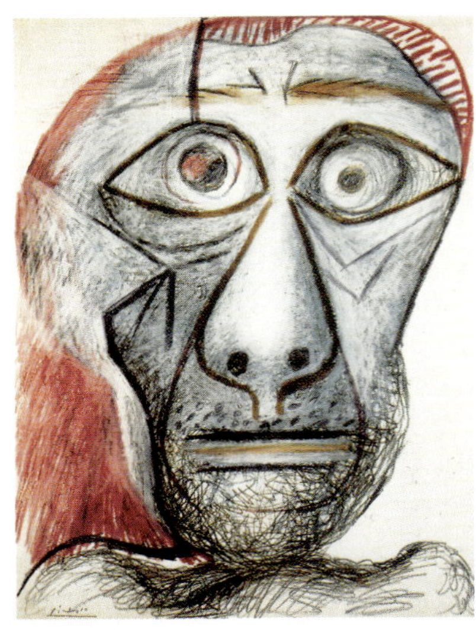

Self-Portrait, 20 June 1972
Wax crayon on paper; 60.7 x 50.5 cm
Tokyo, Fuji Television Co. Gallery

For the English edition:

Editorial Coordination
Philippa Hurd

Production
Meike Weber and Hugues Charreyron

Graphic Design
Philippe Ducat
in memoriam Elephstratios Eleftheriades

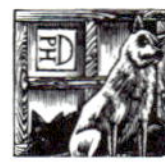

Set in Aldus, Grotesque and Modern Script.

Origination by
IGS (Ingénierie Graphisme Services) Angoulême.

Paperback ISBN: 3-7913-2530-2
Hardcover ISBN: 3-7913-2561-2

Printed by Aubin Imprimeur, Poitiers, France, March 2001.